T0367518

Also published by the author (*Chas J. Vale is a pen name).

THE MATHEMATICS OF THE ENERGY CRISIS (1978) by Richard L. Gagliardi & Samuel W. Valenza, Jr. ISBN 0-9366918-01-2.

GEOMETRICAL THEOREMS IN SLIDES (1979) by V.P. Madan, Designed, illustrated and edited by Samuel W. Valenza, Jr.

LOTTO GAMEPLANS AND SYSTEMS: WINNING STRATEGIES (1985) By Norman Peden and William Lawrence, Designed and edited by Chas. J. Vale.* ISBN 0-936918-06-3.

SWEDISH LOTTO SYSTEMS: Guaranteed & Tested Strategies (1986) Thomas Ollson Designed and edited by Chas J. Vale.* ISBN 0-936918-08-4.

CREATION OF NOTHING: SUPPLEMENT TO THE US PATENTS #4,616,556 & #3,601,077 (1989) the Meilmans and Samuel W. Valenza, Jr. ISBN 0-936918-12-8.

PEIRCE MEANS BUSINESS: A HISTORY OF PEIRCE JUNIOR COLLEGE, 1865-1989 (1990) by Carl Fassl, Design by Samuel W. Valenza, Jr. & Bonnie Hoffman. ISBN 0-962501-0-9.

THE LOTTERY NUMBERS BOOK (1990,1995) LCC No. 95-72664 By Samuel W. Valenza, Jr. with Ron Shelley ISBN 0-936918-14-4

PROFESSOR GOOGOL'S FLYING TIME MACHINE & ATOMIC SPACE CAPSULE MATH PRIMER (1974, 2009), Story and illustration by Samuel W. Valenza, Jr. ISBN 0-036918-00-4.

THE MATHEMATICS OF LOTTERY GAMES: HOW THE GAMES WORK, (2012) By Samuel W. Valenza, Jr. ISBN 0-936918-11-2

Cover: The casino at Red Men's Hall occupied the third floor of this building in 1941 and operated with impunity, entertaining mobsters from New York and other major cities as well as local gamblers "in the know." Photo by the author, circa 2003.

The Secret Casino at Red Men's Hall

Samuel W. Valenza Jr.

iUniverse LLC
Bloomington

THE SECRET CASINO AT RED MEN'S HALL

iUniverse books may be ordered through booksellers or by contacting:

iUniverse
1663 Liberty Drive
Bloomington, IN 47403
www.iuniverse.com
1-800-Authors (1-800-288-4677)

ISBN: 978-1-4917-1846-9 (sc)
ISBN: 978-1-4917-1845-2 (hc)
ISBN: 978-1-4917-1844-5 (e)

Library of Congress Control Number: 2014904566

Printed in the United States of America.

iUniverse rev. date: 04/29/2014

To Bessie

CONTENTS

ILLUSTRATIONS

ACKNOWLEDGEMENTS

THIS memoir owes much to a host of friends and relatives. I am extremely grateful to Jacque Navieux, retired Marine flyer and buddy for his inspiration; Ray Hoagland, former teacher and coach, B-17 commander and friend for 65 years; and Ev Turner, former SBD2 pilot and photographer extraordinaire of Mt. Holly's history. Others to whom I am indebted include Frank Smith, who introduced me to Ev Turner and Buck Watson, Rancocas historian. Also thanks to Tom Ross of the Coconino County Sheriff's Department; Jim Cheevers, Curator of the USNA museum; Rich Hathcock, LA Times photographer; Joanie Henderson Hodges, a historian in her own right; Deanna, Las Vegas historian (last name unknown) who led me to discover the Meadows Casino; Sam and Cindy Muro, among the few remaining cousins from the family club; Patti, of the Wheeling Historical Society; and of course, my wife Dotti and our children, who lived through my telling of the story. Additionally many thanks to the Mt. Holly Historical Society; Larry Tigar for his assistance; The New Jersey Pinelands Association; The New Jersey Division of Fish and Wildlife; and the librarians at the Burlington County Library for their patience. The telling has been long (I started on the project in 1995) and traumatic, as I have been plagued by childhood memories throughout my adult life, and seem to have been blessed (or cursed) in remembering far too many details.

PREFACE

So much has changed... in today's society, TV, email, twitter and the internet have created a new awareness that in the 1930's was dampened by the printed page and a polite society. A society in which practically everyone paid their taxes, attended church on Sunday and garnered information from the newspapers and radio. The fellow next door that appeared to be a friendly neighbor may have been a drunk and a wife beater or had a Boo Radley chained in the basement. It was none of your business.

It was an era when a few smart fellows discovered that markets existed that could be statistically defined and attacked with branding and mass advertising. Thus, Elsie the Borden cow became a national icon and bovine milk joined the required food groups. Mickey Mouse endorsed everything from Ritz Crackers to throw rugs. The Wizard of Oz, the 1939 film musical broke all box office records in bringing to life Frank Baum's 1900 novel that was the Harry Potter of its day, selling millions of copies worldwide. And everybody, even ladies smoked cigarettes.

In that society less than a dozen states allowed church bingo; all other forms of gambling were outlawed activities, and those who operated gambling establishments were criminals. An exception was made for pari-mutual wagering at a few racetracks scattered across the land. In the statutes, a bookmaker was as much a criminal as an armed robber, but frequently was treated with largesse by a local magistrate, who might be his neighbor or client. The real criminals were the "Big Time" gamblers.

The society was shell-shocked in the aftermath of a great depression and the obliteration of millions of acres of farmlands in the Midwest, bereft of topsoil and called “the dustbowl.” The social norms that we accept today evolved from years of painful struggle and subtle changes in behavior and social mores. One fifth of the working population was unemployed. The mafia didn’t exist; J. Edgar Hoover said so.

This story begins in 1989 when I, a middle aged son am shocked from routine by the revelation that my father left me a stolen car when he passed away nine years before. The seriousness of the situation (I was arrested on three felony counts) causes a re-evaluation of my childhood and a new curiosity of exactly who my father was.

Flashbacks detail my childhood during World War II and maturation in the wash of the Korean and cold wars. Until 9-11, the current society had no idea of what real fear was about. Only a very small segment of our society really knows the emptiness of hunger, the fear of eviction or the scorn of contemporaries; what it feels like to be a victim in a society where people are ashamed of their poverty and unemployment. You didn’t talk about your troubles.

Although the 21st Amendment was already two years old when I was born, the affects of its target legislation were devastating to the population. Drinking and alcoholism were major problems in society; the crusaders for a return to Prohibition had good cause to hope for a revival of a drunk-free society. Drunks were killing themselves and innocent victims at an alarming rate, beating their wives and children without any fear of interruption or jail.

But the 18th amendment had only curbed the *selling* of branded liquors and beers, putting many honest workers out on the street, while it created a subculture of criminal activity and financed the creation of the American mafia through the import and sale of illegal whiskey and beer. After repeal, the hoodlums that had made hundreds of millions during prohibition were seeking new sources of revenue. They needed to continue the lifestyle to which they had become accustomed.

This was the milieu in which my father grew to maturity. His dexterity at games funneled him into the fast crowd that offered games of chance, and he soon became a master player and a leader. How much influence Simone “the Count” DeCavalcante may have had on dad’s immersion in a life of crime is unknown, but it was considerable and combined with the mentoring of Enoch "Knucky" Johnson, my father became firmly entrenched in a life outside ordinary society.

As a child and young man, I had only glimpses of dad's activities. When we became older, I asked my father about these events and in some cases, he filled in details. After he passed away, I tried to reconstruct as much as possible by querying dad's surviving brothers, and finally by researching his escapades in newspaper archives.

While the old adage is true; you can't choose your relatives, so is the truth that it is often impossible to evade the backwash of their lives. In this story we follow Tuck, my alter ego, as he tries to achieve respectability in spite of the reputation of his father. And although I realized that my father was different, I had no real appreciation regarding his life amongst some of the most nefarious of gangsters of the era. Until I did the research as a 78 year old grandfather, I naively believed that dad had been a minor player in the Mafioso scheme of things.

Two relationships changed everything for me: The first was the revelation that Simone DeCavalcante, dad's lifelong best friend became a member of the Commission, La Cosa Nostra's governing body in the 1960's. This occurred when Joe Bonanno was purged from the commission for refusing to settle the war he created with Chicago's Tony Accardo. Bonnano demanded a share of the skim from the Las Vegas Tangiers and Stardust casinos. DeCavalcante, a long time friend of Bonanno was brought in as a liaison with the exiled Chief. Dead bodies and blown up Cadillacs on the Las Vegas Strip were bad public relations.

Secondly, as a six year old, I remember the night that standing in the kitchen behind the secret casino in Edie Maye's grasp, hearing about the Murder, Inc. assassin that robbed the casino, broke Johnny Marinella's nose, and murdered Freddy Fosciano as a warning. It was this 72 year-old memory of the name "Carbo" that triggered my research and revealed that man to be Frank "Paulie" Carbo. A soldier in the Lucchese family of New York, Carbo was a Murder, Inc. assassin who was indicted for five murders and suspected of at least 12 others. Dad was messing with the big boys!

The story essentially follows the chronology of my life, and in that journey, I describe many of my father's adventurous and illegal escapades.

Much of dad's life will remain a mystery, but it is not lost on me that many of his exploits have already appeared in films like "Goodfellas," "The Sting," "Coogan's Bluff," "Casino" and "The Cincinnati Kid" glamorized of course by Hollywood.

The writing has been difficult. Can anyone really understand another person? By the end, I reluctantly understood that dad probably loved me, his youngest son, but his personality simply didn't have the means to express that kind of feeling. My brother summed it up best. "He's Popeye! 'I am what I am!' Take it or leave it…he doesn't mean anything by it."

So in the end, my father's story tells itself. Some of the events of our lives were quite fantastic, and in retrospect, I felt almost embarrassed to relate details about our often desperate situations. Writing it in the first person was impossible for me. Our peers had no idea that we lived on the edge of poverty, almost at the same level as the "sneaky Pete" alcoholics who slept in the alley behind the Arcade Bar on Main Street. But we knew it, and we feared that if everyone we knew didn't know it, someone would tell them about the ragtag family of the frequently arrested local jailbird, bookie and gangster associate.

Thus, Tuck and Sal Falconetti are the alter egos created to bring the story to the page…I often looked at my life as an outsider watching events unfold before me, unable to change or affect the outcomes. Thus I found it a useful and productive way to relate painful memories. Some characters are conglomerate personalities, but most are as historically accurate as I could make them.

The sequence of events depicted may be a little shaky, and I may have added some embellishment to some for literary purposes, but the history is true. Since dad never told anyone where he was going or when to expect him back, I have tried to reconstruct events by correlating to the places in which we lived. I'm sure that I've made some errors. He operated in so many important places in the formulary of the mafia in its heyday that it's been impossible to pin him down to exact dates. So if the chronology may be a little off, I apologize, and wish I had been more attentive.

The Author, September 2013

PART 1:
YOUNG TUCK

1

PAROLE

WAITING at a stoplight in one of the better areas of Camden, Salvatore Tucker Falconetti, Junior checked his door locks when the black man at the curb stirred from his sleeping position, arose and stumbled toward his car. The man paused momentarily to hoist a brown bagged bottle to his lips, jeered at Tuck through the windshield, and staggered on. Camden, New Jersey, wasn't what it used to be.[1]

Tuck rolled into Kinney's Parking Lot, across from the county Administration Building, parked the Jaguar and braved the early morning snow flurries without his topcoat. He was a little excited, since this was to be his last visit to Danny Silverstein, his Parole Officer.

Tuck wasn't much more than five-eight in height. Like most of his family, his head seemed abnormally large. He thought that this misfortune of birth was exacerbated by his hair: curly and thick. For most of his life, he kept it cropped short, except for a period in the sixties when he taught high school mathematics and was swept up in the anti-Vietnam war movement. An irreverent "sweathog" had once remarked in Geometry class that "you've got a big head like Einstein," which Tuck would have taken as a complement from any other source.

He trotted across Market Street, musing to himself that he was grateful that he could still jog fifty yards without noticeably wheezing. The date was January 17, 1989, exactly nine years to the day from his father's death. And now, at 54 with problems of his own, he was finally going to bury the legacy of his iniquitous father, a mystery to all that knew him.

Ironically, Tuck's dad Sal had missed the 80's decade. The period which resulted in the destruction of his domain, the most powerful crime syndicates across America: the mafia. The Organized Crime Control Act of 1970, RICO and the Witness Protection Program brought down many of Sal's friends. His boyhood companion, Sam DeCavalcante, "The Plumber:" serving a 15 year sentence; Joseph Columbo, paralyzed by three bullets in his head in 1971, now dead; and his Chicago godfather Sam Giancana, murdered in 1975 while making pasta. Now, in his ubiquitous way, Sal had reached out from his grave to remind Tuck that his father still remained a score for the son to settle.

It's a blustery, blustery day, Tuck thought as he crossed the lobby and peeled from his leg a page of the Camden Courier Post that the wind had attached to him. He felt a little giddy, being blown uncontrollably by the winds of his life. But he also felt optimistic, having an end in sight to this particular windstorm.

When the elevator appeared, he couldn't resist musing that this was the only building he had been in since his 20's that still had elevator operators. *Goddamn waste of taxpayer's money,* he thought, smiling at the overweight uniformed pilot for his two-story trip.

There are few places left where offices also still feature frosted glass windows, but the PTI, "Pre Trial Intervention" offices, like all others in the aging county building, had them. As usual, inside the door in a narrow corridor leading to a receptionist's desk, the four wooden chairs were filled, and several other unfortunates stood waiting. They were a mixed representation of Camden's streets; at least two easily identifiable hookers, bleary eyed with filthy hair and caked-on make-up, some younger blacks, sullen and tight-lipped, an overweight construction worker, and one very pregnant and pleasant looking young lady.

Tuck was wearing a tie, uncommon, but necessary for the meeting. As he pushed forward, one of the hookers gave him a wink and made sure that her ample cleavage was available for a glance.

Tuck knew that he was on time as he squeezed through the crowd and announced himself to the black girl behind the desk. He also knew that she would immediately send him over to Danny's desk, and although he wanted to get it over with, it angered him to be pushed ahead.

What the hell am I doing here anyway? He mused, *I thought I was on the good guy's team...a Midshipman doesn't lie, cheat or steal or tolerate one who does. And it's bad enough being the white honky in a Camden parole office, let alone being pushed ahead of everyone else.*

Tuck had matriculated here, at Rutgers, Camden, a tiny university campus surrounded by a city buried in corruption. The neighborhoods where Walt Whitman and Enrico Caruso once trod were now rubbled and teeming with drug gangs. Tuck, who spent a lifetime trying to be the good guy, incorruptible and honest to a fault, was so naive that he now was just another parolee among other unfortunates in a city that had become the murder capital of America.

Tuck was amused by Danny Silverstein, who might have been cloned from Woody Allen. He repressed the urge to tell him of the resemblance on every visit. Danny looked up from his bent over position, pushed his glasses down his nose, smiled, and asked how Tuck was doing. He even talked like Woody Allen.

"Your book, please," Danny asked.

Tuck extracted his parole "book" from his shirt pocket. A bi-folded piece of cardstock about the size of a wallet photo, it had columns in which Danny could ceremoniously record the date and time of Tuck's reporting. It was pretty tattered from Tuck's back trouser pocket. The "book" was big stuff to Danny. Danny wrote in the book, explaining that Tuck still had to carry it until his record was expunged. If arrested without it, the PTI was null and void; Tuck would be automatically thrown into the Courts with an additional charge of breaking parole. Tuck went through a litany of explaining how he had provided the Court with the records of his punishment served, 250 hours of "teaching" an assortment of downtrodden African Americans and Latinos as much English and reading as he could. Tuck could have served five years for grand larceny, auto, and 10 more on the two other felony counts. Thanks to his father, Sal, the "old man."

Tuck had hired the best criminal lawyer in South Jersey the day after the State Police surrounded him in his company's parking lot. They had escorted him off to a gas station to check the VIN numbers on the Cadillac he had been driving for eight years. The one that dear old dad left in his sister's driveway when he died. Of course, it *was* a stolen car! Stolen from a Trenton entity in 1980, just *months* before Tuck's dad died. Tuck was told this by Sergeant Killarny while he was fingerprinting, photographing and booking him on three felony counts at the Princeton barracks of the New Jersey State Police.

Tuck wasn't sure which he found more amazing, the fact that he was being arrested, or how a 69 year- old man, dying of prostate cancer, would be stealing cars. But that was his dad, Sal. For Tuck, a large portion of his existence had been spent broken-field running through his dad's game of life, while trying to make something of his own.

Killarny was almost apologetic about the arrest.

"How long have you been driving this car?" he asked.

"Eight years, off and on," Tuck said, "it sat for a long time after my dad died, and I tried to get title to it."

"Yeah, I can see that," Killarny said, "we've got your gas receipts going back four years."

"I've got nothing to hide," Tuck responded, "I turned this whole thing over to a lawyer after I couldn't get it titled myself. Unfortunately, this Lawyer and his friends were in the process of trying to steal my business, so he used the titling of the car as leverage against me." Tuck wondered if he could possibly explain the situation in a way that made sense, the way that it happened.

"What do you mean by that?" Killarny asked.

"Well," Tuck continued, "I was dependent on these guys for startup money for the business, and when it got going, they tried to secretly sell it out from under me. The lawyer, he used the titling process to keep me dependent. He stalled it for three years until I finally faced them down, and then he submitted the papers to Trenton."

"But you knew the car was stolen," Killarny said, "from the start."

"No, I didn't know that. I suspected that, because my dad had been convicted for auto theft back in the seventies," Tuck said, "but, I didn't know it. He was a registered auto dealer in a lot of states, and always had different cars. That's why I called you guys and gave you the serial number to check out."

"Who did you call?" He asked.

"A Sergeant in the Mantua Barracks. I've got his name in my files. He said he checked it out and it was not a stolen car, but I still called all the states that my dad had worked in, from Jersey to Florida, and the Auctions, too, but nobody knew anything about this car. And there were no papers in his personal effects."

"So why didn't the lawyer have us inspect the car?" He asked.

"You were supposed to," Tuck said, getting more frustrated, "before you issued the title. I offered to take the car anywhere you wanted, but you guys didn't respond, and I got the title, issued by the state. In my mind, everything was resolved. That was four years ago, for Christ sake."

"The papers you submitted to the state had errors," Killarny said, "that's one of the charges against you: falsifying records."

"Hey, look." Tuck's demeanor was now becoming defensive, "My lawyer submitted those papers; I never got to see them before he submitted them, and I told you what his game was, he was after my company."

"You didn't even spell your sister's name right, on the affidavit," Killarny waved a copy.

"I'm still not sure how you spell it," Tuck said, "I don't see my sister much."

"Nevertheless, you're responsible." he said. "But that's not the only issue here; you're in a lot of trouble. These are serious penal charges. You could be locked up because of this."

"Yeah, I see that. That bastard lawyer can submit bad work, and lay off the blame on me. I didn't misspell anything. Are you responsible for your work? Jesus Christ, Sergeant, I'm no criminal! I'm a former Marine and I attended the Naval Academy. I taught for ten years here in this state, I've got a degree in mathematics and hold patents. The last time I got a traffic ticket was over twenty years ago. I'm the President of a public company, for God's sake, and I belong to Press Associations and Alumni Boards."

"Yeah," Killarny seemed impressed, but unmoved, "you've got a lot in your favor if you go to trial, but right now, the state is cracking down on stolen cars. They're really being tough on these kinds of cases."

"Jesus," Tuck said, standing up and walking to the window, "I've spent my whole life trying to get out of the shadow of my old man. Now he's dead nine years and the son of bitch rises out of the grave to smack me down! I thought I was finally rid of him, and all the crap that was associated with him!"

"But you hung around with him, drove across country with him, right?" Killarny asked.

"Well, yeah, I did that a couple of times, at least" *Christ,* Tuck thought, *I wonder if that Caddie convertible was stolen, too?*

To Killarny, he said, "It was the biggest mistake of my life, the day I took that lawyer and his friends as partners."

Tuck's mouth was very dry, and he felt a little lightheaded. He could still feel the cold steel of the handcuffs on his wrists, although Killarny had removed them after stewarding him through the booking ritual.

"How so?" Killarny asked.

"Well, don't you see? They all knew about my concerns about the car, and I had told them about the old man, his record and all. That's a fault of mine; I tell it like it is. What you see is what you get. I didn't hide anything from those guys. When I caught them trying to sell the Company, they would have been violating SEC law, so I stopped them, and I threw them out of the Company. I had to buy their stock back, and I just finished paying for it, so obviously, they called you guys, hoping just to harass me. They'd really be enjoying this, if they knew about it." Tuck shook his head in disbelief as he watched the traffic on Highway One.

"We acted on an anonymous tip; a telephone call." Killarny said. Tuck wanted to ask him if the caller had a lisp. Tuck's most aggressive and least intelligent partner had a lisp.

"Well, they got lucky. The goddamn car was stolen, after all, but they didn't know it any better than I did. I guess I should have, though, knowing my old man!" Tuck sat down again, next to Killarny's desk. His throat was dry and constricted, and he couldn't keep his hands from shaking.

2

THE ARREST

Tuck never knew his dad well. His relationship with him alternated through periods of hero worship, fear, hate and finally, tolerance. Tuck was relatively certain, although his sister sometimes vehemently denied it, that his dad, the "old man" was intimately connected with the most notorious mafia gangsters of his era, and that he was part and parcel of their activity.

When Tuck was older and found himself in his dad's company, he often delicately probed his relationship with the mob, but the only definitive answer he could recall was the time that the old man said, "Sure, I know all those boys. I've known them all my life, but I never got married, and I never killed anybody."

In his reference to "marriage," one had to assume that he was saying he never took the blood oath popularized in the many gangster films[2]. However, Tuck no longer believed his statement. Tuck often mused that he wouldn't be surprised to learn that sometime, in his incredible past, that the old man had killed someone, either.

Tuck hadn't spoken to his sister in about six years. When he first started his Company, she had come to work for him. She was divorced and been through a series of jobs as a medical secretary, and usually ended up in some kind of fight with the Doctor that she worked for. Every doctor she worked for was an Albert Schweitzer when she hired on and in about six weeks she would be describing him with four letter words.

She was working for Tuck for about four months when he realized that she was grabbing cash out of the incoming mail orders. It wasn't much, twenty bucks here and there, but he was sick about it. Tuck wasn't even taking a salary, but he was paying her a competitive wage. Since he usually worked past midnight, he didn't make it in the following morning until about ten. By then the mail had all been opened.

The business was failing miserably, losing a lot of money and Tuck was under tremendous pressure. The potential was there, but the means to make it happen, capital, wasn't. Paying the bills one evening, he noticed that there was a heavy increase in the long distance calls.

It didn't take much investigation to see that the increase was synonymous with his sister's employment. She was spending 45 minutes to an hour every morning talking to friends in Pennsylvania and to her daughter in Colorado. Tuck called the numbers just to make sure.

Making matters worse, he had hired her at an hourly rate, but had been paying her for forty hours. Tuck was lucky if he could get thirty hours out of her in a given week. She pleaded that she had some emergency to take care of, some dental appointment or something that required her leaving early.

"Look," Tuck said, "The accountant tells me that you should be handing in a time sheet to support his making up your payroll check. So, could you just fill this in every day with your hours, and I'll send it over to him on Tuesdays, O.K.?"

"What do you think you're doing?" She bristled, "are you calling me a cheat?"

"No," Tuck responded, "he told me he needs this, that's all. It won't change anything; he just needs it for his records."

"You're trying to cheat me," she screamed, "I should have known it!"

"What are you talking about?" Tuck asked. "I'm not accusing you of anything; it's just an accounting procedure."

"Like hell it is, you bastard!" She stood up from her desk and was really screaming at him, now. He had never seen this side of his sister before. Tuck thought of Marlon Brando in the film, "One Eyed Jacks," kicking his chair backwards and calling his antagonist "a scum sucking pig."

"Look," Tuck said very calmly, "I don't think you're a cheat. Where did you get that idea?" He was amused and shocked at the reaction, but he knew that he was lying.

It's obvious that she's a cheat, and a liar to boot, he thought.

"You told Vic I used the phone too much!" She screamed her face crimson. Tuck could see that she really hated him! Vic was her new live-in boyfriend. He had stopped in and asked Tuck how she was doing, to which he had replied, "Great, but I wish she wouldn't make all those long distance calls in the mornings." They had laughed about it.

"Well, yeah," Tuck said, "I did, but that's not the point. He asked me, and it's not fair for you to make all those calls, when I can't even afford to take a salary, and you're getting paid, but that's got nothing to do with this."

"Well, you take your god damned job and stick it up your ass, you son of a bitch," she screamed, "nobody calls me a cheat, and I don't have to put up with your fucking lies about me, either!" She slammed the door to the office. Tuck stood staring at the door, stunned.

A few weeks later, Sis called Tuck and invited his family for dinner, but he declined.

Best to let a sleeping bitch lie, he thought.

Six years later, on the day that the police confiscated the car, Tuck had borrowed his wife's Pontiac and driven up to see his sister. She opened the back door of the big Colonial house on the lake, and invited him in.

He sat down at the kitchen table with her and her daughter and her boyfriend of some twenty years, Frank. It was her affair with Frank that drove out Stringy, her first husband, and alienated her two other children. She offered him some coffee, and he struggled through two hours of patter before Frank finally left.

"The State Police came to my office today," Tuck said, "and took dad's car. They took it down to a gas station in town and inspected it, and told me it was a stolen vehicle."

"Oh, God," she said, showing real concern, "what are they going to do?"

"They're going to charge me," he said, "I could go to jail. Have they contacted you?"

"No," she said, "I knew that damn car would get us in trouble. What should I do, if they call me?"

"Well," Tuck said, "If they contact you, just tell them the truth as we know it about the car."

"I can't do that," she said, "we know that car was stolen!"

"No we don't. Think about it. All we know is that story that dad told you," Tuck said, "about getting the car up in Newark from the docks, where he said he bought it from a guy he knew. And, we don't know if that that's a true story, either."

"But daddy said that Duby drove him up there to get it," she said, "and it was part of a whole fleet that was stolen."

"Well," Tuck said, "I happen to know that Duby didn't ever drive dad to Newark, so I don't believe that story. The truth is that we don't know where that car came from, or whether or not it was stolen. That's the real truth, and that's what you should tell them, if they call you." Duby was a cousin, and Tuck saw him once a month at a family gathering in Trenton.

"Are they going to charge me?" she asked.

"No," he said, "I don't think so, because they don't know that you kept the car here when dad was in and out of the hospitals. I told them he left it here, and I drove it down to my shop when he died, where I could leave it until I found out who owned it or I got papers for it. So just say you turned it over to me and I took it because I had a space to store it, Okay?"

"They can be intimidating," she said.

"Yes, they can," he said, "but, remember, we don't really know where that car came from. Can you honestly swear as to its origins? I can't, and I don't know if it was stolen, or bought or what. I'm getting a good lawyer, so I'm worried, but I think they'll let the whole thing drop when they realize that we didn't have anything to do with it."

She went on about the car and how "bad" "daddy" was. It never ceased to amaze Tuck how everyone else in the family thought he was some kind of Robin Hood. He left feeling that if they stuck to the story, which was the truth, everything would work out.

Tuck's lawyer listened to his story, and quickly turned the case over to a junior associate.

"You don't want to be paying my fees." he said, "If Joe can do everything I can, it would be a waste of money." Joe is a well-built, but small individual, and a graduate of the same College where Tuck got his degree in Mathematics and served on the Alumni Board of Directors.

"It seems pretty straight forward," he said, after listening to how the car came into Tuck's possession, "I don't understand why they're even wasting money on this. I'll know more after I talk to the prosecutor."

The following week, Tuck met with the lawyer again, and the news was not good.

"They're taking a hard line on this," he said, "and I can't get a lot of information out of them, but they intend to go the whole way, if they have to. Is there something you're not telling me?"

"No," Tuck said, I've told you everything. I've got nothing to hide."

"Listen, they're contending that you knew all along that the car was stolen from the first day."

"That's not true, Joe," Tuck said, "They probably think they've caught some mafia chief or something. I told you that my dad got convicted two or three times in Burlington County, once for Grand Larceny, Auto. It must be some of his old enemies figuring 'like father, like son'."

"That's unlikely, since most of these guys weren't around when your father lived in this area. I hate to keep harping on it, but did you know that car was stolen?" Joe asked.

"No," Tuck said, "I suspected that it was, that's why I went to all the trouble to check it out with the State Police, and when they gave it a clean bill of health, I figured it was just one of those cars the old man drove back to Florida; that he had just purchased. The only difference was that it was brand new. He usually didn't deal in new cars.

"Look, the car had Florida dealer tags on it, like most of the cars he had in those years leading up to his illness and death. Lots of times, he would look in the papers when he was up here, and if he got a deal on a Cadillac, he would buy it, take it back to Florida on dealer tags, and sell it. He did that all the time. And plenty of times he took those cars on consignment, without any papers, and then did the paperwork after he had sold them. I had no reason to suppose any of those cars were stolen. Plenty of times, he worked on them in my shop, cleaning them up and such."

"Did you change the VIN?" Joe asked.

"Hell, no," Tuck said, "but I suspected that he did, after I got the title."

"How's that?" Joe asked.

"Well," Tuck said, "the car had a few scratches and dings on it, because I had driven it a little before I got the title and after my car crapped out. I couldn't afford to buy a car, and it seemed stupid to let it sit.

"Anyway, after I got the title, I took it to the local dealer and told them to put it back in new condition, because even though I had title, the real owner might still come forth. I mean, we had never established where the car came from, and I figured it might be one of those deals where he still owed money, or something.

"So, the Service Manager, when I took it in, he looked at it and said, 'this is one of those bastard caddies.' I asked him what he meant and he said that the serial number wasn't right for the paint color or accessories, or something.

"I told him that my old man died and left me the car, and that the state had issued me a title, and he said, 'you got nothing to worry about, then.' "

"Well, I can't figure it," Joe said, "I mean; you're not exactly a criminal. They shouldn't even have written these charges up on you, they should have just confiscated the car and let it all go."

"I'm telling you, Joe," Tuck said, "My dad was a bad guy. He knew all those big mafia chiefs, from New York to Chicago; he ran illegal casinos for them. He did two stretches in the state Penitentiary and I don't know how many times he was convicted and given suspended sentences with parole. I've spent my life trying to live down his influence. These guys probably think that I'm connected with the mob, too. That's got to be it!"

The following Tuesday Tuck met Joe at the county courthouse and stood mute while accepting an indictment on three felony charges.

3

SAL

Tuck was your typical good hearted fellow. Growing up had been tough, and he often felt lucky that he was able to get to the age that he was. He didn't have a bone of snobbery in his body, and usually forgave anyone who did him wrong. Because he was reserved, people often mistook his attitude, thinking him judgmental and opinionated, but he wasn't. Tuck just never got over the fact that he was alive and participating in a life.

He was terribly shy, and often felt that he didn't deserve being in the company he kept. In truth, he found something admirable in just about everyone he knew, a failing in the business world, which demanded a more realistic approach. Even his new wife, Dotti, never realized how shy he was.

For Tuck, existence was a delicate and quite temporary, too precarious and unpredictable.

As a result he careened through life, reacting to his situations and circumstances instinctively, and finding the courage to display his persona as required, as expected. He was good at it, the acting out of other's expectations, and was observed by others to be quite a competent and interesting person.

His reaction to Sis was atypical, but she had been fueling a fire within Tuck for years, and finally he had enough of it. Not enough that he would actually confront her, but enough that he would simply avoid contact.

Tuck's father was another enigma for him. He knew little about his life until Tuck was in his late forties, and because of circumstances, "the old man," as he called him, began to show a little interest in his surviving youngest son. He lived in Florida, but frequently came to New Jersey for, among other things, treatment of the cancer which eventually killed him.

On these occasions, he would drive up to Tuck's home unannounced, or call him from the Philadelphia airport, asking for a ride; to Trenton, to his sister's house, or to Tuck's sister's house, where he often stayed.

Facing the reality of his cancer, he would sometimes have dinner with Tuck, and after dinner, sipping VO, share with him stories from his past. On more than one occasion, he remarked to Tuck that he, Tuck, should write these stories down, since they were unusual, to say the least. But Tuck was too shy to take him up on it. The last thing he would want to do is put Sal in an embarrassing situation by asking an inappropriate question.

Of course Tuck didn't know that his father had cancer. Sal would never tell him, and it was the kind of thing that Tuck wouldn't suspect. The old man moved around a lot, and his more frequent invasions into Tuck's world were accepted by Tuck as recognition that he, Tuck, wasn't so bad after all. Tuck took the visits as they came, never forcing or inquiring, but openly happy to see his father when he showed up.

During these episodes, Tuck was able to begin to collate the various adventures in his father's life. He had some general knowledge of some of these escapades, his father having shared with Tuck when they were driving out west together, and when something had occurred in Tuck's presence, when he was a youngster in Mt. Holly, or during the brief interlude Tuck spent with him in Phoenix, Arizona.

Tuck's father had known most of the big time gangsters of his era. Sam DeCalvacante, known as "The Count, or Sam the Plumber;" Sam "Momo" Giancana, who succeeded Accardo in Chicago; the Gambinos, Bonnanos and Colombos and Tommy Lucchese of New York; Angelo Bruno of Philadelphia; Santo Trafficante of Tampa and Atlantic City's "Knucky" Johnson were some that he mentioned to Tuck. Tuck realized later, in chronicling his father's past, that he must also have known the various bosses in Oklahoma City, Louisville and other large cities as well, although they were never mentioned to him. In researching Sal's past, Tuck came gradually to the belief that he must have been someone quite special in the mafia community because of the many different venues in which he plied his trade, and the ease with which he accessed these hot spots, assimilating into to a local "family" environment apparently without a hiccup.

Sal at age 23. He was a handsome and charming man and according to some, the "unofficial mayor of Mount Holly."

One of the first recollections Tuck had of his father brought to his mind hot sandy beaches of the New Jersey shore and encounters with jellyfish. All of his memories of those early days related to personal tragedies of one kind or another.

One of Tuck's particular memories related to a black and white photograph; one of those old brownie box camera square prints with serrated edges. It depicted Sal emerging from the front entrance of a tiny wooden beach bungalow somewhere at the New Jersey shore.

Not only had Tuck been overexposed to sun and sand on this occasion, but an encounter with the jellyfish had left blue welts on his already crimson legs. Visits to the shore were a necessity, however, part of his mother's ongoing natural cure for his various maladies, which included whooping cough and incredible attacks of poison oak and ivy in the summers.

Not that Tuck's father was there as part of the family at the beach. That was not it at all. In fact, Tuck couldn't recall seeing him on the beach, only briefly at night at the kitchen table.

It must have been about 1938 or '39, and Sal was there because he was running blanket games ("floating" craps games) in Seaside Park. Of course, Tuck learned this later, from his mother and others who each had a version of the story of Tuck's father, and over the years he pieced it together in the best way he could.

The Bath and Turf Club was probably the most unique illegal casino on the Jersey Coast. It was owned in partnership by the 'boss' of Atlantic City's illegal games, "Knucky" Johnson, who had recruited Tuck's dad in the early days of prohibition.[3] The additional partners were Charlie Schwarz, who was the Manager, and Meyer Lansky, the Jewish mobster. Entering the Bath and Turf, gamblers would pause in front of lobby mural, press a button which opened a disguised door, and traverse a bridge to an adjacent house, which contained the casino. The nearby 500 Café, razed by fire like much of the old city, is revered as the Club that launched the careers of Sinatra, Jerry Lewis and Dean Martin, and other big name show business personalities. Its casino was next door in the Garibaldi Club, a hotel that was popular with Italians.[4]

Only sixteen, Tuck's father was already loading booze for Johnson on the trucks that ran regularly from Gardner's Basin in the Atlantic City inlet to Trenton, Camden and the other cities in New Jersey, New York and Pennsylvania. Over the years, Tuck heard tales of how the rum runners would brave the Atlantic City inlet at night; offload their cargo to Johnson's trucks that would then stream inland on the narrow highways through the pines.[5]

In the fifties, when Tuck was attending high school, a national argument raged as to whether or not "organized" crime even existed. Estes Kefauver, heading a Senate Committee to investigate illegal gambling in America, unwittingly opened a Pandora's Box. Kefauver's Committee heard testimony in fourteen cities, and the information was overwhelming. In Miami, the "mob" controlled more than 100 hotels, and operated in most cities and towns across America, as well as some Caribbean countries.

Some cities, like Covington, Kentucky and Phenix City, Alabama, had become ruled by the gambling and prostitution racketeers. They were identified as sinkholes of depravity, overrun with illegal gambling and widespread prostitution; "Sin Cities." Nearly every major city in the nation was affected.

The problem was that local governments, mostly of the Democratic Party persuasion, were so intricately embedded in the illegal activities that politicians feared Kefauver's investigations would cause irreversible damage to the Party, as more and more evidence emerged linking local governments to the mob. The pattern was clear, local politicians on the take, allowing the gambling parlors and ancillary activities to operate.

Making matters worse, the radio coverage of the Crime Committee hearings became the most popular entertainment of the day as gangster after gangster appeared, denied all charges and invoked the Fifth Amendment privilege of immunity from self incrimination. It became apparent that young Senator Kefauver had opened a door to a huge criminal empire. Many Americans were purchasing their first TV sets at the time, and the hearings were boosting sales of the new technology.

A bitter political war ensued, which was somewhat dissipated by the McCarthy hearings, when the nation's interest was diverted from illegal gambling to the threat of communist infiltration in government and cinema. The revelation of the 1957 Appalachin meeting, a gathering of the bosses of the major crime families in Appalachin, New York that accidentally was stumbled upon by law enforcement officials finally brought the nation and the skeptics in line. Organized crime was for real. J. Edgar Hoover,[6] who for years had been assuring the public and several Presidents that Organized Crime was a myth, was totally wrong!

4

MT. HOLLY

Tuck's Grandfather on his dad's side, Giovanni, emigrated to the U.S. in 1883 from Villalba, tiny village in central Sicily. A cousin, Mario, is the last remnant of the family in the Country and the village that claimed birthright with Corleone, Sicily to much of the nightmare of modern America, the mafia.

Giovanni, Gaspara, two brothers and a sister immigrated from the old country in 1893 and 1905. The sister, Tuck learned from a cousin, eventually married an ancestor of Carlo Gambino, whose descendant eventually became the head of one of the five New York families.

Gaspara eventually settled down in southern New Jersey and his descendants established a thriving produce business in the breadbasket of the area, Hammonton. The two remaining brothers moved to New Orleans and established branches of the family in the south.

When Tuck's son, a Marine embassy guard in Rome, visited Villalba in the late 70's, he said, "It looks like the set from the Godfather movie. Everything is exactly as it was in that movie. Mario's family was just like the family of the young woman courted by Al Pacino. They were nice to me, but it was eerie."

Tuck never knew Grandfather Giovanni, as he died in the 1920's, but he was a baker, and ran a tiny, but successful shop on Roebling Avenue in the Chambersburg neighborhood of Trenton, "the Burg." When he first arrived in this country, he settled, like thousands of other Sicilian

Italians, in Brooklyn. He and his cousin Salvatore Frocione opened a bakery there.

For some reason Tuck never discovered, the families decided to come to Trenton, New Jersey, and the Frocione bakery was re-opened on Roebling Avenue, in the basement of the brick row home they rented. Granddad then sent for his cousin, Rosalina Frocione, to whom he had been pledged in marriage since the age of five, and they were married when she arrived in this country.

They moved back to Brooklyn once, but returned a few years later, and Trenton became the home of that branch of Tuck's family. Grandmom was a minuscule gray-haired matron in Tuck's early memory. She featured the large head and nose characteristic of the family, and sported several large hairs on her cheeks and upper lip.

The family name is not really Sicilian, and perhaps more Spanish than Italian. But there is a tiny town near Milan of their family name on a major river in northern Italy, a center to the European jewelry trade.

Tuck's Grandmom never mastered the English language, but nevertheless raised four boys and two girls in that deeply rooted ethnic neighborhood of one of New Jersey's most successful cities. She was intensely religious, and all of the trappings and rituals of Sicilian Catholicism were evident in her life and her home.

All of the boys, of which Tuck's father was the second oldest, attended mass every morning, learned to play musical instruments, took their turns as altar boys and did what was expected of them. All of them except Salvatore, Tuck's father.

Early on, he drifted away to the more exciting world of billiard halls, floating craps games and anything that he could learn to "hustle". Perhaps one of the reasons he didn't follow his brothers' paths to middle class blue collar Itlo-Armericana was his extraordinary dexterity.

Blessed with physical skills and intelligence, Sal was an exceptional game player. As a pool shooter, he gained a city wide reputation shortly after quitting school at the eighth grade. Eventually, he went on to shoot exhibition pool with the Willies; Hoppe and Mosconi, Minnesota Fats and other renowned hustlers of the day.[7] As a young man, he used his skill to make money.

His constant exposure to older men and the gambling environment of the billiard halls developed in him a maturity and social ease far greater than his years. He spoke little, but what he said was on point and never offensive. He exuded the style of a perfect gentleman and as much as his earnings would allow, dressed the part.

With a quick mind, he easily mastered the rules of craps, roulette, blackjack, poker and other games. Later in life, Tuck, a mathematician by training, envied his father's easy grasp of detailed statistical schemes related to gaming, and his complete familiarity with and instant recall of the changing odds of casino games.

Sal, and other friends from Trenton including Johnny F., frequented a resort on the Rancocas Creek called Kate's Island Store[8] and Canoe Retreat, near the town of Smithville, the home of the famous inventor and bicycle manufacturer, Ezekial Smith.

Saturday nights at Kate's featured a live orchestra in the screened in "ballroom," and refreshments, including illegal liquor, flowed freely. For the boys from Trenton, Kate's "Island Store" was a great place to meet the girls who lived with their families in the summer cottages and cabins clustered along the creek from Mount Holly to Pemberton. It also conveniently met all the requirements of a perfect spot for illegal gambling; hidden in a wooded area, accessible only by a dirt road leading to a single walking bridge, and near a populated area.

Kate's Island Store, on the Rancocas Creek near Smithville was accessible by land only by crossing the bridge from Kate's tract, private property near Shreve Street in Mount Holly. This photo was taken by Ev Turner, noted Mt. Holly photographer, from a small plane, the wing strut visible on the right side of the photo.

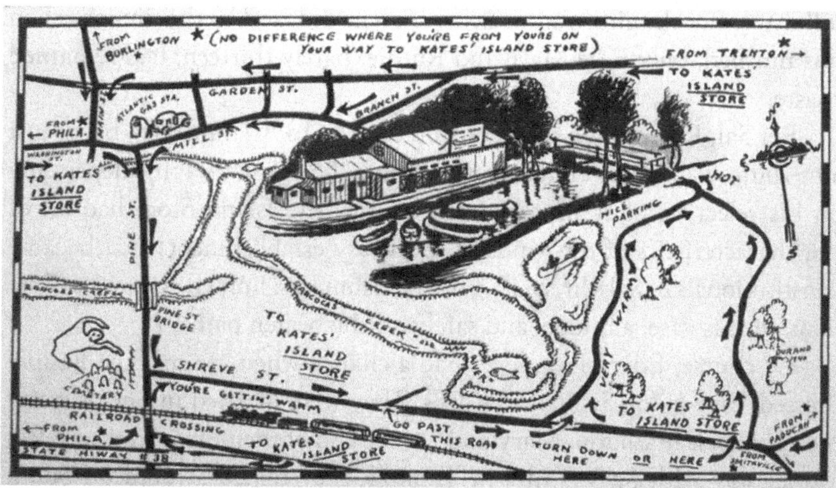

This postcard map was an advertising item to assist customers in finding the way to Kate's Island Store, which featured "refreshments" and live music during the summer months on Friday and Saturday evenings. According to Sal, floating craps games were also popular here, where he was arrested in May of 1947 by State Police. "Every one in two counties knew about the games at Kate's," according to Sal.

Among the few photographs of Tuck's mother is one that showed her perched atop a dock piling at Kate's, strumming a banjo ukulele and dressed in a light summer blouse and shorts. Unlike the other girls that frequented the Saturday night dances, Edie Maye was neither rich nor "well placed." It just so happened that a well-to-do friend of Tuck's Grandfather, Emma Marshall, took her in for the summers to work in her creek side home, and she, like the Marshall's daughters, became a summer regular at Kate's.

'Chip' Ellison, Tuck's Grandfather on his mother's side, was a cabinet maker of considerable skill, but left with the unenviable task of raising four daughters on his own when his wife Bessie, stricken with diabetes, died at the age of 37. Chip, well known to Emma Marshall because of the various furniture pieces he had built for her, was grateful to let the third youngest daughter, Edith Maye, earn her keep with the wealthy Marshalls on Sunset Lake.

Two of the four daughters almost immediately were compromised by local youth after Bessie had died. Chip had little control over the brood of ripe teen-age girls left to his care. He built a workshop behind the house and started taking in work part time, hoping to build a business so that he could be at home more than his job allowed and perhaps exert some influence. But the girls worked faster than he did, and by the time the shop was finished, only Edie Maye and Ruthie, barely thirteen, had remained chaste.

For Sal, Kate's was a frequent stop on trips to Atlantic City, being just a medium walk from Highway 39 (Route 206) or Mt. Holly, depending on his selection of transport, train or car. The Island Store had all of the characteristics of the kinds of speakeasy establishments that became constitutionals in Sal's life of illegal establishments: limited access, a private door, in this case, a bridge, and safely off the beaten path.

Of course, Edie Maye never had a chance when she met the flashily dressed, easy going Sicilian at Katz's. They were married in one of many motel chapels in Elkton, Maryland[9], at the end of their first summer. After a brief stay with Sal's family in Trenton, they rented a room on Spout Spring Avenue, at the edge of Mt. Holly, the first of more than 27 different residences that Tuck, his brother, sister and mother would be removed from over the next fifteen years as they became homeless squatters.

For Sal, those hovels and spare rooms were only stopovers in his adventurous life, places to shelve his cumbersome family, or storage for illegal gambling furniture and equipment. He chose his path in his teens, and the action was in Atlantic City and the South Jersey pinelands. Mt. Holly was a convenient way station.

In 1926 the roads of the "pines" were narrow, unlighted strips of concrete or hard sand winding through millions of acres scrub pine and oak. For Sal, one particular night was even darker than usual due to a heavy September rain, and because of the events that unfolded.

Sixteen-year-old Sal was riding in the passenger seat of the heavily loaded 1925 Reo stake body truck they had loaded with hundreds of cases of Canadian rum. The driver, one of Knucky Johnson's regulars, was a heavy set Italian man. In the middle of the cab was Johnny Frescetti, or "Johnny F.," as he was called in the Trenton billiard parlors where he and Sal had become close friends.

Sal felt a little uncomfortable, squeezed against the door. He had to move his legs to accommodate the door and window handles, and the rain blurred the windshield. There was only one windshield wiper, swinging frantically back and forth, suspended from the bulky vacuum motor mounted inside the cab on the driver's side. Sal was tired and had a sore knee; cracked on the gunwale of the fishing boat they had just unloaded at Atlantic City Inlet. His trousers, shoes and socks were soaked from wading in the inlet to unload the whiskey cases.

Squinting through the droplet covered side window, Sal could barely discern the grotesque shapes of the stunted pine tars and scrub oaks.

This would be a hell of a place to break down, Sal said rhetorically, thinking of all of the stories about the pines, the crazies that lived there, interbreeding, and the Leek's thirteenth child, which became the Jersey Devil,[10] a legendary winged giant that allegedly consumed unfortunate travelers into the vast pinelands.

The big REO thundered through the woods, its solid front axle bouncing them hard on the corduroy sand road. The door handles dug into his leg with every bounce. In another twenty minutes, they'd be on concrete, the driver remarked in Italian.

Sal was making five bucks for the trip. It was big money, and he knew it was an entree into the Atlantic City crowd, the boys who worked for Knucky Johnson. Johnny F had brought him down and introduced him around. Johnson just nodded when he was told his name.

"His aunt, she married Gambino," Johnny had said, and he was in. The flamboyant Johnson ran Atlantic City, but little was done without the acquiescence of the "boys" in New York. Johnson controlled all the illegal booze and operated the games in a half dozen carpet joints (clubs). His people controlled prostitution and ran the policy game, the numbers. He was a big deal.

But being a cousin by marriage to an in-law of a Gambino wasn't enough. Sal knew he had to show his stuff, to make good, if he was going to get anywhere. For a kid his age, he already had a pretty good reputation. By far, one of the best pool hustlers in the Trenton area, he had pretty much cleaned out the sucker action in the billiard halls of Burlington and Mercer Counties.

To his advantage, he was taken for twenty years or older. His heavy beard and quiet manner belied the fact that he was still a teen, and he never volunteered his age or spoke of it. His ability to be pleasant without revealing anything about himself was a major asset, and it didn't go without notice.

Johnny F had been after him for months to get in on the easy money with Johnson's outfit, but he'd resisted, knowing it meant hell to pay with his family. His brothers and sister were all well behaved, and he was usually in a pile of trouble when at home. Still, the family was not far removed from the old days in Villalba, where allegiance to a Godfather was a necessary and vital part of survival. His mom and dad said a lot of rosaries for him.

Thus far, the trip was working out pretty well. He had caught the Camden and Amboy morning train down to Camden, switched to the Atlantic City Railroad and made Atlantic City in four hours, where Johnny F met him at the station.

They had spent the afternoon in a billiards hall on Atlantic Avenue, sizing up the action, but not getting involved in any games. By ten o'clock, they had eaten on the boardwalk, and Johnny F had led him to a small beach in the inlet, near Gardner's Basin. Johnson and about eleven other guys were there, and they just sat in the trucks until Midnight, when the runner's boats nosed up to the beach.[11]

Theirs was the fifth and last truck loaded. The inlet was empty by 1:30 and the rumrunner had nosed out into the heavy current and disappeared, too. Johnson came over to the cab and Sal thought he overheard "Camden" in his conversation with the driver, and he figured that's where they were headed.

They were about thirty minutes out of Atlantic City when they hit the roadblock. Rounding a curve in the downpour, the headlights suddenly revealed two large sedans angled nose-to-nose across the road. Several dark figures could be seen silhouetted by their headlights. They were armed with shotguns and rifles. In the passenger side rear view mirror, Sal saw the lights of a following car appear and bear down on their truck. The truck ground to a halt, and they were ordered out of the cab by one of the hijackers with a heavy Neapolitan dialect. Standing in the pouring rain at the side of the road with hands in the air, they watched as a new driver entered the cab, the sedans were backed off the road, and the truck was driven up the road a few hundred yards.

"Fuckin' hijackers!" Johnny F had exclaimed when they stumbled out of the REO. Sal was scared.

The heavy-set hijacker waved the barrel of a twelve-gauge shotgun in Sal's face and told the three of them to line up at the road's edge. He hadn't ordered it, but all three of them had their arms in the air.

Sal was surprised when the hijacker produced a large pistol from under the driver's coat. Told by a companion to frisk the "two kids," the man confronting them responded, "These two little dagos are so scared they're gonna' crap their pants ... forget it. Let's get goin'."

Sal winced when he heard the racial slur. He knew that Johnny F had no tolerance for that stuff; that he couldn't hold his temper. Instinctively, Sal inched back toward the trees. He thought that if everyone stayed calm, they were just gonna' drive off and leave them. All they really wanted was the booze. The worse thing that was going to happen was that there'd be a long walk, and Knucky Johnson was going to be ticked off at losing a truckload of rum.

As the hijacker turned away, Johnny F. pulled a pistol from his belt, and screaming obscenities, fired wildly. Gunfire erupted all around, and Sal instinctively leaped backwards into the brush and scrub pine, and ran for his life. As he ran, he heard bullets whistling through the wet pine trees. He ran until winded, stumbling through the coarse tar pines and scrub oak, and when he didn't hear any more shots, or anyone coming after him, he crawled under some brush and just sat there, as quiet as the dripping boughs of pine. After a while, he heard the cars and the trucks start up and drive off.

Sal hid in the pines until dawn, when driven by hunger and a chilling cold, he braved the gravel road, walked to the highway and spent all day hitchhiking back to Trenton. The following day, he learned that Johnny F. had been killed.[12]

Two weeks later, Sal identified the hijacker who held the shotgun, pointing him out to Knucky Johnson. He was in a crowd at Johnson's Turf and Bath, and Sal's official status immediately took an upswing, and his education into to the intimacies of table games by Johnson's casino operators was begun.

By 1928, the depression was just around the corner. Tuck's sister, the oldest of the three children, was born in a Spout Spring Avenue boarding house, delivered like his brother four years later, by Mrs. Rossell, one of the town's numerous midwives. Before long they were in another house, now called the San Domingo mansion[13], a huge old brick house next to the town dump. Cholly, Tuck's older brother was born there.

Edie Maye' s life evolved about the trips with two babies in tow to Quigley's billiards hall down town, nearly a mile in bitter ice and snow of the cold South Jersey winters, to beg Sal for money for canned milk, or at least, some tea. He always had enough money to gamble, or to hustle a little pool.

The pickings for Sal were slim after the crash. Most men were out of work, but a few had pocket change and some pride, which was what Sal counted on. On the whole, there were a lot of families in as much trouble as Sal and Edie Maye, so that 'making do' wasn't a badge of dishonor. Unemployment was peaking at nearly 20 percent, and congress was flirting with social programs to supposedly supply some relief to the distraught population.

Sal was getting some work with Johnson and the boys in Atlantic City, but without moving there, it was sporadic. So many people were out of work that Johnson easily grabbed his crews from Atlantic City, although he gave Sal work when he showed up. Soon he was working on the casino floor at The Bath and Turf Club, running money or performing other chores necessary to the smooth flow of casino action.

Tuck's brother was born in the San Domingo Mansion, in a room that Edie Maye had located after they were thrown out of the boarding house on Spout Spring Avenue. The large brick home was built by a William Richards in 1820, and is now listed as one of Mt. Holly's historic buildings. When Tuck was a boy, he remembered it empty and boarded up, adjacent to the town dump. Mrs. Rossell did the honors, delivering Cholly, Sal's second, on a cold October day in 1931.

The Richard's house was called the San Domingo mansion. It was a landmark, four stories of brick and mortar on the southeast edge of town overlooking the dump, St. Andrews Cemetery and Iron Works Hill.

Tuck joined the happy little group in the back room of a tiny house at 10 Brainard Street. It, like the San Domingo house, is now a historical site also, being only a few houses away from the state's oldest schoolhouse. The room in which he saw first light had a dirt floor, and young Doctor McDonald dragged him, unconscious, breathless and completely blue, into the world on March 11, 1935.

Tuck must have been one of Doc McDonald's first deliveries. Midwives had accounted for at least half of all New Jersey births when Sis was born, but when Tuck arrived, only about 12 percent of births were attributed to midwifery. Edie Maye must have somehow scraped together enough money to pay the youthful and handsome six foot four inch Doctor.

By the time he was seven, they had lived in a half dozen of the worst hovels in town, but Tuck was seeing enough of his father during his occasional visits to at least know who he was. Of course, children never make the connections, and Sal's flashy cars and nice clothes didn't seem to Tuck to be in juxtaposition with his family's poverty-ridden lifestyle.

5

THE TAILOR SHOP

THE various houses that the family lived in around the town were Tuck's time references of those early days. Tuck could recall Sal living in only one of them, the White Street Creek house, which was near the main business intersection of town.

Tuck found that his memory was sometimes clouded regarding these various houses, a mixture of water-filled cellars, cracked plaster walls, rooms that he couldn't exactly match to a particular house. While some of these locations were clear pictures in his mind, others were confused by their desperate lives in them.

The Pennsylvania & Reading Railroad was an integral part of the life of most towns in South Jersey. Rolling out of the main yards in Philadelphia, it crossed the Delaware River in Camden and followed a nearly straight line due east toward the sea through the New Jersey pinelands.[14]

Pennsylvania Railroad also operated the ferries that plied the Delaware between Camden and Philadelphia. The fleet, at one time, numbered more that 60 large ferry boats, and enjoyed considerable passenger trade. The Ben Franklin Bridge, opened in 1929, was the death knell for the ferry operation which dwindled each year until its demise in 1952.

Camden City's demise also could be correlated to the improved access to Philadelphia in the 50's. Ben Franklin was followed by the Walt Whitman Bridge in 1957, only two miles downstream, and a decade later, the Betsy Ross and Commodore Barry Bridges, serving the areas north and south of central Philadelphia.

Tuck remembered Camden as a thriving city when he was a teenager. Thousands of workers commuted there to work at RCA, New York Shipbuilding, Campbell Soup, Whitman Chocolates, Hollingshead Wax and hundreds of other prosperous businesses. The city was serviced by two railroads and hundreds of buses provided transit to the South Jersey peninsula. The Pennsylvania and Reading Railroad serviced most of South Jersey and the Rancocas Valley as well. Every town had evolved around its rail station; Moorestown, Mt. Holly, Pemberton, Wrightstown, which serviced Fort Dix, and New Egypt. Even tiny Chatsworth was a stop for the local.

The Pennsy line intersected the Tuckerton Railroad and the Jersey Central deep in the pines in Whiting and then proceeded on to Tuckerton. A roundhouse there turned the trains around after disgorging their passengers and turned them over to the other carriers, including the famous Blue Comet[15], which connected Atlantic City with Jersey City. Most of the shore area was accessible by rail with Philadelphia and Trenton. Many of these places were reachable by autos only on dirt roads, so these rail lines were a key element in the growth of the area. Seaside, Asbury Park, Ocean and Atlantic City and Cape May, all with large resort hotels, were all easily accessible by train.

In the early 1700's, Somers Point was a bustling port in Egg Harbor, sheltered by coastal islands and accessible by a shallow inlet, was nevertheless a major anchorage for passengers and cargo destined for Philadelphia or Burlington, sixty miles west.[16] The tides and currents of the Delaware made the river passage in a sailing ship a long and tedious tacking and towing drill for captains and crews. The Egg Harbor Road Stage Line which ran west through the pines could deposit passengers in Camden or Burlington, the bustling capitol city of the South Jersey region, where they could ferry across the Delaware to William Penn's city, the entire trip doable in a few days.

The stage lines meandered on the Manahawkin Trail and Tuckerton Stage Road through the Lenni-Lenepe settlement at Indian Mills, with lodging and stops at Harrisville, Batsto, Medford, Mt. Holly, Bordentown and other towns. In the early days of colonization, the Pinelands flourished as a center for the production of "bog" iron and glass. These industrial centers were serviced by the stage routes, which eventually became the lines of the PRR and Jersey Central railroads, or highways.

The scrub oak and stunted pine of the Pine Barrens, more than a million acres of the southern part of the state, only give way to hardwood and larger growth where a river or creek is present. In 1605 Henry Hudson sailed into the shallow bay rimmed by dense forests and loamy soil and inhabited small tribes of natives and multitudes of wildlife. The areas surrounding tributaries of the Delaware became the settlements; Salem, Hammonton, Browns Mills, Lakehurst, Medford and Mt. Holly. Traveling due west from the ocean, these were among the first areas encountered that were really rich in immense hardwood trees, fertile farmland and an abundance of fresh water.[17]

The Rancocas Creek winds through several towns, but in Mt. Holly, the creek is wider and deeper, and it creates islands. From Mt. Holly, the creek was navigable by large barges to the Delaware and thus, the Philadelphia market. With all of these natural advantages, the town became a Quaker settlement, originally inhabited by lottery draw by Quakers from nearby Burlington. With its ample hardwood forests, fresh water fishing, tillable soil and central location, it must have been a major Indian site as well.

Early settlers in New Jersey experienced few problems with the Nanticoke Lenni-Lenepe peoples. Lenni-Lenepe, translates to "grandfathers" or "common people," and they, like many Native Americans erroneously were named "Delawares" by early explorers. They were a loose confederation of peaceful and friendly bands, and are considered by historians to be the ancestors of all Native Americans of the region. Much of the Indian land settled in New Jersey was purchased, paid for in some part with lottery money. When the two remnants of the tribes left the settlements in Burlington and Indian Mills for resettlement to New York, the tribal leadership published a statement commending the fairness of the State in purchasing their lands from them.

A nobleman, De La Warre, allegedly visited the fertile bay and river in the late 1600's and the unfortunate natives there were stuck with his name. De La Warre had come to Jamestown and heard of the large and beautiful bay to the north. At the time, the largest settlements were on the "Virginia," or south side of the Delaware, principally in the areas between New Castle and Lewes, Delaware.

It is thought that Rantkote, the leader of a band that hunted and fished the wetlands and forests bordering the Rancocas river, was the namesake for that tributary, but the Lenni-Lenape called it "Ancocas," having no words in their language that begin with "R". The influx of English and Quaker settlers wrested control of the valley from the Dutch and Swedes, whose trading for fur and skins had already seriously decimated the wildlife populations on both sides of the river, a daunting task accomplished largely by trading trinkets and grog for pelts.

The Quakers who settled Mount Holly created a community of small farms, producing a variety of crops; tomatoes, potatoes, peppers, squash and nearly every variety of vegetable, all of which took exceedingly well to the fertile soil. Further out, where the soil became more sand than loam, the blueberry farms flourished in later years, and deep in the pinelands, in the swampy bogs, cranberries were cultivated and blueberries invented.[18]

By 1930, Mt. Holly was a growing town. It was the county Seat, the site of the county courthouse and Jail, and had several large manufacturing companies that shipped their products to market on the Rancocas or the Pennsylvania and Reading Railroad. Ancocas Mills, a large textile mill dominated the west end of town, and there were other manufacturing companies spotted haphazardly throughout, including the area's major manufacturer of ice, Hollyford Ice and Coal Company. Two banks and a good library, as well as Mt. Holly High School, which eventually drew students from the entire region, as far away as Indian Mills, Chatsworth and Ong's Hat made it a bustling center of commerce and business. At the west end of town, a fairground with grandstand and a mile track, featuring trotters and pacer horse and auto races.

One of the places Tuck lived was only a few hundred yards from the PRR trestle near its main station. The "Station Trestle," as it was called, had a reputation for local "winos" careening from its beams into the creek below, attempting to navigate it while under the influence. Chip Ellison, Tuck's Granddad, did "a couple of headers there ..." one resulting in a broken leg.

A siding from the main track brought freight cars into the GLF, which was immediately across the back yard fence of one of Tuck's houses, only a few hundred yards from the trestle. The front of that house faced Bispham Street; the back door opened to the PRR's grain collection facility. Called the "GLF" by locals, its long barn featured grain conveyers and two large silos at the far end of the building, which exuded the fragrant aroma of fresh com and oats.

It was from the apex of this building that Tuck's brother, Cholly, about seven at the time, attempted a jump with a homemade parachute. His leg was broken in two places. These houses were very close to the demarcation line between Mt. Holly's white and black population. Their back yards shared with GLF the other bank of the creek from Mrs. Shoupe's chicken yard and the barn that housed her milk cow, Elsie. Once Mill Street crossed Madison Avenue, it became Washington Street, but was called "Sand Hill" or "Nigger Hill," in the insensitive vernacular of the day.

Mt. Holly, like most of its surrounding towns, was immersed in the racist culture of 1930's America. While lynching was still an occurrence of the South, Mt. Holly's cultural bias was only evident in the arrest record of the town's Police. Hardly a week passed without the misdeeds of several "Negroes" reported on the front page of the town's weekly newspaper. The Negro population had its own grammar school, although black people were tolerated in the town's stores, restaurants and other businesses. "Nigger Hill" not only duplicated many of the necessary businesses that the black population required, but also featured its own black night club, called of course, Cotton Club.[19]

It was a statement of the social pecking order to note that one of the town's two Catholic Churches was also located just across the line in "Nigger Hill". Tuck remembers only a few black students in high school, perhaps 10 in a white population of nearly 800. The Catholics numbered about twice that. Italian Americans were also few in number, and obviously the prejudices of the day were directed towards the "Guineas" also.

Tuck's one additional glaring memory of the GLF house was the night that, in Uncle John's car, with his Aunt Flossie, Edie Maye, his brother and sister; all rode out to the Fairgrounds at the west end of town. There, parked on the side of the highway, they watched in fascination as the Klu Klux Klan held a rally, complete with the burning of three very large crosses. There were more than thirty thousand white robed clansmen in attendance.

Tuck couldn't remember Sal ever being at either of two GLF houses they spent short residences in. He surmises that Edie Maye was drawing a lot of support from Aunt Floss, her younger sister. She had a daughter, Jeannie, almost exactly the same age as Tuck's sister. When they moved on from that house, life became rather difficult, or at least Tuck's perception had grown to the point where he was beginning to understand how desperate they were.

Tuck seldom made a point to friends and acquaintances of his early childhood. He realized early on how fashionable it was for people to describe their childhood poverty. He grew up in late thirties, amid the great depression. He concluded that only those who lived it can really appreciate it. There was no social structure to support people without incomes; no welfare, no food stamps, nothing except the charity of friends and neighbors. Times were tough.[20]

And the depression didn't end with Roosevelt's election in 1932. In fact, it never ended; it was merely supplanted by the Country's gearing up in 1939 to provide assistance to Britain and Russia, and by the eventual entry into the War in 1941.

Hoboes were common. Living in the least desirable parts of town, near the tracks, they were an acceptable part of Tuck's life. Even in their condition, Edie Maye made it a point to never refuse a hobo food of some kind. Often it was only a cup of soup or coffee, but she never turned one away hungry that had asked for food.[21]

The "Bo's," as Tuck came to call them, congregated near the railroad yards and tracks. There were several sites, back in the woods, that they used constantly, and some lean-to shelters had been erected there, as well as a large rock lined fire pit. For the most part they were white men, depressed but not really old, and usually polite and pridefully ragged.

Along Madison Avenue or Pine Street during the evening, one could see their campfires down in the woods, and smell the smoke from a nearly permanent "Hooverville," east of the railroad trestle and next to the creek.

The town also had its incumbent population of homeless, largely the town drunks, a corps of ragged and bent beggars whom everyone knew by name and reputation. They purchased their cheap wine at the Arcade Bar & Grille, slept in alleys and abandoned barns, and were as much a part of the town's trappings as it historic Friend's Meeting House and 200 year-old prison.

Many townsfolk went out of their way to provide these unfortunates with small jobs, paid for in food. When Tuck was seven, he discovered one of them, Old Bill Clancy, lying dead in the pasture between Cherry Street and Mt. Holly Avenue, early one winter morning. Old Bill was covered with a half-inch dusting of morning snow, curled into a fetal position and frozen solid. He looked to Tuck like he was sleeping. Tuck tried to shake him awake, but Old Bill's rigor and frozen snow rendered him unshakeable.

Tuck ran home with the news of his discovery, and Cholly had ridden his bike downtown and told Policeman Bucky Squires that, "Bill Clancy froze solid, in the pasture ..."

Later in life, Tuck learned from his Uncle John that during this period, when Edie Maye dragged her family from hovel to hovel, that Sal lived in Burlington, in one of his 18 apartments and rooms he rented around town. Although Edie Maye never had a phone until Tuck's brother came home from the Navy in 1953, Sal had phones in all of these places.

6

ELSIE, THE MILK COW

For more than a year Edie Maye and the children lived in the second floor and back room of a store front on Mill Street next to the south branch of the Rancocas. This was a creek house, and Tuck remembered it as Mrs. Shoupe's place. Tuck, just past being a toddler, decided that his new mobility required freedom, and began to wander away at nearly every opportunity. The store front was used by Sal and his younger brother, Santo, for a tailor shop and dry cleaning business. They even had a 1932 Ford panel truck with the family name painted on the side by "Peanuts" Rossell, the town's brilliant, but alcoholic sign painter.[22] Of course, Edie Maye did all the work. This exacerbated the problem with Tuck because Edie Maye had to tend the store when neither of the men were there, which was most of the time.

Tuck called this stopover in their gypsy existence Mrs. Shoupe's because she owned the newsstand nearby, away from the creek, separated from Tuck's building by Mr. Byer's Lock Shop and a dirt alley. At the end of the alley Masie Shoupe had a small barn which housed her milk cow, Elsie, and a large run which contained several dozen chickens. In the back; a vegetable garden. Only a short block from the Pennsylvania railroad station and yards, the station could be accessed through Mrs. Shoupe's yard, which was bordered by the creek.

Masie Shoupe had two sons. The older, Bucky was huge and as far as Tuck could ascertain from Mrs. Shoupe's conversations, fairly worthless to the stout farm lady and businesswoman. The younger, Maynard, helped her out in the store, but had his drawbacks, too.

"He can make change, but don't have the common sense that God gave a goose," Masie said, when discussing her younger son. Masie was a successful widow, having sold their farm in Buddtown and moving into Mt. Holly. Mr. Shoupe died after opening the news shop and creating a successful business. In addition to papers and magazines, Shoupe's sold rifles, shotguns and ammunition.

Having suffered a burglary at the store, Maynard responded to his Mother's concerns by rigging a shotgun to the ceiling connected by a piece of twine that looped through the store and was tied to the front door. Customers were somewhat intimidated by the overhead vision of both barrels of a 10 gauge staring them in the face when they entered. The little brass bell mounted on the door frame drew their attention to it, mounted on the ceiling and pointing directly at the door.

Maynard forgot one night that he had set his "burglar alarm," and opened the front door from inside. The resultant explosion blew off his hunting cap, punched an oval opening in the lower door panel and flattened the front tire of Mr. Byer's Model A truck parked at the curb.

To make matters worse, the recoil knocked the long barreled shotgun from its moorings. Maynard had pancaked on the floor immediately when he realized the gun was going off, and as he stood up the heavy gun dropped barrel first on his head and knocked him cold.

Masie responded to the blast and ran to the front door of the shop. Seeing Maynard unconscious, she assumed he had been shot and swooned next to him.

A crowd soon congregated in the news shop, including Edie Maye, Tuck and his siblings and Mr. Byers, and circled the prostrate forms on the floor. No one wanted to investigate, fearing they had both been done in by the burglar alarm.

Everyone breathed a sigh of relief when they stirred and finally got themselves erect. Masie brushed herself off and turned to her son, who as yet hadn't uttered a word of explanation.

"Now that I see that you ain't dead, I suppose I ought to thank the good Lord for my luck," she said, chuckling while hugging the boy tightly, "If you ain't a splinter off your dumb Pa's log, I'll be last in the pew."

The incident became part of the town's legend, which pleased Masie, because her business increased as a result. She had so many questions about it that she had Maynard remount the shotgun to its perch, but never allowed it to be loaded. Nevertheless, they experienced no more burglaries.

Tuck continued to utilize every ounce of determination and guile to continue his runaways. He never really went far, and was usually found along the creek or up at the railroad yard, wandering along the tracks. It was a serious enough problem that Edie Maye took to tying him to the front porch with a rope, like a dog.

Tuck, age 3 contemplates an escape from Sis (in background) near the GLF siding and behind the Tailor Shop. His constant wanderings caused Edie May to tie him "like a dog" to the front porch.

Edie Maye was desperately trying to find means to protect Tuck from himself. In the spring, he had wandered out the back door, down the alley and right into a baseball game. Maynard Shoupe never saw the boy as he walked into the locus of a lazy swing of the bat.

Tuck, bleeding from the nose and one ear, was unconscious for several hours. For the next several weeks, he was quite subdued, but by summer's end Edie Maye had her hands full again, and began tying him to the front porch.

Tuck found the experience humiliating, and would sit with head in hands, elbows on knees on the front step and cry for most of the time he was lashed there. He hoped that he could appeal to the sympathy of passersby, who might untie him, but everyone knew of his escapades and the tears went unfulfilled.

His self pity was interrupted one day by Tom Farley, a tin drummer. Tom was one of the frequent horse and wagon salesmen that worked towns in those days, and on this particular occasion he was abusing his horse in the street in front of the tailor shop.

This was a common occurrence, and nearly everyone agreed that something ought to be done about the way Tom treated the old mare. Having to pull Tom's heavy wagon with wooden wheels and iron rims, stuffed full of pots, pans, tools and every conceivable kind of merchandise was bad enough. It was obvious that the man probably never fed her.

Edie Maye emerged from the house in a rage and began hitting Tom with a broom she had brought with her. In her entire life, Edie Maye never scaled more than 90 pounds.

In fact, Edie Maye had purchased the broom from Tom only the week before.

"That man has the personality of a post," she told Masie, "and I'm sick of the way he treats that poor horse."

Her assault was so sudden that Tom, confused and frightened, dropped to his knees next to the wagon and covered his head with his hands. Edie Maye continued whacking him about the head with the broom and then stepped back and lectured him about the way he treated the horse, one hand on her hip while using the broom to accent her diatribe.

A crowd soon assembled and began adding commentary to Edie Maye's lecture. Still incensed, Edie Maye punctuated several expletives with additional swats to Tom's shoulders.

Eventually, two policemen showed up and led the wagon away, the drummer firmly in their grasp, after telling Edie Maye that she couldn't just "beat the hell out of old Tom because he mistreats his horse."[23]

But Edie Maye took her causes in support of any underdog to the extreme. When she befriended a woman named Muriel who lived in a room over Mr. Byer's lock shop, Tuck heard Aunt Flossie call her "nuts," and "stupid." Muriel was a known whore and dying of syphilis, incurable at the time. It would be another 12 years before the miracle of Penicillin would become an effective treatment for this widespread and problematic disease.

Mrs. Shoupe called for Tuck every morning, as it was his chore to accompany her down the alley. While she milked Elsie, Tuck fed the chickens, splattering grain from a tin bucket onto their excited backs. He then helped to gather eggs, and occasionally, Mrs. Shoupe let him help her milk Elsie.

Even when the weather turned cold, Mrs. Shoupe insisted on Tuck helping.

"This rapscallion needs things to do, Edie, and you don't need to pamper him. Cold air never foundered a growin' colt." So Tuck, bundled in an oversize hand me down coat with a big belt about his waist, excitedly toddled after.

Bucket of grain in hand, Tuck attempted to squeeze between the four foot wire fence and the side of the bam, while this narrow corridor was occupied by Elsie. She was a gentle old beast, but as he slid by, Tuck inadvertently hooked the big belt on her horn. Elsie, namesake of the famous Borden's Milk cow, responded with a head shake that sent Tuck soaring cleanly over the fence and into the Rancocas creek.

Fortunately for Tuck, Masie Shoupe caught the sight of the arcing brown coat in her peripheral vision. She blinked twice, wondering if she had really seen the spread-eagled boy with grain bucket still in hand soaring towards the creek. In her late fifties at the time, she scaled the wire fence, and balanced on the stones at the creek's edge, hauled Tuck to safety.

Life at Mrs. Shoupe's was one series of adventures after another. Playing with the trains was one of them. Tuck often placed crossed pins on the track and returned them proudly to Edie Maye as "a pair of scissors" after the Chatsworth local had smashed them flat.

Tuck's biggest thrill, however, was to scramble up the bank as the train bore down on the trestle and to squeeze between the beams at rail height. The trains, being steam locomotives, roared over his bent head dripping water, spouting steam, and blowing smoke and cinders. The trestle shook and swayed as the train wheels, only inches away, clanged against the steel rails. The noise was thunderous. This was the first of what Tuck recollected as 'death wish' episodes. As he grew older, he found himself in many such situations.

Playing alone one day in an open boxcar, half filled at one end with sacks of corn grain, Tuck was startled by the sounds of two men entering the car. He was out of view, behind the stacked sacks.

Tuck scrambled to a position where he could see them when he heard their angry voices. Dressed in the ragged hobo fashion, they shouted obscenities at each other and began fighting. They were young men, not more than thirty, Tuck estimated, in looking back on it.

Suddenly, one man brandished a large hunting knife and plunged it, on an upward swing, into the other's stomach. The stricken hobo dropped to his knees and grasped the other man's waist. They seemed suspended in that position for a long time; then the knife was withdrawn, and while the victim stared in Tuck's direction in disbelief, his attacker calmly walked behind him and pulling his head back, slit his throat with a deliberate crossing motion.

Tuck was frozen in time by the scene in front of him, riveted by the stare of the dying man. It seemed to the boy that the dead man had been looking directly at him when his life's blood pulsed from the severed artery and puddled across the dusty floor of the boxcar.

He had seen Buck Shoupe do a similar thing to chickens, tying them by their feet, hanging them from a low limb in the alley and chopping off their heads. The blood puddled into the sandy gravel as the chicken did a fluttering dance while swinging to and fro.

Tuck slid down the grain bags and huddled in the dark comer of the boxcar, terrified. He could hear the noise of the body being dragged, and grain sacks being moved. With a great deal of effort, Tuck pulled and tugged at a sack until it nearly covered him.

He stayed in the boxcar, under the corn sack, for a long time after the attacker had hidden the body and jumped out of the open door of the car. It was dark when he emerged and returned home to a frantic Edie Maye.

Edie Maye could see that this time, the boy may have bitten off more than he could chew, and she spared him the customary whipping. He was covered with corn dust and had been crying copiously, the tears having left ample evidence on the boy's dirty face. Tuck was strangely mute, and Edie Maye wondered if he had been abused in some way, but he offered no clue and on inspection, everything seemed normal. She cleaned him up and fed him and was surprised when he asked if he could sit on the back step.

For the next several days, Tuck was very quiet and sat on the back porch staring toward the rail yards, and the boxcar. Then a tender pushed it down the siding to the GLF where it was completely filled with sacks of grain, and the next day when Tuck looked for it, it had disappeared with its grisly cargo.

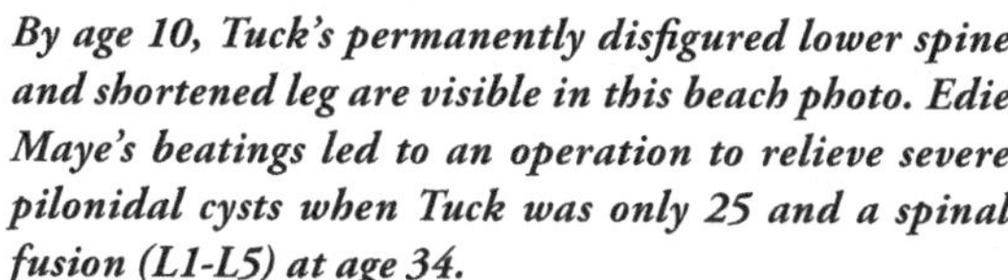

By age 10, Tuck's permanently disfigured lower spine and shortened leg are visible in this beach photo. Edie Maye's beatings led to an operation to relieve severe pilonidal cysts when Tuck was only 25 and a spinal fusion (L1-L5) at age 34.

Edie Maye, concerned because he wasn't sleeping well, and because of the unexpected swing in behavior, probed the boy with questions about what had happened, and then threatened him with whipping, but Tuck had already decided that any amount of whippings weren't worth it. He would never tell anyone about what had happened; what he had seen, but for a while, he stopped running away.

Santo, Sal's younger brother, was a partner in the tailor shop and dry cleaning business. This was mostly due to the fact that he owned a steam press. For the most part, Sal tolerated him and gave him all of the hardest jobs. Of course, only Santo could run the steam press, since he feared someone else might break it. Edie Maye found this ridiculous, since he introduced extra creases in everything he pressed, and she often redid his work after he had left each evening.

Santo was a small individual and had a penchant for generally screwing up anything he was involved in. When confronted with the results of his incompetence, he would smile and say, "Gee, did I do that? I don't understand how I could have done that, do you?"

Edie Maye didn't much like having Santo around the shop. It wasn't that she didn't think he was pleasant enough, and he was a good tailor; he was that. Santo worshiped his older brother, so anything that happened at the shop was relayed immediately to Sal. It also irritated Edie Maye that they spoke together in Italian, which she didn't understand and considered a peasant language.

After Bessie had died, Edie Maye had found herself pretty much adrift. Chip, her father, was deeply affected by Bessie's death, and he literally turned his back on the brood of girls left in his care. He seldom spoke to them, and gave up questioning their activities. He simply couldn't be home all day and hold down a full time job, too.

Although Hazel was the eldest daughter, it was Edie Maye that took over the household affairs. She was terribly saddened by her mother's death. It wasn't fair that she should be gone; Bessie being only 37. But Edie Maye soon learned that running the house without the cooperation of her sisters was nearly impossible.

When Mrs. Marshall came by and asked her to help with the chores at Sunset Lake for the summer, she took her up on it, without even asking Chip. Then she met Sal. He was handsome and charming and a great dancer and she was in love with him before their first evening together had ended.

Edie Maye hadn't thought twice about his Sicilian background. She had no idea about the Italian culture and never gave it a thought. But she soon learned that Italian men had definite ideas about marital responsibility. They had eloped to Elkton, Md., and Sal had taken Edie Maye back to Trenton to live with his parents. Within two days, he had disappeared for the better part of two weeks without explanation. When Edie Maye mentioned this, she received a scathing rebuke from Sal's mother and sister.

Sal's mother spoke to her family in Italian in Edie Maye's presence, and this infuriated her. She knew they were speaking about her, Sal's anglo wife, and she was certain by their sidelong glances that they disapproved of her. That she wasn't Italian could probably have been forgiven, but not being Catholic branded her forever as an outsider.

Bess Lawrence had taught her daughters that propriety and manners were everything. If one couldn't behave properly in the company of others, and make others feel comfortable, then life had little to offer. It was quite possible to state an opposing opinion without giving offense. To Edie Maye, the behavior of Sal's family was ignorant and peasant-like.

Soon the relationship reduced itself to suppressed hostility, and when Sal returned, Edie Maye began a relentless campaign to get away from them and all their strange customs and ignorant manners. Although Sal had none of the offensive mannerisms of his family, blood is thicker than water, and he recognized that the marriage may have been a mistake from his perspective.

But Sal had recognized early on that being Italian was a two-edged sword. He didn't think in terms of his ethnicity or of his family, but rather looked at the world as a place of opportunity in which either of these elements could help or hamper his advance. He loved his family, but thought that their dogged routine of work, morning mass and intense family loyalty to be petty, nonproductive and stifling.

His mother often talked about the old country, and as far as Sal was concerned, she had brought it with her. In his young life, he had branched out, met other people with varying viewpoints, had seen that there were seats of power; connections, influences to be had. There was action, and it couldn't be accessed from the family pew at St. Judes or in the Chambersburg bakery.

Edie Maye wouldn't dignify the family's behavior by verbalizing the problem. In her mind, that would be sinking to their level, and she was too proud for that. Sal had fallen in love with her not only because of her beauty, but he was taken by her innate dignity. She exuded pride and self confidence laced with sufficient femininity to make it non-threatening. In the end, he acquiesced to her pleas, realizing that the very reason that he had fallen in love with her made it as impossible for her to fit into the family circle as it had been for him.

The result had been their move to Mt. Holly, where he installed her in one rented, borrowed, or bartered room after another, returning only long enough to get her pregnant between gambling and business adventures, and move her out when their 'landlord' demanded. He resented how she felt about his family, but in fairness, he recognized why she felt the way she did. He had turned his back on all of that when he was fourteen and began to understand that the world was made up of more than Italians. Edie Maye felt it was the better of a bad bargain. She was hopelessly in love with Sal, but anything was better than the scorn of his family.

She loved Sal deeply and held the conviction that his intelligence and charm would eventually payoff. She didn't mind that he never considered working for someone else in a regular job. She could sense that he knew it would be a hopeless endeavor, to be accountable to someone else. So with each new venture like the dry cleaning store, she hoped for the best and dove in feet first, taking on as much as he allowed and sometimes more.

The day that the dry cleaning business took a downturn, Santo fell asleep at the wheel of the '32 Ford panel truck.

Somehow the truck traversed about a quarter mile of pinewoods, miraculously avoiding trees until it crashed into a stand of scrub oak and wedged itself between two trees slightly less far apart than the truck was wide.

Santo was jolted awake to find himself locked in the truck, no highway in sight. Since the back door lock had been broken, the brothers had mounted a hasp and lock which could be opened only from the outside. Both doors and windows blocked by the sturdy oak trees, Santo spent the better part of a day and a half sleeping in the truck until Sal found and retrieved him.

Although he had had hours in which to make up a story, no one believed that a steering rod had broken. It was the best that Santo could think of, but after that Edie Maye took to calling him "Leatherstockings."

"You can really find your way in the woods," She said. Santo took it good naturedly, but Sal didn't think it was funny. The truck was a total wreck.

Edie Maye worked day and night at the dry cleaning and mending that the store brought. Judging from Sal's activities in later businesses, she must have given all the money to him, which he probably used for gambling. In any case, after the loss of the truck, the dry cleaning store was a failure, Sal disappeared again, and Edie Maye and her brood were forced out and moved on to worse housing.

7

THE COUNT OF KENILWORTH

EVEN if Sal only got occasional work from Knucky Johnson in Atlantic City, there were side benefits to hanging around his operation. Sal had noticed a flashy well-dressed young man whom he knew casually from the old Chambersburg neighborhood. Before long he was formally introduced to Simone "Sam" DeCalvacante, "the Count."[24] Sal knew him from his early days in the "burg" where he was one of the young men idolized by Sal and other youngsters on Roebling Avenue.

Sam was a rising star in what was to become The DeCavalcante Family, then a gang loosely operated by Stefano Badami. Nick DelMore, a Badami underboss, who had contacts with the Gambino family in New York, was Sam's uncle. In the 'burg,' DeCavalcante often surveyed the neighborhoods, asking residents if they in any way needed help. Many residents told tales of the young man's assistance, contributing to his almost legendary status, when he became boss of the family's operations.

When Sal mentioned offhandedly that the action in Mt. Holly was pretty slow, Sam suggested that they meet in Burlington, where he had a few things going, and could use some help.

"I've heard some good things about you," he said, "you know how to keep things quiet and you're a good hand." DeCavalcante was acting on advice from Enoch "Knucky" Johnson, who had recommended Sal as a "problem solver and quick learner."

In a matter of days, Sal was taking numbers bets for Sam and he soon was installed as his chief bookie for Burlington.

Sal ran his "policy" game from the first booth of the Burlington diner, diagonally across the street from the town's biggest Chevrolet dealer. He kept his books there, entertained and paid off customers and Police.[25] It was his office. Stefano Badami, through DeCalvacante, backed his action. Under Sam's tutelage, Sal expanded his operation to include booking the races running in states with legalized handicapping at horse and dog tracks.[26]

Sam DeCalvacante, from central Jersey, gained mafia recognition in 1955 when Stefano Badami was murdered, his successor and uncle, Nick DelMore died, and Sam became the leader of the family that would afterward carry his name. As one of the first targets of the Federal government's newly acquired skills with wire tapping; his phone was bugged for more than two years, while the FBI listened in to his every conversation. He was called "The Count" by his mob associates, as he claimed Italian royal ancestry. The "Plumber" moniker was attached to him by the FBI, since he owned and operated a successful legitimate business, "Kenilworth Heating and Air Conditioning." The two years of wiretapping being inadmissible in court (without warrants), the FBI released the transcripts in 1961, and Sam became a national figure because of some of his quotes. Complaining about bribed judges, he said, "Those guys just won't stay fixed!"

New Jersey was loosely controlled by the big New York families throughout prohibition and into the thirties by their avatars. Gaspare D'Amico in Newark and Stefano Badami in Elizabeth were the most powerful of the gangs operating in the north with ties to the New York families. In 1937, the Commission looked at the garden state and in an effort to stop assassinations and internal feuding, declared the combination of the Newark and Elizabeth families to be paramount, under Badami's control. But Badami was assassinated over a plate of linguine with clams in Vito's Clam Bar in Newark in 1955. He was followed by Phil Amori, who immediately looked for safer employ in his native Sicily, and finally by Nicholas Delmore, Sam's uncle, who represented the family at the Appalachin meeting in 1957.

When Joe Bonnano, head of one of the New York five families, was removed from the "Commission," DeCavalcante became liaison between Bonnano and the Mob's Board of Directors.[27]

During WWII, the "little" family was low key, maintaining a status quo that kept it out of the newspapers. DelMore's flashily dressed, handsome and intelligent nephew was noticed by all as an up and coming star. DeCavalcante strengthened his position in the family power structure throughout the 1950's and as the leadership changed hands, he patiently awaited his election as boss, which occurred in 1964. Further wiretaps during the 60's eventually led to DeCavalcante's arrest, conviction and incarceration in early 70's. Although his reign as Godfather was brief, DeCavalcante became known as an "old style" godfather and often is cited as the role model for Vito Corleone, the Mario Puzo character in the "Godfather" movie, and the head of the DeMeo family in the Sopranos TV Series.

During his tenure as underboss and Godfather, Sam expanded his New Jersey family and his leadership, skill and ambiance earned him a position as a member of the "Commission," the oversight body controlling Mafia operations in the United States. Later in life, Tuck learned from his Uncle John that during this period, when Edie Maye dragged her family from hovel to hovel, Sal lived in Burlington, in one of his 18 apartments and rooms he rented, supporting his "portable" horse parlor. Although Edie Maye only briefly had a phone until Tuck's brother came home from the Navy in 1953, Sal had phones in all of these places. When Tuck viewed 1973's blockbuster movie, "The Sting," he told his wife Dotti that it was Sal's story.

"Sal had a setup like that bookie parlor, only it was smaller and portable, with just one cashier's window and small chalkboard. He moved it around in Burlington and Riverside...they were hooked up with the Annenberg wire in a downtown business, and he told me he had 18 apartments, and said they moved the whole setup about every four to eight days. I saw it once when it was in Burlington, he took me over there and after we went to the bookie parlor, I sat in the Burlington diner with him, in the first booth next to the door...he said that was "his office."[28]

The Count was pleased with his new protégé, who had increased his business considerably. The kid had class, an easy manner with people and was a good organizer.

One area in which the Count had a problem was the numbers "book" in Bristol, the Pennsylvania town immediately across the Delaware River from Burlington. Something "fishy" was going on, but Sam couldn't tell what was happening. Sales were down, and something just didn't make sense. Could Sal take a ride over there and see if he could straighten it out?

"So, what did you do?" Tuck asked his father.

"Well," Sal said, "I packed some iron, because I knew about this guy. He was a wise guy, you know, one of those guys who never gives you a straight answer. I'd heard about him before, because other guys had tried to figure it out, to catch the guy, but they couldn't." Sal went on, "so I drive over there, this guy operates out of a barber shop, and I go in and get a trim, and I ask this guy if I can put some money on some numbers." Sal told Tuck this story from behind the wheel of a 1957 Cadillac convertible, hurtling across the New Mexico desert in the middle of the night.

"He don't know me, of course," Sal continued, "He thinks I'm some mark. So he says sure, and then he gives me this big sales pitch. And the guy was good, a real good salesman, and I let him talk me into a fifty dollar bet. He thought he had a real mark."

Sal told Tuck he had figured out his strategy in advance. It was the first time Tuck had ever heard Sal admit that he carried a gun, although he had seen him with guns many times. He continued with the story.

"So, I peel out the fifty, and he turns around to mark down his bet. See, Sam's got a system. All of those markers have to go back to Sam with the take, and this guy is really stupid, because he marks up $10. I had turned in the chair so I could see what he was doing in the mirror, so I see him make up this phony marker.

"That's how he's doing it," Sal said, "really stupid, because anybody with half a brain can see what he writes down. He writes down $5 on a $10 bet and keeps five for himself. If the player wins, he pays him on the ten, and he charges back on the five, cause that's what Sam thinks the bet is, but he's way ahead, cause you don't get that many winners, and he's gettin' it from both ends. But he marks up the difference on the stub, so's he won't forget if the bettor wins!

"So, I get up and he's brushing off my coat, and I open it up so he can see the shoulder holster. He sees it and he gets real nervous. I tell him who I am, that Sam the Count sent me, and I know what he's doing and it's going to stop or next time I come back, it's not going to be for a haircut!

"Now the guy's all apologies. He thinks Sam sent me over there to rub him out, so I don't tell him any different.

"He confesses he took some money, his mother's sick, and all kinds of bull shit like that. I don't want to hear it. Get the money and the stubs, I say, and he goes in the cabinet under the mirror and comes out with a bag of money. I grab his coat and tell him to shut up, because now he's crying and I haven't done anything to him, but he's sure I'm going to shoot him now that I've seen the money. He's got about $300 in this sack, so, I sit him down in his chair and tell him, don't make me come back. In all this conversation, I never touched the gun."

The "Count" was really grateful for this favor because sales in Bristol climbed right back to where they should have been, and from then on, he relied on Sal whenever he or his friends needed something straightened out.

Edie Maye, Tuck and his brother and sister were in the Creek house on White Street. The whole left side and rear of the house projected straight down and became the walled banks of the Rancocas creek. The Rancocas meanders all through town, and it was once called Bridge Town because of the many crossings of the two branches of the creek that joined there.

The one room Creek House, during the 1938 flood. Edie Maye and the children lived here for more than a year before this flood. The normal creek level was 12 feet below the street, which is covered by approximately two feet of water. Photo courtesy Mt. Holly Historical Society.

The house only had one room. A toilet, complete with water closet and chain, and a porcelain sink stood against the back wall. In the corner, an oaken icebox. There was no bathtub or hot water. Near the front door, the inevitable kerosene heater. The ceiling was open beams to a flat tarred roof that leaked.

The right wall of the Creek house was joined to a stable that ran perpendicular to it. Of course, they had the rats and roaches to deal with. Edie Maye said that Buddy Aiken's horses next door were better off than they were, in one of her weaker moments. The makeshift wall between the horse stalls and their living space was incomplete, wide boards with openings between. At one time in its dismal history, the one-room shack served as the town's Police Station.

Tuck remembers the Creek house because that was where he saw Sal punch Edie Maye. It was a hard punch, bloodying her nose and knocking her to the floor.

Sal had just returned from Burlington where he had been for several weeks.

"If you would just stay with something," Edie Maye said, "we wouldn't be living in this stable. It's terrible here, in case it's escaped your notice."

"I'm doin' the best I can, Edie. This will have to do for now," he said.

"But you never stay here," Edie Maye began to cry, "You don't see what it's like. We could have made it with the shop, the dry cleaners."

"We did the best we could. It wasn't in the cards, that's all," Sal was agitated by the directness of her comments.

"But if you had stayed with it, instead of letting Santo …" Edie Maye never finished the statement, knocked against the wall by his punch.

"Don't talk about my family," he said, picking up his jacket from a chair and walking out the door.

Tuck walked across the room and stood next to his mother. She had assumed a seated position, back to the wall and was holding her bleeding nose and crying. Tuck sat down next to her in the same position. Edie Maye put her arm around the boy's shoulder and drew him close. He grasped his nose and began to cry, too.

It was winter and soon Tuck's lungs filled and he was under attack by the whooping cough. A constant threat, it lurked in the background of Tuck's life, waiting to pounce. Edie Maye's remedy was a hot mustard plaster pack on the chest, scalding hot towels over a layer of black tar-like medicinal paste. She fed him a tonic that she heated on the stove, a thick licorice tasting cough medicine. Tuck hated the mustard packs, but was usually too weak to resist, and they did break up the congestion in his lungs.[29]

They weren't there long, in the Creek house. The next stop for Tuck was the Red Men's Hall. Edie Maye and her brood got to the Red Men's

Hall because Sal took a "fall". The Burlington operation was cooking along, but somehow the whole numbers game was jeopardized. Everyone, including Sal, got named in the indictments.

"I'm going away for a while," he told Edie Maye, "it's no big deal."

"But why you," Edie Maye asked, "everyone else got caught, too. Why does it have to be you?"

"That's the way it is, that's all," Sal was irritated by the questions, "I take the fall, that's the way it works this time. Don't ask no more questions about it."

"It's not fair," Edie Maye said, "what about us?"

Numbers writing was considered largely a benign recreation that pervaded every town in South Jersey.[30] Tuck knew the numbers writer in almost every neighborhood that he lived in when growing up. They made their rounds like the Postman, and in some cases, were the Postmen, and collected bets from nearly everyone, from one cent up to several dollars. The winning number appeared each day in the newspapers, the last three digits of the national debt, published on the financial page, or sometimes the combination of the numbers of three winning horses in three different races at a particular track.

Sal spent nine months in the New Jersey State Prison in Trenton, and was released three months short of the full term for "good behavior."

Edie Maye was mortified. She went out of the house only when necessary and when she saw someone on the street that she knew, she made a conscious effort to avoid meeting them, for fear they would ask about Sal. But everyone in town knew about him anyway, it had been in the paper. The few friends that she had sympathized with her plight, knowing Sal and realizing that she could only try to live through it.

Typically, she told the children that daddy had to go away on business. They were young enough to accept it, and if any of the two older children's peers brought it up, Tuck never noticed it. Sal was in out of their lives so much that they accepted Edie Maye's explanation without question.

But Edie Maye had been raised in a Christian home, and when her mother was alive, they attended church together and were respected members of the community. Within a few short years, she found her social position completely reversed, married to a convicted felon, living in the worst of conditions and trying to raise three small children without the slightest hope of an income.

She knew that he had somehow conspired in it, that there was a reason for him going, part of some kind of deal between others, and she resented that he wouldn't confide in her. He had left her with a small wad of bills, but even with her best efforts it soon ran out.

Sal was a free spirit, she knew practically no one else who lived as independent of responsibility as he. How could he give himself up to a jail cell, what kind of reward or incentive was worth the price he would pay?

Tuck could not think of another contemporary of his early years who had a relative in jail. Crime was not a street affair. In a sleepy little town like Mount Holly, even an arrest was front page news; a conviction and jail term were sensational.

Edie Maye's life, and the children's, as a result of Sal's "fall," immediately took on an entirely different direction. While a penny-ante gambler and numbers writer might be considered by local society to be somewhat of a character, an ex-convict was not. Although Sal never really lived at home for any extended period after the punching incident and the "fall," it was nevertheless sufficient to cast a cloud over their lives. He did the time, and they had to live with it.

Sal told Tuck that he was more concerned about his bookie operation in Burlington than spending time in jail, and the Count had told him, "Don't worry, we'll take care of you when you get out."

"That was the deal," Sal told Tuck, "I was protecting the Count by taking the rap, and he was going to take care of me when it was over. It was no big thing. Doing time wasn't that bad, and Sam had some influence up there, at the pen."

Sal served his sentence, but when he got out, Sam told him, "This guy, Jerry, whose been running your operation, he doesn't want to step down, and we owe this guy a big favor." But Sal didn't want to hear it. He was mad. He told Tuck,

"I was really mad as hell. I built that operation and this asshole won't step aside. And Sam, he doesn't want any trouble, but I did the time, and I was going to get it back. So, I go and get a shotgun, and I'm headed towards Burlington (from Trenton), and Sam the Count catches up to me over on Route 130 in Florence, and they pull me over.

"Now Sam is really mad, 'No guns,' he says, 'no killing. You'll screw up things for everybody.' So he calms me down and he takes the shotgun, and that night, he saved me from committing murder. But still, I want my operation back, so I say, look, what if I take this guy Jerry for all he's got, if I set up a sting; you got any problems with that? And Sam says no, because the horse book is getting hot, and the police are hitting the apartments, trying to shut it down.

"This guy Jerry, he doesn't know much about the wire side of it. We couldn't move the teletype around since that was in a business downtown. Normally, one of my guys would read the race results to the book over the phone. So your Uncle John and me, we set up a delay in the relay for the Annenberg wire. Joey Cocetti reads the wire in the office and holds it for two minutes. Normally he would read it directly on the phone to the book as it comes in. Joey used to read the wire for me, so he replaces Jerry's guy, who we offered a little incentive to be sick, so to speak, and the change is not noticed. So we interrupt the first race of the day and put his whole day on a two minute delay. He doesn't notice 'cause we also changed the big clock in the race room. Jeannie Rich, she goes into the book to lay the bets, play the horses on the races we've picked in advance.

"I'm sitting out in the street behind the wheel signaling the race results to Jeannie. She's on the second floor next to the window. We're getting the winners two minutes ahead of the wire on the telephone, thru walkie talkie radios. Johnny's an expert with these things, and he's in the back seat telling me who wins. I'm holding newspapers, two fingers, second race, signing to Jeannie like that, with my fingers. She's signaling back that she gets the message, and then she goes and places the bet. We took him for $14,000 on one Saturday afternoon, and he owes us another $12,000 and can't pay.

Midshipman Tuck with Jeanne Rich (left) and Mary, both former showgirls in Las Vegas. Mary's son, an idiot savant, assisted Sal in the "Baltimore Sting." See Chapter 43.

"You set this up in a couple of days?" Tuck was curious about how it all worked.

"No way," Sal said, "it took the better part of a month to put it all together. A lot of people were involved, and I had to coordinate it with the boss. He had to know everything, too."

"But how could you get the results before he did? Didn't he have a radio, too?"

"Sure, but those tracks didn't broadcast the races live. They telephoned the results to the central wire - Moe Annenberg's wire service - and then it got sent out from there, so there was already a delay. Get the picture? We did a dry run on it, a rehearsal, so we knew it would work.

"So, the next day I go in with Jeannie, because so far he's only dealing with Jeannie, and we take the $24,000, and I tell him, you're out of business, now. But he says no, Sam the Count will back him up, but he calls Sam, and Sam says 'You're out of business, we're even, we gave you a good operation and you screwed it up.' He still doesn't know we short wired him, or who we were.

"So, the Count is pleased with this, because the only reason he put Jerry in there was to settle an old debt, and that was taken care of. And that's how I got set up in the casino at Greentree Inn and Red Men's Hall, that's where the money came from."

8

CHIP

WHILE Sal was in jail, Edie Maye and the children were evicted from the Creek house, and they moved down Mill Street into a large building which contained the Red Men's Association Hall on its third floor. They had a second floor three room apartment at the front of the building, overlooking Mill Street. This was the first time that Chip, Edie Maye's dad, came to live with them, and his pension was the source of their affluence.

Twice while they lived here, the Rancocas overflowed its banks and flooded the town, an annual occurrence for several years. Tuck watched from the apartment window as people rowed boats up and down Mill Street. Had they stayed in the Creek house, their floor would have been under two feet of water.

The First New Jersey Volunteers, Camp Alger, Virginia. Tuck's grandfather, Chip Ellison, is thought to be the third trooper from the left. Unsanitary conditions resulted in outbreaks of malaria and dysentery. The unit never left Virginia, but had casualties due to illness and bad drinking water. Photo courtesy spanamwar.com

Tuck's Granddad, whom everyone in town called "Chip" because of his wood carving skills, had broken his leg. Having indulged in too much red wine, he fell from the Station trestle over the creek on his way home to his cabin workshop. He recuperated in the living room of Edie Maye's apartment with the cast leg supported by a kitchen chair.

"Oh, he falls off that trestle about once a week," Edie Maye explained, "but this time he landed on a rock." Edie Maye had to provide a spittoon because Chip chewed tobacco at the time. He later gave it up, switching to pipes that he made himself.

Chip was Scotch Irish and one of four brothers whose family had settled in Buddtown, near Pemberton, in the late 1700's. Tuck knew this because Chip was proud to claim that his Grandmother was a full blooded Indian, making Edie Maye one sixteenth Indian. Indian Mills, only 10 miles east, was the last site of the Lenni-Lenepe settlements purchased by the state, and the home of "Indian Ann," supposedly the last of the original tribe[31], who lived there and wove baskets until 1904.

Chip had worked for a carriage maker where they built heavy wagons, and that's where he learned his trade. Tuck's Grandmother, whom Chip married when she was sixteen, was a Lawrence, from the family which claims ancestry back to the original pilgrims. On her mother's side, she was related to the descendants of Alexander Hamilton. This was an important thing to Edie Maye, and she mentioned it often.

Chip was a town character. He counted doctors, policemen, lawyers and the half dozen town "winos" among his friends. A free spirit and blessed with a disability pension from service in the Spanish American war, he only worked when he felt like it, or the project challenged him.

His home was a tiny cabin in the woods about a mile from the town's center. It was off the beaten path, on a dirt road ambitiously called Randall Avenue, overlooking Iron Works Hill and the Pennsylvania Railroad's track to Chatsworth. He had added to the cabin probably one of the first house trailers ever conceived, a nifty little 20 footer, sheathed in metal and aerodynamically designed. He designed and built it sometime in the late 20's, long before they became popular.

When Tuck asked him why he never took the trailer anywhere, Chip responded by tapping out his pipe bowl on his heel.

"Why, it's too damned heavy, Pup. My old Ford wouldn't pull it more'n twenty miles an hour. Need a damn truck to move it, that's the problem."

"Well," Tuck rationalized, "it makes a good bedroom."

The cabin featured a cast iron, pot bellied stove directly in its center. Tuck spent many hours huddled in front of that stove with his Granddad and his wino friends, listening to their stories as they passed the bottle, excluding Tuck of course.

Many times when Tuck appeared at the door of Chip's house, the old man would break into tears as he introduced Tuck around to his friends.

"Edie Maye's son," he'd exclaim through the tears, "the youngest, and the only one who comes to see his old Granny."

Chip Ellison had been an Army dispatch rider in the Spanish American war, one of those figures on an elongated Indian motorcycle with leather aviator's helmet, long gloves up to his elbow and knee length laced leather boots. He loved motorcycles and there were frequently two or three, in various stages of disassembly, in the bushes at his place. He wasn't wounded, but crashed his bike and received severe damage to his groin. His Regiment, the 1st New Jersey Volunteers, was located in Camp Alger, Virginia, outside Washington, D.C. for the entire period of the war. Their swampy encampment was overrun by mosquitoes and epidemics of malaria and diphtheria claimed many lives.[32]

Chip had gained a reputation in the community because of his war experience and his easy grasp of new technologies. Talented with his hands, he understood machines and how they worked, and this didn't go without notice as the automobile became the favored form of transportation. He met the demure Bessie Lawrence at Church and fell hopelessly in love with her. Over her parent's objections, she married the dashing and talented motorcycle rider when she was merely sixteen.

He received a partial disability check from the government every month as a result of his war injury, although Tuck never heard any complaints about his disabilities. When he turned 75, the check automatically doubled in amount, and that gave Chip a chuckle.

"Those bastards never thought I'd make it," he said, "but I did, and now they gotta' pay me double." Chip's drinking started when his beautiful and young wife, Bess, died of diabetes. She was only 37 and he was crushed.

He knew he had been lucky to live through the war, surviving malaria and the motorcycle accident, and he philosophized that when Bessie died his luck had run out. He would never be even slightly interested in another woman. He had had the best that life could offer in Bess, and he was grateful for the time she was with him.

Chip never knew if it was good fortune or not that his family all lived long lives. When he passed on at age 79, his three older brothers were still working carpenters. Tuck met John, Chip's next older brother on the street one day and he said, "Sorry about your Grandpa, Son, but I told him that that wine would get him, sooner not later. It's his own damn fault, dying young like that."

John was 83 at the time.

"Tell me about Grandmom," Tuck had once asked Chip. He never spoke about her. Chip went into the trunk he kept in the room with the stove and showed Tuck a brown tinted photograph, he standing and Bessie seated in a formal pose.

"That's your Grandma, Pup," he said, "She was beautiful and had high manners. She was a classy lady, and your Mom is just like her, 'cept she didn't get her blonde hair." He held the photo at arm's length, and tears rimmed his eyes. Removing his glasses, he handed the photo to Tuck.

"I'll never know why she married a rough cog like me, but she did."

Chip had the pension, and he rationalized that the wine kept him from thinking about Bess. But it didn't. He missed her every day and thought about her constantly. He hadn't the slightest interest in the daughters, except for Edie Maye, who was so much like Bess in spirit that he always cried when he spent any time with her.

It didn't bother him that none of his daughters except Edie Maye would allow him in their homes, principally because one of the regulars at his cabin was a woman named Frances. Often she stayed on there. In today's world, Frances would be called a "bag lady." She appeared ragged, and had ugly blue splotches on her legs.

But Chip liked her, and Tuck did, too. She was nice to the boy and when he went to visit Chip's place, she often held long conversations with him in front of the pot bellied stove. She had a gravelly voice and smoked a corncob pipe. To this day, the aroma of Old Rum pipe tobacco brings Tuck a vision of Frances bent over towards the stove, elbows on knees, puffing on her pipe with a bottle of "sneaky Pete" in hand.

Edie Maye's sisters were repulsed by the drinking. They all attended church and called Chip a drunkard and whore monger, as though they hardly knew him. Although Chip never ended up prostrate behind the

Arcade Grille like some of his friends, he was nevertheless a member of the "Sneaky Pete" gang, named for their choice of cheap wine.

Chip and Edie Maye in a serious discussion in front of Chip's cabin on Randall Avenue. The cabin was taken from Chip by eminent domain by the township when they paved the street.

Chip's skill as a wood worker was palpable. He constructed grandfather and grandmother clocks from scratch, buying only the movements. He also made guitars and mandolins, which he played, as well as the violin. Tuck owned only one thing that he made: a twelve gauge bolt action shotgun with a Mauser stock. Edie Maye's sisters stole everything he had when he got older. He knew they were doing it, but didn't have the heart to stop them.

His wood shop, a separate building behind the cabin, was filled with woodworking machinery. A workbench ran the entire length of one wall, and a shelf behind it held a 30 foot display of chisels of varying design and function. In one corner, the shop contained a forge. Nestled up the outside back wall was a chicken coop, which, as long as Tuck knew of it, contained a still.

The floor was covered with a layer of sawdust, and the aroma of fresh cut cedar, oak and pine prevalent, mixed with the more pungent smells of linseed oil, burnt metal and brazing pastes. Several of his machines; planer, table and band saw were operated by overhead belts, connected to an auto engine outside the workshop.

For Doc Fahrenbruch, Chip completed a set of Louie 14th chairs for his antique table, copying the one chair that Doc had. People told Tuck when he was older that Chip's antique reproductions were virtually indistinguishable from the originals, complete with wear marks and worm holes. Behind his workshop and in it, he kept barrels of different kinds of oil, with selected pieces of wood immersed in them, awaiting use on some project.

Occasionally, Tuck would accompany him on a walk in the woods, where he would mark certain trees with a ribbon or vee cut, for future use. Chip carried a tree saw, trapezoidal in shape, and after studying a particular tree and fondling it with his large hands, he would cut the desired piece and allow Tuck to lug it back to the shop.

Chip was leading Tuck down a hill near a bog on one of these occasions, when he suddenly turned to the boy and gestured for silence. Leading the boy around a tree and under some bushes, Chip whispered for Tuck to sit tight and quiet. Chip sat down cross-legged next to the boy. They were overlooking a boggy clearing through which a dark stream wound. On the far side of the bog, deep green moss covered the bank where the stream turned into it.

The two sat in absolute silence for what seemed an eternity, and then Chip nudged the boy's side and nodded his head in the direction of the mossy bank. A white-tail doe had emerged there, and after taking a drink, she elevated her head and surveyed the clearing in a series of head movements. Her huge ears were erect, probing for unfamiliar sounds.

Within minutes, two speckled fawns pushed their way between her legs, and she nudged them down to the water.

Chip and Tuck watched in fascination as she unsuccessfully attempted to teach them to drink from the stream. The fawns wanted nothing to do with it, and they continually sought her teats, nosing under her back legs.

Tuck couldn't suppress a giggle when the larger of the two slid awkwardly down the bank backwards, landing in the stream with long spindly legs awry. In an instant, they were gone, the only evidence that they had been there being the swaying ferns where they disappeared into the forest.

"If you're quiet," Chip had said, "you can see them here nearly every day about this time. Did you like them?" Tuck told him that he thought they were beautiful.

When Chip got older, he altered his old belt power engine and built a saw in the side yard. It was an elaborate system of levers and ramps that enabled him to cut firewood with minimum handling of the wood, his woodworking machines now powered by electricity.

His furniture was specially known for the carved feet that he created, four talons clasping a large round ball. He told Tuck that they represented a dragon grasping a great pearl.

9

RED MEN'S HALL

SITTING on the front porch, Tuck was called inside by his brother, and they huddled about Mrs. Mueller's Philco radio in her living room to hear the newscast, and the next day, to hear President Roosevelt speak to Congress. Everyone was agitated and excited.

The Japanese had bombed Pearl Harbor! The country was at war!

They were now living in the shed and downstairs of a small frame house on Paxon Street, about one half block from Mill Street, directly across from the Red Men's Hall. Mrs. Mueller owned the house, and Tuck didn't know the circumstances, but he later surmised that they probably were living there free of charge, since the boys slept on cots in a large shed. Edie Maye spent a lot of time taking care of Mrs. Mueller, who was quite old and couldn't get around too well.

Mrs. Mueller's Grandson, George, also lived there. He was sixteen, and in spite of having somehow lost his parents, appeared to Tuck to be a jovially mature teenager. George tried to enlist in the Navy on the Tuesday following Roosevelt's "day of infamy" address, but they spotted him for 16, and sent him home. He then tried the Army, Marine Corps and the RAF, but they weren't fooled either.

By March, George had been accepted into the Merchant Marine, and before Christmas of the following year, 1942, his ship was torpedoed by a German submarine in the eastern Atlantic. It was the first of three ships that would be torpedoed from under him, ferrying war supplies to England and Murmansk, Russia.

Although he continued to try to enlist each time he came home to be assigned a new ship, the armed services wouldn't touch him, an experienced seaman in the Merchant Marine. When the War ended, George had lived one of the most daring and dangerous careers of any soldier, but like all other Merchant Marine sailors, he was ineligible for veteran's benefits.[33]

This was the year of Tuck's introduction to school. Edie Maye took him to Mrs. Fowell's kindergarten classroom for registration, where they sat with other Moms and kids, waiting their turn. They were to be the last to receive the attention of Ms. Fowell in her Brainard School classroom. By then, Tuck was sitting alone in the back of the room, as Edie Maye filled in the necessary forms.

When called forward, Tuck stood up and stepped into the aisle into a large pile of excrement, left there by some other aspiring student. A memorable first day of school.

But he managed to survive grammar school, mainly because of one of his Paxon Street neighbors, "Umpe" Downs. Umpe didn't attend regular school with Tuck; he was assigned to Mrs. Zanone's Room, which was in its own four-classroom building located in the schoolyard. Everyone in Mrs. Zanone's class was in the same grade regardless of age, and it was common knowledge among the school population that anyone in Mrs. Zanone's class was crazy, and should be avoided. Umpe's real name was Raymond, and he and Tuck became fast friends.

Everyone in school was afraid of Umpe. He was a nearly a teen-ager, muscled and almost bearded, with a kindergarten intelligence. His cleft palate gave him a menacing appearance. Living on the same street, Tuck and Umpe played marbles together a lot, and Tuck never made fun of the way he spoke, which gave him the name, "Umpe." When other kids called Tuck a guinea or wop and got on him about being a jail bird's son, Umpe would shut them up, usually with just a glance. The hair lip had given him a sensitivity to name calling.

This was a problem that would plague Tuck throughout grammar school. Tuck could only remember two other Italian families, the Pallantes and the Marcianos, with children in public school. Any Italian worth his salt and with any kind of money sent his kids to the Sacred Heart Catholic School on High Street, placing them safely in the arms of Jesus and the other Italians of Mt. Holly.

But the problem was that Tuck was neither Italian nor acceptable. Edie Maye, with her deep dislike for Sal's family, avoided that side of the family altogether. In her mind, they were Scotch-English-Irish who by some freak of nature, happened to be burdened with a Sicilian name.

Early on in their marriage, Edie Maye and Sal had lived in Trenton at Mama Falconetta's. Edie Maye often related the story of how Grandmom would serve the chicken with the head still on the bird, and how she even cooked the intestines. Everyone thought this to be a delicacy, but Edie Maye found it revolting.

Tuck quickly learned that "wops" or "guineas" were unacceptable as playmates or visitors at most kids' homes, and gravitated naturally to others with the same social standing in looking for friends.

As a result, his friends were either Italian or Negro (in one case, both), or dirt-poor white kids. Edie Maye was usually mortified by Tuck's choice of companions, since she, of course, considered them not to be of Italian descent, but rather, directly descended from the Pilgrims at Plymouth Rock.

School marked the beginning of Tuck's understanding that other people in the community didn't appreciate his dad very much. There were jibes and insults and early on they usually referred to race, but in later years, Sal's escapades as a convicted felon, numbers writer and draft evader were added. In a society where only 11 states permitted church bingo, gamblers were criminals. As a result, Tuck became a very defensive kid, with a real chip on his shoulder. He fought bravely to defend his honor, but it wasn't long before he started acting out his tormentor's fantasies.

Tuck took his first "hookey" from kindergarten. A middle aged woman, finding him in the alley behind the old post office at the top of Paxon Street, inquired, "Why aren't you in school, little boy?"

Recalling this, Tuck can hardly believe that, at five years old, he was already cutting school. But he was, and soon he was steadfastly entrenched on the county Truant Officer's "top 10" list.

Soon after this, Edie Maye and the kids were tossed out by Mrs. Mueller's relatives, who moved in and took care of her until she died. Sal had been released from prison and Edie Maye moved her brood to the building which contained Red Men's Hall, to a third floor apartment.

10

THE CASINO AT RED MEN'S HALL

THE Red Men's hall occupied the third floor of a large building at 30 Mill Street, right in the center of Mt. Holly.[34] Entering from the street through a door to the right side of Hurley's first floor furniture store, two long flights of stairs led to a third floor upstairs hallway. At the first landing was the door to the apartment Tuck's family had occupied briefly when Tuck's Granddad had broken his leg. At the top of the stair, a hallway stretched the half the width of the building to the door to their new third floor rear apartment.

Halfway down the hallway on the left was a closet door. This was the entrance to Sal's casino, the "Young Men's Social Club." Upon opening the closet door, one was confronted with what appeared to be an ordinary closet, with a hanging bar and shelf on its back wall. Garments were hanging from the bar and boxes occupied the shelf. However, the entire back wall of the closet, including garments and boxes, was itself a door. In fact, it was a steel door. On the other side of the door, two large "L" brackets supported a hinged 2 x 4" bar that was removed to open the closet wall.

Next to the door inside the casino a wooden stool with legs at least five feet in length was positioned. On this stool, the "doorman" controlled a small hatch in the roof of the closet and raised and lowered the bar according to his observation of the potential customers standing in the closet. This critical position was usually occupied by "Little Pete" Pro, a long time associate of Sal's. Little Pete was the armed gatekeeper, in command of the daunting security system for the illegal activities behind the fake closet wall.

Peter Pro on his high stool controlled the entrance door to the casino, which was disguised as the back wall of a hall closet. Customers parked their cars behind Eckman's Atlantic Station on the north side of Mill Street. The casino operated for some time with the cooperation of local law enforcement until it was threatened by New York mobster Frank "Paulie" Carbo, who robbed the customers and the casino at gunpoint in April of 1941, using Thompson sub machine guns. Freddy Fosciano, the casino handyman was taken by Carbo and found dead the next day in the Pines. Illustration by the Author.

Players came from New York, Philadelphia, Atlantic City, north Jersey and surrounding areas. On any night the casino was open, limousines with license plates from surrounding States could be seen behind Eckman's Atlantic Station, less than three hundred yards north and across Mill Street from the casino. Among the out of staters frequenting the casino, certain selected locals could be found, having passed Little Pete's scrutiny.

The Red Men's Hall was a large room, and one end of the room was elevated, presumably for the most important of the "Red" Men, who had conducted meetings here in complete Indian costume and with great ceremony. On that dais, Sal had two craps tables. Down one side of the room, several poker tables; and the other side, blackjack and roulette tables. Along three walls, 36 shiny "Chief" slot machines stood awaiting use.

The casino must have been a big success. From their bedroom, Tuck and his brother would drop off to sleep, straining to understand some of the words amidst the clatter of slot machines and the low roar of activity that permeated the common wall.

For a change, there was lots of food, hot running water and a real bathtub. The sun poured into the living room and kitchen in the morning. Tuck remembered it as a warm place and Edie Maye laughed a lot. But Tuck's life in the improved surroundings was dampened by another major bout with the whooping cough, one so severe that Doc McDonald had to be called.

On this occasion, Tuck suffered the hot packs and licorice medicine for several weeks. Delirious for several days, he lost considerable weight, and when it was over, it took months for him to fully recover. Despite his weakened state, Tuck looked forward to Saturday Mornings, when Patrolman Bucky Squires would pay his weekly visit.

An imposing figure in his blue tunic coat, Sam Brown belt, blue jodhpurs and high black boots, Bucky would knock, come in and sit down at the porcelain topped table in the kitchen with Edie Maye. She poured him coffee. On occasions, he would, after some nagging, show Tuck his pistol. They laughed and joked for a while, and then Edie Maye would get up, take a white envelope from the icebox, and slide it across the porcelain topped table to Bucky.

Bucky enjoyed these visits. He used his position and contacts with the county politicos wisely, and made a nice extra income by doing their collecting.[35] He enjoyed the Saturday morning chore even more because it gave him the opportunity to spend time with Edie Maye. She was quite beautiful and a most interesting and intelligent conversationalist. He knew the wives of all of the county bigwigs, but they couldn't hold a candle to Edie Maye, even with all of their money and position. Bucky had never met a woman like her before.

Bucky would unbutton two buttons of his blue tunic and stash the envelope inside it. He would then readjust his Sam Brown belt, stand up, put his gloves in his hat, which he then stowed under the crook of his elbow, and with a pleasant comment, stride out the door.

On Saturday and sometimes Sunday, Tuck and his brother were given the chore of sweeping the casino. They could keep any coins found on the floor, mostly quarters and nickels from the slot machines. They were supervised by a bow-legged little Italian man, Freddy Fosciano. He was the casino's 'gofer,' janitor and odd jobs man; a distant cousin on Sal's side of the family.

Sal had two partners in the casino, the Marinella brothers. John Marinella was a huge but gentle man. At least six foot four; he displayed an easy grin and liked talking to kids. Tony, his older brother, was another matter. Although quietly friendly, he dressed in black and his red-rimmed dark eyes were piercing. Tuck often reflected that in his adult life, he never met anyone with eyes like Tony Marinella's. Like his brother, he was tall, but slim, and his face was pock-marked. He looked like a dangerous person; a man who had never loved anyone.

And Tony was a "mechanic." That is, he was skilled at manipulating cards. At Tuck's request, he would spin a "gambler's rose," and the boy, completely mesmerized by his legerdemain with the cards, was appropriately astonished. Sal once told Tuck that Tony was a "master mechanic." He could "deal bottoms, stack a deck during a shuffle, hide cards" and perform all of skills of the master cheaters.

"Apples," Sal's full-time bodyguard, added to the casino's ambiance. Tall and thin, dressed in a black suit and turtleneck he wore a shoulder holster complete with a Colt .45 caliber automatic pistol. He seldom spoke, and Freddy told the boys he was a notorious "cat burglar" and best known for his knife-wielding skills. All of these men, whom Tuck looked on as idols, super humans, god-like beings, could turn him to stone with a glance or a comment, actually too frightened to speak, frozen.

But Tuck was a happy kid living at the Red Men's Hall. He had new store-bought clothes at Easter time and on other holidays, Edie Maye cooked real dinners, and the relatives came to visit. Sal was around a lot, and they were almost a family. At Christmas Tuck got more store-bought clothes, a snare drum, a red enamel push train that he could sit on and ride and lots of picture books. But he was constantly sick with the whooping cough, and almost died a several times while living in the sunny apartment.

Hazel, Edie Maye's oldest sister, visited them at Red Man's Hall with her daughter, Patsy, in tow. Patsy was four or five at the time. Unlike her three sisters, Hazel was a large woman with great full breasts, and Tuck was astonished on one of these visits when she casually pulled one out of her dress and shoved it unceremoniously into Patsy's mouth. Patsy slurped at the huge gland while Tuck stared in bug-eyed amazement.

Hazel and Edie Maye were sitting at the kitchen table, having coffee.

"Don't you think she's a little old to be breast feeding?" Edie Maye asked the obvious. Patsy, standing next to her mother and tall in her own right, had to bend a little to get a good suck on the huge teat.

"Well, it's only natural," Hazel said, "and I still got the milk."

"Maybe if you weaned her, it would stop," Edie Maye said, "She'll be having boyfriends pretty soon and what will they think?"

Tuck had seen his Aunt Hazel add a healthy portion of milk to her coffee, and she picked up the cup and sipped as Patsy slurped away at her breast. He tried desperately to reconcile the scene. Was Patsy slurping milk or coffee? He wanted to ask Edie Maye, but her raised eyebrow and deliberate glance stifled the question before he could get it out.

This was the winter when Joe Horn, an older boy who lived nearby, shot Tuck's brother. Cholly, four years older than Tuck, played with boys much older than himself. This tendency followed him throughout his life. Joe Horn at the time in question, had his five younger friends stand in a circle, and using his father's police revolver loaded with one blank cartridge, pointed the gun at the chest of each of the boys in sequence and pulled the trigger.

Cholly was an unlucky person, so of course, the blank exploded against his chest, embedding black powder and paper fragments in it. He carried the circular mark for his entire life. Another emergency for Doc McDonald.

The "old" Post Office was located at the corner of Murrill and Paxon Streets until 1935, when the new building was erected on Washington Street. Both Edie Maye and Sal worked in this building; she during the war years manufacturing parachutes on Singer sewing machines, and he operating "the oldest permanent floating craps game in Mount Holly" before and after the secret casino. Photo courtesy Mt. Holly Historical Society.

The few times that Tuck went somewhere with his dad occurred during the years when they lived behind the casino. Tuck recalled that Sal regularly took him downstairs to the street and past Krupnick's next door, where they sat in a booth in the Palace Restaurant, and Sal entertained friends or business acquaintances.

Of the people who came to the restaurant one was a little man who wore riding boots and had a ruddy complexion. His name was Giddle, at least that's what Sal called him, and he was at one time, a jockey. Sal told Tuck that he and Tony and a man named Rosie owned a race horse, and that this man, Giddle, trained it and rode it in races at New Jersey's fledgling new turf arenas, the Garden State and Atlantic City Tracks.

"Rosie" also came to the restaurant on some occasions. He was a very soft kind of person, in Tuck's memory, quite unlike most of the people Sal knew.

Years later, when Tuck mentioned Rosie's horse to his dad, he said, "Oh, yeah, that nag couldn't get out of its own way. We fixed the race one time and the damned horse fell down and lost anyway. Six other jocks pulling their mounts so this horse can run by, and as soon as he gets the lead, down he goes. I guess he was so surprised to be in front that he didn't know what to do."

Since Sal seldom used swear words, Tuck assumed that it was a sensitive subject and dropped it. On the way home from the restaurant, Sal often bought Tuck an ice cream cone from the adjacent Mr. Stavres Greek deli.

"You want nigger babies?" Mr. Stavres asked. Tuck nodded and the vanilla cone was covered with chocolate sprinkles.

Tuck's family lasted almost four years at Red Men's Hall before Paulie Carbo showed up. It all happened on a Saturday night when John Marinella was left to run the casino. Sal, Tony and Apples were out of town, running "blanket" games in the pines near Vineland, Tuck found out later.

Frankie Marsala, a local taxi driver, brought a man to the closet, and the Little Pete let him in because Frankie said, "It's Okay, he's a friend of mine." As soon as the door opened, the man jumped into the casino and knocked the big stool and Little Pete to the floor.

Armed with Thompson submachine guns, five more men followed into the casino. They lined up all the customers, took all the cash from the tables and cash boxes, nearly $3,000, and relieved the customers of their personal jewelry and cash. One man smashed Johnny Marinella's face with a gun butt, and made an announcement.

"My name's Carbo and this game is over. I run all the games around here. Tell that to your brother and his partner."[36]

He directed his comment to John, who was semi-conscious and bleeding on the floor.

Frank "Paulie" Carbo was a prize fight promoter from Philadelphia who was known for his violence. A soldier in the Lucchese crime family of New York, he ran games, the numbers and brewed illegal beer in nearby Camden, but apparently had been given orders or decided unilaterally to quench the activity in Burlington County. He had been unsuccessfully indicted for five murders and it was later reported that he was likely responsible for 12 others, including the murder of Dutch Schultz in New York. Of course, all of the commotion was heard in the apartment, and after Carbo and his thugs left, Bucky Squires showed up, and brought John into the kitchen where Edie Maye cleaned up the ugly gash on his forehead. Everyone was frightened, and no one could find little Freddy Fosciano, the "gofer."

Sal got back early next morning, and he, Tony and Johnny had a big argument in the kitchen, Apples leaning against the window overlooking the creek. Carbo's reputation as a brutal killer and a gunman for Dutch Schultz and Albert Anastasio's Murder Incorporated gang was spelled out by Sal and Tony. It was unknown if Carbo had acted alone or on the orders of higher ups, but his incursion into Burlington County was taken at considerable risk. Any number of important Mafioso from various cities might have been there.

Edie Maye cried a lot, and finally, everybody left. They had decided to reopen the casino that night, and they did, permitting only a few well known customers to enter. At noontime, Bucky Squires had shown up again. The State Police had found Freddie Fosciano in the pines, near Ong's Hat, his throat cut and pennies on his eyelids.

Tuck was within earshot when Bucky spilled out his story. He saw that Sal literally slumped at the news. Edie Maye gasped, tears rimming her eyes as she backed into the kitchen window frame. She pulled Tuck backwards against her legs. Tuck couldn't understand why he was so frightened, but he knew that Sal and Edie Maye were afraid, too. The casino at Red Men's Hall had obviously operated under the auspices of the "Eastern" Syndicate, approved by Sam DeCavalcante's uncle, Nick DelMore, and thereby under the auspices of the "New York Boys." The casino had originated, like many of Knucky Johnson's in Atlantic City, in the back room of one of Mt. Holly's classier restaurants, the Greentree, located on Route 38 on the edge of the town. It had flourished there for two years and was then moved to the Red Men's Hall when it outgrew its original surroundings. Even then, its existence was largely a secret, shared only by certain politically approved citizens and gamblers, but fairly well known outside the town and state to insiders, mob associates and big money players. The murder of Sal's distant cousin was of some significance and would have to be dealt with by the higher ups in Sal's circle of "friends" because of the adverse publicity. Sal made calls to North Jersey and Philadelphia, and it was decided to continue operations with the Casino. Sal told Tony and John Marinella that "The Count says that he (Carbo) was operating on his own: he's a loose cannon, and the problem would be taken care of."

And while Sal's standing with his bosses was sufficient to solve the immediate crisis, another emergency lay in wait for the proprietors of the

Young Men's Social Club. Although news of the raid and Freddy Fosciano's murder did not make the papers, gossip about the Carbo robbery seeped out in the otherwise sleepy and inattentive town and pricked the ears of law enforcement at the state and county level. A State Police Detective was assigned by Supreme Court Justice Perskie to infiltrate the Casino and gather evidence for an upcoming Grand Jury on "big time" gambling in New Jersey.

At 2 a.m. on a Sunday morning in early April, 1941 the State Police raided the Casino, rounding up Sal, Tony, Little Pete Pro, two croupiers and 32 "guests" of the Young Men's Social Club. The young detective, dressed in a snappy blue suit and tie and sporting a fedora hat had been a steady customer for several weeks, completely bamboozling Sal and his partners.

The arrests made the front page of the weekly Mt. Holly Herald, displacing the Soap Box Derby trials and the 'Possible Pea Crop Failure' stories. The story had life as the suspects first pleaded "not guilty," then weeks later recanted and put themselves on the mercy of the Court. Since Little Pete and one of the croupiers were armed when arrested, their charges became more serious. Another front page story. The bail for all suspects combined nearly topped $20,000, a huge amount when a new Buick cost only $600 and gas, nineteen cents per gallon.

There were several postponements as the town folk watched the unfolding drama in each week's paper. Every story carried every name of the "suspects" and "guests." By the end of summer, Tony Marinella emerged as the fall guy, sentenced to 1 ½ to 3 years in prison. Sal, defended by the father of one of his future best friends, somehow was identified as the club "Secretary" and escaped with a $2,000 fine; not exactly an innocent bystander. The other principals paid fines from $200 to $4,000. But the story had occupied the front page, carried over to page 8, for the whole summer.[37]

The night of the day when Tony reported for his incarceration at Lewisburg, while the children slept, Sal and Edie Maye packed up. Edie Maye was frantic, but Sal with his typically laid back persona, kissed her lightly.

"Don't worry, this will all blow over," he said, "and maybe we'll be able to open up again. For now, we're going across the street." The Casino at Red Men's Hall closed its closet and became part of the Mount Holly's secret history. What followed was Sal's only attempt to join the work force that Tuck knew about. Uncle Len showed up, Sal's brother in law from the 'Burg' and the pair apparently attempted to find work in construction, which was Len's specialty.

Edie Maye took no solace in Sal's assurances. When Sal opted to join the workforce, it was his first real introduction to the remnants of the depression, and the way ordinary people had to cope with it. With no previous work experience, he was a lost soul. Uncle Len, drafted into the Army, soon disappeared.[38] Sal was left with Edie Maye to experience the hard times that they had lived before the Casino at Greentree and Red Men's Hall.

Sal soon disappeared with Apples, quickly frustrated by the prospects of earning money legally. It was the last time that Edie Maye and the children would see him for two years. It wasn't long before her money ran out, and she was taking in sewing and washing. Soon her credit ran out with Dave Fisher, the butcher at the corner of Mill and Paxon Street, and they were back to oatmeal for dinner. Finally evicted, Edie Maye and the children settled into the abandoned Stone House, where she knew the casino furniture and slot machines had been hidden, and their lives hit rock bottom.

11

MEETING HOUSE ALLEY

EDIE Maye introduced Tuck to Morte d'Arthur and the Knights of the Round Table when they lived in the "Stone House." Huddling about a pot bellied stove that she continually fed with rolled newspapers, soaking in the warmth from its iron sides, either Sis or Edie Maye read to them nearly every evening. Tuck's brother, sister and he each were wrapped in blankets, their feet propped on towel wrapped bricks that were periodically rotated to the top of the stove for reheating. There was no other heat in the Stone House.

Edie Maye, in a heavy coat, hunched over to enhance the stove's grille light with the light from the single bulb hanging overhead. The bulb, controlled by a long chain, dangled by electrical wire from the remnants of a chandelier bobeche. She read them the entire book, as well as Ivanhoe, that winter.

They were living in a huge abandoned masonry home on Mill Street, which Tuck named, over the years, the "Stone House". A tributary of the Rancocas ran under the house in a walled sluiceway, separated from the cellar by its concrete wall. The little creek crossed under Mill Street in a tunnel and joined the South branch of the Rancocas that ran behind Red Men's Hall. It was the outflow of Woolman's lake and meandered under Branch Street, Mt. Holly Avenue, Cherry and Buttonwood Streets before crossing Mill under the Stone House. There were lots of rats, big rats, and the usual battalions of cockroaches and spiders.

They had moved across the street and only a few hundred feet: from middle class comfort to abject poverty, hunger and fear.

Tuck can't recall any detail of the other rooms of that house, since replaced by an Acme supermarket and then, an office building, except for that one huge room with its cast iron stove, and another large room off the wide hallway that led to the unused front door. That room was filled with disassembled poker tables, slot machines, blackjack and craps tables and at least one roulette wheel, the remnants of the casino. It took Tuck years to comprehend the importance of the gambling paraphernalia and slot machines in that front room, but eventually he came to understand that the tables and particularly the slot machines probably saved their lives.

The Stone House was torn down sometime in the fifties and replaced by an Acme grocery market. The site is memorialized by a bronze plaque on the building that occupies it now. It reads,

"On this site stood John Woolman's tailor shop. Here he probably tended shop and kept books in 1740, when a lad of 20. He bought the property in 1747 and deeded it to his mother, Elizabeth Woolman, in 1753. The Second Friend's Meeting House in Mt. Holly was built in the rear of this lot in 1763. It was in use until 1776 and was reached by a passageway from Mill Street known as Meeting House Alley."

Appropriately, although Edie Maye had no knowledge of the historical origins of the stone house, they ate a lot of Quaker's oatmeal. The black hatted farmer was a constant visitor at their supper table, smiling from the big round box. But Edie Maye did have a few fresh eggs, since in the back yard; she kept several hens under the shed where they lived in stolen milk cartons, (the hens) gifts from the Rhodiers next door. Nevertheless they were very cold and very hungry in the Stone House. Hot water, like the Creek houses, had to be heated on the pot bellied stove. They took their baths in turn, standing up and shivering in a washtub.

She had moved in with the help of Mr. Jones, who had previously moved the casino tables, games and slot machines into a front room of the Stone House. Unknowingly, Edie Maye and her brood had become the caretakers of the slot machines and gaming tables. This unwanted assignment would provide them with intermittent housing and unwanted benefits and dangers in future days. Carbo's incursion into Burlington County only highlighted what was already obvious to the big time gamblers of the New York families: New Jersey was a pothole of feuding groups, some of whom owed allegiance to one or another of the big families. Something would have to be done about New Jersey, sooner or later. While the Italians in New Jersey jockeyed for power, the portable casino, Sal's $10,000 investment, awaited the outcome.[39]

Edie Maye had no idea where Sal had gone. She knew that some of his friends knew, but now that the casino was done, she never saw them, and if she had, she knew that they wouldn't tell her. It took all of her wits and skill to survive. She made coats for the children from blankets and took in whatever sewing she could get paid for, even if it was pennies.

Yet she didn't blame Sal. She knew that the new element that he had become afoul of were bad men. Not just gamblers, but killers, too. She had liked old Freddie, he had been kind to the children and had treated her with courtesy and respect, and she was unnerved to think that they had murdered the old man as a warning.

She was somewhat disappointed in Bucky Squires, whom she thought should have been able to prevent what happened. She knew that the money that she had passed to him every Saturday morning was to allow them to operate, without interference from the county or people like Paulie Carbo. But she also knew that Bucky was more form than substance. He had never really done anything brave after the Farmer's bank robbery, but he was smart enough to trade on the reputation.

When he came to the apartment on Saturday mornings, she often had to suppress remarks about how he had lost the end of one finger, shooting a tied dog.[40]

If Paulie Carbo wanted to avenge himself on Sal's family, Edie Maye knew that they were easy prey. There was no way to make the stone house secure, anyone could come in through several loosely boarded windows.

She had been very happy when the casino was bustling with customers, and she could see that Sal was a popular man. She knew that the money in the envelope every Saturday morning wasn't just for Bucky Squires, there was far too much, a healthy stack of $50 bills. A lot of people in town got rich from Sal's Casino at the Red Man's Hall.

One thing that Edie Maye had inherited from her spirited mother was an eye for practicality and distaste for hypocrites. She couldn't find it in herself to blame Sal for her plight without including half of the town's political hierarchy, too.

But Bessie Lawrence's grit and Edie Maye's pride couldn't dispel the abject poverty evident in the Stone House and to its desperate occupants. The town had buzzed over the Carbo raid on the secret but seldom mentioned casino. Before Carbo, it had been the subject of humor and mildly entertaining, but now it was realized that it had been a threat to the community, drawing thugs armed with Thompson Sub Machine guns into their lives. It took all of Edie Maye's courage to expose herself to the street and townspeople, who often went silent and turned away as she approached.

The Stone House, constructed of large granite building blocks with a slate roof, had been standing empty for some time. It had no heat and was pretty much over run with insects, mice and rats. The windows were missing on the third floor and the rest were boarded up. The open area behind it, lost acreage between Mill and Paxon streets, bisected with the little stream, was strewn with trash and overgrown with briers.

The war had descended on them like a blanket. With so many soldiers in town from nearby Fort Dix, everyone knew that the Movietone News propaganda was a pack of lies. Georgie Marshall came to visit Edie Maye, having lost his second ship to a German wolf pack off Nova Scotia. He told them of the carnage, hundreds of ships being sunk, some within sight of the New Jersey beaches. The German U-boats owned the eastern shore of the United States. In one week, the S.S. City of Atlanta, a passenger steamship and four other cargo vessels were sunk. Before the Navy responded, more than 400 ships would be sunk within sight of the east coast, the Nazi's greatest naval victory of WWII[41]

That was the winter of the soldier's Christmas, the winter that Doc McDonald's wife brought a soldier on Christmas Eve day. Tuck had to assume that Mrs. McDonald befriended them because of Doc's frequent emergency visits, which must have been free of charge, in keeping Tuck from succumbing to the whooping cough.

From Doc's perspective, he was continually amazed at Edie Maye's ability to survive under the worst of conditions. He had known her since he first hung out his shingle, and had seen her cope with the most serious kinds of illness and poverty with class, humor and dignity. Sharing these observations with his wife Doris led her to try to help Edie Maye. Although she and Doc would never admit it, she knew that the husbands of many of her bridge partners had done well on Sal's casino. She had to maintain the professional decorum of a young Doctor's wife, but like Edie Maye, she despised hypocrisy.

For whatever reason, she appeared on their snowy doorstep on that day before 1942's Christmas with a sandy haired, tall young man in Army uniform. He was from Oklahoma, some small town with a funny name, and a real cowboy.

"Edith," Mrs. McDonald said, "this young man is from Oklahoma, a long way from home, and he's about to be sent overseas. He asked me if I knew of someone with whom he might share his Christmas."

"That's right, Ma'am," the soldier said, "I'd consider it an honor, if I could help you' all out." Tom "Sandy" Marston had enlisted with two of his cousins almost immediately after Pearl Harbor. He had felt badly about leaving his dad short of help on their spread, handling nearly 300 head of cattle and with the next oldest brother just turning twelve.

"Doris," Edie had said, beginning what Tuck was sure would be a "no, thank you."

Edie Maye was too proud to accept charity. She had never done it before, and something had always turned up, although they had experienced some hungry spells.

But the Stone House was taking its toll. They literally had nothing to eat, and she knew that the children had experienced a taste of the ordinary life during the years behind the casino. They wouldn't understand the bleak and poverty-stricken Christmas she was about to bring them. And then there was Sal, running away like a scared rabbit and disappearing down a hole somewhere. Edie Maye could understand why he did it, but he could have left them with some resources. And now she was confronted with this youngster, and she didn't want to hurt him, either.

She could read loneliness in the boy's eyes and instinctively felt that he was sincere. Edie Maye was tired of the grind, trying to find a way to feed the children, to keep warm, to keep from collapsing from the strain. A man had approached her on the street the day before, menacing in a black topcoat. For an instant, she had thought it was Paulie Carbo and her heart seemed to jump into her throat. She found herself trembling with fright when he left her after only asking directions.

"Look, Ma'am," the Cowboy said, "I know just how you'll must feel, me bein' a stranger and all. But, see, I got six brothers and sisters at home, and Christmas is a big time for us, and I sure miss being able to give my kid brothers and sisters their gifts, if you know what I mean."

Edie Maye, for once, was reduced to tears. The image of her leaning against the door frame, back lighted by the morning sun on a light snow, hands clasped tightly under her chin as tears streamed down her cheeks, was etched in Tuck's memory. She agreed as Mrs. McDonald's heavy arms tightly embraced her.

Doris McDonald was relieved. She had been sure that Edie Maye would turn them away. She knew how badly off they were and she agreed with Horace that Edie Maye was unique and deserved better.

Tom, the soldier, stepped into the room and squatted down, and holding Tuck by the shoulders, began speaking directly to the boy with his soft, funny accent, asking him what he expected Santa to bring, and what kinds of games he played. He did the same with Tuck's brother and sister, and drawing Edie Maye aside, Tuck saw him take some bills from his pocket, pressing them into her hand, closing his fingers over hers, insistent and smiling. He called her "ma'am."

Mrs. McDonald and the soldier left, but he returned later that afternoon with a Christmas tree, which in Tuck's memory, more than filled the dark expansiveness of that huge room with its high ceiling. And there was another trip, to Dave's butcher shop and to the A & P grocery. Edie Maye and "Sandy," as he wished to be called, returned with brown bags full of foodstuff.

Edie Maye found the cardboard box that contained ornaments and they trimmed the tree on Christmas Eve. As was her custom, she flattened every piece of tinsel between her fingers before carefully positioning it so that it would hang freely.

The following morning, of course, was Christmas, and among the several presents under the tree was a two-wheeled scooter that Tuck had yearned for. His sister got an immense doll with blonde curly hair, and his brother, a baseball glove. The scooter was red enamel, with cream wheels, solid rubber tires and black rubber handle grips.

That night, the soldier returned and Edie put a roasted chicken dinner on the table, which he enjoyed immensely. The children proudly showed him their presents after the dinner, and within an hour he was gone, having pressed another wad of small bills in Edie Maye's hand over her objections.

They had plenty of food for the next several weeks. It was a Christmas that Tuck remembered for the rest of his life.

Tuck again survived another serious bout with the whooping cough that winter, but in the spring, trying to keep up with his brother and his friends crossing the brook that ran under the Stone House, he fell on a broken bottle, nearly severing his right hand at the wrist. The cut, six inches in length, exposed the bone and nicked the artery. Edie Maye passed out when she saw it, and Tuck's sister, thirteen at the time, took him to Doc McDonald's office, his wrist wrapped in a blood-saturated pair of ladies panties.

Doc stitched the artery, and using Band-Aids that he cut down to about an eighth inch in width at the middle, closed the gaping wound. He wrapped the lower arm in gauze and covered it with heavy tape, creating a cast of sorts to prevent Tuck from moving it. He would have liked to stitch the outer wound, but Tuck was uncontrollable without anesthesia of any kind. It was a major wound, and in his weakened condition, healing took the rest of the summer.

In spite of their own desperate straits they, like everyone else, were frightened and confused over the progress of the war. Most of the news to date had been depressing, General Wainwright captured at some place called Corregidor and thousands of American boys starved and bayoneted to death on the Bataan Death March. The Japanese had taken Wake Island, Guam, Singapore and dominated the Pacific with a huge and modern navy. They had occupied the Philippines and General MacArthur had made his getaway in a PT boat.

The soldier, Sandy, never returned, one of the millions who left Fort Dix to fight the war that Sal evaded. In 1944, Mrs. McDonald came to Edie Maye's house again, bringing the news that the young cowboy had been killed in Italy. She thought they might want to know.

They were thrown out of the Stone House the following winter. The owner, a Mr. Scattergood, threatened Edie Maye for several months when she couldn't produce a penny for rent. He finally brought Bucky Squires with him and told Edie Maye to "get the hell out, you're nothing but a bunch of squatters, no better than the hoboes behind the tracks."

Edie Maye looked to Bucky for something, a reprimand, some help of any kind, but Bucky characteristically played with his Sam Brown belt and let the old man vent his anger.

An early snow accompanied their move, which was assisted again by the black man with his stake body truck, Mr. Jones. He moved the heavy stuff for Edie Maye. It seemed impossible that Edie Maye and her brood could survive if their new home was as inadequate as the Stone House, but it turned out to be worse.[42]

12

WAR YEARS

AT the end of the row on the corner of Cherry and Pearl Streets, the Cherry Street house was covered with ugly red asphalt tiles. The rooms ran front to back, living, dining, kitchen with linoleum and a shed with a hard packed dirt floor. Upstairs, two bedrooms and a toilet. There was no hot water, and the toilet usually overflowed when used. The basement was filled with water to the level of the second step from the top. Big rats and lots of spiders and roaches abounded. The back yard still featured an outhouse, unused, but covered in the same ugly tiles, leaning precariously against the fence. The building, which included a duplicate half house on the other side, had already been condemned by town officials.

They lived there for some time. Edie Maye had gained a reputation for her ability as a seamstress, and she made several wedding gowns for customers. Tuck's brother had a paper route, and aside from that, Tuck had no idea where Edie Maye got the money to put a meager fare on the table.

It was worse here than in the Stone House, having no chickens. The kerosene stove was also a problem, causing several small fires, which they managed to put out. In the winter, Edie Maye wrapped hot bricks in towels and put them in the children's beds, under the covers, to get them through the night.

Even when they could afford kerosene, the warmth of the stove brought legions of insects out of the walls. One evening Edie Maye ran across the kitchen and crushed a huge spider in the middle of the linoleum. Before she could move her foot, hundreds of baby spiders radiated across the floor and scampered up the walls.

Opening the cellar door caused the rats to jump into the fetid water filling the cellar to the top of the stair. Edie Maye nailed the door shut and stuffed its crevices with newspaper. They could hear scratching from behind the door, and avoided that area of the kitchen. They all felt better when Edie Maye took in a stray cat, a little calico which they named "Mousie."

A lot of people in town knew of their condition, and Tuck supposed that they attempted to help out on occasion with food or money, or both. Except for the one lapse of the soldier's Christmas, however, Edie Maye retained her independence. She knew that her position in the community's eyes had changed. She was a woman alone, but neither a spinster nor widow. And Bucky Squires was sure to have told people about Paulie Carbo.

She had never ventured into the casino when it was operating, Sal having forbidden it, but most of the patrons knew who she was, and she had many admirers. Her good looks, wit and intelligence posed a definite threat to any married man who might have offered her help. A single parent family was the object of a lot of gossip and scorn, let alone Sal's activities, which had been featured as front page news in the local paper for an entire summer.

At least the war seemed to have taken a slight turn for the better when news of the Dolittle raid on Tokyo was announced six months after the attack at Pearl Harbor. The incredibly brave little squadron of B-25's had flown a one-way trip from the deck of the USS Hornet and dropped a smattering of small bombs on the Japanese capitol and other cities. But the Navy had yet to gain control of the waters off the east coast and to sink U-boats with any regularity. Citizens in shore communities, shocked by occasional bodies washed up on the beaches, were finally convinced to use blackout curtains, thus preventing U-boats from using the shore lights to silhouette their helpless targets.

Henry Kaiser had been commandeered by President Roosevelt to "build ships like Model T's," and he did just that. The burgeoning fleet of Kaiser's Liberty Ships, built in yards from Maine to Seattle, began to ply the North Atlantic with thousands of tons of war supplies for the British and Russians. It became a race to build more ships than the Nazis could sink. By 1943, 15 Liberty ships were being launched every week. By the end of the 1943, one shipyard built and launched a liberty ship in four days, from keel up, just to show they could do it!

Georgie Marshall, again the victim of German torpedoes, told Tuck and Edie Maye of the attack on his third ship in the Denmark Strait, near Greenland, out of reach of either American or British air support.

"There were 400 ships in the convoy," Georgie said, "but we were the third from last. It's better now, in the convoys, but only if you're in the middle. The wolf packs, they get the last ship first, and then work up the line."

George had suffered burns in this sinking, having had to swim through burning oil to reach a life raft.

"We heard the last ship get it about midnight," he said, "and then everybody got real nervous. We knew we would probably be next. They got number two about an hour later, and then we got it about four in the morning. I had to swim through a lot of oil, all on fire, and when the sun came up, I found a life raft floating and climbed on it. It wasn't even from my ship. A Canadian Navy corvette picked me up the next day. I was lucky!"

One evening, Tuck's brother burst in the front door, shouting excitedly, "Mom, look, some guy is throwing money away down on Mill Street." He emptied his pockets on the kitchen table, and Edie Maye quickly stacked the coins and two one dollar bills, counting three dollars and sixty-five cents, a huge windfall, when 5 cans of Carnation condensed milk cost only 23 cents.

To make matters worse, the town was nearly fully employed because of the tremendous war effort. The Navy employed thousands at New York Shipbuilding in Camden, where cruisers were being built. Across the river at the Philadelphia Navy Yard, the newest of the Iowa class battleships, the New Jersey, was launched on 1942's Pearl Harbor anniversary. Down river, behind Fort Mifflin, a huge defense yard was turning out tanks and other vehicles in record times, and up river, Camden's Cramp Shipyard was building wooden hulled minesweepers. The Philadelphia area was becoming the "Arsenal of Democracy." A parachute company opened in the old Post Office on Paxon Street. Stores were overflowing with customers.

Tuck supplemented the food supply by sneaking out early in the morning and stealing milk and pastry from neighbor's porches. Everything was delivered to the door in those days, and simply left there until one arose and claimed it from the front step. Tuck, the urban guerilla, brought these items home and put them inside the front screen door, where Edie Maye would discover them. His early morning pursuit of food ranged across town, even to the Fairgrounds and as far out as the Eagle Dye Company in Claremont. A considerate thief, he didn't like to steal from the same home twice in one week.

Tuck supposed that Edie Maye would think that the foodstuffs were left at the wrong door by mistake. She never offered an explanation of the unexpected food's origins. In the midst of prosperity, they were starving.

Santo showed up at the Cherry Street house one day, saying to Edie Maye that he had heard about Sal, that he was okay and somewhere down south. He had heard this from a friend of the family in Trenton. Edie Maye pressed him for more information without results.

This postcard depicts the Yorkshire Club's facade, dining room and main bar as it was when Sal became interim manager. This and most of the other clubs were closed when nearly the entire town management and police force were named in 193 indictments for their part in sustaining the illegal activities.

It was on Cherry Street that Tuck's nightmares began. Although they featured a variety of monsters, one in particular, a huge man dressed in a tattered tuxedo, with a gaping wound sometimes in his stomach and other times, his chest, stayed with Tuck through high school, the Marine Corps and the Naval Academy.

Chips from the Yorkshire Club are now collector's items. All of the "major" clubs had their own chips. Photos courtesy of "When Vice Was King: A History Of Northern Kentucky Gambling 1920-1970", by Jim Linduff with Roy Klein and Larry Trapp

Tuck named him the "Tuxedo Man." When Tuck's brother took him to the Saturday matinee of "Frankenstein," the movie monster so resembled his dream nemesis that Tuck ran out of the theater and didn't stop running until home.

The monster chased Tuck relentlessly, and no matter what kind of superhuman feats the boy produced to evade him, he eventually turned up in the least expected place, reaching for Tuck just as he would awake in a crying sweat. Eventually, Tuck grew to accept the phenomena, and stopped bringing attention to it when he awoke during the night. It was simply part of his life. As he got older, he anticipated the nightly horror and went to sleep hoping for it soon to be over with, so that he could finish out the night in peace.

Tuck's constant battle to survive the whooping cough continued, and fortunately for him, Doc McDonald's office was now only a block away, at Cherry and Garden. During these bouts, he would drift in and out of consciousness, feverish and straining for breath. Edie Maye packed his chest with a hot pasty concoction of medicines and fed him a syrupy cough medicine by spoon.

When his breathing became really shallow and liquid, she'd send Cholly or Sis for Doc, who would probe his throat with his fingers and try to clear a passage for air.

His brother and sister just didn't seem to get sick, but Tuck was a continual problem, never really getting rid of the congestion in his lungs, and usually running a fever.

The tuxedo man visited Tuck one night when he was fully awake, but feverish and weak. He appeared at the front window of the upstairs bedroom, grinning at Tuck through the wavy glass, his leaking intestines pressing against the lower panes. Tuck's screams, interrupted by coughing spasms, brought Edie Maye running into the room, but he couldn't convince her that the Tuxedo Man was there.

As an adult, Tuck could never remove the scene from his mind, the grotesque intruder plastered against the glass behind her shoulder. Edie Maye obliged Tuck and looked at the window, but she couldn't see him.

She tucked the boy in, renewed the heated bricks at his feet and along his legs, and left him to cope with it. He stared in terror at the apparition for what seemed hours before falling off into a fitful sleep.

Years later, a lady psychologist whom Tuck dated briefly told him that the tuxedo man was a manifestation of his latent homosexual tendencies. Tuck thought he was Sal, or the murdered hobo, asking for retribution. Edie Maye remembered the incident at the Cherry Street house.

"That was the time that your fever was so high, for so long, that all of the outer skin, a thick layer of it, peeled off the bottom of your feet, like they had been burned," she said, "You were nearly comatose for the better part of a week. Everyone thought surely that you would die, even Doc McDonald, but you survived somehow."

About the second year they were in the Cherry Street house, Edie Maye landed a job in the Paxon Street sewing factory, making parachutes in the old Post Office. The work was hard, and they used the industrial model Singers, heavy machines. Edie Maye often came home with fingers bandaged where the needle had passed through, but life became infinitely better, now that they had an income.

Edie Maye was able to talk the manager into letting her have rejected parachute sections, which she then used to make wedding dresses. It was pure silk. There were occasions when she actually gave Tuck coins to spend as he chose. He usually bought an orange or a "delicious" apple, which he considered the greatest luxuries, at the Deli across from Doc McDonald's.

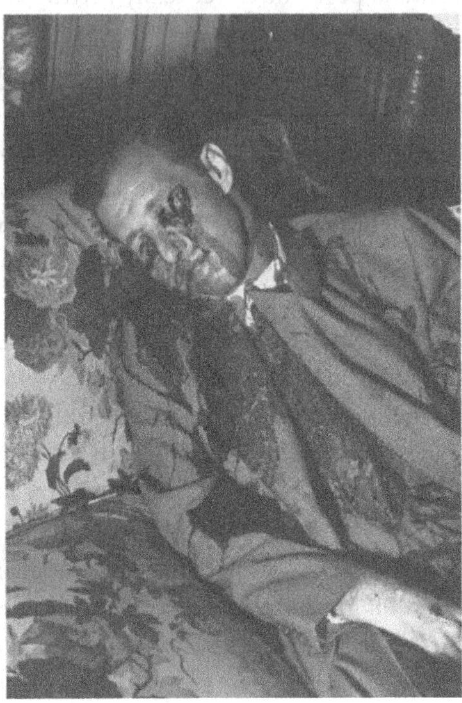

Meyer Lansky, top left, and Bugsy Siegel, bottom left, were alleged to have shared hidden ownership in the Yorkshire Club in Newport, KY, where Sal became an "interim" manager. The picture on the right was taken by Dick Hathcock, a photographer and the first photo journalist from the LA Times to arrive at Virginia Hills home after Bugsy was assassinated. Note that the handsome Bugsy was shot in his "baby blue" eyes, irritants to his mobster friends who resented his publicity with the Hollywood celebrities. Some sources say that Paulie Carbo, Sal's nemesis, setup and arranged the murder. According to Dick Hathcock, this photo was not circulated due to its gruesomeness. Photos by Dick Hathcock and gamblingbeat.com

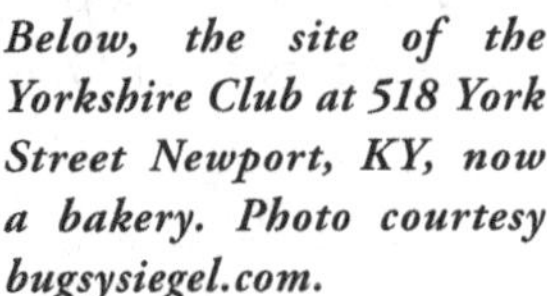

Below, the site of the Yorkshire Club at 518 York Street Newport, KY, now a bakery. Photo courtesy bugsysiegel.com.

13

COVINGTON

WHEN Paulie Carbo's gang marched into the casino at Red Man's Hall waving Tommy guns, it evidenced the chaotic disorganization of what Judge Perskie had described as "big time" gambling in New Jersey. Knucky Johnson, presiding over a flourishing Atlantic City, the Lucchese muscle, Carbo, in Philadelphia/Camden and Sam the Count's family in Elizabeth were constantly struggling for control. There was also a significant group in Newark with ties to the New York families.

Tuck never got the details from Sal. It was one of the items he occasionally asked Sal about without success. Since Sam DeCalvacante apparently ended up in control of the area, assisted by the New York Gambino Family, which later established residency in Cherry Hill, Tuck assumed that "the Count" had prevailed. In fact, the Commission, in solidifying the structure of the new mafia, had decided what to do about the chaos in New Jersey.

The demise of the Casino at Red Men's Hall left a vacuum in the south Jersey gambling marketplace, and as the war effort moved into high gear, Burlington County became a battleground of illegal entrepreneurship. Joseph Brennen, a Philadelphia racketeer, opened the Penn Jersey Athletic Club, a casino in a "big white house" at 22 Alden Avenue in Roebling, and was murdered for his efforts. Brennen, who lived in Philadelphia's Rittenhouse Square neighborhood, was killed by a shotgun blast while still in his car, having just returned from Roebling. The police blamed the shooting on "unknown Burlington Country rival gamblers," who had warned Brennen to "get out of their territory." Vincent "China" Scola, a veteran Camden thug, was the listed suspect.[43]

Joe Bonanno, a close friend of Sam DeCavalcante, became the boss of the Marazano family of New York, and the youngest mafia don at 41. Other members of the Commission often used the smooth talking and respected DeCavalcante as liaison between Bonanno and the rest of the Commission, which had ejected him (Bonanno) from his commission seat of power. Eventually, DeCavalcante would be invited to join the Commission, after being elected boss of the combined families in New Jersey. Thus, Sal's lifelong friend became extremely powerful and his (Sam's) influence would reach as far as the west coast, Florida and the Caribbean.

There were no further killings that Tuck knew of. Freddy Fosciano's demise in the pines being enough warning that things had become serious. Sal had disappeared, as Shorty Rogers would say to Naval Academy seamanship classes, "Faster than a Jewish foreskin." Tony was incarcerated, and the lesser felons associated with the Casino at Red Men's Hall had paid their fines and merged back into the booming WWII society of 1942. Joseph Brennen may have been a victim of Paulie Carbo, but the case went unsolved.

But nothing that happened in South Jersey went without scrutiny of the real "Mafiosos" in New York City. Nicholas DelMore's family was considered a little brother of the New York syndicates. They called the Jersey boys "farmers." DeCavalcante's family grew out of the old Sicilian tradition of a neighborhood Godfather looking after his "flock," his family and friendly neighbors. It was a joke among the New York mobsters that to contact DelMore, DeCalvacante or his men, you had to wait until after five o'clock, since they all had full time jobs. So while they couldn't "make" a member without approval, and had no direct inclusion in the "Commission," their interests were conjoined with the New York gangsters. This all changed with DeCavalcante's rise in the organization.

A minor crisis in Covington, Kentucky required an ingenious solution. Sal, who had solved problems in Burlington and Bristol, was a natural selection to temporarily manage a casino in Covington. At the time, Covington was a gambling Mecca.[44] Cincinnati's sister city featured a half dozen casinos that would be respectable by modern standards; "Carpet joints." They were loosely controlled by the Giancana's Chicago mob; the

Cleveland boys with Moe Dalitz and the Eastern syndicate; Meyer Lansky and Bugsy Siegel of New York. Giancana had become head of a major crime family that had been ruled by Al Capone, "the Outfit."

Casinos and the mob were so firmly entrenched in Covington that Sal's place, the Yorkshire Club, featured pit bosses and dealers who were the third generation croupiers in the same profession and casino. The casinos drew their customers from as far north as Cleveland, their operations completely protected by local law enforcement. The mob's gambling operation supported the city, and was an accepted part of the social structure. There were more than 40 such casinos, most featuring table games and whorehouses in the Cincinnati, Covington, and Newport area. Intrinsic to all of the Casino operations were the associated prostitutes. Even the smallest operations featured a "stable" of girls. One operator claimed to have more than five hundred "ladies" under his control on Milwaukee Avenue.

It was break for Sal, since these positions turned out to be training grounds for Las Vegas, Paradise Island, and eventually even Atlantic City for those who played their cards right. According to Sal, it was a "piece of cake," even dull, but his placement as a Kentucky Casino manager had a purpose and a finite term.

Tuck eventually met some of the executives in Atlantic City casinos who had come there from Las Vegas. They confirmed that the "old salts" in Vegas were those casino managers who had emerged from Covington, Biloxi, and Phenix City, Alabama. One Vice-President of Resorts, the first New Jersey licensed casino, Butch Wixter, told him his story.

"That's who got me started in this business, one of the old Covington hands," he said, "we became great friends, and I was fascinated by the stories of the old days in Covington. There aren't many of those guys left."

"You know, my dad was still alive the day that Resorts opened," Tuck told him, "and I went into the (Resorts) casino with him.[45] We walked around a bit, and then my Dad said, 'That table's doing about $8,000 per hour; that one, about $5,000. Back on the first row, a mechanic just made a switch on the dealer at the first table near the door. I've seen about seven guys in here playing that are banned in Vegas, mechanics, counters and bunko guys …'"

"Those guys like your father; they got their training on the floor and in the streets. They knew what they were doing, all right. He was right, there was a switch on opening day, but we never caught the guy." Butch responded. Tuck heard these words with a heavy heart, as Sal was in the last stages of a terminal cancer. It was a confirmation that his father's understanding of gaming, quick wit and charming personality could have catapulted him into a respectable life as a casino executive in the modern world of gaming in the U.S. The opportunity for respectability grew greater as gaming became a leading industry in the late 80's. But Sal, who had never had a social security number or a regular job, had opted for a life on the edge, and now with a criminal record and no history of legal employment, had cemented his position in the shadows of society.

Sal told Tuck that he had two box men (croupiers) in his Covington casino, the Yorkshire Club, who were the "greatest mechanics he had ever seen." Each of these men, in their sixties at the time, were so deft at switching dice that they could fool an expert, even if he were told they were going to make a switch.

Among the regulars was a young and obnoxious college student who liked to come to the casino, throw money around and in general, behave badly. Since he was the son of the local Mayor, he was tolerated by the previous management. Sal, however, after observing with the young man's behavior for several weeks, understood what he was brought there to do.

"This kid was a real pain in the ass," Sal said, "and he had no class. He was loud and always yelling 'cheat' when he lost in a straight game. He was rough on the girls, embarrassed them in front of other customers, that kind of thing. He needed to be taken down a peg or two. So, I was to figure a way to fix his wagon *without really hurting him*. Nobody wanted to hurt him physically, because of his old man...it was a touchy thing.

"I got hold of a friend of mine, Tommy Cassio from the old days in Atlantic City, and he came out to give me a hand. Tommy was an older guy and he knew how to set up a mark on a long con; that was his specialty. You know him...you stayed with him in Wildwood that summer I took you down the shore; the redheaded guy. He was an old hand at all of the bunko and short cons, too. That's all I needed, because the casino had enough float that I had all the money I needed on a given night.

"So, Tommy comes out, and nobody but he and I and the box man know about the sting. Tommy starts shilling the kid's game, and making up to him while he's losing. Of Course Tommy's losing the casino's own money, but the kid don't know that. All he knows is that every time

Tommy's in his game, Tommy loses a bundle and he, the kid, he wins a few hundred. All this is being done by Tommy and the old man handling the dice.

"So this goes on for several weeks. The kid thinks Tommy is some kind of oil baron, because he's got the pointed boots and ten gallon hat and talking about oil rigs and Texas, while he's losing lots of money. Then Tommy got the kid aside, and after a few weeks of gaining his confidence, tells him that together, they could take the game for a big hit. They need about $20,000 stake money. Tommy says he'll put up $10,000 and if the kid wants in, he'll let him put up the rest, and they'll split the winnings. Tommy was dangling the bait, and the kid goes for it, hook, line and sinker.

"See, this kid thinks he's better than us. His old man's the Mayor, and they don't like Italians, and all that bull shit.

"Course, his old man's on the take just like the rest of the town, and his old man is getting all the best girls in the place free of charge, but he thinks he's something special. Without us in there, the town's just a bunch of hillbillies, but that's the way people are, once they start collecting the bucks, then all of a sudden, they're too good for you.

"So the sting is all set, Tommy tells the croupier that they're playing together tonight, and he gives the kid the money to buy chips and tells him to make the bets. Then he buys drinks and starts kibitzing the croupier and cheering for the kid every time he wins. Tommy's a good actor!

"It's on a Saturday night and the old man takes the $20,000 from the two of them. I'm watching the whole thing and I can't even see it happen, these old guys are so smooth. And Tommy sets it up so's it's the kid's fault... he makes the wrong bet after Tommy tells him what to do. I mean Tommy did it in a way that was slick, so that after you thought about what he said, it could have been either way, but the kid, because of the way the game was set up, did it the wrong way … for him! Then Tommy jumps on his case, saying "You dumb bastard, you bet it the wrong way! I told you to never play black after odd!"

In a few plays, the old man wiped them out!

"So the kid, he starts raising a stink, and I take them in the office and try to settle him down, 'cause now he starts blabbering that he lost his old man's money, and the Mayor, he doesn't know about it, and he's scared shitless that Tommy's gonna' beat the hell out of him, and all this stuff.

Tommy's making out like he wants to kill the kid! The Mayor can make trouble, even though he knows his kid's an asshole, and he will. Now we know it's the Mayor's money the kid lost. This is the touchy part; now the heat is on me.

"So I call my boss, and I tell him what happened. He knows the Mayor and the kid and the situation, and he thinks it's funny as hell, but he says, 'O.K., great job. You better clear out of there, we'll give the Mayor some of his money back, and throw the kid out for good, and we'll blame it on you.' So he sends me out to L.A. and tells me to call him from there, cause he's got something for me to do in Hollywood."

"What the hell did you do that for, I mean, the casino makes plenty of money playing it straight, doesn't it?"

"Oh, sure," Sal said, "you can't beat the house. The house always wins, no matter what."

"That's what I thought," Tuck said, "so, why bother to go to all this trouble to get a guy?"

Sal was picking his teeth with a toothpick. He usually had a supply on hand, and without looking Tuck's way, he settled down in the seat, and put the toothpick away.

"Sure, it's a gold mine when you're the house," he said, chuckling, "but playing it straight's no fun, and that little bastard had it coming. He never knew what hit him, and that's what I was there for, to take his money and make him think it was his own fault!"

14

HOLLYWOOD

TUCK had the opportunity to attend the press party for a revival of one of the old movie musicals at an Atlantic City casino. Milling around with the guests and suddenly confronted by Donald O'Connor the musical comedy star, he introduced himself and asked O'Connor if he remembered Sal. He said no, but he remembered the circumstances Tuck referred to, "the convertible restaurant" across from the main gate of the Paramount studio, and they shared a couple of laughs about it.

Sal left Covington, Kentucky, in a hurry. As it turned out, it was just the right time, too. A few short years later, Estes Kefauver, his Senate Committee and Bobby Kennedy, assisted by Elliot Ness, completely shut down illegal gambling in Covington and Phenix City, Alabama. Sal often used swear words when he referred to Kefauver and his Committee.

In Los Angeles, he assumed management of a restaurant/casino in a building across the street from the Paramount movie lot's main gate. When Tuck was in LA on business years later, he took the time to find the only major studio having a restaurant across from its main gate; it was Lucy's El Adobe restaurant directly across from Paramount Studios main gate, and it had been there since the 1940's, although its ownership had changed several times.

Tuck had to assume that this particular escapade, like many of his others, was financed, approved and encouraged by the 'boys,' as he called them, back east in response to a particular crisis. He told Tuck that the "furniture," came from Vegas and the craps tables were built by the

Paramount set carpenters. When Tuck asked an aging Santo about the Hollywood casino at the family viewing for Sal, he said,

"Hell, no, most of that stuff in the banquet room was made by the set carpenters at Paramount...we only got the roulette wheels from the Vegas people. The craps and blackjack tables were made with folding covers so's you could pull them out and cover up the play; they folded out and rotated over the game with a table cloth and place settings glued on it and looked like a banquet. The fake flowers, dishes and silverware were glued in place, like a movie set or the money on Count Felix's Bar in the 'burg'."

Bing Crosby, Fred Astair, Dorothy Lamore, Betty Hutton and other stars of the fabulous musical comedy era were his customers. They came across the street to eat and play in the casino between takes. Sal got a chuckle out of telling Tuck that the studio gate guard was also on his payroll as a lookout, and if any cops showed up, he immediately called on the phone, and the casino was instantly transformed into the harmless looking banquet room of a restaurant.

Sal never mentioned meeting or knowing Sinatra, but he, like Frank Sinatra, also wore a blue sapphire pinky ring dating from about this time on, which was the friendship gift of "Momo" Giancana, the Chicago mobster who supposedly took over the "Outfit," the Capone/Accardo Empire.

Tuck remembered Sal showing him the ring, and straining to see the star in the stone, as he rotated his hand in the light. He said that a "friend from Chicago" gave him the ring, but never offered any further information. But all of Tuck's uncles confirmed that he got the ring from Giancana, and said Sinatra was there when it was given to him.

Sal made it a point to never ask for favors.

"I can make things happen if I want, but it's not good to always be asking for favors. If you know someone who can really help you, he's not going to keep doing you favors unless you do something in return, then you owe favors, so it's better not to ask. Sometimes you can get the same result without asking, but just by telling somebody you can," he said.

The Hollywood casino, furnished with roulette wheels from Vegas, had support from Jack Dragna and higher ups, and apparently was quite successful, for a time. The café was operated by Jimmy Utley, a lifelong rival of Hollywood's notorious mobster, Mickey Cohen. Cohen, former prize fighter and a long time resident of LA, aspired to take over the rackets there, replacing his new boss, Bugsy Siegel, who had been sent out to LA by the eastern bosses. Jack Dragna, a cousin of Tommy ("Three Fingers Brown") Lucchese, was a competitor of Cohen, and also had other New York ties. Lucchese was a member of the Commission, and his cousin (Dragna) was furious about Siegel's intrusion into his territory.

Los Angeles was just emerging from the Tony Cornero era, when gambling ships had adorned the shoreline. State Attorney General and Governor Earl Warren, later to become Chief Justice of the Supreme Court, led the fight to close down Cornero's operations.[46]

Cornero bought three old freighters, converted them to casinos and anchored them three and a half miles offshore in Los Angeles harbor. Never in bed with Chicago or the eastern mob, Cornero avoided trouble with both Mickey Cohen and Jack Dragna by operating offshore. Dozens of smaller craft acted as ferries and supplied the ships with customers. It was also about this time that Bugsy Siegal was murdered in Los Angeles by his Eastern partners. Siegal had created what became the first major hotel/casino in Las Vegas; the Flamingo. His partners assumed he was skimming the construction money when his girlfriend, Virginia Hill, was discovered depositing large sums in Swiss banks and leasing an apartment in Geneva.

Las Vegas, at that time, was a cow town stop over for travelers crossing the deserts of Nevada, the only state with legalized gambling and prostitution. The murder of Siegal spurned a control scrum as his potential successors, Mickey Cohen and Jack Dragna, vied for power. Siegal's arrival in L.A. had relegated Cohen to a subordinate role, where he festered awaiting the opportunity to replace his new boss. Los Angeles became an "open" city, and the gangster elements were creating enough trouble that the law cracked down on organized crime. Two of Cohen's thugs walked into Lucy's restaurant and one pistol whipped Jimmy Utley to near death in front of a crowded room of diners, while the other held the movie star onlookers at gunpoint. Some reports say it was Mickey himself that blackjacked Utley. They casually walked out as Utley slumped to the floor. Spectators, including Joel McCrea and Shirley Temple thought it part of a movie scene, or rehearsal for one, and resumed dining. Utley operated the Bingo game on Cornero's ship, the Lux, and several Bingo joints in Venice Beach, and Cohen, with his police connections, got them shut down. Lucy's promotion to a carpet joint (they had previously only taken policy and some horse bets there) replaced Utley's lost revenue and assuaged his broken head as his fractured skull healed.[47]

Lucy's El Adobe Café in Los Angeles, about 1935, featured a different spelling of the name. It was located at 5535 Melrose, directly across the street from Paramount Studio's Main Gate. According to Tere Tereba, author of "Mickey Cohen, the Life and Times of LA's Notorious Mobster", it was owned by Jimmy Utley, a longtime rival of Cohen's. Utley was associated with Jack Dragna and operated the café as a bookie room until Sal transformed the banquet room into a "carpet joint," with a full range of casino games. Photo courtesy of eatingla.blogspot.com/2008/03/historic-la-mexican-restaurants

At this time, Los Angeles was a cauldron of boiling police corruption, underworld killings and mysterious disappearances of critical witnesses in murder trials. Dragna and Cohen were locked in combat over the lucrative illegal businesses across the city. There were five unsuccessful attempts on Cohen's life.

In Sal's words, he "got the hell out of L.A. in a hurry." It must have been pretty hot, because he went down to Mexico and stayed there for almost a year, when, tempers cooled, he returned to New Jersey. Cornero, busted by Governor Earl Warren, moved on to Las Vegas where he eventually created the Meadows Casino resort and the Stardust Hotel and Casino. Jack Dragna, although a member of the Commission, was minimized by factors beyond his control. He avoided a deportation order to Sicily, but was harassed, indicted and jailed for "lewd acts" recorded by bedroom cameras in his home.

Neither Tuck nor Edie Maye knew that Sal had holed up in Mexico for a year. He discovered this when Sal was very sick, and traveling periodically to Trenton from his home in Reddington Beach for treatment of his prostate cancer. Tuck was teaching school and one hot Saturday in early June, he received a phone call from the mother of one of his students.

She lived in a more eloquent part of town, and invited Tuck to a pool party that was in progress. Puzzled, but sensitive about parent/student relations, he drove over, only about a mile from his home, to discover that the party was in Sal's honor. He was sitting comfortably by the pool, immaculately dressed in his Florida sports coat and white shoes, sipping a shot of Seagram's VO.

Mrs. Favill filled Tuck in, not knowing that Sal hadn't shared his life with his son, telling him that she had met Sal in L.A., where she was trying to get into films, and she had accompanied him to Mexico, where they lived in an expensive hotel for a year. Sal verified her story with an occasional chuckle or clarifying remark. Her husband, sitting opposite and listening intently to the story, pretended that he was completely aware of all this and not bothered by it all.

When Sal left Mexico, she stayed on, having gotten a couple of small roles in Mexican films, and eventually moved back to Los Angeles. Tuck was flabbergasted. He felt very uncomfortable about his student, Judy Favill, who obviously knew more about his life than he did.

Tuck made a conscious effort to avoid any reference to his family at the high school where he taught. When the conversation in the faculty lounge or cafeteria drifted that way, he never joined in. Even when his brother died of cirrhosis, Tuck only missed one day of school, and made no effort to inform any of his colleagues.

"Jesus Christ, Dad," Tuck said to Sal the next time he stopped at the house, "why didn't you tell me about the Favills? That little girl knows more about you than I do."

"Well, it never occurred to me," Sal said, "that you needed to know about it."

"She could spread all kinds of shit around school," Tuck said, "and whether it's true or not, it could be a problem for me, with the kids that I teach, and maybe with the staff."

"She won't say nothin'," Sal said, "the kid just thinks her Mom and me are old friends. Don't worry about it."

Sal had returned to New Jersey with flair. He rolled up to the Cherry Street hovel in a royal blue 1941 Lincoln Zephyr limousine, complete with jump seats, driver partition, driver/passenger radio, electrically operated windows, V-twelve engine and white wall tires. It was the middle of World War II. Nobody drove cars like this, or could get enough gasoline ration stamps to run one.

It wasn't long before they were moving again, to a nice little bungalow on Garden Street, in one of the better sections of town. Four years later, when they were forced out of the bungalow, Edie Maye told Tuck the story of how she was told that they got it. She had to, in order to explain why they were moving. Sal had "lost the house in a poker game, and four years previously, he had won it" as part of a pot in another poker game, but it was all a lie. The truth was that the slot machines and gaming tables from Red Men's Hall Casino were stored in the basement, and Edie Maye and the children were there to give some semblance of security, protection from Carbo, who still coveted the equipment.

But Tuck believed this story, because the unfinished upstairs of the bungalow, when they moved in, was filled with boxes of sporting goods, which they assumed were also part of the winning pot. They took a few of the things that they could use, and the inventory soon disappeared, sold off to someone. The Lincoln Zephyr also had disappeared, and Sal now was driving a 1941 Oldsmobile convertible, a very rare commodity during the war years.[48]

The Oldsmobile was gray in color with a black canvas top. One morning, Tuck noticed Sal pointing out something to Uncle Santo at the rear of the car. There were four bullet holes in its trunk.

Shortly after the Favill incident, Tuck drove Sal back to Florida, using the opportunity for a short vacation for his three daughters. With the girls sleeping in the back of Tuck's station wagon, Sal told the story of the Oldsmobile convertible.

Sal was beginning to open up a little to Tuck as of late, as though the Favill revelation had convinced him that Tuck ought to know a little more about his father. Tuck welcomed the information and treated Sal with respect. Occasionally, he felt real bitterness, but he didn't let it interfere with learning more about Sal's life.

"Tony and I were running a big game down in the pines, south of Vineland," Sal said, referring of course, to Tony Marinella, "and we dropped the take at the Vineland Hotel, in the center of town about two in the morning, when the game was over. This was a pretty good game, lots of action. Sometimes we had three, four layouts going at once, forty or fifty players, so the take was pretty good.

"We had this big cinder block building way out in the woods. This place was really back there, no farms, nothing around, it was one of those gun clubs, and we had some help to run the games, park the cars, that kind of stuff.

"So, that night, the night the Olds got the bullet holes, we go into Vineland to drop off the take, and this is how it works. The guy who we drop to, he stands outside the hotel with a newspaper, and we've got signals. If the paper's folded, do this, if he's got it open, do that. And we always make two passes on the front of the hotel before we stop, just in case.

"And, he's standing there, like usual, but something's fishy because he's standing really stiff, like a statue, instead of his usual Dan Duryea pose. And he's standing in the wrong place, not where he usually is when we come by. He's making the right signal, but he looks at us real funny. Now, Tony's driving and I've got this big paper bag of cash, Several grand, all small bills, in my lap, so I say, 'Slow down on this pass, but don't stop. Something looks fishy.'

"This time as we go by, Tony slows down almost to a stop and our guy starts shaking his head, no, no. Then we see a couple of guys coming running out of the front of the hotel, and Tony says, 'Let's get the hell out of here!'

"So we take off and head out of town, and in no time, these guys from the hotel are right behind us in a big Cadillac sedan. But they can't stay up because Tony dips down some alleys and back streets. We had an escape route scouted out, see, just in case somebody ever tried to jump us. We figured we'd lost them, and we beat it up through the pines to Hammonton, where we stop for gas. So, we're filling up and talking about who these guys might have been, and bam, bam we hear shots! It's these guys in the Cadillac, they caught up, and now they're rolling into the gas station, shooting at us.

"They had us scouted pretty good and as soon as they lost us, they must have headed for Hammonton, too. Tony backs out of the station and rips the hose right out of the pump, and we take off up Route 206, dragging about 40 feet of gas hose. The hose stretched, you know, and sort of unwound into a long coil, and it's flopping around like a kite tail. The Cadillac is right behind us and we're jumping curbs and throwing gravel like the Keystone Cops. I jump in the back seat and start shooting back, and we're having this gun battle all the way up 206, flat out for about 15 or 20 miles, doing about a hundred and ten.

"I can hear the bullets whistling by, and when they hit the trunk, they make a funny kind of 'plop' sound. All I can see behind us is their headlights swerving back and forth, but I guess I got lucky and hit the front of the Caddy, because the hood pops up and folds back on their windshield, somewhere around Indian Mills, and they go off the road. It's four o'clock in the morning, so nobody knows anything about it but us."

"So what happened to the game?" Tuck inquired. Later in his life, Sal would ask Tuck to ask more questions, saying, "You ought to write all this down, you can write."

"Well, we couldn't sit around with all that cash," he said, continuing the story, "It wasn't our money, so we drive back down to Vineland that morning, and we locate our guy in the diner, and we give him the money.

"He tells us they were a couple of guys who were in the game regular, from South Philly, and when he describes them, we know who they are right away. They had their guns on his back for two hours waiting for us, so he was pretty scared. They're friends of that god damned Carbo, the promoter. That morning, we call the boss, and that takes care of the problem."

"What happened? Did those guys get killed?" Tuck asked, realizing that these kinds of opportunities, where details were revealed, were far and few between.

"I don't know," he responded, "all I know is that they never bothered us again."

Shortly after the bullet-riddled Oldsmobile episode, Sal disappeared again, but this time, unlike others, his escape impacted directly on Edie Maye. Tuck didn't know any of the details of where he had gone or why, but, once again, they were back to oatmeal for dinner, and Edie Maye percolating coffee in an old pretzel can.

The bungalow property included an empty corner lot, which was occupied largely by weeds. One afternoon, after Sal had disappeared, a large black sedan with three menacing figures inside, all wearing overcoats and Fedora hats, drove up in front of the empty lot on the opposite side of the street, parked and turned off the engine.

The car, with its occupants, remained there for nine days. Occasionally, it would pull away, only to return within a half hour. Whenever it left, one of the occupants would slide out the street side door and walk into the bushes and trees in the vacant lot on the other side of the street, next to Bill Grady's garage.

Edie Maye got pretty scared, and kept the kids in the house, not allowing them even to go to school. After a couple of tense days, she went next door and using the Parker's phone, called Bucky Squires. The following day, Edie and the children watched as Bucky approached the car and talked to the occupants. He waited while they started up and drove away, but they were back as soon as Bucky was gone. Edie Maye tried not to let the children see how terrified she was. She was certain that the ominous car was somehow connected to Paulie Carbo.

Tuck and his brother slept in bunk beds in the front bedroom of the cottage, Edie Maye; upstairs in the unfinished attic, and Sis, now in high school, in the rear first floor bedroom. In the middle of the night, all were all awakened by a scream from Sis's bedroom. A large crash followed, and then only the sound of Sis crying.

Sis had awakened to discover one of the men from the car in her room, just about to open the hallway door. She immediately screamed, and the man jumped onto the bed, kicking her in the side as he did so, then stumbled and crashed out the back window. He smashed the entire window, taking the lower half frame and glass, Venetian blind and curtain with him.

Not having a telephone, Edie Maye ran next door to the Ellis Parker house, and they called the Police. When the police came, Tuck followed them outside where muddy footprints, shattered glass and wood verified the story. Some old tires and crates had been stacked against the house to provide the intruder means to enter the window, a good five feet from the ground.

Of course, Tuck never discovered who the men in the black car were, or why they were after Sal, and he never volunteered an explanation.

The following morning, Tuck's brother, anxious to protect them from other such incidents, went into Sal's dresser, where several guns were kept. Standing just inside the bedroom, holding a .45 automatic upside down and trying to figure out how to insert the clip, he discharged a round left in the chamber.

The bullet passed through Tuck's pajama sleeve and the bedroom wall, crossed the living room, ricocheted from a folding top table, its path deflected by 45 degrees, and departed the house through a perfectly round hole in the middle living room bay window glass.

Anyone sitting in either of two constantly used living room chairs would have been killed instantly. Tuck, knuckling his eyes, trying to wake up, was unharmed. Fortunately, it was only seven o'clock in the morning, and only Tuck and his brother were up and about. Terrified by the black car, no one slept very well after that in the bungalow, but at least the car and its occupants had disappeared.

The lack of money and food was even worse than the fear for personal safety. With Sal gone, Edie Maye was back to sewing dresses and mending clothes for people. This house had some amenities, a coal stove in the basement, hot water and such, but they were soon reduced to using the old kerosene heater, set up in the dining room, to keep them warm.

One day, Tuck and his brother discovered a large ring containing hundreds of keys in the attic, in a suitcase belonging to Sal. Three dozen slot machines, from the casino at Red Men's Hall lined the walls of the cellar. The boys tried for weeks to fit keys to machines, hoping to find some money in the coin boxes. Failing to match any key to a machine, they attempted without success to open the machines with tools, and Edie Maye wouldn't let them smash the one-armed bandits with an axe, as New York's Mayor LaGuardia had done in the MovieTone News.[49] In later years, Tuck added the keys/slot machine problem to his Algebra II class presentations, seeking the probability of matching one of the 300 keys to one of the 36 slot machines.

15

TAXI, TAXI

SAL returned in a few months, the crisis apparently over. He concentrated on the taxi business, and the house was often filled with several of the drivers, and of course, their stories. Fort Dix, McGuire Air Force Base and Wrightstown, only 15 miles away, were overflowing with soldiers and the object of Sal's newest adventures.

Edie Maye, now accustomed to his arbitrary comings and goings, accepted him back without question. She knew that it was useless to ask where he had been, or to suggest that they ought to try living an ordinary life. There were lots of jobs available, since most of the working force was under arms.

She couldn't help admitting to herself that she still loved the flashy Italian, in spite of the pain and suffering he had caused her. Even with all she put up with, he was a hell of lot more interesting than most men she had met. But she resisted his sexual advances. Sis had been a love baby, no question. Cholly and Tuck were burdens that she neither anticipated nor wanted, and she certainly didn't want any more. Life could change on a dime, she knew, and it was hard enough as it was.

"Sleep with Jeannie," she told him, "if you want sex. Everyone in town thinks she's your wife, anyway." Since Sal was doing exactly that, he acceded to her wishes. He noticed that each time he returned she seemed to be stronger of will, and he begrudgingly admired her for taking the abuse he was generating in her life.

The Marinella brothers showed up again, Tony on a brief respite between jail sentences, and soon Sal had a thriving Taxi business, headquartered in Wrightstown. A telephone was installed, with a party line to be used exclusively for the business. His customers were GI's, trying to get home on weekends before being shipped off to Europe to face the Germans. In addition to the 1941 Lincoln, his fleet also featured a 1930 Cadillac Limousine.

The Cadillac was an incredible vehicle, close to 23 feet in length; it was powered by a V-16 engine, had a huge luggage rack on its roof, and a rack mounted trunk extending from its rear. The hood featured 5 chromium plated door vents on each side, a white walled wire-wheel spare tire inset into each of sloping front fenders, radio communications between driver and passenger, a convertible top over the driver's compartment and jump seats and a bar in the passenger compartment. The chromium hood ornament, a winged lady, was nearly ten inches high.

On occasions when the Cadillac was off duty, Edie Maye used it. Sis being a cheerleader at the high school, it was enlisted several times to transport some of the school's band, a comical sight with kids, drums and tubas protruding from every window and tiny Edie Maye behind the wheel.

War Cars. These cars, a 1930 Cadillac V16 Imperial Limousine and a 1941 Lincoln V12 Zephyr Limousine were the nucleus of Sal's taxi fleet during WWII. The business was made possible by black market gas rationing 'C' stamps secured through his New York mob connections. The seven passenger limos were designated for long hauls. The V16 Cadillac was very similar to the armored V12 Cadillac 341A Sedan that President Roosevelt absconded from the Treasury Dept. after its owner, Al Capone was arrested. Photo courtesy of flikr.com

The Cadillac and the Lincoln were used to ferry groups of GI's on long distance trips, as far as Albany, New York, and Paducah, Kentucky. Eventually the fleet included a half dozen other cars, everything from 1935 Fords to a 1938 Chevrolet sedan.

Having no meters for his cabs, keeping the drivers from skimming was a problem. Tuck overheard Sal and Tony talking about this one day.

"That sonofabitch McFarland's got slippery fingers," Tony said, "I know he's pullin' down more than we are."

They were referring to a driver named Tom McFarland, who was at the house often. He was very polite at all times and dressed in stereotype; leather jacket with a bowtie, black leather cap with visor, and pencil stub behind his ear. He always made a big deal about turning in his bank, and elaborately describing his fares to Sal.

Tuck, belly down in the Sunday Bulletin's Prince Valiant, knew he shouldn't be in range of this conversation, but Sal didn't seem to notice him in the corner of the living room.

"Is that so," Sal responded uncommittedly to Tony's comment. Edie Maye had never liked Tony, and once told Tuck that Sal often argued with Tony over the taxi business. One day he knocked the bigger man out cold, the argument having progressed beyond words.

"Yeah," Tony continued, "and I think he's into some action on the girls, too." Sal glanced at Tuck, who was concentrating on Prince Valiant. He began speaking in Italian, and the words were harsh. Then he finished up in English.

"My brother-in-law, Lenny, he can handle it," he said, "We'll take care of this my way."

About a week later, Tom McFarland came to the house about eight o'clock on a weekday evening, when he should have been working. He was obviously upset, and his face flushed and breathing heavily. Sal lead him into the dining room, where they sat down at the big table. Tuck again was involved with the evening Bulletin comics in the living room.

"George just left, he told me you were coming in. What happened?" Sal asked Tom, "Did you see this guy?"

"Not very good. He jumps in the cab while I'm at the light in front of the Dix Hotel, and says he wants to go to New Egypt." Tom is very apologetic as he continues, "Jeez, I'm really sorry about the take. I gave it all to him. He had a pistol to my head before I got out of town. I didn't want to get pistol-whipped. I know a guy got killed by a pistol whipping. I'm sorry about the money, but you understand, right? I mean, you didn't want me to not give it to him, did you?"

"Did he hit you with the gun?" Sal asked.

"No, I just gave him the whole take, all fifty bucks. I'd had a pretty good day until then," Tom was dejected. Sal was sitting across the corner of the table from Tom. His legs were crossed and he was leaning forward, with his left hand on Tom's shoulder, looking directly in his eyes as the story unfolded.

"Did you go to the police?" Sal asked.

"No, I come right to you. I figured you'd know what to do. Jeez, I'm real sorry about it, about the money, I mean, but what was I going to do? I wasn't going to take a pistol whipping for no fifty bucks." Tom had a way of making you feel sorry for him.

"How much?" Sal said softly. Tom was having trouble returning his gaze.

"Fifty bucks," Tom responded again, looking down at his shoes.

Without changing his position or his stare, Sal said, "Len, come on in here," and Tuck's Uncle Len sauntered through the doorway between the kitchen and dining room. He had Tom's money pouch in his left hand. Len was Sal's brother-in-law, and was more inclined to Sal's business ventures than his blood brothers.

"Jesus Christ," shouted Tom, "that's him! That's the bastard that robbed me!" He was staring first at Len and then his money pouch, after Len tossed it on the table.

The pouch hit the dining room table with a clanging thump, and Len said, 'a hundred thirty bucks!" There was dead silence in the room and then a moan.

"Oh, shit," said Tom.

Sal let the silence sink in. Len, leaning against the doorway, clipped the end of a big cigar, spun it around against his tongue, reversed it and lit up with a Zippo. The lighter made a loud click when he closed it.

"Now I think there's been a mistake made in your addition, Tom," Sal said, "and I think you miscounted your take. Is that what happened?" Sal still had his hand on Tom's shoulder, but tighter. Tom was fidgeting around in his seat, and when he looked in toward the living room, Tuck noticed a streak of tears on his cheek. Tuck had abandoned all pretense of reading the paper.

"Jesus Christ, you set me up!" Tom said.

Sal continued, ignoring Tom's observation. "Tony thinks you're a bad guy, Tom, but I don't think so. I think you're a good guy that made a bad mistake. I'm going to overlook your mistake, Tom, because you're a good driver, and I know it's not going to happen again. Am I right, Tom?"

"Oh, shit," Tom said, looking everywhere except at Sal, who was about ten inches from his nose.

"Tom, I've got to tell Tony what the score is, you understand? I'd like to say that this was just a bad mistake that won't happen again. You tell me, Tom." Sal was very serious.

"I was stupid," Tom blurted out, "to try and cheat you. I'm sorry, I was stupid." Sal stood up and patted Tom on the back. Tom jumped up as though Sal's hand contained an electric charge.

"What about Tony, Sal?" He was one of several people who called Sal his real Italian name. "You'll square it with Tony, right? I mean, it's all there, all the money. It'll never happen again, I swear."

"Don't worry about it. It's all over. You'll be O.K. I'll fix it with Tony," Sal said as he walked him to the front door, "Everybody can make a mistake now and then." Tom was stumbling over his own feet, apologizing and thanking Sal as he backed out the door, his face lined with tears and contorted with fear and relief.

Sal and his brother-in-law laughed hard about the episode. Tuck had never seen his father laugh loudly and the affair stuck in his memory. Tuck heard later that the McFarland incident led to another big argument between Tony and Sal, according to his sister,

"Tony wanted to kill Tommy. He was a mean person, but Dad wouldn't hear of it. He said Tommy was his best driver, and he straightened him out."

About a year later, Tom McFarland had ferried six GI's to upstate New York in the big Cadillac, and on the return trip, had pulled off the road to get some sleep. A Greyhound bus rear ended the parked car, crushing the whole passenger compartment. The car was so sturdy that Tom, sound asleep on the seat in the driver's compartment, only received minor bruises. The whole front end of the bus was demolished and the Greyhound driver killed.

The half demolished limousine sat in the back yard under the willow tree for a few years, until Edie Maye sold it to a local farmer, Mr. Milich. He cut off the back end and bolted a flat bed directly on the chassis. When When Tuck left town to enlist in the Marine Corps ten years later, he was still running tomatoes to Campbell Soup in Camden in the Cadillac V-16.[50]

Sal was running blanket games down in the pines while his taxi business was flourishing in Wrightstown. A lot of the GI's wanted to gamble, and he was eager to please them.

"I never asked anybody to do something they didn't want to do," he said. It wasn't long after the Tom McFarland incident, however, that the State Police made a huge raid on a pinelands game, taking in about forty people.

The story even made the Philadelphia papers, and Sal told one of the drivers that he and Tony had left the place through a back window minutes before the State Police rolled in. It didn't make a lot of difference to the outcome, though. He and Tony ended up in Trenton State Prison again, this time for a year, Tony on a 3-1/2 to 5 year sentence.

Over the years, in various conversations, Sal would occasionally express bitterness about the fact that he did time in Prison, and most of the people involved in the operation, never even got a mention in the press.

"The problem is that I never did nothin' on my own." he explained. "You can't just open up a place, and start games, and you can't just book horses or numbers, either. Half of the cops and lawyers are in on it, up to their ass, but they never get caught."[51]

Another of his favorite pieces of advice to Tuck concerned lawyers.

"You want to make money, be a lawyer. Being a lawyer is like getting a license to steal, they're all crooks." One of the few times that Sal ever spoke harshly to Tuck was the day he returned home from that prison stint, and the dinner table featured honest-to-god sirloin steak. Tuck couldn't eat it.

"Eat that goddamn steak, boy." Sal finally shouted in frustration. It didn't work. The piece of steak on Tuck's plate, neatly surrounded by green peas and mashed potatoes, was as alien to him as a caviar pate. He didn't even know what it was, having never seen such expensive meat on the table before.

Edie Maye was shocked when Sal yelled at the boy. It was uncharacteristic for him to raise his voice to anyone. She assumed that this time, the stay in prison hadn't been as easy as the first sentence. She could see that he was harder; there was a toughness that showed around his eyes that wasn't there before. It pained her to think of him locked up, caged like an animal.

But she was happy that he was home. Maybe this time he'll stay. Sal seemed to be concerned for the family's welfare. He gave Edie Maye money and told her to stock up and get some decent food in the house. She sensed that he wanted to make a go of it, to try being a family man.

But the taxi business was over, and nobody looked after Sal's interests while he was away, and his indefatigable source of counterfeit "C" stamps (gasoline rationing stamps) was gone.[52] In a few short weeks it was obvious to Edie Maye that he was going to disappear again, and he did. She chastised herself for being so weak, and being taken in again, but she knew she couldn't help herself.

Sal showed up again on Thanksgiving Day with a fifteen pound turkey. Not only did Edie Maye not have a roasting pot big enough to hold the bird, but she couldn't fit it the oven of the tiny gas stove in the kitchen, sans pot. She ended up cooking it in parts, and they were thankful. She didn't tell Sal that she was pregnant again.

A few weeks later, she stumbled on the stair and tumbled from her bedroom to the first floor. Tuck came home from school that day to find Doc McDonald at the house and Edie Maye flat on her back.

"Your Mom took a bad fall," Doc said, "and she's going to be laid up for a while until she gets better. She needs your help, now, son."

But Tuck wanted to hear nothing about it, and he continued his defiant ways. When Sal disappeared again, it was as though war had been declared. Edie Maye yelled at Tuck a lot, and by the time he was five, bare handed spankings on his bare buttocks were pretty common. Later, she replaced her hand with a porcelain hand mirror.

It was during this period that Edie Maye miscarried, and somehow she felt Tuck had to share some blame in it. He was such a trial. Neither of them could explain their behavior. Under the intense pressure of desperate poverty, Edie Maye took out her frustrations on the Tuck, and Tuck, in defiant humiliation and pride, continued to frustrate her. Cholly and Sis kept out of the way of it, amazed at the punishment that Tuck engendered. Edie Maye realized that the boy was struggling with his emotions over his father. It was obvious that he hated Sal, but at the same time desperately wanted to love him. Sometimes she wondered how Tuck kept hanging on, having nursed him through a half dozen brushes with death. And she knew that the boy was as stubborn and proud as herself, more like her than she wanted to admit.

Tuck never cried during those daily beatings, although Edie Maye did, in rage, frustration and pity. Sometimes the beatings would occur in front of other people, and on some occasions, she had them join in. Aunt Floss, in particular, seemed to enjoy punishing Tuck.

But the truth of the matter was that Tuck had almost no control of his bowels; if a toilet were more than a minute or two away, he was in trouble. And it wasn't that Tuck held back his tears and then, when alone, indulged in himself in pity and sobbing. His only defense to the beatings was to outlast Edie Maye. He simply didn't cry, when taking the blows or afterwards, but he had no idea how to prevent or avoid the cataclysmic disaster of a spontaneous bowel movement.

Subconsciously, he began to believe that he *was* despicable, and if Edie Maye had turned on him, who was left? He was beginning to direct a lot of fear and hatred inward. Obviously he was wrong in hating Sal. Edie Maye never gave an inkling that he should feel this way about his father. She didn't hate him, but Tuck knew that there was something wrong. Why didn't she hate him? Tuck had been to Donny Well's house, his father lived there all the time. He was a carpenter. And Billy's dad, he was never home, he was in the Army, but there was no question that he took care of Billy and his Mom.

Tuck, invested with his mother's innate intelligence, couldn't find the answers to the questions. It was too confusing for him. He thought that he must have loved Sal, but he hated him at the same time and Edie Maye, she was everything to him, but she wouldn't hear any sass about Sal. He was usually in trouble for something. And of course, there were the beatings. The force of her blows sometimes propelled him across the bathroom in six inch slides as he stood rigidly defiant. She started beating by the door and ended up with Tuck bent over the toilet, faint headed with jaws locked in bitter defiance.

Tuck couldn't understand the reasons for his hatred and fear of Sal. He assumed that his father's actions toward them were out of necessity, that they were always broke and starving because he was, too. Otherwise, Edie Maye would do something about it. During the frenzied punishment, he sometimes fantasized that it was Sal being beaten. But he was never told by Edie Maye why Sal didn't live with them, like other fathers, or that it was wrong for him to flaunt his relationships with other women. Edie Maye never said a bad word about Sal or his behavior.

He rebelled against nearly everything, frustrating and enraging everyone except Cholly. Sis's boyfriends knocked him around on occasion, when he drove her to distraction with his taunts. One of them knocked him unconscious in the front yard one day, and that was too much for Edie Maye. She forced the teenager to apologize to Tuck and told him he wasn't welcome at the house anymore.

But for Tuck, it was too late. The only person he could relate to in the family was Cholly, and even he excluded Tuck from his escapades with the older boys he ran around with. It seemed to Tuck that he had been chasing his big brother all of his life, just trying to be with him. His life was a trail of misery and pain, nightmares and fear.

So he sought refuge in the acres of woods that edged up to the back of the house, and began to develop a love of the outdoors, camping and fishing.

Ashurst woods featured two fascinating groves of trees, one of cedar, about ten trees, each more than three feet in diameter, completely surrounded by briers and being choked by huge vines that reached nearly to the top, and the other, nine long needled pine trees in a nearly perfect circle, each of them at least one hundred feet high. Tuck spent a lot of time in the tops of these trees. On one occasion, he fell while climbing one of the pines, bouncing from limb to limb for nearly forty feet before landing on the soft pine needle carpet below, unhurt.

There were many times, little capsules of involuntary, almost compulsive reflex, when Tuck had the urge to simply leap clear from the uppermost limbs of these trees.

"*Just jump!*" he told himself, but grabbed fast at the last instant.

Tuck was awakened about two in the morning and stumbled sleepily into the kitchen. Edie Maye and Sal were there, talking. Tuck's head was just above the level of the kitchen table and, as he knuckled his eyes and yawned, he watched Sal count eight one-thousand dollar bills into a pile not ten inches from his nose.

At 1943 prices the stack would purchase at least a three-bedroom house or a dozen brand new motor cars. "Here, take care of this." he said to Edie Maye, picking up the pile of bills. He rolled them into a tight coil, Edie Maye produced a rubber band, and he snapped the rubber band around the bills several times to keep the roll tight. She took the roll and opening the icebox, removed a half-pint Carnation Milk can which had been sliced open around the bottom. She bent out the bottom of the can, inserted the roll, and then bent the bottom shut again and placed the can back in the icebox, right side up.

The evening of the following day, they had Kellogg's Cornflakes with watered instant milk for dinner, the only food in the house. When Edie Maye was terminally ill and staying with Tuck in North Jersey, he questioned her about the incident.

"I remember that night," she said. "He came back later and got that money, which was for a game at the old Post Office. You only saw that once, but there were many nights when I slept on thousands and thousands of dollars under my mattress."

"But, Mom, for Christ's sake," Tuck responded, "why didn't you take some of it? We were starving."

"I couldn't do it; that would have been stealing. That wasn't his money, and I wouldn't steal from your father, no matter what he did," she said, "but I wish now that I had a nickel for every thousand dollars I slept on."

By the time Tuck was in seventh grade, he was getting in a lot of fights on the way to and from school, and on the playgrounds. In most of them, he was on the losing end. In one of them, he took on an eighth grader nearly twice his size. The bigger boy beat on Tuck most of a Saturday afternoon until dark when Cholly happened along and stopped it.

In Junior High, he had his run ins with the faculty. In music class one day, Mr. Loose, the teacher, was playing Schubert's Unfinished Symphony.

Sis had been one of Mr. Loose's best students, and he expected as much from Tuck. But Tuck had heard this story all through school, and the moment a teacher made the comparison, Tuck reacted negatively.

Tuck's chair, with one uneven leg, occasionally rocked, and as it did, it creaked. On that particular day, Tuck was in a reflective mood. Music was his first class, and Edie Maye had sent him off to school with a belly full of white bread dunked in cocoa water.

Tuck liked the music, it had a melody that he could hum and remember. Lost in the sounds, his chair began rocking with the beat of the symphony's refrain. Mr. Loose warned Tuck about it, but it was difficult to prevent, and Tuck ended up in the Principal's office.

Outraged and defensive because it was one of the few times when he was innocent, Tuck struck back with defiant and caustic language. Mr. Holbien, the principal responded by inflicting a beating on the boy, using his fists. He blackened Tuck's left eye and bruised his side and shoulder when he knocked Tuck over a chair. The crashing of furniture brought the secretary into the office, which saved Tuck from further damage.

A week later, Tuck revenged the beating by shitting in a paper bag, placing in on Holbien' doorstep, lighting it and ringing the doorbell on Broad Street. He watched from a safe distance as he stomped the fire out, but still hated him.

Bucky Squires had been elected County Coroner and a new group of cops were added to the force, and they had no sympathy for the feral son of the local bad guy. Any time windows were broken or anything occurred that looked like kid's doings, the patrol car rolled up to the bungalow. On a couple of occasions, they brought Tuck down to police headquarters and banged him around the office quite a bit, before Bucky happened by, and let the boy go.

Edie Maye watched it all in quiet desperation. What was going to become of him? He was so defiant and confused; helpless in a way, and courting his own destruction. She feared for the boy, realizing that it was only luck that he was even with them. Somehow, being near death as often as he was had hardened him, he had a will of iron, a reckless defiance that was beyond reason. As tough as it was on her, she thought that Tuck had it the worst of all of them, being cursed with his vision of Sal, and the impatience and inexperience to deal with it.

He cut twenty three days of school in the eighth grade, spending most of them fishing on the Rancocas or camped out in Ashurst woods. Paradoxically, he almost never went fishing or camping without books. Sis had taken him to the town library and gotten him a card when he was seven, and Tuck tore into the town's meager collection.

Holbien only allowed him to pass on to high school when Edie Maye went to his office and threatened to report him to the police for the beatings he gave Tuck, of which there had been several. She lied and told him that she had reported it but she hadn't signed a complaint.

Tuck kept some books at Chip's cabin, where he would sit with him in front of the pot bellied stove reading, while Chip listened to the radio and smoked his pipe and drank sneaky Pete. He prided himself in the fact that he could get from his home to Chip's, almost two miles across town, without ever stepping on a paved street, cutting through alleys, yards and woods and walking the Pennsy railroad line. This was necessary when he was playing hookey.

Like Edie Maye, Chip never said anything derogatory about Tuck's dad, except on one occasion, when the boy showed up with a nasty cut on his eyebrow as the result of a rock fight, and Frances cleaned it up.

"Your old man's a no-good sonofabitch," Chip said.

"Chip, be quiet, you shouldn't say such things," Frances rebuked.

"Nevertheless," Chip said, "look at the pup. Every time he comes here, he's got bumps and bruises. His old man just don't care, never did, not for Edie either, and that's the God's truth."

For the most part, Tuck's contemporaries were largely protected by their parents from his influence. Anybody who took up with Tuck was vulnerable to being talked into not coming home on time, cutting school or wandering far from the neighborhood that was his play area. Tuck was philosophical about the fears of his friends' parents; he held no grudges and would spend time with anyone who would enter his domain.

Kids from the "other side of the tracks" drifted in and out of his life, and he sampled some of their lifestyle before the parents caught on. For kids from the more affluent and stable element, Tuck was a Huckleberry Finn character; wildly independent, shrewd and tough; an urban guerilla. He was living what they thought were their dreams.

Billy Brenneman was from a quite respectable background. His mother taught elementary school and his dad was a Colonel in the Army, attached to Eisenhower's staff. Billy had a map of Europe on his bedroom wall on which he plotted the progress of the war, using thumbtacks and flags that he made for each Army and sometimes, certain Divisions.

Unfortunately for Billy, he was considered by most of Tuck's acquaintances to be a sissy, and was the subject of frequent plots by them to catch Billy unaware and give him a beating. But no one could catch Billy Brenneman. He was the fastest runner in Tuck's world, and Tuck, with his crooked back and shortened leg was the slowest, and he admired him for it. From Edie Maye, Tuck had acquired the penchant for believing the best about anyone and completely ignoring anything else.

Tuck had recognized early on that Billy was as fleet of foot and elusive as a scared rabbit, so he enjoyed his company until someone else showed up and Billy took off. They enjoyed an unwritten covenant, Tuck didn't join in the chase, and Billy didn't let it interfere with their relationship. They remained close friends until Billy died in 2010.

Tuck and he became experts on identification of aircraft, including axis power's fighters and bombers. Billy had books on all of the machines of war, sent by his father with regularity. His mother, who manned a coast watcher tower, let them use her Aircraft ID Manuals. The war was the topic of the day, the subject of every radio news broadcast and Movietone News at the movies. Everyone in town had some member of the family in the Service, and almost every house exhibited a star in the window.

By the time Tuck squeaked into high school, he had devoured all of the Sherlock Holmes series, the sports oriented boy's readers, Web Adams, a lot of Dickens and anything else that struck his fancy. He studied books that related to the outdoors.

There was a brief stint with the Boy Scouts that ended as a result of a fight between Tuck and one of the older "eagles." Tuck never returned, having suffered a humiliating rebuke from the Scoutmaster and the Minister of the Baptist Church, where the troop met. Tuck and the larger boy had locked themselves in each other's arms and careened across the church basement, where Tuck was smashed into the blackboard mounted against the wall. The large slate, loosened by the blow, rotated slowly out of its frame and struck Tuck squarely on the head, shattering into hundreds of small pieces.

Tuck, staggered by the blow, walked dizzily from the room, telling the Scoutmaster to "go to hell" when he tried to assist the boy. He was too proud to go back, but had been in the scouts long enough to attend a jamboree held near town and to appreciate the skills and knowledge of the outdoors that were offered.

Tuck began to fancy that he was an Indian. He spent huge amounts of time in the woods and on the creek in both summer and winter. Edie Maye felt even more helpless when Tuck began to disappear into the woods. Cholly was entirely different, easy to get along with and receptive to practically everything she said. But Tuck was another matter, and she knew his attitude focused entirely on Sal's activities. Sometimes she wondered how the boy, with so little experience, could react to Sal the way that he did. She wondered why she didn't have the same feelings on occasion.

But Tuck had decided that the beatings were worth it. A beating was only temporary, even the dreaded hand mirror and he deserved it! In the woods, he was competent and self confident. He was Ankote, leader of a band of Nanticoke Lenni-Lenape; no disapproving adults to tell him how terrible he was, or to remind him of Sal's exploits or the fact that he was a "wop."

When winter came, Tuck's world was covered by a fresh blanket of snow, and the trails and activities of all of the animals were clearly revealed. His "secret places" along the Rancocas and in the woods were dappled with the tracks of deer and raccoon. The great horned owl, which often sat in a small sapling and stared at the boy, appeared more frequently to Tuck when the snow was fresh. The pair sat contemplating each other for long stretches.

Another sparse Christmas passed. Tuck brought home a scraggly spruce sapling that he found in the woods, and Edie Maye decorated with her usual dexterity. Edie Maye had cut down and re-sewn one of Sis's coats for Tuck to replace his woods-torn hand-me-down. They burned rolled newspapers to keep warm that winter, which featured snow cover for 79 consecutive days.

Tuck was a very lonely and troubled boy, but he remembered those days with the realization that his childhood was something rather special. In some ways; magical, and in other ways, tragic. His back and shortened leg were problems that he endured for a lifetime. As an adult, Tuck believed that he must have been a very unusual kid to survive his childhood, although at times, he never was sure that he did.

16

ASHURST'S MANSION

THE "poker" bungalow, as Tuck came to call it, was on the edge of town. Driving east on Garden Street, it was the next to last house considered "in Mt. Holly." The next structure encountered, nearly a mile further up the road, was the Ashurst Mansion. Built in 1857 by the first president of the Philadelphia Trust Company, Lewis Richard Ashurst, the Ashurst Mansion dominated the east end of town.

Sal's "poker win" had deposited the family in a part of town they would have never otherwise occupied. The houses leading up the street toward the poker bungalow were large well-kept Victorians.

One of these showpiece homes was occupied by Mr. Scattergood, who had purged Edie Maye from the Stone House.

Mr. Scattergood, dressed in business suit, topcoat and derby hat, walked his white Pekinese pair every day. As they passed the poker bungalow, he waited while they made their daily deposits in Edie Maye's front yard.

As Edie Maye stood in the front doorway with cigarette in hand, Mr. Scattergood would nod his head and smile. "That son of bitch brings those dogs here deliberately," she said, stomping off to the kitchen, "to shit on my yard!"

The big mansion at the top of the street was no longer occupied, but watched over by Mr. Cunningham, a caretaker. Connie, his son, was one of Tuck's favorite companions because of his knowledge of the mansion and the Ashurst tract. And he was a negro. In Tuck's mind, that alone qualified him as a kindred spirit.

Connie was thin and had suffered polio resulting in a left leg that was permanently stiff, withered and nearly useless. He wore a "club foot" shoe on his left foot, which added five inches to the length of the skinny bent leg. In spite of this handicap, he could outrun nearly everyone with his peculiar hopping gait. Only Billy Brenneman could best him in a straight out race.

Connie and his family lived in the servant's quarters of the mansion, which was an attached small cottage and featured its own kitchen. They were the only African American family in town that did not live on "nigger hill." The servant's quarters of the building was a house in its own right, but was only a wing of the 14 bedroom main house. The four-story Victorian brick mansion had another wing that featured a ballroom and drawing room. There were more than a dozen fireplaces, a main stair from the foyer, a secondary stair from the library and a circular back stair from the servant's quarter.

The Ashurst Mansion (circa 2008) now houses professionals and businesses in apartments. Photo by the Author.

When Connie and his family moved away, the mansion fell into disrepair and became one of Tuck's haunts. He would enter a window and could explore the mansion for hours. In the servant's quarters, a long line of brass bells, each mounted on a large helical steel spring, were connected by pull ropes to every room in the mansion. In each room, a tasseled rope hung from a pulley half embedded in the wall.

Roaming the empty rooms, Tuck tried to contemplate what kind of life people lived who could own so much; people who could tug a tasseled rope and have their wants satisfied by servants. Even the imagining was beyond his comprehension. Connie had told Tuck that there was a secret passageway in the mansion, and it became his quest to find it.

Eventually, after many visits, he discovered a doorway cleverly concealed in the milled panels of the library fireplace. It had to be pried open with a knife blade. The door was about four feet high and eighteen inches wide and opened to a ladder affixed to the chimney.

Exploring it, Tuck found that it went directly to the top of the structure and intersected several tunnels that reached every chimney in the mansion. Several of the other chimneys had doors concealed in the trim, although they were not as large. These tunnels were about two foot square. One of them led to a crawl space under the eaves that could be followed all the way around the huge structure. There was also a laddered chimney that ended in the cellar.

The mansion occupied the northeast comer of the huge tract, which was mostly covered with dense woods. The woods featured two fascinating groves of trees, one of cedar, about ten trees, each more than four feet in diameter, completely surrounded by briers and being choked by huge vines that reached nearly to the top, and the other, nine long needled pine trees in a nearly perfect circle, each of them at least one hundred feet high. Tuck spent a lot of time in the tops of these trees.

The cedars were called "The Vines," for the huge vines that covered them and made ascent easy, once the thick briars and brush at their base had been negotiated. To access them, it was necessary to skip from cedar knob to cedar knob through the marsh that was called "Knobby Swamp," and "Skunk Hollow," for the skunk cabbage that grew there.

Tuck's neighbors, the four Pierce brothers, and he had names for every identifiable feature of the woods. Connie had assisted them in establishing these names as they related to the history of the estate and the region.

A stream, which was named Cheyenne Creek, meandered through the mile square tract. Its one tributary ran due west for about a half mile to the "Indian Pond," a circular lake of approximately 40 feet in diameter. The concentric shape of Indian Pond, as well as the circular granite walls that surrounded one end, set in a rise in the ground, suggested that the site had been a meeting place for Indians and later, an amphitheater for the estate.

Not far beyond Indian pond, covered in underbrush, a granite foundation, rectangular in shape, was called "the ruins." There was also a well, walled with the gray granite stones, grown over and partially covered, but quite deep. This portion of the woods yielded many arrowheads if one broke ground in the right places. Mr. Cunningham had told Connie that the woods contained many ceremonial and sacred Indian sites.

Ashurst Woods. The author's sketch of the Ashurst estate in 1944 and its relationship to the "Poker House" at 507 Garden Street. Tuck and his friends named all of the important landmarks in the woods as shown. The Fowell School, named for Tuck's kindergarten teacher, and its playground now occupy most of the western part of the property, behind the "Circle of Pines" while the "Graves of Chiefs" and the "Fences" are the site on which Clover Hill Gardens was built.

At the fork in the stream, Tuck had uncovered a war ax, and that place was named "Tomahawk Fork." The war ax was nearly six inches in length, and Tuck cherished it for years before losing it in one of his many moves around the country.

Frank, the oldest of the Pierce boys, claimed that a boy who had found a blunderbuss in this area, but the story was never confirmed. At Tomahawk Fork, Tuck and the brothers constructed a teepee, using canvas tarpaulins. Most of the materials were stolen from the back yards of those unfortunate enough to live on the edge of Tuck's domain. In the center of the teepee, a circular rock-lined fire pit was dug, complete with forked holders for pots warming over the fire. Tuck camped in this shelter many times, alone and with friends.

The "Circle" was the name for the circularly placed nine pines, a favorite meeting place carpeted with years of fallen pine needles. These were the tallest trees in the woods and very old. The pine needles at their base were more than several feet deep. The trees were obviously planted to form the circle.

The south edge of the woods, which bordered Garden Street, featured four mounds of earth nearly eight feet high. Connie Cunningham related that these were redoubts built by British soldiers during the Battle of Iron Works Hill. That was plausible, since it was common knowledge that a diversionary battle had occurred in Mt. Holly, and the Colonials had occupied high ground and stayed overnight in the Quaker meeting hall. Some reports place the British battery on the Mount, but they could have been on this hill on Garden Street. It was thought the revolutionaries occupied the hill across the creek at Pine Street at the St. Andrew's Church Cemetery, called Iron Works Hill. It was even rumored that a cannon had rolled down the hill, dislodged during the battle, and still rests at the bottom of the Rancocas Creek there. An artillery position at Ashurst would have defended the main artery to the east; the Monmouth Road. In any case, the Battle of Iron Works Hill diverted a contingent of troops that would otherwise been available to Trenton, thus assisting Washington in his stunning victory over the Hussians on Christmas Eve, 1776.

North of the mounds, a straight line of very large pine trees pointed the way to the mansion. Those trees were collectively called "the Fences." In the deep forest of tall elms and oaks at the northwest corner of the woods, "Red Indian Mountain" and "Little Indian Mountain" were the landmarks. These were two huge tree stumps which had assumed a deep red color and shapes similar to the mesas seen in the Monument Valley of Arizona.

It was possible to traverse great distances in the woods by walking the trunks and climbing the many trees that had been felled by storms and lightning over the years. It became a great game to discover who could travel the greatest distance in this fashion.

The Pierce boys had lost their father just after Tuck had moved to the Poker house. He was a stumpy little man with limited intelligence who made most of his living by clearing land and chopping wood. Their only income was whatever Frank and Russ, the two oldest boys, could bring in by serving papers. Between them, they serviced eight different paper routes daily. Like Edie Maye and her brood, they lived at the edge of desperate poverty.

The Ashurst tract was their world, as it was for Tuck. It was a society with its own pecking order, free of adult meddling and full of adventure.

When grown, Tuck passed the Ashurst mansion occasionally returning from business appointments in the northeast and often wondered if the fireplace passageways were ever discovered. As for the woods, only about a third of it remains, a huge apartment complex occupying most of the land between Skunk Hollow and the Mansion. Tomahawk Forks was buried beneath the athletic fields of a large school complex, and although there is nothing occupying the place where the Circle once stood. It, too, suffered the bulldozer.

In the summer of 1944, anyone who wanted work could get it just up the road in Fort Dix. Tuck's brother, then 14, had amazed everyone in the family by having to shave every day. He had the course beard of a Sicilian, and looked about 20.

Cholly had no trouble in securing a job in the warehouses at Fort Dix, and every morning, he waited on the step for his ride to pick him up and take him to work. Tuck's sister, now graduated from high school, had a job at the local paper. Each of them contributed money to Edie Maye for necessities, Cholly simply turning over his entire paycheck.

They were on their own again, Sal having moved permanently to Wrightstown where he opened a Pawn Shop.[53]

Tuck saw him around town now and then, driving a convertible, usually with a blonde in the passenger seat, who Tuck soon learned was Jeannie Rich, a former Las Vegas showgirl. On one occasion, Sal even pulled over the curb and asked Tuck how he was doing. Fool that he was, Tuck greeted him like an old friend, and blurted out some lie.

Pawn Shops being illegal in New Jersey, Sal's Wrightstown pawn shop had a sign that said "Wrightstown Jeweler's." Any soldier needing money could sell Sal nearly any item of value for five bucks and buy it back for seven. The purchase price and buy back figure increased with the value of the item, up to a fifty, seventy five ratio. All of these hocked items made up his "jewelry" display. Some GI's even hocked their gold fillings and false teeth.

Suffering through another cold winter and looking forward to a bleak Christmas, Tuck decided that there was at least one thing that would make the holidays bearable. He sneaked out of the house on a cold and rainy late December night and relieved Mr. Scattergood's manicured garden of a perfect blue spruce. He deposited the tree in Cherokee creek and hid it with brush. On the Saturday before Christmas Tuck dragged the tree home.

"It's so perfect," Edie Maye said, "it's hard to believe it was growing out there in Ashurst woods."

"Sure, Mom," Tuck lied, "there's lots of them out there like that, near the swamp. You just gotta' know where to look."

"Well, it looks a lot like those blue spruces in Scattergood's yard. That's what it looks like." Edie Maye was trimming limbs from the tree's base and getting it ready for the Christmas tree stand. She looked directly at Tuck.

"And if it was one of those spruces, then it would be stealing, wouldn't it, Tuck?"

"Well, yeah, Mom, it would. But it isn't, Okay? And besides, don't he bring his dogs here every day to crap in our yard? So I figure, even if it was one of those spruces ... then it would serve him right, wouldn't it?"

Edie Maye suppressed a smile and let the subject go.

The war, of course, occupied everyone's attentions. Little occurred that didn't, in some way, relate to it. In a way, it diminished problems that in another time would have been the center of attention.

For two years, even the carefully managed Movietone News reports hadn't disguised the truth; that the Pacific Fleet had been destroyed and the Japanese were running rampant under the Southern Cross. Until mid 1942, little except Jimmy Dolittle's raid on Tokyo had happened to booster the idea that the Allies could win the war. Now the American navy had great victories under their belt, having defeated the Japanese at Guadalcanal, in the battle of the Coral Sea, Midway and other engagements in the Pacific.

Tuck had never seen a Japanese person, except at the Saturday afternoon movie, where John Wayne, John Garfield and James Cagney were winning their version of the war. When the Philco radio had broadcast the news that Guadalcanal had fallen to the Marines, Edie Maye ran into the street with most of the town folk. Until then, everyone had expected the worst, even an invasion of the west coast.

Across the nation, Japanese Americans had been rounded up and sent off to concentration camps, their property and assets soon becoming product for the growing legion of carpetbaggers. Italian Americans were also cause for suspicion; Il Duce bellowing forth in the newsreels, conquering Ethiopia. But the Japanese and their highly publicized rape of Nanking; newsreels showing babies speared on bayonets, heads being chopped off in contests, civilians executed in groups directed a disgust and hatred toward the Japanese people that pervaded American understanding of the war, and for Tuck, lasted the rest of his life.

Many of the boys in Sis's class in high school enlisted as soon as they turned seventeen, abandoning their senior year. This became the standard practice throughout the war. As some of these early enlistees returned home disabled or discharged, they re-entered the school system and finished out their high school educations. The 1947 graduating class included nine war-seasoned veterans.[54]

Mt. Holly had a particular penchant for the Marine Corps and the Navy. No one seemed to want to wait to be drafted into the Army, and recruiters of the other branches of the service did well in town. Military uniforms were common on the streets, as were the long convoys of jeeps and trucks that rolled through town frequently on the PRR line.

Everyone went into the Service. Tuck wished that he were old enough to go. They were heroes. And it was a disgrace to be turned down; rejected four-F. Tuck sought out the returning vets and unashamedly asked them about their exploits.

Every home had blackout curtains, required to be pinned over the windows when the air raid siren sounded. Cans had to be stripped of paper and flattened for recycling, and paper, string, tinfoil and other salvageable items were saved and turned in to assist the war effort. Each car owner was allowed only five tires. Tuck collected the pods of the cat-o-nine-tails plants from Skunk Hollow in Ashurst woods and turned them in to the Post Office be used to make life jackets for the Navy.

On the east coast, there was a real fear of attack. Several ships had been sunk by German submarines within view of Long Beach Island, and four German spies had been caught in Philadelphia after coming ashore in Long Island from a German submarine. Mount Holly had a Civil Defense Patrol, and airplane identification towers had been built on several of the farms east of town, and were manned during daylight hours by "coast watchers." The Jersey beaches were patrolled by armed Coast Guardsman, accompanied by trained dogs[55]. Stores hung window posters that said things like "Loose Lips Sink Ships," and pictured Uncle Sam with a finger to his lips.

Sal never mentioned the Service. It was during this period that he was "recruited" to run games for the mobster, Columbo, in New York. This was the mafia man who, in the sixties, gained popularity with the "in crowd" of New York society. He formed the Italian American Anti Deformation League (IAADL), generating protests against the FBI and Hollywood. Eventually, he organized the Columbus Day Rally, a gathering to supposedly celebrate the Italian Americans who were "good citizens," and not associated with the mob. This was in response, he said, to the FBI's bias against Italian Americans. The rally got a lot of national coverage, too much in fact, because Columbo was shot by his less gregarious associates amidst the crowd at the 2nd Annual IAADL rally at Columbus Circle in Manhattan. The youngest boss of the five NY families lingered on for seven years, paralyzed by the three bullets in his head.

Commenting on the Columbo killing to Tuck, Sal said,

"Oh, yeah, I know that guy. I used to run games for him in Brooklyn and Queens." In later years, Tuck came to realize that this casual reference to the head of one of the five families of New York, trivialized Sal's intimacy with the most notorious Mafioso of the era. Sal's boyhood friend and best buddy was a member of gangland's ruling commission.

Although nearly everyone else his age, regardless of family status, ended up in the Service, Sal evaded serving his country. He told Tuck later that a New York doctor supplied him with the necessary deferment for some kind of eye problem. Until he was 60, Tuck never saw him wear a pair of glasses, although he did use a jeweler's glass to inspect rings, gems and watches.

"I couldn't go in the Service," he told Tuck, "there was too much money to be made, too much going on."

17

THE FOX OF THE PINELANDS

WITH the war economy providing a lot of growth, Mt. Holly was becoming somewhat of a little city, the population growing to nearly 8,000. "Give 'Em Hell, Harry" had succeeded Roosevelt, and Edie Maye had been thrown out of the Garden Street bungalow, the Poker house, supposedly because Sal lost it in another poker game.

Movietone News eventually had begun to report the response to the two-front war by the industrious Americans.

Patton and Montgomery took on and beat Rommel's desert Army in North Africa, and the Navy scored more resounding victories in the Pacific. Tuck took it all in at the Saturday matinees between the double features. Billy Brenneman's wall map now had flags in North Africa, Sicily and southern Italy. Things were going well for the Allies.

Rationing had been in place for some time, the little green stamps having become as much a part of the society as currency. Edie Maye thought that it made little difference. She seldom had enough money to use her quota of stamps anyway.

This time Edie Maye had a little warning before being evicted. She had been working for a couple of years clerking Ruman's dry cleaning store and tailor shop on Main Street, and with the help of Doc McDonald, she was able to swing a mortgage on a large old house on Mt. Holly Avenue. This was the only time that Tuck knew her to stand up to Sal. Apparently, she had gone to Wrightstown and demanded that he give her some money to help them find housing. Sal must have come up with five hundred bucks, which she used as a down payment. It would be a couple of years before Tuck found out what she traded off for his help.

The house was a twin, dissected out of an old farm house, and part of the deal was that the best side would be immediately sold to Peg Leonard. Peg was an old friend from Edie Maye's Rancocas Creek days who currently rented the southern side of the house. The end result was a $2,500 mortgage with a 25 year payout and payments low enough that Edie Maye could handle it, if they managed every cent.

It was the first place that Edie Maye lived in where she couldn't be evicted by a landlord or simply thrown out as a squatter. By Tuck's and Sis's reckoning, it was their twenty-seventh move.

The last year on Garden Street had been rough, but they survived. Sis had graduated high school, and the bungalow, only a mile from the high school, had been the meeting place for her crowd. Every day after school she and her friends danced to the music of Benny Goodman, the Andrews Sisters, Frankie Carle and Tommy Dorsey. Her social life dominated the house.

Amazingly, Edie Maye managed to conceal from everyone just how meagerly they managed to live. "Hunky" McDonald, Doc's oldest son, had devoured an entire box of Wheaties, sitting at the kitchen table while talking to Sis. It was near the end of the week, and Edie Maye had no food and no money.

"You can't just let him sit there and eat all of our food," Edie Maye said, confronting Sis, "he'll eat anything you offer."

"Hunky," whose real name was Gerald, was a six footer as a high school freshman, and was pushing 260 pounds by his senior year. Cholly said that he would eat anything that didn't move, and some things that did, if it was close enough to dinner time.

"Just tell him 'no' if he asks." Edie Maye said. Sis was unimpressed by this argument.

"He's my friend and I'm not going to insult him." She retorted. Edie Maye had also concealed from her how poor they really were. She was immensely popular in school, and wearing Edie Maye's creations, usually better dressed than the other girls. It didn't bother her that Edie Maye worked until late hours of the morning to make her wardrobe nearly every night. Of course, Sal favored her. When he showed up, she wasn't afraid to ask him for anything, and he usually produced.

Tuck found this startling. His pride prevented him from ever asking anything of Sal. Better to go without than be refused. Since Sal rarely spoke to the boy, it took more courage than Tuck could muster to initiate a comment, let alone a request.

The next door neighbors at the bungalow were the Parkers, Ellis and his sister, Jane Brown, and Ellis' family. Ellis was the son of the famed "Fox of the Pinelands," and bore his name. Ellis Parker, Sr., was legendary as the detective that always got his man; "America's Sherlock Holmes." He had an international reputation that disintegrated with the Lindbergh kidnapping case.

Ellis, Jr., ran a hamburger and shakes restaurant, formerly called Kennedy's, on Route 38 at the edge of town, and gave Tuck his first job. Working there in the summer of his eighth grade, he became acquainted with an ex-prize fighter, Lou Domillo, who delivered to Ellis' and had known him (Ellis) for a long time. Lou's claim to fame was that he had been knocked out by Battling Nelson in a lightweight bout in California. One day, Lou filled Tuck in on Ellis' dad's part in the Lindbergh case.

"The old man," Lou said, referring to Ellis's dad, "he caught those crooks, because he whupped 'em."

Tuck was fascinated by Lou, who sometimes took the boy out behind the restaurant to teach him boxing techniques. Lou weighed about 250 and was both paunchy and a little punchy. He had cauliflower ears, and had fought under the name Kid Dominick.

"How's that?" Tuck asked, "I thought he was like a Sherlock Holmes, a real smart guy." thinking that Lou was referring to the fact that, in catching the criminals, Ellis Sr. had outsmarted and defeated them.

"Oh, he smart, O.K.," Lou said, "but just to make sure he got 'em, he use the hose on 'em. He get the confession every time from dem crooks. Dat's why they sent him to jail; him and Junior." Having seen his share of Eddie Robinson and Humphrey Bogart gangster movies, Tuck understood what Lou was talking about; body beatings with rubber hoses, but Parker's reputation was so widespread and positive, he found it hard to believe.

"Ah, get out, Lou," Tuck said, "The Fox caught those guys fair and square." Edie Maye had indoctrinated Tuck with the legend of the Fox, and how he always got his man. And Ellis himself had on several occasions testified that he (Parker, Senior) had never "coerced" a confession.

Lou was rolling a root beer barrel across the restaurant cellar. He stopped the barrel and deftly spun it with one hand, causing it carom upright to a standing position.

"Look, kid, Lou tells you straight," he said, "The Fox, he get Lou for some of dem jobs, but don't you say nothin' to no body, understand? Dem crooks, they all sing like birdies for Lou and the Fox."

The prosecutors in the Lindbergh kidnapping case, stymied by lack of hard evidence, built a case against Bruno Hauptmann, an immigrant Brooklyn handyman, based on circumstantial evidence and newly introduced "scientific" techniques. One of the major points of the Hauptmann trial was the Prosecution's evidence linking the saw blade marks on the ladder found at the scene to saw blade marks on lumber found on Hauptmann's property in New York. Hauptmann had been discovered when he passed one of the traceable ransom notes. Since the crime and subsequent trial took place in nearby Flemington, it was a major topic of conversation in South Jersey years after Hauptmann had been executed.

There were people in town that actually knew Charles Lindbergh, and had been to his home. Edie Maye said that when the child was kidnapped, his father was probably the most famous man in the world. Everyone had a position on the case, for or against Hauptmann, and Ellis Parker, Sr. was right in the middle of it.

The case was sensationalized in the newspapers as the evidence was presented to the public in a daily barrage of reports from within the Courtroom. Edie Maye had all the clippings relating to this case in a shoe box. One night, talking about the Parkers, she got the box out and went through them, commenting on each one to Tuck and Cholly.

"He was railroaded," Edie Maye said, referring to Hauptmann, "He didn't kidnap that baby." It was Edie Maye's experience that most prosecutors were crooks and the evidence, in her eyes, was too far-fetched to be believable.

Amidst all the uproar at the end of trial, Ellis Parker, Sr., the "Fox of the Pinelands," emerged with a suspect he claimed to be the real killer of the famous aviator's infant son. Parker had a signed confession!

Later reports revealed that the suspect, an alcoholic and disbarred lawyer named Paul Wendel, down on his luck and poverty stricken, had the confession beaten out of him by Parker and his "associates." Parker had kidnapped the man, stashed him away in the New Jersey Home for Feeble Minded Males[56] in the pinelands and he and his associates had simply beaten him until he signed a prepared confession, according to Wendel. Some reports even placed Ellis, Jr., where the beatings took place, and stated that he took part.

Ellis, Jr., was widely respected in the community for his athletic ability. According to Newt Ruch, the high school football coach, he was "a tough halfback who was never brought down by the first tackler." Tuck's experience with Ellis, Jr. led him to believe that he could be quite ruthless. The first day Tuck worked for him, he had the boy hang oak screen doors. By the time Tuck had finished the first of four doors, his hands were bleeding and raw from the effort, but Ellis persisted and Tuck's hands were a mass of bleeding blisters by the day's end.

The subsequent trials and publicity about the phony kidnapper ended Parker's career as a modern day Sherlock Holmes. Brooklyn Detectives soon uncovered the means that Parker took to achieve his end, and the unfortunate confessor was released. The Police brought charges against the 40 year Burlington County Chief of Detectives and his son. One source stated that nearly all of the hundreds of cases the Fox had solved had been solved with his "rubber hose confession" method. Of the 304 murder cases that Parker had solved during his storied career, more than half were confessed, a suspiciously high statistic even by today's standards.

But detecting, trying and convicting were vastly different in the 1940's than in today's complicated forensics driven system of law enforcement. Arnold Schenck, a Hopewell fish seller, was also set upon by detectives shortly after the kidnapping.[57] He was taken to Pennsylvania and held for 76 days while his captors attempted to force him to confess, then let go when they finally realized he would not do so. Oops!

Both Ellis and his son were convicted in New York; the famous detective receiving a six year sentence, his son: three years. Appeals were unsuccessful and a petition to President Roosevelt, signed by thousands of Mt. Holly residents for a pardon, was denied as well. The Fox of the Pinelands died while serving his sentence at Lewisburg Prison. He was granted a full pardon posthumously by Harry Truman. Ellis Jr. served his time and returned to 509 Garden Street a folk hero, his old job and a legion of fans awaiting him.

Jane Brown, Ellis' sister, was a stunningly beautiful brunette. She and Kay Parker, Ellis' daughter, rode a palomino horse called Sharky, which was kept in small bam at the rear of the property at 509 Garden Street. Jane's problems related to the crowd of suitors who pursued her. One of them, a local businessman, asphyxiated himself in a 1935 Ford coupe in front of the Poker house because she had rejected him. He left a love note to Jane pinned to his chest. "Dearest Jane, I can't live without you!" it said. The whole neighborhood was there when Bucky Squires removed the garden hose from the window, opened the car door and dragged him out, puffed and blue. He lay there, in Tuck's front yard until the Coroner retrieved the body.

Jane Brown's influence on Sis was considerable, who came to believe that she ought to have a horse so that she could canter through Ashurst woods in a riding outfit, as Jane did. Sis nagged Sal every time he showed up at the house, asking for a horse.

Cholly made no comment about this, but Tuck was convinced that Sis had lost her sanity. They couldn't even feed themselves, but a horse, the idea, was important to her.

Sal obliged Sis, showing up one day at the house with a horse so old and sick that everyone feared it would keel over before it was re-loaded into the trailer that delivered it.

"He's real gentle," the little man who drove the truck was saying, "anybody can ride him." Sal, standing next to Sis, was concurring.

Edie Maye, standing on the porch, was absolutely furious. She wouldn't even look at Sal, but everyone assembled knew that these were her first and last comments on the subject.

"You get that goddamn nag out of here! Put it back in the trailer before it dies in my front yard!" That to the groom, and to Tuck's sister, "If you ever mention a horse again, I'm going to brain you with a frying pan!" Sis, of course, immediately burst into tears because she couldn't keep the animal.

Knowing absolutely nothing about horses, Tuck was nevertheless concerned if this one could make it back into the trailer, and not being old enough to really appreciate the situation, he felt sorry for the horse. Cholly, less sentimental about animals, collapsed in laughter.

They did have chickens, though. Their little flock was the result of Easter presents Sis got from one of her high school boyfriends. Tuck got up one Easter morning to see six fuzzy chicks, all dyed different colors, scurrying about the kitchen floor as Edie Maye tried to catch them.

Only five of the Easter flock survived, the one dyed bright red keeling over after a couple of days. Four were roosters and the fifth was a "banty" hen. The bantams were much smaller than ordinary chickens, and this one became a house pet. Edie Maye named her Gertie, and until she was run over in the street by a passing motorist, she delivered one tiny egg every day on the folded blanket at the foot of Cholly's bed. To get the egg, Edie Maye slipped a ping-pong ball under Gertie, and she would nestle down and happily try to hatch it, while Edie Maye stole away with her prize. When she wanted in or out of the house, Gertie flew against the front door, the signal to oblige and open up.

Three of her four compadres grew up to be ordinary roosters, with no distinguishing features, and as they matured, they ended up on the dinner table. The last of the four, however, was different. Edie Maye named him "Alexander the Swoose," from his annoying habit of hiding behind the shed, and then swooping down on her as she attempted to hang the wash.

He was very large, almost two feet high, nearly all black and mean as hell. It hurt when he attacked, which was any time someone wasn't watching for him. The worse thing about his attacks were that he usually charged from hiding without making any noise, except the sound of his wings, spread widely, flapping in the air. No one was spared; Postman, hoboes, children, dogs and cats all became victims if they wandered into his territory. They all bore scars of his vicious pecks on arms and legs. A war raged between Alexander and Edie Maye as to who would control the back yard, and Edie Maye seldom ventured out without a broom with which to defend herself.

Edie Maye would stand at the back door, wicker basket of wet clothes balanced on her hip while she scanned the yard for Alexander. He often strutted defiantly to the back step when she appeared there, anticipating her encroachment into his domain. There was dignity and strength in his approach. Often Edie Maye would put the basket down and find another chore before risking a confrontation.

Arthur "Autsie" Steen, an associate of Cholly's, had been ravaged by the big bird and attempted revenge by trying to pee on Alexander through the wire fence at the back of the yard. Alexander's attack was too quick for the boy when the bird turned to the source of the stream of urine pelting his back.

In a flash the big rooster had inflicted lasting damage on Autsie's penis, getting several vicious pecks on point before the boy staggered backward, screaming. Tuck found this episode delightful, since Autsie was a bully and had it coming. Autsie's family lived across Cherry Street from the hovel they had left a year ago, and the opposite side of their twin house was occupied by Nelson Anderson, Mt. Holly's bona fide strongman.[58]

Eventually hunger consigned Alexander to the pot, his continued attacks finally overcoming their hunger and even Edie Maye's compassion. One of Sis's friends, Bob Carter, did the honors and lopped off his head. Edie Maye roasted him, and he was consumed with sadness. Typically, Alexander got in the last word in the argument.

Sis, chagrined at losing her horse, plotted her next campaign: college. In looking back on these days, Tuck wondered where in the world she got such ideas. The only people who went to college were those who not only had excellent grades, but also could afford to pay for it. Sis did have excellent grades and had wrangled her way into the position of "teacher's pet" in nearly every class she took in high school. Her answer to their poverty was simply to ignore it. Somehow, Edie Maye came through with whatever she needed to maintain a semblance of respectability with her peers. Mostly, Edie Maye sewed a lot, her Singer lulling the house to sleep nearly every night while she fashioned clothes for Sis.

Somehow, Sis made it happen. Edie Maye packed her bags and Sal showed up and drove her out to Reading, Pennsylvania, where she enrolled at Albright College. They gave her a job in the cafeteria, and of course, she did very well scholastically until they tossed her out at the end of the year, when Sal hadn't paid a penny of her expenses.

She returned home crestfallen and angry with the reality of Sal's indifference to her needs and wants.

"At least you got in a whole year," Edie Maye said, "and you did well. You can be proud of yourself; it's not your fault that your father couldn't afford it."

Tuck felt that somehow it would end up being his fault, if his sister had anything to do with placing the blame. He stayed clear of her as much as possible. Her sullen attitude changed for the better when she landed a job at the local paper, but Cholly told Tuck,

"Keep your distance from Sis; she's a cast iron bitch because of the old man." Cholly's work at Fort Dix with older men had given him a better perspective of the situation.

Edie Maye had taken advantage of the Sis's crowd being at the house by enlisting them all in a project to clear the vacant lot next door. Once cleared, the lot immediately became Tuck and Cholly's version of Shibe Park. A baseball game became permanently entrenched there, the nearest school yard being ten blocks away.

Edie Maye and her brood spent several winters at the Poker house. With Cholly working and Edie employed and sewing on the side, they even got to the point where they could afford to have coal delivered and used the furnace to heat the house. The war continued while they lived there, and some of the boys who had left Sis's class returned home. They went back to school; some of them combat veterans who had little time for the niceties of high school discipline.[59]

Sal's Taxi business died with the end of the war in Europe and the reduction of the armed forces, and Wrightstown, once a booming, bawdy hub of activity, began a steady decay that even the Korean War couldn't restrain.

Sal, down on his luck, showed up then to tell Edie Maye to pack up and get out, he had "lost the house" in another Poker game. Tuck never learned the truth behind their separation from the slot machines that had defined their lives for more than 9 years.

Edie Maye was shattered by the news, but she was stronger now. For several years she, like thousands of other women, had found a way to survive in the war economy. It was clear that she and Sal would never be together again. She still loved him, but knew it as the futile exercise it had always been.

With Doc McDonald's help, Edie Maye got the mortgage approved on the Mt. Holly Avenue house, got the down payment money from Sal, and said,

"That's the last time. I'm never going to move again."

18

DAY TRIPS

THE move to Mt. Holly Avenue has been completely blocked from Tuck's mind. Somehow, they were there, and although he lost the recollection of the details, he only remembered that Mr. Jones moved Edie Maye over there with the same rickety old stake body truck he'd used for the Stone House. The slot machines, most likely the stimulus for the move, were last seen in the cellar of 507 Garden Street. Once established at the 'new' house, Tuck was surprised by a visit from Sal. This was obviously prompted by Tuck's behavior.

Tuck's attitude had become decidedly worse during the last days at the Poker house, because of the loss of Major.

Major was a Collie pup that Edie Maye had gotten free from Stanley Dancer's farm. Tuck didn't know how Edie Maye knew Stanley Dancer, but it probably related to her early days on the Creek, or to Sal's interest in fixing races.

Dancer's son was nationally known for his trotters and pacers, and Stanley, Sr., also had a great reputation as a driver/trainer.[60] In any case, a friend, Bob Carter, drove Edie Maye and Tuck out to the Dancer farm in Jobstown one day, where Mr. Dancer told Tuck that he could have the pick of a litter of bouncing Collie pups.

The pups weren't pure collies, the sire being a transient that obviously stopped at Dancer's one day. All of them were fat and lovable except one. Mr. Dancer also liked the scrawny and under sized pup that struck Tuck's fancy.

“That’s the runt, the one you got now, son,” he said. “He’s got the best disposition of the bunch. He was real small when they berthed, but I been feedin’ him special. Nobody thought he’d make it, he was so scrawny.”

Instinctively, Tuck knew that he was a kindred spirit. He picked him and named him Major. He had a perfect white star on his forehead and white collar breaking his tan coat. For the next six months, they were constant companions. He slept in Tuck’s bed and the two were inseparable. Tuck was very happy, as Major lavished love and devotion on him. He could hardly bear to be away from the dog.

But the inevitable happened. The bungalow being on the edge of town, cars and motorcycles usually passed it at highway speeds. Major, whom Tuck couldn’t stop from chasing motorcycles, broke from his grasp one Sunday morning and ran to the edge of the street, anticipating chasing an oncoming rider.

The cyclist, seeing the dog standing there barking, veered his big red flathead Harley and ran him down deliberately. Tuck cried incessantly for several days and withdrew from anyone who approached him. He was alone again.

It was clear to Tuck by this time that not only was he a burden to Edie Maye, who seldom spoke to him at all except to reaffirm his worthlessness, but he was also at the lowest rung of the town’s social ladder. Sis made certain that Tuck understood that it was his negligence that caused Major’s death, taking every opportunity to hammer home what a terrible person he was.

Somehow, in his sister’s eyes, Tuck became the focus of everything that was wrong with their lives. It was the beginning of her lifelong hatred for Tuck. In future years, she would learn to combine this hatred with deceit, and use it relentlessly against him, although it would take Tuck a lifetime to understand that she was the source of many of his problems.

With Major gone, Tuck reverted to the woods and his previously incorrigible behavior. Even a bout with the mumps, a major illness in those days, couldn’t soften his attitude. By the time they were in the Mt. Holly Avenue house, he was a kid on his way to major trouble.

If the fishing was good, the perch were running, or on any other light excuse, Tuck would leave the house for school, wait until Edie Maye caught her ride for work, and then return to the house for his gear and spend the day on the creek.

On many weekends, he would take a can of baked beans and disappear overnight, camping at Tomahawk Forks or on a creek bank east of Smithville and eating the fish that he caught. He told Edie Maye that he would be gone, and when she realized that she couldn't stop him, she acquiesced.

Tuck defied Edie Maye's edicts about homework by never cracking a book in her presence, although books were silent companions on his trips. At night, he simply went out and got into some kind of trouble, breaking windows in abandoned houses, and other kinds of mischief. One night the patrol car intercepted Tuck on High Street, Edie Maye in the back seat, and accused him of destroying a newly poured sidewalk on the other side of town. In this case, the boy was innocent, and proved it by displaying that his sneaks had no concrete on them.

The following Saturday morning Sal showed up at the house.

"You're going with your dad for a couple of weeks, down the shore," Edie Maye said. "I've packed you some clothes."

Still confused about Sal, Tuck's emotions, like a metronome, flipped from adulation to terror with each of his words and actions. He hadn't the slightest idea what to say to him, or how to respond to what he said. Every word he spoke to the boy penetrated his whole being and produced a full range of emotional response, which Tuck was unable to express.

Apparently Sal was combining his fatherly responsibility with "business." He was on parole again, and had to report to the Cape May (County) Courthouse, which is not only the name of the Court House, but also the name of the town in which it's located, a few miles from Wildwood.

Tuck sat in the car in the parking lot while Sal reported to his parole officer, then they preceded on to North Wildwood, where he had second floor rooms across the street from Cozy Morley's Club Avalon. In large neon letters, the marquis stated "featuring Mickey Shaughnessy."[61]

There were two rooms, one being a bedroom with two twin beds, and two temporary cots. That room also had a small enclosed toilet with sink, a closet and one of those large white enameled cabinets, popular then as kitchen storage. A radio and a two-burner electric stove sat on a small table against the wall between the two windows overlooking the street.

The other room was a miniature casino, with four slot machines against one wall, a craps table, and a poker table. With its occupants and equipment, Sal had brought his son to a miniature whorehouse/casino.

The walls featured a half dozen poster calendars with full breasted nudes. These pictures weren't like the ones Tuck had seen in gas station offices; sweater girls. These ladies were completely nude, displaying erect pink nipples, and on one poster, pubic hair!

Tuck slept on one of the cots, which during the day was used by a fellow named Rusty. Rusty got up about five in the afternoon, a tall skinny man with a long thin face and red hair. His face had a lot of red blotches. At night, from the cot, Tuck could hear the games going on. There were two girls; Rusty called them "Ladies," who were in and out of the rooms during the day. One was a blonde and the other a redhead, and each was hard looking and wore heavy make-up.

Coming back from the beach in the afternoon, Tuck burst in the door to find Rusty and the blonde against the far wall in a heavy embrace. His hand was up her dress. The top of her dress was pulled down, exposing her breasts, and he was kissing them. She was holding his erect penis in both hands.

"Jesus Christ, kid," Rusty was zipping his fly and shouting at Tuck over his shoulder, "Knock before you run in here!" The blonde, with one foot up on a chair from the poker table, smiled at him and winked. As he bolted out the door, he could hear creaking sounds from the cot in the bedroom.

Tuck was astonished at the sight of the girl holding Rusty's penis in her hands, as though it was nothing special! And then she had winked at him, actually winked, while he was staring at her breasts, pink and glistening from Rusty's saliva. Tuck, paralyzed by an indigestible smorgasbord of sexual activity, slammed the door and bolted down the stair!

Rusty called Tuck from the open door, and the boy started back up the stair, apprehensive and alert to possible danger. Behind Rusty, another man appeared on the landing, stuffing his shirt tail into his pants. Ordinarily, Tuck would have by now vanished down a back alley, but he was so confused and curious by what he saw that he felt compelled to listen to what Rusty was going to say.

"Don't say nothin' about this to your old man, kid, or I'll have to tell him what you did," Rusty said, fishing in his pants pocket. "Here, go down the boardwalk and take a ride on the rolly coaster, on me. You keep your mouth shut, and I won't tell your old man, you hear?" He handed Tuck a dollar!

"Yes, sir!" Tuck responded, delighted at his good fortune. Tuck still didn't know what he was guilty of. He didn't tell Sal of course, feeling that somehow Sal would tell him what *he* did wrong.

Each time after that when Tuck saw the blonde woman, she smiled at him and winked. He immediately responded by turning red from head to toe. Tuck was told by Rusty and the girls not to hang around during the day, but on the one day it rained and cleared the beaches and boardwalk, Tuck observed the steady stream of men knocking at the door of the small casino and being admitted by the girls. He waited until dinner time to return, hanging out under the boardwalk.

On that evening, Sal took Tuck across the street to the Club Avalon, where they had dinner and watched Mickey Shaughnessy's nightclub act. In the 1970's, Tuck saw Shaughnessy on TV, and the TV/movie star delivered the only line that Tuck remembered from that show in North Wildwood. His nightclub act had not changed in thirty years, in spite of his celebrity as a Sinatra chum. Holding up a dummy rifle, he said, "This is rifle, this is my gun." When he said 'gun', he thrust his groin at the audience. "This is for war, and this is for fun!"

Shaughnessy sat at their table after the show, with Cosey Morley and a couple of other men. Shaughnessy asked the boy if he went to Catholic school, to which Tuck replied, "No." Tuck didn't think he was funny.

Tuck stayed there with Sal for a week, but he spent only a couple of hours with the boy. When leaving to drive home, Sal drove to Sunset Beach, nearly the southern end of the New Jersey peninsula, to show the boy the wreck of the Atlantus, a beached shipwrecked vessel made of concrete. They continued from there to his next visit to the Cape May Court House Parole Office, and then brought him home. The only conversation between them occurred when walking with Sal on the beach when he asked, "What are your eating all that junk for?"

Tuck had purchased some pink cotton candy with the dollar from Rusty.

Sal showed up on a couple of other occasions during the next year. Tuck supposed that he was really making an effort to respond to Edie Maye's pleas for help. Tuck, the urban guerilla, was probably driving her crazy. Her problem was that Tuck's lifestyle, diet of fish and fresh-stolen vegetables, days spent fishing and patrolling the woods, and hours spent at the local swimming hole, "the swings," had shaped him into a very lean and tough individual.

The days of hand-mirror beatings were long since over. Tuck weighed about 120 pounds, had no body fat, and his torso was rippled muscle. She had no recourse if language didn't work. She tried slapping him on occasions, but he simply ducked, or if it landed, just laughed it off. But the boy was still scared of Sal.

One day trip with Sal consisted of a long ride towards Atlantic City, where they stopped at what is now called the Somers Point Diner. They sat in a booth, where Tuck had a piece of apple pie, and eventually were joined by an "associate" of Sal's. The man's name was Irving Meyer. Later Tuck found out he was appropriately called "One-eye Irving." About five feet four inches in height, he was very stocky. An ugly scar reached diagonally across his face, starting at the hairline above one ear, crossing directly through his eyebrow, eye and nose, and terminating at his jaw line beneath the opposite ear.

The right eyebrow featured a hairless half inch gap through which the scar ran. In different places, the healing process had produced a ridge of scar tissue, like one of those three dimensional maps of mountain ranges Tuck saw in seventh grade Geography class. The man had the Appalachian Mountains running diagonally across his face! Tuck couldn't tell which eye was looking at him, and he was glad he had finished his pie by the time One-Eye Irving sat down.[62]

Irving's speech was guttural, laced with swear words, and hard to understand.

"Hey, Sal," he said, "how you doin', dis your kid?"

Sal affirmed that Tuck was his kid, adding that he was the youngest. In later years Tuck would discover that this, too, was a lie.

"How's da pawn shop?" Irving asked, then turning towards Tuck, "You like'a my scar, keed? You wanna' see Irving's eye? Irving take it out for ya, you wanna' see."

"No, sir," Tuck stammered. His attention was riveted on Irving's glass eye, and he was terrified that he might take it out. Suddenly Irving turned in the booth so that he was facing Sal, and his voice dropped to a raspy whisper.

"Get this fuckin' kid outa' here, Sal," he said, motioning toward Tuck with his head. Sal told the boy to go outside and wait in the car, and he responded quickly. Standing outside on the brick porch of the diner, Tuck could see them huddled in conversation, and as he walked down the steps, he saw Sal reach into his inside jacket pocket and pass a bulging white envelope to One-Eye Irving. Ten years later Tuck would meet One-Eye Irving again, almost 3,000 miles from the Somers Point Diner.

"What happened to that man?" Tuck asked on the return trip from the Diner.

"Irving's a Jeweler, he's got one of those places on the Boardwalk in Atlantic City," Sal said, "he got that scar when some guys robbed him. They cut him up pretty bad."

Tuck accepted the explanation. It didn't occur to him that no one in their right mind would buy anything from a salesman who talked and looked like One-Eye Irving. In a way, Tuck felt sorry for the man, cursed with the grotesque mountain range across his face.

Another day trip took Tuck to Burlington, where Sal picked up a man named Tippy Carralenes. Tippy was a huge person, very fat, and smelled badly. Although the weather was warm, he wore an overcoat over a red-checkered woodsman's shirt, buttoned at the collar. He sat in the middle of the back seat and said nothing after Sal had brought him out of his house and led him to the car.

They then drove to Philadelphia, crossing the Ben Franklin Bridge. Tippy and Sal exchanged brief comments in Italian. In the rear view side mirror, Tuck noticed that Tippy looked out the window whenever he spoke. Sal circled under the bridge and drove down to the Society Hill section, near Elfreth's Alley. He parked the car in a cul-de-sac with brick walls, and he and Tippy knocked on the back door of one of the colonial houses there.

A man soon appeared at the door. He was small and wearing a smoking jacket. It was maroon velvet, and the man appropriately was holding a large curved pipe in one hand. The three men talked, and after closing the door briefly, the man reappeared, and handed Sal a key ring.

Soon they were heading south on Fourth Street. Somewhere in south Philly, Sal made several turns and ended up outside a large warehouse near the Delaware River. Sal unlocked an entrance door next to the overhead doors, and they entered. The whole place was filled with boxes and furniture stacked in rows.

Sal wandered around a bit, and finally said, "This is it, all this stuff right here. I'm going to mark it for you, so you get the right stuff. The Judge don't like no mistakes."

Tippy just grunted. Sal took a piece of chalk out of his pocket and starting marking furniture. Tuck noticed that some of the furniture included craps tables and roulette wheels, and under some canvas, slot machines. Tuck noticed that the machines bore the silhouette of Chief Pontiac, the same as the "Chiefs" from the Casino at Red Men's Hall. Finished marking, Sal walked to the door and made a telephone call from a wall phone. They then went out to the car, and Sal said, "You need anything? It'll be about an hour before the truck gets here. You want some smokes?"

"Nah," Tippy said, "I wait, you go. I be O.K. Don't worry, Sal, Tippy do the job OK. Adio, Sal."

"Well, O.K.," Sal said, "Gabby's got the address. Just make sure you cover everything with those tarpaulins. Gas up over here, up on Ninth Street, just to be sure. And don't take no chances, no speeding, nothing like that. You tell Apples Sal said so, O.K.?" Sal pulled a roll of bills out of his pocket and peeled off several, handing them to Tippy.

"I'll have something' for you next week," Sal said, as they entered the car. "Tell Apples the Judge wants his keys back tomorrow morning." Tuck liked this trip because Sal drove down to the river and they caught the river ferry back to Camden before coming home. And for some strange reason that the boy didn't understand, he felt relieved to know that the slot machines from Red Men's Hall were OK and reposing in a safe warehouse in South Philadelphia, being watched over by Apples, the second story man and bodyguard.[63]

19

FUGITIVES

THE war at long last, had ended. At the house on Mt. Holly Avenue, Edie Maye and the children had cried through the trauma of FDR's death and the ascension of the little politician from Missouri, Harry Truman.

"Give 'em hell, Harry," left little to the imagination regarding his Presidency. He moved into FDR's offices and made his presence felt from the very beginning.

Tuck and Billy Brenneman had tracked the Allied forces across Europe on Billy's wall map. Patton, the hero of the day, had spearheaded the rush to Berlin. In the theaters, moviegoers cheered when he, Bradley or McArthur were featured in the news.

The capture of Berlin brought shocking news to the home front - thousands of Jews rounded up, gassed and burned. The scenes were run over and over again in the newsreels, gaunt survivors in the arms of American G.I.'s, piles of bones and corpses. The war had begun with newsreels of Japanese Soldiers bayoneting women and children in Nanking, and ended with the realization of Nazi death camps. It was a war that had to be fought.

And then Enola Gay ended the misery in the Pacific. The great bombs bringing the anticipated horrors of more Okinawas and Tarawas to a halt. No tears were shed for the two scorched cities or their inhabitants. The two bombs together had killed fewer civilians combined than the Japanese army in its ruthless five week attack on the city of Nanking, where they also raped more than 200,000 women and conducted head chopping contests for their officers with their Samurai swords.[64] They had asked for it. They got it. It was over.

It was about this time that Tuck's solitary repasts in the woods and along the creek were interrupted by two older gentlemen. One was a fugitive from Nazi Germany, and the other, a former stock owner, a fugitive from the 1929 crash.

Tuck's fishing buddy, Donny, introduced him to Jan Wilga one day when they met in the woods, picking up bait for a fishing trip. "Wilga," as Tuck came to know him, was in his sixties, a tall, thin angular man with white hair that just "arranged itself" atop his huge head. He had intense blue eyes set in a deeply wrinkled face that was highlighted by a large thin nose and his huge ears. He usually sported two or three days of white stubble and dressed in clean, but ill-fitting clothes.

His speech was thick with a European accent, and he was very friendly. Soon he was accompanying Donny and Tuck on all of their fishing excursions. As they fished, he would ask questions about every aspect of what they were doing, treating the boys as equals. Of course, it wasn't long before Edie Maye found out about Wilga, and this prompted a visit to Donny's house. Bea Wells, Donny's mom, didn't know any more about Wilga than anyone else, but she had met him, he lived across the street from her, and she felt that he didn't mean the boys any harm.

Donny and his family moved away soon after that, and Wilga and Tuck became constant companions. Wilga had a portable chess game which he brought with him, and taught Tuck the game. He had a room in an apartment house at Broad and Cherry Street, and Tuck had free access. On his many visits there, they would play chess or he would share with Tuck some of the hundreds of photographs he had taken in war-torn Palestine during its transition to Israel.

Wilga's entire family, including two sons and a daughter, had been among the millions murdered by the Nazis, his family meeting their deaths in a concentration camp. Tuck knew him for several years before he related the story of his escape from the Nazis. Tuck presumed he waited until he was old enough to understand it.

Because of his reputation as a renowned chemical engineer, his life had been spared and he was used by the Germans as slave labor. Toward the end of the war, he escaped, walking out of Germany through the advancing

Russian lines. He was shot in the shoulder by a Russian soldier, but aided by partisans, still managed to escape capture.

He called the Russians "evil brutes," and told Tuck that the U.S. would have to fight them someday. Eventually, with the aid of fellow scientists in France and Portugal, he was smuggled into Palestine, and finally found his way into the U.S. He was the first Jew Tuck ever knew, and he loved him dearly.

He had come to Mt. Holly because he had a job with the Permutit Corporation, a chemical manufacturer that had a plant in nearby Birmingham, on the Rancocas Creek. Eventually, he got Edie Maye the job that she held there until her retirement due to illness in 1960.

Wilga bought a 1949 Buick Roadmaster convertible, and the fishing trips took on a whole new perspective. Often, they drove to Long Beach Island and spent the day fishing the rock walls at the base of the Barnegat lighthouse. Wilga never fished, but sat comfortably nearby, knees folded up to his chest with arms encircling them, sometimes puffing on an elegant brier wood pipe, and quietly watched. He talked to everyone with an easy grace and genuine smile, and listened with interest to everyone's comments. He told Tuck he was "enjoying freedom."

He often supplied Tuck with money for lures, line and tackle, but one gift that he provided in the first summer of the time at the Mt. Holly Avenue house made Tuck as happy as he ever remembered being during his childhood.

On a Saturday morning, Wilga came by and picked up Tuck in the Buick.

"I tink you should fish in Brown's Mills today," he said. Brown's Mills, near Fort Dix, was a 15 mile drive.

Mirror Lake, created by the dam there, was essentially the origin of the South Branch of the Rancocas, although it was possible to follow a feeder stream all the way to White's Bogs, deep in the pines.

Instead of stopping at the dam, Wilga drove about half way around Mirror Lake and stopped at a cabin. He went to the door, knocked, and followed the woman who emerged to the lake's edge, where he waved for Tuck to join them.

Submerged in the brown cedar water next to the dock was a 16 foot Old Town canoe.

"Ve must empty the boat, and take it wid us," Wilga said. He had bought it for five dollars. Wading into the lake, Tuck beached the bow, and the three of them rocked out the water. It had been submerged for some time, and appeared in pretty ragged shape.

They tied the canoe atop the convertible and brought it back directly to Hack's Canoe Retreat on Mill Street.

Wilga negotiated a complete renovation, including new canvas, with Dick Lamb, the manager, for seventy dollars.

Three weeks later, Wilga and Tuck stood waiting anxiously as Dick rolled it, like new, out of the boathouse. New canvas was painted bright green, and Dick pointed out a half dozen new ribs that he had installed, and the hand woven wicker seats. The entire interior was restored to natural wood color and brightly varnished. It was magnificent.

Wilga handed Tuck the key to the boathouse.

"This is your canoe, to use as you see fit, to care for and keep up. I know you will do this well," he said. "The boathouse costs four dollars each month, which Wilga has paid for one year. Next year, you pay. I hope that you like my gift to you."

Tuck choked back tears, knowing that Dick Lamb was watching. He finally managed a soft "Thank you, thank you, Wilga."

"Now, let's see how you can navigate," Wilga said.

Dick showed Tuck the proper procedure for launching, using the two wheeled boat trolley from the boathouse and the pipe rollers on the dock, and demonstrated proper paddling techniques. It was the beginning of a series of new adventures for him on the Rancocas and other New Jersey lakes and rivers, a new freedom of movement, and the first time in his life that an adult, a man, had extended him a gift of such magnitude.

Tuck soon knew every cove and tributary of the Rancocas from Mt. Holly to Brown's Mills, a ten-mile trip on the creek. He was often on the creek at sunrise, fishing select coves for pickerel and crappie, and developed stalking skills and the ability to "indian paddle," moving the craft swiftly but silently through the early morning haze. The canoe now accompanied him on all trips to the swings, his favorite swimming hole on the Rancocas. He took pride in being able to slip into a cove in the early morning mist, and for the first sound heard to be that of his Dardevil spinner dropping next to a lily pad.

The Swings, Tuck's favorite swimming hole on the Rancocas, during a canoe bombing mission, about 1945. The turn at the Mill Dam and the water company buildings are visible downstream. Color sketch by the Author, pictured on the "20 foot limb."

The Rancocas feeds the Delaware River. The dividing point between that portion of the creek which is tidal and the remainder, which is fresh, is the Mill Dam in Mt. Holly. Below the dam, the creek exhibits daily rises and falls that are recorded in advance in the tidal tables. It was possible to portage at the Mill Dam and access the creek below, but there was a waterfall of about two feet just below the Washington Street Bridge that discouraged Tuck from exploring there.

There were three other portages on the upper creek, at Smithville, Pemberton and Brown's Mills. Smithville, the site of Hazekial Smith's famous bicycle railway, was the easiest. The canoe had to be carried about 40 yards past the dam, where a launch was possible. Tuck often made this portage in order to fish Smithville Lake, just beyond the dam.

Several miles upstream, the Pemberton portage was somewhat of a problem, since the canoe had to be carried about two hundred yards, across heavily trafficked Main Street in the process. In Brown's Mills, the problem was the same, as the dam was located nearly in the center of town.

Mt. Holly's Mill Dam was a favorite place for Tuck, before and after the canoe. The main dam was comprised of seven large wooden gates, controlled by gearing mechanisms linked together across its span. Near these "seven gates" was a small brick building that contained three additional spillways.

The creek spilled through these gates with a steady roar, the race forming a large lake with heavy currents that swirled in circles before flowing into the lower portion of the creek. Each year, in late March, this lake was filled with thousands of yellow perch, which spawned there for about two to three weeks. The Perch "run," as the town folk called it, was a seasonal fishing festival.

Just above the seven gates, where the creek ran very deep, was Tuck's favorite night fishing spot for bullhead catfish. Night fishing for catfish required special skills and patience, and was great fun. Although Tuck now had a canoe, he simply used it as transportation to get to his favorite places, and would often beach it and fish from the banks.

But the canoe opened up to Tuck all of the coves and rivulets of the upper creek that were inaccessible from land.

Sunset lake, Shreve's Cove and other choice fishing spots now fell within his domain. And the canoe also led Tuck to the other gentleman who influenced him greatly and became a friend; Hugh Campbell.

About two miles upstream from Hack's, near Smithville, the creek divides, creating an island. This island is the site of Kate's Canoe Rental and store, the resort where Edie Maye and Sal first met. Kate's still maintained his canoe barn there, but the buildings were abandoned and run down. The Saturday night dances, parties and "blanket games" organized by Sal had long since disappeared, along with any legitimate business he once had.

The south end of the island, near the canoe barn, featured a beach that was a good spot for pickerel, and Tuck fished it often from the canoe and from the bank. One day, ashore at the cove, he was surprised by a man, who quietly walked up on him. His name was Hugh Campbell, a landscape painter. In exchange for keeping an eye on the place, Mr. Katz let him live in the Canoe barn.

Tuck had four fat yellow perch on a stringer, and he offered them as a gift. He wasn't supposed to be on the island. It was the beginning of a relationship that lasted for about five years.

Once Tuck knew Hugh, he made it a point to join him whenever he discovered him on a painting excursion. He was another one of the town characters to most people. He dressed in surplus Army clothes, wore a pith helmet in the summer, was usually dirty and spoke very little to anyone. A small man with bow legs and a bald head, he lived a monk like existence year round in the drafty boathouse. Tuck instinctively knew he was a painter of some distinction.

Most of his paintings were creek scenes. He only painted landscapes, and used palette knives to apply his colors. Every painting was starkly three-dimensional, its perspectives enhanced by color and the thickness of the paint laid on. While painting, he worked in feverish concentration, applying the heavy colors with swift deft strokes. Sometimes the oil paint was nearly a half inch thick on the canvas.

But the paintings were extraordinary. He captured exactly what the creek meant to Tuck in painting after painting. On some days, he would finish four or five canvases, and could be seen laboring down some path or lane, barely able to carry all of his equipment and paintings.

He occasionally included buildings in his works, but mostly they portrayed a particular bend or turn in the creek, overhanging trees reflected in the deep brown cedar water, lily pads blooming along the banks.[65]

In the fall, he liked to paint surrounding farmer's fields, especially those with corn left standing. Tuck particularly liked one painting that featured a dirt road winding through such a field to a one-point perspective, the glorious fall colors of sugar maple, oak and hickory trees framing the scene. The corn was nearly gone, broken stalks mostly on the ground, a few proudly standing near a raggedy weather beaten scarecrow.

About twice each summer, Hugh would set up a display along the cemetery wall on High Street, just below the "mount" for which Mt. Holly is named. He would line up about 30 paintings, and sit there on a folding canvas chair all day, reading and occasionally selling one for four or five dollars.

Tuck didn't really know if he could call Hugh Campbell his friend. He had more or less tolerated the boy, sitting on the grass behind him as he worked. Occasionally, he talked to Tuck, but being limited in experience, Tuck was at a loss to respond. Hugh was a political activist, and by the time Tuck emerged from the military, he had given up painting to pursue activism full-time. He was particularly concerned with industrial pollution.

He may have even been a communist, since he spoke bitterly of the capitalistic system that had caused his downfall and the loss of a personal fortune, wife and family after the 1929 crash. Tuck didn't understand much about his angry commentary, remembering only that the "Goddamn government let those bastards play with the margin."

When Tuck graduated high school, he had taken a day job in Eckman's gas station in the center of town. Hugh showed up there one day, on his way to protest some indignity to the local newspaper. Approaching him, Tuck broached a subject that had been on his mind for some time.

"Mr. Campbell, can I speak to you?" Tuck inquired timidly.

He knew the boy, of course, and after exchanging pleasantries, Tuck continued. He hadn't seen him very often in the past couple of years, being involved with high school, sports and work.

"Would you consider taking on a student? I want to be an artist, and I want to paint. I can pay you, I've got two jobs." Tuck had a vision of himself as a recluse, like he was, traveling the back roads of the pines and painting.

"I don't paint much anymore, son. Not interested." He said.

"But you don't have to paint, just to teach me. Anytime you want. I wouldn't be a bother." Tuck was pleading now, but already extremely embarrassed by his rejection.

"What do you want to be a painter for?" He asked, "There's no money in it, and people think you're a goddamn lunatic."

"I just want to paint." It was the only response that Tuck could think of. "I don't care about money."

"You know what this is?" he asked, rattling a sheaf of about twenty hand-written pages in Tuck's face. "This is a protest against the Permutit, Ancocas Mills and Eagle Dye companies. They're poisoning the creek, killing all the fish, they don't give a damn, you know. The fish, the creek, the woods, they belong to everyone, not just those money grubbing bastards. They're ruining it for everyone."

He was right, of course. That year had featured a fish kill up stream of Mt. Holly that resulted in thousands of dead fish of every variety, floating under the town bridges for several days. Similar kills had occurred many times before.

"They're the power, kid; painting pictures ain't going to change that. That's why I quit. Pretty soon there won't be anything left that's worthwhile to paint. Somebody's got to do something. Just sitting on your ass, painting pictures, that's what they want." He said. Tuck was taken aback. How would you make a Company stop doing something? Confused and embarrassed by his tirade, Tuck's face was now red and he had tears in his eyes. It had taken a lot of courage for the boy to approach him.

"Look, kid," he said, softening his tone, "you're too goddamn young to hole up in the pines and paint pictures. There's a whole life in front of you. Get some education under your belt, see some of the world. There's always time to paint."

"But," Tuck protested, knowing that he needed money.

"Not interested. I don't need any students. Don't need things, kid, you'll be better off. Good luck to you." He dismissed the boy, and strode off up Mill Street and out of Tuck's life.

20

JOINING UP

PEG Leonard's son, Jim, was a constant next door reminder of the war that ended only three years before. He had gone off to the Army a strapping six foot, 240 pound athlete. Commissioned a B-25 bomber pilot, his plane was shot down over Germany in 1943. He came home in 1946, after three years in German POW camps, weighing only 89 pounds.

Jim now walked with a limp, bent at the waist. He had lost all of his teeth and most of his hair, and the remaining corona had turned white. Since coming home, he had regained some of his previous bulk, but looked as though he were 90 years old.

It was the first time in Tuck's memory that the country was not at war. He had celebrated like everyone else when first the Germans surrendered, and then the following year, Harry dropped the bombs. But, there were lots of signs that the country was still engaged in other kinds of strife. Everyone talked of the Rosenbergs, who were executed over the secrets of the A-bomb, and there was a new awareness that Russia was now an enemy.

Tuck found it totally confusing. The Russians had been partners with Hitler, and then the Nazis had attacked them only a couple of years into the war. They then became an Ally. Like the Italians, they changed sides in the middle of the war! Local sentiment never really crystallized against the Italian Americans as it had against the Japanese. When the Army hit the beach in Italy, the many Italians surrendered in droves with great friendship and apologies. Back home, the Italian army was the butt of jokes.

There had been hundreds of German and Italian prisoners at Fort Dix and many of the town folk would drive up there on a Sunday and bring them food and magazines and newspapers and pass the packages over the wire fence. It was a new form of entertainment.[66]

Tuck took little satisfaction in the Italians when they captured the fleeing II Duce and literally mugged him to death. Pictures of his body, hung in a public square with his dead mistress for days, had been in all of the newsreels and papers.

Ike was elected President; a genuine hero. There were lots of heroes, plenty to go around, Tuck thought. They represented all that Tuck had come to believe about his country; fairness and decency and the "American way."

Before the Allies of World War II had signed a peace treaty with Japan, the country was already engaged in another war in Korea.[67] The North Koreans had invaded South Korea, and a United Nations force composed mostly of American troops responded. The draft was initiated, and most of the young men were rushing to enlist before their number was called.

Tuck's brother, just graduated from high school, had developed a severe drinking problem. He had worked every summer since he was fourteen in Fort Dix, and always had a part-time job and money. He and a couple of his friends became known for their hell-raising drinking bouts in several towns along the river, where the bartenders asked no questions. One summer, he had gone with a photographer to the Army base in Watertown, New York, and worked there for the whole summer, sending Edie Maye cash each week by mail.

They didn't talk much, but he was Tuck's idol. He briefly quarterbacked the high-school football team and played utility infielder in baseball. He claimed the sixth man position on his basketball team as a senior, when they won the state championship in Camden Convention Center.

He was undeniably among the fastest swimmers in town, and would dive from any height at the swings, the swimming hole on the Rancocas. He did everything as hard as he could, including drinking. Obviously deeply introverted by Sal's influence, he adroitly avoided every opportunity to be photographed.

Cholly was driven, like his peers, by the knowledge that he was going to be drafted or enlist in the Service. The realities of the previous war; dead, crippled and lost acquaintances, the Jim Leonards, were still very real. He already had been gripped by the alcoholism that would eventually kill him.

He certainly had enough reason to drink. His paychecks had largely supported Edie Maye, Tuck and Sis for a major portion of the past three years, and Sal simply didn't acknowledge his existence. Even when they were small, if Sal brought presents from one of his excursions, he seldom brought anything for Cholly. His one exception was when he returned home from a three month stint in the Cape May County jail, and presented Cholly with a fully constructed but uncovered model of a Piper Cub airplane, made by his "cellmate." Cholly was a complete nonentity in Sal's eyes, where Tuck, at least, existed. But Cholly curried Sal's favor, whereas Tuck had developed a sullen, defiant attitude toward him.

Over the years, Sal took advantage of him in many ways, but Cholly didn't seem to care. As Tuck idolized him, he looked up to Sal as someone quite special.

The previous Saturday night, Edie Maye had awakened Tuck about three o'clock in the morning, and they retrieved Cholly from the front porch, where he was passed out, his head lying in a puddle of vomit.

He weighed about the same as Tuck, about 130 pounds, but it was a struggle for them to get him up the stairs. He threw up, spraying them and his clothing with more vomit as they negotiated the turn into the bathroom. In the bathtub, lying on his back, he continued to vomit as Edie Maye stripped off his clothes and ran cold water. Tuck tried to keep him from choking, unbelieving that anyone could continue to vomit after each explosive episode.

They worked together silently for at least an hour, Edie Maye occasionally giving tight-lipped instructions, cleaning him up, emptying and refilling the tub and feeding him coffee from a spoon. The vomiting was replaced with dry heaves and he began to come around. Finally, he was able to stand, and Tuck dried him off and steered him into his bed. Edie Maye staggered off to hers.

Earlier in that same summer, Edie Maye had awakened Tuck and sent him down to the Police Station on a Sunday morning about three a.m., to retrieve his older brother. He was passed out in the lockup, but able to maneuver, and Tuck staggered home with Cholly draped over his shoulders in a fireman's carry.

Tuck had awakened on other nights to bathroom sounds in the early hours, but that Saturday night was typical of what became a weekly ritual for Tuck and Edie Maye.

On a day following one of the vomit-filled nightly cold baths, Cholly got up about two in the afternoon, dressed and went out to get a drink. He made a remark on the way out about "hair of the dog that bit him."

After the door had closed, Edie Maye made a remark from the top of the stair, something to the effect that "He's nothing but a goddamn drunk, seventeen years old, and he'll never amount to anything."

Stung by her attack on his brother, and completely surprised to hear Edie Maye criticize anyone except himself, Tuck responded, invoking a heated argument. Each of them ended up in tears, Tuck at the bottom of the stairs, she at the top, screaming at each other. "He is not a drunk!" Tuck shouted, hating Edie Maye for what she was saying.

But she was right, and although Tuck was blinded to it, Cholly was a drunk, and a dangerous one. One evening, Tuck came home to find Sis at the house and everyone in a deep depression.

"Your brother's been in accident," Edie Maye said, "he's in the hospital."

"What happened?" Tuck asked.

"All we know is that he and Ronny Taylor were in an accident out on Route 206," Edie Maye said, "we were waiting for you before going out to the hospital. He's all right."

They walked into Cholly's room after a brief argument with the nurses on duty about calling so late. He greeted them with a weak grin. He had a lot of small bandages on his face.

"What the hell happened?" Tuck asked.

"Taylor," he said, "he was driving, and he drove right onto the highway into the wrong lane, into a tractor trailer. We were both pretty drunk."

Two days later, they brought him home, his entire body black and blue. Incredibly, Ron Taylor had broken only his left arm. They had survived a head-on collision with an 18-wheeled tractor trailer. The impact propelled the two drunks under the dashboard and had sheared off the entire top of Taylor's coupe, leaving it looking like a wrinkled, squat convertible.

Leverich's gas station at the top of Main Street displayed the wreck for about a month, until a more spectacularly drunk driven crashed vehicle took its place. A glance convinced everyone that God takes care of stray dogs and drunks. It was a miracle that they weren't both killed. It was the first of five major accidents that Cholly would survive.

On a Sunday of the following October, Tuck returned home from the ice plant about five in the afternoon. Cholly was sitting at the kitchen table, beer in hand.

"I'm getting out of here," he said, "just thought you ought to know." Already drunk, he had stacked a pyramid of empties on the kitchen table. "I joined the Navy," he continued, "and I figured I'd tell you before I take off."

"When are you going?" Tuck responded, amazed at the idea. It should have occurred to Tuck that he would enlist. He had just turned eighteen on October second. Sis, now married, had moved out last year to a small apartment on Garden Street. Tuck knew, like everyone else, that turning eighteen meant that you'd better enlist in the Service of your choice, or accept the inevitable; induction into the Army. Unlike WWII, where inductees would serve in all branches of the service, all draftees for the Korean War went to the Army.[68] But Tuck was still surprised when the draft struck close to home.

"Right now, I already told Mom last week." he said. Tuck was confused, and as usual, at a loss for words when confronted by critical situations. Finally, he stammered out, "Where are you going, I mean, where's the Navy?"

"Trigger's picking me up. Bud's old man is driving us to the Brooklyn Navy Yard[69] in the morning. That's where we report." Trigger and Bud, his two best friends, had also enlisted. As Tuck digested all this, a horn blew out front.

"That's Bud," he said, "I'm outa' here. I can't take any more of this shit around here, anyway. I signed up for a program, so that Mom will get sixty percent of my pay every month. Make sure she uses it, understand? I don't want her puttin' it in any god damned savings account for me, so you tell her, O.K.? You see the old man; tell him I said so long."

He finished off the beer he had been holding, crunched the can, slapped Tuck on the back, and swinging a light jacket over his shoulder, walked to the front door. Without looking back, he said, "See ya' around," and stepped out. Tuck ran to the front door in time to see the door slam on a Chevy sedan. Bud squealed rubber and blew the horn on his dad's car all the way down Mt. Holly Avenue to the intersection of Mill Street, then he was gone. Tuck wouldn't see him again for four years.

"Lucky bastard," Tuck thought out loud. In a way, he was envious as well as hurt. *At least he was getting out of this hell hole.* Tuck knew that life in the Service would be better than at home, and that Cholly, and he, when his turn came, would be judged on their merits and not the reputation of their father.

Edie Maye returned from work at Ted Quay's at six o'clock.

"Cholly's gone," Tuck blurted out, "he just left with Buddy and Trigger. He joined the Navy." She didn't respond, but walked over to the battered couch in the living room and sat down on the edge, put her head in her hands and began to cry.

Suddenly, Tuck felt frightened and confused. He preferred keeping Edie Maye at arm's length as an antagonist, and he didn't know how to react to this turn of events. She looked so helpless, crying in her hands. He suppressed a feeling of anger at Cholly, simply going off and leaving them. How would they cope? Tuck had no idea if Edie Maye's meager salary was enough to survive on. He offered money from his ice plant pay, but she always refused it. But he knew that Cholly intercepted most of the bills in the mailbox and paid them without even asking Edie Maye.

Tuck sat down next to her, wanting to hold her, but not knowing how. Gazing at the floor and choking back his own tears, he asked, "Didn't you know? Didn't he tell you?"

"Oh, God," she sobbed, "I shouldn't have yelled at him, he said he would go, but I didn't think he met it. I called him a drunk, and told him he'd never amount to anything, that he'd end up behind the Arcade with Gus Ward and the other winos." She began to regain her composure, and producing a handkerchief from her bag, wiped her face, saying, "Maybe they'll straighten him out, in the Navy."

"Ah, Mom," Tuck said, "Don't worry. He'll be all right; he just didn't want to get drafted." Tuck didn't know what else to say, confronted with Edie Maye's tears.

21

A TREACHEROUS BEACH

LIFE on Mt. Holly Avenue settled in to a pretty acceptable pattern, as far as Tuck was concerned. Edie Maye had a job on Route 38 at Ted Quay's Flowers, where it turned out that her design skills as a dressmaker were easily transferable to floral arrangement. Most of the time she walked there, about a mile trek each way. Since it wasn't far from Granddad's place, she got to see him often.

Jealous of her incursion into his Granddad's domain, Tuck still ended up there a couple of times each month. It was summer and he was absorbed in his life at the local swimming hole, "the swings."

Not just anyone was permitted to swim at the swings, and if Tuck and his friends had been tougher with that policy, they could have saved a young boy's life on one summer day. In order to survive there, one had to be a tough little athlete. Often, Tuck found himself in predicaments that were hazardous, demanding skills as a climber and swimmer.

On this particular day, the boys weren't "bombing canoes," and one of Hack's canoe renters; a woman, had beached her canoe at the foot of the hickory tree. Normally, this wasn't permitted, but it was a very hot day, and none of the older swimmers were around to tell her to move the canoe. Since the swing was almost never idle, it was dangerous for swingers and swimmers if a canoe were beached within the locus of the swing. Tuck and his friends just didn't attempt any roundhouse swings, and worked around the canoe, which was protruding about ten feet into the creek at a right angle to it.

Mrs. Zanphel, who lived on Mt. Holly Avenue, was at the top of hill, sitting on a blanket while her little boy, Charley, played on the beach next to the bow of the canoe. Charley, with a couple of other seven to eight-year olds, was running in and out of the water, and doing little dives. Each time he came up, it took him a long time to clear the water from his face and erase the squint he made before submerging. Afraid that his dives might carry him into deeper water, he was running diagonally and diving towards the canoe. Tuck observed from the top of the hill that on a couple of occasions, he came up very close to the canoe.

Suddenly, Mrs. Zanphel was at the water's edge, calling frantically for Charley. No one had noticed that he was missing! All of the swimmers immediately jumped into the creek and started walking and diving the area and one pulled a little girl to safety, but Johnny was nowhere to be found. Someone had immediately run up to Sapp's house and called the emergency squad, and within a half hour, the creek was overflowing with police and rescue workers and two rowboats were afloat, manned by Firemen working with grappling hooks.

Being ordered out of the water by the Police, Tuck had scrambled up the hickory tree and took a position on the twenty foot limb, over the water, hoping that he might be able to see something of Johnny. An hour later, Tuck was still there, watching the drama unfold beneath.

By then, several fire companies had responded, and there were five rowboats and canoes on the creek, dragging.

One of them hooked Johnny about 150 yards downstream, against the near bank. Quickly pulling him aboard, they raced upstream to the beach and carried him up the hill and to a blanket, where one of the Firemen started artificial respiration.

But Johnny was quite dead, his little body now blue, and exhibiting the black holes left in his neck and shoulder by the grappling hook. Mrs. Zanphel, standing behind the Fireman with hands clasped as though in prayer, cried silently as the men worked. When Joe Anderson, who was doing the artificial respiration, finally gave up, he looked up at Mrs. Zanphel, and said, "I'm sorry, ma'am, he's gone."

Mrs. Zanphel stepped back and became a noise. Tuck couldn't say she screamed because it wasn't a scream, it was a noise, a moan, a scream, a sob.

It contained the words, "My baby, my baby," but there weren't any words, only this animal-like noise from the depths of her being. It went on for a long time, the noise, and Tuck never forgot the sound of it.

Joe Anderson told onlookers that Johnny had a lump on his head the size of a small apple. Everyone knew immediately that he had surfaced under the canoe and knocked himself out. The woman who had beached the canoe there had long since gone.[70]

The swings was a world unto itself. In the early morning, if Tuck sat quietly, he could watch a few fat muskrats doing their business under the hickory roots. He had even seen a raccoon there one morning, vigorously washing his food in the springs.

It was an early Sunday morning in the fall when Tuck was sitting at the top of the hill, enjoying one of Mr. Sapp's apples, that he was surprised by his newly acquired brother-in-law, Stringy, and a friend of his, Walt. Now home from the Navy and getting established in civilian life, the two veterans wanted to see if the swings had changed since the war.

After exchanging pleasantries, they changed into their bathing suits and sat down next to Tuck. They chatted while trying to get up enough courage to go in the water in spite of the chill in the air. Tuck was acutely aware of Stringy's reputation as an athlete. He was one of the better halfbacks to ever play at Mt. Holly High School. On returning to school from the Service, he played as a punt returner for Mt. Holly's semi-professional team the following year, the Mt. Holly Moose. He ran back two of the opposition's punts for touchdowns in their first game. It was the only game he played for them, Sis prevailing upon him to quit for some unknown reason.

Tuck was reluctant to go in the water, for fear he would embarrass himself in front of Stringy, but events transpired that eliminated that worry entirely.

A clatter of inefficient handling of canoe paddles was heard from downstream, and out of curiosity, Tuck strained to see who might be coming up creek at this time of year. Many of the trees had already taken on fall colors. A canoe came into view, rounding the bend from the Mill Dam. In it were two couples dressed in sweaters and light jackets. The two girls sat on the canoe's bottom amidships, facing each other. They had a portable radio and picnic baskets and blankets piled there.

Suddenly, without any apparent reason, the canoe just flipped over, about twenty feet from the opposite shore. By the time the trio on the bank heard the screams for help, Stringy and Walt were already sprinting for the water, and Tuck was running to his right along a seldom used path that led to the water company and mill dam. The path would bring him nearer the foundering canoe. Instinctively, Tuck had decided that the quickest reaction would be to run down the bank and then swim to the canoe.

As he ran, Tuck glanced back and saw Stringy and Walt swimming strongly down the middle of the creek. They were still a hundred yards from the upturned boat. Ahead of him, through patches in the trees and brush, he could see a woman in a pink sweater splashing wildly and screaming. She was out of view of the two swimmers, blocked by the overturned canoe. One person had pulled himself up on the bank and was yelling, "hurry, hurry!" The woman and the canoe were swinging in the current toward the seven gates of the Mill Dam, less than 200 yards downstream.

Tuck crashed through some briers and dove for the water, striking a low hanging limb as he did so. Swimming frantically to the last spot he had seen the pink sweater, he surface dived and collided with the woman underwater.

She was still screaming, and Tuck could see her eyes bulging out at him as she grabbed him in a bear hug. He was surprised and a little frightened at how deep the creek was here. Afterwards, he realized that they were not far above the Mill Dam, and this was the point where the creek got gradually deeper until, at the dam, it was nearly twenty-five feet deep.

She was dragging Tuck deeper with her, and his feet were reaching frantically for the bottom, but it simply wasn't there. Wrestling with her underwater, Tuck managed to somehow to break her grip and get behind her just as his feet touched the sandy bottom. His lungs bursting for air, he sprang for the surface, using the bottom to push off. He was holding her by her waist, and her weight dissipated the momentum of his jump.

In a near panic and swimming desperately with one hand, Tuck finally broke the surface. Fortunately, the drifting canoe was only a foot or two away, and he quickly swung the woman's arm across the upturned bottom. Coughing and gasping, she grabbed the keel.

Tuck swam under and surfaced on the other side, putting his hands on top of hers. Stringy had the other end of the canoe, and was swimming it toward shore. The three other canoeists were now sitting on the bank, in various stages of throwing up and coughing. The other two people hadn't gone under, and Walt and Stringy each had grabbed one and brought them to shore.

The couples thanked them profusely. Only one of them could swim, and Walt asked rhetorically, "What the hell are you doing on the creek if you can't swim?" Stringy retrieved their radio from the creek bottom, but the other items had been carried downstream and disappeared in the roar of the Seven Gates into the tidal portion of the creek.

Walking back up the path on the far side of the creek, Stringy patted Tuck on the back and said,

"You did a nice job. You saved that woman's life. Not bad for a skinny kid!" With that, he and Walt grabbed the boy, ankles and arms, and gave him a one, two, three, heave about ten feet out into the creek. It was the proudest moment of Tuck's life.

When Tuck came home from the Service in 1958, he took a bathing suit and went over to the swings on a hot day. The rope was gone, and no one was there. The far side of the creek had been cleared of underbrush and a new town park and athletic field backed up to the three jumping trees.

He could tell from the condition of the bank and the steps on the hickory tree that no one had been swimming here for some time. There was now a guarded beach below the dam in the Mill Dam Park. The big limb still showed polished grooves, signs of the rope that had swung there for years; the rope that Edie Maye had swung from. The fork was as smooth and bright as Pocahontas' fingers in Jamestown Park.[71]

Tuck pulled on his suit and climbed the hickory, walking out on the twenty-foot limb. He sat down there, in the same fork where watched little Charley Zanphel grappled out of the creek. From his vantage point, he could easily see the turn where the tourist's canoe had capsized, and how close it was to the dam.

Upstream, Tuck saw that the third of several jumping trees had been struck by lightning, and the entire trunk that had ended with the fifty-nine foot jump, was gone. Tuck's brother, Cholly, Trigger Forbes and Bud Horner were the only ones who would make that jump. The tree swayed so much when they jumped, that its backward reaction negated their arc towards deeper water. Everyone else was afraid of it.

It was a nice day, and Tuck sat there for about an hour, just watching the creek and thinking. A little wind came up, rustling the leaves around him and producing a slight sway. In spite of the warm sun, Tuck felt a little chill.

A couple of canoes paddled by. The people in the first one didn't even notice that he was sitting there, twenty feet above the water. Tuck reflected that people seldom look up. The occupants of the second canoe had spotted him, and he returned their wave. Later, a water snake emerged from the lily pads to the left of the beach and made a serpentine trail of ripples as he crossed the creek directly in front of Tuck. The current carried him downstream, and he made his landing forty yards below his entry point.

Tuck thought about the woman in the pink sweater. He hadn't remembered the current being as swift as it appeared from where he now sat. There was absolutely no doubt in his mind that he had saved her from drowning. He had taken a life from the creek, but in the end, the creek had taken little Charley. The two dramas were strong memories, but they didn't cancel each other out. Tuck could still hear Mrs. Zanphel's tortured cry echoing in the trees.

Tuck thought about another time, when he and Sammy Powell engaged in a wrestling match on the twenty-foot limb and both had plummeted to the creek below, locked in combat. Tuck had lost his wind and been tumbled along the bottom of the creek in a panic. He recovered and surfaced with Sammy, each of them laughing about it, but surely the creek had prepared them to face emergencies in the water. Finally, Tuck climbed down, unwilling to risk the twenty foot dive into five feet of dark cedar water.

22

MEGARA, WIFE OF HERCULES

CHOLLY had found a home in the Navy. From Brooklyn, they immediately shipped him to boot camp at the Great Lakes Naval Training Center, Great Lakes, Illinois. Being the only 18 year old that required two shaves a day; he was soon elevated to Platoon Leader.

The promotion snapped him out of his nervous depression. Without admitting it, he knew that boot camp was drying him out and the balanced diet was contributing to his well-being. He thought that Sal probably didn't even know that he had left home, and for the first few days, he had to keep himself from falling into the funky mood that he usually drank himself out of.

His easy manner with older men stood him in good stead and he breezed through boot camp, making a lot of friends in doing so. To his own surprise, he found himself considered a leader and looked up to by his peers and the Navy bos'n mates who conducted the camp. Soon all thoughts of Sal had been erased from his consciousness.

Unlike Tuck, Cholly had more of Sal's attitudes than Edie Maye liked to admit. He made friends easily, but never committed himself totally. He didn't care a whole lot about others' opinions about himself, if one were voiced that he didn't like, he confronted it with a challenge. He was a fearless combatant regardless of his small stature and that gained him respect.

Surprisingly, he became a wonderful correspondent. Not only did his allotment checks arrive with monthly regularity, but at least one letter a week was found in Edie Maye's mailbox.

Tuck found this amazing, since the last thing his brother ever wanted to do was talk. Another first: he sent pictures. Cholly had never permitted himself to be photographed. Tuck wasn't sure he was even in his high school yearbook, as Cholly had never purchased one.

His letters were remarkable, and Tuck wished that he had some of them, now that he's gone. He decorated every letter and envelope with cartoon characters in various stages of the activities described in his message. And the cartoons were excellent. He didn't say much, just factual descriptions of Navy life, the base, some of his instructors and other patter, but Tuck devoured them several times a week, waiting anxiously for the next installment.

From Great Lakes, he was assigned to Aviation Electronics Repair School in Memphis, Tennessee, for ten months of training. Although he had leave time between assignments, he didn't come home, explaining that the train rides back and forth would use most of it up.

Instead, with duffel bag on his shoulder, he hitched hiked from Great Lakes to Memphis, Tennessee; sampling life in the towns and cities he passed through.[72]

He did well in Memphis, as Tuck expected. Tuck was convinced that his brother could do anything that he put his mind to.

After graduating his school in Memphis, he was assigned (as an "Airdale, third class") to a ship under overhaul and redesign in Pensacola, Florida, the U.S.S. Megara. He was proud that he became a "plank owner," having been with the ship when it was re-commissioned in 1949. Megara, originally laid down in 1944 and namesake of the wife of Hercules had served during WWII, missing the D-Day landings by 21 days. He served his entire remaining enlistment of three years in that ship. In 1972, she was decommissioned and subsequently sold to the Mexican Navy.

The Megara was a converted LST, "Landing Ship, Tank." Essentially these ships were shaped like cheese boxes, 300 feet long and thin with flat bottoms that permitted them to beach the bow. The bow featured two huge "clamshell" doors that opened like French doors, a ramp was dropped, and the tanks could drive into the surf and onto the beach. A huge anchor, deployed on the way in, winched the ship off the beach.

Cholly's ship, the U.S.S. Megara,(called the "Mighty Meg" by its crew) anchored in the harbor at Monte Carlo and being attended by ship chandlers. U.S. Navy photo.

The Megara's clamshell doors had been locked shut, and the cavernous hull filled with workshops. The mission of the ship was to precede the Sixth Fleet in the Mediterranean from port to port. Inoperable electronics equipment from the fleet's carrier planes would be delivered to Megara, and this equipment would be repaired as the ship moved on the next port, ahead of the fleet.

When the fleet pulled into a port, the repaired equipment would be exchanged for new work, and the Megara would depart for the next destination. To Cholly's delight, this gave the Megara's crew first crack at the best girls and best bars in every port, with nearly a six day repast before any of the rest of the fleet showed up.

In order to test the various radars and other aircraft electronics, dozens of antenna structures had been added to the ship's superstructure. With all the additional weight topside, and essentially empty below except for compensating ballast tanks to assist in stabilizing the ship, the Megara was a very unseaworthy ship.

On her first passage from Pensacola to Naples, Italy the Megara set a fleet record. It took her 115 days to cross the Atlantic. In one severe storm encountered, she averaged minus 12 knots in speed, and recorded a fifty-five degree roll. Daily averages of four knots, fighting wind and sea, weren't unusual, nor were 25 or 30 degree rolls, in only moderate weather.

In one letter, Cholly wrote, "We've been in the same place for four days, all engines ahead, full." The envelope bore a cartoon of the Megara fighting the sea, crewmen in portholes paddling furiously.

The crew was small[73] and closely knit, and because they were all "plankers," navigational information, as well as all "scuttlebutt" concerning ship operations, was quickly made general knowledge.

Like destroyer sailors, who lived under similar conditions, the sailors of the Megara became "old salts" very quickly. And like destroyer sailors, for whom every venture out of port was fraught with the perils of the high seas, they were hell-raisers when ashore.

Ordinary standards of dress and housekeeping were difficult in such a ship, and photos received home pictured Cholly with a full beard, frayed and whitened dungarees and "two-blocked" white hat. And although they lived like old China hands on board, one hand for your chow and one hand for the ship, they took the privilege of their status as real sailors, and dressed to the hilt for liberty. Cholly soon had all of his uniforms tailored with "liberty cuffs," which required silk linings, extra flare to the bell bottoms, taking in the blouse and upper pant legs, embroidered dragon designs on the inside of the blouse cuffs, zippers to replace the 13 button fly, and Chinese silk embroidery on the inside of the neck flap[74]. He soon began to accumulate stripes for his achievements in his specialty at sea, and a medical record for his achievements ashore.

Barely in service for six months, Megara showed the highest percentage rate of venereal disease of any ship on station. She was enviously called the U.S.S. Gonorrhea by the rest of the sailors in the fleet.

23

BESSIE

It was some time after they had moved to Mt. Holly Avenue before Tuck learned the price Edie Maye had paid to get down payment money from Sal. He arrived home one evening and she was sitting in the kitchen at the table with a letter in hand. He could see that she was upset.

"What's wrong, Mom?" He asked.

"I got this today, from your Father," she said, unfolding the two page document and turning it so he could see it.

"What is it?" Tuck asked. He could see that it was some kind of official thing. It had some kind of Mayan decorations at the top of the first page.

"It's a divorce. Your father's divorcing me, us." She corrected herself, but showed no emotion as she continued, "It's the only way I could get money out of him - the $500 down payment for the house, but I didn't think he'd do it. I have to sign it, because I promised him I wouldn't contest it."

"What do you mean, contest it?" Tuck asked, very curious about this piece of paper that purported to be a "something," a divorce. He knew what the word meant, although in the forties and fifties, it wasn't a word that was bandied about. Divorced women weren't very well thought of.

"It means I won't fight it. All I have to do is sign here and send it back, and it's done. I might as well sign it," she said, "since it's probably illegal anyway. It's probably not worth the paper it's printed on."

"Mom, what are you talking about?" Now she was getting Tuck confused. "What do you mean about it's illegal?"

"Because it's Mexican, he got this in Mexico somehow. I suppose he went down there, or sent to somebody down there to do it for him, but look at the top of that page, and look at those names at the bottom, they're all Mexicans," she said, pointing out the law firm's logo on the first page.[75]

"These things are a big joke, it's in the papers all the time how these movie stars get them, and then they're no good up here in the U.S. Leave it to your dad to think of something like this."

"So what, Mom?" Tuck said, a little exasperated by the fact that he'd sent an illegal divorce paper, "Who the hell cares what he does? I don't care," Tuck angrily replied. "I hate the son of a bitch. He doesn't even know that Cholly went into the Navy. He treats Cholly like shit! Granddad was right, he's a no good sonofabitch!"

Edie Maye was taken aback by the outburst, the first time that Tuck had ever verbalized his feelings about Sal. She looked at him and thought how much he was beginning to look like Sal did when she met him, but Tuck was all muscle and a rough stone, where Sal had been soft and slick. The boy has done more physical work in the past year than his father had in his entire life, and in spite of his rough manners and the way he treated her, she knew he had more character than Sal could muster if he lived to be a hundred.

His trouble is, she thought, *that he's just as stubborn as I am.*

Edie Maye looked over her glasses and said calmly, "Don't talk about him like that. He's your father, and it's not your business to criticize. I'm going to sign this and send it back, because I said I would, and I will. I've never broken a promise to him, and I'm not going to start now."

Tuck's feelings toward Edie Maye were now largely negative. Perhaps he blamed her for their condition. He couldn't take any criticism that she might offer. She was more miserable than he; Tuck realized when he was older. She ate very little, smoked incessantly and seemed to live on coffee. She was a beaten woman. He was little help to her.

Tuck did blame her in a way. It wasn't as though a better life wasn't available. She was still quite beautiful, one of those women who actually grow more attractive as they age, and she had many admirers, men who made their feelings and intentions known to her. But she never responded to any of them, which Tuck felt was unfair. With one exception, she was totally attached to Sal, who hadn't give her ten minutes of his time even on those few occasions when he did live at home.

It was too much for Tuck. He didn't think about Sal anymore. The only time he entered Tuck's consciousness was when somebody else mentioned him. He didn't care about any papers that he sent to the house. As far as Tuck could see, they made no difference in their lifestyle. It was just another one of his shitty little incursions into their lives, something to be forgotten as soon as possible.

It was about this time that Bob Carter started showing up a lot around the house. Bob was a tall slim young man who had been in Sis's class in high school. He was one of the fellows, like the fellow that Sis had married, that had enlisted in the Navy right out of his junior year. He'd served in destroyers for four years as a Machinist's Mate, and was home again. Now he was coming to the house pretty regularly.

Bob had a job at the local Chrysler dealer, and was learning to be an auto mechanic. Everyone who knew him said he was very good, and they were right. He had grown up on Mt. Holly Avenue a few blocks away, raised by his dad after his mother died when he was twelve.

His dad was an independent construction contractor and Bob had worked at his side from the time he was old enough to tote a hod of bricks, but the old man was a tyrant. When Edie Maye lived at the bungalow, Bob used to sleep over when he was recovering from the beatings the old man, a heavy drinker, inflicted on him. When his favored older brother, Jim, an Army fighter pilot, was killed in a dogfight in the Pacific in '42, the old man took it out on Bob, and had been doing so ever since. Edie Maye used to patch him up, and they'd spent a lot of time talking.

Over that year, Edie Maye and Bob started taking some trips together. Bob had a big Harley Davidson "Flathead" motorcycle, and she sewed herself a set of riding leathers. She'd climb up on the back and they'd take off and not reappear until late at night, and on some occasions not until the following day.

Tuck thought nothing of it. He really liked Bob, and he taught the boy a lot of things, simple little lessons that have stayed with him; like sawing a piece of lumber. "Keep your cut straight," Bob said, "and let the saw do the work. Get your rhythm and listen to the blade as it cuts. Work with the tool, not against it."

Edie Maye was happy, and best of all, Tuck became less the center of her attention. With Bob around, she found less to nag the boy about. Tuck responded by starting to act somewhat human towards her, although he still did pretty much as he pleased. Most of what he was doing now, however, centered about fishing, the outdoors and the ice plant. He was getting in a lot less trouble in school and with the Police.

Chip was sick, and Edie Maye was making a daily trek every evening out to his place with a hot dinner, wrapped in tin foil and insulated with towels in a big wicker basket. Sometimes Tuck would take the food, and often, Bob drove Edie out there on the Harley.

Hazel, Edie Maye's older sister, only lived a quarter mile from Chip's, but she wouldn't help him because Frances might be there. Floss lived closer, too, but she was the same. Ruth, Edie Maye's younger sister lived over in Merchantville, which might have well as been in a foreign country.

The relationship with Bob was pretty steady for about a year. One day, Tuck came in the front door to find Edie Maye sitting on the couch, head in her hands. At first, he thought she was sick.

"What's wrong, Mom?" he asked. She still had her coat on and she was clutching a crumpled letter and envelope in her hand.

"It's Bob," she said, "he's going to marry Anna Watkins." With that she started to cry, sobbing heavily. This time, Tuck had the presence of mind to sit down and put his arm around her. When he did, she collapsed on his shoulder, heaving uncontrollably. Tuck felt a deep, gut wrenching sickness in the pit of his stomach.

"Christ, Mom, she's in my class. I see her every day." Tuck said, realizing who she was referring to. "She lives in Hainesport, near Eddie's Bar." He felt terrible that they were losing Bob, whom he really cared for. "She's just a kid, like me," he continued, trying to apply logic to the situation.

"But she's young and pretty," Edie Maye coughed out, "she's everything I'm not. She continued to cry, but more softly and under control. Then she said, "I love him so, he's the best thing that ever happened to me. I practically raised him, and I always knew I would love him, but I never expected him to leave me."

Tuck was at a loss for words, so he just sat there, holding her and marveling at how small she was, and delicate, and how hurt.

A short while later, in the spring, Edie Maye told Tuck that she was pregnant. She did this without shame, in a matter of fact way that made Tuck think that she respected him. She told him that Bob was the father, and she wanted to have the baby.

"I don't care what anybody thinks; for all anyone knows, it could be your father's baby," she said,

Soon she was beginning to show a bulge, but was able to disguise it well with her wardrobe, which she still created completely from scratch. She was making monthly visits to Doc McDonald, but she didn't look good.

For a change, they talked occasionally, usually about the baby. Edie Maye was convinced it would be a girl. "I'm going to name her Bessie, for your Grandmother," she said. "You never knew her, but she was wonderful, and a beautiful young woman when she died."

"Was she part Indian, like Grandpop says?" Tuck was really curious about that. "Or is it Grandpop that's part Indian?"

"Your Great-great Grandfather married an Indian, on Grandpop's side," Edie Maye said, "that's truth; I saw a photo that my Granddad had of her, an old Indian woman in buckskins and beads."

"What was her name, Mom?" Tuck asked, "Let's name the baby like her."

Edie Maye laughed, and said, "We couldn't do that, she had one of those names like 'Little Woman Who Walks on the Snow,' or something. I don't even know what it was."

"Maybe Indian Ann would know her name," Tuck said, not wanting to give up the idea. Indian Ann was erroneously referred to as the last remaining descendant of the Lenni-Lenepe, and she lived in an old cabin in Indian Mills, according to rumor.[76]

"Nobody's sure if she's a real Lenepe," Edie Maye said, "and besides, this woman wasn't one for sure, she was a northern Indian, one of those New York tribes; Iroquois, Seneca, or something like that. We'll name her Bess, for the Lawrence's who came here from England with the Pilgrims."

One evening when Tuck came home from the ice plant about eleven o'clock, he found Edie Maye standing in a dark corner in the kitchen, supporting herself with one hand on the porcelain top of the gas stove and clutching her abdomen with the other. He could see she was in great pain.

"Quick, run over to Doc's," she said, "and tell him the baby's coming." Tuck grabbed his jacket, about to bolt for the door.

"Wait," she said, "help me upstairs first." Throwing down the jacket, Tuck picked her up and carried her up to the front bedroom. He was surprised at how light she was. As he deposited her on the bed, she eased herself down, "Now go, hurry!"

Doc came to the door in his pajamas, and Tuck blurted out his story.

"Anybody else home?" he asked.

"No," Tuck said, "just me."

"O.K., son, you scoot back there, and see if you can get Peg to come over," he said, "I'll be right there."

Tuck ran home, covering the three blocks in record time, and went next door and awakened Peg Leonard. Then he raced upstairs and sat next to Edie Maye, who was moaning on the bed.

As soon as Doc got there, he chased the boy out and invited Peg in. About three hours later, he came downstairs, and put on his coat.

"Edie's had a tough time, you're going to have to help her out now, because she's pretty sick, and will be for a few days." He put his hand on Tuck's shoulder. "Where are your brother and sister?"

"Sis is married, and Cholly's in the Navy," Tuck blurted out, "What happened, Doc? What about the baby, my little sister?"

"Your Mom had a little girl, but she only lived a few minutes. Peg's going to take care of everything with respect to your mother. You help her out with the baby. For your Mom's sake, I want to keep this quiet, Tuck[77]. I'm not going to do any official reporting on the baby...you can find a nice spot for her out back tonight. I've given Peg instructions, too, but you'll have to find a spot for her. I'll be back tomorrow," he said.

Tuck gagged on a response, and he could feel tears welling in his eyes.

"The baby died?" He finally got it out.

"Yes," Doc said, "it wasn't time yet, and she just didn't have enough strength. She was very tiny, only a few pounds."

Tuck didn't know what to say. They had been so happy when she talked about little Bessie, and Tuck had spent hours dreaming of how he could be her big brother. Doc read the anguish in his face.

"Don't worry, son," he said, slipping on his coat, "Edie will be all right. She's a tough customer. I'll be back tomorrow."

He started for the door, then turned.

"Your Mom's had a tough life. As tough as anybody I know in this town. I don't know how she's survived, or you either, for that matter. I've counted you out several times since Edie delivered you. I'm real sorry about the baby, Tuck." The door closed quietly behind him.

Tuck leaned against the cold glass of the front door, watching Doc climb into his big Chrysler convertible. He cried silently for a few moments, then found a dish towel in the kitchen and dried his face and climbed the stair to the front bedroom.

Stepping in to Edie Maye's bedroom, he watched her for a moment, drawn and white and lying very still in the bed. She was asleep. Peg motioned Tuck to come over to her, where she was sitting at the dressing table. Peg had tears in her eyes as she said,

"Your Mom had a real hard time, but she'll be O.K. This poor little tyke never had a chance."

Peg had Granddad's wicker basket on her lap, and it was filled with rolled up towels, just like Edie Maye arranged it with Granddad's dinners. But it wasn't a hot dinner in the basket; Tuck realized as Peg started to move the towels about, it was the baby. As she spoke she folded back a comer of a towel to reveal the tiny bluish white body of his dead half-sister, perfectly formed and quite beautiful, with a large shock of jet-black hair.

"Doc says I should take care of her," Tuck stammered, "I'll make a nice grave out back."

"Make sure it's good and deep, Tuck. God bless you, son."

The back yard was a graveyard of dead cats and dogs, but Tuck knew where every one was buried, and quickly selected an appropriate spot. As he shoveled the moist earth, he found himself unable to stop the flow of tears. It was hard to breath. He had found a boot box in Edie's closet and emptied it. Peg had let Tuck hold the tiny girl, swaddled in a bath towel, before covering her with a torn sheet and a small woolen blanket. Under a setting crescent moon, Tuck took another look at Bess before placing her gently in the waist deep hole he had carved. He raised the box and kissed her cold forehead, sobbing a soft "goodbye, little Bessie."

It was after 5:00 a.m. when Tuck finally came in from the back yard. Exhausted and emotionally drained, he woke Peg and told her she could go home now, and he fell asleep in his clothes on the floor next to Edie Maye's bed.

The next day, Peg stayed with Edie Maye, and after school Tuck went in sat down next to the bed. She was still weak and Doc had given her something that made her drowsy. She turned her head towards him and smiled faintly.

"It was a little girl and she died," she said softly.

The lump in Tuck's throat, that he had taken to school, and struggled all day to contain, suddenly burst as Tuck began to cry, unable to control himself.

24

A MOUTHFUL OF MONEY

THE years on Mt. Holly Avenue went by quickly while Cholly was in the Navy. He kept up his correspondence and the checks came with regularity. Edie Maye, through Jan Wilga's recommendation, got a job at the Permutit Company, where an employer finally began to reward her for her loyalty, dedication and hard work.

Chip came to stay with them for a while during those years, having suffered a stroke. The stroke caused the left side of his face to sag, and he had a difficult time eating and talking. By 1954, they had purchased a television, and Chip loved to sit and watch the Hopalong Cassidy movies.

Tuck struggled through high school, doing as little studying as possible and constantly in trouble. Being a fair athlete, he made both the football and basketball teams, and ended up as a starting quarterback his junior year. The team was terribly small and lost a lot of games, and of course, Tuck rebelled against the Coach as a matter of course, making his life more miserable.

Tuck's thought processes were developing to a point that he found frustrating. He defended his slovenly school habits by drifting into a convoluted logic about lying.

Edie Maye's rigid independence had imbued his personality with defiance. For years, he had simply lied about everything, and often couldn't recall the reality of a situation if pressed. But he outgrew that and substituted a rigidity of purpose that he felt reflected his station in life.

With Cholly gone, Tuck's world was work, the woods and school. At home, he had little to share with Edie Maye, who herself had receded even further from life. The memory of baby Bess permeated the house. Neither she nor Tuck could stop thinking of her. Edie managed to keep enough coming in to meet the mortgage payments, and Cholly's subsistence check kept them in a meager condition with respect to food. Tuck was earning now, always having one kind of job or another, but Edie Maye refused to take any of the boy's money. She insisted he spend it on clothes or whatever he felt he needed.

She could see how lost he was, but saw no way to help him. Now that he could interact in the community and earn money, she saw that he would cast his own course. It would have helped if she let the boy contribute to the household funds, but she continually refused him, adding a measure of guilt to his problems. He entered the high school community every day with peers who had opportunity, who could see something ahead of them. All Tuck had, Edie Maye thought, was the realization that he had survived this far; nothing more.

She felt that she had failed him. He deserved more, but that was how it had happened. He was bright, intelligent and sensitive and most of the kids his age couldn't hold a candle to him, she thought, but he's got little chance in this world. In her confused despair, she still harbored resentment towards the boy, who had contributed greatly to her misery.

The old house was dark most of the time, Edie Maye sitting with coffee in the kitchen, Tuck off at work or on one of his escapades or at school. When the opportunity afforded it, Edie Maye sometimes made a goulash or spaghetti for the boy's dinner, but for the most part, they simply didn't eat meals. They existed, each heartbroken, lonely and desperate and without the understanding to talk out their problems.

He no longer lied, and he refused to cheat, but he did no work, either. Knowing for certain that he would never go to college, he rationalized his attitude by considering himself practical.

What the hell's the point? I don't need Problems of Democracy or Algebra class for the Marine Corps, he thought.

His peers saw him quite differently than he knew himself to be. He was quickly assimilated by the group that ran things and his athletic ability and easy ways with friends made him quite popular. But he was still the gambler's kid; his old man was a felon; an ex-con and a bookie. Everyone recognized that there was an element of danger in associating with Tuck, but that was part of his charm. They found it remarkable that he did what he wanted to; he seemed under no parental restraint whatsoever. They envied his lifestyle, knowing little about it.

Although he was working at the ice plant, he couldn't even scrape together enough money for a class ring. He refused to let Edie Maye buy him such luxuries out of her meager salary.

Tuck held the job at the Ice Plant, which eventually paid fifty-five cents an hour, for seven years. By the time he acquired his Driver's license, he was subbing for the delivery men who didn't show up for work in the summer or on weekends in the spring. He didn't like baseball, and went directly from school to the plant during the spring, where he often worked alone, crushing and bagging ice until eleven or twelve o'clock.

At work, he handled himself well, making only the stupid mistakes of youth and inexperience, but at school he was completely at a loss. Constantly hammered about how well Sis had done, he found himself on an emotional roller coaster with faculty and administrators. He responded with defiance. As tough as he was, an adult could easily bring him to tears.

He failed completely to understand how competent he was. Ralph Flanagan, his boss at the ice plant, gave him run of the facility, where he operated the crushers and scorers and monitored the manufacturing process without supervision. Tuck memorized all of the delivery routes and could be called on to load out a truck and run anyone's route on a moment's notice, or deliver a 10 ton load to Pemberton or Toms River.

The town routes were especially difficult, requiring 100 pound blocks of ice to be delivered to second and third floor apartments. Tuck enjoyed the work, the reaction he got from customers when he knocked on the door, ice block on his shoulder, tongs in his free hand; pick in its holster on his belt. They knew him by name and sometimes gave him a tip when he collected.[78]

The customers were open and friendly and represented a cross section of the town's inhabitants. Only the rich could afford refrigerators. When he delivered crushed ice to the town's bars, the bartenders often drew him a draft beer, or at least a cold Coke-Cola. There were usually a few early morning customers at the bar who would query Tuck about the latest football or baseball game.

The Hollyford ice plant was an integral part of the farm production cycle that affected all of the county's farmers. When the cabbage or lettuce harvest came in, tractor trailers lined up on King Street, awaiting a sprayed load of crushed ice to assist their refrigeration in preserving their truckload of fresh vegetables. Tuck and the crew working the service dock would crush and spray ice until the early morning hours, rushing to accommodate anxious drivers. Icing the summer crops would empty the plant's storage; a 60 foot square room of 300 lb blocks stacked 15 rows high, the work of an entire winter's ice making.

Tuck felt comfortable in his role, among his kind of people. At school, it was "them" and "me;" the have and have nots. He couldn't correlate or transfer his easy assimilation in his world of work to the school environment.

Sal still had his pawn shop in Wrightstown. Tuck and Edie Maye knew he was there, but never heard from him.

Having a steady girl friend, and with the Junior Prom coming up, circumstances evolved that left Tuck without transportation. Tuck's first car, a 1929 Model A two-door sedan he had bought for forty dollars, only ran when it wanted to; was prone to catching fire, and usually had to be hand started with the crank.

"Are you and Sally going to the Prom this year?" Edie Maye asked.

"Yeah," Tuck said, "I got the tickets, but I'm going to have to double up with somebody. The Model A won't make it, and Sally won't sit still for me hand-cranking it on a prom date."

Sally was Tuck's steady girlfriend, which introduced another pressure-packed element into his life. Her parents were dead set against him as a steady. She was a Rita Heyworth look-alike and Tuck adored her: it was their first great love, and for Sally, his status as quarterback on the football team was an entree into a popular group that was a year ahead of her in age and class. Being love sick and afraid of losing her, Tuck ignored her sometimes blunt behavior. A cheerleader and extremely attractive, Tuck thought her to be someone very special, and she cared a lot for him.

"Why don't you borrow your father's car?" Edie Maye said, "He's got one of those big Hudsons, a black one. I saw him in it last week, downtown."

The idea had Tuck excited, but he was afraid to ask Sal for the car. The newly designed Hudson Hornet was the hottest car in the marketplace, and the big Commodores, eight cylinder sedans, were even faster on the top end. The thought of lowering himself to ask him for assistance was revolting to Tuck. He had never asked him for anything that he could remember, but he had promised Sally that they were not going to the prom in the Model A.

"Are you kidding?" Tuck said, "He won't lend me his car, and I don't want to ask, so he can just say 'no'. He knows what I think of him."

"He's always known what you think of him, Tuck," she said, "because you've never had the guile to hide it. Maybe he'd like to make it up to you, to show you that he's not so bad, after all."

Tuck digested this comment slowly. It never occurred to him that Sal knew how much Tuck hated him. Not that he cared. It was just a thought that never entered Tuck's mind.

"Yeah, well, he'd have to do some goddamn back flips to show me that, that's for sure. I don't want anything to do with him." It was getting close to a fight, but Edie Maye persisted.

"So what's the harm in trying?" she said, "Go over there and just ask him. Maybe you'll get lucky, and he'll let you have it. It's only for an evening."

"Nah," Tuck said, "to hell with him and his god damned Hudson."

But Edie Maye knew how to get to Tuck. She felt that the worst of it was over, it wouldn't hurt Tuck to get to know Sal now. She hoped that Sal could do something for the boy, but she knew he never would unless Tuck asked. He's a chip off of my block, she thought.

"What's the matter," she asked, "are you afraid of him?"

"No," he lied, "he doesn't give a shit about us, that's all."

But circumstances evolved that changed Tuck's mind. The couple that Tuck had agreed to double with, "Piney" and his girlfriend, "Urp," each from wealthy families, apparently thought better of doubling with Sally and Tuck. Sally's dad owned a tavern in Hainesport, so she wasn't at the top of the social ladder, either.

About four days before the prom, they bailed out on Tuck, and Tuck and Sally were left without a ride. Tuck had thought that Piney was his friend, it was only years later that he realized that his fascination with Tuck, like others, was based on the thrill of hanging around with a "dangerous" element, one of the bad guys his dad, the County Prosecutor, put away regularly. He came from a world that Tuck knew nothing of. It was at his house, where Tuck had stayed over for a weekend, that the boy first discovered that other people actually sat down to a cooked breakfast. Tuck had never experienced a complete breakfast as a morning meal! That could've been a Thanksgiving at Tuck's house.

His life was ordered. He had his own room, clean sheets, books and his own radio. In the back yard, a backboard on the garage created a basketball court. They had a television set in their den, and another behind a full bar in the basement "recreation room." Piney's family was rich. His dad was the County Prosecutor and had dominated county politics for years. He had made a name in county politics by going after Sal and his "big time gambler" friends and associates.

Like most of Tuck's associates, Piney's house had a man in it. Someone who, at least on the surface, brought order and the small luxuries to life. Tuck and Edie Maye seldom sat down to eat anymore. She lived on cigarettes and coffee with an occasional fried tomato thrown in. He ate on the run with his ice plant money, a White Castle hamburger here or there, a sandwich from the school cafeteria or handouts from mothers of his friends.

Sally's mom usually fed Tuck when he showed up at the tavern on Friday and Saturday nights. She saved him platters of cold ham and succotash from their dinner and sat smiling while the boy consumed it. Edie Maye made a goulash with ground meat on the weekends and occasionally kept a pot of spaghetti sauce going so that if the boy did come home, she could put something in front of him.

But their life was too tenuous, too desperate and lonely for Edie Maye to put on the pretense. Since the death of little Bess, she had receded further from the boy than usual. She wondered what would become of him, but felt useless and unable to help him. He had such a chip on his shoulder, such defiance.

Tuck knew he was missing out. He envied how his peers lived. They had aspirations where he knew he could have none. They would go out in the world, to colleges, jobs their fathers helped them with, some to family businesses. Tuck knew that his future lay in the Marine Corps, he could see nothing else. There was nothing else for him.

And now it was the Senior Prom, his Senior Prom, and he was class President. He had scraped and saved and thrown ice to put together enough for the tux, tickets and corsage. And now, no ride! He couldn't let Sally down, and he was outraged that he'd been betrayed and used by Piney. In desperation, Tuck cranked up the Model A and headed to Wrightstown.

Walking into Sal's "pawn shop" on Ft. Dix Street, he could feel the dryness in his throat.[79]

"How ya' doin'?" Tuck asked.

"O.K.," Sal responded. He had a jeweler's glass in his eye and was picking little bits of metal out of a cup on his glass counter. The store was only about fifteen feet wide and twenty feet long, and had two display counters running down its sides to a third one, which ran across the back of the store and had a cash register on top of it.

"What are you doing in this neck of the woods?" He asked.

"I came to see you," Tuck said, but afraid to venture into the reason for his visit. "What are those things?"

He had one of the nugget-like objects in a pair of tweezers and delicately placed it on a balance next to the cup. He then selected a tiny weight from a wooden tray at the base of the balance and deposited it on the other side in the little brass saucer. He did this several times until the balance was perfectly level.

"They're gold. I'm weighing it," he said, "before I send it off and get some money for it." Tuck had never seen gold before, in clumps, and his curiosity was aroused.

"Where'd it come from, the gold?" Tuck asked.

"They're fillings, from teeth. Caps, that kind of thing. These G.I.'s, they'll hock anything. They bring these in here, get some money for them, then they go to the dentist on base, and get amalgam fillings put it. Here, look at this."

He turned to the back wall, opened a cabinet and extracted a gray cardboard box. Opening it, he handed Tuck a set of false teeth. Each tooth had been rimmed at the artificial gum with a ring of gold.

"These guys get the gold fillings and special work overseas, where it's real cheap. When they get home, they need money; they can get dental work free from the Army, so it's like insurance. They've always got a mouthful of money. I send it up to Connecticut, and this Company, Handy and Harman; they boil it down, get rid of the impurities, and send it back to me in a gold bar."

This was amazing to Tuck. Sal continued talking, showing the boy some German cameras, bayonets, watches and other items he had "bought," and the customers had never reclaimed.

Reaching down to the bottom of the display case, he deposited a flat wooden case about ten by twelve inches in front of Tuck.

"You like to draw, right?" He asked.

"Yeah," Tuck said, wondering how he knew that. He filled pads with drawings all the time, and had even once created his own comic strip called Willie Wabbit.

"Well, here, you can have this," Sal said, opening the polished wooden box. The box contained a complete set of drafting instruments of German silver, each tool lying in its perfectly shaped niche of green velvet. Complete with bar compass, railroad pens, four compasses of varying function, it was obviously a very expensive and professional set.

"You're kiddin', aren't you?" Tuck asked, completely taken back by this incredible gift.

"No, you take it," he said, "and learn how to use it. The guy who left it, he's a Master Sergeant and he got shipped out. He'll never come back."

Holding tightly to the drafting instruments, Tuck blurted out, "Dad, can I use your car for the prom on Friday night?" Sal paused before he answered, continuing to fiddle with the gold fillings.

"Jesus Christ, that's a brand new car," he said, "I hardly had a chance to use it yet. And I need it on Friday nights. Get a ride with somebody else."

That was it, no car. Tuck knew he should have never even thought of the possibility. It was the gift that threw him off, for a minute, he was starting to feel like Sal really liked him. Tuck knew he shouldn't have come to see him.

"I had a ride, but it fell through. I was going with Piney. Piney Parker." That caught his attention.

"And what happened?" He asked, with definite interest.

"I guess the bastard figures he's too good for us. He waited until the last minute and then said he couldn't take us. I wouldn't be here, I wouldn't have asked you if I had some more time, but everybody else is already doubled up."

"You had some trouble with him, didn't you?" Sal asked.

Christ, Tuck thought to himself, *how did he find out about that?* A few months before, Piney and Tuck had been chosen as "Student Legislators," and had gone to Trenton on an overnight trip. This was one of the first positive things Tuck had done in high school. Assigned the task of writing a bill to introduce into the schoolboy legislature, he had composed legislation banning the dumping of pollutants into the creeks and lakes of the State.

Mr. McCann, an English teacher who invested a lot of time in Tuck's buried potential, had urged the boy on and helped him with the work. He had even invited Tuck to his apartment once, and talked to him, asking Tuck about Sal. With his urging, Tuck came up with the pollution idea and he inspired the boy to work hard on it. Tuck felt that he could trust him and responded to his suggestions.

Piney, however, treated the idea as a big joke, and although he was supposed to help Tuck as co-sponsor of the bill, he did nothing.

Staying in a hotel with the other boys, Piney had called a friend of his from Pennsylvania who came over and brought beer into the hotel. Tuck had resisted the whole affair, since he never drank beer unless it was a free one when delivering ice and he didn't like Piney's friend, whom Tuck considered a rich snob. Tuck had wanted to go to the legislative session in the morning and introduce the bill he had written.

Piney and his friend raised so much hell in the room, spraying beer around and eventually breaking the glass window in the transom that the hotel detective threw them all out. No one would believe that Tuck wasn't totally involved in the whole fiasco. Tuck called Piney's friend a rich fucking faggot and challenged him to fight after he drove them home, and he guessed that's what led to the prom problem. He wouldn't fight, of course.

The following day, Tuck went to Piney's house to try to smooth things over and his dad answered the door. "What do you want?" He asked.

"I want to talk to David," Tuck said.

"Young man, you're not going to talk to David," he said, raising his voice. "I should have known better than to let him hang around with a *little guinea bastard* like you. You got him in a hell of lot of trouble. I don't want you coming around here again. You're going to end up in jail just like your old man!"

"What?" Tuck stammered, as the door slammed in his face. Tuck related the story to Sal.

"So Big Piney blamed it all on you, right? His kid did nothin'?" He asked.

"Yeah," Tuck said, seeing the prom slip away.

"And he called you a guinea bastard?" Sal asked.

"Yeah, he said I got Piney in trouble, but it was the other way around," Tuck said, "I don't even like beer."

"You pick up the car on Friday, after lunch. Bring it back on Saturday morning, because I need it for the afternoon," he said. "Now get going, and take that with you. I have to close up the shop for a little while. I'll see you on Friday."

"Geez, thanks, Dad. I'll be real careful with it, you'll see," Tuck said, grasping the wooden case, and thanking him about every third step as he raced out the door.

The black Hudson sedan, with its in-line eight cylinder engine and sloped back, was a big hit at the prom. At the last moment, another couple, George and Shirley, who were left in the lurch by their ride, doubled with Tuck and Sally. They were farm kids and the foursome had a great time.

On the way back to Wrightstown the following morning, Tuck stopped at the Pemberton sand hole, a large gravel pit lake that was a popular swimming spot. He took a swim in his underwear, and washed the Hudson, realizing that he wouldn't have gotten it if the county prosecutor hadn't called him a guinea bastard.

PART II.
COMING OF AGE

25

GRADUATING

THE lights in the Arcade's Billiards parlor were dim. Men clustered about the four green felt topped tables in quiet concentration. There was a stink of stale beer and wine, and a couple of the town winos were slumped on the oak benches along the wall.

On the front table, Bud Parker was running his third consecutive rack, cigar stub protruding from the stubble on his craggy chin. His opponent, a young lawyer from uptown, leaned against the wall in impassive frustration. No one had beaten Bud Parker in a game of points in the past five years. An appreciative crowd had gathered.

At an adjacent table, Tuck was pondering. Umpe Downs had left him no shot. He was directly against a rail with two balls blocking his line on the eight ball.

"Bank it," Umpe said, turning to spit on the dirty wooden floor. Tuck lined up the shot, a two cushion bank, and dropped the eight ball in the corner. The cue ball continued on, caromed off the side rail, rolled lazily across the table and dropped into the side pocket.

"Shit. Your game, Umpe." Tuck dug in his pocket for a quarter and flipped it on the table. "That's it for me. I can't win for losin'."

It was the spring of his senior year in high school. Outside, the trees were in bud and a balmy breeze swept across South Jersey. Tuck and Umpe left the poolroom together. Standing on the wooden porch they surveyed Main Street on a late Saturday afternoon.

"How about a beer?" Tuck asked.

Umpe grunted and they made their way around the building to the back door of the Arcade Bar & Grille. Tuck disappeared inside and returned in a couple of minutes with two bottles of Ortleibs. They cracked the tops against the door jam and walked down the alley and sat down on the creek wall, feet dangling over the dark cedar water of the Rancocas.

"How'd ya get the beer?" Umpe asked. He wiped his sleeve across the cleft palate.

"I deliver ice there every Saturday. George sells me a couple any time. He gives me a cold draft when I deliver, too. He's O.K. It's the old lady you've gotta' watch out for.

"You graduatin' from school?"

"Yeah," Tuck said, "last week. I glad I'm out of that fuckin' place. Probably go in the Marines, now. Ain't nothin' here, that's for sure."

"De said you got big trouble. Got throwed out." Umpe's hair lip got in his way when he spoke. He looked middle aged, partially balding with a huge head and pale skin. He was working at Arrow Safety, sweeping floors and carrying trash. It was hard for Tuck to believe that they were nearly the same age.

Tuck had managed to graduate from high school, having finally decided, in his senior year, to try to learn something. This was due largely to another friend, Richard, an over achiever from the Medford farm community. Richard and his Mother convinced him that if he applied himself, he could do as well as anyone, and surprisingly enough, they were right. The realization was too late to correct a mediocre high school record, but in time for Tuck to recoup a failing senior year. He had been elected President of the senior class, and was to give a speech at graduation.

Graduation wasn't without its problems, however. The class had taken its "Senior Trip" to Washington, D.C.

Tuck didn't go, the prom and trip being mutually exclusive for his pocketbook. As expected, Piney and his crowd got drunk and caused damage to the hotel, the result being that the school administration threatened to cancel the baccalaureate service, unless the culprits came forward.

Some innocent kids were being accused, including Tuck's friend Billy Brenneman from grammar school days. As class president, Tuck undertook to negotiate the problem with the principal, Mr. Butler.

Tuck found himself in Butler's office, sitting uncomfortably in the green leather chair across from his desk.

Everybody hated Butler. There were locker room rumors going around about him and some tales about his comments to Bill White, a Negro youth who had played tackle. It was generally acknowledged locker room lore that White had the biggest penis in the county. Butler often showed up in the locker room toilet when the team was showering.

He listened while Butler went on about the serious crimes the class had committed while on the trip. Butler wanted to know the names of the kids who had done the damage. He had fifteen names, and all were going to be suspended and denied graduation privileges. Half of them were completely innocent.

Tuck offered to tell him the names of those who did the damage, in exchange for a promise that no letters be sent to the parents of those who were unjustly accused, and all parties are allowed to graduate as planned, with the baccalaureate service reinstated. The guilty parties would get suspensions, as required, but still graduate.

Butler agreed to the terms, and Tuck gave him the names. By the end of the school day, all fifteen had been promptly suspended, guilty and innocent alike, and Butler had sent letters to all their parents, refusing to reinstate the baccalaureate service.

Butler was in the superintendent of schools office the next morning when Tuck stormed in, unannounced.

"You lying bastard," he shouted, "you promised you wouldn't do this if I gave you the names, and then you turned around and did it anyway!"

"Just a minute, Son," Butler said, "I made no such promise."

"He did," Tuck said to the superintendent, tears in his eyes, "I should have known better than to trust him, he's lying right now!"

"We wouldn't lie to you, son," the Superintendent Evans said, "we teach high moral and ethical principles, and your classmates acted very badly. They've shamed the school and our names, and ruined class trips for the classes behind them!"

"You guys are really something," Tuck said, regaining some control, "you're lying like a couple of bandits right now, and that's what you teach here, a bunch of goddamn lies!"

"Young man," Butler said, "if you don't curb your language, you won't graduate next week."

"Yeah," Tuck said, "that figures. If you suspend me and throw me out of school, you think nobody will know about your lying, but it's too goddamned late, everybody knew what the deal was before I came in to you yesterday."

Tuck stormed out of the office, hurt and angry by the deceit of adults, something he was unable to understand. He feared most of the adults he knew, but that fear was not associated with treachery. He still had a mistaken assumption that maturity and fairness went hand in hand.

The following day Tuck was told by the guidance counselor that he couldn't graduate unless he agreed not to speak at graduation. They gave the honor to "Didi" Golf, whose mother taught in the English department. Edie Maye pleaded with him to go to graduation, and he accepted the diploma in line, like everyone else. Sal didn't come, but that didn't surprise Tuck. He hadn't come to Cholly's graduation either.

Umpe listened to the story while tossing pebbles in the creek. When it was over, he smacked Tuck on the shoulder.

"Ya dumb ass," he said, "everybody know dat Butler's a queer. You shoulda' stayed outta' the mess. Even Umpe knows dat."

"Yeah, I know," Tuck said, "but half of those guys didn't do anything, they just happened to be staying in the same rooms."

Umpe stood up, pegged his empty into a trash can, and started walking back toward the street, "How do ya' know they didn't do nothin? Because they told ya' so? Dat sounds like bullshit to Umpe!"

Tuck watched him jog up the alley and wondered if he had really been that stupid. Even Umpe Downs had a better perspective of reality than he.

Tuck had been dropping into the pawn shop in Wrightstown occasionally and one day Sal asked him if he needed a job for the summer.

"You looking for another job?" he asked.

"Yeah, I guess so," Tuck said. He had a day job at an Atlantic gas station and was working four or five nights at the ice plant, but still couldn't accumulate enough to buy a decent car.

"I know this guy, he's a shop steward. He might be able to get you on over at Dix," Sal said. He was referring to the big expansion program at Fort Dix. Hundreds of new buildings were being constructed to accommodate the swelling number of draftees for the Korean war.

Tuck stopped back on a Saturday, and Sal introduced him to a small skinny fellow named Mickey. "You ever do any construction work?" Mickey asked.

"Sure," Tuck said, "I can lay block, and I've done a little framing."

"O.K.," Mickey said, "let's take a ride, and I'll fill you in and show you the place."

Tuck said so long to Sal, and sitting in Mickey's Ford convertible, they drove on to Fort Dix. Mickey talked.

"Here's how it works, kid," he said, "you'll be in the construction worker's.(union) You report to me every morning, seven sharp. You're late, you're done, no bull shit."

Tuck was beginning to get the idea that this was not going to be an easy job.

"You don't take no orders from anybody but me," Mickey continued, "any of these college shit engineers tell you to do something', you tell 'em to go fuck themselves, and see me, or the union supervisor. Got that?"

They were driving now on dirt roads lined with flagged stakes. Piles of lumber were spaced about and flat bed trailers loaded with reinforcing steel rods loaded eight feet high were parked at intervals.

"This is where you report, over here," Mickey said, pointing to a trailer office, "Just tell them at the main gate that you're with the construction workers, and they'll pass you through. Wear steel toed boots. You can't work without boots."

"I don't have any steel toed boots," Tuck said.

"Then get 'em before Monday," Mickey said, "or you don't work. No bull shit here, kid."

That afternoon, Tuck borrowed fourteen dollars from Edie Maye and bought a pair of steel toed work shoes, and some heavy socks at Green's army and navy store. On Monday morning, he found himself standing in front of the trailer with about fifty men of varying ages and colors. Mickey called names and assigned them in groups of two and four to various supervisors.

Tuck was assigned with another young fellow, Bobby Brown, to digging footings. The holes had to be six feet deep, and ten by ten feet square, with the bottom and sides flat.

Tuck liked Bobby immediately. At five-eleven and about 180 pounds, he looked like a movie star. A brown shock of hair fell across his forehead. He was handsome, had a deep tan and an easy grin. He took to Tuck immediately, also. The two worked like demons. Tuck's years at the swings and handling 300 pound blocks of ice had conditioned him. Bobby, like Tuck, enjoyed challenging the job, digging as many footings as they could in a day. The earth was soft and pickaxes were only used occasionally. The older men didn't like it, of course, but the two young men ignored their complaints and charged ahead.

They dug from seven to nine, took fifteen minutes for an ice cold coke, and continued digging until noon, when they had a half hour for lunch. After lunch, back in a hole until a fifteen minute break at two-thirty, and continue digging until four forty-five.

The pay was $1.80 an hour, an outrageously high amount for laborer's work; Union pay. On pay day Mickey came around to the hole, and paid them in cash, already counted and neatly tucked into a brown envelope.

"Count your money on your own time," Mickey growled one day when Tuck paused to count his pay before jumping down into his hole. You slacked off or gave a shop steward any guff, and you were gone, no questions asked, none answered.

In a few weeks, they became known as the "crazy banjos," for the short-handled shovels they used, and for working so hard. The supervisors vied to get them for various sites each morning. On pay days, which were Thursdays, they drove down to Wrightstown to Lou's Bar, across the street from Sal's pawn shop, after work. Mickey required the return of the pay envelopes to him there and there had to be a ten-dollar bill inside. union dues, but they never received membership cards.

Working without shirts, their tans deepened to nearly black. The hot New Jersey sun was relentless, and many men simply couldn't take it. Some fainted. Mickey brought salt tablets around throughout the day, and made sure everybody drank plenty of water. One fellow in particular, who worked with only for a few days, removed his shirt the first day on the job despite repeated warnings.

By the third day his back was covered with massive liquid-filled blisters, peeling skin and various tones of pink and scarlet. He had several children and this was his first good job in a long while. On the fourth day, he collapsed, a victim of sun poisoning, and Tuck didn't see him after that.

The "crazy banjos" created the holes into which the carpenters placed forms for the foundations of the barracks buildings. After the carpenters, the steelworkers lay in the reinforcing rod, and then the entire foundation and all footings and foundations were poured at once. Next, the carpenters created forms for the concrete walls and floors and the cycle was repeated, resulting in a complete barracks building, sans roof.

One morning Mickey called Bobby and Tuck away from the hole in which they were digging.

"Go over to unit three," he said, "and see Scaglia, the foreman for the steelworkers. He needs ya'."

The last thing they wanted to do was to work for the steelworkers. From Brooklyn, they were members of a New York local and tough looking men. Scaglia, their foreman, was huge and had more hair on his body than any three men Tuck had ever seen before. When they got to unit three, they could see that Scaglia was beside himself with anger. He and a couple of engineers, along with most of his "gang," were grouped at one corner of a barracks unit. The carpenters had just begun breaking wall forms when the problem was discovered.

The entire two hundred foot barracks had been poured at an angle. Each corner of the building was rotated about two feet past its alignment point with the foundation.

"We have to get a ball in here," one engineer said, "knock it down, move the forms and pour it right. It's the only way."

"What the fuck are you talkin' about?" Scaglia screamed, "you think those goddamn walls are just gonna fall down? We got iron in there, for Christ's sake. The goddamn carpenters should put it right; they put the fuckin' forms in the wrong place!"

"You ever look at a blueprint, you Sigi bastard?" Vince Motto, the carpenter's crew chief, chimed in, "you iron workers strung the iron wrong, and my crew had to form where you worked it."

"Bull shit," yelled Scaglia, "we ain't takin' no heat for this. We're gonna finish the goddamn thing on schedule."

"What are you talking about, Scag?" said the engineer, "I can't sign off on this."

"You'll sign off, all right." Scaglia said, and he walked to a pickup truck and picked up a ten pound sledge and twelve inch steel chisel. Pushing through the group, he handed Tuck the chisel, and said, "Get down there, kid."

Tuck, confronted by the big Sicilian and so flattered by being selected for some unknown assignment, he quickly obliged Scaglia and jumped down into the ditch.

Scaglia followed Tuck, jumping down into the six foot trench next to him. Pushing Tuck forward to a point where the foundation began jutting out from under the wall, he wacked the protruding concrete with the sledge, and turned to Tuck.

"You're Sigliano, right?" he said.

"Ah, yeah," Tuck said, "I guess so." He had never thought that he would be considered a Sicilian, a special kind of Italian. It never occurred to Tuck that there was a difference. He knew Granddad's family was from Sicily, but had never before heard the term, Sigliano.

"Hold that thing like your dick, firm, but not tight." Scaglia continued, "Keep it steady, and lean back." As he said this, he grasped both Tuck's hand and the chisel and placed the point where he wanted it. Tuck kneeled down with his right arm extended, realizing that he intended to slam the chisel with the ten-pound hammer. An involuntary chill ran down Tuck's spine. He forced himself not to think about the damage the hammer could do to his wrist or forearm if Scaglia missed.

Scaglia stepped back, spit in his gloves, and after tapping the end of the chisel twice with the sledge hammer, he said, "Hold it steady, kid," and let fly with a full roundhouse swing.

The sledge struck squarely on top of the chisel, driving it into the fresh concrete with a ringing sound. The force of the blow bounced the chisel from Tuck's grasp as particles of concrete peppered his face and arms. Tuck's arm felt like it was vibrating and he noticed that he was sweating profusely.

"That's one!" Scaglia said.

"That's my boy there, Scag, he don't have to do this," Mickey shouted from the edge of the hole, "he ain't no steelworker!"

"Fuck you, Mickey. He ain't afraid, so forget it. He's workin' with me," Scag said.

"You miss, you're gonna' break his fuckin' arm," said Motto.

The sledge arched again. Now Tuck's arm was vibrating, and the shock of the blow made his balls tingle. Tuck lost concentration for a moment, wondering why his balls would tingle at such a time.

What's this got to do with my balls? He asked himself.

"What the hell are you doing, Scag?" The engineer asked.

"You all right, kid?" Scag asked.

"Yeah," Tuck said, "go for it." Scaglia had him mesmerized. He was afraid, but confident that Scaglia wouldn't miss the chisel. He knew that he couldn't back down, walk away from it, although he sensed no one would blame him for it.

"I'm gonna' knock these two corners down," Scag said, swinging the sledge, "and put the fuckin' foundation … under the wall, ... where you dumb bastards … should have put it...in the first place!" He punctuated about every third word with another swing of the hammer.

With each successive blow, Tuck's hand began to sting more, as though he were catching a fast ball without a glove. Tuck was holding himself so rigid that his shoulder began to ache. He covered his face with his remaining hand, warding off the particles of shredded concrete.

"O.K., kid, that's ten," Scag said as he bent down and grabbed the chisel. He pushed the sledge into Tuck's hand, knelt down next to the wall, placed the chisel and said, "Now, it's your turn!"

Earth stopped dead in its orbit! Tuck could feel the sweat pouring down his back and armpits; but his tongue was dry, the inside of his mouth like cotton. His right arm was numb, and the echoes of the ringing blows were still resounding in his ears. The fear that Tuck had of being hit by the hammer was nothing compared to the thought of driving ten pounds of steel into Scaglia's hand or wrist.

"He's gonna knock your fuckin' head off, Scag," said Motto. He was grinning widely, hands stuffed in his pockets, and thoroughly enjoying the show.

"Come on, kid," Scag said, staring at Tuck, "you got ten licks comin' but don't miss, or you'll be kissin' fishes."

Tuck tried to swallow unsuccessfully, and ended up coughing up some mucous and spitting it on the ground. Everyone was watching him.

"Knock his fuckin' block off, kid," Tuck heard Motto call.

"Leave him be, Scag," Mickey said, "It ain't his fault."

"Don't chicken out on me, kid. Hit the fuckin' thing," Skag said. Tuck hefted the hammer, stepped into position and measured his swing, tapping the chisel twice, like Scag had done.

"You ready?" Tuck asked. His voice was raspy.

"Go for it," Scag replied with a grin.

Swinging with all his energy, Tuck struck the chisel perfectly, driving it into the foundation. The hammer, bouncing back, struck Scag in the shoulder. Tuck felt his heart skip a beat.

"Oh, shit," Mickey said from the edge of the trench.

Scaglia sat back on his heels and rubbed his shoulder where the errant hammer had struck. Then he wiped his nose with the back of his glove, and looked Tuck directly in the eyes. Tuck could see tears rimming the steely blue stare.

"Watch the goddamn hammer, kid," he said, "and lay into it." The earth jiggled a bit and slowly re-started its orbit as Tuck's focus returned. The crew, above them and rimming the hole began chanting with each swing, "two, three, four." By the fifth swing Tuck's fear gave way to a feeling of power, and he began to grin a little more with each successful blow. The foundation wall was crumbling and Scaglia was cleaning away the broken concrete with his free hand.

"Good job, kid," Scag said after the tenth blow. He grabbed the hammer, and climbed out of the hole. Tuck glanced up at Bobby, who was grinning like a Cheshire cat at the edge of the trench.

"There's hammers and chisels in the truck," Scaglia said, "now get your jerk offs moving and let's clean this up before it's too late," he said to Motta. He reached down and offered his hand to Tuck as he climbed out of the hole.

"You and your buddy clean out under the corners that stick out, and give me a base for a new footing," Scag said, "You did O.K., kid. Stop down the Pioneer on Friday night and I'll buy you a beer and get you laid." He punched Tuck lightly on the shoulder and strode off, shouting orders laced with obscenities.

"You got solid brass balls," Bobby said as they picked up their shovels, "I woulda' told him to go fuck himself."

"I wanted to," Tuck said, "but I was too scared."

Tuck's status on the job improved greatly after that day. Soon he was coming in on Saturdays, the only man on the job, and wetting the newly poured concrete while it was still setting up. Time and a half, $2.80 an hour, for running a garden hose!

Tuck appreciated the special status and when Bobby suggested one day that they take off and get a nap behind one of the foundations, Tuck was upset.

"What the hell for?" he asked Bobby, "We'll get fired for sure if we get caught."

"I'm tired of all this digging bullshit," Bobby said, "it's boring as hell."

"Hey, Brownie, it's a laborer's job...that's what laborers do, dig holes! Just the same," Tuck said, "I'm making four times here what I make for throwin' ice, and that's a damn sight harder than diggin' holes in the sand.

You go, if you want to, but if Mick comes around, it's your ass, not mine. I ain't gonna' lie for you."

Bobby took off and soon it became a daily occurrence. Each time, Tuck refused the offer to join him, but it didn't take Mick long to figure out that the crazy banjo brigade was only putting out about half as much work as they had in the beginning of the summer.

On payday, Mickey told Tuck that he was going to work alone from now on; he had things for Bobby to do on the other side of the project. Tuck was relieved. Bobby had returned from each little escapade grinning. He would then proceed to goad Tuck for the rest of the day.

"You must be gettin' tired," Bobby said, "not gettin' a nice long break like me."

"When shovelin' sand tires me out," Tuck said, "I'll quit. I don't take somethin' for doin' nothin'."

"Yeah," Bobby said, "you're so god damned honest you'll break your balls so Mickey can get his cut and go down to the Dix hotel and get a blowjob, on your sweat. He takes plenty for nothin', old Mickey, don't he?"

"Listen, Bobby," Tuck usually got irritated by day's end, "lay off of me and layoff of Mickey. I've got no complaints here, I never made this kind of money and I ain't gonna' fuck it up."

After Mickey moved Bobby Brown out of Tuck's hole, he only saw him in the morning when the men gathered at the trailer for assignments. Tuck noticed that Bobby stopped showing up around the beginning of August. By this time Tuck was working with the carpenters, stripping forms, so he didn't miss him for a few days. On pay day, Mickey came by with Tuck's money.

"Where's Bobby working, Mick?" Tuck asked, "I haven't seen him around."

"Dintja' hear?" Mickey asked. "He got himself all fucked up over in Burlington."

"What happened?" Tuck asked.

"He held up a gas station," Mickey said, "got himself caught doin' it, the dumb bastard."

Bobby had told Tuck that he had spent some time in the Jamestown Reformatory for stealing a car when he fifteen, so the story seemed plausible. Tuck asked what was going to happen to him.

"I dunno," Mick said, "I got some of his pay yet, so I'm going to be seeing him or his folks. I'll let you know." Two weeks later, when paying

Mickey his cut at Lou's Bar, he told Tuck that Bobby had been sentenced to two years in the state penitentiary, but the Judge gave him an option to take a four year enlistment in the Marine Corps. Bobby took it and was now at Parris Island, South Carolina, in boot camp.

Tuck told Edie Maye what happened to Bobby. He had brought Bobby home a couple of times, since he had to pass through Mt. Holly to get to Camden, where he lived. Tuck was cutting the grass in the back yard when he mentioned this.

"I'm not surprised," she said, "he seemed to be headed for trouble." Watching Tuck push the mower, she felt a surge of pride. He was brown as toast, and holding his own in what she knew must be a tough environment. "Your back's all muscle," she said, "you've lost any semblance you ever had of baby fat."

Tuck blushed at the complement. At the end of the summer, Mickey offered Tuck an inside job in the barracks; a chance to learn finish carpentry, but he declined. He had already made his plans. Coach Hoagland at the high school had promised to let Tuck assist him in coaching the first freshman football team in the school's history. Tuck still had his part time job at the ice plant for spending money, and had decided to enlist in the Marine Corps right after football season was over. He'd be eighteen in March and was sure to get drafted.

He never did take Scag up on his invitation.

26

DRAGGING ANCHOR

Tuck's commitment to enter the Marine Corps before his eighteenth birthday somehow made him reflective about his future, and in September, he enrolled in a night school in Philadelphia that offered a course in drafting.

Answering a want ad in the Philadelphia Bulletin, he was hired by the Drum Company, an explosives manufacturer in Bristol, just across the river in Pennsylvania. Tuck took the job because they worked from seven in the morning until three-thirty, which gave him time to make the freshman football practices.

The drafting school was one of many new schools taking advantage of the G.I. Bill, which paid for veteran's training. Tuck was the only non-vet enrolled. He drove his '41 Ford over the bridge five nights a week for the four-hour sessions.

The instructor, Mr. Williams, was a pleasant 60 year old man and Tuck took to the work easily. Every paper came back marked "E," for excellent. The vets thought he was a little crazy, paying the tuition out of his own pocket. Tuck quickly came to appreciate the set of tools Sal had given him.

One Saturday morning in September, Tuck answered a knock at the front door. A sailor, in dress blues, was standing there; white duffel bag at his feet.

"This Cholly's house?" he asked.

"Yeah," Tuck said, "I'm his brother."

"I'm Matty," he said, "Matty Beers. I just come from Cholly, in Naples."

"Come on in," Tuck said, and holding the door open for "Beersy," as Cholly referred to him in his letters, he shouted for Edie Maye, who was upstairs.

Matt removed his hat when Edie Maye came down stairs.

"It's Matty Beers, Mom," Tuck said, "Cholly's shipmate. He said Cholly's in Naples." Their last letter from Cholly had been posted from Spain or Portugal, and he said they were heading to Sicily. Edie Maye put some coffee on, and they all sat down in the kitchen.

"I'm on my way home," Matt said, "to Circleville in Ohio, but I thought I'd better stop in to see you." Obviously, something was wrong. They waited for Matt to continue.

"Cholly's real sick, Ma'am," he said, "I think he might die."

"What do you mean, sick?" Tuck asked, "What's he got?"

"Yellow jaundice, and hepatitis," Matt said, shifting uncomfortably in his chair. "Everybody but five guys got it. I was lucky. Three guys died before we hit port."

"Where is he?" Edie asked.

"He's in Naples, in the Cardarelli Army hospital, but I was just there and he just keeps lookin' worse. They ain't doing nothin' to help him. The hospital's all screwed up," Matt blurted out. "He's as yellow as that saucer."

"What can I do?" Edie asked.

"I dunno, Ma'am," Matt said, "Maybe the Red Cross. I thought you ought to know. I brought you the hospital address."

Matt turned up his blouse and pulled out his wallet, which had been folded over the top of his bell bottoms. He extracted a slip of paper and handed it to her.

"How did he get sick?" Edie asked.

"We had a rough time, Ma'am," Matt said, "three years at sea and I never seen nothin' like it. We were in Naples and this storm came up, a real doozy. They called everybody back to the ship, and lying at anchor in the harbor, we could see the Army trucks being washed off the quay. The storm settled down a little after a couple of days, but the Skipper was afraid we were gonna' start dragging our anchor, so we headed out for Tripoli, our next port."

Edie poured Matt some more coffee, and he continued.

"Trouble was that our resupply was on the quay when that storm hit. We were short on supplies. We were supposed to take on food and water, but the loading area was all screwed up with wrecked trucks and buildings half torn up. Megara began dragging anchor and we couldn't stay in the harbor any longer. We went aground a couple of years ago in Tarragona, in Spain, and I guess Skipper figured we couldn't chance stayin' there. The ship's really light, and two days out we hit another storm, only this one's worse.

"We must have done this crossing seven times before, it usually takes about eleven days. Eleven days out, we're all sea sick and just being blown around the Med. The goddamn Megara's taking forty degree rolls, nobody can sleep, and we run out of food."

"You had nothing to eat?" Edie asked.

"Well, for another week," Matt said, "we ate anything that Cookie had left, canned peaches and stuff, but pretty soon he even ran out of flour. Couldn't even make bread. We even ate the Crisco cooking grease when there was nothing else left. Now, some guys are gettin' sick. I mean the storm, it comes and goes, but we didn't see the sun for twenty days. It was a worse storm than I ever saw in the ocean. The wind never stopped, even when it stopped raining. And then cookie tells us he even ran out of coffee. Two days out of Tripoli, the storm's gone, but we're gatherin' water with tarps on the radars topside, just to stay alive. Everybody but about five guys is sick, and two guys from the quartermaster crew, they died in sick bay. Another guy, Frenchy, he died in Tripoli. He was a good friend of ours. We dropped anchor in Tripoli twenty-eight days out of Naples."

"Why didn't the Fleet send help?" Edie asked. Her lips were creased tight, and Tuck could see her getting angry.

"They tried," Matt said, "they said they sent out a flying boat, but he couldn't find us in the storm, and he couldn't have landed if he did. The Fleet was way behind us, and they were having problems, too. We could hear it on the radio, off and on.

"As soon as we hit Tripoli, they loaded the worst guys on a plane and sent them back to the hospital in Naples. Cholly was real sick and they put him on the first plane out. We picked up some supplies and headed right back. We had lost part of our superstructure and had to lay in to Naples to fix it, so we come back with a skeleton crew. Even the Skipper's sick and the First Officer brought us back."

"Jesus Christ," Tuck shouted at Matt, "how the hell could this happen?" He had been sitting in stunned silence. Cholly may die because the fucking Navy ran out of food? Tuck couldn't believe what Matt was saying.

"It's not Matt's fault," Edie said, "he was lucky not to get sick."

"I dunno," Matt said, "the Skipper fucked up, ah, excuse me, Ma'am, for the language, but he should have laid back into Naples instead of tryin' for Tripoli. Anyway, I get back to Naples and get a pass and I go right to the hospital to see Cholly. He looked real bad, and nobody's changing the sheets or feedin' those guys or anything. It's a fuck-, it's an Army hospital. So I just kept comin' back every day, bringing food and doing what I could for about two weeks. When the Fleet came in, me and the First Officer, we went over to Roosevelt, an aircraft carrier, and got a Doctor that's a pal of the Skipper and brought him to the hospital. After that, most of the guys got better, but Cholly, he just kept gettin' worse. Then I got my papers. I'm out now. And I had to go, but I figured I'd stop and tell you what's going on. I flew in on MATS[80] to McGuire Air Force Base, and caught a bus down here."[81]

"Matt," Edie said, getting a sweater out of the front closet, "I want to thank you for being my son's friend, and coming to us like this." She had walked back to him, and she leaned down and kissed him. "You can stay as long as you like," She said, "I'm going to see somebody who may be able to help us."

"Where are you going, Mom?" Tuck asked, wondering who could help his brother, dying in an Army hospital half way around the world.

"Drive me up to Doc's," she said.

Tuck drove Edie up to Doc McDonald's and waited for her in the car. Pretty soon she came out and stood next to the car.

"You go on back to the house," she said, "Doc knows some people at the VFW and American Legion, and we're going to see them."

Tuck went back to the house, and Matt asked him to drive him over to Camden so he could catch a bus. Tuck told him he could stay, but he said no, he wanted to get home.

"Look," Matt said at the bus station, "I didn't tell your Mom this, because I didn't want to upset her any more than she already is, but your brother is in real bad shape. When I came into that fucking Army hospital, nobody had changed his bed in four days. He was laying in his own shit and piss, and was too weak to help himself. I raised a lot of hell around there, but still couldn't get anybody to even bring him food. If I hadn't come up there, he'd be dead now!"

"Jesus," Tuck asked, "what the hell's the problem? Why isn't he getting any care?"

"It's the fucking Army guys. The guys off the Megara are the only white hats in the place. They got 'em all stuck together off in a dirty ward with no windows, the mother fuckers! They don't figure they should have to take care of any sailors, see, especially Megara's. I ended up taking a Doctor up there from the carrier Roosevelt, when the Fleet showed up. He finally got things moving, so's I felt safe to leave. Otherwise, I was gonna' stay on until Cholly could walk out of there."

"What the fuck is wrong with them?" Tuck asked. "Why are they doin' this?"

"Because they all know us." Matt said. When we hit Naples, they lose all their whore girl friends to us white hats. All the G.I.'s, Army, Navy, Marines they all go to the same places. After we leave, the fleet comes in and works over all the liberty spots, so these guys all got hard-ons for sailors."

"Yeah," Tuck said, "but they'd let a guy die lying in his own shit just because of some whore in a bar? It don't make sense to me, Matt."

"A lotta' things that happen in the service don't make sense, kid," he said, "so, when you go in, watch your ass and be careful who you trust. And don't go in the Army, they're nothing but scum bags, all of them."

Matt's bus came in and they shook hands. He left his address so that they could contact him.

Edie came home later that evening. The guys at the VFW and American Legion both had contacted the Red Cross and sent telegrams to the Navy Department and to the hospital in Naples, but no one knew if they would do any good.

The following days were tense with apprehension. Edie Maye was on the verge of tears most of the time, and Tuck knew she wasn't sleeping much. She talked to the fellows at the VFW and American Legion every day, and they came around to the house on a couple of evenings.

Fifteen days after Tuck had put Matty Beers on the bus, Edie Maye got a telegram from Naples. It read,

YOUR SON, CHARLES J RECOVERING AND WILL BE SENT HOME AS SOON AS AMBULATORY STOP ASSIGNED TO PATUXTENT RIVER NAVAL STATION WASH DC STOP YOURS IN CHRIST STOP SIGNED REV J H CONDEL CMDR USN.

Edie Maye cried again as she read it to Tuck when he came in from work that night.

Three weeks later, Cholly called Tuck from 30th street station in Philadelphia. Tuck drove over, parked at a meter, and went inside to the bar, where Cholly said he would be waiting.

From the door of the bar, Tuck watched him for a few seconds. He was facing away from the entrance, duffel bag at his feet. Tuck noticed that he couldn't stand without gripping the bar tightly with one hand. He seemed to be swaying slightly.

As Tuck shook his hand, he couldn't hide his shock. He was an ugly yellow color under his normally tan complexion. His eyes had yellowed whites and were sunken into a drawn face. Black circles under them added to his gaunt appearance. He couldn't have weighed more than 100 pounds.

"Pretty bad, eh?" he said, stepping back, "they wanted me to stand a parade today, but I told 'em to go fuck themselves, I can hardly stand up."

"You sure in hell aren't gonna' win a beauty contests," Tuck said, shouldering his duffel bag.

27

SEMPER FI

TUCK's brother's return from the service coincided with Sal's apparent move into the legitimate business world. He opened a Ford's Jewelry store in Mt. Holly, at the foot of Main Street, on Mill, facing up the hill into the town's principle shopping area.

Sal had been taking a mail order course in Gemology and received a diploma and certificate declaring him a "registered Gemologist." However legitimate the school was, he learned a lot about gem stones, and in his new location, he was soon doing a lively business in diamonds and other jewelry.

Sal added to the jewelry with an expensive line of kitchen counter appliances and cutlery, which led to another arrest and release on parole for possession of stolen property. Cholly expressed ignorance on the stolen property charge.

"I don't know anything about it," he said, "Cherry called me the other night to tell me that the cops came to the apartment and arrested him... they took out a bunch of stuff he had stored in the closet, I guess they were all stolen goods. The old man said he was innocent, he bought the stuff from another jeweler in North Jersey."

Sal had mastered the intricacies of estimating the value of diamonds, calculating their weight and worth, and combining that with his natural business savvy, the store was an immediate success. Cholly worked for him in the store, and picked up a secondary job tending bar at the Washington Hotel, which enabled him to continue with his drinking.

Knowing that he was reporting for the Marines in January, Tuck began a running and conditioning program in the fall. He did calisthenics with the freshman football team, and a lot of extra pushups and sit-ups. Tuck had heard about Parris Island, and was determined to be ready.

When Edie came home from work one evening, he told her the news.

"I enlisted in the Marine Corps today," Tuck said, "I report on January 24th."

"I knew you would," she said, without revealing her feelings.

"Mom, all the guys are going in. Eddie, Doug, Abie and I went over to Philly and signed up," Tuck said, "but those guys are going after me, in March."

"What did your brother say?" She asked.

"He said what everybody says; don't end up in the Army." Tuck said, "Besides, if I hang around here until March, I'll get drafted, just like Larry DeVaro did, as soon as he was eighteen." They had drafted Larry right out of high school.

"I'll be all right, Mom," Tuck said, "I can handle myself."

"I know you can, I just don't like to see you go, is all, but you will be drafted if you don't go now. You're right, but just the same, I don't like it," Edie said.

"You don't like anything I do," Tuck said.

"That's not true," Edie responded, "but the Navy almost killed your brother, and the Marines, they always send them wherever it's the worst."

"What the hell do you expect me to do," Tuck shouted, "throw ice at Hollyford for the rest of my life? Piney Parker and those guys, they don't have to worry because they're deferred, 'cause they got enough money to go to college! Even if we had the money, they wouldn't let me in no college, an ex-con's kid!"

"You're sister got into a college," Edie was unimpressed by his outburst.

"Yeah, big deal," Tuck responded, "and then they threw her out when they found out who she was! I'm just sick of this whole god dammed town, and everybody in it, I've got to get out of here!"

"Maybe you're right," Edie said, "I'm just afraid for you."

"Ah, don't worry, Mom," Tuck said, realizing that she had tears in her eyes, "I'm tough."

The marine recruiter told Tuck that he would report on January 24 to the Philadelphia Customs House. He was part of a 300 man recruitment, called the "Independence Company." What he didn't bother to tell him was that 260 of the other recruits were taking an enlistment in the Corps as an option; four years in the Corps or two or three years in prison, depending on their crimes. The Corps needed warm bodies.

A marine Master Sergeant administered the oath to the group, assembled in Philadelphia's Customs House hall.

Tuck was sitting next to a very small person, Bill Vogt. They had struck up a conversation during the initial processing. He seemed to know a lot of the guys in the group from haunting the boxing gyms in Philly. Billy had fought in Golden Gloves as a featherweight, and he couldn't have weighed more than a hundred twenty pounds.

"Watch out for those two guys," Bill said, nodding towards two very large fellows in the front row, "McDonald and Culleo. Mac had a couple of pro fights, and they're both mean as shit. Culleo, his old man's a drunk, beats the shit out of him all the time. He's been sparrin' with some pros."

"You going in on an option," Tuck asked, "like most of these guys?"

"Nah," Billy said, "My old man was a career marine. He got killed on Tarawa, in the Pacific. I enlisted, just like him, but my Old Lady, she's been havin' a fit. She didn't want me to go in."

"Yeah, I know what you mean," Tuck said, "my brother damn near died in Italy, so my Mom thinks the same thing is gonna' happen to me." He told him the story of the Megara.

The Master Sergeant made them all stand up and raise their right hands and he swore them in to the United States Marine Corps. They repeated the oath.

Then three additional Non Commissioned Officers came into the hall. Tuck noticed that they were all wearing sidearms as they spaced themselves around the group, and the Master Sergeant began speaking.

"As of two minutes ago, all of you girls became the property of the United States Marine Corps. You will no longer have your Mamas to take care of you. I will take care of you. You will do as I say." As he spoke, he strutted back and forth in front of the now seated recruits.

"It will be my job to escort you to Parris Island, South Carolina, where other unfortunates will have the herculean task of turning you misfits into United States Marines! Until that moment, your asses belong to me!

"Becoming a United States marine is a privilege. Not all of you will enjoy this privilege. Some of you will not even make it to Parris Island,

and of those who do, some will not graduate from there. Some of you may die in the process! That will be your problem. My problem is to deposit you in Parris Island.

"From here on, you are on your own. You will answer for your mistakes. You have sworn an oath, and you will live up to it!" At this point, he paused, and walking down the aisle between the rows of chairs, he pointed at one unfortunate fellow to Tuck's left, jabbing him in the chest with his swagger stick.

"At-ten-hut," he bellowed. The youth, a tall black, stood up slowly, grinning at his neighbor as he did so. The Sergeant grabbed him by the scruff of the neck and quickly marched up the aisle, the bigger youth being pushed along in front of him at arm's length. He stopped and positioned the boy in front of the table at the front of the room. The boy's grin was gone, replaced with a concerned look. Tuck was impressed by the ease with which the smaller man had handled the larger youth.

"Empty yo' pockets, boy!" He screamed into the boy's face.

The black, prompted by the Sergeant, emptied all of his pockets. Among the coins and papers that cascaded onto the table; a switchblade knife and a deck of cards containing pictures of various sexual activities.

The Sergeant picked up the switchblade, and turning to the group, said,

"Now, some of you girls may have an idea that you are some kind of bad asses. You may think this is true because you come from the City, from so-called "rough" neighborhoods.

He paused to let this sink in.

"You pussies don't know what a bad ass is, but you soon will learn. And you will soon learn what a rough neighborhood is."

He snapped open the switchblade, and with the open knife in his raised hand, continued.

"Any recruit that has in his possession a knife or weapon or sharp object of any kind will not go to Parris Island, but will be placed on a train straight to Portsmouth Naval Prison. In a few short hours that person will wish he never heard of the Marine Corps or the mother that gave him birth; but however difficult you girls may think that the Corps is, you do not want to go to a Naval Prison, where they will lock you up and throw away the key!"

He put the switchblade on the table, and held up one of the cards, displaying it to the entire group with a slow sweep of his arm. With his other hand, he still had a firm grip on the negro youth's shirt, now pulled out of his pants and bunched up at the back of the neck.

"Furthermore, any recruit who has in his possession any lewd or obscene literature of any kind, any condoms or any kind of sexual device, will be placed directly on a train to Portsmouth Naval Prison," he said. Placing the card back on the table, he turned and slapped the boy with his open hand.

The motion was so smooth and deliberate that neither Tuck nor the rest of the attentive audience realized what had happened until they heard the resounding slap. Several of the recruits in the front row jumped involuntarily. He hit him so hard that the boy's knees buckled. The sound echoed in the large hall. There was dead silence.

"Now take that fucking knife out of your boot, boy!" The Sergeant yelled, *"And put it on the table!"* He had pulled the boy's face against his own. The boy was terrified. Reaching down with his left hand, he extracted a deadly looking dagger from his boot.

"On the table!" The Sergeant bellowed. The knife clattered on the table.

"You will now proceed by rows past this table and empty your pockets of any such material," the Sergeant said amiably, releasing the boy and motioning him to sit down.

By the time Tuck got the table, it was piled high with lewd magazines, hunting knives, switchblades, a half-dozen hand guns, dirty cards, condoms and even a couple of blackjacks. Tuck had nothing to contribute to the pile.

"How the hell did he know about that guy's knife," Tuck whispered to Billy, after they filed back to their seats, "in his boot?"

"I don't know," Billy said, "but he's got a mean right."

They bussed the Independence Company over to Thirtieth Street Station, where Edie Maye and Sis met Tuck and spent a half hour waiting for the order to board the waiting train. Tuck said goodbye when the order came, relieved to get started, and found a seat on the train.

Tuck, in a window seat, dozed on and off as the train crept slowly through the worst areas of Philadelphia, Wilmington and Baltimore. Through the dark rainy night, he admitted to himself that he was frightened, apprehensive; but nevertheless happy that the adventure had begun.

Sal didn't even know that he was gone. Unless Edie Maye told him, but that was unlikely. And Tuck knew that he probably didn't give a shit, either. That was his way. Sally had turned him away after he graduated high school. He was no longer a part of her life, separated from her teen-age world by his jobs. He was alone, but then, he thought, It's pretty much the same as always… the only difference is that I'm on my own for real, now.

At a snail's pace, the train continued its thirty-hour run to Parris Island, South Carolina.

28

P.I. PONIES

Tuck found a home in the Marine Corps. Staff Sergeant Flowers had made everything crystal clear from the moment he lined them up at the Yammassee rail station, then loaded them onto several busses for the short trip to Parris Island. At the marine base, they were grouped by several NCO's who had lists in their hands, and finally arranged in a ragged formations.

Staff Sergeant Flowers stood rigidly at parade rest directly in front of Tuck's group. He was small, no more than five six, Tuck estimated. He wore the blue trousers with red stripe, gabardine shirt and a "Garrison" hat, similar to a cowboy hat except the brim was flat. In his hand he carried a "swagger" stick, a variety of riding crop particular to his position as Chief Drill Instructor.

He calmly uttered a command, "A - ten - shun!" Some of the recruits responded as best they thought was appropriate. Tuck simply stood still. Flowers walked up the nearest recruit.

"What the fuck's the matter with you, boy? Are you deaf? Are you dumb? Can you see me, boy? He screamed this, barely four inches from the recruit's face. Confused and shocked, the recruit began an explanation.

"Shut your face, peckerhead! No explanations! Yes sir or No sir, that's your answer. Now what is it, peckerhead?"

The recruit, thoroughly confused as to which question he was to answer, mumbled a 'no sir.' Flowers moved to the next man, circling him and jabbing him with the swagger stick, hurling obscenities and at the same time bringing him to the proper form. He stepped quickly to the back row, and approached a recruit from the side.

"Are you in love with me, peckerhead? Do you want to fuck me? Answer me, boy! The recruit repressed a giggle and responded negatively.

"Then why are you looking at me, you asshole?" No answer.

Flowers moved back in front of the group. "You people are disgusting. You are filthy. You have ugly facial hair, and you stink! You are lower than dog shit! I am not pleased." He stepped back, turned and consulted with another NCO, who had been standing behind him.

Tuck was now standing at attention. His mind was reeling. He had never heard such verbal abuse used by one person against another. He thought some of the comments amusing and a little theatrical, but felt instinctively that laughing was not going to be an appreciated response.

If nothing else, this starchy little Staff Sergeant seemed deadly serious. "Take this bunch of misfit pussies to chow," Flowers said.

The group was marched to a chow hall, open and staffed at two in the morning specifically for the "Independence" Company. The menu was fish and stewed tomatoes with potatoes. Tuck, hungry after the long train ride with only a box lunch, loaded the aluminum tray, sat and went to work on the food while others filed into the mess line.

Harold Fishberg weighed exactly 263 pounds and most of his bulk was distributed from his shoulders to his thighs. With beady eyes aglow, he pushed his tray toward the mess hand ladling out stewed tomatoes. Flowers, who was patrolling the food line with intensity, rapped the back of his hand with his swagger stick, and Fishberg nearly raised his entire bulk off the floor.

"You do not eat stewed tomatoes, boy," Flowers bellowed, "you do not eat potatoes. Nor do you eat stringed beans, beets, corn or any other vegetable. Do you hear me, peckerhead?"

The flat brim of Flower's hat was making a crease in Fishberg's forehead.

"You are a fucking whale, peckerhead." Flower's back was arched, his hands on his hips. "Obviously your Mama fed you pogy bait and let you suck teat until you were seventeen." He was suspended over Fishberg's ample stomach.

"I am not your Mama! We do not feed whales in the Marine Corps, peckerhead," he continued, "and we are not going to feed you. We cannot afford to feed you! You are done sucking tit!

"You will not eat cake, ice cream or pogy bait of any kind. Do you understand me, peckerhead?" Flowers now began punctuating his words with his swagger stick, the tip of which disappeared into Fishberg. Fishberg was crying, tears tumbling over his mountainous jaws.

"You are permitted one portion of meat or fish only at midday and evening mess, one portion! In the morning you may eat one slice of toast. One slice, no butter!" Flowers now prodded a stumbling Fishberg to the fish. He watched carefully as the mess hand ladled a small filet onto Fishberg's tray.

"You are permitted one glass of milk, whaleface, one at each meal." This was bellowed into Fishberg's ear as he filled a glass from the milk pitcher.

"Somewhere in that blubber there may be a U.S. Marine, peckerhead, and if so, I will find him, and I will bring him out!" Flowers led Fishberg to a rear table where several other corpulent recruits had been seated, each with a lonely portion of fish on their tray. All had received the same abuse.

Tuck was about half finished, when he realized two things. First that he had taken far too much food, and second, that Flowers was standing next to him. Flowers tapped Tuck's tray with his swagger stick.

"You take what you want, son," he said, "but you eat all you take."

Tuck ate every morsel. He had noticed that those that had food on their trays upon reaching the exit door were being spirited outside, where he could see various kinds of calisthenics being forced upon them.

Flowers then led the group off to a supply facility, where uniforms, shoes, backpacks, pup tents and various other required items were stacked on their outstretched arms.

Lambasting the ragged group with obscenities, Flowers marched them across the base, until they arrived at what they later came to know as "tent city." The group was then unceremoniously divided into sets of six and each group assigned to a 20 by 20 foot pyramid tent, their home for the next 13 weeks.

Several recruits had already marked themselves for special treatment, not being able to carry their gear or keep in step to Flowers' cadence. Tuck's arms were aching from the prolonged walk and heavy load. It was obvious to him, even at the customs hall, that many of his fellow recruits had never done a hard day's work.

Once they had settled into the tents and been given a brief course in bunk make-up by the Junior DI's, Flowers began calling every man individually to his tent. By then, it was four a.m., and they were pretty well exhausted, as well as confused and quite intimidated by the little Texan with all the ribbons on his chest.

Flowers tent, unlike the rest, had a wooden door and frame. As instructed, Tuck pounded the frame with closed fist three times as hard as he could.

"I can't hear you." A lilting voice came from inside.

Tuck pounded three more times, this time hurting his hand.

"Enter, and identify yourself," Flowers barked. Tuck stepped in, whipped off his cap, stood at attention and shouted; last name, first name, followed by "reporting as ordered, Sir!"

"Get back outside and do it right, asshole!" Flowers screamed. He was sitting in a chair facing the door, and his foot catapulted Tuck out into the street. He had forgotten to precede his name with his rank; "Recruit." On the third try, he got it all right, but by then was quite shaken, intimidated and afraid.

Flowers sat and stared at Tuck for a full minute. "What kind of shape you in, Mister?" he asked.

"Good shape, Sir!" Tuck shouted.

"We'll see," he said, "hit the deck and do pushups."

Tuck complied, thinking to himself that he'd show him what kind of shape he was in. He knocked out the first fifty in no time. Flowers called in the next recruit and began abusing him. Tuck was slowing down, his shoulders beginning to ache. Occasionally, Flowers glanced his way and shouted.

"Who told you to stop, asshole?" The other D.I. used his swagger stick to keep Tuck's back straight or chin up, tapping him with it.

By the time the fourth recruit had been in and out, Tuck's whole body was trembling. He was sweating profusely, and each pushup seemed like it was the last that he would ever do. He realized that he was making funny noises from deep inside as he forced first one arm, then the other to straighten. Finally, he collapsed, face against the boards.

"Get out of here, ass hole," Flowers said, "I thought you said you were in good shape."

Collapsing in his bunk, he realized he wasn't such a tough kid, after all. He must have done 300 pushups, but had never been taken to the limit of his physical ability before. Tuck got the point. Survival here depended on listening and doing exactly what was told, exactly. Arms and shoulders completely numb, he immediately fell into a deep sleep.

An hour later, Flowers was screaming at them to fall in. Life in the Marine Corps had begun.

For someone as rebellious as Tuck, it was paradoxical that he quickly fell in line. By some subconscious trick unknown to him, he detached his normally overemotional response mechanisms. He became a quick learner.

Parris Island, surrounded on three sides by South Carolina tidal swamps and on the fourth by a large bay leading to the Atlantic, experienced thirty to forty degree temperature swings during the winter months. The solitary USMC blanket wasn't enough for the near freezing nights, and fatigue uniforms were sweated through under the summer-like noon sun.

Late February brought an indication of spring's more humid air. Tuck's upbringing in New Jersey had accustomed him to heavy humidity, but the near tropical heat of South Carolina was a different experience.

Somehow Tuck found that he was tolerating not only the weather, but all of the petty nitpicking, calisthenics, long hours, short nights and abuse from Flowers and his assistants. Even his shaved head, the ground mosquitoes and gnats were manageable.

He was in boot camp seven weeks when he made Platoon Leader. They were Platoon 81, one of 120 such groups assigned to the tent city at P.I. With the largest contingent of Marines active since World War II, there were simply not enough barracks to go around. They spent the entire thirteen weeks in pyramid tents with kerosene heaters at their center, six men to a tent.

A fire watch was mounted every night. The damply chilling nights being what they were, the tendency was for people to turn the heaters up after the lights out bugle call. If left on the "hot" setting, first the stove, and then the stove pipe soon began to glow crimson as the night wore on. The crimson eventually turned to yellow, just before the tent would catch fire,

There were several such fires in tent city, so each platoon had a watch that patrolled its area during the night. As soon as Tuck went on duty a two a.m., and walked the area once, he saw that he had a problem. Walker's chimney was turning yellow.

Walker was a black tough, and a lot of the recruits were afraid of him. Another of the Philadelphia gang thugs, he was always trying to intimidate people.

Drill Instructor Staff Sergeant John William Flowers, holder of the Silver Star with a cluster, and a Bronze Star with two Oak Leaf Clusters, was explicit regarding talking back. Walker was the example of this lesson in marine discipline. If you did it, you were dropped, no questions asked, with a quick punch.

Walker had talked back twice, and paid dearly for it. The second time that Flowers dropped him, he was unconscious for at least a minute. Flowers had made him Platoon Leader, but he lost the position with the first punch, the second week of boot camp.

Tuck had his M1 at the "sling arms" position, resting behind his right shoulder, when he entered Walker's tent. It wouldn't have mattered much anyway, since they had no live ammo. Walker was responsible for the stove, being bunked on the first cot on the left of the entrance. Tuck shook him by the shoulder, a little apprehensive because of Walker's reputation.

"Walker, wake up and turn your stove down," Tuck said, "or the tent's gonna' catch fire." He was lying on his side, with his back to Tuck.

"Fuck you, man," he mumbled, "turn it down yourself, you don' like it."

"No way, Walker. Your job," Tuck said, "I'm not touchin' that stove. Now drag your ass outa' there and turn it down. If I have to do it, you're goin' on report."

"You ain't puttin' me on report, fuck-up, you're turning' down that stove yourself or you're gettin' the fuck outta' here and leavin' this black boy alone, hear?" As he spoke, he rolled over and Tuck could sense the bayonet in his hand, without looking down at it.

"The son of a bitch always had his bayonet handy, either sharpening it or just using it to punctuate his sentences."

"Turn the stove down, Walker," Tuck said, "and I'll forget about the bayonet." Tuck knew that he was in some trouble, but he wasn't going to back down. Back down wasn't one of the lessons in Edie Maye's repertoire. Walker rolled out of his bunk, holding the bayonet in his left hand, low and pointed at Tuck's stomach.

"Get the fuck outta' my tent," he hissed.

"Turn the stove down, for Chrissakes, it's no big deal and it's your job!" Tuck said, "You're the tent leader."

"Get outa' my fuckin' tent, Guinea Boy," he said, rotating the bayonet in a circle, "or Walker gonna' open yo' gut."

Son of a bitch. Tuck thought, *This guy's crazy, and now I'm in it all the way!* Obviously, Weber, whom Tuck had relieved, was afraid of Walker, and wouldn't even try to make him turn the stove down. The bastard would have let the camp burn!

"Look, Walker," Tuck was trying to sound reasonable without pleading or showing fear, "all I have to do is call for the OOD, and your ass is going to the brig. Now put the knife down and cut the shit." All he could think of was the hoboes fighting in the boxcar.

"Yeah," Walker said, "but yo' ass be dead." Tuck moved his left hand across his chest to unsling his weapon.

When he did so, Walker jabbed with the bayonet.

This is it! Tuck thought, *Do something!*

Tuck went for the bayonet with his right hand. He felt the cold steel against the top of his left wrist, but managed to get a firm grip on Walker's thumb and wrist.

Turning the knife towards his chest, Tuck pivoted behind him, and got a choke hold around Walker's neck with his left arm. He was choking him as hard as he could, twisting his head backward.

Tuck could feel blood on his arm, but there was no way in the world he would let go of the thumb and hand holding the bayonet. He had felt the blade scrape bone, and it made him a little nauseous. They crashed backwards over Walker's cot and bounced off the tent wall. Tuck was underneath, but still had Walker tightly in his grip. The bolt return lever of Tuck's M1 was digging into his back. In his mind's eye, Tuck could see the blood squirting from the hobo's severed jugular in a boxcar a million years ago.

"Get Sergeant Flowers," Tuck yelled to Simmons in the next bunk. He had been awakened by the clatter.

"You're in deep shit, Walker, you son of a bitch!" he heard himself shouting in Walker's ear, and pulled the choke hold even tighter. Walker responded with a funny gasping sound.

"You cut my arm, you son of a bitch," Tuck shouted, realizing that he was crying, feeling tears on his face, and a little light headed..

It seemed like an eternity before Simmons got out the door. Tuck's shoulders and back were aching, and the blood was streaming under his shirt cuff and leaking into the crease of his elbow. Walker was twisting and clawing with his free arm. Tuck didn't know how long he could hold him.

"Let him, go, Private!" Sergeant Flowers commanded. He was standing in the tent door, flashlight beaming in Tuck's eyes.

"No, Sir," Tuck shouted, "I ain't lettin' go until he drops that bayonet."

"He can't drop it, you peckerhead, you're breaking his thumb, and he's already unconscious!" Flowers said.

"Let him go, goddamit, that's an order!"

"Aye, aye, Sir," Tuck released his hold. Walker didn't move, and Sergeant Flowers dragged him from Tuck's chest. Corporal McGaughey, the Junior DI, appeared at the tent door, and Flowers told him to check Tuck over. He was shining the light in Walker's eyes.

"You're lucky, mister," he said, "he ain't dead, but you damn near put his lights out for good."

"He wouldn't turn down his stove, and pulled his bayonet on me," Tuck said, forgetting that his left arm was bleeding profusely.

"Corporal," Flowers said, "get the watch down to our tent and take care of that wound. Call the mainside OOD and get an escort over here for this spear chucker. Simmons, turn that fucking stove down, now!"

Simmons was galvanized into action. He and the rest of the recruits in the tent had formed a semi-circle and were staring at Tuck's bleeding arm and Walker's unconscious form on the tent floor.

"Right, Sarge," the Corporal said, and he led Tuck off down the alley between the tents. While McGaughey was bandaging the arm, Tuck heard a jeep drive up to the area, and Flowers talking to someone outside. The jeep drove off, and Flowers came into the tent. He stood in front of Tuck, arms crossed. Tuck stood up and came to attention. His left wrist was throbbing, but the cut was only superficial, behind the thumb on top of the wrist.

"Why didn't you call the watch Commander," Flowers asked, "when he pulled that knife?"

"I never saw him pull it, Sir," Tuck said, "he was sleeping with it."

"Why not when you saw it, then?" Flowers asked.

"I figured I was gonna' have to handle it, Sir," Tuck said, "I didn't think he'd try to use it."

"You want a man like him in your fox hole?" Flowers asked.

"No, Sir," Tuck said, "the stove was his responsibility. He shoulda' taken care of it. Five other guys were depending on him."

Flowers looked over at Corporal McCaughey, who coughed and looked away.

"You like Fifth Avenue bars?" he asked, grinning at Tuck. This was one of his standards. Tuck tightened his stomach muscles, sensing that he had passed some kind of test, and that the Corporal had somehow predicted it.

"Yes, Sir!" the expected response.

"So do I," Flowers said, "but you ain't allowed to have 'em," punching Tuck hard in the solar plexus. He took the blow, as required, without flinching.

"Get back on the watch," Flowers said, "tomorrow you take the Guide on; you're the new Platoon leader. But first thing, after piss call, you report to the hospital and get that wound dressed right, and get a tetanus shot."

"Aye, aye, Sir," Tuck responded. He stepped back, did a about face and marched out the door, amazed and flattered at his new status, and by the fact that he had handled Walker, who was on his way to the brig.

Back on watch, Tuck immediately went to Weber's tent. He was from North Philadelphia and had a buddy, Ginsburg. They were constantly together and acted like a couple of tough guys. Weber sat up as soon as Tuck opened the tent flap. Tuck placed the muzzle of his Ml right in the middle of Weber's sweat shirt.

"Pretty fuckin' cute, Weber," he said, "but I'm gonna' tell you somethin', and you'd better listen good. Walker's on his way to the brig, and the next time you slack off, you're gonna end up his cell mate, 'cause I'm Guide On now, and I'm gonna' watch your ass."

"I didn't do anything," Weber said.

"That's the point," Tuck said, walking out of the tent.

He knew that his new position as Guide On was a precarious one. Walker had been the first and Slade after him.

Each had screwed up, being unable to demand respect from the troops. Culleo and McDonald keyed the Guide On's success. They wouldn't cooperate with either of the first two appointees, and they had intimidated half of the Platoon into following their lead.

Each from south Philly, both Culleo and McDonald had fought in the Golden Gloves tournaments, as well as some pro fights, according to Billy Vogt. They were heavyweights, weighing about 200 pounds. McDonald was lean, with a sculptured torso; Culleo was a broad Italian type like

Tuck's Sicilian cousins. The following day, after evening chow, he went to their tent.

"Well, looky here," McDonald said, "It's the new Play-toon Leader."

"How ya' doin', Mac," Tuck said, sitting down on a footlocker.

"How's the wrist?" Culleo said, pointing the trigger mechanism of his Ml at Tuck's bandaged wrist. He was trying unsuccessfully to reassemble his rifle.

"O.K.," Tuck held it up, "he didn't get a full cut on it. The medic put a couple of stitches in it."

"Fuckin' spades," Culleo said, "always got to fight with a knife."

"Yeah," Tuck said, ignoring the racial slur, "he was sleepin' with his. Had it in his hand when I woke him up."

"Yeah," McDonald said, "one hand on his knife and the other on his cock."

"That nigger's gonna spend his time in Portsmouth," Culleo said, then pointing the trigger housing assembly at Tuck, "you know how this thing works? I can't make the fucker fit."

"Let me show you something," Tuck said, "There's a trick to gettin' that trigger mechanism in. Here, hold the piece in your left hand, and make sure you get that little tip under, then push down easy."

He shifted the rifle, and the trigger mechanism clicked into place. "Where'd you learn to fight?" McDonald asked.

"A guy I knew, Lou Domillo, that showed me some stuff," Tuck said, "He fought under the name Kid Dominick back in the 30's."

"Come on," Mac said, "let's do some body shots."

"Yeah, sure," Tuck said, getting up.

"Nothin' to the head, no kidneys, no low blows, O.K.?" Mac gave him the rules, and they began circling. Tuck had come here for this, everybody talked about the body shot matches. Mac had knocked out Slaughter with a straight right to the heart.

They closed and began slugging, each looking for an opening. Most of the blows were landing on their arms.

Mac was moving Tuck simply by hitting his arms. They went at it for about a minute before Mac got a good shot to Tuck's left side. He took it, realizing that he was holding his own, and managed to retaliate with a short right to Mac's chest. He felt that, Tuck thought.

After about two minutes, Mac Said, "That's enough; you're bleedin' on my fatigues." Tuck's wrist bandage was leaking, the cut reopened by the activity.

"Yeah, I'd better get this redressed over at the infirmary." Tuck put his fatigue shirt back on and rolled the sleeve to keep it from getting blood on it. Starting out the door, he stopped when Culleo spoke.

"Listen," he said, "you need any help with the troops, you let us know. See ya' later."

"Yeah," Tuck said, "we'll give 'em some boxing lessons. Take it easy." He knew he had passed the test, but had an intense pain in his side where Mac had caught him with a heavy left hook.

29

BETRAYED

THE technique used by the Corps at Parris Island is simple; "break 'em down and build 'em up right." Fear is the motivation. Not simply the fear of failure, but the consequences of failure; the brig, dishonorable discharge, a punch in the face, calisthenics until you drop, verbal humiliation and personal intimidation.

Inwardly, Tuck was terrified for nearly his entire boot camp, but outwardly, he responded as expected.

There were things about the Marine Corps that Tuck had never considered. For the first time in his life he ate three "squares" a day, and he could find no fault with the food. In fact, it never occurred to Tuck that one should ever complain about having food. He couldn't remember any meals that he didn't eat.

Living in tents, taking classes in the woods, double timing through the damp lush South Carolina forest; these things were a treat.

At night, musing his way to dreamland, he thought about his footlocker, crammed full of clothing; uniforms, shoes, socks and underwear as well as 782 Gear, canteen, ammo belt and bayonet, and of course, the vintage MlAl Garand rifle stacked between the bunks with five others. Tuck had never experienced the feeling of having his own belongings, things that were only his, and for the most part, new things. He felt 'complete'.

And he felt like he belonged. He heard the other recruits, continually complaining about chow, about their shoes, about not getting enough sleep. Typically, Tuck listened sympathetically, but really didn't understand their problems.

The only complaint he had, he thought, was that the toilets were all open, lined up at even intervals along the back wall of the Company "latrine." Tuck couldn't get used to sitting and shitting in the presence of thirty others.

Flowers became the father figure Tuck had unknowingly longed for. He respected him as much as he feared him, but he had solace in that he knew that Flowers knew what he was about. The platoon became Tuck's family, and he was no longer confused about who he was, or what was expected of him.

Except for the comment by Walker, Tuck never heard a racial comment or any reference to his civilian family. Hard work paid off in more responsibility and recognition, mistakes were dealt with swiftly and the record swept clean.

After the rifle range in the eleventh week, 81 had to take its turn at the Mainside Chow Hall. The platoon was divided up into groups that each took a task, servers, clean up, warehouse or garbage detail. Flowers put Tuck in charge of the garbage detail.

The garbage detail was required to remove the thirty gallon cans used for trash and garbage from the mess hall as they filled, take them to the rear of the building, empty them into the dumpster, clean and scour the cans and return them. Weber was assigned to Tuck's group, along with his buddy, Ginsberg. It was back-breaking work, as the cans easily weighed more than a hundred pounds.

Mainside chow hall was used by the Parris Island brig to feed prisoners. When prisoners were coming, all hands were on alert. The shuffled clanging of their leg irons could be heard from a block away, an ominous quick step restrained by the eighteen inch chains that linked each prisoner's foot to his partner in front of him. They wore irons on their wrists that allowed six inches of movement between the hands.

They were not allowed to speak, or to remove their gaze from the man's neck directly in front of them. They wore the shaved heads of first day recruits, and remained chained as they filed through the mess line, sat down, ate, stood and shuffled out on command. Many of them exhibited what Flowers termed a "1,000 yard stare;" beaten men with little or no future.

The prison chasers brought them into the chow hall at a double time step, a curiously swaying centipede as they shuffled up to the chow line. Their entrance brought complete silence to the drone and chatter of hundreds of men at mess, and everyone quickly stepped back to allow at least six feet of clear space. Anything less would invite a chaser to claim his territory with an M1 rifle butt or billy club, no warnings or questions asked.

Tuck had by this time taken a leadership role in Platoon 81, not only carrying the Guide on, but literally. His few private moments were filled by other recruits. How to spit shine dress shoes, how to field strip the Ml, even helping McCarthy, a illiterate black from Alabama to write letters home, and teaching Simmons, the rich kid from Toms River, how to peel and eat an orange.

Even Flowers recognized his natural and easy way with his peers. He lifted the "speak only when spoken to" rule for Tuck and often passed the time of day with him as they waited for the platoon to finish mess.

After the first day at Mainside mess, Flowers approached Tuck in the barracks, where they were temporarily assigned.

"How's the garbage detail going, Mister?" he asked.

"O.K., Sergeant," Tuck said, "but a couple of guys are sloughing off."

"What are you gonna' do about it, son?" Flowers asked.

"I'm telling you about it, Sir," Tuck replied, realizing at once that he had made a mistake.

"Not my problem, boy," he said, raising his voice, "it's your detail, and it better get done right, or your ass is on the line, you savvy?"

"Yes, sir," Tuck said, "but these guys are making it hard for everybody on the detail." Weber and Ginsberg had been fucking off from the first minute, finding places to hide and refusing their turns at carrying the heavy garbage cans.

"Well, I can't help you, boy," Flowers said, "but I ain't gonna' be upset if somebody falls over a garbage can lid."

The following morning, Tuck told Weber and Ginsberg that they had the first shift on the cans.

"I ain't carrying no cans," Weber said.

"Me, either," said Ginsburg, "go fuck yourself."

They were standing inside the little brick building where the cans were scoured. It had a concrete floor with a drain in the middle of it. Weber was the leader, and the bigger of the two, so Tuck instinctively directed his comments to him.

"You're gonna' carry cans," he said, "just like everybody else, or I'm gonna' kick your ass."

"Yeah?" Weber said, doubling his fists and hunching towards Tuck, "You and what goddamn army?"

Tuck punched him in the stomach as hard as he could. It felt to him like he didn't hit Weber very hard, but he dropped to his knees immediately. Adrenalin flowing and outraged by their behavior, Tuck hit Weber twice more before his eyes rolled back and he splattered face down on the concrete floor.

Spinning to his right, Tuck pushed Ginsberg's shoulder hard, causing him to stagger backwards.

"You want some, too," He said through clenched teeth, "or you gonna' do your job?" Ginsberg picked up a can and headed for the mess hall. Tuck grabbed Weber by the arm. He had a nasty cut on his cheek and a thoroughly confused look on his face. The skin was split and the one-inch cut was bleeding. Marching him across the street, Tuck presented him to Flowers, in his office in the barracks.

"Got a man that needs some first aid, Sir," Tuck said, after knocking and presenting himself.

"What happened to you, Weber?" Flowers asked.

"He tripped over a garbage can lid, Sir," Tuck replied. Flowers sat back, tapped his pencil on the desk and grinned.

"O.K., you get back to your detail, Mister," he said, "I'll take care of this."

A half hour later, Weber came back to the detail, face bandaged and eye now black. He and Ginsberg pulled their weight for the rest of the week.

The following day, Flowers was patrolling the mess hall when the prisoners were brought in for evening meal.

He was standing behind Tuck, near the front door, as the prisoners loped through, chains clattering. In the silence and above the clatter, Tuck heard his name called out twice, in a loud whisper.

Six feet in front of him, Bobby Brown was shuffling by, eyes staring straight ahead at the neck of the prisoner in front of him. The prison chaser near him whacked him on the shoulder with the butt of his M1, without speaking. Tuck noticed that Bobby was making a "thumbs up" signal with one hand. Flower's voice startled him.

"You know that fuck up?" he asked.

"Yes, Sir," Tuck said, "we used to dig footings together, at Fort Dix."

"He'll get his ass kicked tonight," Flowers said, "for talking. You keep your eyes in the boat and don't say a fucking word to your Buddy. Do I make myself clear?"

"Aye, aye, Sir," Tuck replied. As he swept up near the door, he risked a glance at the two long tables where the prisoners were standing at attention, trays in hand. He found Bobby's face in the line and thought, *Christ, look at him, he looks like he's been through a meat grinder.*

It was the last day on garbage detail. Tuck had just replaced the breakfast cans next to the front door and stepped out on the porch. The early morning sun was showering Parris Island with a crisp clean light. You had to squint to look to the east.

In front of him, a marine in gabardines was leaning against the brick pillar of the porch. The back of his uniform, dark in the contrasting light, appeared to be moving! Stepping closer, Tuck realized that there were two large Palmetto roaches scrambling up his blouse and making a beeline for his collar.

Tuck restrained an involuntary shudder. He had lived with cockroaches all of his life, but these beasts were unbelievable. He instinctively struck out, knocking them to the deck.

The force of Tuck's blow sent the marine staggering forward. He grabbed the pipe railing to prevent himself from falling down the porch stair.

When he turned to face his unknown assailant, Tuck's knees got wobbly. He was an Officer, a Captain, the first that Tuck had ever encountered.

"Just what the hell do you think you're doing, mister?" The question came out low and steady, but there was real steel in it. Speechless, Tuck pointed to the floor, where one of the roaches was now a four-inch circle of squashed ooze.

"Was that P.I. Pony on my back?" he asked.

"Yessir!" Tuck croaked, finally finding a voice.

"Thanks, son," the Captain grinned, "I can't stand those big bastards, either. You know, Private, that there are locals here in Beaufort that claim this whole island is supported on the backs of thousands of those roaches. Do you believe that?"

"Ah, No, Sir," Tuck said, grinning at the picture of Parris Island floating on a sea of palmetto roaches. "Neither do I, son," the Captain said, "Carry on, and thanks."

That night, Tuck related the story to Billy as they packed up to return mainside.

"Jesus Christ," Billy said, "you should have let them fuckers run right up his nose. Didn't you think about it, smackin' an Officer?"

"Hell, no," Tuck said, "all I could see was those P.I. Ponies crossin' his back. I didn't know I was gonna' do it and I couldn't see any bars or nothin'. It was an instinct. I grew up with those mother fuckers."

"Well, those instincts are either gonna' kill you or save you, one of these days." Billy said, "Just like Flowers always says." The fulfillment of Billy's prophecy was imminent, only a week away!

Back in tent city, Platoon 81 was readying its gear for final inspection and graduation when Flowers called Tuck to his tent just before lights out.

"This is Leatherneck Magazine and this here's the Marine Corps Gazette," he said, tossing two magazines on his desk, "every recruit signs up for a subscription. It comes out of your pay automatically. Here's the order forms, I want 'em all back signed in the morning."

"No, Sir," Tuck replied. He knew he was getting into trouble. Flowers got up and walked around the desk. He placed his nose about four inches from Tuck's face.

"What's your problem, Mister?" he growled, "don't you like the Corps?"

"Begging the Sergeant's pardon, Sir," Tuck responded, "but I ain't giving up any of my pay for a magazine, Sir."

McGaughey, cleaning his Colt automatic at his desk, coughed.

"O.K., pin head," Flowers said, still grimacing, "I'll let you off just this one time. You don't have to buy 'em yourself, just take the forms and turn to and make sure everybody else buys 'em." He turned back toward the desk.

"No, Sir," Tuck responded, knowing he had been given a big break.

There's no way, he thought, *that I'm selling those goddamn magazines to the troops!* Tuck had a sick feeling in the pit of his stomach.

"When I was in the AF of L, I had to kick back to my shop steward, Sir, but I figure that the Marine Corps ain't no labor union. Besides, what the hell does selling magazines have to do with being a good Marine, Sir?"

"What the fuck is the matter with you, boy?" Flowers shouted, enraged, "I'm telling you to do this!" Tuck tensed for the punch, but he also noticed that Flowers had said 'telling' and not 'ordering.'

"With all due respect, Sir," Tuck said, "if I wanted to sell magazines, I woulda' joined the fucking Army, Sir."

"Goddamn it, Goddamn it! Goddamn it, boy!" Flowers was now beyond reason, his face an angry red, "sometimes I think you're the best fuck-up I ever pushed through the Island, and sometimes I think you oughta' spend your enlistment in the brig, with your fucked up buddy! What the fuck are you defying me for? What's your fucking problem, you Peckerhead?"

"Sorry, Sir," Tuck said, "but ... "

"Shut your shithole, pin head," Flowers shouted, "and address the door!"

Tuck about-faced and stepped up to the door. Flowers planted his foot in the small of his back and catapulted him into the street, where, missing the step, he landed on his face.

"Get back to your tent, Asshole," Flowers shouted. Tuck knew he was in deep trouble. The only consolation was that there were only two weeks to graduation.

I can take anything for two weeks. He thought.

"Jesus Christ," Billy Vogt said, back in the tent, "you shoulda' sold the magazines. What's the difference, and now he's gonna' be on you like stink on shit."

"It ain't the fuckin' magazines, Billy," Tuck said, "It's him; I thought he stood for somethin', but he's just usin' us boots to make a little cash. I thought he was something special." Tuck had no forgiveness in him. His image of Flowers was shattered.

"Yeah," Billy said, "but what's the big deal, they all do it. That's what I hear."

"The big deal is that I took on Walker and damn near got killed, or a bayonet in the stomach," Tuck said, "Because I believed what the mother fucker's been telling us. And it ain't fair to the troops. Half of these guys can't read, for Christ's sake. What do they want with a magazine? That's the big deal." Tuck had been writing letters home for Salva and McCarthy, recruits from Pennsylvania.

"You're right," Billy said, "I wouldn't read no magazine about the Corps, no way."

"I never figured the bastard would stoop to forcing magazines on the troops just to make a few bucks." Tuck said, "That Silver Star don't mean shit to me now, the son of a bitch probably got it for kissin' some Officer's ass. He wants to get rich selling magazines, let him quit the Corps and get a job, for Chrissake."

The next morning, Flowers threw Tuck's M1 at him so hard after inspecting it that he missed the grip and it dropped on the dirt, a cardinal sin. Tuck was forced to march with the rifle over head for the rest of the day, holding it with one hand, since he carried the Guide On with the other.

For the next week, Tuck polished toilets with a tooth brush for two hours after lights out and pulled fire watch three nights. Flowers was on his case for every minuscule item, and Tuck was beginning to crumble under the pressure and lack of sleep.

Tuck sensed that Flowers had lost face with McGaughey and that was the reason that he was laying it on. Some of the other recruits, watching the vendetta anxiously, said it was because Flowers lost money, since all of the D.I.'s got a cut on selling the magazines.

Platoon 81 then went on bivouac. It was the last major test before graduation. They moved into the Carolina swamps loaded with sixty pound back packs and full 782 gear; bayonet, canteen, k-bar knife and extra empty ammo clips on a web belt. The first night, 81 made camp and pitched and trenched pup tents after a ten-mile forced march through woods and swamps.

At two in the morning, Flowers had them up breaking camp and marching in a pouring rain. The tidal creeks were running very fast and they had to be forded in total darkness. Everyone in the platoon was dog tired, wet to the skin and fearful of the gators and water moccasins in the swamps. Tuck was operating on adrenalin and rage, having had only about eight hours sleep over the past week.

Flowers put Tuck on point, and entering the tidal creeks had him more than a little nervous. He hadn't seen any alligators, but had witnessed several incidents where one recruit or another ran across large snakes. McGaughey stalked to Tuck's rear, following him and occasionally correcting his choice of direction.

Tuck came to another creek and hesitated, squinting in the darkness to get a glimpse of the far bank. The creek was menacing, rushing black water dimpled by the heavy rain. It wasn't clear to Tuck that he should proceed across, but he slid down the mud bank, and stepped into the water, knowing the McGaughey would correct him if he wanted him to follow the shore.

Tuck could feel immediately that the current was stronger than in the others, none of which had been more than waist deep. The other creeks had been rivulets compared to this one.

"Sir," Tuck backed out of the racing sluice, "this creek's really running, and it looks deep as hell."

"Bull shit, Mister," McGaughey said, "we cross here all the time. Get your ass moving, it's only fifteen feet wide!"

Three steps into the creek, with rifle elevated over his head, Tuck felt the bottom disappear. The current caught his back pack, turning him sideways and suddenly, he was under water, being rolled over by the current.

Tuck's helmet ripped off when it struck something solid. Panic stricken, he struggled to stop rolling. He tried turning to the current and to right himself, but the pack felt like a 400 pound anchor. With considerable effort, he managed to turn himself belly down to the bottom, facing the current.

Tuck clawed at the muddy bottom as it raced under his body. He could feel his lungs burning for air, and he had already swallowed several mouthfuls of the brackish water. He knew that he would surely drown if he couldn't somehow get to the surface, but each time he raised his head, the current caught the pack and threatened to roll him again.

Trying to stop himself with his hands, Tuck realized that the muddy bottom was just too porous! He could feel that he was moving very rapidly down the creek, propelled by the current. He began feeling nauseous. His chest seemed about to explode, and in his mind's eye; a slow motion view of himself sliding backwards on his belly down a big rain spout! For one delirious second, he saw the scene.

Somehow he managed to make some crab like movements and push himself sideways up the angled bottom. Feeling the steeper angle of the bottom, he lunged for the surface, but the current immediately tumbled him backward again. For a brief second his head was above water and he heard his own scream choked off by swallowed brine!

Tumbling again, he felt limbs whipping against his body, and then he collided with a large tree limb, hurting his legs. Scrambling for the surface, Tuck emerged, gasping for air, entangled in debris and pressed against a fallen tree limb by the onrushing current. The current held him against the limb as he retched convulsively.

Crawling up the tree limb, he collapsed on the muddy bank. Tuck lay there for a few moments; face down in the course grass, fighting off the dizziness. The only sounds were the drumming rain and pounding of his heart.

Miraculously, he still had all of his gear except the helmet, which had disappeared with the first collision with the bottom. Except for the pouring rain and the rush of the tidal current, there was dead silence. Tuck had been carried a good distance, out of hearing of the Platoon. He cried for a couple of minutes, and then began laughing at a picture of himself, tumbling uncontrollably down the creek and screaming under water. His pack was so heavy with accumulated water that he had to wriggle out of it to stand up. Tuck emptied it out, and began wringing out his soaked clothes and repacking them when he heard the Platoon approaching. The NCO's were searching the bank with flashlights.

"Over here," Tuck shouted. He was beginning to shake with shock, exhaustion and cold, and the realization of how close he had come to drowning. Thinking about it, he realized the creek must have been ten or twelve feet deep at the center, a really dangerous sluiceway with sloping sides. It was only luck that he had hit the tree.

Flowers strode up to Tuck and slapped him in the face, hard.

"You think we came out here so you could go skinny dipping, you ass hole?" He shouted, "get that pack on and move out. What the hell made you think you could ford this creek?"

"I was following orders, Sir," Tuck said, shivering and struggling to mount the water-logged pack.

"No way, Sarge," McGaughey said, "he was trying to be a smart ass. I told him to follow the bank."

"Bull shit..." Tuck started to respond to McCaughey's lie, but was stopped by another hard slap. This one split his lip. Tuck could taste the blood.

"Don't give me no Bull shit, Mister," Flowers shouted into his face, "take the point and follow this creek, and no more fuck-ups."

Tuck saw the futility in arguing, and moved out. He felt sick to his stomach, and McCaughey's grinning face, the lying bastard, was etched in his mind as he marched. Further down the creek, the Platoon crossed on a fallen tree, and they marched until early light. The rain stopped and by morning, Tuck's clothes were still clinging wet.

Back at tent city, Flowers eased up a little for the last few days before graduation. In drill, the Guide On is the first man to execute a column left or right command, being in front of the Platoon in his own row. Tuck's mind started playing tricks on him, and he began to execute exactly the opposite command issued, in spite of intense concentration. Flowers took it as defiance, but Tuck couldn't help it. The more he thought about it, the more convinced he was that he had been set up for that tidal creek!

The son of a bitch tried to kill me, Tuck thought, and he was tight as a bowstring by the time graduation rolled around.

Platoon 81 graduated on schedule, minus four original recruits. Walker, who went to Portsmouth Naval Prison, Pugh and Keery, who decided to desert and almost drowned in the tidal swamps before they were caught and reassigned to another platoon, just starting its first week, and Fishberg, who went berserk at the rifle range and tried to kill several tent mates before being subdued by Billy Vogt, Tuck and several others. He ended up in a mental ward at the hospital, a Section 8 discharge in his future.

Tuck had gained thirty pounds, all muscle, and felt really proud of his accomplishment, of having survived. He would be a marine for the rest of his life, as most men are who complete boot camp in the Corps. Platoon 81 took GCT tests the day after graduation, but nearly everyone was designated 0300, basic infantryman, and assigned to the Second Division, Camp LeJuene, North Carolina. Tuck was assigned to 2nd Division, 3rd Marine Regiment, 3rd Battalion Special Weapons Communication Company, and Flowers made a big deal out Tuck's assignment to basic infantry.

"You don't have to worry about selling magazines, Private," he shouted while dancing along next to the marching platoon and waving Tuck's orders in the air, "you'll be digging foxholes!"

They placed 81 in Casual Company for a week, awaiting transfer. The first day in Casual, Tuck lay around the barracks like everyone else. On the second day, he stood the morning formation, changed into fatigues and headed for the swamps on the western side of the island. By noontime, he had located the bivouac area and after getting lost a couple of times, he forded three tidal creeks and found himself standing where McGaughey had urged him to cross the big creek.

In the daylight the creek was more menacing than at night. Walking along the bank, Tuck stepped off the distance from his entry point to the tree limb that had saved his life, nearly 900 paces! It was easy to see how he could have tumbled that far, the creek was filling rapidly with an incoming tide that must have been running at about six or seven knots. Large pieces of driftwood and other debris were being carried rapidly by the current.

Sitting on the tree limb, Tuck extracted his Pall Malls from his pocket and lit one, and watched the tide racing into the creek. He heard a slight noise in the woods behind him and turned to discover an NCO standing quietly in the shadows, watching. He was carrying a hunting bow and quiver of arrows. As near as Tuck could make out, he was a Tech Sergeant.

"What are you doin' out here, Mister?" he asked.

"I lost a helmet around here," Tuck said, "when we were on bivouac, when I fell in this creek."

"If you lost it in that creek," he said, "that hat's halfway to Savannah by now. Your outfit didn't try to ford this crick, did it? Ribbon Creek is the worst goddamn tidal sluice in the swamp. Everybody crosses on the tree, upriver from here."

"Well," Tuck said, "a Junior DI told me to ford it, and it damned near killed me. This tree limb here saved my ass, when I crashed into it. The tide was running the other way."

"Nobody fords this creek; everybody knows it's treacherous,"[82] he asked, "what's the DI's name that told you to do that?

"If you don't mind, Sarge," Tuck said, "that's my business. I'd rather not say the mother fucker's name."

"Sure," he said, "no skin off my nose. You must be a pretty good swimmer, though, to get the hell out of that sluice in full gear."

"I've been in trouble in the water before," Tuck said, "That's for sure. I thought I'd had it this time, though. I think I was just lucky."

The subject turned to the double action bow he was carrying, and after chatting for a few more minutes, Tuck started the long hike back to Casual Company. When he told Billy where he had gone, he was incredulous.

"You mean you found that place?" He asked. "I couldn't find that place again if you paid me to do it. What the hell did you go out there for?"

"I just wanted to see it in the daylight" Tuck said "to satisfy myself that what happened was no accident."

"You satisfied now?" Billy asked.

"Yep, I meant a Tech Sergeant out there, a DI. He said anybody that tried to ford Ribbon Creek was a looney. All the Dl's know about it, it's a killer, all right," Tuck continued, "and Flowers was trying to kill me, sure'n shit. I'm positive about that, now!"

"You didn't tell that Tech Sergeant that, did you?" Billy asked.

Tuck's USMC boot camp graduation picture (March, 1954). His adventure in Ribbon Creek was prophetic. Two years later the Corps would be changed forever when a D.I. took his platoon through the same tidal sluiceway as a 'disciplinary action,' resulting in six drownings.

"Nah," Tuck said, "he asked me who ordered me into the creek, but I didn't tell him. He told me that there's a half dozen of those killer creeks out there, and all the Dl's been warned not to put recruits in 'em."

But all the way back to Casual Company Tuck had wondered if he could figure it out; that he was in Flowers' Platoon. There were only about four Platoons in Casual. Everybody else had shipped out except the guys assigned to Second Marine Division.

The next day Tuck found out where the brig was and hiked across the Island again. The Master Sergeant in charge looked up when Tuck entered his office.

"'Scuse me, Sarge," Tuck asked, "Can I see a prisoner?" Tuck was still nervous about talking to NCO's.

"Who's the prisoner?" he asked.

"Bob Brown, Private Brown," Tuck said, noticing the two Corporals seated at the other desks. They were big mean looking guys and had stopped what they were doing to stare at him. Everybody was armed with

Colt .45 Automatics and had billy sticks. Tuck had no doubt that they were carrying live ammo.

"What do want to see him for?" the Sergeant asked, adding, "No visitors except relatives is allowed."

"He's my cousin," Tuck lied, "I just want to talk to him."

The Sergeant nodded his head toward a big Corporal, who walked over to Tuck. The other got up and went through a door at the back of the office.

"Put your hands over your head, Private," he said, and began to frisk Tuck, making a point to do it roughly.

Confident that he wasn't concealing anything, he pointed to a chair and told Tuck to sit down and wait.

After a half hour of complete silence, the second Corporal reappeared and told Tuck to follow him through the door. They walked down a narrow hall and Tuck was led into a windowless room separated down its middle by a heavy wire mesh. Bobby Brown was standing on the other side of the wire, wearing leg and wrist irons. The Corporal shut the door behind him and took position outside looking through the single pane window in the door.

"Jesus Christ, Bob," Tuck blurted out, "you look like shit."

"Don't do nothin' to get in the brig," Bob said, "They're killin' guys in here." He stood back from the wire and glanced nervously at the door as he spoke.

"What the hell did you do?" Tuck asked, "How did you get in here?"

"Big fuckin' deal, I put a D.I.'s lights out the first week, and I been here ever since," he said. "That day I seen you at the chow hall, they hosed me that night. They hose somebody every night, the mother fuckers, they enjoy it."

"They hit you with rubber hoses?" Tuck asked.

"Rubber, shit, they use them billy sticks and their fists, but they never hit you in the face, where somebody can see it," Bob said, "the first time, I pissed blood for a week. Now I'm gettin' used to it. I'm gonna' get hosed for this."

"For what?" Tuck asked.

"For havin' a visitor, but I don't give a shit anymore," he said, "even if they kill me, I just don't give a shit anymore. I'm gonna' break outta' here, before they kill me."

"Look, Bob," Tuck said, upset about the news that he would cause him to be beaten, "I got a leave coming. You want me to contact your Mom, or somethin'? I'll be right near Camden."

“Nah,” he said, “fuck her, too. I don’t need nobody. I’ll either be dead or over the wall in a few weeks, anyway. Forget it.”

The Corporal opened the door and said, “Time’s up, that’s it.”

“I’ll see ya’, Bobby,” Tuck said, “take care, don’t cause no trouble, and you’ll get out of here.” Walking toward the door, Tuck heard him sob.

“Go see Mom,” he cried. His voice broke and was almost a whisper, “Tell her I’m sorry, hear?” Tuck looked back as he went through the door. Bobby Brown’s head was bent to his shackled hands and he was crying uncontrollably.

Tuck stopped at the Sergeant’s desk on the way out.

“Is he gonna’ get his ass kicked because I came here?” he asked. The Master Sergeant looked at him with disgust.

“Get the fuck outta’ here, or you’ll end up in the cell next to him,” he said. Tuck swung on his heel and left, sensing it wasn’t an idle threat.

30

STOPPING A RUNNING TANK

He was six months out of boot camp, and standing in the office of a Marine Corps Brig again, only this time, the brig was located at Camp Lejuene, North Carolina. It struck just as much terror in Tuck as P.I.'s brig. Being located mainside, near the base movies, the entire base was witness to the daily beatings that the prisoners took in the yard.

The Master Gunnery Sergeant in charge was about sixty years old, his chest a mass of ribbons with battle stars and his weathered face lined with wrinkles. His left sleeve was covered with hash marks from cuff to elbow, and he had a gravelly voice. He looked a lot like the fifty pound bulldog, Chesty, that was lying next to his desk. Chesty wore a marine green coat with Master Sergeant stripes and sported a red leather spiked collar, his chin laying in a drool pool on the hardwood deck.

"You're one of those goddamn football players, eh?" the Gunny asked.

"Yeah, Sarge," Tuck answered, "but I'm assigned to Casual Company now, awaiting transfer to Naval Academy Preparatory School."

"I got your 501 here, son," he said, "I know all about you. Your ass belongs to me from now on until you get your papers, you savvy? You'll report here directly to me every morning, oh-eight hundred hours, to chase prisoners."

"Aye, aye, Gunny," Tuck responded with a sinking feeling. Prisoner chaser was a job that could get you in trouble very quickly. Obviously, the Company Commander was getting back at him for making the base football team, getting out of regular duty, and passing the test for Naval Academy Preparatory School. The Officers did their level best to maintain the status quo. They wanted everybody to be a grunt, no special privileges.

Tuck had been assigned, along with Simmons and Vogt, to 2nd Marines, 3rd Marine Regiment's SWCC, Special Weapons and Communications Company. In no time, he had been trained in the use of the field radios, ANGRC-9's, PRC-10's and EE8's, as well as the art of setting up field telephones, tree (utility pole) climbing and wire stringing procedures.

SWCC was responsible for communications with other units, including the 4.2 mortar Company; the jeep mounted Anti-Tank Rocket Company, the 105 mm and 155 mm Howitzer Companies and Regimental Headquarters. The mortars and rockets were actually part of the unit.

In a month, Tuck had learned everything he needed to know and the boredom sat in. He ran into MacDonald at the base movie one night, and pretty soon he was working out with the boxers down at the regimental gym, just to kill time.

They hit Onslow Beach every weekend, sometimes picking up some women marines, which they called BAMS for "Broad Assed Marines," and would spend the day drinking 3.2 beer and swimming in the surf. Tuck discovered that the base had a sailing facility on Onslow Bay and quickly qualified in the Rebel class boats, which gave him a nice way to spend the day with a date, with the opportunity to be alone on a secluded island in Onslow Bay.

Second Battalion mess was a disgrace, serving fried rabbit four nights a week. Often there were only soup spoons to eat with. A treat of being in the fleet was Sunday morning mess. For those who made it, the cooks would fry as many eggs as one ordered. Tuck usually tried to make it, regardless of how drunk he got on liberty the night before.

On the fourth consecutive Sunday morning that Tuck was told "no eggs today, we're all out," he decided to find out what the hell was going on.

"Goddamn it, Billy," Tuck said, "this ain't right." Tossing his tray on a table, he walked through the kitchen and opened the door of the office at its rear.

"What the fuck do you want?" asked the Captain behind the desk. He was out of uniform, without a tie and needed a shave.

"Begging the Captain's pardon, Sir," Tuck said, "I wondered how come we're outta' eggs all the time when all the other Battalions got 'em?"

"Who the fuck do you think you are," the Captain responded, getting up from his chair, "some goddamn IG? We're outta' eggs because we're outta' eggs, you asshole. Now get out of my face, before I figure out some way to throw you in the goddamn brig."

Billy Vogt had followed Tuck, fearing that he would get into trouble. He was standing just outside the office door, which Tuck had left ajar. Tuck could smell whiskey on the Captain's breath, and he was immediately sorry that he had decided to do something about the eggs. The Captain was weaving noticeably, staring at Tuck with bloodshot eyes.

"Thank you, Sir," Billy blurted out from the kitchen, and they spun on their heels and raced out of the mess. An African American cook followed them outside, a Sergeant.

"Don't fuck around with Captain Brophy," he said to the two Privates, "or he'll find a way to screw you white boys over."

"What the hell's goin' on, Sarge?" Tuck asked, unwilling to let it go, "This mess is all fucked up. It ain't right."

"Don' ask no Montford Point black boy about what's wrong," the Sergeant said, "I just cook an' keep my mouth shut, and you'll be better off if you does jus' the same."

When fall rolled around, Tuck had no trouble making the Regimental football team as starting quarterback. As a result, he moved into the team barracks and was able to access the Fourth Battalion mess hall, where the team had eating privileges. Having relieved his immediate problem with food, he forgot about the incident at the Second Battalion's mess.

He took up tennis, which filled in some evening hours, but on the whole, the Fleet was a big disappointment. He was drinking a lot of beer, and couldn't see himself going anywhere. This all changed just before they loaded the Regiment on six-by's and took it up to Fort Bragg, North Carolina, for maneuvers for a month.

Tuck reported directly to two Technical Sergeants, a big Swede named Swenson, and Dale Bird, a full-blooded Cherokee Indian. Bird was crazy, it was generally thought. He wore a Purple Heart and bronze star from Korean combat and was friendly to Tuck.

Tuck pulled liberty with him one night and he drove his car into the surf at Onslow Beach! Tuck liked him a lot, but socializing with him could be dangerous.

Swede was altogether different. He was really serious about everything the 'replacements' did, a real taskmaster.

Tuck had a couple of run-ins with him, mostly over how to do things, but over all, they had a good relationship. He'd had Tuck over to his quarters a couple of times for dinner with his family. His wife was a beautiful Korean girl, and they had a couple of fat, happy babies.

"Listen, Si, you ever heard of NAPS?" he asked one day, when they were cleaning up some radios. Swede and Tuck were sitting in the shade of some big oaks behind the motor pool. Everybody had picked up on calling Tuck, "Si," because of the Sicilian name. It stuck harder when he objected to it, so he just accepted it. Everybody had a nick name of one kind or another.

"Nah, Sarge." Tuck asked, "What is it?"

"Naval Academy Prep School. It's up in Maryland. They give a fleet-wide test for it every year. If you pass, you go to NAPS, and if you pass the test there, you get appointed to the Naval Academy," he said, "could mean a free college education and a commission."

Swede knew that Tuck had been volunteering for everything on the bulletin boards, ReCon Marines, Arctic Force, NavCad, anything they put up, but the Company Commander, who processed all the requests, just shit-canned them.

"When's the test?" Tuck asked.

"Dunno'," he said, "but it ought to be coming up soon."

When the Company Clerk couldn't help him, Tuck talked to the CO, who was a Reserve Captain.

"They don't give that test anymore," he said, "forget about it." He was a real prick, and everybody agreed to that. Swede and the other NCO's were with him all the way, and they urged him to see other officers. The lieutenant who ran the 4.2 mortar platoon was more helpful. Tuck usually carried his radio, a PRC-1O, on maneuvers, and he was pretty friendly.

"Yeah," he said, "I've heard about that, but they've never given it here at Lejuene. Why don't you go over to Battalion and ask some of those Officers?"

Tuck tried several Officers at Battalion headquarters with no luck. No one had ever heard of the NAPS test at Lejuene. Tuck figured, *Nothing ventured, nothing gained,* and took a shot at Regimental Headquarters.

A Sergeant there said, "Try Captain Tight-Ass, he's a ring knocker." The Captain's name was Titus, and he was a graduate of the Naval Academy. Standing at attention in his office, Tuck waited a full two minutes before the Captain swiveled his chair to face him. Tuck couldn't help notice the huge gold ring on his left hand.

"I was wondering, Sir," Tuck said, "If you might know anything about the NAPS test, and how I would go about taking it, Sir."

"You just watch the boards for the announcement, Private," he said, "and then follow instructions."

"Begging your pardon, Sir," Tuck said, "but there won't be any announcements, they haven't been giving the test here. I've been over the whole base, and nobody knows anything about it, Sir."

"Is that right, Private?" he asked, "Where have you inquired?" Tuck rattled off the list, naming the Officers he had talked to.

"I see," he said, "we'll just have to look into this." He looked at Tuck curiously. "Do I know you, Private, from somewhere else?"

"Yessir," Tuck replied, "I almost knocked you off the porch of the mainside mess at Parris Island. You had some big roaches on your back."

"Of course," Titus smiled, "you looked like you were going to faint. I recognize you, now." He asked Tuck a little about his duty assignment and Company and then dismissed him.

"I'll see what I can do," he said.

Two weeks later, the Company Clerk handed Tuck a message from Captain Titus. It said the test would be given at the Mainside Special Activities Center on August 14, two days after the Division returned from four weeks of maneuvers at Fort Bragg.

The following Saturday was just after pay day, and most of the troops had taken off for a weekend liberty. Tuck was getting dressed to hit the base library and see what kind of review books were available, when the somber beat of kettle drums caught his attention. He had a good view of the parade ground from the second floor. Walking to the front of the barracks, he was surprised to see the adjacent Battalion in full formation in front of their barracks. Most of the Companies were in dress blues. The Battalion was formed in an unusual formation, like a big "U," and the Commander was at the top of the "U," facing towards its bottom, with his staff behind him.

Standing at attention at the bottom of the "U" was an officer in dress blues, flanked by armed guards! On command, the drums began a slow cadence, and the guards marched the prisoner up the middle of the formation, where he came to a halt in front of the Battalion Commander.

The Commander then produced a set of legal sized papers and began to read from them in a loud voice. Tuck couldn't hear the words, being several hundred yards away. He read for some time, then stopped, handed the papers to his Adjutant, and stepped smartly up to the prisoner.

The Commander drew the prisoner's sword and broke it over his knee. Throwing the sword to the ground, he then reached over and tore first one set of captain's bars, and then the other, from the prisoner's shoulders. He then ripped the brass buckle and belt from the jacket, and the red stripes from his trousers. Finally, he pulled the ribbons from the prisoner's chest, and then plucked each brass button and the Marine Corps Eagle, Globe and Anchor collar emblems from his tunic. Removing the prisoner's hat, he ripped the quatrafoil from its cover.

Each item was removed with a drum roll from the trap drums, and cast on the ground. Having finished, the Commander stepped back, did an about face, and maneuvered his staff to one side. He gave a command, and four additional guards fell into line behind the prisoner, behind them, the four kettle drums. The final insult; the entire command did an about face, showing their backs to the drummed officer!

On command, the unit stepped out to the kettle drums, which were sounded for every other step, like a death march. The unit marched to the middle of the street, did a column left, and headed for the main gate, four miles distant. The prisoner, his uniform now stripped of all distinguishing features, marched with his head down at the front of the formation.

Billy Vogt happened to be at the main gate when the prisoner reached it. Tuck saw Billy later that evening.

"Did you see what happened?" Tuck asked. "They drummed some Officer out of the Corps today. They marched him to the main gate with a guard and drummers!"

"Fuckin' A I saw it," Billy said, "I was just coming back to base. Don't you know who it was, the Officer?"

"No," Tuck said, "I saw the whole thing, from the barracks window." He told Billy about the ceremony. "Who was it? Did they really throw him in the street?" he asked.

"Yeah," Billy said, "a big MP actually kicked him in the ass so hard that he landed face down on the street, outside the main gate! And you say they marched him four miles that way?"

"Yeah," Tuck said, "it was First Battalion, right next to our barracks, where they started. It was some ceremony, each time they ripped something off of his uniform, they had a drum roll. It was eerie, it took about five minutes to strip him, and all you heard was these drums, every time the Commander ripped something else off."

"Jesus, I talked to the Sergeants, the guards," Billy said, "and they said it's the first time they ever saw that ceremony, and they both been in the Corps for fourteen years! It was that goddamn Second mess Officer, Brophy, his name was."

"The Captain that gave us all the shit?" Tuck asked.

"None other. The MP's said he had some kind of scam goin', selling the food instead of serving it and he got his ass caught." Billy was delighted at the turn of events.

"When you get drummed out of the Corps," Tuck said, "it's an automatic dishonorable discharge, that's what I heard."

"It's a goddamn wonder with what that bastard did," Billy said, "that they didn't take him to the brig."

At the base library Tuck began boning up on everything he had ignored in high school. The Navy had created a series of self study books for the high school equivalency test, and when the 2nd Marine Division took off for Bragg, Tuck's knap sack contained Algebra and Geometry texts, and review books on literature, poetry and history. Tuck knew how to study in the woods, and there was plenty of time available after stringing wire and setting up field phones.

Back at Lejuene, Tuck took the test with 23 other marines and one Navy Corpsman. They learned the same afternoon that fleet wide, of the 300 applicants, only eleven had passed, and that Tuck was the only one from LeJuene. He had moved out of Company barracks when he made the football team, and now he was moved again to Casual Company at Mainside.

Tuck called Edie Maye that evening, from the pay phone in the barracks hallway. "Mom, it's Tuck. How are you doing?"

"I'm fine, Tuck," Edie Maye realized that something had happened. He had told her about the test in his last letter before going on maneuvers. The letter had been bitter about the Corps and the boring assignments and lack of opportunities. Since she had listened through a dozen other applications he had made and expected to get, Edie was curious but pessimistic.

"I passed the test for NAPS, Mom. Three hundred guys took it from the Fleet, and eleven passed. I made it!"

"I thought that you would, Tuck," she said, "from the very beginning. What happens now?"

"I'm going to NAPS, Mom, Naval Academy Prep School, in Maryland. They'll be cutting my papers next week."

Edie Maye felt her heart skip a beat.

"Oh, Tuck," she said, "I'm so proud of you! I knew you could do it. You're going to the Naval Academy. My son, at the Naval Academy!"

"Whoa, Mom, not quite." Tuck reacted strongly. "I'm just goin' to the prep school. I still have to get through that. It's not easy, you know, everybody doesn't make it!

"But you will, Tuck," she said, "I know you will!"

Tuck hung up from the conversation after inquiring about Chip and Cholly. He felt proud of his accomplishment, but a little frightened about the aspect of competing with college kids on an academic level.

Edie Maye hung up the phone and sat down at the kitchen table. Chip shuffled in from the living room when he realized that she was crying softly over a cup of coffee. The stroke had made it nearly impossible for him to speak. He placed his hand on her shoulder.

Edie Maye covered Chip's hand with her own and without looking up, said, "It's Tuck, daddy, our Tuck. He's going to go to the Naval Academy. He's going to be an Officer!"

Suddenly, the Corps realized that they would have to give Tuck dental care, NAPS requiring it for entrance. For months, He had tried to get an appointment, but few PFC's got taken care of by the dental technicians. With his transfer staring them in the face, Tuck reported to the infirmary and two dentists filled 26 teeth in one day, the first time, except for an examination at Parris Island that he had ever been in a dentist's chair. He was recovering from the dental episode when they assigned him to prison chaser duty.

"Now I want you to understand something, private," the Brig Commander said, "you'll be chasing these Bo's all over the base. You are responsible, completely responsible. If your man breaks and gets away, you will finish his sentence. Is that clear?"

"Yes, Sir," Tuck gulped, knowing he was serious. It was common knowledge in the ranks that a prisoner chaser who lost a prisoner took his place. No trial, no questions asked.

"No one talks to them; they are not permitted to speak. No one touches them and no one gets within six feet of them," the Sergeant asked, "is all this clear in your mind?"

"Aye, aye, Sarge," Tuck said. He handed Tuck a full clip of live ammo.

"If your man breaks, you shoot, savvy?" he said, "you out rank any man, woman, child on this base when chasing, if anyone interferes with your prisoner, you understand?"

"Aye, aye, Gunny," Tuck said. It was the first live ammo he had handled since boot camp.

"Here is your schedule, and a map of the base," the Gunny continued, "you give your man a piss call every two hours, and a drink. He feeds at the chow hall nearest. You don't eat. Any questions?"

"No, Sir," Tuck said.

"Don't call me Sir, Private," he said, "and watch your ass, some of these Bo's are hard cases."

A Corporal brought Tuck's prisoner out, a big kid with a pocked face and irons on his wrists. He was wearing the gray brig fatigues with a big white "P" in the middle of the back. While the Corporal was removing his wrist irons, Tuck unslung his M1, inserted the clip, and did a "lock and load," the bolt banging home a live cartridge with a loud clatter in the small office. Tuck told the prisoner to move out at a quick step and stay four paces in front.

His first stop was the Infirmary, but as soon as Tuck had cleared the Mainside compound, he took his prisoner behind a barracks and put his back to the wall.

"I'm tellin' you this one time," Tuck said, "and one time only. I'm locked and loaded with live ammo, and sittin' in Casualty Company waitin' for my walkin' papers out of here. You run, I'm gonna shoot you in the back. I shot expert at P.I., and I can drop you at 500 yards, and I'm not letting any brig rat fuck me up. I've got no intention to finish your sentence. You savvy?"

"Aye, aye, Sir!" he responded.

"O.K.," Tuck said, "move out, and no bull shit!"

The trouble came at lunch. Tuck took him into the Fourth Battalion mess hall. As chaser, he could take the head of the line, which was considerable. Everybody gave way, knowing the rules that chasers are under. Tuck saw a table in the back of the hall that was empty, and when his prisoner had filled his tray, he headed him for it, marines parting in front of the prisoner as they crossed the hall. Tuck's M1 was at port arms when a Technical Sergeant with a full tray tried to walk between him and the prisoner.

Tuck instinctively planted his left foot, pivoted towards the Sergeant and smashed him in the chest with his rifle butt. He sprawled backwards on the floor, the tray turning over on his chest. Tuck shouted.

"Prisoner, halt!"

The mess hall went completely quiet. Tuck now had taken a semi crouched position with the M1 waist high in a firing position, pointed directly between the Sergeant on the floor and his prisoner, who was frozen in his tracks, and shivering. Several marines in the line of fire left their meals and stumbled out from the mess tables, seeking safety.

The Sergeant got up, brushing accumulated food from his blouse, and looked at Tuck. He read the tenseness in his face and body. Tuck's finger was on the trigger, and he swung the muzzle of his M1 slightly in his direction.

"What the fuck do you ..." he started to lay in to the obviously nervous Pfc. with the loaded M1. Tuck had made a real mess of his gabardines.

"Stow it, Coopers," a Gunny Sergeant said from a nearby table, without looking up from his tray, "or that chaser will blow your ass away, and he'll be right to do it!"

"Son of a bitch!" Coopers said, and kicked his tray, sending it spinning. Tuck's M1 was now pointed directly at his stomach, an instinctive reaction to the clatter of the tray glancing off his foot.

"Back off, Sarge," Tuck said, finding the words somehow, "you're interfering with my prisoner."

"Son of a bitch," he muttered it this time, spun on his heel, and headed out of the mess.

"Sorry, Sarge," Tuck said, turning to the Gunny, who was now studying him. Tuck had no idea that he would have reacted as he had. It had been completely instinctive. He could see that the men in the mess hall had accepted it as a normal and expected reaction, but Tuck was afraid, nevertheless.

"No matter," the Gunny said, "he was stupid. Any ass hole that walks between a prisoner and chaser deserves to get knocked on his ass. Move your man out."

Tuck moved his prisoner to an empty table and stood behind him while he ate. As he escorted him out of the chow hall, he was afforded an even wider berth than when he came in. When Tuck brought him back to the brig at 1600 hours, the Commander had heard all about it.

"Had a little trouble today, didn't you, Private?" he asked. Tuck had worried for the rest of the day about the consequences of knocking down an NCO. He had reacted instinctively. A millisecond before it happened; he had no idea that he would do such a thing.

"Yessir, Sarge," Tuck said, "some Tech Sergeant tried to split me and the Bo in Fourth Battalion mess."

"And you dropped him, right?" the Commander asked, chuckling a little.

"Yeah, damn right I dropped him," Tuck said, "but until the minute I did it, I had no intention of knocking him down! I figured you were serious about taking the prisoner's sentence if he breaks."

"You're goddamned right I was serious, Private," he said, "and don't you forget it! But did you have to deck a Tech Sergeant?"

"There was a Fourth Batt Gunny who saw the whole thing," Tuck said, "he can tell you what happened. The son of a bitch strolled right between me and the prisoner, and we were only about twenty feet from the open front door. I couldn't risk losing sight of him, in the crowd."

"That was Coopers, the Gunny. He's a drinking buddy, and he called me when he got back to his office. He says you're a tough little son of a bitch."

"I ain't so tough, Sarge," Tuck said, "I was scared, and that's the truth of it, and I don't mind telling you so. I'm not ashamed of it."

"Well," the Gunny said, "it took brass balls, boy, but you did the right thing. You're goddamn lucky that you're transferring out of here in a few days, though. That Coopers is a mean bastard."

Tuck felt the relief wash over him. Under any other circumstances, striking an NCO was a brig offense!

The second and third days as prison chaser went without incident. Tuck was beginning to feel fairly comfortable, moving his prisoners around the base, but he was still acutely aware of the situation he was in, and tried to maintain a sense of alertness at all times. It was his fourth day on the job that was filled with drama and tragedy; a Russian novel.

The Corporal brought out Tuck's prisoner, and it was Tank Clegall. Of all the aspects of the Marine Corps that agitated Tuck, the single thing that he abhorred the most was the penchant of the Corps to accept nearly any volunteer.

That aspect of recruiting had laced the Corps with hundreds of illiterate and dangerous men. Every outfit had their share, sullen and unpredictable, with few moral or ethical principles. Only severe discipline and the fear of the brig kept these types at least sociable. Many had prison records and were capable of nearly any act. Tank Clegall was one of these men.

Clegall had been in the headquarters outfit with Tuck, and was assigned to the 4.2 mortar group. He had a 22 inch neck, weighed 250 pounds, and engendered fear from everyone around him. Everyone in the outfit tread lightly around Tank, who was as close to a Cro-Magnon man as any living human being could be. When Tuck and the other replacements from 81 joined the unit, Clegall was finishing up a four-month stint in the brig for stealing a .45 automatic from the armory. His upcoming release was a daily topic of conversation in Special Weapons. Most of the men in the outfit were clearly terrified by Tank Clegall.

Nearly retarded, he had a mean streak and became violent at the drop of a hat. No one ever knew what would set him off, and everybody actually whispered when they were close by, fearing that a simple comment would elicit an outburst of violence.

He came back to the outfit about a month after Tuck had arrived, released and returned to regular duty. The first evening that he was back, Tuck watched in amazement at an outburst of Clegall's temper when he threw Luzerne, another big marine, completely over a top bunk, separating Luzerne's shoulder when he hit the bulkhead.

Tuck soon discovered that Clegall liked to stalk the barracks in the nude, challenging anyone to require him to follow regulations. His body was an amazing sculpture of muscular bulk, huge bulging muscle everywhere. Nobody fucked with Tank Clegall. Only a couple of the Sergeants could handle him, and that was with kid gloves. He'd been in the Corps for six years, and had spent half of it in brigs, and was still a private.

He was on his way to Portsmouth Naval Prison now, having wrecked a bar in Jacksonville and put four marines in the hospital in the process. He beat up the MP's that arrested him, dumped them in the woods near the main gate, turned the jeep over and set it afire. One guard was so badly damaged that the scuttlebutt was that he was getting a medical discharge, if and when they ever released him from the hospital.

He was fairly well subdued now. It was obvious that they had been beating him for some time, but the beady eyes in that broad inscrutable face still suggested danger. Tuck was really terrified of the prospect of running him around the base. He had adroitly managed to avoid any contact with him when he was in the outfit, but Clegall often hung out at the regimental gym, and Tuck knew that he seen him there, working out and sparring with the boxing team.

Tuck took him behind the barracks and gave him his speech about running, making sure to stay about ten feet away from him. Clegall could see that Tuck was frightened, and like a feral dog, he sensed it. He listened, staring at Tuck stupidly.

"You better be ready to shoot," he said, "Tank's gonna' run. You can bet yo' ass on it." He grinned, squinting up his prodigious face and then spit noisily against the wall.

"You run, Clegall," Tuck said, "and I'll shoot you. You can bet on that, so don't try it!"

But he ran, anyway. Coming out of the Infirmary about ten-thirty that morning, he just dropped his file folder and took off, straight away from Tuck in a sprint. He was heading out across the broad lawn that was used as a parade ground, towards the street, about 400 yards away, running with his head down, like a sprinter in a track meet.

"Prisoner, halt!" Tuck shouted, but he kept running. Tuck's legs turned to water when he saw him break. Cold fear gripped him, and he felt an involuntary shudder down his spine.

Shit, you're in big trouble now, Si! Tuck heard himself saying out loud, "Do something, for Christ's sake!"

Without intending it, he was already working the catch on his sling, releasing the buckle, the weapon now upside down with butt on his thigh.

"Jesus Christ," Tuck could hear himself shouting, "Clegall, halt, goddamn it!" He sounded like a contrite pet owner railing after his dog. A terrible feeling of helplessness came over Tuck. He could see that Clegall had no intention of stopping. He was going to run straight across the parade ground, across the street and into the woods on the other side! His feet were raising little clouds of dust.

Tuck realized that he was going to have to shoot him! His future was running away in front him.

React, for Christ's sake! Tuck thought.

Tuck shoved his left arm up to his armpit into the sling and looped his elbow, wrapping the sling onto the back of left hand. Keeping one eye on Clegall, who was now beginning to zigzag across the broad lawn, he popped up the rear sight and slid the range bridge to the 400 yard mark. Clegall was getting close to the street! A full twenty seconds had elapsed since he started his run.

Dropping to a kneeling position, Tuck forced the butt of the MI into his chin, pulling the sling so tight that it cut off the circulation in his left arm and fingers. He pulled the sight down on Clegall's fleeing form. Each time he turned, he looked back at Tuck. He saw that he was in the kneeling position, pulling down on him.

"Halt, prisoner!" Tuck screamed it this time, and when Clegall didn't stop, he squeezed off a round. The M1 rocked him back, ejecting the casing on Tuck's foot and noisily ramming home the next cartridge.

Tuck saw a puff of dust in front of him, about ten yards long and to the left. Clegall was nearly on the street now.

There was a dense wood on the other side, it was now or never!

Tuck waited this time for his next turn and re-ran the training litany; *breathe out, and squeeze easy, don't lead him so much.*

He had jerked the first shot, and realized it the moment the M1 went off. This time he squeezed steadily and the report and recoil surprised him, as it should have.

That's it, Tuck thought. A half second later, the running Tank Clegall threw his hands up in the air, and tumbled to the asphalt.

Tuck heard the brakes of a car, and noticed that there was a black sedan near Clegall. It had screeched to a halt. Some voices behind him caught his attention. The shots had brought some Corpsmen out of the Infirmary. Tuck turned as he began to run across the broad lawn.

"Call the OOD, somebody!" he shouted. As he ran, he was conscious of feeling very cold. He tasted bile in his mouth and his legs felt like posts. Eyes still riveted on Clegall, he saw the big man roll over onto his side and realized that he wasn't dead.

The bullet hit him in the left thigh and must have passed through his leg. He was lying on his side holding the thigh with both hands when Tuck ran up to him. There wasn't much blood.

"Goddamn it, Clegall," Tuck said, gasping for breath, "I told you not to run, didn't I?" He was still keeping his distance. The car was stopped in the street about 40 feet away. There were a couple of civilians in it.

"Get over to the curb," Tuck ordered.

"I can't move," Clegall said, "my leg burns."

"Get over to the curb, Clegall, or I swear I'll pump one into your other leg!" Tuck was really agitated, obviously more frightened than Clegall was, and was beginning to get the shakes. Using his massive arms, Clegall dragged himself back to the curb in a sitting position, leaving a smear of blood on the black asphalt. Waving the car through, Tuck motioned the driver, a woman, to stop.

"Ma'am," he said, "will you notify the first MP that you see that I've got a prisoner here who was shot trying to escape?" Looking as frightened as Tuck, she nodded and moved on. Clegall had dropped right in front of her car. Tuck sat down cross legged in the street about ten feet away from him, his M1 across his knees and pointing in Clegall's general direction. He was propped up against the curb.

"Christ," Tuck said, more to himself than to Clegall, "I'm probably in a lot of trouble now, because I had to drop you! This isn't funny, goddamn it, I knew I was gonna' get into some kind of mess the first day they put me on this detail!" In the back of his mind, he was marveling at the shot he had made, nearly 400 yards and he had hit him in a non-fatal spot.

Tank Clegall was grinning. He didn't seem to care about his wounded leg, or anything else, for that matter. Tuck thought about Simmons, who had come to Tank's attention when he was in the outfit. Simmons was always running to the "Gedunk," the battalion's PX cafeteria. He'd bring back orders for anybody who'd pay him an extra quarter. Clegall picked up on it, and would give Simmons a big order, and when Simmons asked for the money, Tank would say, 'use yours.' Clegall took Simmons for about three or four bucks a week, and Simmons came to Tuck, asking him to talk to Tank.

"What the hell do you think I am, Crazy?" Tuck responded. "He's insane, for Christ's sake. What makes you think he'll do anything for me?"

"Well," Simmons said, "you helped me with those other guys."

"Yeah," Tuck said, "but those guys were just playing around with you, they didn't want any trouble. This guy's an animal, a sociopath. He's dangerous as hell, and the scuttlebutt is that he's got another .45 in his footlocker. Go see Sergeant Bird or the Swede, they'll talk to him, but I'm not going to, no way. I'm sorry."

Somehow, Tuck had become Simmons' caretaker, but he wouldn't help him with Clegall. Too risky. He had faced down a couple of black guys who were agitating Simmons, challenging them to a fight. They didn't want to fight.

Clegall was another matter. He enjoyed inflicting pain!

"You got a smoke?" he asked amiably. Tuck nodded, and took his butts out of his sock, lit two, and tossed one over to him. Tuck needed to do something to conceal his hand's involuntary trembling. Clegall sat there smoking and holding his thigh. Tuck could see Corpsmen coming from the infirmary now, jogging.

"Your leg hurt?" Tuck asked, "Don't you feel any pain?" It was like they were old buddies, now.

"Nah, it just burns a little, but it hurts to bend it," he said, "Tank is tough, you can't hurt Tank with one little bullet."

"What the fuck did you run for?" Tuck asked, "Where the hell did you think you were going? You couldn't get off the base, for crying out loud! I told you I would shoot."

"You shoulda' killed me," he said, still grinning, "I don't want to go to no fuckin' Portsmouth, no way. Too bad you're such a lousy shot." He showed no pain at all from the wounded leg.

"You think I want to go, in your place?" Tuck asked.

"I figured you'd be too scared to shoot," he said, dead serious, now. "You ain't hardly outta' P.I."

"That's where you figured wrong, Clegall," Tuck said, "I was too goddamned scared not to shoot!"

"Anyway, I ain't going to no Portsmouth now," he said.

"Well," Tuck said, "you'll go the hospital now, before you go anywhere else. I can't blame you, in a way. I know I couldn't take the beatings you've been getting." The two Corpsmen slowed to a walk, and Tuck stood up and swung the M1 their way.

"Keep your distance; nobody touches him until the MP's get here!" he said.

"He's got a serious wound. He needs treatment," the first Corpsman was indignant.

"Just the same," Tuck responded, "you aren't getting near him. Not until I turn him over to some MP's." They stayed put. In about five minutes a jeep rolled up with the two big Corporals from the brig. Lenny, the biggest one, got out and walked over to Tuck.

"Took off on you, eh?" he asked.

"Yeah," Tuck said, almost happy to see Lenny, "just outside the Infirmary."

"How many rounds did you use?" He asked.

"Two," Tuck responded, "I think I warned him four times. He coulda' stopped after the first one. It was a little long, but I know he heard it, and he saw me pulling down on him. He had plenty of chances to stop, that's for sure. He told me he was gonna' run, this morning."

The other Corporal drew his .45 automatic.

"Good shot, Private, must be about 300 yards," Corporal Lenny said, and then walking over to Clegall, he stood over him and addressed the Corpsman while they placed irons on Clegalls wrists. "You guys patch him up. We already called for an ambulance."

Tuck took Clegall's folder from the Corpsman who had picked it up on the way over. The ambulance arrived shortly thereafter, and they loaded Clegall into it with a temporary splint on his leg. Tuck rode back to the brig with the Corporals.

"What kind of trouble am I in?" Tuck asked. "Is this going to screw up my transfer?"

"You'll be all right," Corporal Lenny said, "you were under orders. You'd be in deep shit if he got away, though." The Master Sergeant was waiting for them at the brig door.

"Goddamn it, Private," the Master Sergeant shouted, "You must have Joe Blsphk[83] for a father! You've been nothin' but trouble since they sent you over here!"

"Sorry, Sarge," Tuck said, "but there's no way to stop that guy without shooting him. He was in my outfit. I've seen him pick up a whole 4-duece mortar, fully assembled.

The Master Sergeant just stared at Tuck for a moment. A 4.2 mortar weighed over 450 pounds when fully assembled. "He'd carry the barrel around like a goddamn walking stick," Tuck blabbered on, "everybody in the outfit was scared shitless of him; you could never tell what he'd do. He's crazy."

"Of course he's crazy! Anybody that ain't crazy when they get here is certifiable by the time they get out. That ain't the point, Private. The point is that I haven't had any incidents like this for damned near a year," he shouted, "now you're involved in two inside of a week!"

"Sorry, Sarge," Tuck said, following the big man inside.

"Fill in this statement," the Master Sergeant said, rifling through his desk drawers and finally tossing a form on the desk, "and describe the incident. Make sure you put in all the details, where, when, number of warnings issued, number of shots fired. Fill in the bottom with serial number, rank and outfit, and sign it. You savvy?"

Tuck sat down at the Corporal's desk and filled in the form. The Gunny looked it over when he was done, and signed under his signature. Tuck sat nervously while he reviewed the document, worried sick about the whole affair. It must have been obvious.

"You got nothing to worry about," he said, "Clegall's been here more than in his outfit over the past year. We know about him. Somebody's gonna kill the sonofabitch someday. It woulda' been okay if you had killed him! You were just lucky you didn't. You were shooting to kill, weren't you?"

"I shot at his legs, Sarge," Tuck said.

"Then you're either the best goddamn shot in the Crotch or the luckiest," he said, "and don't feel sorry for the bastard. He's tough as nails. If you hit him anywhere but in the leg, he'd still be running." Then after a pause, he asked, "feel like stayin' around here? I can get you on, here at the brig."

"No, thanks, Sarge," Tuck said, "I feel a little sick, if you want to know the truth. Shooting people in the back isn't my idea of fun."

"Yeah," the Gunny said, laughing, "You'll never forget your last days at Lejuene, I'll bet on it."

He leaned back in his swivel chair and stoked up a big cigar that was half-smoked and laying in the ashtray. This one was different, that's for sure; he takes orders like a priest. No fucking around. You tell this kid what to do and he does it, or busts his ass trying.

The Master Sergeant was a good judge of character. He had kicked around the Corps since he was sixteen. He had walked from his family's sharecropper cabin twenty seven miles to Atlanta, Georgia, and joined up. The Corps didn't care if he was white trash; he could walk, talk, shit and spit and a war was cooking up in Europe.

He'd been among the first marines to confront Japanese prior to World War II. He'd been a China hand, briefly served on the Panay before it was sunk by the Japanese, and was with Chesty Puller in Shanghai when he rounded up 22 Marines and demanded the release of 200 Chinese civilians the Japanese Army had taken.[84] He knew men. This kid had reacted like an old hand without even thinking. Twice. The Gunny wanted to keep him around.

"You've done a good job here," he said, "you can take the rest of the day off, and don't bother to report tomorrow. I don't know if we can take another day of your luck!"

"Thanks, Sarge," Tuck said. He popped the clip out of his Ml, cleared the round in the chamber and laid them on his desk. "Thanks a lot, I appreciate it."

"Yeah, sure," the Gunny said, shaking Tuck's hand, "now get the fuck out of here, and if I don't see ya' next week, good luck to ya'" The next day, Tuck lay around Casual Company, and then his transfer came in. He hustled immediately down to Regimental Headquarters to get the signature of the Sergeant Major of the Marine Corps, as required on the document. The Sergeant Major, grisly as the brig commander, but with more ribbons and hash marks, told Tuck that he had done a "good thing" and "not many grunts get this chance...make the best of it, son."

The word had gotten out to that he had decked a Technical Sergeant, and shot Clegall, and was surprised by the difference this made to the NCO's around the base.

Tuck wondered if he were making a mistake, striking for Navy. Life in the Corps had surely gotten interesting in the past few weeks. He had found out that he was pretty good marine. He was willing to bet that he could make Sergeant's stripes in no time if he stayed on with the Second Division.

31

NAPS

TUCK had more than a week to report to Bainbridge, Maryland, the site of the Naval Academy Preparatory School. He turned his M1 in to the armory, stopped by the gym and shook hands with the boxers, walked over to Special Weapons Company and said goodbye to the few friends that happened to be there on a Saturday morning.

Swede, on duty for the weekend, wished him good luck and shook a groggy Dale Bird out of the sack.

"I hope you're up to taking shit by the shovelfuls," Dale said, "cause you're going where they give it away free."

"Don't listen to a crazy Indian that's still drunk." Swede threw Dale his gabardines and they sat on a bunk watching him shave and get dressed.

"You'll be bangin' heads with a bunch of uppity white folks that think their shit don't stink, Si, so keep a crease in your pisscutter … and don't let it get to ya." Dale tapped his chest with his straight razor. "It ain't easy bein' a Tonto with a bunch of lone rangers. This here Indian knows that score."

"1 don't know if I want advice from somebody who goes surfin' in a '49 Chevy," Tuck said, "but I'll keep in mind what you said."

They insisted that Dale ride him into the bus station in Jacksonville, where he caught a Greyhound up to Raleigh and boarded the train to Philadelphia. It was Cholly's turn to pick him up at 30th Street Station.

Tuck had spent a solitary ride on the train, reflecting on what had happened to him since riding the same rails south.

At this point, he felt pretty good about managing a way out of Special Weapons Company. The life expectancy of a radioman in combat was 30 minutes. His self confidence was such that he was ready to face what was ahead, but he really hadn't begun to understand what he had accomplished.

Tuck had always been certain he would never go to college. Until Swede had mentioned it, he had never entertained a serious thought about the United States Naval Academy. He had heard of it, and knew about the Army-Navy game, played in Philadelphia every year since he could remember. He had seen a couple of Navy officers at Camp Lejuene, medical types, and thought that their uniforms looked funereal, compared to Marine Corps dress.

Tuck had no idea that the Academy received as many as 20,000 applicants each year and typically accepted only about 1200. Until 1943 they had seldom accepted anyone from the fleet. Looked down upon by the academia, USNA nevertheless required more study and academic discipline than nearly all of the big colleges, offering students fewer options to lessen their academic load through course selection. The institution offered a curriculum packed with engineering, math and physics courses, with a smattering of the classics and world history as well as seamanship, leadership and navigation. Everyone took the same track, with a few exceptions for extremely talented individuals.[85] If you got in, you were among the nation's top 10 percent.

Edie Maye was beside herself. She regaled Chip with the news several times each evening and probed Cholly about it.

"Look, Mom," Cholly said, "don't get your hopes up too high, that's a tough school down there. Tuck's gonna' have a tough time getting through it."

"He can do it! I know he can. He's smarter than he knows himself, you know." Edie Maye was flushed and excited each time she talked about it.

Tuck found her exuberance depressing. She had him an Admiral already and he hadn't even reported to the Prep School. He got together with some high school buddies and spent each evening getting as drunk as he could, thinking about nothing but the impossible prospect of finding a willing female companion in any of the bars they frequented.

He sat down with Chip one morning and interrupted his Hopalong Cassidy TV show.

"Granddad, I shot a man two weeks ago; he was trying to escape from the brig."

Chip placed his hand on Tuck's knee. He had retrained himself enough to make his speech understood.

"Is he dead?" Chip asked.

"No, I hit him in the leg, but it was only luck. I was shooting to kill, under orders." Tuck's subconscious had been working overtime ever since Clegall ran.

"You're a marine now, Pup," Chip squeezed Tuck's knee, "you got to do what's right. It's the only way. Don't worry about it, hear?"

"It scared me, Grandpop. I didn't like doing it..." Tuck said, squeezing back tears of self-pity.

"I know, Pup." Chip settled back in the rocker and closed his eyes. Although he couldn't express it, his heart had been lifted by the incredible news about Tuck. It was Edie Maye that had done it, he thought. She raised this one straight as an arrow in spite of the ass she had married and all that they had gone through. He only hoped that Tuck could see the opportunity for what it was.

Cholly drove Tuck the ninety miles south to Bainbridge the following Sunday and he strode through the Main Gate of Bainbridge Naval Training Center with duffel bag on his shoulder. The base, layered into rolling Maryland hills and tucked onto the peninsula formed by the Susquehanna and Elk Rivers at the head of Chesapeake Bay, was awash with sailors as they formed up for midday lunch. Nearly 18,000 of them in neat ranks filled every street.[86]

Tome Hall was the centerpiece of the The Naval Academy Preparatory School, which is the Navy's fourth oldest school; only the Naval War College, the Naval Postgraduate School, and the Naval Academy are older. In 1918, the Secretary of the Navy signed a provision that sailors from the fleet be eligible for the Academy. As Undersecretary of the Navy Franklin D. Roosevelt allowed for a school to prepare Sailors and Marines for entry to USNA. In early 1943, as President, Roosevelt acquired the location in Perryville and created the United States Naval Training Center, Bainbridge, with NAPS its centerpiece above the Susquehanna River. In August 1974, NAPS returned to its permanent home in Newport, RI.

As Tuck skirted the formations on his way to the school barracks he ignored the catcalls and remarks from the ranks, "Looky, another fuckin' jarhead … fresh meat!" By the time he had checked in with the school's Officer of the Day, Tuck had heard enough to convince him that life was going to interesting, to say the least.

Tuck found a room with another new marine, a tall cowboy from Kansas[87]. The other two occupants were two white hats with hash marks. He picked the room because the OOD told him that they were football players. The Cowboy, Jack Phillips, was the stereotyped tall, dark and handsome westerner, with movie star looks and easy charm that disguised his ruggedness and seriousness of purpose. Tuck soon discovered that he was a magnet for good looking women, and even in the leanest environment for finding a date, Jack usually ended up with not only the prettiest, but also the richest available girl.

Tuck had settled in at the school and immediately began to appreciate the Marine Corps more each day. The school was populated by all branches of the service, and as far as Tuck could see, none of them were as squared away as the marines enrolled there.

Within a few days, Tuck was totally engrossed in a routine of classes, football practice and study. By the end of his second month, the school was buzzing about their newest student.

Half of the 150 sailors, marines, soldiers and Coast Guardsmen at the United States Naval Academy Preparatory School were afraid of him, and the remaining half resented Richard because he was a jock. The word was out when the swarthy Hawaiian-Filipino marine Corporal settled in; special privileges, recruited for the Navy football team.[88]

It didn't help when he didn't come out for NAPS team, being regularly crushed each week by the small college schedule it played. He stashed his gear on the lower floor of Tuck's barracks, in the only room to have only one occupant.

Richard Dagampat was five-foot eight inches and 185 pounds. His broad flat nose, deep set eyes, high cheekbones and full lips gave him an awesome appearance. He looked like a very serious person, if not smiling. Even marine green trousers with their full cut legs were tight on his huge thighs and calves.

About halfway through the football season, Tuck was in the barracks corridor, and heard some rather intricate ukulele plucking coming from one of the rooms. Opening the door, which was slightly ajar, he stood for a moment watching Richard play. He was sitting on his desk in a pair of scivvies.

"How ya' doin?" Tuck asked. He didn't look particularly menacing, strumming a ukulele. He looked up and put the ukulele down.

"All right," he said, "but I'm not used to this cold."

"Yeah," Tuck said, "but it gets a lot colder in the winter around here."

"I ain't talkin' about temperature, Man," he said, "I'm talking about the guys in this here school!"

"Yeah," Tuck said, "I know what you mean. The scuttlebutt's out that you won't play with us, that's what's bothering some of them."

"No fuckin' way," he said, "I've got me a shot at Navy, and I don't want to blow it. Anyway, Coach Hardin told me I'd better not, if I blow out a knee, it's back to the FMF."

"Hey, Man," Tuck said, "you've got your reasons, and they're none of my business." He introduced himself, "Everybody calls me Si."

"Shit, Man," he said, "that's a Jewish name, and you're some kind of Italian. You're the quarterback, aren't you?"

"I don't know what the hell I am," Tuck said, "except a Corporal in the USMC, I'm a mongrel just like you, I guess, and yeah, I'm the quarterback."

"You got it," he said, "my Mom's a pure Hawaiian, six foot five inches, and my dad's mostly Filipino and five-four. Nobody messes with Mama!"

They talked for a while about previous duty stations. Richard related that he was one of four brothers and grew up in a Los Angeles barrio. He was All-City in football, basketball and track. Two weeks later, he moved his gear into a room with Flesner, Sklenar and Tuck, all marines. They installed a sign over the door, "NCO Quarters." Flesner was a Sergeant with one hash mark, and except for one other Sergeant, a Texan and former D.I., their room outranked the whole school. Phillips, a tackle on the team, moved in with two other linemen.

Richard and Tuck became fast friends, taking liberty together and teaching each other routines on the uke. Tuck had a baritone ukulele that he had picked up in a North Carolina pawn shop. Edie Maye had taught him to play on her banjo uke. They helped each other with the school work, and pulled liberties together.

Cruising bars in Maryland and Delaware was interesting to say the least, since Richard's appearance was a riddle for a lot of the places they walked into. He was totally confused by the east.

"Shit," he said, "I got off the bus in Atlanta and went to get a drink. One fountain said 'white only' and the other, 'colored only.' I didn't know where to drink, or to shit, since I'm not either!"

When they ran into the same problem in Maryland and Virginia towns, they told everyone that Richard was Hawaiian, the son of Duke Kehanamoka, and of the royal family. The bullshit usually worked. Tuck invited him home every time he took off for Jersey, but Richard usually declined, hanging around the barracks for the weekend.

The United States Naval Preparatory School at Bainbridge, Maryland, was a completely new environment for Tuck. Bainbridge, itself, was a Navy specialty schools camp and accommodated NAPS as well. There were thousands of sailors at Bainbridge, and Tuck soon learned that he was one of the seventy-four marines stationed there.

The NAPS students were housed in the last two barracks far up a hill towards the west end of the base. Following the street that ran past their barracks to the west, the base changed dramatically as the vestiges of the old Tome School campus at the top of the hill were actually the centerpiece of the Navy schools complex.

NAPS was housed in what was once an expensive boarding school for sons of rich fathers, the Tome School for boys. Built in French Renaissance style, the campus featured winding paved streets with brick sidewalks and overhanging sycamores, a parade ground and athletic fields and two streets of lovely "Presidents" homes built previously for students. Absconded by the Bainbridge brass as Officer's quarters, they formed one side of the school's quadrangle and faced Tome Hall, the principle school building.

To the east, a beautiful nine hole golf course meandered around the back of the campus, and to the north, beyond the parade ground, a ridge that dropped away 300 feet to the Susquehanna River. Tucked into the convolutions of that ridge was a tiny town, Port Deposit, which looked more like a village in the European Alps.

Classes were held in Tome Hall, the main building which featured a golden dome nearly 100 feet high, twin marble staircases in its lobby leading to the second floor auditorium, intricately patterned parquet floors in the large classrooms, and an atmosphere of rich tradition. The school was appropriately called "Little Navy" throughout the fleet.

Their routine consisted of a minimum of military activity. They stood watches at the school and in the barracks, and held morning formations, but other than that, went to class and studied and participated in the athletic programs.

The curriculum included a pressurized review of high school subjects, interlaced with practice sessions with previous CEEB exams. The school even offered a social calendar. A ball on the Marine Corps birthday offered the opportunity to wear dress blues, and there were several other formal dances attended by young ladies from Goucher College and other small schools nearby.

Making NAPS brought pressure of a kind Tuck had never experienced before. As far as Edie Maye was concerned, he was already the Brigade Commander of the graduating class at Navy. It lead to a lot of fights when Tuck was at home on weekend liberties.

"Jesus Christ, Mom," Tuck said, "I've still got to pass the test! This test isn't easy, and I'm not the brightest guy in the world. It's the College Entrance Examination Boards - CEEB test."[89]

"You'll do it easy," Edie Maye said, "I know you will, and none of these snobs can turn their noses up to us, anymore."

"Look, Mom, I have to study all the time," Tuck responded, "just to hold my own with these guys. A lot of them have already been to college, just to warm up for NAPS and the test. It's not guaranteed!"

"But you'll do it," she beamed, "I know you will."

Every time she launched into this, Tuck cringed. He didn't feel very secure with his studies, and the curriculum at NAPS was geared to the test. He remembered Cmdr. Jones, standing next to his desk in his previous Tuesday's math class, asking,

"Good lord, son, don't you know how to clear a polynomial fraction?"

"Mom, for Christ Sake," he said, "they've got every test ever given by Navy at the school, and that's what we study a lot of the time."

"That's why I know you can do it," she said.

"But don't you see?" Tuck asked, "That being able to pass the test, even if I'm lucky enough to do that doesn't mean I can do the work at the Academy."

"They can't look down on us," she said, "anymore." She just couldn't fathom that something could go wrong, and the more she harped on it, the more depressed and angry Tuck got about it.

"Look, Mom, there's a guy at school from Morrisville named Walsh, he's failed the goddamn test twice already. If he fails this year, he's washed out, back to the fleet."

"But if you have a problem," she said, "then you can take it next year again."

"He's not a marine, Mom," Tuck said, "he's a Navy Corpsman, and he helps out at the base hospital, that's why he's been able to hang around. I'll be back at Lejuene so quick that it'll make your head spin, if I miss on the test. That's the way the Corps works."

Tuck was home on a long weekend, and Cholly agreed to drive him back to the base, having nothing else to do on a Sunday afternoon. It was a two-hour drive down routes U.S. 40 and 13 on Maryland's Eastern Shore.

"You ever meet a guy named 'One-Eye'?" Cholly asked.

"Sure," Tuck said, "One-Eye Irving, from Atlantic City. I was with the old man one time in a diner, down the shore somewhere, Somers Point, I think." Tuck remembered the ugly scar the man carried on his face. He asked Cholly what brought him up.

"I met him a couple of years ago. He's some kind of character, isn't he?" he said rhetorically. "I'd been driving the old man around the pines and down the shore about three, four days a week that summer."

"You ever meet an old man named Manny?" Cholly asked.

"No," Tuck said, "look, the old man and I haven't exactly been bunk buddies over the past few years."

"Yeah, I know," Cholly said. After a long pause, he continued, "I drove him down in the pines one day, way down in South Jersey somewhere around Vineland or Millville. I couldn't find the place again if I had to. Anyway, we're running around on these dirt roads, and we come up to this place with a big iron gate, right out in the middle of the woods. We go in, and here's this big Mansion, stuck out in the middle of the pines, and dad goes in and talks to this old guy, Manny.

"Then this One-Eye comes out and asks me if I shoot pool, and takes me inside the place, and I'm shooting eight-ball with these guys and having a few beers for a couple of hours. This place has two tournament tables and a full bar in the library. Some place, like a palace inside. Finally, the old man comes in and we take off.

"So, for the next three or four weeks, I'm driving the old man all over the Jersey Shore. He's got these maps of all the towns, from Wildwood to Asbury Park, and we go to every town and rent space for casinos."

"Like Red Men's Hall?" Tuck asked.

"Well," Cholly said, "a lot of the places are real small, but in a couple of towns, we got the Moose lodge hall, a couple of bigger places.

"You mean, one or two room casinos, like the whorehouse he put me in, in North Wildwood?" Tuck told Cholly the story about Rusty and the prostitutes. Cholly said,

"Yeah, little casinos, like that..." He laughed about it, and continued,

"Every town we hit, the old man pays off the cops. He's got this book that Manny gave him, and calls them up before we get there, and they meet us and have a drink or coffee and they get paid off. Some of 'em have already got the places picked out for us. It's a goddamn riot. I mean the old man's got an envelope with their name on it. It's like a milk delivery route. Sometimes it's the Police Chief or the Mayor, but there's a name for every town."

"Jesus," Tuck said, "you mean they're running games all over the shore?"

"Not quite," Cholly said, "but it was all supposed to start in the fall of '53, after the election. The old man, he was going down to each place and telling them how to set up the tables and stuff. He's had about fifty guys lined up to run the games."

"Was Tony in on it?" Tuck asked.

"Yeah, Tony and Johnny both," Cholly said, "and this One-Eye Irving from Atlantic City and Moe Schwarz some guys from North Jersey. I didn't know who they were, but they were a mean looking bunch of characters."

"Jesus Christ," Tuck said, "I hope nobody finds out about this. I've got an appointment to the Naval Academy if I pass the test in May. I've got to pass an FBI investigation, too. He could fuck the whole thing up, as usual. Did you say Moe Schwarz? The old guy that ran that little restaurant next to the Pawn Shop?"

"Yeah," Cholly said, "the old man said the whole State was in on it, from the Governor on down. Moe's one of the guys from the old days in Atlantic City. He wouldn't miss this under any circumstances! All the politicians were all gettin' a cut of the action. Everybody was paid off. He said nothin' could go wrong this time, 'cause everybody's in on the take. The cops were treating us like we were some kind of rich investors."

"Get out. How the hell could the Governor of New Jersey have been in on it?" Tuck asked, "He's always in the papers against gambling, and I think that's one of the things he ran on, 'Clean up New Jersey with Driscoll,' something like that."

"Yeah," Cholly said, "but he wasn't gonna' get re-elected. They had the election fixed, and this other guy, Troast, the Union guy that built the Turnpike, he's all paid off. He's going to let them operate the places as long as he gets his. It's all fixed. It's a boat race."[90]

"What?" Tuck asked, and, thinking to himself,

"Forget the Naval Academy, you dumb ass. Either way, the FBI is going to find out about this, and Tuck will never see the front door of USNA with this stuff in his 501 file."

"A boat race, a fixed race," Cholly said.

"Was he payin' you for all this driving?" Tuck asked.

Christ! he thought, *Now he's pulling Cholly into it, and sooner or later, he'll have him in trouble, too.*

"Yeah, he filled up the car with gas and he gave me forty or fifty bucks every time I took him down there," Cholly said, "I don't give a shit what he's doing. He wanted me to run one of the places, but I said no, I'm still looking for a good job in Holly or around there. I'm running his jewelry store for him, but right now I'm still looking around."

"If I were you," I wouldn't even run his fucking jewelry store," Tuck said, "you don't owe him anything."

"Yeah, I know," Cholly said, "but what are you gonna' do? He is our old man." He punched Tuck on the shoulder and popped his pisscutter from his head into his lap.

"You couldn't prove it by me," Tuck said.

"Don't worry about it," he said, "just get that appointment."

Years later, Sal confirmed the whole story for Tuck. He was back in New Jersey for treatment of his cancer, and in a talking mood, so Tuck just asked him outright.

"Dad, Cholly told me once that you had the election fixed in Jersey, for the Governor's race," Tuck said.

"You knew about that?" Sal asked.

"Well, I don't know the whole story, just a little that Cholly told me one time," Tuck said.

"It's true," he said, "Sam and the Boys had everybody in the State paid off or on the take for the '52 election. It was a big deal; we had forty-five places set up, from Wildwood to Asbury Park, and every politician down the shore and half of 'em in Trenton and Newark were in on it. The boys had a big slush fund in Trenton to pay off the politicians. We paid off all the cops, like a big payday. Cholly drove for me while I did it. Did he tell you that? You were still in high school."

"Yeah, well, he told me he was driving you around, because of some business at the shore," Tuck said.

"I brought all the furniture in from Vegas," Sal continued. "The election was fixed for Driscoll to get beat, and the new guy, Troast; he wasn't going to bother us. He was gonna' look the other way. I ladled out close to 150 grand that summer."

"Was he in on it?" Tuck asked, "Was he paid off, too?"

"Oh," he said, "I don't know about that, but he was gonna' let everything happen right on schedule. He's the guy that built the New Jersey Turnpike, and he knew some of the boys through the labor unions. You know that project was done in record time-no troubles with Unions; that was no accident. So, we were going to open all those clubs the day after the election. What do the lawyers call it? Quid pro quo or something? The next day, the Jersey shore would've been wide open, just like Atlantic City in the old days."[91]

Paul L. Troast, left, was going to "look the other way" regarding illegal gaming at the New Jersey shore according to Sal, if elected Governor in 1953. Robert B. Meyner, right, prevailed when the 6th district, traditionally Republican, elected a Democrat by only 2000 votes, triggering a Democratic victory in the State that Eisenhower had swept in the 1952 presidential election. Troast, Chairman of the NJ Turnpike Commission wrote NY Governor Tom Dewey requesting leniency for his friend, Joseph Fay, a convicted racketeer. Troast's request was made big news, and coupled with an inept campaign led the way to a sound thumping at the polls, destroying the mob's plans for a gambling renaissance at the New Jersey shore. Photos courtesy of The New York Mirror and meyneralum.lafayette.com

"Forty-five places?" Tuck asked, just beginning to realize the scale of the operation.

"Yeah," Sal said, "I had them all set up, all the furniture in place, food and liquor concessions lined up, ladies for each place, all the box and pit men hired, everything ready to go."

"What happened, then?" Tuck asked, "Because I know you didn't open up like you wanted to."

"It was some kind of fluke," Sal said, "one of those Districts in South Jersey went the wrong way and swung the election, and then our guy didn't even get elected. I mean, this District, I think it was always solid Republican, so nobody worked on it, figuring it was no problem, and goddamn if it didn't go the wrong way, and that was the whole deal! It was just a few thousand votes, but the election was real close. All the payoffs in the other Districts didn't help."

"And you got caught, right?" Tuck asked.

"Yeah, as usual, all the politicians, all of the sudden they don't know nothin' and they're pointing the fingers at us," he said, "so we all get indicted for Aiding and Abetting."

"What's that, Aiding and Abetting?" Tuck asked.

"That's what they try to get you on," he said, "Aiding and abetting a felony, or gambling. But they couldn't make it stick, or didn't want to, because I had records of everybody I paid money to as well as witnesses, and so did the guys in north Jersey, who had a guy in the Governor's office and if they took us to trial, we were gonna' lay them all out. Heads woulda' rolled from Newark to Trenton, so they changed their minds, and I ended up with some kind of misdemeanor charge and some parole again.

"One Eye Irving, he almost got sent up anyway. He tells the Judge to go fuck himself right in the Courtroom. He says to the Judge, 'You bastard, you were gettin' yours, too,' and the Judge really gets mad. Because he *was* getting his, just like all the rest. Politicians, they're nothin' but crooks, and they ain't even honest crooks, if you know what I mean. Sam always said, *'Those bastards just won't stay fixed!'.*"

"Yeah," Tuck said, "I know what you mean."

After the Christmas holiday, Tuck was in math class and Commander Jones, the instructor, called him forward to his desk.

"Corporal," he said, "I've been given a message that you are to report to the Commandant's Office immediately.

Take your gear with you, here's your pass."

"Aye, aye, Sir," Tuck responded, wondering what the problem could be. Tuck was a squad leader, quarterback of the football team and had been getting straight 3.2's in all of his school work, but you didn't get called to the NAPCOM's office for just doing well.

The Commandant was a Lieutenant Commander, a veteran of Iwo Jima. Tuck had never talked to a man of such rank before, and now he was standing at attention in his office.

"At ease, Corporal," he said, "I have your record before me, and it appears that you are doing well here. How do you like the school?"

"I like it very much, Sir," Tuck responded.

"I see that you did well in the Second Marines when you were there, also. Expert marksman, you played football and made an early jump to Corporal. Your CO recommended you highly. Any comments?" He asked.

"I was the headquarters' radioman, Sir, so we got to know each other, so to speak."

"What is your intention for the Naval Academy, son?" he asked, continuing to leaf through Tuck's 501 personnel file.

"Marine Aviation, Sir," Tuck said, "I want to be a carrier pilot."

"You like the Marine Corps, then?" he asked.

"Begging the Captain's pardon, Sir, it's the best." Tuck responded.

"You wouldn't have been involved with the Marine Corps flag that the Perryville Hook and Ladder Company had to remove from the hall, would you?" he asked.

So that's it, Tuck thought. On the Marine Corps birthday, November tenth, five unidentified marines had climbed the dome of Tomb hall in a rainstorm and raised the marine Ensign there. They had to call in a hook and ladder to get it down the following day.

"No comment, Sir," Tuck answered, stifling a grin.

"Son," he said, "I have to ask you this. Do you know anything about this affair, or who this person is?" He handed Tuck a newspaper clipping. The headline read, "GAMBLING CHARGES DROPPED," and someone had circled a list of names. Sal's was included. It was on the front page of a Maryland newspaper, the Baltimore Sun.

Tuck's heart skipped a beat as he scanned the article. The color drained from his face and for a second he felt a little lightheaded. The Commander was clearly in focus, yet Tuck sensed that he was hundreds of yards away, beyond his reach.

"Sir, this, ah, this is my Father listed here," Tuck stammered, figuring it was all over, "but he doesn't live with us, and I don't know him very well. I haven't seen him in over a year, and I don't like him much when I do see him. That's all I can say, Sir. He gets in a lot of trouble."

"I see," the Captain said, "is he aware that you're striking for the Academy?" Tuck was hearing the words clearly, but they sounded as though the Captain was talking in slow motion.

"I can't say, Sir," Tuck responded, "but..."

"But, what, Mister?" the Commander said, "Finish your sentence."

"I don't think it would make much difference to him if he knew, Sir," Tuck said.

"I see," the Commander Thompson said. He reached for the clipping and sat back in his chair and stared at Tuck, now rigidly at attention. When the silence became unbearable, Tuck mustered his courage and spoke out.

"Am I going to be able to stay on, Sir?" he asked, fearing the worst. Even if he did stay, he realized that the old man would now be common knowledge.

The Officers were like a bunch of fucking old women when it came to gossip! Tuck figured he'd end up with Sergeant's stripes and a bus ticket back to Camp Lejuene, if he was lucky. Tuck's face was now flushed. He felt totally humiliated and embarrassed.

"Young man," the Commander said, "none of us has the luxury of choosing our relatives. For most people that is never a problem, but for some, it's a serious burden. This is your record that I'm holding here, the results of your efforts and your sweat, and no one else can change that. You keep up the good work, Corporal, and if you have any problems, my door is open to you." As he spoke, he shuffled the papers and replaced them into the personnel folder. Tuck noticed that he put the clipping back into the folder, also.

"You're dismissed," he said.

"Thank you, Sir," Tuck responded, saluting, and after doing a precise about face, marched out of his office. Tuck had a queasy feeling in his stomach for the rest of the day.

Son of a bitch, this is my chance and he's going to fuck it up for me. Tuck's mind raced and he could feel the anger and frustration throughout his entire body.

When he got back to quarters, his roommates, Ted, Tom, and Richard, asked what had happened with the Commandant. The word was out that Tuck had been called down. The last guy who was called down packed his duffel bag and went back to the fleet the following day.

"He had a fucking clipping from a newspaper. My old man's on parole again for some goddamn gambling thing up in Jersey," Tuck said. "It was all in the paper." He was embarrassed by the tears welling up in his eyes.

"Those bastards," Tom said, "did you tell him your old man's totally fucked up?"

"Well," Tuck said, "I tried to, but I think I might be a short-timer as of today."

"Like hell," Ted said, "Look at Greg Boyington, for crying out loud. His old man is a drunk and has a dishonorable from the Corps, and they don't give Pappy any shit."

"Yeah," Tuck said, "but his old man was an ace with the Flying Tigers and he holds the Medal of Honor. His appointment's guaranteed by law. My Old Man's a goddamn draft evader and an ex-con."

Tuck heard nothing further from the Commandant's office, and after a week or so of worry, he hoped that the incident was buried and forgotten. Tuck often brought some of his buddies home on weekends to South Jersey, to Edie Maye's delight. She would rise on a Saturday morning to find a half dozen marines asleep in various parts of the house.

Banging a fry pan with a heavy spoon, she'd roust them out like a drill instructor, collect a bunch of bills from everyone and send someone off to Southwick's Deli for five or six dozen eggs, lots of bacon, coffee and bread.

Within fifteen minutes she would have a breakfast feast organized and would be trading insults with the whole group. Sklenar, the big Swede from Minnesota, was particularly taken with Edie Maye. Picking her up as though she were a feather, he would turn to his audience and say,

"Boys, hold off the Golden Guinea while Edie and I go topside for some Rand R."

Edie Maye flushed and laughing like a teenager, would then swat him and demand to be put down. When they were piling out the door to return to base, Edie Maye would invariably pinch Sklenar on the butt.

"Take care of my little boy, Tom," she would say, "or I'll track down your Swedish mother and you'll be sorry."

"Hell, Edie Maye," Tom answered, "that little boy of yours is one ornery sonofabitch. He's been taking care of us for a year now."

Richard taught Tuck that year how the game of football ought to be played. They talked about it incessantly, and Tuck came to realize that attitude was a great part of the game. Richard punctuated his verbal lessons with occasional physical examples, subtle little events that rammed home his philosophy; think that you're the meanest guy on the field, believe it and relax, the rest will follow.

Tuck's play had improved steadily under Richard's influence. One game in particular gave him a preview of big-time college football, and subconsciously made up his mind regarding playing at Navy, if he were lucky enough to win the appointment. On a Saturday morning, the team loaded on the Bainbridge Commodore's bus, borrowed for their biggest game of the year; Anacostia Naval Receiving Station.

Anacostia was a Naval Station with over several thousand enlisted men and hundreds of Naval Aviation Cadets to draw a team from.[92] They played in the Inter Service League with the Bainbridge Commodores, Quantico Marines, Fort Dix and the other big teams. These teams were nearly professional, staffed from the ranks of college players who had been previously deferred and then drafted into the Service after playing college football.

Bobby Williams was the quarterback of the Bainbridge Commodores, and many of the teams had ex-pros and college All-Americans as players. Tuck and some of his teammates occasionally were invited to mess on the Commodores training table. Like most of Little Navy's games, the Anacostia game was an incredible mismatch, a Tony Galento vs. Joe Louis "bum of the month" affair for the Anacostia team.

NAPS won the toss and took the ball. From his position at the thirty yard line, Tuck picked out the biggest lineman on their team, a brute who must have weighed 275 pounds. Everyone on the field had made note of his presence. It was obvious that he had played a lot of ball, and he looked mean as hell.

Might as well start there, Tuck thought, still harboring anger and frustration with Sal's intrusion.

Tuck cut blocked him from the side at mid field, taking his foot in his ribs. The monster sailed about five yards before he hit the ground like a derailed freight, and when he got up, he said, "Pretty cute, you little mother-fucker. I'm gonna' bust your ass up!"

Tuck couldn't respond because his ribs hurt so badly, and he was having trouble getting his breath. It turned out that he was their defensive left tackle, and Tuck figured he'd take the game to him. For three quarters, Tuck ran options to his right side. Every time the big fellow had a shot at Tuck, he took it on his left thigh and pitched out to Erickson, the halfback.

Tuck scampered out of his grasp a half dozen times and completed sixteen of eighteen passes, one for a touchdown. Near the end of the third quarter, Little Navy was leading 6-0, and the Anacostia coach and team were frantic on their sideline.

Dropping back for another pass in the third quarter, Tuck failed to elude the monster. He drove into his Tuck's chest with his helmet, and when Tuck was pancaked, his head bounced off the frozen ground. Leaping to his feet, his antagonist did a little dance, his hands above his head.

"I finally got the little mother-fucker!" he shouted.

Tuck got up, walked to the huddle and called the next play, then dropped to his knees in a state of semi-consciousness. He spent the fourth quarter lying unconscious in the locker room, and when the team filed in and shook him awake, they told him the final score was 14-6, a major showing by Little Navy and nearly an upset!

By the time the bus got back to Bainbridge the next day, Tuck's left thigh had turned black and was nearly thirty inches in circumference. They had to cut off his best greens at the Infirmary.

"You've got a real nasty blood clot in that leg, Corporal." the Doctor said, "We're going to have to draw it off."

"What do you mean, draw it off?" Tuck asked weakly. His leg hurt so badly that he would have entertained the idea of cutting it off. It had turned crimson everywhere except directly on top of the thigh, where it was an ugly black from hip to knee.

"I'm sending a technician in here to get some of that blood out," he said, "it's going to be painful, but you could be in a lot of trouble if we don't do this!"

Tuck let his head fall back on the pillow. The Corpsman showed up later with a tray full of huge hypodermic needles, which he then used to probe into his leg and draw off black vials of blood. Tuck passed out four times during the affair and heard himself talking in tongues, but the next day a lot of the pain was gone.

Released after a week, the pain and discoloration had subsided, but the leg remained swollen and stiff, and Tuck couldn't bend his knee or wear his regular uniform or left shoe until the season was nearly over, six weeks later.

The following week, Cholly brought Edie Maye down to the school to watch Tuck play. It was the first game of Tuck's that she ever attended, and they had to sit in the stands with his stiff leg and watch the team hand Western Maryland Freshmen a beating, 33 - 2.

Tuck got in shape again by going out for the wrestling team. The team only had about four matches, and being completely ignorant of the sport, he only qualified to wrestle in one match, with the Navy plebes, where he was decisioned 2-0.

In the spring, Richard talked him into going out for track. Being too slow to even compete in running events, Tuck tried throwing the javelin, but never was able to throw well enough to even place. Track was a joy, however, because Richard was on the team, in fact; he was the team.

Richard high-jumped and long jumped in the field events and ran the 100 yard and 220 yard dashes and the quarter mile. In one match, he scored 28 of the team's 30 points. They called him Little Navy's Jim Thorpe.

"You should go out, Si," Richard said, trying to talk him into going out for Navy football when they made it to the Academy, "you're as good as a lot of these guys they go after, Man."

"Shit, Richard," Tuck said, "they don't give you any special privileges down there, you know, for playing football. I'm afraid that I'll mess up my studies, and I don't know if I can take the beating."

"Look, Man," he said, "if I can do it, you can do it. Don't be putting yourself down all the time. The Coaches, they know who you are. You made a reputation with that Anacostia game." Richard had visited twice already this season with Navy coaches Eddie Erdlatz and Wayne Hardin.

"Ah, I don't know," Tuck said, "we still got to pass the test to get in there, and don't forget, I couldn't walk for nearly three weeks after that game, and it cost me in grades, too. I don't want to think about it 'till I have to."

Home for a weekend, Tuck stopped over to the Washington House Hotel on a Sunday afternoon to have a few beers and shoot some pool, before returning to NAPS. Cholly was tending bar. Tuck sat down at the bar, having just lost a game.

"You see that guy at the end of the bar?" Cholly asked, "In the brown jacket."

"Yeah," Tuck said, wondering who the fellow was. He was middle aged, and dressed in dungarees with cowboy boots.

"The old man introduced him to me," Cholly said, "he comes in here about once every two weeks, and every time he's here, he gives me the winner of a race at the (Garden State) track!"

"What do you mean?" Tuck asked, "Is he one of those handicapper guys?"

"No, no," Cholly said, "he doesn't give me the name of a horse that he *thinks* will win; he gives me the name of the actual winner, two or three days in advance."[93]

"Get out," Tuck said, "how can he know who the winner will be? He's just giving you lucky picks, that's all."

"No way," he said, "this guy and some of the old man's friends, they're fixing races down at the track. He gives me the boat races, and the horse that's gonna win! Sometimes he gives me horses at Monmouth and other tracks, too, but I don't feel like driving all over the state."

Tuck knew nothing about the track, but he could see that Cholly was serious.

"How can they fix races?" he asked, "don't some of those races have ten or eleven horses in them?"

"Listen," Cholly said, "I've made about four thousand dollars in the three months he's been coming in here. I'm telling you that they fix certain races, and he knows which ones, and who the winner is going to be."

"But how can they do that?" Tuck asked, naively.

"They get the jocks in on it," Cholly said, "and then they make it happen. They don't need all the riders in a race, because some of 'em are riding nags that wouldn't win anyway. They just need the right ones on the right horses in the right race, and they (the jockeys) do the rest!"

"Is the old man in on this?" Tuck asked, fearing the worst, "I mean, is he involved in it, or did he just know about it? He's on parole, isn't he, for that other thing?"

"I don't know," Cholly said, "I don't ask him what he's involved in. He is on some kind of parole, though. This guy came down to the jewelry store a couple of times in the summer, and he and the old man went out. Now he stops in here, and gives me the horse and the race, and I go down to the track on that day and put in a bet for the old man, and a couple for myself."

"Jesus!" Tuck asked, "Aren't you afraid you'll get in trouble?"

"What trouble?" Cholly asked, "Guys come in here and give me tips all the time. As far as I'm concerned, he's just another guy giving me tips; like a lot of other customers. You want to make some money?"

"No way, I don't know anything about horses or tracks and you know I don't gamble on anything." Somehow, Tuck thought that this information would eventually result in some kind of problem for him. Cholly returned from taking care of some customers.

"You might as well take advantage of it," he said, "you're always short of dough, and you always need some, in the service."

"Forget it," Tuck said, "I don't want anything to do with that kind of stuff, with anything the old man's mixed up with. You know that thing with the casinos down the shore? A clipping about that showed up in my 501 file, the Commandant called me in on it, and asked me what I knew about it."

"No shit!" Cholly asked, "Those bastards, what does it have to do with what you're doing down there? What did you tell 'em?"

"I told him what I'm telling you." Tuck said, laughing, "That our old man is a shit head, and there's not much that I can do about it; that's just about what I told him."

"You're too tough on dad," Cholly said, "He doesn't mean any harm to us. He is what he is, that's all. You can't change it so you might as well accept it."

"I've accepted it all right," Tuck said, "but I don't have to like it, and I don't. What you do is your own business, but I just can't cozy up to the bastard, that's all."

"Christ!" he said, "Mom doesn't hate him. Why should you?"

"I don't understand Mom either, or you, for that matter." Tuck said, realizing that this was a rare opportunity. Cholly seldom talked about personal matters. He continued.

"The son of a bitch has shit on all of us for all of our lives, especially you! And Sis, she thinks he's some kind of All-American father. And you sound like you're workin' with him in anything he wants you to, next thing you know, you'll be in some kind of mob, or something. It doesn't make sense to me!"

"You're too much of a square shooter," Cholly said, "like Mom. That's your problem. Ease up, for Christ's sake, everybody makes mistakes. As for me, I do what I want; I couldn't be in any mob anyway."

"You're probably right," Tuck said, "the only problem is, is that everything he does, it ends up in our laps, one way or another, and everybody assumes 'like father, like son'."

Tuck reflected on his brother's statement for a minute, he had never seen him so animated and willing to talk about the old man.

"What do you mean; you couldn't be in any mob?" Tuck assumed that Cholly was making a judgmental statement about some of the old man's friends.

"Because I'm just like you," Cholly said, "only half."

"Half what?" Tuck asked, with a laugh. "Half-assed? What the hell are you talking about?"

"Sicilian, half Sicilian ain't good enough; you've got to be 100 percent, like the old man. You're just rattled because the Commandant found that clipping in the paper, that's all," he said."

"That's enough, isn't it?" Tuck asked, "That means I can't be just like everybody else. It means I've got to be better than everybody else, and I can't give anybody an excuse to get on my case, otherwise, they've got an excuse to get rid of me."

"You're exaggerating," Cholly said, "The Commandant told you that you couldn't choose your relatives, he's not holding it against you."

"Then why didn't he tear up the fucking clipping," Tuck asked, "instead of putting it back in my file?"

It seemed to Tuck that he couldn't simplify his life. Everything he was working towards in the Service seemed to somehow be tainted by Sal's activities. Every small accomplishment he made seemed to take a back seat to something else he learned about the old man. Everything Sal did caused him more worry, since it was always outside the law. Tuck thought sometimes that he'd be better off if the old man were dead.

He thought that when he was at NAPS, that Sal was out of his life and out of his mind. But then, a conversation with Edie Maye, Cholly or Sis would bring back the reality. He was always there, in Tuck's subconscious. And he still had the wounded giant to contend with in his nightmares.

The population of NAPS swelled to about 350 students by June when all took the CEEB test for Navy. Nearly all passed and little Navy graduated them, awarding a diploma and orders to report to the United States Naval Academy with an honorable discharge from the USMC or their respective branch to be effective prior to swearing in at Navy.

For nearly two years, Tuck had been a regular in the marines, holding the rank of Corporal for half that time. He had learned how to be a responsible NCO, and been through a lot. Twice, at Lejuene, they had mobilized the Second Marines, once loading the Division on AKA attack transports in full battle gear, when Lebanon was the center of world crisis, and the second time, when Greece was embroiled in a civil war. In both cases, the Division was at the ready for a couple of days and then stood down. Flesner, a Sergeant, had seen combat, and many of the guys were saltier than Tuck. Now they were heading for the world of Officers, and would be Plebes, subject to the whims of younger kids who probably couldn't fathom a murderous D.I., let alone fighting for your life with a knife-wielding loony or shooting a fleeing prisoner. They were all a little apprehensive.

The successful graduates piled their duffels atop a fleet of school buses and were convoyed south to Annapolis. The buses lined up along the wall and deposited them at the Main Gate to the United States Naval Academy an hour later.

"Jesus H. Christ, Tuck, take a look at this place," said Sklenar, who was marching next to Tuck as they crossed the yard. There had been a previous visit by the Nappers, but Tuck had missed it while in hospital with the blood clots.

"Yeah, man," said Tuck, "it's pretty god damned awesome."

The group threaded their way across the manicured grounds of the Academy, past the golden-domed chapel, the Herndon Monument and Tucumseh statue.

Tuck noticed that nearly every bench, every walk and monument bore brass plaques of dedication. They dropped their duffel bags on the esplanade of Bancroft Hall. It was the biggest and most impressive building that Tuck had ever seen.

A Navy Captain administered the oath to them as a group. He stood directly under the John Paul Jone's Serapis[94] battle flag in Memorial Hall. Tuck recited the words automatically; his whole attention riveted on the flag, tattered and burned by musket fire. Richard, Sklenar, Perry and the other marines in the group found each other and shook hands.

Flesner declined taking the oath, and having served more than his required four-year enlistment in the marines, packed up and headed for home; to St. Paul, Minnesota. Tuck gave him his Marine Corps ring as a souvenir of the NCO quarters at Little Navy.

32

THE YARD

SINCE Plebe summer was largely military indoctrination, the "NAPPERS" in the Class of '59 rapidly took on positions as Company Officers. Classes were conducted by Junior Officers of the regular Navy and Marine Corps and each Plebe Company had a First Classman of the just graduated Class of '55 as a Company Liaison Officer.

A little known fact to the general public is that the United States Naval Academy is in nearly all facets of its operations run by the Brigade of Midshipmen. While Admirals, Generals and high ranking officers of all the services may serve in executive roles and as instructors, the Brigade is governed and supervised by the Midshipmen officers selected from its own ranks.

The Navy had provided buses to transport the NAPS graduates directly to the Academy. Officially, they were civilians and under no obligation except their own promise to report to the Naval Academy. Several members of the group took advantage of the loophole and disappeared, having served only a few months in the Army. Tuck was glad to hear of their defection, as he had them spotted as goof offs when they reported to NAPS. Their defection was noted by some members of Congress, which passed legislation requiring enlistees who decline entrance to an Academy to return to their original units and complete their originally contracted term of service.[95]

Tuck and Richard Dagampat were billeted with two young fellows in the west wing of Bancroft Hall. Each came from a wealthy family, and

The Author (front, center) conducting close order drill with his Plebe Company at the United States Naval Academy during plebe summer 1955. US Navy photo from "Historic Photos of the United States Naval Academy," page 176.

their fathers were professional men. Tuck and Richard soon became their mentors in everything they needed to know about existence in the Service. Each of the new roommates had spent a year at college, but was without any appreciation of what military life would require of them.

"Did you ever happen to think that you may be sleeping in the very bunk that Admiral Halsey or Admiral King slept in?" Watley, the more precocious of Tuck's roommates was beginning one of daily philosophy lectures. He had spent a year at Delaware University.

"No, man," Richard said, after walking to the bathroom door and opening it with a flourish and hand salute, then pointing to the toilet bowl, said "but I think I took a shit on the same toilet that Halsey used, just this morning." Richard and Tuck got tears in their eyes as they watched Watley stammer for a reply. The civilians had some difficulty understanding the marines and their extraordinary sense of humor.

Plebe summer passed easily for Tuck and the other NAPS graduates. They had quickly assumed leadership roles in their various units. Jimmy Brown, a NAPS marine sergeant, became the Commandant of the

Plebe class. Tuck was Plebe Commander of his company, and felt fairly comfortable in his new environment. He quickly understood that much of the training during plebe summer was quite mild compared to USMC boot camp and FMF (Fleet Marine Force) standards. For the civilians, it was a mind-blowing change to a lifestyle they had never contemplated.

In the beginning of September, the plebe class of 1959 awoke one morning to find the Chesapeake Bay east of Annapolis filled with an armada of fighting ships; cruisers, destroyers and two battleships, barely discernible at distant anchor in the lee channel off Thomas Point Light. The brigade was back, and the moment they dreaded was upon them.

With the brigade's arrival, all plebes would be reassigned equally to the twenty four companies that comprised it. Richard and Tuck, assigned to the Twelfth Company, wrangled the same room assignment and managed to get one other NAPS graduate, a former marine named Roger Erickson, who was one of the halfbacks on the NAPS football team, as one of their roommates. The fourth bunk was occupied by a nice kid from Chicago named Osborne.

The schedule was intense; seven major subjects, with classes and quizzes in each every day. Physical training for one hour every day; in addition to the requirement that everyone participates in an extracurricular sport, stand watches in Bancroft Hall, and give the "morning call" on a rotating basis.

Every morning, a plebe in each company was required to rise early at 0530 hours and stand at attention in the corridor, shouting all of the orders (instructions) of the day at the top of his lungs, until the company moved out for formation and breakfast at 0600. In this way they absorbed all of the pertinent temporary information, such as names of the Officers of the Day, number of days left to certain events, and so on. This duty was rotated among the plebes, by room assignment.

On top of that was the hazing by the upper classmen. As a plebe, the privilege of walking the centers of the corridors in Bancroft Hall was denied them. They were required to hug the walls, marching at attention, and to double time all stairs, two steps at a time. Any upper classman could ask a plebe any question, to which they were required to respond. "I don't know," as a response, was removed from their vocabulary, replaced with "I'll find out, Sir!"

Former marines were fair game for some of the upper classmen, who felt threatened by their previous military experience.

Most of the harassment took place at meals, where the four plebes on a table of 12 were required to eat sitting on only three inches of their chairs at a "brace," every fork full of food making a right-angled approach to the mouth, and eyes "in the boat" for the entire meal, staring straight ahead, chin tucked tight enough to hold a pencil under it. The additional eight upper classmen would be entertained by requiring the plebes to recite from memory any number of responses to questions asked previously, or passages from the plebe's bible, "Reef Points," a 330 page book they were required to memorize.

Within two weeks, Tuck knew that he was in over his head. Tuck had only gone as far as Algebra 1 in high school, and done poorly. Now he was digesting Trigonometry, Physics, Chemistry, English Literature, History, Engineering, Spanish and Seamanship and Navigation, as well as the unending flood of mundane questions from upper classmen.

"What's up, Mister?" First Classman Foote always asked simple, easy questions. He just wanted to get it on record that he harassed a plebe, but coming from the Fleet, the former submariner didn't want to usurp any extra time.

"Sir, Fidelity is up, and Obedience is down on my bayonet belt buckle, Sir!" It was one of about forty standards plebes had to have on the tip of one's tongue, along with the number of days left to the Army game, graduation and the next holiday. Of course, they had to know the names of the president, his entire cabinet, the chiefs of staff, all of the administrators at the academy, the Officer of the Day, his staff, and all of the Midshipman officers for the twenty-four companies in the brigade, the complete starting offensive and defensive line-ups of the football and other varsity teams and the complete schedule and scores of last year's contests, among other things.

First Classman Foote, like many of the more mature upper classmen, was just as likely to ask a plebe for 59 pushups as to ask him to answer a question. The physical abuse was nothing. Tuck could knock out 59 pushups, pull-ups or sit-ups without blinking an eye, and had no reservations about doing so. One "firstie" had 'braced' him for two hours and forty minutes, until the other plebe unfortunate enough to be caught with him, a big fellow who eventually made the varsity football team and an all-America recognition,[96] passed out. Even an occasional ass-taking, where the plebe had to "assume the position," grabbing ankles with his hands while an upper classman whacked his butt with his 15 pound yearbook, was okay.

If they dropped the book, the plebe got his chance, and it was in good fun more than harassment. Three meals a day brought a barrage of questions from the upper classmen. Many questions had easily memorized answers.

"HOW'S THE COW, Mister?" A common question at mess; to determine the status of the nearest pewter pitcher of milk at the table. The response:

"Sir, she walks, she talks, she's full of chalk. The lacteal fluid extracted from the female of the bovine species is highly prolific to the nth degree! (Where n = the approximate number of glasses of milk remaining in the pitcher).

WHAT ARE THE LAWS OF THE NAVY, MISTER? The response;

"These are the laws of the Navy, unwritten and varied they be,

And he who is wise will observe them, going with his ship down to the sea.

As naught can outrun the destroyer, even so with the law and its grip,

For the strength of the ship is the service, and the strength of the service the ship,

On the strength of one link in the cable, dependeth the might of the chain,

Who knowest when thou mayest be tested, so live that thou bearest the strain."

"WHAT TIME IS IT, Mister?" First Classman Montieth always asked something that was difficult or required research, a very squared away midshipman who felt obligated to treat plebes without mercy!

"Sir, according to the great sidereal movement ..." Tuck responded, giving the 350 word explanation of how time is kept according to the movement of celestial bodies. These kinds of questions were a "snap," once you committed to memory the required litany. The hardest question among them was "How do you bring a full-rigged ship about?" That question invoked an answer that contained all of the commands to tack a square rigged barkentine through the point of the wind, identifying and resetting all 21 sails, halyards and braces. Another very difficult standard was the answer to "Are you from Ar-kansas?" This question had a salty 450 word response that traced the historical origins of Arkansas as a part of Kansas, and why the citizens of the former resent the pronunciation, "Ar-Kansas."

These standards made up a whole section of the plebe's bible, "Reef Points." Plebes were required to repeat from memory any of its 330 pages.

The tough questions were the research questions. They usurped energy and study time. One meal's worth of questions could bury a Plebe, creating a never ending cycle of more questions if answers were insufficient. If the upper classmen on a table were feeling particularly vindictive, a plebe could come away with a dozen questions to be answered by the next meal.

It was serious, because bad answers or forgotten questions would lead to "come arounds," visits to an upper class room and eventual demerits and more lost study time marching off the demerits, or "fraps". With the academic load and continual testing in every class, grades were a direct function of study time. Mixed in with all of this were snap (unannounced) inspections of plebe rooms, lockers and desks, in addition to daily personal inspections at all formations.

Natividad Valdez, the Navajo Indian who played guard on the NAPS team walked into Tuck's room one evening in civilian clothes. He shook hands with Tuck, Roger and Richard and announced he was on his way home.

"I just stopped in to say goodbye, I still don't know any of those guys in my company," he said.

"What happened?" Tuck asked. Natividad had been in the Marine Corps, a rifleman.

"I bilged out, man; I haven't passed a test since we came down here. They don't give a shit; they just keep throwin' it at you. It's back to the reservation for me." He laughed at the old joke, but couldn't disguise the tears rimming his eyes.

"Jesus," Tuck said, "I thought they had to keep you around here until exams, at least. What'd they do, send you some kind of letter or something?"

"No, Man, they had me up before the Review Board; a bunch of starched scivvie admirals and generals, and told me I couldn't cut it. A bunch of other guys got it, too. Wesley, Stardall, Mite, Smitty and McMaster. I saw 'em waiting to go in when I came out."

Natividad shook hands again all around and they wished each other luck. The door swung shut to a quiet room when he left. Tuck got back to his math problems and tried not to think about it. The NAPS graduates were dropping like flies.

"Describe the Gearing Class Destroyer, Mister" It was Pistotnick, a second classman with an attitude, asking the question. Tuck responded.

"Sir, the Gearing Class is a class of destroyers, Sir. The main function of the ship is picket, anti-submarine operations, and rapid deployment, Sir. The Gearing class is armed with three five-inch thirty-eight caliber rifles, and eight quads of forty millimeter anti-aircraft Bofers automatic rifles, and the Hedgehog anti-submarine depth charge, Sir. It is 330 feet in length, 45 feet abeam and draws 22 feet of water, Sir. its displacement is 14,500 tons, and has a crew of two hundred men, and a top speed of 30 knots, Sir." Tuck responded with what he remembered from the "Jane's Fighting Ships" encyclopedia.

Tuck was familiar with the gearing class destroyers, since Frank Donovan, one of the ends on his NAPS team, had served in one, the USS Timmerman, DD828, and the ship's experimental boilers operated at extremely high pressures. Standard at the time was 600 psi and Frank had related that serving in TIMMERMAN was sometimes a little scary. Her boilers became the prototypes for the 1200 psi boilers in later DDG and DLG class ships that reached speeds near 43 knots.

"Some of that information is incorrect, Mister," Pistotnick shot back. Tuck knew that most of it was totally accurate, but was willing to bet that Pistotnick was less sure of it than he was. He knew that an "I'll find out, Sir" would evoke a "come around," and Tuck couldn't afford to give up the study time. He was leery of Pistotnick, since one of the football players had told Richard that he had made a big deal out of making sure Tuck ended up on his table at mess. Only five responses were permitted if a plebe didn't know the factual answer to a question. They were: "I'll find out, sir"; "Yes, sir;" "No, sir;" "No excuse, sir;" and "Aye, aye, sir."

Come arounds were requirements to report to the upper classman's room during study hours, where they would then find more crap for the plebe to do to satisfy them. Some of the more sadistic bastards would "brace" them up for an entire study period of two hours, order them to out scream their stereos, or sit their butt in the sink and open the hot and cold taps and "thermocouple" balls. The upper classmen that exhibited this behavior, in Tuck's eyes had lost all focus on the reason for the question/answer hazing. They acted like spoiled college students at rich ivy league school.

"You will find out the correct specifications of the Gearing class destroyer, Mister, and you will report this at morning mess, along with the name of every ship in the class."

"Aye, aye, Sir," Tuck replied, thinking to himself that *the bastard just stole tonight's two-hour study time.* He knew that the Gearing class to be one of the bigger classes of destroyers, the last design of WWII. *I'm going to have to memorize the names of 128 ships before breakfast tomorrow,* he thought. He already had seven other questions to answer for the First Classmen at the table.

"I don't know how much of this bull shit I'm willing to take," he said to Richard after evening mess, "I've got seven fucking questions for chow tomorrow and one of 'em is a list of 128 ship's names, for Christ sake. I know I'm gonna' fail Chemistry; I don't understand that stuff at all. I could make it if these little mother fuckers would layoff of all this fraternity shit!"

"Yeah, I know," Richard said, "you should have come out for ball, Man. These guys give me too many questions and Smitty tells them to layoff."

Bill Smith, an all-East end, was in their company, along with a half dozen other varsity players.

"Shit, Richard," Tuck said, "you've still got about 30 demerits already. They can only protect you so much, and you've got to take all the same tests I do, and as soon as the season's over, you'll come off the training table."

Having made the first string plebe team, Richard ate at the training table with the other football players, and didn't get all the bull shit handed out in the rest of the mess.

"Yeah," Richard said, "but somebody's after you, and I think it's that goddamn Monteith. He was a NAPPER (NAPS graduate), and I think he wants to prove how tough we marines are, you know; semper fi."

"I know how tough I am," Tuck said, "half of these fuckin' guys wouldn't last a day in the Second Marines; they'd get their asses kicked. That's not the point. The point is, I can't do all this shit and keep up with the classes."

Tuck had already taken to hanging a blanket over the shower door in their room, and studying there as long as he could stay awake after taps. The problem was that he got caught several times by the Midshipman Officer of the Deck, and each offense was 15 demerits, or "fraps," which had to be marched off, 10 fraps to the hour, during study hour or before reveille, at five in the morning. A plebe was allowed 300 demerits before being politely thrown out.

Tuck realized that being caught regularly studying after hours would soon result in his dismissal, unless he worked off a portion of the demerits as they accumulated. He arose early most mornings at 0500 and marched off ten before morning chow. On Saturdays, he could negate thirty fraps by three hours marching, one hour before reveille and two after lunch. On average, he was being caught studying after hours three to four times a week, and of course he was picking up the ordinary run of fraps that all plebes got for dusty shelves, improper haircuts, etc. The overall result was that he was able to reduce the rate of accumulation, to slow it down, but it was costly in sleep, time and energy. It was a problem in differential calculus.

Tuck usually called home on the weekends, on Sunday afternoon just before evening mess, to see how Edie Maye was doing. One Sunday Sis was at the house when he called.

"I want to come down and visit you," she said, "this weekend."

"Well," Tuck said, "look, I've only get Sunday afternoon, four hours each week, out of the yard, and we usually just relax and take in a movie in town, or I crew on a boat for some upper classman, and then come back and study."

"It's only for an afternoon. You'll let us, won't you?" She turned on her charm, and Tuck figured he might as well give in.

"Yeah, sure," he said, "I'll meet your at the main gate about one o'clock."

"Oh," she said, "I knew you'd do it. That's wonderful. Uncle Santo is bringing me down."

"Who?" Tuck asked.

"Uncle Santo, Aunt Mary and Aunt Josephina," she said.

"What the hell are they coming down here for?" Tuck asked, "The last time we saw them, we were starving on Garden Street and they ate all the food in the house! What the hell are you bringing them for?"

"They just want to see," she said, "they've been nagging me about it for weeks. Don't be nasty about it."

"They want to see the yard," he said, "they can do that anytime. It's open to the public, they don't give a shit about me, or at least, they didn't, until I made the Academy."

"I knew you'd act this way," she said, sounding hurt.

"All right," Tuck said, exasperated at having to give up precious time, "come on down, I'll meet you at the main gate, okay?"

They showed up on Sunday. Tuck was surprised that Edie Maye was not with them. When he asked Sis about it, she said that she was busy and couldn't make it. It was a nice day, and Tuck spent the four hours showing them around and sitting in the yard. When they were leaving, he pulled Sis aside.

"Why did you say mom didn't come?" he asked.

"She was busy, that's all," Sis replied.

"Come on, Sis," Tuck said. He was getting angry and she could see that he wasn't going to let the subject drop. "What's mom doing on Sundays all of the sudden? That's taking all her time up?"

"She didn't think we should come," Sis said, dropping into her defensive mode, "she thought you were too busy to spend time with us."

"Well," Tuck said, "she was right. I'm having a tough time here, and I need every moment to be productive. I don't mean to be rude, but I could be studying right now, so don't pull this kind of thing again. I only agreed because I thought mom would be here. Next time, I'll tell you when to come, okay?"

"You're such a shit," she said, smiling.

When Tuck said good bye to Aunt Mary she let the cat out of the bag.

"I'm so glad your sister invited us," she said, "I would have never thought of coming down here if she hadn't insisted."

On Sunday afternoons, Tuck often volunteered as crew for upper classmen who had dates and had signed up for a yawl. This was called "drag sailing." The 44 foot Luder yawls in the academy fleet required a crew of five to sail in comfort, and he found that sailing was something that he really enjoyed.

Hanging around the yacht basin early Sunday afternoon could easily get you a crew berth, but Tuck was soon crewing every opportunity he could on the Highland Light, a 68 foot cutter rigged sloop. Retired Admiral Kasker commanded her, and he was in charge of selecting crews and captains for the Bermuda race each summer.

It took a 20 knot wind to heel the "Light," since she had an 8,000 pound lead keel. When the wind was there, it was an absolutely thrilling experience. Designed by Belknap and Skene, she had set a record to Bermuda in 1936 that had never been broken. The admiral took a liking to Tuck. He thought the boy a natural sailor. He had enthusiasm and was a fast learner.

There was no subterfuge in the boy, he loved the boat and the sea and was oblivious to the ribbings of his classmates when asked to do even the most menial chores. He often gave Tuck the helm while he gave the commands to trim sails and instructed the crew. Within a few weeks, he asked Tuck if he would crew in next summer's Bermuda race.

The Highland Light was boiling down the Chesapeake at the time. Forty feet of her lee rail buried in rushing water as she heeled nearly 30 degrees, sails filled and causing her sixty foot mast to flex against the straining stays. Tuck was holding her tight on the wind with both hands on the five foot diameter wheel, wiping spray from his face.[97]

"You'll have to give up two weeks of your summer leave, Tuck," the Admiral said, "and I'll work you hard all through the spring."

"I'd consider it an honor, Sir," Tuck replied.

Towards the end of the quarter, Tuck found a message in his room after sports activities period. It said to call home, urgent. At the beginning of study hour, he headed for the pay phones in the basement, five floors down, but got caught by a first classman from the Eleventh Company on the third deck.

It was always dangerous outside your company area after evening mess. The upper classmen in other companies considered a "stray" plebe fair game, and they pulled a lot of hazing that they would answer for if the harassed plebe was in their own company.

The firstie and his roommate had Tuck brace up for a half hour, then they organized some "carrier landings," and he had to play airplane in his scivvies, running down the corridor and belly flopping on a mattress with a bunch of other plebes they had caught. The 11th Company officer, an army captain named Al Haig, emerged from his office and broke up the hazing, but Tuck had lost the study hour and had to get back to his room for lights out.

As soon as the hall settled down after taps, he chanced the stairs, made it to the basement and made his call. It was nearly eleven thirty on a Thursday night.[98]

"Your Granddad died yesterday," Edie Maye said, "the neighbors looked in on him because the front door was open, and he had had a heart attack."

"Oh, Jeez, Mom," Tuck said, "poor grandpop. Wasn't anybody there at all?"

"No," she said, "I feel so terrible, because I was going to take him something to eat yesterday, but I was so tired, I laid down after work, and fell asleep."

"When is the funeral?" Tuck asked. He couldn't understand why he wasn't crying, but he sensed it was going to be a problem to get home.

"Tomorrow night and they're burying him Saturday morning," she said, "at the Odd Fellows Cemetery in Pemberton. The VFW is giving him a military funeral, with a color guard and rifle salute. Can you come home?"

Tuck could hear the hurt in her voice, and he was beginning to get depressed.

"I don't know, Mom," he said, "I'll try and find out, tomorrow, and I'll call you back as soon as I know."

"If you can't, it's O.K.," she said, "Granddad would understand."

"Mom, for Christ Sake," Tuck said, choking a little, "I loved Grandpop. He was the only father I ever had."

Tuck sat down in the phone booth after he hung up and just stared at the wall for about ten minutes. The following day was the Friday before the Columbia game. The two upper classes would ride a train to New York and attend, the two lower classes stayed home. His company advisor was a Marine Captain, and Tuck figured he would help him out, so the following morning, before breakfast, he presented himself to his office.

"Captain, my Mother called last night to tell me that we've had a death in the family," Tuck said.

"I'm sorry," Captain Dickey asked, "your father?"

"My Grandfather, Sir." Tuck said, "He had a heart attack on Wednesday. I'd like to request a weekend pass, Sir, so that I can attend the funeral tomorrow morning."

"Not possible, son." he said, "Unless it's a member of the immediate family, parents or such."

"But, Sir," Tuck pressed, "the brigade's going right past Philadelphia. I could ride up with them on the train and be back here at Bancroft Hall by 1900 hours!"

"Sorry, son," he said, "that would be highly irregular. I couldn't approve it, especially since it's a grandparent."

"But, Sir," Tuck said, starting to feel even more depressed, "my granddad, he was like my father. I never really had a father around. He lived with us."

"Not according to your file, son," he said. He had pulled Tuck's folder from his file cabinet and was leafing through it as he spoke. "You're from Second Marines, aren't you?"

"Yes, Sir," Tuck responded, noticing the newspaper clippings in his file.

"Well, son," he said, "this is the Naval Academy. This kind of story may have worked in the Fleet with some Gunny Sergeant, but it won't work here."

"Begging the captain's pardon, Sir," Tuck said, "but I'm not lying! Could I have my mother call you, Sir, to verify what I've told you?" Tuck couldn't believe what he was hearing. *The son of a bitch thought I was cooking this up to get a weekend off!*

"You could," he said, "but I still can't guarantee anything. Now, you better get to formation for morning mess, Mister."

"Aye, aye, Sir," Tuck responded and hurried out the door. He was furious that the son of a bitch thought he was lying about granddad. Typical Officer bullshit, Tuck thought, but at least he'll approve it when Mom calls.

At mess, Pistotnick nailed him for the 128 names of the destroyers in the Gearing class, and he had to give him an "I'll find out, Sir." He tongue lashed Tuck and gave him a come around for that evening's study hour. Tuck couldn't hide the expression of disgust and depression on his face.

On the way back to Bancroft Hall from PT, Tuck's last class of the morning, he grabbed a phone in the basement and called home. Sis answered.

"Look," Tuck said, "I've only got a minute. Tell mom she has to call Captain Dickey today so that I can make it home for the funeral. The bastard doesn't believe me that granddad died. Tell her she's got to call, today!"

Sis said she would tell her, and he hung up and rushed to his room to change for afternoon mess. He cornered Captain Dickey that evening on the way out of the mess hall.

"Excuse me, Sir," Tuck said, "but I wanted to know if my mother called you this afternoon, about my grandfather."

Dickey turned away from the two first classmen he was talking with. "No, she didn't, Mister Falconetti," he said, "I'm sorry, but I've checked my messages and I was available all afternoon."

"Thank you, Sir," Tuck said, crushed. He couldn't believe that Edie Maye had let him down, but there was no way that he was going to be able to make the funeral, unless he went AWOL.

"Richard," he said, back in his room, "I'm gettin' the fuck out of here tonight. My granddad died and they're burying him tomorrow, and that fucking Dickey thinks I'm lying about it."

"Don't do it, Man," Richard said, "they catch you and you'll be back at Lejuene in the brig in a week. Besides, how in the hell can you get to Mt. Holly by tomorrow morning without a car?"

Tuck knew he was right. He remembered one trip when he had hitchhiked from Lejuene and got a ride to the produce terminal in South Philly. It took him four hours to walk to Cherry Hill in Jersey where he finally got a ride to Mt. Holly.

The marine in Tuck remembered the gray brig fatigues with the big white "P" in the middle of the back, and Bobby Brown crying uncontrollably, rubbing his eyes with manacled wrists.

"Ah, shit," Tuck said, "you're right, as usual, but it ain't fair, goddamn it! "You're right about that,"

Richard said, "I'm sorry, man."

Sunday morning, Tuck got up early and fell in with Richard for mass at the Chapel. He had a pass to attend the Unitarian Church in Annapolis, which he usually did, taking advantage of his lack of a real church affiliation and turning it to an advantage. The Sunday morning trek offered an opportunity to meet some local girls and grab a cheeseburger on the way back to the yard.

Tuck needed the chapel that morning, he thought, as they filed in with some 300 others and waited for the mass to begin. He listened to the sermon and thought about Granddad and Edie Maye as the chaplains performed the mass. Tuck never really understood religion, and had never been baptized nor attended church at home, but he liked the services in the chapel, and came here when things were getting him down, to John Paul Jones' sepulcher in the basement.

Ever since Edie Maye had called, Tuck's mind had been flashing little movies to him, vignettes of granddad in his workshop, on his electric bike, telling the young Tuck a story by the pot-bellied stove. Now that he was gone, he felt cheated, because he hadn't known him better, and empty, because he was so isolated from his death and burial. The last hymn of the mass, as usual, was the sailor's hymn. As the voices filled the chapel, Tuck felt Richard pat him on the back, and realized that he was crying, tears streaming down his face. Sunday afternoon he got Edie Maye on the phone.

"Jesus, Mom," he said, "why didn't you call Captain Dickey for me, I wanted to be there."

"What are you talking about?" She asked, "Was I supposed to call someone?"

"Didn't Sis tell you?" Tuck asked, "I called back on Friday. Dickey wouldn't believe me, but I had a chance if you called and told him, too."

"He wouldn't believe you that Granddad died?" She asked, and said, "That's terrible, that they wouldn't believe you. It's not fair!"

But she never answered his question.

First quarter grades came out, showing Tuck failing to make the required 2.5 average in both chemistry and physics. Pistotnick was becoming a real problem, going out of his way to think up outlandish questions for Tuck at each meal. For some reason, he was really on Tuck's case. The other plebes could see it, so Tuck was sure that he wasn't feeling sorry for himself. On one occasion, he had more in mind than plebe "indoctrination."

"What's the measurement of Olympia's bust, Mister?" he asked at an evening meal.

"I'll find out, sir," Tuck responded, wondering what the hell Olympia was. He found out, after mess was over, that Olympia was the bronze bow figurehead of the "protected" (armored) cruiser, U.S.S Olympia, launched in 1901 and famous for its part in the Spanish American war; Dewey's flagship. The huge bronze replica of the Greek goddess Olympia was displayed in Memorial Hall. Tuck rushed down to the hall to survey the situation, knowing that he couldn't touch it with anyone around. It took him a while to find another plebe that had a tape measure, and after taps, about two in the morning, he pulled on a navy blue turtleneck, got his black watch cap, and made his way to the basement of Bancroft Hall.

Tuck emerged from the basement near the steps leading up from the rotunda, where the watch stood duty. The Midshipman on watch was far enough away from the entrance to Memorial Hall that it would have been easy to sneak by him and up the curved marble steps. As Tuck prepared to do this, however, something moved in the shadows to one side of the main doors, in one of the alcoves.

Son of a bitch, they're laying for me! He thought. He crouched in the shadows for several minutes and identified three figures in the alcove. Like him, they were dressed in black, but he couldn't tell who they were. Moving back the way he had come, he dropped down to the basement and found his way out onto one of the small patios that separate Bancroft from the King Hall, the mess hall. He climbed to the roof of King Hall, easily scaled the wall that was the back of Memorial Hall, and entered through a window he had unlocked, just in case, when he was there earlier in the evening. As he climbed he thanked Sgt. Dale Bird, who had taught him to always have a backup route up or down a tree.

Climbing Olympia's pedestal, Tuck got her measurement and slipped away the same way he had come in. Pistotnick could hardly contain himself at morning mess.

"Report, Mister," he said, "on Olympia's bust measurement."

"Fifty-two and one half inches, Sir," Tuck replied.

"That answer is incorrect, Mister," he said, "You will come around to my quarters after evening meal."

"That answer is correct, Sir, and I challenge!" This was a privilege which was largely given lip service; if the questioner was wrong, and the plebe correct, the plebe could take his ass, no penalty. Pistotnick looked around the table at the other upper classmen, savoring his power, and figuring that he had Tuck.

"Mister, I know for a fact that you did not measure Olympia's bust last night," he said, "as is required by this question. Since you did not measure Olympia's bust, you must have extracted the answer from someone who has, and therefore you are lying."

Tuck broke his brace, and reaching into his pocket, tossed the tape measure onto the table, thinking, *What kind of asshole would spend all night in an alcove just to see if a plebe made a measurement?*

"I will not be accused of lying, Mr. Pistotnick," he said, "and I have challenged you to refute my answer!"

"Brace up, Mister, you're out of line," shouted Hanley, the first classman in charge of the table, "and Pistotnick, I want to know what the hell is going on here!"

"It's nothing," Pistotnick said, "I don't think he went to the hall, that's all."

"You don't capriciously accuse anyone of lying, Mister," Hanley said to him, and then to Tuck, "Did you go the hall?"

"Yes, Sir," Tuck said, "at about 0230 hours, Sir, where I observed three men hiding in the shadowed alcove to the left of the main entrance. I entered from a window by scaling the wall from the roof of King Hall and got my measurement, Sir."

Pistotnick's face reddened when this information came forth. He shifted nervously in his chair. "Who were the men, hiding there?" Hanley asked, looking at Pistotnick with disgust.

"I was not able to identify them, Sir," Tuck said. "Sir, may I suggest that the veracity of my measurement may be easily checked by measuring Olympia right now?"

"That's not necessary, Mister," he said, "I happen to know that your answer is correct. Accordingly, you may report to Mr. Pistotnick's quarters this evening to extract your revenge."

"I'd rather not, Sir," Tuck said.

"It's your privilege," Hanley responded.

"Just the same, Sir," Tuck said, "I need all my time for studying, and I'd prefer not to dignify this episode by prolonging it, Sir."

Tuck didn't know where the words came from. It was though he was listening to someone else talking. He could feel the redness in the back of his neck, and he knew this was going to cause more trouble.

"Mr. Pistotnick," Hanley said, "your conduct has been less than exemplary this morning. You are hereby prohibited from asking this midshipman any further questions at mess, and I will expect a full explanation of this matter asap."

Pistotnick nodded, his face crimson with embarrassment and rage. *A midshipman will not lie, cheat or steal.* Those eight words were the entire honor code of the Academy, and Pistotnick had violated all ethical and moral standards by unjustly accusing Tuck of violating the code, a dismissal offense. The bastard deserved whatever he got.

Tuck enjoyed a brief respite, getting only an average load of questions for the next couple of weeks. He sensed that Pistotnick's classmates thought he was way out of line, and he lost a lot of face. But even with Pistotnick off his back, the pressure was still intense, and the football team didn't help things, either.

Navy, at the time, was the leading Division I offensive football team in the nation. Quarterbacked by George Welsh, All American, they rolled over every team in their path. Army, on the other hand, had struggled through a mediocre season.

The Plebe class knew what was at stake when Army played Navy at Philadelphia. A win meant that plebes could "carry on" until Christmas holiday, eating like normal human beings with no harassment. A loss meant that every upper classman in the brigade would vent his frustrations on the plebes. It was traditional; the plebe class paid for all losses to Army.

Of course, they lost the game. The class of '59 stood stunned in the stands at Philadelphia Municipal Stadium, unbelieving that the team that had beaten Notre Dame, Duke, Georgia Tech, Penn State and the other great teams of 1955 had been put away by Army and a squat fullback with some kind of polish name (Kyasky). By Christmas leave, Tuck had accumulated nearly 230 demerits.

Edie Maye had forgotten about the details of Tuck getting away for granddad's funeral, and he was so relieved to get away from Bancroft Hall for a ten day Christmas leave that he didn't bother to pursue it. He figured that Sis had told her and she forgot to call, or that she was afraid that she might get him in trouble by calling. He brought all his books home and spent the mornings studying, hoping that he could catch up over the holidays. Edie Maye kept nagging him to wear his uniform around town.

"Look, Mom," Tuck said, "it's supposed to be a holiday. Nobody wears their uniforms when they're home. We have to wear them every day, and I just want to relax."

"I know," she said, "but you look so nice in it. I want to show you off"

"Mom," Tuck said, "If you only knew how hard it is... I don't know if I can make it. Every day is a big struggle."

"Oh," she said, "but you'll make it. I know you will."

"Mom, for cryin' out loud;" he pleaded. "It's not that simple. The work is really hard, and I'm always behind. I'm trying as best as I can, but please stop acting like it is so simple, because it isn't. Just saying I can do it won't make it happen, so please, lay off with the uniforms and stuff! Just let me be here without all the fuss, please!"

"You can't fault me for being proud of you," she said.

"Mom, I'm not," he said, "I can't explain it, it's so hard, and I'm trying so hard, I just don't like to think ahead too far, that's all. I have a lot of trouble with some of this stuff."

Just after Christmas, Eddie, Tuck's friend from high school, called to tell him that there was a party in the Lakes, at "Urp's" house. Why don't we go over? "Urp's" real name was Jeanne Brinkley, and she and Tuck had always been friendly, each having an interest in drawing, but he'd never really been accepted into that Medford Lakes crowd. She was now attending the Philadelphia Museum School of Art. He figured he might as well go.

Standing in the comer of her den that night with a bottle of beer in his hand, Tuck was surprised to see a Second Class Midshipman, in uniform, approach him. It was Gene Radcliffe, who had graduated high school two years before Tuck. He and Tuck had never gotten along, after Tuck had kicked him in the ass one day at football practice. In a Junior Varsity game the previous day, Radcliffe's intentionally missed blocks had gotten Tuck splattered all over the field.

Radcliffe had another Second Classman with him, and he was gloating. "Brace up, Plebe," he ordered.

"What?" Tuck asked, incredulously

"I said," he repeated, "brace up, mister. We're going to show everyone what it's like to take a plebe's ass." Tuck had heard about Eugene. It was scuttlebutt that he and several other second classmen from his company had formed some kind of sadistic club, and they went out of their way to give plebes major heartache. Their favorite sport was "taking your ass," a beating on bare buttocks with the navy yearbook. The scuttlebutt was that a couple of guys had been taken so hard and so many times that they ended up in sick bay with swollen genitalia.

"Look," Tuck said, bristling, "if you think you're going to humiliate me in front of these people, you're full of shit!"

"Listen, mister," he said, "you're still a plebe, even if you aren't at Bancroft Hall. I've heard all about your insubordination and big mouth. You'd better do as I say!"

"I'll tell what I'm going to do," Tuck said, "I'm going to let you off. I'm going to let you walk away from me without busting your nose, that's what I'm going to do!"

His buddy was getting nervous, seeing that Tuck was deadly serious. Several other people, within earshot, had turned to the conversation.

"Eugene," he said, "this isn't such a good idea. It is Christmas, after all, and you can catch up with him back at Bancroft Hall."

"That's right, Eugene." Tuck said, "You want to play games with me; that's your prerogative back at Bancroft Hall. I can take any of the shit that you can dish out, and you know it. But we aren't at Bancroft Hall now, so back off, before I do something I may regret!"

Tuck was exerting all the self control he could manage. A feeling of rage was engulfing him, and his entire body was tense. He knew that if he decked him here, nobody here would hold it against him. He had always been a jerk, trying to impress everybody with his family's money. Tuck was certain, however, if anything happened between them, he would make it a point to come after him when leave was over, and Tuck would be vulnerable.

"You'll regret talking to me this way," he said, "I've got friends in the twelfth company. But it's exactly what I'd expect from you, with your father's record! They should have never let you in the Naval Academy, your type doesn't belong!"

Tuck felt his temperature rise as the words sunk in.

"That tears it, you bastard; you want to go outside, right now?" Tuck asked, putting his beer on a nearby table and bringing his nose inches from Radcliff's face. He glared at Radcliffe for a moment, who then turned and quickly walked away. Tuck tracked down Eddie, who was in another room, dancing.

"Let's get out of here," he said, "I've had it, and if I stay any longer, I'm going to break Radcliffe's face." He excused himself, and they got his car and left.

"What happened?" Eddie asked, as they drove back to Mt. Holly. Tuck was certain that Radcliffe and Pistotnick were asshole buddies, and if that were true, it would explain a lot of things, but it wouldn't make life any easier.

"I found out who my real enemy is," Tuck said, "by accident."

33

P -WORKS

THE plebes returned from Christmas leave feeling refreshed, but after a couple of weeks, the hazing was back at full strength again. Tuck found himself wondering if it would ever end. Pistotnick was now laying for him in the corridor every day. Hanley said he had to lay off at mess, so he was always standing at the door of his room, watching for Tuck to emerge. He would then grab him on some pretense and load him up with questions, or require some other stupid routine. Tuck noted that he was afraid to come into the plebe room, although it was his privilege as an upper classman.

Tuck managed to pull the chemistry and physics grades up to passing at the end of the second quarter, but failed math with a 2.25 grade average. There just wasn't enough time to go around. A new option was offered on marching off demerits. Ten demerits could be worked off by running the 700 yard obstacle course at 0530 hours in lieu of one hour of marching. Tuck jumped on that, knocking off twenty demerits every morning he went out.

He needed to, as the demerits were piling up fast. He was getting caught studying about three or four times a week after hours, each new hiding place being discovered by upper classmen.

On top of his regular studies, Tuck had to take a re-examination in math, which he passed with a 2.7, enough to give him a total average for the semester which was one-tenth of a point in the black, a 2.51.

One Saturday morning, Sal showed up at Bancroft Hall. Tuck found the message after noon meal, and went down to say hello.

"You want to take a ride?" he said.

"I'm not permitted to ride in a car," Tuck said, "but if you drive down past the main gate, I'll jump in. I wouldn't mind getting a cold beer." It was a defiant breach of regulations, but Tuck was bordering on exhaustion with the pressure and willing to risk the potential demerits that could result if he were seen.

They drove up to Baltimore, and Sal wound his way around the suburbs and parked at a little row house. Inside, he introduced Tuck to Charles, a huge fat person, and his mother, Martha. They sat in their living room and drank a couple of beers, talking. Riding back to the Annapolis, Tuck asked Sal where he knew Charles from. It had been immediately evident that Charles was retarded.

"I know his mother," he said, "from the old days."

Back in his room after the ride to Baltimore, Richard asked Tuck where he had been.

"My old man came by," Tuck said, "so I took a ride with him up to B-more, and visited with some of his friends and had a couple of beers."

"Is that right," Richard said, "I thought you and your dad didn't get along."

"I don't know what to think of him, Richard," Tuck said, "He really fucked us over when I was a kid, I mean we nearly starved while he living high on the hog, but you know, I don't think he meant to do it."

"What do you mean," Richard asked, "he didn't mean to do it?"

"Well," Tuck said, "I just don't think the bastard ever thought about it, or something. It's hard to explain, he's really a nice guy to be around, if you know what I mean."

"Yeah, Si," Richard asked, "but where the fuck was he when your granddad died? He should've called down here and set things right."

"Yeah, you're right," Tuck agreed, "but he probably doesn't even know that Chip is gone. At least, he didn't mention it. He's in his own little world and nobody else gets in, unless it's for his reasons, if you know what I mean. The son of a bitch forgot I existed until I got the appointment. My brother says, 'Don't expect anything from him, because you're not going to get it.'"

"That's what I mean, Si," Richard said, "I don't think things are any different, but it's none of my business."

Tuck was a member of the plebe wrestling team, but was unable to beat any of the top wrestlers in the 168 weight class and get a chance to compete in the matches, so he dropped in weight to 158 and then to 148 pounds. He finally won the opportunity to wrestle against the Slippery Rock University freshman, but was decisioned 2 - 0. The dieting was too much at that weight, and he started getting dizzy spells on top of everything else.

The third quarter finally ground to an end, and Tuck had brought the math grade up to a passing 2.5, but failed physics again with a 2.30 average. He had found a good study spot in the "mokes" closet at the end of the corridor, so he was able to get in some late night studying.

The "mokes" were the black, Latino and Puerto Rican sailors that were assigned to the academy to cook, wait tables and do the janitorial work. They were housed in the Reina Mercedes, a barracks ship anchored at the quay, which was the answer to one of the standard plebe questions. In spite of Doris Miller's heroic actions at Pearl Harbor, few minorities were found in the 1955 specialty ranks in the U. S. Navy[99]

"What's the fastest ship in the Navy, mister?" An upper classman would ask.

"The Reina Mercedes, Sir!" was the required answer, since it was "fast" to the dock, tied up with hawsers and chain, and had been so for as long as anyone remembered. It was years before Tuck realized how blatantly the Navy had practiced racism as a matter of policy against blacks, Puerto Ricans and other Latinos and even Italians.

Pistotnick was now increasing his vendetta against Tuck, and the ban had been lifted from him at mess. He was very careful at the table, however, to ask appropriate questions without going overboard. Hanley's ears perked at every question he directed at the marine.

The problem was that he now had access to Tuck again, and he was soon coming around to Pistotnick's quarters almost every night. On Fridays, the twelfth company put its laundry out in the corridor, each neat little canvas bag of dirty clothes stenciled with a room number.

The laundry crew would pick up the bags while midshipmen were in class, and the following Tuesday, Tuck or Richard would pick up the cleaned garments, re-packed in the appropriate bags in mother Bancroft's basement outside of the laundry door. Richard and Tuck rotated picking up for each other; two bags being about all one person could carry.

On a Tuesday early in the fourth quarter, Pistotnick nailed Tuck coming up the stair with the laundry bags, prior to evening meal. He called him in his room and braced Tuck against the wall.

"What is my little fucked-up marine doing today," he asked, "with two laundry bags?"

"Picking up my laundry, Sir," Tuck responded. He was feeling a little desperate, having received the results of a P-work, a test covering two weeks of work, in chemistry. He had failed miserably, in spite of intense late hour studying in the mokes' closet.

"I believe that you have more than just your own laundry, Mister," Pistotnick smirked, knowing that he had him breaking a regulation. His roommate was sitting at his desk, studying.

"Yes, Sir," Tuck responded, "I have my roommate's laundry also." Regulations stated that one could retrieve only your own laundry bag, but of course, the upper classmen all made plebes do it, so this was a bull shit regulation that no one obeyed.

"And you know that that is against regulations, don't you?" He was gloating now, as it was the first time in about three weeks that he found an opportunity to give Tuck some demerits. "I'm from Texas," he continued, "and in Texas, we follow regulations, mister. Do you know the song, 'The Yellow Rose of Texas?'"

"No, Sir," Tuck responded. His arms were aching from holding the two laundry bags, and he felt very tired, drained. Tuck could feel despair; wanting to scream, completely disgusted with the whole goddamned Naval Academy and a system that let a little prick like Pistotnick steal his study time with bull shit like this, and wouldn't let him go home to his grandfather's funeral!

"I think you do know it, Mister," he said, "and you will now sing it while you swing those laundry bags about your head."

Tuck wanted to comply, but found that he couldn't do it. He had tears in his eyes now, and was at the limit of his endurance.

"No, sir," Tuck said, holding himself in check, but knowing he was right on the edge of an explosion.

"Listen, mister," Pistotnick said, "You will not defy me. I know all about you and where you come from."

"I beg your pardon, sir?" Tuck said, not believing what he was hearing. He thought, *Jesus, Radcliffe must have filled him in on my old man and his reputation.*

"The Yellow Rose of Texas," he said, "sing the song. I can cause you to bilge out of here, Mister, and you'll end up in a marine brig, behind bars, just like your ***mafia father***!"

Tuck's brain dropped into slow motion, the words echoing into oblivion. Internally, he heard himself saying, *No fucking way, no fucking way that I'm taking this!*

"I will not sing your fucking song," Tuck shouted, dropping the laundry bags and stepping forward, fists clenched, "and if you don't get off my case, I'm going to break your fucking neck!"

"Stand at attention, plebe!" he responded, stepping back and turning white in the face.

"Fuck you, you little prick," Tuck shouted, crying now. He hit the upper classman on both shoulders simultaneously, knocking him backwards onto the desk, "I'm failing courses and you're fucking around with me, talking about my family! I'm done with you, you little bastard."

His roommate stepped in front of Tuck and grabbed him in a bear hug. Tuck was beside himself, and ready to damage Pistotnick, regardless of the consequences.

"Let me go," Tuck growled, "I'm going to teach this little prick a lesson he won't forget!"

Propelled by Tuck's shove, Pistotnick inadvertently performed a backward roll and fell off the desk sideways on his hands and knees, scattering books and paperwork. In a frightened crouch, he ran around the desk and stood against the far wall, in some kind of white-faced shock, knees together and hands on his cheeks; like a girl!

"You've, you've, done it, now," he stammered, "you're in big trouble, plebe!"

Tuck pushed his way out of the roommate's grasp, picked up the laundry bags and walked out of the room. Back in his room, he threw the laundry bags in a corner, sat down on his bunk with elbows on his knees and head down, and tried to keep from completely breaking down.

"What happened, man?" Richard asked.

"That goddamned Pistotnick," Tuck said, "he grabbed me with the bags and started his fucking games, talking about my family, and I knocked him over his desk." It was hard getting the words out, and although Tuck wasn't actually crying, he couldn't stop the flood of tears.

"You punched his lights out?" Richard was incredulous.

"Nah," Tuck said, "I just pushed him, on the shoulders, but he went over anyway, the little piss ant."

"Shit, Si," Richard said, "That little prick has been trying to get you. He's gonna' make trouble now, man!

What'd he say about your family?"

"The son of a bitch knows my old man's an ex-con; Radcliffe must have told him. It's probably all over the fucking brigade by now. I've had it, Richard," Tuck said, "I couldn't take any more of his shit. When the son of a bitch made that remark about my old man and the mafia, I let go." Tuck lay back on his bunk and put his forearm over his eyes, which were burning. "I didn't even know I was going to do it. I guess I really blew it, now!"

"Son of a bitch!" Richard said, and Tuck heard him go out the door. In a few minutes, he was back with second classman Wes Phenegar. Wes was a 148 pound wrestler and had taken a liking to Tuck. They often worked out on take downs and other holds on Saturday afternoons, which would normally be free time. Tuck believed that Wes came from a lot of money, but you wouldn't know it by his personality and attitude, which was exceptional. He had often helped Tuck with his calculus work, even if he couldn't spare the time.[100]

Wes listened to the story, told Tuck to sit tight and left the room. He returned shortly with the Midshipman Company Commander, First Classman Hart. Hart gave Wes a 'thank you, Mr. Phenegar,' dismissing him, and sat down on the bunk and asked Tuck what happened.

Tuck related the whole incident, reciting the conversation word for word. He was very upset, and having difficulty speaking.

"How many demerits have you?" Hart asked.

"One-ninety, as of this morning," Tuck said. "Give me your grades, course by course," he said.

Tuck told him his averages, all just above passing, except Spanish, a solid 3.0, and PT, which was a 4.0, perfect, and of course, the failing chemistry grade.

"And when, in your estimation," he asked, "did Mr. Pistotnick begin showing an extra interest in you?"

"Day one," Richard said, "Smitty told me that he insisted on getting on Si's table."

Hart looked at Richard with a puzzled expression.

"That's right, Sir," Tuck said, "I don't know what his problem is, but he's buddy-buddy with a segundo from my home town, Mr. Radcliffe."

"Just relax," he said, "this little vendetta of Mister Pistotnick's hasn't gone without notice. What you did was wrong, of course, but I don't think you're entirely to blame. You have my permission to skip evening formation and mess. Just stay here and relax. I'm going to talk to Mr. Pistotnick."

Hart came back to the room during study hour. Tuck was working on his chemistry assignment, but unable to concentrate. He felt like his world had collapsed, and was completely depressed. Richard and the other two roommates had diplomatically avoided talking about anything since they returned from mess. Hart told Tuck to follow him to his room, which he did.

"I've talked to Mr. Pistotnick," he said, "he will not be bothering you any further, and if he does, I want to know about it, understand?"

"Yes, Sir," Tuck responded.

"I took the liberty of looking at your file. Were you in the MP's?" Hart asked.

"No, Sir," Tuck replied, "but I did some temporary duty as a prisoner chaser at Lejuene."

"Did you kill someone there, an escaping prisoner?" Hart asked. "Your record is not clear on this."

"No, Sir," Tuck said, "I had to shoot a prisoner who attempted to escape, but only wounded him, in the leg."

"Well," Hart said, "you have an excellent record, which shows that you reacted well under pressure while an enlisted man."

"I stopped him. I did what I had to do, Sir," Tuck said, "I'm not particularly proud of it, and not even my roommates know about it. The Marine Corps is specific on prisoner chasing, Sir. If you lose a prisoner, you take his place. It's always been that way; a tradition. I'd prefer to keep it - that episode - private."

"I see," he said, reflecting on Tuck's response for a moment. "The problem here," he continued, "is that it's sometimes difficult for some Midshipmen who had never had your experience in the Fleet to understand the balance between positive and negative leadership. I have been expecting something of this nature to occur for some time, so I was not surprised by what happened here."

"Mister Hart," Tuck said, "I want to apologize for involving you in this. I'm ashamed of myself for losing my temper. I feel terrible about it, but just the same, he had no right to make personal remarks."

"You're correct and your reaction is understandable," he said, "but you should put it behind you now and concentrate on your academic subjects. There will be no demerits associated with this event, and Mr. Pistotnick has been assigned to another table at mess. It would help, though, if you would apologize to him."

"That's not in me, Sir, after what he said," Tuck responded, "I'm sorry."

"Very well," he said, "I won't require it. If you have further problems, my door is always open."

"Aye, aye, sir," Tuck said. He felt drained, exhausted both emotionally and physically. He had read Hart correctly the first day he introduced himself to the twelfth company plebes. A perfect gentleman, he was firm, but completely fair. He wasn't easy, he had given Tuck some tough questions, but plebes never felt threatened under his hazing, it was somehow always instructive.

With Hart, the question of where Tuck came from was never in the background. Most of the brigade came from solid family situations; bilging out of the Academy would mean taking their degree from Georgia Tech, Harvard or Penn instead. Richard and Tuck, and a few others among the plebes, especially the Nappers, were exceptions. Success on the outside was not guaranteed, or assumed in any way. Tuck had no support structure at home to fall back on. He had to make it here; it was the one chance for a future. Richard was banking on his talent as a football player; his ace in the hole.

"That Hart's a good man. He's going to make a good Marine Corps Officer," Richard said, when Tuck told him of the conversation. He still didn't tell him about shooting Clegall.

"Yeah," Tuck said, "but I don't understand what the fuck I'm doing sometimes, blowing up over somebody finding out my old man's an ex-con. The way he's treated us, especially mom, I shouldn't give a shit. He's not worth the aggravation."

"He's your father," Richard said, "it's not your fault, but you can't take anybody else talking against him. It's like my brother, Jimmy. He was a bad kid, but nobody could call him 'nigger,' or I'd kick their ass."

"Jimmy was black?" Tuck asked.

"Yeah," Richard said, "Mama took him in when he was a baby. He was abandoned. Here's a picture, taken just before he got killed in a car accident. He was sixteen."

Looking at the picture of Richard with his arm around his brother's shoulder, Tuck realized how much he envied him his family. For the remaining few weeks of the quarter, Tuck was treated like the rest of the plebes in the company. He took his share of abuse, and even enjoyed some of the good-natured pranks that they had to endure. He had elected not to participate in a spring sport, so after going out to the athletic field each day and participating in a mandatory mile run, he was free to return to his room and crack the books.

The last quarter in English required a research paper on some aspect of philosophy. Tuck selected Dewey's "stream of consciousness" theory, but in doing the research, ran across another lesser known philosopher, Edgar Fahs Smith, who had a similar theory that preceded Dewey's.[101]

With the assistance of the librarian, Tuck cracked the oldest stacks, many of the books simply piled in crates in the library's storeroom. Amazingly, everything was there, even a copy of Fahs' monograph. He became completely fascinated by the idea, and by the research, finding himself taking notes from books published in the early 1800's, original editions.

The professor, a civilian, handed Tuck the paper. It contained no grade, only a comment, "see me." Approaching his desk after class, Tuck held the paper out and asked him if there was a problem.

"The problem is, young man, that I'm not convinced that you wrote that paper," he said.

"I beg your pardon, sir," Tuck said, in a state of shock, "but I wrote and researched every word. Why would you think otherwise?"

Tuck's mind was reeling.

Here it goes, again! He thought. *What is it that makes me stand out to these bastards? Why doesn't this happen to other people?*

"It's simply not your work, that's all," the Professor said, "it's far too scholarly. Look at this bibliography. I'm willing to bet that half of these books don't exist."

"You're accusing me of plagiarism," Tuck said, his emotions only skin deep," and that's goddamned unfair!" He had spent weeks scrounging in the stacks at Mahan Hall to do the paper. "If you think I copied it, then you better be ready to produce whatever it is you think I copied it from!"

"I've never even heard of this theory, or this man, Smith," he said, "and I believe that I have more experience than you in these matters."

"Plagiarism is moral turpitude. It's the same as cheating! You're accusing me of cheating, and you don't even know what the hell you're talking about! This man Smith was from Philadelphia, and he's a famous scientist there, and was President of the American Philosophy Association." Tuck's voice was higher, strained. "I know where every one of those books is located, in the bibliography," he said, "and I'm signed into those storeroom stacks on the ledger at Mahan Hall, and I've got all the notes associated with this paper, and I am not a cheat!"

"There's no need to raise your voice, Midshipman," The professor responded, "I'm sure we can work this thing out."

Tuck could see that he hadn't expected a rebuttal, and was now unsure of his position. Unfortunately, he was in a position that required a loss of face, if he was to rectify it.

"I'm sure we can work it out, also," Tuck said, "because if we don't, I'm going straight to the Commandant and put this whole affair on the record, Goddamn you! You're trying to get me thrown out of the Academy on a moral turpitude charge, but you're wrong, dead wrong, and I can prove it! What's your motivation? Who's been telling you lies about me?"

Tuck wondered what the hell else could go wrong. He had worked diligently on the paper, writing and re-writing it, and now the son of bitch was accusing him of stealing it. He was enraged by the accusation, and at the same time, completely discouraged and depressed by it.

"I'm not accustomed to being spoken to in this way," the Professor said.

"That's too goddamned bad, because I'm not accustomed to being called a cheat!" Tuck responded. He had no other alternative but to challenge him.

This was plagiarism, moral turpitude! Good bye to the Academy. On these kinds of charges, I could wake up bouncing outside the Main gate, with a blemish that couldn't be erased in a lifetime, Tuck thought. He had built a wall of armor against Pistotnick and the hazing. The last thing that he expected was an attack on his ethical behavior from a Professor.

A long pause ensued; the Professor tapping his pencil on Tuck's paper on his desk. Tuck was standing immediately in front of him, rigid with rage and indignation. He could feel that his neck and ears were red, flushed.

"I'll hold on to this, and talk to the librarian," he said, "and if what you say is true, I'll reconsider my remarks and grade it."

Tuck turned and left without comment. In the room that night, he told Richard the story. "Jesus, Si," he asked, "What the hell did he assume that for?"

"I don't know," Tuck said, "unless it was the fact that nobody ever gave him a paper on this guy Smith before. But I don't understand why he would think I copied it. I'll bet nobody's written a paper on that guy's philosophy since about 1830. If he pushes me, I can nail the bastard to the wall. Hell, half the librarians thought it was great that I was doing this paper. We had to move crates and everything else to get at some of the reference books, they were so old. This guy Smith was a genius, made contributions in a lot of fields, and was a big deal at the University of Pennsylvania"

"Somebody must have a voodoo curse on you, Si," Richard said.

The following Monday, Tuck received the paper back, marked with a 3.83, an "A" minus grade. The Professor made no comment, nor did he.

When final grades were distributed, Tuck had passed all subjects except Chemistry, and his appointment to the Third Class was contingent on passing a re-examination in August, after the Brigade returned from summer cruise. He would lose ten days of leave time and his position on the Highland Light's crew for the Bermuda race, but he was still alive. Unknown to Tuck, three of his best buddies, all Nappers, were selected to the Light's racing crew and would sail the big cutter into history in the next three years.[102]

On graduation day, Tuck watched the gang of Plebes climbing the greased Herndon monument, a pyramid of shouting squirming bodies. A plebe from the Ninth Company made the top of the pile and placed his cap on the point. Plebe year was over! Tuck knew that he couldn't have survived another week without losing his self-control or sanity, or both.

34

HOLYSTONERS

RICHARD and Tuck had been assigned to the U.S.S. Healy, a sleek new destroyer, for the eleven week summer cruise. Because he had failed chemistry, Tuck was re-assigned to the U.S.S. New Jersey, BB-62, an Iowa class battleship. Chemistry classes would be conducted throughout the cruise in preparation for the re-exam back at the academy in August.

The fleet was anchored in the Chesapeake, east of the yard. The U.S.S. New Jersey and U.S.S. Iowa, the largest ships, were anchored furtherest out. Eight destroyers and two cruisers, in addition to the two battleships would carry half of the brigade during the cruise. Ports of call were to be Oslo, Norway, Portsmouth, England and Guantanamo Bay, Cuba.[103]

The USS New Jersey ploughing heavy seas in the Pacific in 1944, then flagship of the Third Fleet under Admiral Halsey's command.

The Midshipmen settled into crew's quarters just forward of the number three turret on the main deck level. The Jersey represented the ultimate in surface ship naval warfare. She and her sisters, Iowa, Wisconsin and Missouri were the last of the great battleships. New Jersey was built in Philadelphia when Edie Maye worked in the parachute factory, her main deck was 887 feet long, all teak laid over steel, and a half foot thick. She was 129 feet at the beam, required 36 feet of water to float her, displaced 45,000 tons, and her hull was protected with up to eighteen inches of steel armor plating, from deck to keel.

With the Midshipmen aboard, the ship's normal complement of 4,000 men was nearly reached. Since the Korean War had cranked down, the Jersey was running on a skeleton crew of only 2,500 men. But it was still a small city, with its own laundry, Post Office, slop chute (cafeteria), ship's store, movie, newspaper and all the amenities required for a group that size.

Her three main turrets, two forward and one aft, each carried three 16-inch rifles, capable of throwing a 2,000 pound projectile more than twenty miles. A man could crawl down the forty-foot barrels, and did, when cleaning and inspecting them. Her eight steam turbines drove four propellers, two seventeen feet and two eighteen feet in diameter, and she could steam 33,000 miles at 15 knots, with a top speed of 33 knots, nearly 40 miles an hour. Her ship's generators could power a city the size of Seattle, Washington. She was awesome.[104]

Midshipman regimen on the ship was divided into two week segments with the various divisions; engineering, armament, fire control, etc. They were treated as Seaman third-class by the sailors who ran the divisions, standing watches and doing the chores required. As soon as the crew that Tuck worked with discovered that he had been in the fleet, and a corporal, he got along great, regardless of the assignment.

Of course the regular crew enjoyed having the midshipmen to order around. The bos'n mates, mostly young blacks, lined them up in rows, gave each a "holystone," a brick-sized piece of pumice with a hollow cup in its center, and a broomstick. With their rhythmic chant for timing, the "wogs" (midshipmen) would then "holystone" the teak decks, swaying in unison, side to side, grinding the pumice block on the smooth teak. The bosn's would keep the chant going and slop water on the deck as necessary.

Tuck enjoyed all the work, even chipping paint. A good job just required elbow grease and minimum concentration, cathartic after the intensity of plebe year. But the ship in general was working on him. He spent every moment of free time exploring its bowels and climbing the superstructure. She throbbed with a mighty pulse, the gigantic drive shafts turning slowly deep inside her hull.

Since reporting aboard, Tuck's "tuxedo man" nightmares had slacked off. Throughout the entire academic year, a night without the terrifying visit from his nightly childhood nemesis had been rare. Now he was seeing old bloody chest only about twice a week. He even enjoyed the starchy food, a far cry from the abundant gourmet at the Academy.

In engineering, they learned to run the boilers, changing nozzles in a "hot" tub, and responding to the ship's telegraph, lighting up boilers and putting them "on line." Tuck found "shaft alley" fascinating, and would sit next to the giant drive shafts, turning slowly in their wooden bearings, while studying chemistry. Using a pocket knife given him by Chip, Tuck carved a small "T-1956" in one of the starboard inboard oaken bearings.[105]

They had steamed down the Chesapeake Bay and laid into Norfolk, where the "Jersey" took on fuel and supplies for the cruise at Pier 7, and a day later, the huge ship cleared Cape Henry and steamed north by northeast, heading for the Arctic Circle and the North Sea. The destroyers ran in front and behind with the cruisers on the flanks.

The Jersey took the sea like a grand old lady; with a matronly roll. Tuck spent a lot of time topside, catching the sunsets and sunrises, if he were awake or on a watch. In a couple of weeks, they were scattering schools of thousands of flying fish all around the ship as she plowed northward. They had settled down to a routine, and Tuck loved it!

The seas began to lengthen, the swells deepening, and the word was that they were approaching the Arctic Circle. From topside, Tuck could perceive the earth's curvature on the horizon, which appeared so close that it was no longer flat, but the ocean's swells could be seen on it.

One morning, coming off watch in the engineering section, where Tuck had been below decks for four hours, conducting flashpoint tests on fuel samples, he found a favorite spot between the stacks about 40 feet above the main deck. He sat there quietly, enjoying the fresh breeze in his face. Off the starboard side, about a mile distant, he noticed dark forms in the blue green water. Bruce Shoemaker, a Napper who had played on the football team, was with him.

The destroyers and cruisers had left the line, and would rejoin the New Jersey on the run from Norway down to England.

"Hey, Shoe," Tuck said, "Take a look out there. I think I saw a whale!" Tuck pointed in the direction, standing up.

"Shit, Si," Shoe said, "you're seeing things."

"Like hell," Tuck said, now convinced, "that's a couple of whales out there." Tuck's vision was 20-10 in both eyes. He often saw things at distance that others couldn't. Ten minutes later a bos'n pipe sounded.

"Now hear this," the ship's speaker bellowed, "the crew is informed that we have whales on the starboard beam. Watch captains may release crew in shifts to observe. That is all."

The Jersey coughed black smoke from her stacks and her throbbing slowed as she began to turn toward the whales. There were two of them, blues, porpoising along side by side and clearly visible. The ship steamed by them, within a few hundred yards, and keeping the helm over, began to make a series of slow circles around them.[106]

Tuck had read of the great blue whale. The largest creature ever to have ever lived on the earth, and master of the seas, his domain included all the great oceans of the world, which he crossed leisurely in annual migrations. Moby Dick had accompanied him on many a fishing or camping adventure. But even Melville couldn't put into words the thunderous grace, power and beauty of these wondrous animals, when seen in their element.

"Look," Shoe said, "there are three of them."

It was so evident. Tuck only had to watch for a moment and he could see it plainly. "That isn't just three whales, Shoe," he said, "that's a family."

The female, the cow, was well over 100 feet in length. She was magnificent, and no matter where the ship was located, she positioned herself between it and the male and the baby. Each time she porpoised, Tuck could see her eye, watching with curiosity and caution. Her skin was deep blue, so deep that it appeared black and rippled with shimmering highlights of red and purple when the sun's rays reflected from it. She ran next to her mate, about forty yards distant. He was smaller, perhaps only eighty feet in length, and slimmer.

Tuck's memory paintings of his time aboard the Battleship New Jersey. Top, the ship battling a north sea storm, middle left, Tuck observing from the signal bridge a nearby destroyer being tossed by the same storm, which caused many injuries aboard the smaller ships, center right, the ship being visited by a family of blue whales, and bottom, the Jersey in Oslo Fjord (Norway) surrounded by mountains.

The pair broke the sea together, huge geysers erupting from their dual blowholes. Tuck could easily hear the great "whoosh" that accompanied their water spouts. The infant, the calf, was about 25 feet in length, and typically, he was giving his parents fits, swimming between them and frolicking in their tail splashes. His geysers were miniature versions of his parents', only more frequent, and the sound, like a little sneeze for the adults; comical. Whenever he headed for the ship, the bull or cow would head him off and lead him back to a safe position between them.

Most of the crew was topside now, and each time a parent intercepted its frisky offspring, they cheered and clapped.

"Give him hell, pop," someone shouted.

"Watch him, dad, he's a pisser!" another shouted. As the ship circled, its huge propellers created a half-mile long wake, and soon all three behemoths were playing in it.

Tuck thought that they acted like kids in the surf at the shore. All three rolled over in the wake, exposing their gleaming white bellies, and the calf, on several occasions, actually leaped clear of the water!

When the three rolled in rather close to the ship's stem, Captain Brooks let go on the fog horn, a loud blast of sound. The whales reacted quickly, turning out of the wake and moving a safer distance away, where they re-entered the ship's churning trail, and continued to frolic.

Tuck watched them in breathless silence, awed by their size and intelligence and amazed by the human quality of their behavior. Their eyes were exactly like human eyes, only larger. Tuck thought he even saw eyelashes! In a nimble leap of his imagination, Tuck realized that the 25 ton calf was exactly like the many 5 ounce kittens he had observed, continually teasing their parents and the adults reacted in kind, nosing the baby away or prodding him in the direction they wanted him to go.

"They stay with their parents for at least two years," Tuck commented to Shoemaker, without losing his focus on the family.

The skipper circled for two hours and finally, Jersey resumed their original course northward. The whales followed along for another hour, then turned southeast into the Atlantic, their destination probably below the Equator. Tuck remained topside watching them until they were out of sight, savoring the experience.

"Shoe" had long since gone below, bored and restless. Tuck only half heard his comments as he went down the ladder. The whales had captured him; his entire attention and concentration was focused. He felt attached, an inexplicable feeling of being lost, yet found, engulfed him. It was as though he was swimming with them, a part of their family.

He thought about Chip, crouching in the glen, watching the doe and fawns. It would have been nice to tell Chip about the whales. He would understand it. And he thought about Hugh Campbell, a Don Quixote fighting useless battles. Tuck pictured his favorite painting of the creek forays, "Corn Left Standing."

For the next several days the Jersey plowed through the lengthening dark swells of the North Atlantic. Tuck spent hours aloft, hoping without success to see more whales.

Tuck came topside after a turn on the dog watch; midnight to four a.m. He was curious because the turbines had slowed to stop and the ship was relatively silent. He was surprised to find the ship laying about a mile off a dark, rugged coast, which he assumed must be Norway. They were so far north that it no longer got dark at night, and it was easy to see the craggy granite cliffs covered with green pines in the twilight. They had cruised inside the Arctic Circle and were now in the land of the midnight sun.

The ship was lying to while it took aboard a Norwegian pilot from a small fishing trawler. He would guide them up the 70-mile fjord to Oslo harbor. The pilot, dressed in a long leather coat and black hat, climbed the sea gangway lowered for him. He stopped at the rail, banged his pipe empty against a lifeline stanchion, pocketed it while slowly rotating his gaze from one end of the ship to the other, and then shook hands with the skipper and the Officer of the Deck.

About a half hour later, Tuck felt the vibration of the big drive shafts, and the Jersey swung her nose toward a narrow opening in the cliffs. The opening of the fjord was about a half mile wide, and the big ship glided into it with her screws barely turning over. They left behind the vastness of the Atlantic, with its infinite horizon, and were now completely surrounded by mountainous cliffs.

The cliffs fell directly to the water on both sides, like walls, and soon they began to narrow. By 0530, most of the crew had come topside and lined the rails. The fjord had narrowed in some places to less than 300 feet.

The New Jersey, with her 129 foot beam, was so close to the walls that Tuck could have thrown a rock and easily hit them.

Everyone was talking quietly, apprehensive about the close fit. Occasionally, the walls would give way to sloped meadows, some with thatched roof homes on them. They saw some people next to a house. Tuck wondered how they could not look at a 45,000 ton battleship quietly stealing by their front yard.

One such meadow appeared on the starboard bow, and all could see a man walking down toward the shoreline.

Here's a fellow, Tuck thought, *that's going to take a morning swim.* The man never even glanced toward the gargantuan ship as it glided by. Instead, he turned his back, dropped his pants, and defecated in the fjord!

Everyone on the starboard rail let out a big cheer, and the Norwegian responded by turning, after pulling up his pants, and waving back with a toothless grin.

Welcome to Norway, Tuck thought.

By 0900, the fjord had opened up into Oslo Harbor, and they dropped anchor directly in its center, surrounded by a sparkling city of brick and pastel buildings. The bosn's pipe preceded general announcements. No liberty today. All hands would turn to readying the ship for visitors on Monday morning. Daily liberty would commence at 1600 hours tomorrow afternoon.

Being in a fortunate position of not having any particular assignment, Tuck took a place along the rail on the fantail with a lot of others just looking at the city.

"Damn," someone said, "if that ain't a nudy beach, over there, to port!" One sailor had a pair of field glasses.

"Son of a bitch!" He said, "Look at that pair of tatas!"

Tuck headed for his battle station, a 40 millimeter anti-aircraft gun control center. It had a pair of binoculars in it that you actually sat in! Everybody else had the same idea. Jumping into his seat in the little turret, Tuck powered up and grasping the control wheel, he put his face in the binocular and started swinging the shoreline in the direction the sailor had been pointing.

Tuck soon had a beautiful brunette under the cross-hair in the scope. Her heavy breasts were bouncing up and down as she batted a volley ball back and forth over a net. Her partner, a thin blonde, was quite beautiful, too! They were absolutely naked! Unlike Tuck, the two guys on the other side of the net didn't appear affected as they were nude as well.

Suddenly, Tuck's turret powered down, and with the swing of the ship at anchor, he lost his view.

"Now hear this!" the speaker blared, "All hands secure from topside gun mounts and battle stations."

Every gun in the forward and aft port quadrants of the ship, eight turrets of five inch thirty-eights and ten 40 millimeter quads, had rotated with their aiming radars and were targeted on the beach club!

The following morning, Shoe and Tuck made the acquaintance of two lovely Norwegian girls when they came aboard during the open house. For the next seven days, they drew their daily liberty, met the girls at quayside and spent the days and evenings taking in the sights. In spite of everyone's later bragging, like Tuck, most ended up spending the week as perfect gentlemen and left Oslo with their dates' virginity in the same state they had found it.

Marit, Tuck's date, spoke perfect English as a second language and had learned no vernacular, slang or colloquialisms, she used "thee" and "thou," and it was a delight to hear the English language spoken in this way. The city was sparkling clean and the Norwegian people very friendly. They were the first American sailors in port since 1939.

The Jersey pulled her fifteen ton anchor after ten days in the Harbor, and threaded Southeast through the fjord into the North Sea and steamed South towards England. The Officers were signing everyone up for tours of either Paris or London, and Shoe and Tuck picked the London tour.

Tuck and Marit in Frognerparken, Oslo. Frogner Park is the largest park in the city. The sculpture Arrangement is the world's largest sculpture park made by a single artist, Gustav Vigeland.

Gunnery practice was scheduled during the run south, which meant Tuck would have the opportunity to fire the 40 millimeter quadruple Bofers that his turret controlled. The third day out, they were called to battle stations, and the speaker system informed the crew that they could expect the target to be towed into the line from the Southeast. The destroyers and cruisers had rejoined, and they were now steaming in line, the twelve ships covering six miles of ocean.

In a short while, radar picked up two blips on the horizon, closing at better than 400 knots! Hearing the radar report in earphones, Tuck swung his mount forward, and picked up the tiny dots skimming the ocean. They were two delta wing Cranberra fighter/bombers, the cream of the English Air Force, and they came at the line flat out, less than a hundred feet off the water. As they approached each ship, the pilots tilted the inboard wings upward, and then level again, after the fly by.

Tuck backed out of his mount in time to catch them as they buzzed the Jersey with a thunderous roar. He could see the rivets and every detail of the skin structure, they were so close, even a grinning blue-eyed pilot with a gloved "thumbs up" signal in the cockpit. The Cranberras banked out to sea at the end of the line, and in broad sweeping turn, buzzed the Jersey again, coming from abeam and putting their inside wings down, they figuratively flew between her stacks!

The Avro Lancaster that followed, towing a tube target at about 5,000 feet, was somewhat of a disappointment after the Cranberras. The Healy, the last destroyer in line, was the only ship that could hit the targets, and she knocked five of them down. She was equipped with the brand new three-inch fifty caliber guns and a new computer controlled fire system. Tuck found it incredible that anything could fly through the wall of lead the first 10 ships put up, without noticeably being hit, but each time the target came into Healy's range, the first few rounds blew it to shreds and parted the towline.

The ship nosed up to a buoy in Portsmouth Harbor the following Sunday, and everyone debarked for their tours.

Tuck found London a huge disappointment after spending time with the Norwegians. The American sailors were heckled by communist sympathizers everywhere they went, and the downtown area, particularly Picadilly Circus and Trafalgar Square, was filled with prostitutes, who constantly tugged at their sleeves with propositions. The city was filthy, and the merchants anxious to rip off the sailors, and get American money.[107]

Tuck made it point to take in the changing of the guard at Buckingham Palace, and found the Sherlock Holmes house on Baker Street, which he toured. Aside from that and a medieval dinner at the Gore Hotel, he spent most of the time drinking with some British Marines that frequented a small pub near his hotel. He grabbed a train a day and a half early and returned to Portsmouth, figuring he'd just as soon spend the last couple of days back aboard the Jersey.

Walking from the train station in Portsmouth, a British Naval Officer approached him. Tuck offered to buy him a beer, and he agreed, but instead of entering the pub they were standing next to, he grabbed a cab and took Tuck to the British Officer's Club at the Portsmouth Naval Yard. Tuck was welcomed like an old friend, and all insisted that he stay on there until the ship was ready to sail. He attended a garden party, played cricket and snooker, and had a great time for two days. Back on the Jersey, everyone bragged about how many times they got laid, etc., but Tuck knew that he had experienced the best slice of British life.

The Jersey steamed out of Portsmouth and took a heading past the white cliffs of Dover north towards the Arctic Circle for maneuvers with the rest of the fleet, after which they would steam south for Cuba. Tuck's battle station was changed from the 40 millimeter gun control center to number one turret, where he became a "powder passer."

Each turret was contained in its own "barbette." The barbette was essentially a perfectly round 40 foot barrel that extended from the deck to keel, sealing off the turret so that it could rotate freely. This meant that, under combat conditions, the turret could only be entered from topside, inside the gun housing. It was a self-contained unit.

The job was a little tricky. The turret had horizontal half barrels protruding from its circular walls at intervals on the fifth and sixth level down. These half barrels would align with their counterparts outside the turret. A signaling telegraph told the man on each side what needed to be done, since only one side of the barrel could be open at a time.

The passer stationed outside the turret would open his side of the barrel. A heavy lever activated the curved steel door, and once it was started, it was virtually impossible to stop. He would then load a 100 pound charge of powder, a mixture of dynamite and ammonia nitrate, into the barrel. Slamming home the door, he would then signal the Passer on the inside, who would open the inside door, remove the powder charge and place it on a lift, slam home the door, and signal his partner outside the turret.

The danger lay in getting your signals mixed. Opening one side automatically closed the other, the door slamming down without warning with a guillotine effect. The door could, and had, severed men's fingers and broken arms. For the first time in the Jersey, Tuck was frightened. It wasn't so much the passing of the powder charges. He had worked with explosives before. There was virtually no way, should an emergency arise, to get out of the turret. They were stationed six decks below the main deck. Thirty feet under water, and the only escape for the 30 men working at different levels, and all the men in the turret above, was one vertical ladder shaft, hardly wide enough for a man's shoulders. The shaft dropped forty feet straight down into the base of the sixteen inch gun's housing. During battle a station, the entry to the shaft was dogged down, the last clanging sound before the work began.

"Hey, Sigi!" the "bos'n" training the new crew was calling to Tuck, but he didn't realize it. When the passing drill was finished, he came over.

"You're a sigi, ain't you?" he asked. He was reading Tuck's name which was stenciled on his cap.

"Yeah," Tuck said, "I been called that before."

He was a huge fellow, swarthy with black curly hair. He asked where Tuck was from, and he told him. Extending his hand, he said, "My name's Vince, Vince Scaglia, I'm from Brooklyn."

The following day, Tuck saw him at chow and sat down at his table.

"Hey, Vince," Tuck said, "I met a guy named Scaglia once. I worked with him; he was an ironworker, from Brooklyn."

"Get out," Vince said, "that had to be Joey, my older brother."

Tuck told Vince the story of the crooked barracks, and they had a laugh about it.

"Joey's a tough guy," Vince said, "he served in the Jersey, too, in the big war. He got a medal for saving some guy that went overboard in the Pacific. Joey dove off of a pom-pom tub when he saw this guy go over, and he saved his life before he got sucked into the screws. There's a couple of Chiefs still aboard that was there when it happened."

"I'll never figure out why he picked me that day, to hold the chisel," Tuck said.

"He figured you was one of the boys, that's all. There's a couple of Falconettis around home that's connected," Vince said, "that's why he picked you."

The Jersey crossed the Arctic Circle again and this time, she paid for the privilege. About a week out of Portsmouth, they plowed into a North Sea storm that sailor's legends are made of. The ship was taking water on the bridge, nearly forty feet above the main deck and two hundred feet aft of her bow! The seas were nearly three hundred feet from crest to crest, and with decks continually awash, all hands except essential personnel were confined below decks.

Tuck stole out to the signal bridge, and watched the storm from there, amazed to see Jersey's bow completely buried in the huge swells. At times the entire front third of the ship was under water.

The destroyers were taking a terrible beating, since the distance between swells was too great for their length. Tuck watched one off the beam and was looking right down her stacks one moment and then seeing nearly her entire bottom the next, with propellers turning uselessly in air, thirty feet above the sea! Watching the destroyers, he thought about the

Megara. It was easy to understand what could happen to less seaworthy ships, facing the power of the sea.

They steamed northward for four days, their course dictated by the wind and seas, until the storm blew itself out.

Reversing course, two destroyers came alongside and transferred personnel who were in serious condition from seasickness and the battering of the storm. Breeches bouys were rigged and the sick men hauled to the battleship, which had hospital facilities. Two men were so ill that ten days later, they lay off Bermuda and put them over for treatment in a land-based hospital.

Steaming south into the Caribbean, the water became clearer and clearer, a light green in color, and the ship picked up escorts of spinning porpoises. They played in the bow wake on and off for several days, sometimes as many as a hundred of them.

Topside on the superstructure one day, Tuck discovered a huge shark swimming in the shadow of the ship, his long slim body hardly moving as he matched their 20 knot speed. He told a couple of sailors, and they quickly marked his length, using the life line stanchions on the main deck. Tuck got the distance from the waterline to their observation point from engineering, and doing the trigonometry, calculated the shark's length at thirty-two feet!

They dropped anchor in Guantanamo Bay after two days of firing the sixteen inch guns at Viegas, the Navy and Marine Corps firing range in the Caribbean. Castro's revolution was in flux and the situation in Cuba was unsettled and somewhat tense. Jersey hauled anchor after a couple of days, and steamed north for Cape Henry and the Academy.

Entering the Chesapeake Bay at Hampton Roads, a high pressure steam line burst in a compartment next to turret number one's sixth deck magazine, where Tuck had worked as a powder passer. The bulkhead got so hot from superheated steam at 750 degrees that the Skipper secured the crew aft of bulkhead 94, fearing an explosion. Several destroyers came alongside and picked up the Midshipmen, and ferried them to the anchorage at Annapolis, where they debarked in motor whaleboats to the Academy. Jersey headed for the Philadelphia Navy Yard and mothballing.

It was the last major cruise for the USS New Jersey prior to decommissioning and scheduled mothballing at Philadelphia, where she was built. Tuck was proud to have served in her, and sad that she would disappear from the seas of the world. Like the great blue whales, she had roamed the seas and sailed in harm's way, the most decorated ship in the Navy, but the day of the battleship was apparently over.

Tuck stepped ashore on the Academy quay amidst hundreds of excited parents and families. The grounds were awash with activity as other Midshipmen met their loved ones, loaded up the family cars and debarked for thirty days' leave. Tuck sat on his duffel bag, waiting for the crowd to subside. He would live at mother Bancroft for ten more days, during the re-exam period.

The late afternoon sun cast long shadows on the dock before Tuck hoisted the duffel bag to his shoulder. He looked out on the Chesapeake where a few of the destroyers were still visible on the silvery surface. They were steaming south; towards Cape Henry. He watched them for a while and then strode off towards Bancroft Hall, thinking about the whales.

35

THE SWORD

FOR the two week re-exam session, Tuck bunked in with Bruce Shoemaker and Norm Bednarik, two ex-NAPPERS, and they studied arduously for the upcoming tests. A major summer storm, a hurricane named Betsy, hit the east coast that year, flooding the Academy grounds.

The "fastest" ship in the Navy, the Reina Mercedes, broke her chains and drifted down the Severn River and smashed into the Route 50 Bridge, removing that question from the plebe lexicon forever. A large and famous staysail yawl, the Vamarie, part of the sailing fleet, broke from her mooring and was smashed between the quay and the tug that was trying to save her, and sank. Tuck watched helplessly as the sailors did everything wrong...he was sure Vamarie could've been saved simply by towing her out to deep water, but the tug crew trapped her in a "lee shore" situation and crushed the smaller hull as the tug smashed against its rail.[108]

Tuck passed the chemistry re-exam with ease, packed his gear and hitchhiked to Baltimore, where he caught the PRR to Philly. He had twenty days leave coming and he needed it. Cholly met him at the Philadelphia station in his '55 Plymouth. Tuck was driving a '53 Plymouth when he enlisted, and Cholly had taken over the payments and traded the car on this one, which was red and white and loaded with chrome. With a big V-eight engine, it was very fast and powerful, and its likeness would later be made famous in film as the possessed restoration "Cristine".

He was still at the foam rubber plant, and now managing the whole works. Working sixty hour weeks, he was making great money, but drinking heavier than ever. Tuck was home only a week when Cholly totaled the car and nearly drowned as a result.

He left work late one evening, stopped at a local bar and drank until closing. In a heavy downpour, he dozed at the wheel and went off the road at about sixty-five miles per hour, cutting a utility pole in half fifteen feet from its base. The car rolled 240 feet into a corn field, but Cholly had been thrown clear at first impact with a drainage ditch.

He was lying face down in the ditch when a passing motorist stopped and pulled him out, and then drove to a telephone and called the police. Black and blue all over, but this time with a broken right arm, he was home from the hospital in three days.

Bill Evans, a NAPPER from Trenton was a good buddy, and he drove down from his home in Trenton to visit Tuck. They dated some girls Bill knew from Ryder College and Tuck spent a few days in Trenton. Sitting in Count Felix's bar in the 'burg' one afternoon, Bill switched the subject from the baseball game on TV.

"Did you hear about Radcliffe?" Bill asked.

"No." Tuck said, "The less I hear about him, the better. Why, what's the scuttlebutt?"

Bill was in the Third Company, and his roommate had connections through his father, who was an Admiral.

"He and six other guys are up before the Review Board," Bill said, "and they may get scuttled completely."

"What's the story?" Tuck asked, "What did they do?"

"Well," Bill said, "one of the guys in the Fifth Company. He told his folks about the ass-takers. He had to, he was in the hospital for six days with blue balls, and they wanted to know what the hell was going on."

"Son of a bitch," Tuck said, "you mean that story was true? Those guys were putting plebes in the hospital?"

"Yeah," Bill said, "and as soon as the one guy spilled the beans, a whole bunch of others came forward. Guys they had been beating up on."

"I'll tell you, Bill," Tuck said, "I heard some scuttlebutt, but it seemed impossible to me that it was true."

"Those guys were real sadists," Bill said, "Tony's old man said they kept a list of 'undesirables' that they were trying to bilge out. It was like some kind of secret society. They called it 'The Sword'."

"I'll be damned," Tuck said, "but it figures. Some of these guys are real snobs. So, Radcliffe has got his ass in a wringer, eh?" The news was not unsatisfying.

"Your name was on it!" Bill said, "That's why Tony called. He knew we were buddies."

"What?" Tuck asked. It took a minute for it to sink in.

"Yeah," he said, "a whole bunch of the NAPPERS; you, Fernandez, Powell, Casamante, and a big bunch of guys who came in from fleet appointments, all black, Asian, Puerto Rican or Italian."

"Come on, Bill," Tuck said, "You can't be serious! They had a list based on race?"

"No," he said, "it's all true. These guys are in deep shit, and there's a bunch of segundos from other companies involved, too, but they don't know who they are."

"That fucking Pistotnick," Tuck said, "he's got to be one of 'em."

Tuck told him about plebe year, and how he had lost control and attacked Pistotnick.

"The thing is," Tuck said, "he was such a pussy. I swear he almost peed in his pants when I went after him. If he'd belted me back, or held his ground, I would have had some respect for him, at least, but he literally turned white and cowered in a corner."

"All these guys are like that," Bill said, "there isn't an athlete in the bunch, it's really weird."

"Well," Tuck said, "That explains why Hart let me off so easy, after I decked him. He must have known something about it or at least suspected something."

"My roomie says the brass is really upset about it," Bill said, "especially after what happened down at Parris Island with that D.I. on trial. The publicity could raise hell with the Academy; the thing at Parris Island is making news."

"They should throw the mother fuckers out," Tuck said, "can you imagine puttin' your life on the line with one of those guys in command? Giving them commissions is like signing a death warrant for some poor grunts!"

"Tony says they're probably going to set them back," Bill said, "and make them take Second Class year over again, on probation."

"Big deal," Tuck said, "they're still going to make shitty officers. They represent everything that Navy isn't, they're like anti-matter in physics, or something. The thing that pisses me off is that guys like that breeze through the academics, and I have to damn near kill myself just to pass a course."

"You gotta' promise that you won't tell anybody what I told you," Bill said, "My roomie's on the line with his old man. Some scuttlebutt is already out on these guys, but nobody, I mean nobody, knows about the list except the Review Board and My roomie's old man."

Mum's the word," Tuck said, "and Bill thanks, I appreciate this. It clears up a lot in my own mind."

Tuck settled in for the new year with Richard as his roommate. Third classmen could bunk two to a room, at least some of them, and Richard used some of his football influence to make it happen.

He soon discovered that the absence of hazing wasn't enough for him to be able to study like anyone else. Right out of the gate, he was failing electrical engineering. His new status allowed him to study late at nights without repercussions, but he was having a lot of difficulty.

Richard immediately made the varsity, starting on both defense and offense. It was evident that he was on his way to an All-American year. The smallest player on the team, he was the most devastating blocker that Navy had seen in a long time.

Since the team traveled a lot, the football players ended up in their own class sections, lagging behind the rest of the brigade in studies. They got a lot of personal attention, being in smaller sections, but otherwise, had to contend with the same work load.

Captain Dickey nailed Tuck the first week back, calling him into the office.

"I was looking at your personnel folder," he said, "and I noticed that you fired expert with the .45 automatic during plebe summer."

"Yes, sir," Tuck said, "that's correct."

"In fact," he said, "you fired the fourth highest score ever recorded at the range, a 374!"

"Yes, sir," Tuck said, seeing some study time disappearing.

"We're organizing a Company competition," he said, "and I'd like you to represent the Twelfth."

"Is that an order, sir?" Tuck asked. He had no interest in shooting a pistol in competition.

"Well, no," he said, "but certainly you'd want to comply, it wouldn't be in the correct spirit to refuse. It's for the company."

"I don't care to compete, sir," Tuck said, "I haven't time to practice, and I haven't handled a pistol since plebe summer."

Captain Dickey struck a little pose with his swagger stick, scratching his chin with it.

"Well," he said, "let's put it in terms of a personal favor, you could give up a couple of afternoons."

"Begging the captain's pardon, Sir," Tuck said, "but I seem to recall asking the captain for a favor of a very urgent nature, and being refused, when my grandfather died!"

He got up from his desk and walked around it, facing Tuck down.

"Now that's out of line, Mister," he said, "you will fire in this competition; that is an order, now!"

"Very well, Sir," Tuck said, "I'll fire, but I'll be goddamned if I'll give up one minute of study time to practice, and if you try to make me, I'm going to the Commandant."

Tuck was enraged, but controlling his anger. This was practically the only time he had ever spoken to Captain Dickey, except when Chip died, now the bastard wanted him to give up study time.

"I'm failing EE, Sir," Tuck said, "I need all the time I have to stay up with my studies. I don't have any extra time to spare."

"Lower your voice, mister, and stand at attention! You'll fire in this competition, representing the twelfth." Tuck could see that Dickey was angry, but he didn't care. The captain continued, "Are you aware that you are very close to the top of your class, in spite of these little anomalies of yours and your poor performance academically? I sometimes think that you're going to make a fine officer, and other times, I wonder."

"My drill instructor said the same thing, sir," Tuck said, "and then he tried to drown me in Ribbon Creek."

"All right," he said, "I'll ignore that remark. Now, get out of here, and do your best in the competition. I won't require you to practice."

That fall Tuck talked Edie Maye into visiting him at the Academy. She came on a Sunday morning and Tuck had arranged for space on the Highland Light, the big cutter. Edie Maye had sewn a special sailing outfit and bought a pair of soft soled moccasin in anticipation.

There was little wind and the boat was unable to show off her speed. They ghosted up the bay to the Annapolis Bay Bridge and made their way slowly back to the Academy by nightfall. Edie Maye talked with Admiral Kasker and everyone aboard, explored it below decks and lay on the foc'sle long enough to get a good burn.

"I'm sorry about the weather, Mom," Tuck said, "she's not a lot of fun when the wind is light."

"Don't you worry about it, Tuck," she replied, "I'm enjoying every moment." Tuck thought that she looked radiant. He decided not to worry her with his problems in Electrical Engineering.

Wes Phenegar[109] tried helping Tuck with the EE, but it might as well have been Greek. He failed it with a 1.7 average the first quarter. What the hell was inductance? impedance? watts and amps? Tuck couldn't grasp it, the attempt to quantify electricity, an invisible thing.

They had a load of new plebes in the company, and Tuck was sympathetically friendly with a few of them, but mostly ignored them. Third classmen could ask questions, but Tuck figured that he'd be the last guy on the planet earth to harass a plebe.

He reported to the range the day of the pistol competition and shot a miserable 200 score. Dickey made no comment about it. He would like to have done better, but knew it to be impossible to hit anything with a .45 caliber automatic unless you practice with the same weapon for a period of time.

Navy played Notre Dame in Baltimore that year, and the brigade boarded trains early on that Saturday morning and arriving in Baltimore, debarked at the train station and formed up, four miles from Municipal Stadium.

Four thousand, five hundred strong, the brigade marched through the tree lined streets of Suburban Baltimore to the cadence of the drummer's sticks on the rims of their traps. It was a clear and frosty fall morning, and about every twenty minutes, the Drum and Bugle Corps would burst forth with "Anchors Aweigh" or the Navy "Fight" song, the clear tones of the brass and thunder of the big drums echoing through the neighborhoods.

It was the most thrilling experience of all the parades that Tuck had participated in. Soon, the people of Baltimore were lining the route of march, standing on porches in bathrobes, and talking quietly. The brigade moved with extraordinary precision that morning, everyone swept up in the grandeur of it, the huge line of 4500 blue uniformed midshipmen, moving in silent cadence through the sun speckled autumn colored streets.

Navy beat Notre Dame that day on a muddy field, Richard intercepting a Paul Horning pass and running it back fifty yards for a touchdown. When the game ended, the Irish were backed up to their one yard line, uniforms so muddy that it was impossible to read numbers.

With Wes's help, Tuck managed to pass the re-exam in EE, and things looked a little brighter for the second quarter. He had gone out for the Battalion football team, since he was required to participate for two hours each day, and soon found that he had missed playing ball. He made the starting quarterback spot, and in the third game, tore his left knee badly.

The infirmary packed it in ice for about six hours, and turned him out. Battalion ball players got cursory treatment. Richard came over to sick bay, which is located in the basement of Bancroft Hall, when he heard what happened. Tuck was sitting outside the closed infirmary and couldn't walk. Richard retrieved a laundry cart from the nearby laundry, loaded Tuck and pushed him to the other side of Bancroft Hall in the basement, then got Bob St. Roberts, a first classman.

"Saint," as he was called, was a 280 pound, All-American football prospect until he tore up both knees, and surgery required the removal of his kneecaps. He picked Tuck up and carried him, like a baby, up the ten flights of stairs to his room. The following morning, Tuck got up at reveille, swung his legs out of the bunk, stood up, and passed out.

The knee put Tuck on crutches for five weeks and was so painful that he had difficulty concentrating on anything, a major setback. Hobbling on crutches to class one morning, he noticed a color guard of marines on a break outside the chapel. One of them spotted Tuck and walked over.

"Hey, Si," he said, "how ya' doin?" It was Weber, the marine whom Tuck had decked in boot camp!

"How are you, Weber?" Tuck said, a little apprehensive. "Are you stationed here, in Annapolis?" he asked. Weber looked sharp in his dress blues, and was sporting sergeant stripes.

"Nah," he said, "I'm with the capitol regiment, in D.C. I just made my third stripe last week. We've got a little ceremony here at the chapel. What happened to you?"

"Busted up my knee playing football," Tuck said.

"I've been hoping I'd run into you," he said, "ever since P.I."

Tuck figured he was going to take his revenge, and he knew that he was helpless. He still couldn't put any weight on his left leg.

"I want to thank you, Man," he said, "for a long time, I wanted to find you and bust your ass, but now I realize, I mean, you did what you had to do, no hard feelings."

He removed his white glove and extended his hand.

"Ah, listen," Tuck said, somewhat embarrassed, but returning his handshake, "you would've done the same, if the situation were reversed. It was nothing personal, you know."

"You squared me away," he said, "and I figured I should tell you. I'm in for the long haul; I just signed over for another four-year hitch."

"Well, thanks," Tuck said, "but I've gotta' get to class, and I'm probably already late. It's been good seeing you."

"My pleasure," he said, "I can't wait to get back to D.C. and tell Flowers I saw you. He'll shit when he finds out you're going to be an officer!"

"You see Flowers?" Tuck stopped, hopped in a circle to face Weber again.

"Yeah, he's in the outfit," he said, and added with a chuckle, "He's still a four-striper. They're wise to him. He's afraid I'm gonna' outrank him pretty soon!"

"The bastard ought to be cashiered," Tuck said, "he and McGaughey tried to kill me on bivouac, in Ribbon Creek. They set me up for that."

"Yeah," he said, "everybody knows about that now; everybody thought you'd drowned. All that shit with the other D.I. that got convicted put the heat on Flowers. About 150 D.I.'s got cashiered eventually. Ours was the last platoon that he pushed through P.I. They pulled him out because of the rumors about Ribbon Creek.[110] He still hates your ass! All the more since the guys told him about Lejuene."

"Tell him for me," Tuck said, "the feeling is mutual. What are you talking about, what about Lejuene?"

"We got a couple of guys in the outfit from the Second Marines," he said, "You're some kind of legend down there. You killed some guys escaping from the brig, right?"

"No way, Weber," Tuck said, waving as he hobbled off, "they must have me mixed up with somebody else. I never killed anybody."

Tuck found himself laughing as he hobbled down the walk, thinking about all the stories he had heard about legendary marines; Dan Daily, Chesty Puller and the others.

If I ever get bars, he thought, *that shot in Clegall's leg will probably have killed a battalion of escaping convicts at Leavenworth Prison!*

He had signed on with the Brigade Hop Committee as an extra-curricular activity, and on the Friday morning prior to the Army game, they were to fly up to Philadelphia to decorate the Bellevue-Stratford Hotel ballroom for the Army-Navy ball that evening.

Tuck boarded a motor whaleboat with the other committee members that morning, and they loaded onto a Grumman Goose, a two-engine amphibian, waiting for them in the harbor. Within forty-five minutes, they were on the ground at Willow Grove, Pennsylvania, where a Navy car was waiting to take them to the hotel.

Tuck was delighted to discover that a number of young ladies from Bryn Mawr College, an exclusive main line Philadelphia school, were waiting to assist them.

Within an hour, Tuck had a met one of the girls, a lovely brunette, and they spent the afternoon working on decorations. Tuck couldn't ask her to dinner, since he was required to attend the dinner preceding the ball, but they promised to meet at the Academy later. They exchanged name and address information, each excited about a future relationship.

Back at the Academy, Tuck made several calls to her home over the next couple of weeks. A servant answered the telephone, but he always seemed to miss her. Her father, an ex-Senator and once the Chairman of the Boy Scouts of America, was very rich.

At the end of the quarter, Richard and Tuck were walking across the yard on a Saturday afternoon. The yard was filled with midshipmen and their dates, who flooded the Academy on weekends. Tuck spotted Denise, the girl from the Bellevue-Stratford, with a second classman, and walked over.

"Hello," he said, "It's nice to see you again …"

"I beg your pardon," she replied, "but I have no idea who you might be, except someone who is very rude!" She hooked the second classman's arm and they strode off, she looking very angry.

"Christ, Richard," Tuck said, "that's the girl I was telling you about. She acted like she really liked me in Philly!"

"Yeah, Man," Richard said, laughing, "she acts like you're some kind of poison, now!"

"Do you know that segundo?" Tuck asked.

"Yeah," Richard said, "that's Abrams, a JV player." A couple of days later, Richard came into the room laughing.

"Hey, Si," he said, "I found out what happened with your date from Bryn Mawr!"

"Okay," Tuck said, "let's have it. I'm ready!"

"Her old man checked you out," he said, "You aren't a member of the right soo-ci-e-ty! She told Abrams all about it, how lucky she was not to get mixed up with you!"

"Jesus Christ," Tuck said, "I thought we had something going there, but she really turned out to be a bitch. Do you believe it?"

"Hey," Richard said, "That's why I never take up any of these nice white chics when they ask me out. It's only because I'm on the team. If they took me home to their Mamas and Papas, it would be all over with. Your problem is you don't look Italian. You should have figured that out."

"Nah," Tuck said, "it isn't because I'm Italian. It's on account of my old man, probably."

"Maybe so," Richard asked, laughing, "But how many Italian admirals can you name?"

"I get your point." Tuck said.

"There's just as many Italian admirals as there are Hawiian-Philippino ones," Richard answered his own question; shaking his head and laughing, "Exactly zero!"

Richard and Tuck each received a note under the door...they were invited to a special luncheon on Wednesday afternoon with all of the other marines in the class and General Chesty Puller! Puller, the most decorated marine in the Corps, was making a retirement tour and had reviewed the Brigade that day at Worden field. Tuck found himself seated directly next to the famed hero, holder of four Navy Crosses, Four Legions of Merit, two Silver Stars, and numerous other awards for bravery and valor.

He asked Tuck how he liked the Academy. Tuck replied honestly, adding that he didn't think he was up to the academics required.

"Don't worry, son," he replied, "I couldn't make at VMI, either. I got my commission in the field." Tuck had mixed emotions about the General's response.

Second quarter grades were posted, and Tuck had failed math. It would be his fifth re-examination, and he was fighting the realization that he couldn't handle the intensity of the schedule. He was able to pass the re-exams, but maintaining a passing grade in all subjects at the same time was impossible.

They were studying advanced calculus, the last quarter of it before moving on to linear math and other courses. It was difficult work, applying theoretical ideas to engineering problems. Tuck studied hard, and reported to take the re-exam on a Saturday morning with about fifty other third classmen who had also failed. As soon as he opened the exam paper, he knew he was in trouble. The questions were much, much harder than those on the original exam. Tuck read it through, and began tackling those problems on which he thought he had a chance.

About an hour into the exam, the midshipman next to Tuck started to cry softly. Tuck didn't know him, but the sound of his crying cut him like a hot blade. Tuck was feeling pretty helpless. Uncharacteristically, the exam room silence had been occasionally punctuated with a long sigh, and once, someone had said "Jesus Christ!" under his breath. No one in the room even looked up when the adjacent test taker got up, and choking back sobs, tossed his paper on the Instructor's desk and walked out, with a full hour and half left to work. Tuck could feel the despair permeating the room.

When Richard got back, he asked Tuck how he'd done.

"Jesus, Richard," Tuck said, really depressed, "it was the hardest fucking test I ever saw. I couldn't believe the questions, they weren't anything like the first exams, or the stuff we did during the semester. I don't know if I made it or not."

Grades were posted, and Tuck had failed the exam by three-hundredths of a point with a 2.47, making his final average for the semester a 2.495, they took it to three decimal points! Tuck was notified that he was required to meet with the Review Board, to discuss his future at Navy.

Tuck was running flat out, through the darkness in the yard behind Bancroft Hall. His uniform was torn and soaked with sweat. He was terrified of what was chasing him, and had a painful stitch in his left side. He had been running a long time, climbing fences and walls and was exhausted. Every time he stopped to catch his breath, there he was, almost upon him! Gasping for breath, Tuck hurdled a hedge on officer's row; fell headlong on the grass, digging holes in the damp turf with his knees. He could feel the terror almost on him, just behind, and he scrambled to his feet and raced to the front door and began slamming the brass knocker.

Doc McDonald opened the door and stepped back.

What the hell is Doc doing on Officer's row? Tuck thought, but he didn't have time to contemplate. He stumbled into the foyer and slammed and locked the door.

"Doc," Tuck gasped, leaning over and grasping his aching side, "you've got to hide me, quick, it's coming right behind me! Please, Doc, hide me!"

"Get in there," Doc said, motioning toward the closet door in the foyer. It was pounding on the front door, thunderous slams that were shaking the door. A piece of the frame trim splintered off and fell at their feet!

Tuck opened the closet door, expecting to dive in and hide behind the clothes, but there he was, standing in the closet!

"Oh, God!" Tuck screamed. He was reaching for him. Tuck could see through the gaping hole in his chest! He had him by the shoulder!

"Si, wake up!" Richard said, "You're having one hell of a nightmare. Wake up!" He was shaking Tuck by the shoulder. Tuck looked at Richard and sat up, his T-shirt and scivvies soaked with perspiration. He was shivering uncontrollably. It must have been the thousandth time he'd had the nightmare since it started when he was a kid in the Cherry Street hovel. This time, however, Tuck felt that he would have been caught for sure, if Richard hadn't awakened him.

"Jesus Christ, Richard," Tuck said, "I'm sorry. I guess you think I'm a fucking looney, or something."

"You want to talk about it?" Richard asked.

"No, Man," he got up and retrieved a towel from the shower, "that mother-fucker's been chasing me since I was about four years old, in my nightmares. He just got a little lucky tonight. It's nothin'. I'm sorry I woke you up, that's all."

Tuck didn't know it, but it was the last time he would ever have the nightmare of the wounded giant, the Tuxedo Man. The next morning, he called Edie Maye and told her about the Review Board. She was crushed, of course. A few days later, Sal showed up. Tuck took him down to the cafeteria in the lobby basement of Bancroft, where they sat in a corner with a couple of cups of coffee.

"What's going to happen?" he asked.

"I don't know, Dad," Tuck said, "They'll probably toss me out, or ask me to resign."

"Look," he said, "I never told you what to do, but you should try to stay on here. This is a good deal."

"What the fuck are you talking about?" Tuck asked, quickly losing his temper, "this isn't a fucking 'deal,' this is the United States Naval Academy!" Other Midshipmen and their parents turned to the rising sound of his voice. He didn't care, for once.

"There is no other place like this, anywhere. This place runs on honor, hard work and dedication. Everybody here, everyone, is special, in the top one percent of the entire country, for Christ's sake. You have to cut the mustard here. This isn't some place where you can push some money under a table and get what you want. You have to do what is expected, or you get thrown out, nobody swings any weight around here. If I can't pass the courses, I can't stay - black and white - goddamit!"

Sal recoiled in his chair. His eyes reflected a look that Tuck had never seen before.

"What I meant," he said, "is this is a good opportunity for you."

"Yeah," Tuck said, "everybody wants me to stay because it's such a good opportunity, but it isn't that simple. It's goddamned hard to make it here! Thirteen hundred guys come in and seven hundred and fifty graduate, for Christ's sake, what do you think happens to the rest? The other five hundred?

"What the hell do you think I've been doing down here, screwing off? I failed at least one course every semester, I've already had more re-exams than anyone in my class, and I study every night until one or two in the morning. I can't make it here; I'm going to have to make it on the outside, on my own."

"It could mean …" he started to argue, but Tuck cut him off.

"Look, goddamn it," he said, not understanding where his thoughts were coming from, "I got here on my own; nobody gave a shit about this before I made it happen. There are ten other guys here that would have never had the opportunity if it weren't for me. I was looking at a career in the Marine Corps, or working in a goddamn factory for the rest of my life, but I made it happen, to get here!"

Tuck never talked to Sal like this before. He meant nothing to him now. All those years of fearing him, worrying about what others thought because of him, met nothing.

"I don't need any goddamn Monday morning quarterbacks now. Where the hell were you with all this advice when I was in high school? If I had some background when I got here, I could've made it. It would've helped if we had something to eat once in a while. It would've been nice if Mom had had some real care and my little sister had lived!"

"What? Your sister?" Sal managed to react to his son's sudden fury.

"Yeah, that's right, you bastard, my little sister that died! The one that you don't even know about! So don't come down here now, and tell me what to do!" Tuck was standing now, leaning over the table into Sal's face, "You don't cut any ice with me, understand? I don't have any choices here anymore, and if I do, I'll do what I want, goddamnit!"

Tuck straightened up and walked out, upset and angry.

Admiral W. R. Smedberg III gestured to a seat next to him at the head of the Review Board's table. There were eight Admirals and two Generals sitting there, staring at Tuck. They all had their caps on the table, with the scrambled eggs turned front, emphasizing their rank and importance.

"Your position in the Class of '59," Admiral Smedberg said, "is 112 of 1350 midshipman. We have read many laudatory comments in your file regarding your qualifications for leadership, and feel that you have the makings of a good Naval Officer. However, your academic performance, as you know, is lacking. Have you anything to say?"

Richard and Tuck had discussed the test. Whomever had graded it must have known exactly what he was doing, since the questions were not graded right or wrong only on the final answer, but on the methodology employed in setting up the problem, the reasoning involved, formula used, and so on. The three-hundredths of a point could have been added justifiably to any one of several responses without any loss of integrity.

"The work is difficult for me, Sir," Tuck said, "I don't seem to have enough time available for study to maintain a passing level in all subjects at the same time, however, when I concentrate on each subject by itself, I'm able to do well enough."

"That is the Board's conclusion, also," the Admiral said, and asked, "Have you anything further to say? Do you wish to continue here?"

"Yes, Sir," Tuck said. He couldn't think of any way to support himself. Essentially they were right. Nearly everyone else, even the shit heads, was able to do the academic work.

The admiral asked the Review Board if there were any further questions or comments. They just sat there, staring.

"The Board would like you to consider sitting back to the Class of 1961, and re-entering with that class in September," he said. If he had slapped

Tuck in the face, he couldn't have felt more humiliated and depressed. A feeling of despair washed over him. He was asking the one thing Tuck knew he couldn't do!

"Sir," Tuck asked, "you mean take plebe year all over again?"

"Yes," he said, "go home, rest up, do some studying on your own, and report in with '61 when they come aboard for plebe summer."

Tuck thought about Pistotnick and the agony of plebe year, and Flowers, trying to kill him in Ribbon Creek. The firsties usually lay off "turnback" plebes, but Tuck was exhausted, drained by petty interferences and constant pressure. The thought of another entire year of being a plebe ... he simply couldn't contemplate it, his brain and being was repelling it.

"I can't do it, Sir," he heard himself saying, "One plebe year was enough for me."

"That's your decision, then?" He asked.

"Yes, Sir," Tuck replied.

Tuck left the conference room feeling relieved and stubbornly belligerent. He thought that they were crazy; to think that he would do another plebe year. He hadn't anticipated the offer, but he was sure that he couldn't do it, that he wouldn't do it.

Near the entrance to Bancroft Hall, he stopped in the shadow of the Tucumseh statue. Like everyone else, he had thrown pennies at it on the way to exams, but it had only worked half of the time. He gazed out over the yacht basin and tennis courts and then walked over to the chapel. Tuck had taken to commiserating with John Paul Jones on several occasions.

Sitting with his back against the circular marble wall of the crypt, he stared at the secarphogus and thought about what had happened to him. He had made a leap of light-years, he thought, an ex-con's kid with no real preparation, to even get here.

Tuck reflected that things had taken quite a turn since John Paul, a British sea captain under suspicion of murder, became an officer in the fledgling American Navy. He took the name of 'Jones' to avoid recognition by the unsympathetic British aristocracy in the Colonies.

Yet, his ideas were the cornerstone of the Academy's traditions and concepts of the "officer and gentlemen" that all midshipmen were expected to become.

The Admirals and Generals, they were a big help, Tuck thought. The bastards didn't even spend ten minutes with him. But he really hadn't expected any help from officers. They were the untouchables. Tuck had been afraid to speak in their presence. It was the haves and have nots, all over again.

"Too much chicken shit," Tuck said aloud. That was the problem, too much unrelated bullshit to the job at hand.

He wasn't going to take anymore, he had made his mind up, spoken his piece. It was done, over with. He was tired, bone weary and depressed. The thought never occurred to him that they had made the offer because he *was* exceptional, that they *wanted him to stay* on, to excel.

Shoemaker had bilged out, too. They hadn't offered him a turn back. He stopped over to Tuck's room that evening.

"Hey, Si," he said, "I'm going down to Tampa University on a football scholarship. You got one, too, if you want it."

"How can that be?" Tuck asked, "I never even heard of Tampa University."

"L. J. Rhodes," Shoe said, "his old man is Dean of men down there. He saw all of our games at NAPS." L.J. was one of the linemen on the NAPS team. "He talked to the coach, and the coach said for both of us to come on down."

"Forget it, Shoe," Tuck said, "I've had it with all this Joe college stuff for the time being. I'm just going home and figure out what to do from there. Tell the coach thanks, but no thanks."

When Tuck told Richard about the offer to play ball at Tampa, he laughed.

"You made the right decision, Si," he said, "I wouldn't play if I didn't have to."

"You don't have to," Tuck said, "this is one school where your scholarship can't be cancelled because of injury. Nobody can do anything about it if you don't play."

"Yeah," Richard said, "but I'd still be sending telegraph signals somewhere in the south if they hadn't looked me up. I made a promise, and I'll keep it. You should think about turning back to '61, Si, it happens to a lot of guys."

"I know," Tuck said, "I've thought of nothing else. I think they'd lay off me for plebe year, they usually do, but there are a couple of things that worry me."

"You're thinking about our age, and I don't blame you," Richard said.

"Yeah, that's one thing. You realize that we're as old as the graduating class right now. In '61, I'd be an old man, for Christ's sake, and then there's Radcliffe and Pistotnick, I'd have to deal with them all over again, and Pistotnick would be a Firstie. The other thing is that they won't bring me back into the twelfth, it'll be another company, in another Battalion."

"Yeah," Richard said, "and your buddies will have to come from the plebe class, because you can't hang around with the upper classmen."

"But it's not all those things, either, Richard," Tuck said. "The truth probably is that I don't have what it takes to make it. There's something that you and all of these other guys have that's lacking in me, or there's something I have that I shouldn't have. I don't know what it is, but it's just not there, a degree of tolerance, a chip on my shoulder, some kind of inferiority complex, I don't know what the hell it is, but I know that I don't have it, or I've got too much of it, that's all.

Everything's a big problem for me, especially the studies. You know how hard I've worked. Nobody could have worked harder, but it still wasn't enough. It's like I'm my father's son, I can't get away from that, and I just don't belong here with the rest of you. God knows I want it, to stay, but I just don't think I can do it. I can't see how EE or calculus is going to be any easier next time I take it. I'll be repeating the same problems, probably with the same results, you know what I mean?"

"You tried harder than anybody I ever saw," Richard said, "that's for sure, man."

"But what did it get me? That's the problem. All that work, all the worry and the pressure of squeaking by and then it starts all over again for the next quarter. I'm tired, Man, exhausted by all the chicken shit that means nothing. You and I know that I could take a platoon onto a beach under fire right now. Most of this bullshit has nothing to do with the kind of officer I'd make."

"That's the truth, man," Richard said, "anybody who's been in the fleet knows what a bunch of asses most officers are, and there's damn few of them from the Academy. I never even saw one before I came here."

"My old man came down, you know," Tuck said, "the other day, and tried to talk me into turning back. I let go on him, Richard, I told him to mind his own fucking business. He's caused me nothing but trouble, his goddamn reputation has been following me all my life, I can't get rid of it.

The CO's still got those fucking clippings in my file. The Admiral told me I was at the top of the class, Man, but he still had the clippings, in my file.

"It's like they're saying, 'You're okay, kid, but we gotta keep this stuff just in case you don't pan out, so we can drag it out.' I'm going to have to make it on my own, on the outside, that's all."

"I can't tell you what to do, Si," Richard said. "All I can say is, that if you leave, I'm gonna' miss you around here. You're my only real buddy."

36

TWENTY BUCKS A NIGHT

Tuck was home only a few days before he was again throwing ice at Hollyford. He'd sold most of his USNA uniforms to a trombone player in the Navy band for a hundred bucks, and when Navy got through with his accounting and he bought a bus ticket, he had about 40 bucks to his name.

Cholly took him over the Tacony-Palmyra Bridge and bought him a '46 Ford sedan, eleven years old but in mint condition. Tuck was flabbergasted by his brother's generosity. He thought they had ridden over to just look at cars, but when he saw the Ford and said he liked it, Cholly made the deal and paid cash.

Cholly was on a temporary layoff from the foam plant, and had taken a job in Wrightstown, managing Lou's Bar, just outside Fort Dix.

"Lou needs another bartender," he said, "at the Pioneer. You want the job, it's yours."

"What the hell do I know about tending bar?" Tuck asked.

"Look, you'd learn it in about five minutes," Cholly said, "it's a shot and beer joint with a band, that's all; all GI's."

Tuck took the job and in a few weeks, Lou Swartz, the owner had him on the day shift, opening at ten and working until six. The Pioneer was a joint, one of two Lou owned on Wrightstown's "strip." The other, Lou's Bar, was managed by Cholly and was the hangout for the NCO homosexuals stationed at Fort Dix.

Cholly hadn't a bone of prejudice in his body and ran the place with an efficient indifference to the sexual preferences of his customers.

"These guys keep givin' me tips like I'm gonna' let 'em give me a blow job," he told Tuck, "so I just keep 'em guessin'." Tuck was embarrassed by his brother's comments about the homosexuals, but had to laugh about it when they got together.

The Pioneer was across the street from the Dix Hotel; twenty bucks a night, girl included. The girls who worked the hotel were a mixed lot, none under thirty and a pretty hard-looking bunch. When they discovered the fresh meat behind the bar at the Pioneer, all made a point of having a "breakfast beer" with Tuck.

Tuck took their ribbing with an embarrassed smile. They were usually his first customers of the day. When Tuck set up Bernice with a boilermaker; a shot and beer, for breakfast, she grabbed his wrist, leaned across the bar and kissed him hard.

"Jesus Christ, Bernice," Tuck broke away, red from head to toe and brandishing a big smear of lipstick slanting across his jaw. Bernice sat back, dumped her whiskey into her beer.

"Honest to Christ, Tucker," she laughed, "I never seen a boy who could blush so easy. Come on over here, and I'll teach you how to French kiss."

"I already know how to French kiss, Bernice. I didn't fall off the Christmas tree yesterday, you know." Tuck had to laugh. She did that every morning, and he really had a hard time avoiding it. He didn't want to hurt her feelings, and he was too shy to make an issue of it.

"Well, this is a new thing for me," Tuck stammered, "I never knew anyone like you girls before."

"You mean, whores, Tuck?" Bernice asked. "You mean you've never been with a whore?"

"Well, no," Tuck was indignant, and still red.

"Hell, no," Betsy chimed in as she saddled up to the bar, "he's been diddling all those cute little high schoolers, right, Tuck?"

"Come on over to the Dix on your way into work tomorrow, Tuck, and I'll fix all your problems in about ten minutes," Betsy said.

"Free!" she added with a chuckle, "Hell, I might even pay you!" That evoked a laugh all around.

"Well, thanks, but no thanks," Tuck was getting tongue-tied. It happened every morning when the trio came in for their boilermakers; jump-starts, they called them. The truth of the matter was that Tuck was still chaste, not because he hadn't tried, but mainly because he was totally inept at pushing home an advantage or even knowing when he had willing partner.

"Well, if you ain't decking the local cheerleaders, and you never been with a business girl, then you're still a virgin." The girls all laughed when Tuck's blush got deeper.

The Naval Academy had ingrained Tuck with a gracious style. And Edie Maye had always enjoyed friends from all walks of life, so Tuck took everyone at face value. He found the girls from hotel Dix a refreshing group, unashamed of their "profession" and completely frank and open. He liked them and always stood them a drink "on the house."

The girls were disappointed when Lou put Tuck on the night shift, when they were working. Tuck was relieved, the morning banter was amusing, but it only accented how far he was from the yard, from being a midshipman; one of the top ten percent.

Edie Maye acted as though nothing had happened, but she was crushed. She was sure that he could have made it.

She never accepted the possibility of Tuck bilging out, but she couldn't bring herself to berating him about it. She knew he had tried his best.

Coming in to the Pioneer at four in the afternoon was a different story altogether. The oval bar was packed all around with GI's and stayed that way until closing at two o'clock in the morning.

Three days out of four, Tuck went over the bar to prevent or break up a fight. Gretchen was usually the cause of it. She was a very attractive redhead and invariably wore a tight-fitting dress. A German war bride, she'd amble in about five every afternoon and drink martinis, sitting near the front door with its two glass panels.

She sat there so that she could see her husband, Horace, when he would drive up to the curb and double-park his Caddy convertible at about five-thirty.

By the time Horace arrived, Gretchen would be surrounded by GI's, all buying her drinks and vying for her attention. More likely than not, they were southern boys.

The trouble usually started when the suitors spied Horace, all six-foot four, 250 pounds of him, very black and a Gunny Sergeant in the Army with a chest full of ribbons. When Horace opened the door and planted a big kiss on his wife, the bar erupted!

It wasn't only the sight of the big black sergeant kissing his sexy white wife, the Caddy convertible just added insult to infuriated injury for the boys at the bar.

Tuck had learned to be ready for it. He was over the bar before a punch got thrown, separating Horace and three or four privates with blood in their eyes. He never had to use the billy stick, but the privates didn't know that, they only saw that he was ready to do so.

"Jesus Christ, Horace," Tuck was pushing him into the Cadillac after he and Gretchen had pushed him out the door, "Can't you just honk the horn?"

"Hell, no, Tuck," Horace said, grinning, "That wouldn't be any fun!"

Tuck wondered how long it would be before one of the boys from Alabama would blow Horace's head off with a sidearm. The bar would buzz about it for about an hour after Horace left. Tuck or Joe, the other night bartender, usually stood drinks for the angry southerners.

Tuck had visited the high school and talked to the Guidance Counselor about continuing with College. He was astonished to find out that his work at the Academy was considered practically worthless. Civilian schools would give no credits for the course work at Navy and all wanted him to start from scratch.[111]

Mrs. Kirkland, the Guidance counselor, finally located a school in north Jersey that would give Tuck credit for his freshman year. Fairleigh Dickinson College was a brand new school and hard up for students, Tuck figured.

Between working at the ice plant and the Pioneer, Tuck had put away $700 by September. He loaded up the Ford sedan and headed north to finish his College education.

On his last night at the Pioneer, the girls from Hotel Dix presented him with a gift box. It contained a gross of condoms and pint jar of Vaseline. Tuck had no idea what he would do with either gift.

37

A LETTER TO EDIE MAYE

It was only three years since Tuck had left Navy, and he had managed to screw up his life even worse than he thought possible. He had enrolled in Fairleigh Dickinson College, fallen in love and gotten his girlfriend Bev pregnant, all within a year.

They married and moved up to Bridgeport, Connecticut, ashamed to reappear on Fairleigh Dickinson's campus and explain their irresponsibility. Tuck had transferred to the University of Bridgeport, encouraged by his physics professor who said,

"FDC has no accreditations - all your work here is of no value". On top of his personal problems, Tuck realized that his quick acceptance at Fairleigh Dickinson was probably because of their lack of status among the university community, but the straw that pushed Tuck and his new bride to Connecticut was his creative writing professor.

When Sputnik, the first man-made object to orbit earth spun overhead on Oct 4, 1957 Tuck was stunned.[112]

The damned Russians; the bastards stole the B-29 and the A-bomb and now this! He thought; practically considering it a personal insult. Frightened for the country and immediately aware of its military importance, he wrote about the Russian satellite for an assigned creative writing paper. The Professor accused Tuck of plagiarism, before she even finished reading the first page. When Tuck protested, she said,

"You couldn't have written this, it's too good."

Tuck, outraged, ripped the paper from her hand. He later shared the experience with Dr. Taylor, his physics instructor, who read the paper, talked to the young English professor and informed Tuck that she had agreed to grade Tuck's work and extended an apology. But Tuck understood that he had made a bad choice in coming to Fairleigh Dickinson, and he and Bev packed up the '41 Ford and moved to Bridgeport, Connecticut. At the end of the first semester at the University of Bridgeport he ran out of money. The Veteran's Administration refused to consider his time at Navy as legitimate service, and with a recession in full progress, they moved back to New Jersey with Bev's folks after Tuck's son, Chris was born.

With the help of his father-in-law, Tuck abandoned the idea of finishing college and landed a job at Picatinny Arsenal, and bought a bungalow in the woods on Lake Hopatcong. Within the year, the marriage fell apart. Bev, Tuck's wife, obviously had married only because she was pregnant. Their quarrels usually ended with her calling Tuck a "guinea bastard, dago son of a bitch" or "perverted wop!"

Soon the marriage disintegrated to a series of accusations by Tuck about Bev's absences from the house. It became apparent that Bev was seeing a fellow that she met at the restaurant where she was waitressing part time.

Tuck followed her one night when she left the restaurant with him. Since Bev had their only car, he was riding an old bicycle and couldn't keep up. When she finally returned home in the early morning she answered his questions with scorn.

Tuck's world was misery and self-pity, but he continued trying. He loved her and she excited him in spite of her obvious disgust. He confronted her lover at the restaurant, shoving him against the wall in front of customers and inviting him outside, but the owner broke it up and Tuck was escorted out.

Tuck thought he made some progress, as Bev lost her job as a result of his outburst, but soon she was seeing the owner of another bar, where Tuck had a part time job, and he simply couldn't cope with it any longer. After another night of trying to find her and a traumatic argument, he packed up the car and took off, driving west, completely depressed by the breakup.

He stopped in at Sis's house to see Edie Maye, who was quite sick. She had put the old house on Mt. Holly Avenue up for sale, and was living in one of Sis's spare bedrooms.

"She never did love you," Edie Maye said, "I could see that from the start." Edie Maye, recovering from chemotherapy had stayed with Tuck for about three weeks in the spring, just to give Sis a rest.

"She was fooling around when I was there," Edie Maye said, "but I thought I had better keep it to myself. I was hoping it wouldn't come to this."

"I still love her, Mom," Tuck said, "but I can't take it when she goes into those rages, and calls me a guinea. I slapped her a couple of times when she called me that, and I feel terrible about it."

Edie Maye gave him five hundred dollars, insisting that he take it.

"It's money from my insurance," she said, "I don't have any use for it, and you're going to need something to get you started."

Tuck decided to head for California, but Edie Maye had told him that Sal was in Phoenix so he figured he'd stop to see him. The trauma of his breakup and the residual despair of his lost career in the Navy still monopolizing his every thought, he drove straight through, 34 hours, to Commerce, Missouri, before grabbing a motel for the night. Two days later, he pulled into a gas station in Flagstaff, Arizona, and called the number that Edie Maye had given him, in Phoenix.

Sal got on the phone, and they chatted for a minute, and he told Tuck where to find him. Sal had come to Tuck's home in North Jersey for his grandson's christening, but other than that, Tuck had said little to him since his explosion at the Naval Academy.

Back in the car, Tuck turned south through Oak Creek Canyon just as the sun was setting and took in the sights as he dropped the 3,000 feet on the canyon road, and emerged in darkness on the semi-desert, still 250 miles and 1,500 feet above Phoenix.

Tuck felt himself recovering, coming back to reality. He had found himself crying silently for the first two days, squinting through tear-laden eyes as the miles raced by. He had long since stopped asking himself how she could have done it. She had done it; it was over, she hated Tuck and he couldn't grasp why. He had never before been so completely rejected or hated, but was still hopelessly in love with Bev.

But his mind was clearing, and the magnificence of the Arizona expanse before him; the millions of stars overhead flooded his senses; cathartic and refreshing.

He found a motel room at midnight on the outskirts of Phoenix, and the following morning, met Sal for breakfast in the dining room of his motel. Tuck, awash in his recent failures; the Academy, the marriage, was beginning to realize how tenuous life's relationships can be. He greeted Sal with friendliness.

Sal gave no reaction to the news that Edie May was very sick and receiving chemotherapy for cancer.

"I've got two suites here," he said, "some friends are staying with me, on business. There's plenty of room, if you want to bunk in for a couple of days."

"I might do that," Tuck said, "It's really beautiful here. The road from Flagstaff is really something. I've never seen Pine trees that big. Have you been up there, to Flagstaff?"

"Yeah," he said, "I go up there a couple of times a week, to Page. That Oak Creek canyon is really beautiful, isn't it?"

They finished breakfast and went back to his room, where his friends were already waiting. Sal introduced Tuck. "This is Irving," he said, "from Atlantic City. Jack, everybody calls him 'Blackjack,' and Paul, from Oklahoma City. This is my son, Tuck."

"One-Eye Irving" hadn't changed since Tuck met him years ago in South Jersey, except he was a little grayer, and perhaps a bit more ugly. He was dressed in a dark business suit in spite of the temperature, which was already 95 degrees and it was only nine o'clock.[113]

"Blackjack" Jones was obviously a bad character, too. He reminded Tuck of Sal's old partner, Tony. Tall, with dark hair and a pock-marked face, he spoke with staccato sentences. Tuck was certain his name wasn't Jones, and within the next 30 minutes, when he saw him handle a deck of cards, he was certain he was Sal's old partner, Tony Marinella.

"The Oklahoma Kid," as Tuck came to know him, was a complete departure from the other two eastern hoods, and was introduced as "Mr. Paul, the Oklahoma Kid" an overdone movie mob alias.

Medium sized, his hair was done like Robert Wagner's, and he bore a close resemblance to the movie star. He was dressed in an expensive western cut suit, alligator boots and had a string tie, fastened with a clasp that featured Indian turquoise jewelry framing a 100 dollar gold piece. He was a smooth talker with an easy grin. His real name was Ray Carson, Tuck would learn years later.

After some chit-chat, Sal told Tuck they had business to take care of and would be gone most of the day. He responded that he wanted to get a paper and see what the job situation was, and he'd at least hang around until dinner time. Sal left Tuck with a room key and they took off in a red Buick Roadmaster convertible that he was driving.

Tuck responded to an ad for electronic circuit designers and by one o'clock had been hired by a subcontractor to General Electric, which was building computers in a new plant on Black Canyon Highway, west of the city. After visiting the Company office and filling out forms, he was told that he could start the following day.

"I've got a job," Tuck said to Sal that evening, "with General Electric. I'm starting tomorrow. Do you mind if I hang around here for a week or two while I find a place to live?"

After about a week, Sal told Tuck that he was a little short of cash and asked him if he had any to spare.

"I can lend you about a hundred," Tuck said, "and I don't mind doing it since I'm not paying any rent. Why don't you find a less expensive motel, without a pool, bar and all the glitz?"

"I gotta' put up a good front," Sal responded, "for the deal I'm working on. We got a guy coming in here, a big money guy, and it wouldn't do to be in anything but a real nice place."

"Oh," Tuck asked, figuring he might as well try to find out what the scam was this time, "what's going on?"

"Well," he said, "I was going to ask you for a favor anyway, since you worked for the government at that Arsenal.

"This guy is coming in here from Ohio, he's a big businessman out there, has a big construction business, and we're working with him on the dam contract, up in Page."

"What dam contract?" Tuck asked.

"Up in Page," he said, "they're building this dam, the Glen Canyon dam[114]. It's supposed to be the biggest in the world; they've been pouring concrete up there for four years."

"So," Tuck said, "that's a government contract, awarded to the lowest bidder, and that's all run out of Washington, probably."

"Well," Sal said, "I know a guy here, in this county, and he's married to this girl whose father is on the congressional committee that makes the contract award in Washington every year. He's the head of the committee, and that's their job, to lay off these big contracts."

"So you think this girl is gonna' get her dad to give the contract to somebody who's not the lowest bidder?" Tuck asked. He knew a little about government contracting awards from his work at Picatinny Arsenal. "That isn't going to happen," Tuck said, "that stuff is all on the up and up, those bids are all published after the awards are made. It can't happen."

"Oh, it'll be on the up and up," Sal said, "only our guy will know what the other bids are, so he can be the lowest, see?"

"Shit, Dad," Tuck said, "I don't like the sound of it. I'm holding a Top Secret clearance with the Army. I don't want to get involved in anything like this; I could get in a lot of trouble."

"Look," he said, "these politicians are all a bunch of crooks. This guy we're bringing in, he's legitimate and doesn't know anything about this. The government's going to get its money's worth. All he has to do is put in his bid, and pour the concrete. It's a five million dollar contract!"

"What's in it for you?" Tuck asked.

"Well," he said, "this guy, Skilkin, that's his name, he'll pay us a finder's fee, one percent, for getting him the job; $50,000. That's how these jobs get done, it's all normal politics. The guy on the committee, he's been gettin' his kickback from the other contractor, now it's somebody else's turn, that's all."

"I don't want anything to do with it," Tuck said.

"No," he responded, "I don't want you involved, either. All I want you to do is to spend some time with this guy Skilkin when he comes in. He's a gentleman, and I can't let One-Eye or BlackJack talk to him, it'll make him nervous."

"Yeah," Tuck said, "they make me nervous, too."

"If it all works out, there'll be something in it for you, too," Sal said.

"No, thanks," Tuck said, "I don't mind spending some time with your guy before or after work, but I don't want anything for it. I'm here, and I wouldn't be rude to the guy, and you've got a real problem with One-Eye and Blackjack, that's for sure."

Tuck picked up Mr. Skilkin at the airport the following Friday. He was a delightful gentleman, about sixty-five years old with a gregarious personality. He took to Tuck right away.

"What do you know about this contract award you're father's promising me?" he asked. They had just finished doing twenty laps of the motel pool, his 'morning constitutional', and were drying off in a couple of beach chairs.

"I don't know a thing about it, Sir," Tuck said, "I worked in publications in the government and didn't get directly involved with subcontractors."

"But I understand that these things always go to the lowest bidder," he said.

"Yes sir," Tuck said, "but sometimes we awarded what was called a 'cost plus fixed fee' contract. In those cases, the contractor bids a fixed amount for his services above the actual costs of the job. Perhaps it's one of those."

"Well," he said, "it certainly has me confused, but it would be grand if Skilkin Construction could get the job. Another swim this evening before dinner, young man, or am I tiring you out?"

"No, Sir," Tuck said, "it will be my pleasure."

Mr. Skilkin stayed a week, and in addition to the pool workouts, Tuck took him out to see Talisman West, Frank Lloyd Wright's architectural school, and ferried him around the city on a couple of evenings. He flew back to Ohio with a fond farewell.

"He doesn't know what's going on, Dad," Tuck said, "but he's suspicious. He doesn't understand how he'll get the contract, and to tell you the truth, neither do I."

"That's okay for now," Sal said, "when he saw the dam, he was drooling. He won't be any problem. Don't forget he flew out here for a whole week, just to look at the job. I'm going to make sure you get something out of this."

"Forget it, I told you I don't want anything out of it. He was a nice person and I enjoyed the time I spent with him. That's why I did it. I don't want any money."

The Glen Canyon Dam in Page Arizona, created Lake Powell, which took 17 years to fill. Construction took 14 years and the town of Page was built by the government to accommodate engineers and workers. Thousands of workers had no place to spend their earnings and Sal thought they would appreciate a small casino, since both Las Vegas and Phoenix were more than 300 miles away. The plans went awry when Sal's confederates brought in prostitutes without his knowledge, after Sal had bribed the necessary politicians and law enforcement personnel, promising "no whores."

Tuck had determined that he had to get out of the motel, and after the third week, he moved into a flea bag rooming house in a rundown part of the city. Sal had grabbed most of his first several paychecks by asking him to cover the motel bills. Tuck bit his tongue about the money, seeing that Sal was really at rock bottom. And it was not unsatisfying to have Sal at a disadvantage, however small. On reflection, Tuck was certain that "Black Jack" was in fact Tony Marinella, Sal's old partner from the Casino at Red Men's Hall.

Tuck wondered how Cholly was making out, since he had told Tuck that Sal was draining most of the Jewelry store money for his Arizona adventure. Cholly had stopped taking a salary when Sal came out here, trying to keep the jewelry store alive.

Tuck met a waitress at a restaurant where he took most of his meals, and she steered him to garage apartment with water cooling, and he moved in there, glad to be away from the mosquitoes in the rooming house. It wasn't much, but he could afford it, and he could make his own meals on a two-burner stove and keep fresh food in a small refrigerator.

Tuck saw Sal once or twice a week. The Oklahoma Kid, Blackjack and One-Eye disappeared, and Sal moved into an apartment with a well-used ex-showgirl named Cherry, near Scottsdale. On a Saturday morning, Tuck answered the door to find Sal.

"You got any tools with you?" Sal asked.

"Not really, Tuck replied, going to his kitchen area and getting his toolbox, "just a few basics."

Sal rooted through the box and came up with a miniature crowbar.

"I bought this thing used," Sal said, referring to the Buick convertible, "and it's got different keys for the trunk. I never got the key from the guy I bought it from." While he talked, Sal attacked the trunk with the crowbar, disfiguring the trunk lid around the lock. Tuck cringed, watching the damage he was inflicting on the beautiful car.

"Dad, why don't you get a locksmith?" Tuck asked,

"Yeah, that's what I'll have to do, I guess." Sal returned the crowbar and they went inside where Tuck made a pot of coffee. Sal was driving to Page a lot, and he asked Tuck if he wanted to drive up with him on Saturday night.

They took the cherry red Buick Roadmaster convertible, and after the four hour run to Flagstaff, Sal drove around some back streets, and picked up the "three stooges," as Tuck had come to call them, to himself. They got something to eat, pointed the Buick north and four hours later, rolled into Page, Arizona.

Page was a tiny town on a high windy plateau. It couldn't have had more than fifteen hundred permanent residents, but it did have eight churches, a tiny business district, and an airfield. Danny's Lounge had been enlarged with an addition at its rear. In the addition, Sal's casino, catering to the fourteen thousand workers living in trailer cities around the town and on the road out to the dam.

Workers were standing in line to get inside Danny's. They were trapped in one of the loneliest places in Arizona, three-hundred miles from civilization, making exceptional money, and had no place to spend it except in Sal's casino![115]

They went through a rear door to a tiny office, where Sal introduced Tuck to the Mayor, who also happened to be the Sheriff and a Pastor of one of the churches and an employee of the federal Bureau of Reclamation. It made him think of Silver City, Colorado, and the boom towns of the old west he had read about. He expected Errol Flynn to poke his head out of a door any `minute, in black western costume wearing a white ten gallon hat and a big smile.[116]

Tuck hung around for a couple of hours drinking beers while Sal talked to various people, did some accounting and money counting, and shuffled in and out of the little office with the Sheriff. Each time the door opened, a blast of sound washed over them from the noisy play at the tables. The three stooges had disappeared into the back room casino.

The Oklahoma Kid and Blackjack were staying in Page and driving back on Monday. Sal and Tuck left with One-Eye Irving, who insisted on driving back to Flagstaff. After about an hour on the road, Sal had fallen asleep in the back seat, and Tuck was dozing in the passenger seat, a little drunk from the beers.

At three in the morning, Tuck awoke to the sound of screeching tires and gravel splattering under the car.

They were sliding sideways on the highway at about seventy miles per hour, the car's rear end fishtailing on and off the shoulder! One-Eye Irving, his face stark white and his good eye bulging, was struggling to keep the big Buick on the road.

The car did a ground loop, rotating 360 degrees. The headlights first played across a solid wall of rock and then probed the infinity of the starlit

Arizona sky. It crunched to rest facing back toward Page, and during the last several seconds of the slide, it was evident that the under carriage was dragging directly on the ground!

"Jesus Christ, Irving!" Tuck shouted, "are you trying to kill us!"

Tuck started to open the door to assess the damage, and the car rocked to his right when he shifted his weight. He moved his arm slowly to the window control and lowered the passenger window. Tuck found himself staring down into blackness, a drop of at least five hundred feet!

"Dad, get on the other side!" he shouted, "we're hanging over a fucking cliff!" Irving went for his door handle and Tuck grabbed his arm.

"Stay put, for Christ's sake," he shouted, "if you get out, we're liable to go over!"

"Only one back wheel is on the road," Sal said, straining to look out the back window without moving. He had been fast asleep.

"Look," Tuck said, "we've all gotta' get out of here at the same time, or this car may go over." He thought of the "Dilbert Dunker" drills at Navy where he learned to get out of an overturned SNJ Texan cockpit upside down in fifteen feet of water while in full pilot's gear.

"Put the top down," Sal said to Irving. By that time, Tuck was practically sitting in One-Eye's lap. He reached up and unlatched the top with the lever just behind the rear-view mirror. Irving hit the switch, and the top folded back, exposing the vastness of the cold night sky.

"Dad," Tuck said, "get up on the seat. Irving, when you open the door, move your ass, because I'm coming out over you if you're still there."

The car shifted a couple of inches toward the drop off, making a grinding sound.

"Oh, shit," Irving said his first words since the spin out. Sal counted to three, and they piled out of the car. Tuck shoved Irving so hard that he landed face down in the gravel under a spread eagled Tuck. Sal easily jumped clear from the back seat.

The car slid another two feet and ground to a halt. They got up and walked around it, eyes adjusting to the darkness. One-Eye groped for a minute on the ground, and located a .38 snub nosed revolver that had spilled out of his coat when Tuck shoved him out. Both right side tires were overhanging a steep hill, the one back wheel still on the road only had another eighteen inches to spare before it, too, was over the edge. They had straddled the edge for a hundred feet before coming to rest!

Sal walked over to Irving and punched him in the jaw, knocking him flat!

"I ought to throw you down that hill, you bastard," he said, "You fell asleep, didn't you?"

Irving apologized about four times in Italian, wiping his mouth with his handkerchief. After they realized the car wasn't going over, they sat down on a blanket that had been in the back seat with their backs against the fender, and waited for about an hour before a truck came by and stopped. They piled in, all jammed in the front seat, and rode down to Flagstaff, arriving there after sunrise. The trucker dropped them off at a gas station with a towing service, and Sal sent Irving back with the wrecker to retrieve the Buick.

Sal made a phone call and Blackjack's girlfriend came over to the station, and Sal drove her home while Tuck waited, and then they drove down to Phoenix in Blackjack's car, a big Cadillac sedan.

"You were a little rough on One-Eye, weren't you?" Tuck asked Sal.

"That's not the first time he almost got me killed," Sal said.

"Well," Tuck said, "it's none of my business, but I wonder why you're doing business with him, with all his drawbacks. I mean, everybody's more or less afraid of him, and his language is so bad, you never know what he's going to say." Tuck didn't mention the gun he was wearing.

"He's got his uses," Sal said. Tuck wondered what they possibly could be, but didn't pursue it, reading in Sal's response that he wasn't going to reveal anything further.

Sal told Tuck the following week that the Buick was ruined, and he had purchased another car, a 1957 Cadillac convertible.

Tuck had made a couple of friends through his job, and had plenty of excuses not to accompany him to Page on any more of his trips.

Tuck's attitude toward Sal was neutral at this point. It was somewhat comforting to know that there was someone in town whom he knew, but every time they were together, Sal hit the boy for more money. Tuck had created a nice little routine for himself, and was trying to send money to Bev every week, along with a letter, but Sal was putting a real dent in Tuck's earnings.

Tuck missed his son, only an infant, barely more than a year old, but he still hurt badly from the emotional beating he had suffered. When he just started to feel like living again, about six months after arriving in Phoenix,

Sis called to say that Edie Maye was really sick, and Tuck had better come home as quickly as possible.

"Mom's really sick," Tuck told Sal at Cherry's place, "she's not going to make it. I'm flying home on Thursday."

"That's too bad," Sal said.

"Are you coming with me?" Tuck asked.

"Sure," he said, "I'll tell you what; I'll get the tickets with my credit card. Do you know the flight?"

"Yeah," Tuck said, "I already checked. It leaves Phoenix at about eight-thirty Thursday morning."

"Okay," he said, "I'll come by your apartment about six o'clock."

Sal showed up on Thursday morning with Cherry in tow. Tuck invited them in, but she just stood in the doorway.

"Look," he said, "I'm not going. I've got to stay here."

"Jesus Christ," Tuck said, "why didn't you tell me? I'll have a hell of a time getting a ticket now!"

"Here," he said, extending an envelope, "I got your ticket. We'd better get going, or you'll miss the flight." Tuck sat in the car in stony silence as he drove to the airport. Cherry tactfully told him she'd wait in the car and they went in. Tuck checked in and found a seat, waiting to board. Sal went into the gift shop, made a purchase, and standing at a display, Tuck saw him write something and put it in an envelope. When they announced boarding, he stood up and extended his hand.

"I'll see ya'," Tuck said, "I don't know when I'll be back, but my apartment's paid up for a couple of months, and my car's in the shop. I'll call you."

"Okay," Sal said, and reaching into his inside coat pocket, he pulled out the envelope and handed it to Tuck, "give this to your Mother."

It was the first commercial flight Tuck had ever taken, and the fellow next to him, a businessman, seemed to be an experienced traveler. Tuck asked him to help him decipher his ticket. It appeared to Tuck that he was going to change planes in Minneapolis.

"No, son," he said, "you're getting off at Minneapolis, that's as far as this ticket will take you."

Tuck had only thirty dollars in his pocket when they touched down at the Minneapolis/St. Paul airport in a blinding snow storm. The ticket counter informed him that he needed another eighty dollars to make it to Philadelphia. He found out that he could make it to Pittsburgh on a Greyhound, but it might be too late, Edie Maye was dying!

Strangely enough, Tuck found it hard to formalize a reaction to Sal's treachery with the tickets. It was typical, something he should have expected. He blamed himself for being taken in by his charm again, and pushed him out of his thoughts. He had to find a way to get home!

He considered hitch hiking, but it was six o'clock on Minnesota's Election Day, everything was closed for elections, and there was already a foot of snow on the ground. Tuck had nothing heavier than a light windbreaker to wear. He holed up in a phone booth and combed the directory until he located Ted Flesner's name in Minneapolis and Tom Sklenar's in St. Paul.

They met Tuck in the airport lounge. Neither had seen the other since graduation day at NAPS. Tuck told them of his problem, and they quickly lent him a hundred bucks. At eight o' clock, the bar opened, having been closed while the polls were still active, and they drank and talked until midnight, when the Philadelphia flight was boarding.

"Listen, Si," Tom said, "why don't you forget your old man? The son of a bitch is still pulling your string. He's liable to get you in real trouble one of these days."

"I've got to go back for my car," Tuck said, "and don't forget, I've got a good job there, that they're holding for me. But you're right, the less I see of the son of a bitch, the better off I am!"

"Semper Fi," Ted said, "and tell your mom we're praying for her." Ted was still wearing the Marine Corps ring Tuck had given him when the NCO quarters split up. The eagle, globe and anchor were so worn that the Marine Corps emblem was no longer distinguishable. Tom shook Tuck's hand, then hugged him, hard.

"Tell Edie Maye," he said, hesitating, "tell her she was special to me, real special, and I miss her a lot." Tuck saw that he was close to tears.

Tuck fell into an exhausted sleep and the stewardess had to shake him awake in Philadelphia the following morning. In three hours, he was sitting in Sis's bedroom, talking to Edie Maye.

"How ya' doin?" he said.

"I'm real tired," she replied, "and they've got me doped up most of the time. Did you get settled out there, have you seen your father?"

She was skeletal, her veins making blue ropes under her skin on tiny arms. She had lost most of her hair and couldn't have weighed more than sixty pounds. Tuck fought back tears.

"Mom," he said, lying for the bastard, "Dad was all set to come with me, he bought tickets for us both, but at the last minute, something came up.

"I had to change planes in Minneapolis, and Tommy Sklenar and Ted Flesner came down to the airport. They sent you their prayers."

Why am I protecting the sonofabitch? Tuck thought. *It's only luck I made it here in time!*

"Ah, that Tommy," she said, smiling, "he was really something. How is he?"

"They're doing fine, Mom. Tom said to tell you that you were special to him. I think he was in love with you."

Tuck saw that she was tiring, and the comment about Tom brought tears to her eyes.

"I know he was," she said, "his mom died when he was just a baby, you know. How is your father, how's he doing?"

Tuck didn't want to give Edie Maye the envelope, but he knew he couldn't keep it from her. He hoped that she couldn't see how his teeth were clenched, the rage in him just below the surface. He couldn't conceive of the envelope doing anything good, he was sure that she would be hurt by it, and he had been thinking about it all day. In the end, he knew he would surrender it, because if the positions were reversed, Edie Maye would do that. It had been a promise, a commitment.

"He sent you this." Tuck handed her the envelope.

"You'll have to read it for me," she said.

Tuck opened the envelope and extracted the get well card inside. Inside, under the printed message, Sal had penned in a line.

"Dear Edie," Tuck read, "I hope that this card finds you on the way to a speedy recovery. Love, Sal."

She took the card out of his hand and clutched it to her breast. Turning her head against the pillow, she began to sob.

"He's the only one I ever loved," she said, crying. When Tuck heard the words, his heart skipped a beat, and he suddenly gasped for breath. He stumbled out of the bedroom and walked outside. It was a cold, nasty fall afternoon in New Jersey, prematurely cold with a chilling fine rain falling from a low gray overcast sky.

Cholly drove up to Sis's house to find Tuck soaked through and sitting on the concrete step in the rain. Putting his hand on Tuck's shoulder, he said.

"I was afraid you wouldn't make it." He could see that Tuck was struggling with himself. "What's goin' on, Tuck?" he asked.

"The old man," Tuck's words were like deep sighs, "the sonofabitch sent her a get well card." He began to cry openly. "A fucking get well card that he bought in the Airport."

"Ah, shit, take it easy," Cholly said, "what did you expect him to do?"

Suddenly Tuck was on his feet and had his brother by the collar of his jacket. He smashed him against the door of his car and snarled in his face.

"Don't defend that mother-fucking scumbag!" Tuck was out of control, "don't say one god damned word! Not one!"

Cholly put his arms around Tuck and drew him close. Tuck's rage dissipated with the embrace and he stepped back and wiped his face. He began to stammer an apology.

"Don't worry about it," Cholly said, putting his arm about his brother's shoulders, "you're right, he's is a no good prick most of the time, when you think of it."

Two days later, Edie Maye went into Hahneman hospital in Philadelphia, where she stayed for three weeks before lapsing into a coma.

Sis, Cholly or Tuck stayed with her constantly after that, for seven days and nights, until she just stopped breathing.

When it happened, Tuck and Sis had fallen asleep in the waiting area next to Edie Maye's room. Cholly had just left to drive home and get ready for work. A nurse shook Tuck awake at four in the morning. He was sprawled in a wicker chair.

"Your mother is gone," she said.

Tuck staggered to his feet and walked to the door of the room, which was dimly lit. As he pushed the heavy hospital door open, a stream of corridor light veed across the floor and then onto the bed where Edie lay, finally out of pain.

As though on signal, a huge cockroach scattered into the light, casting its own shadow as it darted between Tuck's feet, running out of the room and down the corridor.

Tuck gasped, his stomach turning over when he saw the beast. He wanted to scream out when he saw it, to crush it through the floor, to destroy the hospital, the doctors, the snotty nurses who treated Edie Maye like a carcass. But the roach was gone. He sat down next to the bed and took Edie Maye's cold hand in his and thought that although shocking, how appropriate it was, the roach.

Tuck knew that Sis would be furious if he didn't wake her immediately, but he just sat there, looking at Edie Maye. He was exhausted by the ordeal, of watching her die over a three week period. He felt relief now that it was over, relief for her. In some places on her back, the bedsores had exposed raw bone. Her face was relaxed, but the mouth was turned down, the way it was when Tuck saw a beating coming or a rebuke for his ungodly behavior.

He wondered where it came from, the will, the undeniable and unshakeable love that she had lived with. She was so tiny and had been so ravaged by life, fighting continuously for the better part of fifty two years just to survive.

And she had never really had anything except the worst that life could offer. But somehow she made it do, rose above it with an unquenchable wit and a grittiness that everyone recognized. On reflection, Tuck realized that she had no enemies. Everyone who had ever crossed her path liked her and many loved her. Her hospital room had been constantly full, even when she was comatose. To his surprise, some of Tuck's high school buddies had come and sat with her, recalling kindnesses she had done for them, many of which Tuck never knew about.

Near the end, Doc McDonald, now grey and retired, had come to the room. He read her charts and turned to Tuck. "She'll be free soon, Tuck," he had said, "she's feeling no pain now ...I want you to know that I feel privileged to have known Edie, to have been able to help her and you children over the years. Your Mother was someone very special. I know I'll never meet another with character and determination like hers. When the good Lord made Edie Maye, he threw away the mold."

"She was a woman of principle, you know," Doc had choked on his words, "and far too good for your father, who never appreciated her."

"She loved the sonofabitch right to the end," Tuck had said, "and he gave her nothing. She loved him in the unheated hovels with sick kids and no food, with his goddamn goombah girlfriends and hoods that he involved her with, the jail terms and the cockroaches and spiders and rats. It didn't matter. Not to her."

"I know," Doc had said, replacing Edie Maye's chart and caressing her foot for a moment before leaving. Tuck realized that he had been sitting with her for some time, holding her hand.

"No more roaches or rats, mom, no more," he choked. He got up and staggered out of the room and woke up Sis. In her inimitable way, Sis took charge of the funeral for "*her* mother." Cholly never seemed to mind it when Sis referred to Edie Maye as her mother exclusively. Tuck knew it was done for his benefit, to hurt him, and it did. But he bit his tongue. He knew it was just Sis being her bitchy self.

Edie Maye was buried next to Chip and Bess, and Tuck sat around the empty house for a couple of days, collecting his thoughts and wondering how he would get back to Arizona to get his car and belongings. The house was listed, waiting for a buyer. He was watching television, beer in hand, about seven o'clock when he heard Edie Maye call him from the top of the stair.

"Tuck!" she called loudly. She sounded a little upset.

Tuck dropped the beer and realized that he was standing upright, her voice ringing in his ears. He took the stairs two at a time and opened her bedroom door.

"Mom?" He knew it was impossible, it couldn't be, but he had heard it! She ***had*** called. The room was dimly lit by the setting sun. No one was there. Tuck went through the rest of the rooms, even climbing to the attic. He called her name several times without result, then sat down on the top step of the attic stair.

His heart was racing and he felt a chill. Edie Maye had reached out to him; he knew in his heart that it had been her, calling him as she had so many times. He went downstairs and got a towel. Cleaning the spilled beer, he couldn't keep his hands from shaking.

38

BROTHER, WHO ART THOU?

THE day after he had arrived back in Jersey, Tuck had gone job hunting. Having no money, he needed to at least earn enough to get back to Phoenix, and there was no way to know how long Edie Maye would last. His boss in Arizona had told him that he couldn't hold his job any longer, but he knew that there was lots of work there.

In a couple of days, he picked up a job with a small government publications contractor in center city Philadelphia. Tuck told his new boss just what the situation was with Edie Maye, and he said it was okay if he disappeared when things got rough, just to let him know. It was tough riding the Medford 54 buses from Sis's house. Edie Maye's house finally sold, and he was sleeping on a cot in Sis's basement, but in a couple of months, he had enough money to move into a garage apartment in the Gibbsboro woods near a bus line.

Before Tuck moved out, he and Sis were going through some of Edie Maye's things.

"There are some of your things in here," Sis said, opening a large trunk, "left over from the house." As they sorted through her scrapbooks, Tuck came across Chip's obituary notice.

"I've never seen this," he said, "it's Granddad's obituary. I wish I could have made the funeral."

"Well," Sis said, "Mom was really mad at you for that. That's the weekend you went to a goddamned football game, instead of your own Grandfather's funeral!"

Tuck looked at her in disbelief.

"What the hell are you talking about?" he asked, "I tried to get leave, but Mom didn't call the Academy, and they wouldn't let me go. Richard talked me out of going AWOL!"

Sis kept moving things around in the trunk, but he noticed that her face was getting red.

"Wait a minute," Tuck said, the memory flooding back, "I asked you to tell her to call Captain Dickey, and you said you would, but you never did, did you?"

"You never asked me any such thing," she said defensively, "or I would have remembered!"

"No," Tuck said, "I'm pretty sure I asked you. In fact, I know that I asked you, and you promised that you would tell her to call. I talked to you at noon time, on my way to chow."

"I never talked to you at noon," she said, "you're mixed up." Tuck could see that she was really embarrassed.

"Like hell I am. But in any case, I didn't go to any football game; I just sat on my ass at the Academy. They wouldn't let me go, since Granddad wasn't immediate family."

"Anyway," she said, "you broke Mom's heart when you quit. That's when she just gave up; she didn't want to live anymore."

"Jesus Christ, Sis," Tuck said, "where do you get these ideas? I didn't quit, I was forced to resign for academic deficiency."

"But you could have stayed, Mom said you could," she said.

"I could have gone back the following year with the Class of '61," Tuck said, "and started all over again as a Plebe, but I would still have had the same problem with the studies. Also, I would have been 25 years old, an ex-marine, getting shit on by a bunch of teenagers, for Christ's sake. You don't know a goddamn thing about it."

"I know that that's what *killed my mother*," she said, "you quitting the Academy."

Tuck got up and picked up his jacket. Edie Maye was too fresh in his memory; he couldn't digest anymore of Sis.

She's like a pit bull trained for fighting, she doesn't know any other way to act, and she can't help herself, even if she wanted to! he thought.

"Don't you want this stuff?" she asked.

"Keep it," he said, hurt by her accusations, and confused by her attitude. "Maybe I'll get it later." Tuck kept in touch with Cholly, and when he told him about the conversation, he laughed it off.

"She's pissed at you, all right," he said, "because you walked in on her that morning when Harry was there. She thinks you told Stringy about her coffee breaks with Harry."

"I didn't tell Stringy anything," Tuck said, "because I didn't think anything of it. They were just having a cup of coffee."

Tuck had missed his bus one morning and barged in on Sis having coffee with one of her old high school beaus. He thought nothing of it, but it seemed that now, from Sis's reaction, there was something going on.

Cholly told Tuck that Sal had showed up just two weeks after Edie Maye had died, and now was heading back for Phoenix after being home only about a week.

"What the fuck are you telling me?" Tuck asked, "The sonofabitch comes waltzing into Jersey a couple of weeks after Mom dies, but he couldn't make while she was alive? Jesus Christ, I swear that someday I'm gonna' kill that bastard!"

"When are you going to learn?" Cholly asked, "That you can't expect nothin' from him. Nothin'. He's Popeye. "I am what I am!" He doesn't think like you and me."

"No shit," Tuck said, "as far as I can see, he doesn't think much at all, except about himself. That's the way I see it."

"Just the same, you gotta' learn to get what you can from him, but don't expect nothin', 'cause nothin' is what he'll give you," Cholly said, "Look, you gotta' go back to Phoenix, right? Well, he's heading back there, too. So hitch a ride with him, you can't afford to fly."

Tuck thought it over, swallowed his pride, and called Sal from work one day.

"You going back out west?" Tuck asked. He needed to get back to his belongings and car before they disappeared. He decided that paying for half the gas with Sal was doable. He couldn't afford an airline ticket and still have enough to drive back to Jersey.

Tuck had unconsciously made the decision to stay on with the Philadelphia Company. He felt obligated, having missed so much time with Edie Maye's illness and death. They had been understanding to a fault.

"Yeah," Sal said, "next week."

"How about if I ride along?" Tuck asked, "I've got to pick up my car, it's still in the shop, and I've got some stuff at the apartment, yet. I can help you with the driving."

"Sure," he said, "I'm taking the southern route."

A week later, after telling his new boss that he needed eight to ten days to retrieve his car, he was heading south on Route 301 in the Caddy convertible Sal was driving, and the plan was to drive straight through, alternating turns at the wheel and sleeping in the back seat.

They started hitting a lot of rain in Virginia, and the radio was giving weather reports that told of major flooding in Louisiana and the delta region. By the time they hit southern Mississippi, it was evident that they weren't going to make it any further west. The major highways were flooded out.

"As long as we're stalled," Sal said, "we might as well drop in on an old friend." He turned the car north and they headed for Meridian, Mississippi, 200 miles distant. The conversation thus far had been civil, and Tuck decided if the subject of the plane ticket or the get well card came up, then he would open up on Sal. He had no fear of him any longer; he told himself that he just didn't care about the man anymore.

In Meridian, it was immediately evident that Sal was completely familiar with the town. They found a Morrison's cafeteria, had dinner and Sal excused himself to make a phone call. After a few minutes, he returned and sat down.

"We might as well hole up for the night," he said, "we can make a stop in the morning, and the roads will probably be clear if we leave here about noon."

The following morning, they had breakfast in the motel where they had slept, and without explanation, Sal drove into the suburbs of Meridian, finally stopping at a beautiful ranch house in an expensive neighborhood. An extremely good looking woman of about 40 was waiting for them on the porch.

Sal got out, and they talked for a moment. She was obviously controlling her emotions very well, but Tuck could see that she was very happy to see him, and at the same time, on the verge of tears. He brought her over to the car, and introduced her as "Mary."

Sal got back in the car, and then drove about five blocks and pulled up in front of an elementary school. A teacher was waiting for them. She came over to the car, inquired as to Sal's identity, and went back into the schoolhouse. A moment later, a child of about seven years opened the door and walked toward the car.

Tuck found himself staring at the child and realizing that his own mouth was hanging open. He was experiencing a mild state of shock! The boy's features were an exact duplicate of Sal's! He had the same long nose, black hair, sloping shoulders and even walked with Sal's peculiar gait, pushing off with his toes. Sal shook his hand and gave him a hug, then brought him over to Tuck. Tuck had gotten out of the car without intending to.

"This is your half-brother, Johnny," Sal said.

Tuck shook Johnny's hand, and they got back in the car, and chatted for a moment. He was a delightful child, intelligent and apparently well-adjusted, and carried on an excited conversation with them. After a few minutes, Sal got out of the car, opened the trunk and pulled out a box. Opening the box in the car, he handed an Overseas Zenith Radio to Johnny.

"I brought this for you," he said, "you can listen to stations all over the world on it."

They spent another half hour with Johnny, then left. Tuck looked back to see him standing in the driveway of the school with his teacher, waving goodbye with one hand and holding the immense radio in the other. A miniature Sal.

"I guess you're surprised to know you have a half-brother," Sal said.

"You might say that," Tuck said, unable to contain a chuckle, "but, nothing you do really surprises me anymore."

"His old man is a big lawyer, a prosecutor," Sal said, "he'll be pissed when he finds out I was here, but what the hell, she (Mary) said it would be okay."

"You planned to stop there all along, didn't you?" Tuck asked.

"Yeah," Sal said, "but I didn't know that you would be along."[117]

Tuck couldn't find a way through his confusion to respond. The roads were open, and he thought of nothing else for the rest of the 2,000 miles across the southern states.

Even with the stopover, they made it to Phoenix in five days. There were times in the desert when Tuck held the big car at one hundred and ten miles an hour for what seemed to be hours on end. Tuck insisted on driving most of the way, using it as an excuse not to have to talk to his father.

Sal dropped Tuck off at the body shop that had repaired his car, he waved good bye, and told Sal that he would give him a call before he took off to return to the east.

Backing his car out of the parking lot, Tuck's foot went to the floor and he rolled out into the highway backwards.

He had no brakes! Pulling back into the shop, the mechanic quickly diagnosed a bad master cylinder, and he was stuck for at least a day before he could start back. Worse than that, the new master cylinder depleted his meager resources for the return trip. He walked down town to his apartment, explained the situation to his landlord and decided to just take it easy for the day, pick up the car tomorrow and start back the following night.

The following day, after picking up the car and the rest of the stuff from the apartment, Tuck drove over to Cherry's place, and Sal and he went out, presumably to get a beer. Tuck could see Sal's whole attitude had changed; he was really depressed. They got back in the car after having a couple of beers and he just sat there, behind the wheel, staring ahead for a couple of minutes.

"What's the matter?" Tuck asked.

"Ah, shit," he said, "I should have stayed here, I should've never left. I'm in big trouble."

"Why?" Tuck asked, "What happened?"

"That fuckin' Oklahoma Kid," he said, "he and the other two assholes blew the whole thing sky high, in Page. They brought a bunch of whores in there from Vegas, and the Sheriff shut the whole thing down. I should have never trusted those bastards, with all their big-time bull shit about New York and Oklahoma City. They're a couple of second-rate punks."

"You mean with all the shit going on there," Tuck asked, "he objected to a few B-girls?"

"Yeah," Sal said, "he said from the start, 'no girls' and I agreed to it. Those people are all real religious, you saw all the churches. They didn't mind the games because they were getting a cut, but right from the start, they said 'no girls' and they meant it! And those guys are all government bureaucrats – they all work for the Bureau of Reclamation. They built the whole damn town, when they started the dam back in '54. It's not even a real town."[118]

He laid his head back on the seat and sighed.

"I wouldn't care if it was only some bunco scheme, or short con," he said, "but I spent months setting this up. Every goddamn sheriff and prosecutor from Page down to Maricopa County had to get paid off, and I did it, I meant every fucking one of them and gave 'em their money.[119] They got paid good, and a lot of them pushed for extra money. That little back room casino was pulling in a plenty on big nights, it was a goddamn gold mine, and it wasn't even set up yet!"

"What a bunch of hypocrites," Tuck said, feeling a little schizoid. He found it somewhat amusing that the sonofabitch was in trouble, but at the same time was sympathetic, "what's going to happen now?"

"Well," he said, "the big guy, here in Maricopa County, he's saying it's my fault entirely. I'm the fall guy. It's his father-in-law that's on the Congressional Committee, so the dam deal is shot, too."

"There's nothing you can do to repair the damage?" Tuck asked.

"I could have," he said, "if I was here. I could have gotten rid of the girls and smoothed it over with the Sheriff in Page and the big shots with the (Reclamation) Bureau, but it was the congressman's daughter, she screwed everything up. She was fucking around with this guy from Washington, who worked up at the dam site. He worked up there a couple of days a week, and the rest of the time here in Phoenix. So she's up there in Page, and she sees him talking to the girls in Danny's, 'cause she likes to go in there and lose the old man's money. She run right back to Phoenix and tells her daddy, the congressman, about the whores she saw."

"What the hell did she do that for?" Tuck asked, "How did she cover up being there, in Page?"

"She wanted to get back at her husband, the prosecutor," he said, "I could see that the first time I met her. She's a real bitch, and you could see he was only married to her because of her old man being in Congress, and she knew about the payoffs, she was right there when I paid him and that god damned Senator, in his own fucking house!"

"Christ," Tuck said, "what a mess! So the congressman won't do the contract deal, either."

"Not now," he said, "he can't afford to be associated with his screwed up son-in-law now. This gives him an excuse to lay that whole thing off on him. It would have been okay, but half of these prosecutors have been telling everybody about it like it was a big joke. They're saying they met me and told me off, and stuff like that. According to them, nobody took any money. I set the whole thing up by myself, that's what they're saying, the fucking liars."

"Blow the whistle on the whole bunch of hypocritical bastards," Tuck said, "let some of them take the fall with you."

"I can't," he said, "it's too big. It goes all the way back to New York, through the guys in Vegas. I can't make trouble for them, and damn near every prosecutor in the state that was in on it, or knew about it. They can bring the feds in because the furniture came across the state line, from Vegas. They're holding all the aces, they'll gang up on me in Court and I'll never see the light of day. I've already got two federal raps, they can throw away the key on a third conviction, and they will, to cover their own asses."

"Jesus Christ," Tuck said, "it looks pretty bleak. Are they looking for you now? Is he going to let you go, let you get out of the state?"

"Yeah, he told me to get the hell out of Arizona, and if I ever come back, he's going to put me away and throw away the key!" Sal said this with a chuckle, "I paid him ten thousand bucks, the bastard, but he didn't give any of it back. He's puttin' me on a list, an all points bulletin - like dragnet on TV - banned from the state. He ought to be banned, the crooked bastard!"[120]

Deputy Sheriff Coogan (Clint Eastwood) was sent east from Arizona to extradite Jimmy Ringerman from New York in the movie "Coogan's Bluff," in 1968. In 1961's real life version, Deputy Sheriff William Steele (above) of Sedona flew to the east coast to represent Arizona at an extradition hearing for Eli Newmark and Sal. Sal, whose whereabouts were unknown, was the subject of a nationwide bulletin by Arizona law enforcement agencies at the time. The extradition hearing was so important to Governor Meyner of New Jersey that he announced that he intended to preside over it himself. Eastwood and Director Don Siegel made the popular film based on a Warren Miller script. Photo courtesy of Coconino County Sheriff's Department.

"What about Blackjack and the Kid?" Tuck asked.

"They took off when they heard I got back," he said, "and it's a good thing, too. I would have killed the bastards if I caught up to them yesterday. If I get the chance, find out where they are, I'll put One-Eye on 'em, anyway. Especially the Kid, he's the one who ratted us all out."

"Why, what can One-Eye do?" Tuck was fascinated by the expose'.

"He can break their fucking legs," Sal said, "with a baseball bat, that's one of his specialties." It was Tuck's turn to put his head back on the seat. He was amazed by this outburst of information. Usually Sal only gave him enough to shut him up.

Tuck surmised that Sal felt guilty about the short ticket, and the way he came home only weeks after Edie Maye's death. He thought that this must be his way of apologizing, sharing some of his problems, and opening up for once.

One-Eye Irving. Tuck wondered what the envelope was for that Sal gave to One-Eye Irving in the Somers Point Diner that day, when he was a kid. The scope of what Sal was telling him was incredible, but Tuck knew he wasn't making it up. He had seen the casino in operation. There was no doubt in Tuck's mind that everything he was telling him was the truth.

"What are you going to do?" Tuck asked, "Can I help you out in any way? I don't have to leave tonight; I can stay another couple of days if you need me."

Tuck suddenly felt sorry for him in a way. He really did work hard in what he did, and there didn't seem to be any difference in the culpability, in Tuck's mind, between his activities and the elected officials that were always available with their hands out.

"Nah," he said, "you get going. I'll stay while Cherry closes up the apartment, then we're heading east. There's nothing you can do to help me out, but thanks, anyway."

Tuck started back that night, driving Northeast through Salt River Canyon and the Indian reservations. By the time he got half way across New Mexico, his car was losing power, and only running on two of its four cylinders. He turned south out of the mountains and barely made it into Sweetwater, Texas.

The mechanic at the City Garage said it would take a couple of days to get new valves from Fort Worth, so Tuck holed up in a rooming house. The new master cylinder had shot his budget, and he had to call Cholly and have him send the twenty-eight bucks to pay for the valve job.[121]

Sitting on the porch of Emma's boarding house, Tuck thought about his half brother, Johnny. It would be great to have a younger brother, but how could Tuck relate to this situation? Sal hadn't even told Tuck Johnny's last name, and apparently, none of them would be welcomed by his step-father. Tuck had to assume that they had waited until the following morning so that Johnny's stepfather would be away from the house, at work.

Tuck reviewed his aborted career in the Service. If everything had gone right, he would probably be a first lieutenant in the Marine Corps right now, assigned to some VMF, or perhaps flying from a carrier. How would this situation look, he thought, to my superiors? The FBI tracks all this shit, he had found out at Picatinny Arsenal, when he finally got the TOP SECRET clearance. He got it all right, but only after six months of waiting and two personal interviews in which it was revealed that the clippings about Sal's adventures were still following him.

"I would have never made it," Tuck said out loud, musing about the situation.

"Eh, what's that, sonny?" The old Texan, sitting in the rocker next to him on the front porch of Emma's Boarding House, looped a spit of his tobacco over the porch rail, "Whatda' say?"

"Nothing, Pop," Tuck said, "just day dreaming."

When the valve job was finished, Tuck took off again and finally pulled into his apartment in South Jersey, thirteen days after leaving to get his car. He was exhausted by the trip, not so much from the 6,000 mile drive, but more from trying to sort out what he had learned about Sal and his new half brother.

Tuck was back on the job only a few days when Richard Dagampat called him from a phone booth at the airport. He was lying over for a few hours and wondered if Tuck wanted to have a beer. Tuck told the boss he had an emergency and met him in a little bar overlooking the passenger terminal at Philadelphia airport.[122]

Tuck told Richard about Edie Maye and filled him in on his job. Richard responded, bringing him up to date on the beginning of his career in the Military.

"I went down to Quantico, Man," he said, "and all they wanted me to do was play ball in that Inter Service League. "I took a clue from you, Tuck, and told them no way. I swore after the last Army game, no more football for me!"

"Why," Tuck asked, "what happened?" Richard had All-American mention that year, and scored the lone touchdown in Navy's 7 – 7 tie with a powerful Army team.

"My knee went out," he said, "against Georgia Tech. Every game after that, I played with a couple of shots of Novocain in it. In the Army game, I hurt it again, but they made me play. I had seven shots of Novocain before the game was over. It wasn't any fun anymore, so no way I was going to play for Quantico."

"Those bastards," Tuck was incensed, "but, anyway, you made it, you graduated, Goddamnit, at least one of us did! So what are you doing now, up here?"

"I'm getting out of the Marine Corps," Richard said, "I've had it with the chicken shit. I'm resigning my commission and going over to the Air Force."

"You'll probably be the only Navy graduate in the Air Force," Tuck laughed.

"Yeah," he said, "probably so. Everybody says I'm crazy, because I'll lose my class number. But I don't give a shit. I was only a piece of meat to the Navy and the Corps, that's all. I'll start out fresh in the Air Force."

"We never figured you'd make Admiral." Tuck said, "So what's the difference?"

39

THE RIGHT ROCK

LIVING in Germantown, PA, Tuck was half way between his night job at Tech Services in downtown Philadelphia and his day job at General Electric in Paoli, PA, preparing illustrations on GE's bid to send a man to the moon. Long hours on drafting stools exacerbated a dull pain on Tuck's coccyx, which eventually festered, and pilonidal cysts emerged, requiring surgery.[123]

Dr. McAuliffe, a huge Scotsman, removed the cysts, telling Tuck,

"I had to remove a lot of muscle. They were a couple of monsters, as far cysts go!"

Tuck took three weeks to regain enough strength to return to work at Tech. GE had lost the bid for the moon project while Tuck was hospitalized. Offered a management position at Redstone Arsenal Alabama, Tuck packed up his Austin Healy Sprite and left for Huntsville on two day's notice.

Tuck's life took a turn for the better about a year later, when he met Dotti, his present wife. They fell in love at first sight at a friend's wedding, and the fact that he was running a NASA project for Tech Services in Huntsville, Alabama, didn't deter them. Within another eight months, he had divorced his first wife and married Dotti in a civil ceremony.

He was transferred to Columbus, Ohio, and they moved into a big mobile home Tuck had purchased in Alabama and had hauled to Columbus. A daughter was born there, in St. Francis Hospital. Tuck ran half of a publications contract for the Army DCSC[124] in Columbus, until the Company lost the job to a lower bidder, after a year and a half. The

Company brought them back to Philadelphia. Tuck worked out of the main office designing and managing a project for the U.S. Army Biological Warfare Lab. When the big cutbacks in military spending threatened the industry, he quit and moved into the commercial side of publications.

Tuck took a job as an Art Director in a small advertising agency, and moved on from there to a bigger agency headquartered in Philadelphia's Society Hill district.

He saw very little of Sal any more. Once he had stopped in Columbus, driving another brand new Buick convertible. He still had Cherry in tow, and she, her two obnoxious Siamese cats. Tuck knew that he had acquired an EconoCar car rental agency, the first in New Jersey. It was a new idea, and doing well. He soon had agencies in Trenton, Wrightstown and New Egypt. The jewelry stores had died with the advent of the big mall discount stores, but Sal still sold a little jewelry from the car agencies, and diamonds from his shirt pockets.

In Columbus, Tuck had injured his back moving some darkroom equipment, and for about a year, the condition got continually worse. He was running the publications department for Tech Services in Philadelphia when it finally just fell apart. Dr. DiPalma, the foremost authority on these problems in the Philadelphia area, did a spinal fusion, and Tuck was nearly a year recovering. The finance company with which he had mortgaged the mobile home allowed him to make interest only payments, and Dotti's family kept them in groceries. By that time, they had a second daughter, and having finally received dispensation from the Pope, Tuck and Dotti were married again in a Catholic ceremony; their daughters in attendance.

DiPalma told Tuck that he had a "congenital defect," several of his lumbar vertebras being curiously flat.

"These 'wings,' if you will, on the vertebra, are defective." He said, showing Tuck his X rays, "you can see how flat they are compared to the others. Once the muscle was torn away, the geometry isn't there for a successful reattachment. Of course, the condition was exacerbated by the muscle removed when you had the pilonidal cysts operation. That caused an unbalance. Did you ever fall from a height and land on your lower back?"

"No, Doc," Tuck said, "I never hurt myself falling on my back."

"I can only surmise that this misshapen vertebra is congenital, then," he said.

Tuck remembered standing in the bathroom, his pants about his ankles, defying tears while Edie Maye flailed at his coccyx with the porcelain hand mirror.

"Yeah, I guess so, Doc," he said.

Cholly was still running Sal's businesses, and when Tuck's car gave out, he sold him a reliable Dodge, very cheap, that had been a rental car. Tuck went up to Trenton on the bus to pick it up.

"Where's dad?" he asked.

"You really want to know?" Cholly responded with a question. "Of course," Tuck said, "unless it's some big deal."

"He's in Switzerland," Cholly said.

"You've got to be kidding," Tuck responded, thinking that something was going on, "what's he doing in Switzerland? Has he taken up skiing?"

"I don't know," Cholly said, "some kind of deal with jewelry."

It was nearly fifteen years before Tuck got the details on the trip to Switzerland. Sal was up from Florida and made an unexpected visit to his house. He seemed in a talkative mood, and after Dotti made dinner, Tuck got out the VO, and they sat at the kitchen table, and Sal told him the story.

"Did I ever introduce you to Harry Woodruff?" He asked.

"No, I don't think so," Tuck said.

"He lives over here in Bristol," Sal said, "I knew him in the old days, from Burlington. Well, Harry's been working for the government for the past few years, and he knows this guy who invented an airplane that takes off and lands in fifteen feet. The inventor, he's a guy I meant in Covington. That's where he's from, and he used to come into my joint. The guy has been trying to sell his plane to the Air Force and Harry knows him from that.

"They can't sell this plane to the government, so Harry makes up this factory down in Florida, and he's trying to get people to invest in this airplane. He says it's like the Model T was in 1925, everybody will have one in no time." Sal's chuckling about the story, enjoying it while he's recalling the details.

"What do you mean," Tuck asked, "made up a factory?"

"Well, Harry makes a deal with this guy who's got a big empty manufacturing plant, which went out of business, and he can rent the place a day or a week at a time.

So, when he's got some investors coming, he has all these guys lined up from unemployment, and he pays them to sit at these drawing tables and look like they're working. And he hangs parts of these planes all over the manufacturing part of the plant, where they used to make baby carriages, or something, so it looks like they're manufacturing these airplanes. But they don't have order one!

"Any way, everybody down in Florida thinks they've got another Howard Hughes[125] in the back yard, and Harry's gettin' enough money to keep up the show, but not enough to make the thing go. One of the people that Harry gets to know through this airplane thing is one of the prosecutors of Dade County. Harry gets to know him pretty good; he takes him fishing on his boat all the time.

"So this airplane is just a big hoax?" Tuck asked.

"Oh, no," he said, "the airplane is for real. It was called the Lanier Paraplane. Harry flew one at the Paris Air Show one year. It's got these funny wings, and it flies at fifty miles an hour and lands and takes off on a dime at fifteen miles an hour, but nobody wants it for some reason. Some German guy, Lanier, invented it. He also invented the ice cream cone and that's how he got the idea for the airplane...he noticed that when you drop an empty cardboard ice cream cone, it always lands on its tip, and that gave him the idea for the airplane.[126]

"Anyway, Harry's got the prosecutor out fishing one day and the prosecutor asks him if he knows anything about diamonds. Harry says no, but he knows somebody who does, meaning me. It turns out that this prosecutor knows about a prisoner in the Dade County jail. This guy is doing twenty years for something, and he tells the prosecutor that he knows where there's a couple of million dollars worth of diamonds buried."

"Like a buried treasure?" Tuck asked. He was fascinated by the story. It had everything, almost like the Count of Monte Cristo.

"Well," Sal said, "not exactly. These diamonds were stolen by the Nazis, or taken from Jews during the War and the guys who stole them, they were all German SS officers, and they got stuck with them, when the Russians came in. According to this guy in the jail, they sneaked them into Switzerland and buried em, figuring they'd come back for them later, after the war."

"So, what happened?" Tuck asked, intrigued by the story.

"They all got caught by the Russians," Sal said, "except this guy, who got away first and eventually came to the states. He forgot all about it, because he didn't know the other guys got caught until this year, when some distant relative came to the jail, and happened to tell him they all got caught and executed by the Russians. So, all of a sudden, he realizes that the diamonds are still there, and he's the only guy left who knows about it! He thought the other guys got away, too!

"So, this guy gets word to the prosecutor, and he tells him the story, and if he'll get him out of jail, he'll tell him where the diamonds are. The prosecutor tells Harry this story, and he says he believes it, because he's been talking to this prisoner for nearly a year, off and on, and he believes the story about the diamonds. He says this Nazi is a likeable guy!"

"This sounds like a James Bond movie," Tuck said, laughing.

"Yeah," Sal said, "but it's true. Harry calls me up and asks me if I want in on it, because they need somebody to look at these diamonds. They could be fakes; it could be just a big bunko scam just to get this guy out of jail, see.

"Now the prosecutor, he thinks Harry's loaded, that he can pick up and fly to Switzerland after supper, any time he wants. Harry can't let on that he's broke, and the airplane factory is a big fake, so he says sure, he'll get me and we'll go get the diamonds. Only Harry doesn't know that I'm broke, too, and we figure the trip is gonna' take about ten thousand bucks, by the time all the expenses are taken care of."

"Ten thousand to fly to Europe?" Tuck asked, "Isn't that pretty steep?"

"Well," Sal said, chuckling, "the air fare was about three, and we figured we had to go first class. After all, we're gonna' pick up about four million dollars worth of diamonds!"

"So, where did you get the money?" Tuck asked. Obviously he had gone. Cholly told Tuck that the old man was in Switzerland when he bought the Dodge from him, in Trenton.

"One of the investors in the airplane was a widow from a big steel family, from Pennsylvania," Sal said, "You'd know the family if I told you, they got a whole city named after them on the Delaware River. The investor was an old lady, she ran what's left of this steel empire and a couple of banks, and she took a liking to Harry. That's why she bought the airplane stock, because she liked Harry.[127]

"So old Harry, he goes over there and sweet talks Mary, if you know what I mean, and Mary, she puts up the ten grand, and we're off to Switzerland. We flew into Geneva, and catch a train up to Lausanne, and put up in this Palace on the lake. I mean this place was first class all the way."

"You mean it was actually a Palace?" Tuck asked.

"Yeah," Sal said, "a couple of treaties were signed there, ending wars. It was called the Beau Rivage Palace[128]. So, we get settled in, and Harry calls this Swiss lawyer we have to meet, so's I can assess the stones."

"Didn't the guy tell the prosecutor where they were?" Tuck asked.

"Oh, that guy was real cute," Sal said, "he wrote down the directions to this place where the diamonds were buried, draws a map and tore it in half. He gave half to the prosecutor and mailed the other half to the lawyer in Lausanne, so nobody knew where they were until we were together, and put the pieces of paper back together.

"The next afternoon, this little lawyer shows up, and I don't like him the minute I laid eyes on him, but what are you gonna' do, I mean, he needed us the same as we needed him. But still, we don't want him to see our half of the address and he doesn't want to show us his half. It's a Mexican standoff.

"We go down to this dining room with a big domed ceiling and have dinner, feeling each other out, asking questions and such. The lawyer can speak a little German and Italian, so we can talk in Italian. This is driving Harry crazy, because he can't understand either of us, but anyway, I'm getting some real bad feelings about this lawyer. We agree to meet the next day the same time and we go back to the room to talk it over.

"I tell Harry that it's no go, I think this guy is conning us, and I don't like him. I say we put a call or telegram into the prosecutor and find out about this guy from the prisoner and just sit tight until we get somebody else to deal with, 'cause I can smell a trap. I don't like it.

"But Harry says no, this guy is okay, guaranteed. He's related to the guy in jail somehow and the guy trusts him. I say 'yeah, but I don't trust him.' Harry keeps the pressure up, and the next day, I figure, what the hell, it's his gig, I'm just along to look at some stones, so I say, okay, I'll go along with it.

"We find the place; it's one of those swiss farms like you see on the calendars, tiled roof house stuck in the hillside. One end of the house is the barn; this farmer keeps his cow in there, right next to where he sleeps. This little farmer, he comes out and they jabber away, him and the lawyer, in German. The farmer, he's got one of those swiss machine guns slung on his shoulder, and the way he moves it around, I can tell he knows how to use it."

"Sure," Tuck said, "all swiss men have to serve in the military, and they never get discharged, like here.[129] They keep their weapon in their home, so they can respond in an emergency. It's kind of like a National Guard, without any weekend meetings."

"This little National Guardsman, then," Sal said, laughing, "we show him the map, which is now taped together, and he leads us down the hill to another building, like a small barn. It's got a dirt floor and the walls are made out of big rocks, and he goes over to one wall, and after a couple of tries, counting rocks, pulls out this big rock. He reaches in the hole and pulls out an old wooden box, about twice as big as a shoe box, and hands it to me."

"Were the diamonds in it?" Tuck couldn't resist asking.

"I opened the box," Sal continued, "and inside there's this big ball of burlap, about as big as a honeydew melon. I unwrap it, and I'm looking at about eight million dollars worth of the best looking stones I've ever seen!

"Now, I'm trying to look calm, you know, like I see this every day. I take my glass out and start looking at different ones, and they are choice! Really nice stones, I couldn't find one with a blemish, and a lot of them are big; two, four carats, maybe.

"The little farmer, he starts getting nervous. He takes this machine gun off his shoulder, and keeps grabbing at the box, so I look at a few more, and he wraps them back up, puts them in the box, puts the box back in the wall and covers it up with the stone. I'm not forgetting that he's carrying that machine gun, and Harry is really looking nervous. The wall looks like it's never been touched, after he puts the rock back.

"We go out and stand in the yard, and the lawyer starts talking about how hard it will be to get the stones out of the country, and I don't say nothin' because I don't plan to take them out of the country. The little farmer, he just stands there, kicking dirt, and listening."

"You mean you're going to leave them there?" Tuck asked.

"No," Sal said, "I had it all worked out. A couple of my friends, they got connections in swiss banks, and I got the addresses of their bankers and box numbers, so all I got to do is get the diamonds to the bank and put them in a safe box. We'll use them as collateral and wire transfer out the money. Or, we can sell them, without ever taking them out of the bank. We can run the money all around, through the international banks. My friend does it all the time, and you can even make money on the currency differences while you're doin' it.[130]

"So," Tuck asked, the suspense killing him, "what happened?"

"Well," he said, "the banks would all be closed by the time we get back to the city, and this takes a little setting up, and the lawyer, he has to be in all of it. So we decide to leave the stuff where it was. What the hell, it had been safe there for thirty years already. We figured we'd come back in the morning and pick it up.

Harry says to the lawyer, "Tell the farmer to get his hat, we'll take him and the diamonds back to the hotel and he can bunk with us; we'll get him a room in the Palace, and we can settle everything in the morning."

"But the little farmer gets all upset...he won't leave the farm! So, we end up leaving the stones there, anyway!

"In the car, on the way back, the lawyer almost gets hysterical talking about the machine gun. He was scared shitless when the little farmer swung it off his shoulder in the barn, and he's real nervous about getting the stones away from the guy."

"Doesn't sound good," Tuck said.

"Yeah, I guess we were stupid. We should have grabbed them right there, and took off, and left the goddamn lawyer to walk back. Instead, we waited until the morning, and when the guy didn't show up, Harry rented a car, and we drove out there. Christ, we got lost about ten times, but we finally found the place. We walked down to the little barn, and the rock was out of the wall and the diamonds were gone!

"So, we went up to the house, which was open, and we found the little farmer in the kitchen with his head smashed in, dead as a doornail!

"Jesus," Tuck said, "what'd you do then?"

"Harry panicked; he wanted to get the hell out of there right away. I looked around for a minute being careful not to leave any prints, but I didn't find anything, so we took off. We went back to the palace, packed up and caught the next train to Geneva, then the next flight back home. I was pretty sure we'd be okay, because nobody saw us out there except the little lawyer, and he's the guy that must have done in the farmer. I figured he wasn't going to tell anybody."

"That farmer must have known they were there, all along," Tuck said, "I wonder why he didn't use them. Eight million dollars in the wall in your barn. Jesus!"

"No," Sal said, "he didn't know. That's where we made our mistake. We assumed that he knew those diamonds were there. It seemed only natural. After all, he was related to the jailbird, and they had been there a long time. We figured he was in on it with the guy in jail all along, that he helped them hide the diamonds in that wall.

"See, the address had on it, south wall, 6, 2, meaning the sixth rock over, second one up from the floor. I mean, we tried a couple of rocks before he got the right one. That's where I screwed up. I thought he knew about them, too. But when he couldn't locate the right rock, I got worried. Like I said, I figured he was in it with the guy in jail. Otherwise, anybody would have taken them long ago."

"Boy!" Tuck said, "That's some story. What did Harry tell Mary happened to her money?"

"He told her the truth." Sal said, "What else was he going to tell her? I mean, that's pretty unbelievable, isn't it? The problem was that I misread Harry, too. He got too nervous. You can't be nervous or over anxious on a big deal. We should have found out more about the lawyer. We could have stayed there a couple of weeks, if we needed to, see?"

"I guess you have to keep the right balance between greed and caution," Tuck said.

"Yeah," Sal said, "that's right, and Harry screwed up another deal the same way, down in Florida, but I'll tell you about that another time."

"And how about the guy in the Florida jail?" Tuck asked.

"Oh," Sal said, "he's still there, doing his time, as far as I know."

"So, after all that," Tuck said, "you got nothing from it!"

"I got a nice vacation in Switzerland!" Sal said, laughing, "and I got this!" Sal flattened his right hand on the table, showing off another pinky ring, this one highlighting a large diamond, set in silver, "When I palmed a couple of those rocks from the wall!"

40

CAR CAPERS

TUCK lucked out when he was strong enough to job hunt after the spinal fusion, landing a job at the Philadelphia Inquirer as an advertising artist and photo retoucher. The money was very good, it was probably the best job for an artist in Philadelphia, but it was all shift work. Being the junior man in a 33 man unionized department, Tuck got the worst shifts.

He liked the people that he worked with, most of them extremely talented artists, and especially his boss, Cal, who was a graduate of the Girard School for Boys. Stephan Girard had established the school for poor orphan boys back in the 1800's. The school became a Philadelphia icon.[131]

He was there about a year when Cal walked up to him just after Tuck checked in at seven o'clock for an evening shift.

"You seen the early edition?" he asked.

"No," Tuck said, "what's up?"

"I think you'd better take a look at this," he said, dropping an early edition on Tuck's drawing table, "I already took some heat about it at the production meeting with the bosses."

The headline read, "TRENTON MAN INDICTED IN MAJOR STOLEN CAR RING." Sal's name, in good journalistic style, was in the first sentence. The story described how the car ring, allegedly directed by Sal, was selling cars in New Jersey, then stealing them and reselling them in southern states. Tuck could feel his face getting red as he scanned the story.

"What can I say, Cal?" Tuck asked, "It's my old man, up to his tricks again. It's got nothing to do with me."

Did you ever think of being an orphan as an advantage? Tuck kept the thought to himself.

"Yeah," he said, "I know. But thank your lucky stars you joined the (Newspaper) Guild, because management tried to make something of it, mostly because the names are exactly the same. They thought it was you!"

"Christ," Tuck said, "my old man and I, we don't exactly get along, if you know what I mean. I walk to the beat of a different drummer than him."

That's ironic, thought Tuck, *Moe Annenberg's son is queasy about a staff artist's father having the 'wrong' connections.*

"Why do you think I never play in the football or basketball pools? Tuck continued, "It's because of him, my old man...that money, no matter how innocent it appears, ends up with his big time friends and finances their real businesses. I try not to have anything to do with him, or his friends..."

"Well," Cal said, "you're a Shop Steward, so you know what to do if anybody approaches you on this. I just wanted to bring it to your attention."

"Thanks, Cal," Tuck said, "I appreciate it." Tuck called Sis the following day.

"Oh," she said, "did you see the article? Daddy's being bad again. Isn't he something, stealing cars at his age?"

"Jesus Christ, Sis," Tuck said, "this isn't some kind of joke. He's got the FBI after him. It's not funny, and I don't appreciate being told about it by my boss, either."

"Oh, sure," she said, "it's serious, but he'll get out of it. He always does. He just doesn't learn, does he? He just keeps being a bad boy. But, you can't be mad at him, he's our daddy!"

Since Tuck was working nights, he had enrolled again in college, deciding that the only way to really make it would be to finish college with a degree. At Rutgers, Camden, he took a full load of classes during the day, and often left school to come directly to work. He watched for Sal's trial date, but with his schedule, he missed the trial, and had to get the details from Cholly.

"They convicted him on one count of Grand theft, auto," Cholly said, "and fined him ten thousand bucks."

"No jail?" Tuck asked.

"No," Cholly said, "five years probation. The judge really read him out. He humiliated him, called him all kinds of names. He went on for about five minutes."

"How'd the old man take it?" Tuck asked.

"Like water off a duck's back!" Cholly said. Years later, after Cholly's death, Sal told Tuck his story of the car ring. He had asked Tuck and Dotti to attend a dinner with him at a Union hall in Trenton. Tuck didn't really want to go, but had been trying to make himself friendlier towards him, so they went along.

After the dinner, Sal brought an older gentleman over the table and introduced him as Judge Pleriano. Tuck shook hands and they chatted for a moment.

The next time Sal stopped over to the house, Tuck asked him about the Judge.

"He buys diamonds from me," Sal said, "I pick them up on jeweler's row in Philly, and re-sell them. He's always interested in something that's a little unusual."

"How did you get to know him?" Tuck asked.

"Oh," Sal said, "he helped me out on the car thing, with the Feds."

"How's that?" Tuck asked.

"Well," he said, "they had me on seventeen counts, the Feds. Each count would have been five years and ten grand, so I needed a little help, if you know what I mean."

"You could have been in jail for the rest of your life," Tuck said.

"Yeah, I know." Sal continued, "But my Friend Sam, he introduced me to the Judge, the one you met at the Union hall and the Judge, he got the thing pushed over into Judge Wood's Burlington County Superior Court, and then he went to work. By the time the trial came around, I only had one count to worry about."

"What happened to the other sixteen counts?" Tuck said.

"I bought them back, from Judge Wood, at five grand each. Eighty thousand bucks, right in his pocket!" He said calmly. Tuck choked a little on his potato as he listened to Sal's nonchalant explanation.

"Cholly said that the Judge really humiliated you," Tuck said, "in the courtroom. He's the one that took the payoff?"

"Oh, yeah," Sal said, chuckling about it, "he was really pissed at me, 'cause I made him take all that money. Like I really had to twist his arm.

That's the way they are, you know, they like to think they're better than you, *but they always take the money!* They were just lucky that they caught us, anyway."

"How's that?" Tuck asked, still thinking about Judge Wood, who had the reputation in the county of being the toughest straight arrow in the system.

"Well," Sal said, "I had a pretty good system going. I'd go buy a new car at a discount, from one of the dealers I know up here. I'd make a second set of keys, then put it in the paper and sell it to somebody at a good price. I've got this guy who works for me, so after a couple of weeks, I'd give him the keys and he'd go around and pick up the car, easy as pie.

"The guy who bought it, he turns it into the insurance company, and he gets another new car, maybe even makes a little money, 'cause I gave him a good deal on the car in the first place. It's no skin off his nose.

"We run the car down to Virginia, where this friend of mine has a big dealership. He re-titles the car and sells it to somebody right off the showroom floor, and then we do the same thing down there. Hell, we sold one car about five times! Nobody's gettin' hurt except the insurance companies, and I figure they deserve it!

"So, I'm doing this for a couple of years, moving a lot of cars, when this guy from Trenton, he's out at the Bordentown Auto Dealer's Auction with a friend, and he sees his stolen car being auctioned off!

"He starts yelling about it, that that's his stolen car that's being sold, and he tells the auctioneer that there's a scratch inside the trunk, where he loaded a lawnmower, or something. So they take a look, and sure enough, he's right, it is his car that just got stolen a couple of months ago, although it has different VIN numbers.

"Course, when I started this, they didn't have this big computer system that hooks up all the states. So the cops, they start tracing this car back, and it comes back to me. I'm the guy who sold him the car in the first place.

"They come nosing around asking questions and I tell them I don't know nothing. I bought the car legit, and sold it to this guy because I didn't particularly like it, that's all. I don't know anything about it getting stolen. I even took a little loss on it, I tell them.

"But some smart ass, he decides to use this computer and he finds about thirty other cars that I sold, and he starts tracking them down, and seventeen of them got stolen, so he gets a little suspicious. But still, they got nothing on me, because the rest of those sales, they were legitimate, too. So they're suspicious, but they're confused, too. All of those cars got stolen in Trenton and they're figuring that they've uncovered a big stolen car ring!

"The trouble is that they hooked up this computer system, and this guy's looking at the dealers in Virginia because this car at the Bordentown auction, it came up from there. So he starts checking the sales of the cars in Virginia, and he finds out about my friend with the dealership. For each of the stolen cars, there was a duplicate car, same model and color, sold out of this dealership in Virginia, a few weeks later with a legit title. They called them 'cloned cars.'

"So he talks to the Virginia State Police and they get a warrant and they go in and pick up my friend, and he sings like Mario Lanza. They tell him he won't be prosecuted if he tells them everything he knows. So he tells them I made him do it! He didn't know where the cars came from, and all this bull shit, that I threatened him, and a bunch of other stuff. And that's when they bring the Feds in, and have the Grand Jury."

"So, there wasn't any 'stolen car ring,'" Tuck said, "just you and a couple of your friends. No big organization, like they said in the newspaper stories. Did you make the guy do it, I mean, did you put some pressure on him?" Tuck couldn't resist asking.

"Hell, no," Sal said, "the whole scam was his idea. He thought the whole thing up. See, I knew him from the time I was in Chicago, he used to come up to this club I ran there; he liked the boat rides and the casino. After the fire put me out of a job, Momo, my boss, asked me to stop in and see this guy who owed him a lot of money. I was going through Virginia anyway so when I saw his name on the dealership, I dropped in to see if it was him, and it was. I knew that he still owed my friend from Chicago a lot of money, gambling debts from this club, so I asked him if he got that stuff straight yet. That's when he brought up the whole idea, to turn over some cars and get the money to pay his debt to my friend. It was just a couple of us. The reporters, they like to play all that stuff up, you know. It sells papers and makes the cops look good."

But Sal was exploiting his son's naiveté with his cavalier explanation. The truth of the matter was that when organized crime got into the car stealing business, thefts rose almost six fold from one car stolen every two minutes in the U.S. in 1960 to an astounding one car every 36 seconds in 1969.[132] Practically every major city crime family was involved in the "car cloning" business, a nationwide endeavor that was sucking $150 million out of the consumer market and elevating already high auto insurance rates.

Every time Sal told him about one of these episodes, it set Tuck's mind spinning, wondering if there were any honest politicians, judges and lawyers. He seemed to move in an entirely different world than the rest of society, keyed into a different set of laws and responsibilities. It would have been a lot easier for Tuck to continue to hate Sal, had not the authorities been involved in every lawless escapade that he perpetrated.

Tuck remembered the day that they were driving through the Baltimore tunnel, and Sal's car broke down. A police van rolled up behind them, and the officers pushed them through the tunnel. Tuck was driving, and he got out to go back and thank them.

"Give them a couple of bucks," Sal said.

"They won't take it," Tuck said, fearing the cops would respond with a ticket for offering a bribe. "And they're liable to make a stink about it."

"They'll say they won't take it, but give it to 'em anyway," he said, "then, they'll take it!" He was right. They took the five dollars Tuck pushed in the window.

"I never knew you ran a night club in Chicago," Tuck said.

"Oh, yeah," he said, "that was a few years back. It was only for a little while, though. I was an interim manager, so to speak."

"You mean you just ran the place until they got a regular manager?" Tuck asked, wondering about this whole new episode that he had never heard anything about.

"Well, yeah," Sal said, laughing, "something like that. It was a real nice club, right on a river just outside of Chicago, but nobody ate there, they just watched the show. Usually, they just came in one door and out the other."

"What for?" Tuck asked.

"Well," Sal said, "we had these gondola boats on the canal, like in Venice, Italy. The customers would come into the club, get cleared, and then go out the back door. They'd get in a boat and it would take 'em down the river where we had a casino set up in this portable army warehouse, they called it a "hut." You couldn't get to this warehouse, except from the boats, and some special shuttle buses, so it was a pretty safe operation.

"So you ran the casino," Tuck said.

"No," he said, "I helped them out with that, but I ran this swank night club, right there on the canal, until it caught fire and burned down."

"What happened?" Tuck asked.

"Nobody ever really figured out how the fire started," he said, "but it was in the kitchen. Restaurants get a lot of kitchen fires; it's not unusual, Jewish lightning."

"So you were out of a job, then," Tuck said.

"Yeah," he said, "so to speak. That's when I took off. In fact that's when I came down to Virginia and got involved in this car mess."

Tuck got a different story from Sis about the Chicago fire. When he was teaching, Dotti and the kids and he would go up to Medford Lakes and have dinner at Sis's once in a while, having temporarily buried the hatchet. One night they started talking about Sal's escapades. Tuck had forgotten all about the Chicago story, but he mentioned that Sal was in Illinois before he went to Virginia.

"Oh, yeah," Sis said, "that's when he burned down that Chicago night club for Sam Giancana."

"He didn't burn it down," Tuck said, "he just happened to be running it when it caught fire, according to what he told me."

"That's the only reason he went there," Sis said, "was to burn it down!"

"Get out, Sis," Tuck said, "can you picture dad burning a place down? I can't. I don't believe that story."

But Sis was right. The Villa Venice supper club, out of the way on Milwaukee Avenue in Wheeling, Illinois opened its doors in 1960. Its owner, Sam "Momo" Giancana made major revisions to the huge property in 1962, adding canals to the landscape and first class furnishings to the interior. In addition, a casino was constructed in a quonset hut only two blocks away, still on the eight acre property, but hidden among rusting heavy machinery and car wrecks. In November of that year, Momo called in his marker with Frank Sinatra, who had asked him to deliver the Union vote for his friend, Jack Kennedy in the West Virginia primary election. The request had been enhanced by a valise filled with Joe Kennedy cash delivered by Judy Exner, Kennedy's girlfriend.[133] The result was a show opened by Eddie Fisher, featuring Sammy Davis Junior and Dean Martin, followed by head liner Sinatra. They sang and danced and clowned on stage, involving the audience in the act, which was already famous at the Las Vegas Sands as "the Rat Pack."

The Villa Venice Supper Club, where Frank Sinatra and the "Ratpack" lured mafia bigshots and high rollers to a quonset hut casino hidden in a nearby scrapyard. Sinatra cancelled scheduled engagements for himself, Eddie Fisher and the "Ratpack" at the Las Vegas Sands for his friend Giancana. Customers could hire a gondola (with a prostitute) to ferry them to the games. Sal, after briefly working as Manager, burned the property to the ground on Giancana's orders in 1967. "That's what I was there for," Sal told his daughter, "to burn the place down."The casino took in more than 3 million in eight days by FBI estimates. Photo courtesy of the Wheeling Historical Society

Customers were treated to the greatest show in the entertainment business, and if they enjoyed water sports, they could hire a gondola, complete with gondolier and a prostitute for a cruise on the canal just outside the back door. The other feature was of course the casino, serviced by continuous shuttle buses, which reportedly grossed over 3 million during its short life, all profit, since the entertainers were working free of charge. The bright star of Villa Venice Supper Club was turned off quickly; entertainment ceased and the casino was closed after a frantic week of shows, attended by a galaxy of star gangsters. Sinatra's hopes for respectability faded with Jack Kennedys' acquiescence to his advisors' pleadings to shed the association with the singer and his crowd of gangster friends.

Peter Lawford was Kennedy's messenger, first telling Frank that his black buddy his beautiful blonde Swedish wife, Sammy Davis and My Britt, weren't welcome at Jack's inaugural ball, and by the way, Jack won't be coming to stay at Frank's Palm Springs house, after he built a heliport and special wing for the President. The President stayed with Bing Crosby, a republican. Then Momo Giancana was discovered at the Cal-Neva Casino by the Nevada Gaming Commission and Sinatra's bullying and bad language caused his removal from partial ownership there and his thirty percent ownership of the Sands, and it appeared that all bets were paid. The head liners stayed in Vegas with the Villa Venice reduced to a restaurant only with its busty gondolier crews gone, it operated for a few years before it needed to become an insurance adjustment and bust out joint.[134] Momo, pissed at Sinatra and his back stabbing political pals, called on his reliable Jersey boy, Sal Falconetti to solve his problem. There has been speculation that retaliation of Kennedy's betrayal may have included the demise of his girlfriend, Marilyn Monroe.

41

YOU'RE IT, NOW!

TUCK completed his degree work at Rutgers while holding down the job at the Inquirer. In 1972, he received a Bachelor of Arts degree in Mathematics, graduating with the Night School class of 1972. They had a little picnic at the house, but Sal attended neither that nor the graduation ceremony.

Dotti and Tuck now had three daughters, whom Sal never recognized with even as much as a birthday card. Tuck ran into him occasionally, when he was in New Jersey, visiting his family in Trenton, or Sis in the Lakes. He seldom bothered to tell him if he was coming.

Cholly was in deep trouble at the time, drifting from one bartending job to another. He'd been hospitalized for his alcoholism at least once by then. Of course, he wouldn't admit that he had a problem.

But the problem was evident. His thought processes, retarded by the disease, were still in the fifties. His conversations were duplicates of those they had years before. Each time that Tuck saw him, his heart ached, but there was no talking to him about the problem. For him, it didn't exist.

His adult life had been a series of tragedies, one after another. He married a young girl who had worked for him at the foam rubber plant, a pert blonde. Her background was one of abysmal poverty, and Cholly's attempts to build a home were thwarted by a major psychological problem that eventually led to her breakdown and eventual institutionalization.

When Terry, Cholly's wife, was finally released from the state mental hospital, Sis didn't want to give back their infant son, whom she had insisted on taking care of. It was a major problem. Tuck didn't make any points with Sis when he told her she had to give the boy back; it was more fuel for her fire.

Terry continued to have relapses into a state of uncontrollable insanity, and Cholly drank more than ever while she was gone, one time disappearing to the west coast for nearly a year. Tuck called Sis one night to find out how he was doing, since he couldn't reach him, and found out he was in Burlington County Hospital with all the classic symptoms. Tuck drove over to see him and happened to be there when the doctor on the case came into his room.

"Charles, can you hear me?" The doctor asked. He was standing at the foot of the bed, file in hand. Cholly was completely limp, exhausted from attacks of the jitters, chills and alternating sweats. His color was yellow.

"Charles," the doctor said, "you cannot drink anymore. You may not wish to hear this, but if you continue to drink alcohol, you will most assuredly die. You have cirrhosis of the liver, Charles, and it will kill you."

Cholly just nodded. The doctor asked Tuck if he had any influence over his activities.

"No, doc," Tuck said, "he knows my position on this. I want him to stop. He's my brother, but he won't even admit that he's got a problem."

"Charles," the doctor said, "you are in serious condition. You must eat a balanced diet, and you must stop drinking. I'm warning you that drinking will kill you. Alcoholism is a disease, Charles, and it must be treated. Do you understand what I am saying, Charles?"

But Cholly didn't stop. Terry moved back into her parent's place with the baby when she could stay out of the mental hospital long enough for the doctors to permit it, and Cholly moved up to Brown's Mills, near the bar where he was working.

Soon, he was living with a German girl, a divorcee brought to this country by some G.I., and in order to see him at all, Tuck had to drive up to Brown's Mills. Marilyn, his girlfriend, refused to recognize his problem, and encouraged him to drink. She kept the house stocked with all kinds of liquor.

Marilyn had problems of her own, a teenage daughter who was deaf, and a young son with multiple sclerosis.

Cholly took to the poor kid, bent and twisted so severely he nearly couldn't walk, and became his alter ego for almost three years before he died at age seven. Cholly's life was one misery after another.

Shortly after Cholly was released from the hospital after another bout with the DT's, Tuck called Sis to find out if she knew how he was doing. He had gotten out on a Monday, and Tuck wasn't able to locate him. It was Friday when he called Sis.

"Have you seen Cholly?" Tuck asked, "I haven't been able to get through to him, and he hasn't been at the Sky Lounge for a couple of days."

"He drove out west," Sis said.

"What the hell are you talking about?" Tuck asked, "He wasn't strong enough to take a trip. Couldn't you stop him?"

"I didn't know about it until Wednesday," she said, "when he called me from Las Vegas. He was talking crazy."

"What do you mean, talking crazy?" Tuck asked.

"Oh, he went on and on about Terry and little Freddy dying. He was crying, and then he said he was going to kill himself," she said, contritely.

"Jesus Christ, Sis!" Tuck shouted, "Why didn't you call me? Where did he call from? What hotel?"

"He called from a pay booth, along the road," she said, "I thought you didn't want to be bothered." Tuck's heart sank with the news.

She's was playing her little games again. Tuck thought, a*nd she's pissed off because I found out about it!*

"Christ," Tuck said, "Did you call the police? In Nevada? They'll pick him up."

"No," she said, "I didn't think of that."

"Jesus, Sis," Tuck asked, "why do you do things like this? The trail is two days cold now, for Christ's sake. Stay by the phone, I'll get back to you."

Dotti got him a road atlas. He knew he was heading for Los Angeles, where he had taken off for a year when he first ran up against the problems with Terry. Tuck traced the route from Vegas into the L.A. area and circled the towns, and began calling the police in every town en route. Cholly was driving a Mustang GT, a muscle car with a matte black hood with hood locks and a wing spoiler on its tail. He'd be easy to spot.

None of the police had seen him until Tuck talked to a desk Sergeant in Barstow, California. He remembered seeing the car on Thursday morning, but Tuck ran up against a blank wall with the L.A. police. They all agreed to keep an eye out for the Mustang, and said they would pick him up when Tuck told them he was extremely ill, and had suicidal tendencies.

Tuck called Sis back and told her what he was doing.

He had given her number to the police, as well, and they might call there if they picked him up.

"Make sure you call me if you hear anything," Tuck said.

The following morning she called. Fortunately, it was Tuck's day off since he usually worked the weekends.

"A policeman called me from Ventura." she said, "They arrested Cholly last night. He cut his wrists!"

"Oh, God," Tuck said, "give me his number. I want to talk to him."

Tuck called the desk Sergeant who told him that they had investigated a car on top of a mountain with its headlights on. Tuck's brother was lying across the hood of the car, with both wrists opened and bleeding. They had taken him to the hospital, patched him up and he was now in the Ventura County Jail. He gave Tuck the number of the jail, and he thanked him.

Calling the jail, Tuck found out that he was okay, but he would need $500 to bail him out, plus another $200 to get his car, which was impounded. Tuck called Sis back and gave her the information.

"What a mess," she asked, "but what can we do, with him all the way out in California?"

"I don't know what you're going to do," Tuck said, "but I'm going out there and get him, goddamn it. I'm not going to let Cholly sit in some goddamn jail in California."

"I'd come with you," she said, "but Stringy wouldn't give me money for a plane ticket."

"If you want to come, I'll get your ticket," Tuck said. Dotti wasn't too happy about the developing drama. It only took her a couple of years to understand more about Sis than Tuck had learned in four decades.

Monday morning, they caught an early flight to Los Angeles, and then a feeder airline to Oxnard. They grabbed a cab to the county jail, which was in the downtown area. Tuck was directed from one officer to another, and finally managed to pay the bail and get the information on where the car was impounded.

They led his brother out, and he acted as though they had just dropped in for a visit! Under the tan, his skin reflected a yellow pallor. Both wrists were bandaged. It took another three hours to get the car from the impound yard, and as soon as Cholly and Tuck checked it over, they gassed up and headed east.

Stopping to eat, Sis unwrapped his wrists and applied some first aid cream she had picked up in a drug store. Each wrist had about seven stitches in the angry red cuts running from one side to the other. Cholly insisted on driving, claiming that he was okay. They made their first stop in Tucumcari, New Mexico, and grabbed a cheap motel for the night.

Tuck called Dotti and let her know he was on the way back, but he was concerned that they had enough money to make it. Pooling their resources, they had only about a hundred bucks. They traveled the interstates and got off on the old routes to eat and sleep, trading off the driving. The cash ran out in Little Rock, Arkansas.

On Sis's insistence, Tuck asked Dotti to call Stringy and have him wire some money. Tuck was tapped out, having used up all his available resources to get the tickets, pay bail and get them half way back across the country. Apparently, Sis and her husband weren't speaking, but Stringy came across and wired enough to bring them home.

The conversations in the car were bizarre, and Tuck wondered if he had done the right thing. Cholly and Sis talked about everything except the major topic that needed talking about, his drinking. Tuck's attempts to steer the conversation that way were fruitless. A lot of time was spent idolizing Sal, and his various exploits. Sis was on her best behavior with Tuck, however, so sweet that he thought he might throw up a couple of times. It might have been better to leave him in jail, where he couldn't get to any kind of booze.

Cholly did thank Tuck for coming out to get him. Tuck told him that he thought he would do the same under the circumstances, but that he should try to stay alive so that he could return the favor someday.

That year, Tuck left the Inquirer and took a position as a mathematics teacher in a prestigious south Jersey high school. He had received a grant from the state, and using the money, published a little book on number theory that gained him some notoriety. His peculiar background in art, publishing and mathematics interested people, and he found himself lecturing at some local colleges and having one-man shows of his paintings, most of which were related to mathematics.

Each of his achievements, however insignificant, seemed to further alienate Sis and space Cholly further from him. Sal was coming to Jersey, but almost never stopped to see Tuck's family, although he stopped everywhere else.

Soon Cholly was back in the hospital with the DT's, and in the next three years, he was in and out with more and more frequency. Each time Tuck saw him; he tried to talk to him about the disease, but got nowhere. He just dismissed it, and changed the subject.

Tuck had joined the Naval Academy Alumni Association as a matter of course, keeping up with his classmates through the monthly magazine. Now a teacher, he decided to attend the annual homecoming for his class. He drove down to the Academy in time to catch the pre-game tailgate party, but realized immediately that he had made a mistake.

He was completely out-of-place with the close cropped young officers. Their language, peppered with military anagrams, was beyond his understanding. Those classmates who were no longer in Service were dressed neatly in casual sport coats and ties. Tuck, in dungarees and sweater with hair covering his ears, stood out like a sore thumb.

Angelo Fernandez, a Napper marine, was the first person whom he recognized.

"Do you know about Jack?" he asked, referring to Tuck's roommate who was the left tackle on the NAPS team.

"Yeah, Mendy, I read about it," Tuck replied, "in the Shipmate." Phillips had died in Vietnam.

"He was killed in hand-to-hand combat," Angelo said, "I was commanding his Battalion. It was terrible, Tuck, his Company got overrun by a thousand Viet Cong."

"Jesus," Tuck said, "I didn't know about that, they didn't give any details …"

"Yeah," Angelo said, choking a little, "they threw everything they had at them, and then fought with bayonets for the better part of an hour. Jack must've killed about fifteen; they were piled all around him. One of them finally hit him with an RPG. We couldn't get any support in there …" [135]

"Ah, shit, Mendy," Tuck couldn't find any words. After talking briefly to a few other classmates, he got in his car and drove over to the Academy grounds, forgoing the football game. He felt totally embarrassed and depressed. As he parked the car, a fine rain began to fall, pushed in by a cold wind from the Chesapeake. He walked slowly across the yard, noting the new buildings now occupying what had been the small boat marina.

Without thinking about it, he found himself standing on the main walk in front of Bancroft Hall, next to the Tecumseh statue; the god of

2.5. He looked at the huge bronze Indian head, adorned with war paint for the game and noticed that the red under the eyes was beginning to run, a result of the rain, now drumming down.

Tuck sat down on the wrought iron bench and began to cry uncontrollably, head in hands, great wrenching sobs.

He didn't know if he was crying for Jack, killed in the black night by hordes of screaming Viet Cong; Wes, riding a blazing SkyHawk into a rice paddy; for his brother, killing himself with alcohol; little Bessie; or for himself, for walking away from the most infinitesimal chance to be what he saw his classmates had become.

He sat there, soaked through and shivering for a half hour until he felt strong enough to return to his car and head for the Route 50 Bridge.

When he rolled into his driveway that evening, Dotti ran out to the car to tell him that Cholly was hospitalized again. Cholly's personality was now so changed that Tuck felt he simply didn't know him anymore. He was a completely different person than the one he had grown up with. Tuck drove up the hospital every day after school, but the doctors told him it was hopeless this time, his liver was beyond any kind of functioning. It was just a matter of time.

Bud Horner came to see him a couple of days before he died. He stood at the end of the bed, looking exactly like he did when he left for the Navy with Cholly when they were both eighteen. His gray hair gave away their age; each of them was forty-four.

"Hey, Paisano," Bud said, "long time no see."

"Yeah," Cholly said weakly, "you're lookin' good."

Bud nervously twisted his baseball cap and popped gum during a long pause.

"We raised some hell together, didn't we?" Cholly asked with a tiny voice.

"It's been a big game of tag," Bud said. He began crying silently, the tears rolling down his face.

"It'd been nice to see Trigger," Cholly said.

"Trigger cashed it in," Bud said, "a couple of years ago."

"Yeah," Cholly said, chuckling weakly, "you're it, now."

"Good luck to you, Chas," Bud said, "and God bless you."

Tuck walked out of the room with Bud and put his arm around his shoulder. He was having trouble making words come out.

"Thanks for coming, Buddy," Tuck said, "he loves you like a brother."

Bud grabbed Tuck and hugged him, hard, then turned and walked away. Tuck knew that he couldn't speak.

Cholly went into a coma the next day, and they transferred him to the intensive care unit.

Sis was with him the next day when Terry came in. Sis got really angry, seeing Cholly's wife. "She's got a lot of nerve, coming here!" She said.

"Jesus, Sis," Tuck said, "she's still Cholly's wife, she's got every right, for crying out loud! *Can this woman really be this much of a bitch?* he thought to himself.

"Well," she said, "she better not show up at the funeral!"

"What?" Tuck asked, stunned by her outburst, he thought, *I guess that answers that question.* Terry was having trouble keeping herself together. Sis disappeared into the elevator with a menacing stare.

"She doesn't want me to be here, does she?" Terry asked.

"Don't worry about her," Tuck said, "you have every right to be here, and I'll be God damned if anybody will keep you out."

The following evening, Tuck came in and stood next to his bed, watching the weak signal on the monitor above his head. The door was open in the dark room and self consciously, Tuck began to talk to him.

"I don't know if you can hear me or not," Tuck said, "but, you're my brother, my only real brother. We never spent enough time together, you and me. In everything I ever did, I tried to be like you, to be as strong as you, to be as fearless as you were. I never wanted to be like anybody else."

He began to cry, exhausted by the emotional pressure of the past weeks.

"I don't know if you can hear me, but we had a little sister, little Bessie, that you never knew about...she died upstairs in that front bedroom, when you were overseas...I buried her out there in the back, with all the dead animals. She was beautiful and she'd be about 19 now, so when you see her, you take care of her, like you did for us. And tell her I'm sorry, O.K?"

"What the fuck did you do this for?" Tuck asked, angrily, "Now you've gone and killed yourself, for Christ's sake. It isn't fair, Goddamnit, you don't have the right to do this! You don't have the right! God damn you, Cholly, I love you, and now you've killed yourself."

The monitor beeped loudly, two loud beeps and then it stopped. Tuck's heart turned over in his chest and he slumped over on the bed, his head in his hands.

Oh, God, he thought irrationally, *I've killed him, I've killed him! I should have kept my mouth shut!*

The monitor beeped softly again and continued with a weaker signal than before the outburst. The following day, Sis called him at school to tell him that he was gone. That evening, Tuck met her at the funeral home, which was owned by one of the player's on Tuck's 1954 freshman football team. They completed arrangements and Tuck followed Sis back to her house. Discussing details, the subject of Terry came up. Tuck had called her that afternoon to tell her Cholly had died. Terry's only request was that a bouquet be placed in the casket, marked "Dad," from Cholly's son, Chuckie.

Sis had the flower arrangements all worked out.

"There'll be a bouquet of white roses on his chest," Tuck said, "from Chuckie."

"There will not," Sis said, "that bitch is not getting any flowers in the funeral home. Who the hell does she think she is? And I won't have her coming to the viewing, either!"

Tuck stood up so violently that his chair spun across her kitchen, scattering the several bowls she kept by the sink for her cat.

"She's coming to the viewing, and the funeral," he shouted, "and his son is gonna' have a bouquet in his dad's coffin, God damn it! And if I find out that you've tried to do anything different, or to keep that boy away from his dad's funeral, you're going to be the sorriest bitch you ever saw!"

Sis's daughter, Bobbi, had her boyfriend there, a big fellow just out of the Marine Corps. He stood up at Tuck's outburst and came towards him.

"Get the fuck away from me," Tuck growled, "if you know what's good for you!"

He reached for Tuck's arm and Tuck slapped his hand away easily and shoved him backwards towards the table where he scattered cups with his hands. "I'm leaving," Tuck said, "but I'm telling you that Chuckie's flowers will be there, in the casket! And Terry will be there, too, and that's the way it's going to be! Don't fuck with me on this, or you'll be sorry!"

Tuck slammed her back door as hard as he could, but it didn't break, as he had hoped it would.

At the funeral, Sal sat between Sis and Tuck as the old gang from the swings filed by. Tuck hadn't seen most of these people for twenty-five years, but he recognized them all, and they all had something nice to say about Cholly.

Danny Do-die approached the coffin crying copiously. He placed a rose across Cholly's hands and choked out, "So long, chum. I'm gonna' miss you." Danny was mildly retarded and Cholly had given him the name 'Danny Do Die' when he interrupted a masturbation session at the swings.

When Cholly told Danny that, "too much of that will make you die," Danny continued, saying, "I don't care if I do die, do die, do die …"

They had laughed about it many times over the years.

A minister came in and made a few comments, and then read from the Bible. As he began to read, Sal put his hand on Tuck's thigh, and Tuck heard a great sob fill the room. It was the gut-wrenching moan that Tuck had heard from Mrs. Zanphel, and Tuck realized that he was the source!

Everyone went back to Sis's place after the funeral the next day, in a severe snowstorm. Aunt Mary came over to Tuck and offered her condolences.

"How come you don't come to the family meetings?" She asked.

"What family meetings? I don't know what you're talking about," Tuck responded.

"The family club," Aunt Mary said, "we meet every month, all the cousins. You're welcome any time."

"Look, Aunt Mary," Tuck said, "I don't know anything about a family club. Why didn't someone call me about it?"

"Your sister, she comes all the time." Aunt Mary said, "She says she calls you, and you're always too busy to come."

"That's bull shit, Aunt Mary." Tuck said, "She has never mentioned any such thing to me. This is the first I've ever heard of a family club."

"Will you come?" Aunt Mary asked obviously embarrassed that she had opened a can of worms unexpectedly.

"You call me when you're going to have a meeting," Tuck said, "I want to know about it, at least. But if Sis is going to be there, I won't come, no way."

"Why?" Aunt Mary asked.

"Because this is it with Sis," Tuck said, "I'm only here now out of respect for Cholly and everyone who loved him. When this is over, I don't ever want to see Sis again or ever know anything about her. She's impossible. There's no knowing what kind of lies she's told you about me over the years, but I'm done with her now, for good!"

Somehow, Tuck got through the next couple of weeks. It helped to go into school every day, the rigors of mathematics and his students helping him to survive.

42

THE BALTIMORE STING

SAL had moved to Florida at just the right time. With some help from an influential "friend" in the Tampa area, he obtained a Florida Auto Dealer's license, which, in that state, allows the holder to also finance auto purchases. In no time, he had bank credit line and a flourishing used car business. He told Tuck that he bought his cars at auction or out of the papers, had them cleaned up or "detailed," and sold them at a nice profit off the lot.[136]

The Florida economy was booming, and big hotels and condos were being built along the "gold coast," north of Miami. The state's general economic boom helped Sal's business, too, and the little car lot soon became a whole city block. Sal was moving about 500 cars a month.

He began flying to Jersey rather frequently, and Tuck would pick him up at the Philadelphia airport. Tuck didn't know it, but he had been diagnosed with a prostate cancer, and was getting treatments for it in Trenton. Sis knew it, but since they seldom saw each other, she had little opportunity or inclination to tell him of it. And of course, she wouldn't tell him of it anyway, being something that she could use against Tuck with Sal.

On one of these trips, he stopped at Tuck's place, and that's when Tuck heard the story of the Baltimore sting; the story of Charles, the idiot savant.

"That guy, Charles, who you meant in Baltimore," Sal said, "he's got a photographic memory. He can remember the pages of a phone book if he wants to, all by just looking at them, but he's simple."

"What do you mean simple?" Tuck asked.

"Well," Sal said, "he's like a kid, like he never got to be more than five years old, or something. You saw how his mother was, waiting on him and all. That's because of the way he was." On a visit to the Academy, Sal had driven Tuck up to Baltimore and they visited Charles and his mother in a Baltimore row house with white marble steps.

"Yeah," Tuck said, "I think they call that an Idiot Savant. It's a special kind of retardation. A lot of the famous mathematical calculators had it, and in some cases, great mathematicians like Carl Gauss could do it. Savants sometimes can manipulate large numbers, but if they are moronic otherwise, like little children, they're called 'idiot savants'."

"That's Charles," Sal said, "he could remember every hand and every card played in a poker game, and every bet made by every player, even if the game went for a couple of days."

"So how is it you know him?" Tuck asked.

"Well, his mother," Sal said, "she was the girl friend of an old pal of mine, from Vegas, and I looked her up one time when I was passing through Baltimore. We spent some time together and I met Charles and she told me all about him. You met her that day I picked you up at the Academy."

"So, I figured that this ability, the way that Charles could remember stuff, I could use that. See, Tony, he used to come down to Baltimore all the time. There were a couple of big poker games that ran out of the back of a famous restaurant downtown, a big steak house called Morton's, and Tony was a regular player there.

"So, we work a deal with the guy who runs this game, the game at the restaurant. There's this heavyweight businessman who comes in there. He's a pretty good player, but we figure we can sting him for a bundle, because this guy comes from one of those old Baltimore families, with lots of money."

"So, how did Charles figure in," Tuck asked, "he couldn't sit in a big poker game, could he?"

"No, that was the problem; Charles couldn't be away from his mother. What we did was we wired the room where we played with a tape recorder in the basement, and we taped the games. Charles was in an adjacent room, supposedly watching TV, but he could hear a lot that was going on in the game. His Mom was with him, and she was the 'turn'; serving drinks and whatever. We made sure that somebody made a comment about every hand, not so's you'd notice it, so we got all the bets and hands, and most of the folds that this guy dropped. It took about six weeks of playing with the team, couple of times a week. When Tony was the dealer, he made sure the guy won enough to keep coming back, dealing seconds and stuff every once in a while. Then we had the rest of the team as support...all guys who had worked bunko and stings like this in the old days, from Atlantic City."[137]

"Why couldn't you get this guy with just Tony dealing," Tuck asked, "he was a mechanic, wasn't he?"

"Yeah," Sal said, "but this guy insisted on rotating the deal, and he was the biggest player, the mark, so we had to figure a way that he wouldn't suspect a setup. If anybody took the deal, he would've figured it out in no time, and we wanted this smooth, so he wouldn't run to the police. The guy had a lot of connections, all the way up to the Governor, who was his friend."

"Okay," Tuck asked, "so how did you do it?"

"We took the tapes," Sal said, "and we played them for Charles, the next day after every game. If anything was missing, a hand that he folded, or a bet that we couldn't hear, we filled it in. It was really something, amazing, really, how Charles could remember all this stuff. After about ten games, he was able to tell us what the guy was going to do before he heard it on the tape! And he'd be right, every time. And this was with different sets of players in some of the games … but that didn't bother Charles, he was like a big computer.

"Pretty soon, we had this guy down pat. We knew what he was going to do before he did, so we laid out a game where we'd run the stakes up and hit him for one big shot."

"Laid out a game?" Tuck asked.

"Yeah," Sal said, chuckling, "we planned the whole game, every hand, in advance, like a script for a stage play. We ran his winnings to $15,000 and came back at him with a switched deck and popped him for 30 grand!

"You mean you switched the decks on him?" Tuck asked.

"Sure, but he asked us to do it, at just the right time," Sal said, "Just like Charles said he would; he asked for a new deck! That's the beauty of it. He asked for a new deck, only he didn't know it was stacked. Tony was the dealer, and he never had a chance. Tony had three decks prepared and hidden 'because we weren't sure where he would sit...at which seat at the table, and that made a difference."

"How the hell can that happen?" Tuck asked. "Tony had to shuffle, and how can you stack a new deck?"

"That's easy," Sal said, "Tony can riffle shuffle a deck right under your nose and never change a card's position, but it looks just like a real shuffle; he can even stack it while he's shuffling! You saw him do it when you were a kid. You cut the cards, and when he picks them up, he uncuts your cut, with one hand; any good mechanic can do that without you seeing it done. We stacked the deck and repackaged it new, that's all, you can buy all the stuff you need to do that kind of thing from an outfit I know in Chicago; the Casey Card Company. Look, let me show you something; give me that deck of cards. Tuck handed him the deck of cards from the wicker basket on the window sill. Sal quickly turned them face up and ordered the four suits, two to ace

Sal continued as he manipulated the cards, "See, everybody has a pattern to how they play, they might not know it, but they have it…they always do the same thing in certain circumstances. It's human nature.

"Now," he said, "this is how a deck comes when it's new, right?"

"Yeah," Tuck said, "I guess so, I never looked at it, to tell you the truth."

"Just to show you," he said, "I want you to cut this deck, as many times as you like."

"Okay," Tuck said, and made five cuts of the deck, separating it each time into two piles, then putting the portion which was the bottom, back on top.

"Do a couple more," Sal said, "just to make sure."

Tuck complied and Sal then started dealing a hand of five-card poker with five players.

"Now, in this game, every player is gonna' get a real good hand, but the dealer, he's gonna' get the best hand. Watch this."

He dealt out all five cards to each hand, and then began turning them over, one hand at a time. The first player had a full house, sevens over threes. The next player, another full house with eights over fours, the third player; full house again, nines over fives, and the fourth player, tens over three sixes. He paused, chuckling.

"Everybody in this game would be raising sky-high," he said, "since they each have a full house, but look at the dealer's hand!"

He turned over the dealer's cards, one at a time, to reveal another full house, jacks over three sevens!

Sal continued, "So the players, now they're suspecting a cheat! So they demand the dealer keep one and take four cards!

"But now, everybody is really suspicious, so the dealer agrees and keeps one and takes four new cards off the top, to show the players he wasn't messing around. Sal dealt four new cards from the top of the deck to the one that he kept from the original deal, and turned them over to reveal a straight flush in hearts, seven through jack![138]

"I'll be damned," Tuck said, "I cut that deck about nine times."

"You cut it eight times," Sal said, "to be exact. It's mathematical, it will always work with any number of even cuts, but then to beat the players, the dealer has to give himself two bottoms, or to deal himself a whole new hand or four cards from the top. I dealt myself the seven and Jack of hearts from the bottom. I'm clumsy at it, but you didn't even notice."

"Is that how you stung the guy in Baltimore?" Tuck asked.

"Not exactly," he said, "but, it's a variation of it. There are quite a few variations. You should figure it out, it's all mathematical. It goes back to the twenties, called The Exhibition Poker Deal."

"Did this guy make a stink?" Tuck asked, "After he lost the big money?"

"Nah," Sal said, "he never knew what hit him. He still doesn't know he got stung, he kept on coming back, so we hit him again about a month later, and then we got out of there. We didn't want to press our luck."

"And that was when I was at the Academy, right?" Tuck asked.

"Yeah," Sal said, "that's when it happened, when you were a Midshipman, and I came down there and you read me out."

"You know," Tuck said, "I meant the Governor of Maryland, that next week. What did this fellow look like, that you stung? Was he a tall man, partially bald, with a thin mustache?" Tuck asked.

"Yeah," Sal replied, "that's him, all right."

"Well," Tuck said, "I meant him, too. In fact, I rode to Baltimore with the both of them, in the Governor's limousine."

"How did that happen?" Sal asked.

"I had to go up to Baltimore," Tuck said, "to get my status with the Marine Corps straightened out, before they could cut my discharge from Navy. Shoemaker and I each had the same problem, so we walked out to the highway 50 and put our thumbs out.

"We were in uniform, and the first car that comes along is the Governor's limo, complete with State Police escort on motorcycles, and he stops and picks us up."

"No kidding," Sal said, "and this fellow was with him?"

"Yes, he was. He and the Governor were sitting in the back seat, and Shoe and I sat on the jump seats. Governor McKeldon asked us why we were hitch hiking, and I told him, and then he began talking to us[139]. He talked all the way to Baltimore, telling us we still had our future ahead of us, and that everyone eventually finds a niche in life that they were fated to occupy. It was a stirring conversation; he was a very impressive individual, the Governor."

"Did he ask you your name?" Sal asked. "Yes, he did, and I told him," Tuck said.

"And the other fellow, what did he say when he heard your name?" Sal asked.

"He never said a word, from Annapolis to Baltimore," Tuck said.

Sal did well in Florida for a few years, and then the bottom of the economy fell out, and the state experienced its worst depression since 1929. Businesses were folding all over the state, and hundreds of construction jobs were left standing incomplete. Tuck ran into Sal again at the family club meeting in Trenton. He didn't know that he was in town, and after the monthly poker game was put away and the cousins had gone, Tuck sat at Aunt Mary's kitchen table with him, having coffee and talking. Tuck asked him how his business was doing, as the crash of the Florida economy was being predicted in the news nearly every day.

"I've been having a little trouble," he said.

"How's that?" Tuck asked.

"Well, I got it straightened out, but this guy at the bank, he was giving me a hard time, and he pulled my float."

"Pulled your float? What's that mean?" Tuck asked.

"When I go to the auction," he said, "sometimes I'll buy forty, fifty cars. So, instead of paying for the cars, I fixed it up with the bank so they would float me $50,000, and that way, I'd buy the cars, and then pay the bank when I sold them, and they'd get the interest on the money while I still had a car on the lot."

"And the bank paid the auction?" Tuck asked.

"Yeah," he said, "it's the only way to do this kind of business. You use other people's money. It's the same way the new car dealers work, only the manufacturer arranges the float for them. Some of these big appliance stores do it, too."

"So, what happened?" Tuck asked.

"Well, this guy who arranges all this, and keeps track of it, he calls me and says they can't float me any more money, because he says they're scared about the economy. That's not the reason, though; because my friend, he practically owns the bank, and I figure it's something personal. I get pretty upset, because this bank has made a bundle on me in the past three years, and I never stiffed them for a penny."[140]

"But you're not buying as many cars now, right," Tuck asked, "because of the economy?"

"That's right," he said, "I already let a couple of salesmen go, and we're only moving about 200 cars a week now, out of the iron works. All of my auction cars are on float, but they're all gonna' go, and the bank's gonna' get paid, so I ask him what the problem is, because we've been doing good business for three years, now. It's just going to take me longer to make up the float, that's all. The bank is going to make more money, in the long run."

"Yeah," Tuck said, "but banks are weird, they think loyalty is a one-way street."

"That's it," Sal said, "that was the way I figured it. I just needed a little help, nothing special, and nobody would get burned. But this guy, he keeps calling me and threatening me and raising all kinds of hell about the float. This went on for weeks, until I finally got fed up."

"What did you do?" Tuck asked.

"Well, I didn't like to do it," he said, chuckling, "but I went to see a friend of mine, and I asked him for a favor, to have a talk to this guy at the bank."

"And what happened?" Tuck asked.

"Well, this banker, he gets a phone call, and everything is hunky-dory after that," Sal said.

"You could have done that straight out, though," Tuck said.

"Yeah, I could have," he said, "but I don't like to ask for favors because there are two problems with favors. The first is that the one you ask, the first one, might be one too many. That's the first problem, and the second is that now I owe a favor in return. For those reasons I've hardly ever asked anybody for a favor."

This was the night when Tuck asked Sal if he was "connected," a "made" man in the mafia. He said no, that he wasn't, that he had never "gotten married," or killed anybody. It was years later that Tuck learned from Sis that he had told her that Sam Giancana had been his Godfather. In Sam Giancana's Chicago, "made" men didn't get "married" like the New York families, with a Sicilian blood oath, they just shook hands on it at a fancy dinner, Napolitano style.

Of course the "iron works," as Sal called it, went out of business like hundreds of other car dealers in Florida when the big crash came. Sal still had his dealer's license, but was reduced to hustling one car at a time from his apartment. This was the time that he was asked, apparently, to return the favor that he had received.

Tuck got the story on a Super Bowl Sunday evening, when Sal had dropped in on his way to see his friend that lived in Tuck's town, the one he had gone to Mexico with. The Super Bowl prompted Tuck to ask him whatever happened to the crown jewels of England.

Eight years prior, Sal and most of the rest of the Trenton family had gathered at Aunt Mary's to watch the 1972 Super Bowl game.

After it was over, Sal went to the trunk of his car and brought into Aunt Mary's house a complete replica set of the Crown Jewels of England! There were only two such sets in the world, and each had cost over $250,000 to produce in the 1950's.[141]

Using a sofa and coffee table, Sal displayed the most important pieces, the Imperial State Crown, St. Edward's Crown, Queen Mary's Crown, the Orb of England, Royal Scepter, the Sword of State, the Sword of Mercy and various staffs and smaller crowns. Although costume glass was substituted for the real jewels, and gold and silver plate for the solid gold and silver of the originals, the craftsmanship and magnitude of the display was impressive. Sal also showed the group a display of a replicate set of the famous diamonds of the world, which represented over a billion dollars in historical gemstones.

Returning a "favor" for one of his friends, Sal became the proprietor of one of the two existing replica sets of the Crown Jewels of England, shown here in Trenton, NJ at his sister's house on Super Bowl Sunday of 1972. This set was sold to a Las Vegas casino, likely the Tropicana for display in their lobby. Accompanying this set was another display, "46 of the famous diamonds of the world," which replicated the Hope diamond and others conservatively valued at more than 1 billion dollars. In the picture below, Sal enlists his granddaughters (Tuck's children) in showing off the set, valued at more than $250,000.00 in 1960 dollars. Photos by the Author.

"My friend asked me if I would help them out, over at the bank," Sal said, years later when he told him the story of the Crown Jewels, "so, I said okay, since the car business had gone to hell, and I really didn't have anything to do, anyway. The truth is that my friend asked me to help them out, the guys at his bank, as a favor."

"What did they want you to do?" Tuck asked.

"They had been talking to the politicians in Lake Havasu City, Arizona, about the Crown Jewel set," Sal said, and then asked Tuck if he had ever been there.

"No," Tuck said, "all I know about it is that there's a big lake there, and that it a fast developing area, being almost on the California line and there's a tribe of pissed off Apache that live on the shoreline."

"Well," Sal said, "they've got the London Bridge there. They brought it over here in pieces, and re-assembled it over the lake there, as a tourist attraction.

"So these guys have been talking to the bank, and maybe they want the replica set of the Crown Jewels to go with the London Bridge, I mean, it's a natural."

"And what did you have to do, drive out there with the set?" Tuck asked.

"Well," he said, "it isn't that simple. See, this set has three tractor trailers that go with it. Each one sets up and you can file right through them, they got stairs and ramps and special lights inside, and recordings and the whole works. So this is a convoy I've got to take out there, three trucks and drivers and me and my car.

"And that's okay, because the bank is footing the bills. Every time we roll into a gas station, it's about $350 per truck, so when we stop, I'm spending close to a thousand bucks just for gas. The trouble comes when we get to Lake Havasu City."

"Why, what happened there?" Tuck asked.

"They didn't want it, the exhibit," he said, "and they never wanted it. It was this guy at the bank playing games because my friend put some pressure on him about the float with the car business. He was gettin' back at me, at us!

"So, the bank, they claim the people in Arizona lied to them, and they tell me to leave the display there, but the people in Lake Havasu City, they tell me if I don't get it out of town, they're gonna lock me up. I'm caught in the middle. I can't afford to get locked up in Arizona, because of that other stuff with the Glen Canyon Dam. If I get locked up and they put it on the wire, I'm in big trouble.

"The bank, they don't want to send any more money to move the convoy, but I get pretty rough, and they cough up enough money to keep the drivers and get some gas, and we get it on the road, and I take it up to Vegas, where I figure I can get rid of it, sell it to one of the casinos. At least, I'm out of Arizona.

"Were you able to sell it," Tuck asked, "in Vegas?"

"Yeah," he said, "a couple of places wanted it, but the bank wouldn't cooperate. See, they had lent money on this thing, a lot of money, and they wanted to get it back, to cover their losses, but all the offers were lower, because nobody wanted the trucks, they didn't need 'em. Everybody who made offers had display space of their own, inside their casinos. They could set it up without the trucks.

"So, this stuff went on for weeks, offers back and forth, and the bank always screwing it up. The drivers, they walked on me, because I couldn't pay 'em, so I end up stuck in Vegas with three trucks, the Crown Jewels, and no money."

"Jesus," Tuck said, "what a mess!"

"Yeah," Sal said, "that's when I packed up the set and came back east. That's when you saw them, in Trenton. I had to get some help, because the guy at the bank, he was screwing everything up, and he was making it impossible for me to do what I was supposed to do, to get rid of the whole works. So, I had to see my friend again, and try to get this thing straightened out."

"I see what you mean about asking for favors," Tuck said, "it looks like one thing leads to another."

"Yeah," he said, "that's what happens, but what I got going for me is that it's the same guy causing all the trouble down in Florida, and don't forget my friend owns a lot of the bank's stock."

"So, what happened this time?"Tuck asked.

"Well, before I go back to Vegas," he said, "I find out that this guy resigned his job at the bank, and he's gone. I call the bank and they tell me to just get the best deal I can, and not to worry about getting the price they wanted."

"What happened to the guy in Florida," Tuck asked, laughing, "Did he end with cement shoes, or something?"

"I don't know what happened to him," Sal said, "he just disappeared. Anyway, I go back to Vegas, but now nobody wants to deal on any terms, because the bank has screwed everything up so badly, so I'm still stuck with all this stuff. I sold the two smaller trucks, but nobody will buy the bigger one, because it's been built special for this exhibit. You can't use it for anything else. Meanwhile, I'm paying storage on it, and it's costing me a fortune not to sell it."

"Jesus," Tuck asked, "Didn't you have some friends who would store it for you?"

"Nah, I couldn't let on that this thing was breaking my back," he said, "It would have killed any deal I was trying to make. After a while, I got desperate, I had to get rid of the truck, so I put some gas in it, and then drove my car up to Pahrump, on the California border. I caught a bus back to Vegas, and then drove the truck up there and checked into a motel. That night, I drove the truck out on the desert and walked about five miles back to the motel.

"So, the next day, I get up and I tell the guy at the motel that somebody stole my truck, during the night! Call the Police!"

Sal is having a hard time getting through this part of the story. Apparently, the episode was pretty funny looking back on it, even from his perspective.

"So," he continued, laughing, "the local Sheriff comes out to the motel, and he looks like one of these guys from the movies. He's got a big beer gut, hasn't shaved in a week and half of his teeth are missing. This is a little town, and he's a real country bumpkin, I figure. I mean the only thing this town has going for itself is its' whorehouses and rifle ranges. It's where the Chicken Ranch is, you must have heard of that one. It's an old indian town, smaller than Page, without an airport, dam or all the churches.

"So the old Sheriff, he takes me back to his office, and I'm sitting there talking to him, telling him how I drove up from Vegas and all that, and his deputy walks into the office and hands him a sheet of paper. He had filled out a report when I first came in and given it to the deputy.

"So, then he says to me, 'What the fuck do you think I am, some kind of fool? I got your rap sheet here, Sal," he says, 'and if that goddamn truck got stole, then I'm a monkey's uncle. You got a sheet here as long as my leg, Sal,' he says, 'so you better decide whether or not you want to make a stolen truck report, because if you do, I'm gonna lock you up, and start calling the authorities on you to see if there's anything open on you!'"

"So what did you do then?" Tuck asked.

"I got the hell out of there," Sal said, "picked up my car, went back to Vegas and made a quick deal on the replica set for traveling money, and headed east. I couldn't believe that this country Sheriff, out there in the middle of nowhere, could pull up my rap sheet like that!"

"And the truck," Tuck asked, "what happened to the truck?"

"I don't know." he said, "Maybe the Sheriff got it, because I left it there, stuck behind some sand dunes. God damned computers, they got me again!"

43

GODFATHER

EVER since his brother died, Tuck had maintained contact with Sal's side of the family in Trenton. The family club met every third Saturday for ten months of the year, and if nothing else, it was a nice evening of nickle-ante poker. The family club had been originated by Sal's oldest brother, Louis, who felt it was tragic that the brothers didn't know all of their nieces and nephews. Each meeting was a raucous affair with children playing, loud arguments between cousins and a loosely formalized meeting that caused everyone to sing happy birthday and anniversary greetings to various family members. An annual Christmas party featured Tuck's cousin Louis, a 380 pound giant, dressed as Santa, passing out presents to all the children.

As a result of moving back into the family circle, so to speak, Dotti and Tuck soon were attending weddings and funerals in Trenton, and an engagement party for Sal's niece was one of these events. It was in the summer, an outdoor affair in Aunt Josephina's back yard.

Josie's husband, Sam, had recently died and the whole family turned out for the engagement party. Even Aunt Francis was there, who was Louis' oldest daughter, and keeper of the family history. Tuck was delighted to talk to Aunt Francis, because she remembered more about the original family than any of the cousins. She had gathered a lot of old world knowledge from Louis, since she had an inquisitive nature.

Aunt Josie's house was at the end of a row of typical brick houses in a blue collar neighborhood off Trenton's Greenwood Avenue. She had enough side yard for a little driveway and some grass and a modest back yard, where tables had been lined up for the party.

Everyone had filled their plates from the barbecue and there was the usual low roar of conversation typical of the meetings. Tuck was sitting with his cousin Louie, one of Louis' sons, when a white Cadillac limousine pulled up in the street, blocking the driveway. Sal, who was circulating between tables, immediately walked up the driveway.

The driver, a huge fellow in a business suit, had gotten out and walked around the front of the car. Nodding to Sal, he opened the back door, and an older gentleman emerged. Dressed in a white suit with white shirt and white silk tie and shoes, he had a deep tan. His hair was also stark white; he was an imposing figure.

"Who the hell is that?" Tuck asked Louie.

"Don't you know him?" Louie responded, "That's Sam the Plumber, Sam DeCalvacante, the Godfather."

"Jesus Christ," Tuck said, "He looks like he just stepped out of a movie. He's prettier than Caesar Romero!"[142]

"I don't believe it!" Dotti said.

"You'd better believe it," Louie said, "you're gonna' have to pay your respects."

Sam the Plumber had disappeared into the back door of Josie's house, and a line soon formed at the door. Dotti declined, but Tuck followed Louie into the line.

The godfather was seated in a kitchen chair with his back to the sink, the table in front of him. Sal sat on his right and his bodyguard and driver were standing behind him and to each side. Tuck watched as his cousins, aunts and uncles filed into the kitchen, were introduced by Sal, and then shook the godfather's hand.

The godfather offered a little pleasantry with each handshake. Tuck's family, without exception, fawned on his every word. It was as though they were meeting the President or some internationally famous film star!

"And what line of work are you in?" Sam the Plumber asked Tuck, after the handshake.

"I'm a school teacher," Tuck said.

"What do you teach?" he asked.

"Secondary mathematics," Tuck said.

Some of Sal's mobster friends who were mentioned in his conversations with his son include (from upper left, clockwise) Angelo Bruno, the "Gentle Don" of Philadelphia, Simone "The Count" DeCavalcante, New Jersey's mob boss, Salvatore "Momo" Giancana of Chicago, for whom Sal allegedly torched the Villa Venice Supper Club, Enoch "Knucky" Johnson of Atlantic City, who was Sal's early mentor, Santo Trafficante Sr. who controlled Florida and the Gulf coast from Tampa and enabled Sal to create his auto business there, and Tommy "Three Fingers Brown" Lucchese, a member of the mob's Commission, who controlled the black market in rationing stamps during WWII. In the center, Frank "Paulie" Carbo, an assassin of Albert Anastasia's Murder, Inc., who allegedly killed 17 people including Dutch Schultz and was Sal's nemesis for many years. Photo credits: en.wikipedia.org (Bruno, Columbo, DeCavalcante, Lucchese,), filmog.com (Johnson), tampix.com (Trafficante)

"That's very good. My oldest son is a mathematics teacher, also," he said, "he teaches in a University, here in New Jersey."

"I see," Tuck said, "he must hold at least a masters degree, then."

"He's a PhD," he said, "I'm very proud of him, as your father is of you."

"It's been nice meeting you," Tuck said, "I don't want to hold up this line."

"My pleasure, young man," he said, "keep up the good work."

"I don't believe that I did that," Tuck said to Dotti and Louie as they resumed their seats.

"Oh," Louie said, "everybody respects the godfather. You gotta' show your respect, because your dad brought him here. He's a very powerful man. You had to get in line."

"Why does everyone here respect him so much?" Tuck asked Louie, "have you ever asked him for a favor or any kind of help, or has he ever helped you out in any way?"

"No, but that's not the point." Louie said, "It's because of your father. Everybody loves your father, and he's his friend, so everybody respects Sam the Plumber."

"He doesn't even live around here, does he?" Tuck asked.

"No," Louie said, "he lives up in Princeton, in a big fancy place. You'll never find him in Trenton any more, that's for sure.

"He used to live here, when he was younger, in Chambersberg, on Roebling Ave. In those days, he'd go door to door and ask everybody in the neighborhood what he could do to help them out...did they need money? Is the landlord treating them right? That sort of thing, and if there was a problem … he'd fix it."

"Do you know if he ever helped anybody in our family?" Tuck asked.

"Not that I know of," Louie said, "except your father, and he never talks about him, to anybody."

"That's for sure," Tuck said, "you know he's under indictment, don't you, for all kinds of stuff, racketeering, drugs, prostitution, all those nice things?"

"Yeah, I know," Louie said, laughing, "that's why he's got that nice tan. Every time they throw an indictment at him, he goes into a hospital in Florida. Your dad says he's got a suite there like the Waldorf, in the hospital."

"I didn't expect to meet the pope," Dotti quipped in the car on the way home.

"Amazing, wasn't it?" Tuck asked, "Did you see the way they were fawning over him?"

"Life with father is never dull," Dotti said.

"Christ," Tuck said, "I hate to contemplate that all my life I've believed a lie. I asked him once directly if he was connected to the mob, and he said 'no, I never got married,' but what we saw today … I doubt if Sam the Plumber goes to just anybody's engagement parties."

"I tend to agree with you," Dotti said, "but it could be true; that they're just old friends."

"Yeah," Tuck said, "It could be, but now I doubt it. I guess I just don't understand enough about my Sicilian heritage. In a way, I hate my mom's attitude on that. She rejected everything about dad's family and clung to the idea that we were of some of some special lineage, descended from the Hamiltons and Lawrences, who came over with the Pilgrims.

"The problem with that is that we never had any heritage. Being who we were, we were never accepted into the society she thought we belonged to, and we never learned anything about our real heritage from dad's family. I wish I could speak Italian, at least. I must have meant a hundred people over the years who expected me to be able to do so. I mean, even though we go to the family meetings, and we know virtually all the cousins now, we're still not really accepted as part of the family, it's all on dad's presence."

"You're his only surviving son," Dotti said, "that's a big deal to your family, but you know that."

"Yeah," Tuck said, "but his name, and what he did, the reputation he earned in a small town, that forced us into a position where my peers thought I was a sigi, and I wasn't, because mom wouldn't dream of us learning anything about being Italian. I'm willing to bet that most of the kids I went to school with think that I can speak Italian. I never thought about it before, but I bet that they do. Everybody I meant in the service took it as a given. They all thought I spoke it, in the same way I expected Richard to speak Spanish. People perceived that I was my father's son, and mom perceived that we were something else, unrelated and completely different, but that world was closed to us, too. It's a self fulfilling prophecy; worrying about the clippings in my 501 file, midshipmen calling me the son of a mafia hood, and here I am lining up to kiss Sam The Plumber's ass!"

"Your dad's a charmer," Dotti said, "My mom would say that he could charm the ears off an iron pot, and she has said it."

"The thing that's frustrating about it is that we had such miserable lives," Tuck said, "because we never had any money. Never had enough to eat, or to have the normal things everybody else had. If he's connected to the mafia, then why the hell did we have to live like that? I mean, I thought that these guys did all these illegal things in order to get money and power; to be rich. All of them that you read about in the papers, they're all rich. So why isn't dad rich? You see, that's always been a thorn in my side when I've tried to figure out whether or not he really belongs to La Cosa Nostra. He knows all these guys, like Sam the Plumber, Santo Trafficante, Joe Columbo. But he's always broke, and they aren't. I mean, why be involved in it, all the risk, the prison time and all that, if you don't get rich?"

"Maybe that's a myth, too," Dotti said, "that they all make money at being crooks. Maybe we only read about the ones that are the most successful."

"But what is incomprehensible to me," Tuck said, "is that virtually every one of the rest of the family are decent, honest hard-working blue collar people. No one else in the family does anything dishonest, and if their kids do any such things, God help them. I mean, look at Uncle Chas and Louie and Tony, they're all going to or already have retired from jobs that they held for thirty years, with the same companies. They wouldn't do anything dishonest, yet they revere dad and kowtow to this mafia hood, DeCavalcante. I just can't figure it out."

"It's the same thing with Frank Sinatra," Dotti said, "everybody knows that he's mixed up with the mob, but it just seems to make him more popular, especially with Italians."

"But the funny thing to me is that none of my relatives," Tuck said, "including Duby, can give me an instance when dad ever helped them out. It's always been the other way. He comes into town and they put him up. He needs a car and they lend him one. He's down on his luck, and they lend him money. If you look back on it, over the years, he's never done anything for any of them. And it's the same way with Sam the Plumber. Nobody in the family has ever gotten any benefit from dad knowing him, nobody. I asked Louie and Aunt Mary and the Uncles, too. It's the truth.

It's a goddamned legend built on some mythological idea that dad and Sam the Plumber are some kind of Robin Hoods, but they aren't. Dad's just a freeloader, as far as I can see. He's never lifted a finger to help any of his own family, or to help us, that's for sure."

"He gave you your drafting instruments, and he gave us our wedding rings," Dotti said.

"Your right," Tuck said, "that's true. He did give us those things, but everything he gave us came out of stock, of his store, for Christ sake, and might have been stolen! And we're talking about forty years here, forty years! Do you ever remember him giving us a Christmas present? I don't. I don't see any giving in him, just taking, but everybody seems to think it okay, that that's the expected behavior, and they are somehow honored to be used by him. It's strange, that's the only way I can describe it."

"It's that Sicilian thing," Dotti said, "like they say in the movies."

"Yeah, honey," Tuck said, "I know, but none of these people were raised in Sicily. They're all second-generation Italian, at least. Even the third generation, Tony and Santo's kids, though, they acted just like their parents toward the Plumber, fawning over him and whispering and Christ, Dennis is a cop! I can't figure it. It's one of those human mysteries, like the people in Alabama when I lived there, and their attitude towards blacks."

"I'm glad the Irish don't have problems like that," Dotti said, laughing.

"But they do," Tuck said, "with this IRA thing. I can't imagine your dad condoning an IRA member in your family. Honesty is everything to your dad."

"You're right there," she said, "dad wouldn't put up with his brothers doing anything dishonest, and that's the truth."

"Christ," Tuck said, "It's no wonder I've had difficulty with different people all my life. The old man's probably got a file a foot thick with the FBI. Ever since Bobby Kennedy, they've spent millions tracking all these families, who the 'capos' are and who works for them. At the Senate hearings, they displayed whole organization charts, with all the names of the members of these families right on them.

"Sometimes I think it would have been better if he had just said, 'I'm in the mafia, I took a blood oath and I kill people and that's who I am, now's here's the money for college and here's a nice house we can live in and have good food on the table.' It would have been better for us, his family, if that was the case; instead of the miserable life he gave us. The hovels we lived in, no food, people treating us like shit. Mom dying of cancer when she was fifty-one; Cholly drinking himself to death; me having nightmares until I was twenty-four and bilging out of the academy; and Sis turning out to be a bitch. He's destroyed us all, in one way or another, for Christ's sake."

"It would be nice to know just what and who he is," Dotti said, "That would put everybody's mind at ease, I think."

"Yeah," Tuck said, "That's what I mean. All of this mystery. You never know when he's coming or going, or what he's mixed up in, or whether he's telling the truth or not. You're right, it would be nice just to know who the hell he is, because I've known him all my life and I don't. That's the truth. He's like some guy I know, who used to know my mother and brother, that's all. He's never let me love him, like a father. Your father is more of a father to me than my own, for God's sake. We go to ball games, and if I have a problem, I can talk to Joe. I'd like to have that relationship with my own father, but I can't, because I don't know who the hell he is. If the worse case was true, and he is a Mafioso, and he told me, I could still have some kind of relationship, but he won't let that occur, because he won't tell me who he is. He's just a charmer, whom I happen to know better than a lot of people, but not as well as I know my best friends."

"Well," Dotti said, "you don't owe him anything, that's for sure. You know he's never sent any of our kids even as much as a birthday card, let alone brought them a present."

"But we're not alone in that," Tuck said, "he ignores Sis's kids, too."

"Like hell he does," Dotti said, "he never misses their birthdays!"

44

RETRIBUTION

Tuck pushed the down button and stepped back to wait for the Courthouse elevator. The new county courthouse was a breath of fresh air in Camden, but it hadn't brought the revival hoped for. Except for the new courthouse and the Rutgers Law School, Camden looked like Beirut, Lebanon.

The doors opened and Sergeant Killamy stepped out. "Hello, Sergeant," Tuck said, "how are you doing?"

Killarny gazed at Tuck for a moment, then visibly recalled who he was.

"OK, Tuck," he said, extending his hand, "I heard you got everything straightened out." Tuck responded, shaking the officer's hand and they chatted for a few minutes, talking about PTI and expungement, Killarny verifying that his record would disappear after six months. Tuck explained that he was at the court assisting his newly divorced daughter in her custody case. Tuck could see the young man wanted to say more. He invited Tuck to sit down on one of the marble benches in the lobby.

"I shouldn't be telling you this, but I know you'd like to know the details about your situation, and in a way, I think there's some things you really ought to know," Killarny said.

"Well," Tuck responded, "I sure in hell would like to know where that Cadillac came from, that's for sure."

"It came from a guy named Coopersmith, in Trenton. He had a leasing operation and was suspected of having mob connections, but he was the owner.[143] He's dead now. He reported it stolen, and the prosecutor was sure that you helped your father steal it," Killarny explained.

"Well, I didn't, and I never heard of this guy, Coopersmith," Tuck said, "why was the prosecutor so hard-headed about it? My lawyer said he wanted my ass, bad."

"Because everything I just told you, we knew before we picked you up," Killarny was intent. Tuck felt he was trying to communicate more than the words, "From our phone call," he hesitated, "and witnesses …"Tuck characteristically missed the message,

"Sarge, I'm just as confused as ever," he said.

"Well, I've got to go," Killarny said, rising, "I've got to be in court. Good luck to you, Tuck."

"And to you," Tuck said, watching him disappear down the marble corridor.

Tuck mused about the conversation throughout the day, and that evening, from his office, he called Sis. She answered the phone and feigned happy surprise in hearing Tuck's voice. He explained that the ordeal was pretty much over and there was nothing much more to worry about. Then he asked her the question that was the real reason for the call.

"By the way, Sis, did the State Police ever contact you?"

"Yes, they did," she responded, "they got real nasty on the phone and said they were going to come out to my house, but I wouldn't let them. They can be real bastards, especially if they get you alone, so I wouldn't have any of it. And I told them I wasn't coming to their barracks, either, so they could intimidate me."

"So, what happened?" Tuck was feeling a little sick.

"Well, I told them that I would only talk to them if we met in a public place, where there were other people around. So I met these two detectives, Killane and Bronsky, or some names like that at the Sheraton Post Inn one day, on my lunch break."

"And they were real bastards. You know, they tried for a half hour to get me to say that I knew that the car was stolen and that you and daddy stole it, and I wouldn't say it.

"But they kept it up, wording things in different ways, and trying to trick me into saying it, and I finally told them to cut out the shit. I didn't know any such thing and I wasn't going to be harassed any further, and I left."

"And they didn't get anything definitive from it?" Tuck asked.

"Nothing that they didn't already know. You know, stuff like where daddy lived in Florida and that kind of thing, but nothing about the car."

A couple of days later, Tuck dropped off some forms related to the expungement at his lawyer's office. Joe asked him to step inside when he mentioned that he had run into Killarny at the court house.

"Killarny told me about interviewing my Sister," he told Joe, "at the Sheraton Post Inn. Did you know about that?"

"Killarny interviewed your sister at her house," Joe said.

"What did you say?" Tuck was taken aback.

"I finally got to see the case file," Joe explained, "I saw the report, signed by Killarny. It took place at your sister's house, in Medford Lakes." Joe sat down behind his big desk and started fiddling with a pencil. "I guess there's no easy way to tell you this," he said, "but, she's the one that sold you down the river. She told them that you helped your father steal the car. She testified that the two of you left from her house to go steal it, and brought it back there afterward. That's why the prosecutor was hard lining it; she was to repeat that testimony against you in court. She was going to be his number one witness."

"Jesus Christ!" Tuck's color drained from his face, "she said that to those guys? She told them that I helped the old man steal that fucking car?" Tuck fell into a chair in total disbelief.

"This is one for the books." Joe said, "What the hell did you ever do to your sister? To make her do something like that?"

Tuck was deep in concentration, aghast at the revelation. "Of course," he said, "why didn't I see it? When those guys came to the office, on the arrest, one of them kept commenting on the car's inspection sticker...I should have realized it then."

"Realized what?" Joe asked.

"Well, when Sis worked for me, sometimes I would drive the Caddy to work, but I didn't have an inspection sticker, so I made one up and I would stick it on the window when I was driving it and I made sure I had all of the papers, the affidavits and all … from my lawyer with me, in case I got stopped."

"That's a crime in itself," Joe said.

"Yeah, I found that out when my daughter told me of a friend she knew who was arrested with a phony sticker. It was a felony charge, so I quit using the car after that. I don't understand why it's a felony, but it scared me to think that I was doing something that serious. But Sis didn't know that, you see, it wasn't long after that that I got title to the car and got it inspected and got a real sticker from the state."

"So, what's the point?" Joe asked.

"The point is that she told the troopers I was driving the car with a phony sticker. That's why the one cop was so confused at the arrest. He must have said three times, 'There's nothing wrong with this sticker.' Since we didn't speak to each other, Sis had no way of knowing that I had finally gotten the car titled. Sonofabitch, I can't believe this. I could have gone to jail for Christ's sake, if this had gone to trial!"

"Well," Joe said, "it's really not that unusual, for relatives to hate each other, but this one has me shaking my head. She really must hate you for some reason."

"Maybe it's because I never let the old man off the hook for being the bastard that he was," Tuck said, "who the hell knows? All I know is that I've tried to do the right thing and live that bastard down all my life, but you know what?"

"No, what's that?" Joe was obviously moved.

"The bastard ruined all of us," Tuck said, "in one way or another. My brother's dead, an alcoholic, Mom died early, heartbroken, and look at my sister, a vindictive, lying spinster old bitch living up there all alone in her big house, still refusing to believe the old man was what he was. And me, bilging out of the Naval Academy, giving up a once in a lifetime second chance, because his fucking record was following me throughout the service It's sad, isn't it, Joe?"

"You're still saying that you had nothing to do with it...it's over now, you don't have to worry." Joe said.

"She wanted the car, Joe," Tuck shook his head as he spoke; "it was a big thing to her. I've been telling you straight since the first day we met.

"Look, Joe, I don't know if I told you this before, but when the old man first showed up at Sis' with the car, I asked her where he had gotten it. He wasn't there at the time, being back in Florida.

"She gave me this story about how the he had bought it from some guy at the docks in Newark, and it was one of a whole fleet of expensive cars that was stolen from a Manhattan leasing corporation.

"She told me how they brought 80 or 90 guys ..."

"Who are they?" Joe asked.

"The mob, in New York. How they brought like 90 guys and drove away this whole fleet at one time to Newark and were loading them on a ship bound for Kuwait when the FBI caught them, the whole bunch. She even showed me a clipping from the New York Times about the arrests. And she told me that dad was there that night, and my cousin had driven him there and he bought the car as it was sitting in line to go on the ship."

"Well, that's not what the case file says," Joe said, "the car came from Trenton."

"I know, and the reason I know is that when she told me that, the following Saturday I was at my cousin's house, and I asked him right out, 'Did you ever drive the old man to Newark so that he could pick up that Caddy?'

"And what did he tell you?" Joe asked.

"He told me, and listen to this good, Joe, he told me that he *never in his life* was in Newark, nor did he ever drive the old man anywhere to pick up that Caddy. In fact, he had no idea where the car came from."

"Did you tell him the story that your sister told you?" Joe asked.

"You're damn right I did," Tuck said, "and Duby said to me, and these are his exact words, 'That's bullshit. That never happened, I asked your dad where he got it, and he told me that he bought it from a friend'. That whole story is bullshit, there's no question about that. So the truth was, and was until I ran into Killarny the other day, that I didn't know where the car came from, and she didn't either.

"Look, Joe, she's done other things to me over the years, told people lies, all kinds of shit, but this is something that's incomprehensible to me, how she could do this? What's puzzling to me is who made up the story about the docks in Newark, Sis or the old man? And for what reason?"

"It is a puzzle, that's for sure. Why don't you ask her?"

"Not my style, Joe. I'll never speak another word to her." Tuck sat down and shook his head in amazement. "Even the old man wouldn't do something like this ..."

45

PINKY RING

Tuck had to park a half block away from the dam. Woolman's Lake was now surrounded by neat little split levels and their back yards came right down to the water's edge. The big willow trees along the banks were gone, but the lake stretched out in front of him, slate grey in the winter rain.

He thought about the eight pound largemouth he had caught here one summer morning, on a Hawaiian wiggler. The lure was a gift from Wilga, his old friend and fishing companion. Tuck had run home with the huge fish, figuring it would feed everyone for about a week.

"He's the largest bass ever caught in Woolman's," Tuck bragged to Edie Maye, as she inspected the behemoth in the kitchen sink. The big bass was still quite alive and glaring at Edie.

"You've got to put him back," Edie Maye said.

"But why, Mom? You always cook what I catch." But Tuck knew that she was right.

"Because," she said, "look at him. Why, he's like the king of Woolman's Lake. He's beautiful, and he's old. He doesn't deserve to be cut up and cooked. Why don't you let him go? I just think he's very special."

Of course Tuck took the battered old warrior back to the lake and released him. In spite of being out of the water for nearly three-quarters of an hour, he slapped his tail and vanished back into its murky depths. Edie Maye was right. Tuck felt good letting him go.

Besides, he had asked Mr. Southwick at the corner grocery store to weigh him, so his story was substantiated. He didn't need to kill him.

Tuck's first year out of high school, he had bought Sally an engagement ring. When she refused it, they had broken off the relationship. The ring, paid for over a year in weekly installments, layout there in front of Tuck somewhere at the bottom of the lake where he had thrown it in 1953.

He thought about these incidents without realizing that his clothes were now soaked. Motorists passing the dam were wondering what kind of jerk would stand out in the cold rain staring at Woolman's Lake. In a three-piece suit.

Opening his mail at the office that morning, he had received the letter he'd been looking for, from the lawyer.

His record was now expunged, no evidence any longer existed that he was charged, nor was he obligated to tell anyone of the old man's Cadillac, or anything about it. He was free and clear.

Tuck struggled to remove the sapphire pinky ring from his left little finger, where it had resided since the day he took it from Sal's dead hand in the hospital. One of the last things he had said to Tuck was to take the ring and wear it. Sis was all bent out of shape about it since she wanted the ring, and that was just the incentive Tuck needed to comply with his request.

Tuck looked at the ring, cupped in his right hand. It was ten years since he put it on. He was surprised that Sal wanted him to have it. He knew it meant a lot to Sal.

Probably worth eight or nine hundred bucks, he thought. The ring. The sign. It came to the old man from Sam Giancana, his Godfather. Frank Sinatra had one, too. Also a gift from the Mafia boss of Chicago.

Tuck pictured Sal in his mind's eye, laid out in his coffin. Uncle Santo approached him as he looked down on the body.

"I'm puttin' these in his hand." Santo said, "He'll find a way to use 'em." He squeezed a pair of Resorts Casino dice into Sal's lifeless palm.

"Where's his ring?" Santo asked, "You got it?" The whole family knew about the ring and where it had come from.

"Yeah," Tuck had said, displaying his left hand. "But, where's Sam the Plumber, Tony Marinella, Santo Trafficante and all of those big-time friends of his? I don't see any of them here, do you?"

During his teaching years, Tuck had watched with amusement as Mario Puzo and the Hollywood crowd painted the mafia with a sympathetic brush, making heroes of the thugs and sociopaths that really populated the crime families. Shortly after Sal's death, Tuck had stopped for lunch at a local Mt. Holly bar, where Butch Eckman, a classmate, joined him. After offering condolences, Butch said,

"I'm going to miss your old man. He taught me everything I know about hustling and making money. He used to take me to New York and set me up with wholesalers up there..."

"Yeah," Tuck responded with an outburst, "while he was giving you an education, he was letting us starve in God damned hovels with the roaches and rats, living on what Mom and Cholly and I could scrape up or steal...so, shut the hell up, Butch!" Tuck left, fighting back indignation and tears. He had known about Sal mentoring Butch, the object of Tuck's jealousy throughout high school. Under Sal's tutelage he sold watches and rings to high schoolers and even wrote policy during his senior year.

When it was clear that Sal wasn't going to leave the hospital, Tuck had stopped at the Pioneer, a plush bar on the way to Philadelphia. Sal had brought him there a couple of times. Sal told Tuck that Rico, the bartender, was "connected" and could get word to anybody important. They always huddled in the corner for a few minutes before Rico would pour drinks.

"Hey, Rico," Tuck asked, "you remember me, Tuck Falconetti?"

"Yeah, sure," Rico had replied, leaning on the bar, "you're Sally's son, right? Where's your old man? I haven't seen him for a while. He usually stops in, ya' know."

"He's dying of cancer, Rico, over in Burlington County Memorial. I was hoping you could tell some of his friends, maybe Sam, anyway, 'cause I know dad would like to see them." Tuck noticed that Rico was avoiding his eyes.

"Aah, that's too bad," Rico said, "but Sam's down South right now ...I'll pass the word, though. I'm sorry, kid." Tuck had refused a free drink and left; knowing that Rico would tell no one.

"Well, maybe they didn't hear about it," Uncle Santo rationalized with a confused look. Idols are hard to fell. Tuck knew that they didn't come because they didn't care. Unlike the Hollywood stereotypes featured in the films, real wise guys and Dons don't give a shit about their buddies or their families; it's all a myth, perpetrated by Hollywood screen writers and "wannabees." According to a cousin, Sam the Plumber's family was treated much like Edie Maye and the Falconetti kids.

It had taken Tuck the better part of fifty-five years to come to grips with the idea of his father. And now it was over. He wondered how other people dealt with the problem. What would it have been like if he'd just been an ordinary working stiff? But Sal had been far from ordinary, a phantom that lived an entire existence as a familiar to the most notorious criminals in society. He had created a life in the shadows of respectability while making his mark from the east coast to Hollywood, an associate of one big boss after another. Dying of cancer, he somehow became an engineer/bridge inspector for the State of New Jersey, suddenly having a social security number issued to him and instantly acquiring a qualifying background for a position that allowed full medical coverage of his illness and required a civil engineering degree, in spite of having completed only the eighth grade.

Tuck thought about his brother, and spoke, to the lake, the wind, the rain.

"He was more talented, more intelligent, a fearless and better athlete than me, and selfless. If he knew that I wanted something and it was within his means to get it, he simply got it. No obligation. No thanks necessary. That was his way. "Dead at forty-four. And the old man played him like a violin, involving him in his scams, taking advantage of his generosity, and sitting back and letting him drink himself to death. Cholly loved him in an unadulterated way, did anything he asked. Sal could have saved him. He could be here, now.

"In any case, he could have tried. But we didn't matter to him... his family was the circle of smooth talking mob bosses, slick bunko artists, card cheats, policy writers, liars and killers in their thousand dollar suits, Cadillac limos and never ending scams. While in his last week of life, Sal still had scam in progress, asking Tuck if with his nautical experience, naval architecture and engineering training, he could liaison for his friends with the Coast Guard. His mobster friends had their eyes on the Queen Mary as a possible floating casino for Atlantic City.

On his deathbed, Sal asked Tuck if he would be interested in helping "the boys" to bring the Queen Mary I east to Atlantic City and be anchored in the inlet as an additional casino/hotel. The ship, now laying in Long Beach, CA is shown here returning victorious soldiers to the U.S. after WW II. In addition to Coast Guard certification, the ship would have had to meet New Jersey Casino Control minimum requirement of 500 rooms for a casino. In order to meet this and the square footage/room requirement the ship's staterooms would have to be doubled in size by removing a separating bulkhead, engendering a near complete overhaul of the ship's basic structure. Tuck declined, not wishing to work with Sal's confederates and realizing that the cost of compliance to be overwhelming, even for the mob. US Navy photo.

"He just never gave a damn about any of us. My sister, in her fantasy world, thinking he was our father. He was our sire, nothing more, nothing less. Fathers are people who care about their offspring." Sis was dead now, a victim of cancer. Tuck saw her obituary in the local paper and in her own way; she managed to leave Tuck with a little stab wound. She had instructed her daughters to leave Tuck out of the list of surviving relatives in the printed obituary. She had done a similar thing to Sal, giving the surgeon permission to castrate him the day before he passed away. Tuck asked Sal if he had agreed. He replied, "What the hell, I don't have any use for that stuff anymore." Appalled by his sister's cruelty, Tuck never mentioned the affair until he was a sick 75 year old and confessed to Dotti what Sis had done.

Sis had contacted Tuck's half-brother, Johnny. She tracked him down in Thomaston, Virginia, where he worked in a beauty parlor, the complete stereotype homosexual hairdresser. So the old man left his mark there, too.

What kind of tortured childhood had he endured, completely abandoned, but not even near enough to know if the old man was alive or dead?

Tuck and Cholly had ice skated this lake on hundreds of winter evenings with their friends, playing "blackie chase caught" and "foxy, foxy." They built big bonfires on the bank to keep warm and often would skate onto the ice with smoldering dungaree cuffs, feet kept too close to the fire.

Edie Maye sometimes came over, and using Sis's figure skates, joined in. All observers commented on her mastery on skates, performing spins and even small jumps. She had taught Tuck how to ice dance with a partner, the only time he had ever danced with her. He remembered her sitting on a willow log, skates to the fire, hands extended to catch the warmth, a rosy glow in her cheeks while she told everyone of the days on the Rancocas Creek, when she and her sisters ice skated the seven miles to Smithville. As Tuck became older, the dimension of Sal's abandonment became more and more clear to him, the vast loneliness that Edie Maye had lived with; essentially ignored. The bathroom beatings with the hand mirror had faded from his memory years ago, although the results, his disfigured and fused back, shortened leg and arthritic hips plagued him constantly. He had forgiven Edie Maye completely the night he carried her up the stair to deliver baby Bessie, and after that traumatic moonlit night, he was forever bonded to her soul.

He wondered if she were happy now, if they were together. Tuck realized that in her tortured and pained existence, she had never hugged him or told him that she loved him. He recalled the evening that he and Cholly wanted to take her to the movie, Jose Farrar as Toulouse Lautrec in "Moulin Rouge," making a national release. She had refused and the conversation became an argument, ending up in a shouting match.

Tuck wiped his face with his silk hanky. He suddenly felt self-conscious, standing in the rain, crying and talking to no one. He thought about his days on the creek with Wilga and Hugh Campbell and Hugh's painting, "Corn Left Standing." A few remaining stalks ravaged by the wind and storms of winter; brown and broken, but still standing with the raggedy torn scarecrow.

I'm the Scarecrow in that field, he thought, looking down at what was left. A sapphire pinky ring set in sterling. Recognition in the right circles. Chosen by Sam Giancana, one of the Commissions' big bosses.

"Big deal," Tuck said loudly. Stepping back he turned sideways and let the ring go in a high arc toward the middle of the lake. In the rain, he couldn't see the tiny splash it made.

The End

BIBLIOGRAPHY

Annals of Camden, No. 3 (Old Ferries), The Camden County Historical Society, 1900 Park Blvd., Camden, NJ 08103.

Chance of a Lifetime, Grace Anselmo D'Amato, Down the Shore Publishing, West Creek, NJ, 2001, ISBN 0-945582-75-7.

"***Byrd's Eye View,***" Senator Robert C. Byrd, "***Organized Crime and the Stolen Car,***" Syndicated column, Sept. 8, 1971, digitally published on the web (.pdf).

"Final Report of the Special Senate Committee to Investigate Organized Crime in Interstate Commerce August 31, 1951" (legislative day, August 27) 1951, commonly called "the Kefauver Report."

"Fiorello's Foggiani," John T. Correll, Air Force Magazine, June, 2010.

"Flight Tests of Lanier Paraplane; Aeronautical Engineering Report," by C.D. Perkins, James Forrestal Research Center, Princeton University, NJ, January, 1952.

"***From Paperboy to Philanthropist,***" Richard Smith, The New York Times, book review of "***Legacy,***" by Christopher Ogden, July 25, 1999, (Walter Annenberg's life story).

"***Mafia NJ.com presents La Cosa Nostra, Official NJ State Commission of Investigation Report,"*** Published by UrbanTimes.com, Jersey City, NJ, 2008, ISBN 978-0-9777600-4-6.

"Plan B 4.0 Mobilizing to Save Civilization," Lester R. Brown, Earth Policy Institute, Published by Norton & Company, NYC, NY, 10110, 2009, ISBN 978-0-393-07103-0.

"The Great Kentucky Scandal," Bill Davidson, Look Magazine, October 24, 1961

"The History of the 1st New Jersey Volunteer Infantry," Patrick McSherry, from Spamamwar.com, (Spanish American War Centennial website).

"The Impact of Relief and Public Works Programs on Socioeconomic Welfare during the 1930s," Fishback, Price V., Michael R. Haines, and Shawn Kantor from "Births, Deaths, and New Deal Relief during the Great Depression," Review of Economics and Statistics 89 (February 2007): 1-14.

"The Nine Lives of Edgar Fahs Smith," The Schoenberg Center for Electronic Text and Image, University of Pennsylvania Libraries, The University of Pennsylvania, Philadelphia, PA.

"The Survey," Vol XXXI Oct 1913 to Mar 1914, subtitled ***"Pineys - Today's Morons, Colonial outcasts, disowned Friends...revelers from Bonaparte's Court at Bordentown, and other sowers of wild oats,"*** Elizabeth S. Kite. Published by The New York Survey Associates, 105 East 22nd Street, NYC, NY.

"Watson Buck's Presentation," as he gave it to the Rancocas Women's Club in 1962, transcribed by Nora Dunfee. Available on RancocasNJ.org, 2007.

Battleship New Jersey, an Illustrated History, Paul Stillwell, Naval Institute Press, Annapolis, Md. 1986, ISBN 0-87021-029-7.

City of Ambition, FDR, La Guardia, and the Making of Modern New York, Mason B. Williams, Illustrated. 494 pp. Published by W. W. Norton & Company, NYC, NY.

Gangbusters; the Destruction of America's Last Great Mafia Dynasty, Earnest Volkman, Published by Avon Books, 1350 Avenue of the Americas, NYC, NY, 10019, 1999, ISBN 0-380-73235-1.

Henry Hudson Trail, Central RR of NJ's Seashore Branch, Tom Gallo, Published by Acadia Publishing, San Francisco CA, 2001, ISBN 0-7385-0188-3.

His Way, the unauthorized biography of Frank Sinatra, Kitty Kelley, Published by Bantam Books, 666 Fifth Avenue, NYC, NY 10103, 1986, ISBN 0-553-26515-6.

Historic Photos of the United States Naval Academy, James W. Cheevers, Turner Publishing Company, Nashville, TN, 37219, 2008. ISBN 13: 978-1-59652-418-7.

Historical Society of Cecil County, 135 E. Main Street Elkton, MD 21921

Images of America: South Jersey Farming, Cheryl Baisden, Published by Acadia Publishing, Charleston, SC, 2006, ISBN 0-7385-4497-3.

Images of Rail: Steam to Diesel in New Jersey, revised edition, Charles P. Caldes, Published by Acadia Publishing, Charleston, SC, 2002. ISBN 0-7385-1085-8.

Inner Circles: How America Changed the World, A Memoir. Haig, Alexander M. Jr., with Charles McCarry, New York: Warner Books, 1992.

Interference: How Organized Crime Influences Professional Football, Dan Moldea, William Morrow, Publisher, New York, ISBN 978-06880-8303-8

Liberty; the Ships that Won the War, Peter Elphick, Naval Institute Press, Washington, D.C., 2006.

Made Men, The True Rise-and-Fall Story of a New Jersey Mob Family, Greg Smith, Berkley Books, Berkley Publishing Group, 375 Hudson Street, New York, NY 10014.

Mafia Princess, Growing up in Sam Giancana's Family, Antoinette Giancana and Thomas C. Renner, Published by Avon Books, 1790 Broadway, NYC, 1985, ISBN 0-380-69849-8.

Mafia: The Government's Secret File on Organized Crime. 2007, the Bureau of Narcotics, the United States Treasury Department, 2007.

Master Detective. The Life and Times of Ellis Parker, America's Sherlock Holmes, John Reisinger, Published by Citadel Press (Kensington Publishing Company, 850 Third Avenue, New York City, NY 10022).

Meeting the Whales, the Equinox Guide to Giants of the Deep, Eric Hoyt, Camden House , 1991, ISBN 0-921820-25-9.

Mickey Cohen, The Life and Times of L.A.'s Notorious Mobster, Tere Tereba, ECW Press, 2100 Queen Street, Toronto, CN M4E IE2, info@ ecwpress.com.

Mount Holly, Heidi Winzinger and Mary L. Smith, Published by Acadia Publishing, San Francisco CA, 2001, ISBN 0-7385-0908-6.

Pinelands Preservation Alliance, 17 Pemberton Road, Southampton, NJ, 08088.

Shipbuilding Along the Great Egg Harbor River, Richard Roberts Crane, Egg Harbor Township Tercentenary Publications Committee, Laureate Press, Inc., Egg Harbor City, New Jersey, 1964

Special Committee on Crime in Interstate Commerce, Parts 1 - 5, Estes Kefauver, Senator, Tennessee, Published by the Government Printing Office, Washington, D.C., 1950-1951

Steam to Diesel in New Jersey, Charles P. Caldes, Published by Acadia Publishing, San Francisco CA, 2002, ISBN 0-7385-1085-8.

Testing, Testing: Social Consequences of the Examined Life, Hasson Allen, Berkeley, Published by the University of Southern California Press, 1993.

The 1955 Cruise, Yearbook of the United State Naval Academy Preparatory School, prepared by the 1955 yearbook committee, Bainbridge, MD., 1955

The Art of Magic, T. Nelson Downs, Published by Arthur P. Felsman, Chicago, IL, 1926

The Complete Idiot's Guide to the Mafia, Jerry Capeci, by Marie-Butler Knight, Alpha Books, Penquin Group, 375 Hudson Street, NYC, NY 10014, 2004, ISBN 1-59257-305-3,

The Conde Naste Traveler Book, 12th Edition, Published by Penguin Books (USA), 2012, ISBN 13 978-0143112617.

The History of Mount Holly, Henry C. Shinn, Published by the Mount Holly Herald, 1957.

The Lives of Whales and Dolphins, by Richard C. Connor and Dawn Micklethwaite Peterson, Published by Henry Holt & Company, New York City, NY, 1994, ISBN 0-8050-1950-2.

The Lucky Bag, yearbook of the USNA; 1956, 1957 and 1959, published annually by The Brigade of Midshipmen (graduating class Yearbook Committee), USNA, Annapolis, MD.

The Rape of Nanking, Iris Chang, Published by BasicBooks, a subsidiary of Perseus Books, 44 Farnsworth Street, 3rd Floor, Boston, MA, 02210, 1997, ISBN 0- 465-06835-9.

The U.S. Marine Corps Story, Third Revised Edition, J. Robert Moskin, Published by Back Bay Books, imprint of McGraw Hill, 1992, ISBN 0-316-58559-9.

War of the Godfathers, William F. Roemer, Jr., Published by Ivy Books, Ballantine Publishing Group, NY, 1990, ISBN 0-8041-0831-5.

Howard Hughes, His Life and Madness, by Donald L. Barlett and James B. Steele, Published by W.W. Norton & Company, 500 Fifth Avenue, New York, NY 10110, 1979, ISBN 0-393-32602-0 (pbk).

We Are Still Here! The Tribal Saga of New Jersey's Nanticoke and Lenepe Indians, John R. Norwood, Published by Native New Jersey Publications, Moorestown, NJ, 2007, in partnership with the Nanticoke Lenni-Lenepe Tribe, 18 East Commerce Street, Bridgeton, NJ 08032.

The Battleship USS New Jersey, From Birth to Berth, by Carol Comega, (a commemorative volume published on the return of the ship to its permanent berth as a museum in Camden, NJ) Published by Pediment Publishing, presented to crew members by the Camden Courier Post Newspapers, Cooper's Ferry Development Corporation and the Camden Waterfront. 2001, ISBN 1-801395-76-9.

What They Didn't Teach You About World War II, Mike Wright, Presidio Press, 1998.

Wheeling Through the Years, Published by the Wheeling Historical Society, 1987.

When Vice Was King: A History of Northern Kentucky Gambling, 1920-1970, Jim Linduff with Roy Klein and Larry Trapp, digitally published on the web.

Newspapers (Archives)

The Mount Holly Herald	Philadelphia Inquirer	Chicago Daily Herald
The Arizona Daily Sun	Newark Star Ledger	Camden Courier Post
The New York Times	The Tucson Daily Citizen	Lottery Player's Magazine
The Miami Herald	The Flagstaff Arizona Sun	New Jersey Mirror
Time Magazine	Look Magazine	Miami News
Carolina Morning News		

Websites referenced.

www.Americanrails.com	*www.waybackmachine.com*
www.cchistory.com	*www.lcnd.com*
www.healthbeatnews.com	*www.spanamwar.com*
www.usmm.org	*www.redmen.org*
www.about.com	*www.olivedrab/wardogs*
www.wikopedia.com/ (various)	*www.laalmanac.com/history*
www.PreWarBuick.com	*www.Ask/Art.com(Hugh Campbell)*
www.navycollector.com	*www.lexology.com*
www.waymarkers.com (Indian Anne)	*www.togetherweserved.com*
www.nationalgeographic.com (Doris Miller)	*www.answers.com (Alex. Haig)*
www.USBR.com (Glen Canyon dam)	*www.history.NASA.com*
www.emedicinehealth.com	*www.stason.org (Swiss military)*
www.cards-expert.com	*www.bainbridgedevelopment.org*
www.rancocasNJ.org (Watson Buck)	*www.oai/dtic.mil (Lanier)*
www,Thehistoryplace.com (Nanking)	*www.ehow.com (draft)*
www.gangstersinc.com	*www.MafiaNJ.com*
www.rancocasNJ.org(Jersey Devil)	*www.njpinebarrens.com*
www.rupd.org(MaryRoebling)	*www.resortsac.com*

www.Hullnumber.org/arv6 (USS Megara)

www.vineland.org/history/trainingschool/

www.americanmafia.com (Willie Moretti)

www.c141heaven.info/dotcom/matsbook_html.

www.themogh.org (Bath & Turf Club)

www.ehow.com/about_6376851

www.NAVsourceOnline

www.preservinggaminghistory.com(Covington, KY)

www.battleshipnewjersey.org

ENDNOTES

PART I

1 **Camden, NJ**. Although once a thriving center for manufacturing and industry, Camden is perhaps best known for its struggles with urban dysfunction. Three Camden mayors have been jailed for corruption, the most recent being Milton Milan in 2000. Since 2005 the school system and police department have been operated by the State of New Jersey; the takeover expired in 2012. In 2008, Camden had the highest crime rate in the U.S. with 2,333 violent crimes per 100,000 people while the national average was 455 per 100,000. Camden public schools spent $23,770 per student ($19,118 on a budgetary per-pupil basis) in the 2009–10 school year and two-thirds of the students graduate. Two out of every five residents are below the national poverty line. Cite– ***http://www.rupd.com. Rutgers University Annual Statistics. Author's Note:*** *The City has been dubbed the "Murder Capital of America," many times since the 1980's, recently recording 2,333 violent crimes per 100,000 residents, an interesting statistic since the population has been reduced to less than 70,000 residents, as neighborhood after neighborhood has fallen to abject poverty and physical deterioration. The latest incursion by the State of New Jersey in 2013 included an overhaul of the Police Department, which resulted in a complete replacement of all personnel, with a rehire of a selected few, in an attempt to save the city from itself.*

2 **Blood Oath. *Author's Note:*** *When the commission learned that one of the family chiefs had brought in a half dozen new "made men" with a handshake en lieu of the traditional blood oath, they required him to "re-make" those men in the traditional Sicilian way, reciting the oath while holding the burning card of a saint and then suffering a cut of the hand or knife prick of the trigger finger. Tuck's sister claimed that Sal was "made" by Sam Giancana in the Chicago way; a handshake at a formal dinner. See* **"Idiot's Guide to the Mafia,"** Jerry Capeci, page 22 ff.

3 **The Bath and Turf Club,** at South Iowa and Stenton Avenue near the Boardwalk was only one of several "carpet joints" operated by Knucky Johnson and his associates. Its unique hidden entrance and Chinese cuisine

set it off from its competitors. The Managers paid a fee to "steerers" or "luggers," individuals who haunted the bus and train stations and steered customers to their respective clubs. Cite-***"Chance of a Lifetime,"*** Grace Anselmo D'Amato, Down The Shore Publishing, West Creek, NJ, 1927 and The Museum of Gaming History at www.themogh.org.

4 **Organized Crime.** In many cities, large and small, there is evidence of active and often controlling participation by former bootleggers, gangsters, and hoodlums in the political affairs of the community. In some cases this participation extends to other cities and even to the government of the State. Underworld characters do not engage in politics for the good of the community or the Nation. They do so for the purpose of increasing their power and wealth and gaining greater protection for their illegal activities. Cite-***"Final Report of the Special Senate Committee to Investigate Organized Crime in Interstate Commerce, August 31"*** (legislative day, August 27) 1951. ***Author's Note:*** *The existence of Organized Crime, verified by the Senate Committee was a revelation to the American public, which for years had believed J. Edgar Hoover's denials of the fact. Hoover was a closet homosexual and cross dresser, which was known in mob circles and a Damocles sword against FBI interference. See note 3-4.*

5 **Rumrunning** in itself was a risky, but lucrative proposition for Jersey boatmen. Christopher Freind describes the activity in an interview with his grandfather, Jake Freind. "All the boats were kept in Gardner's Basin. Our crew was top notch; we had no choice. After every run, the engines were lifted out and completely overhauled. We owned another set of engines. That way, we would always have fresh horsepower for each trip. In fact, in order to stay one step ahead of the Coast Guard, we even used airplane engines. Boy, did she fly with those babies!" His passion and memory for detail were palpable. But it wasn't just about speed, for several reasons. "First, before we could even think about the run out to the drop-off ships (they were Canadian freighters) we had to cross the sandbar, and let me tell you, that's not easy even in daylight." After that, they would make their way 12 miles offshore, in pitch blackness, into international waters to meet up with the supply vessel. They had no RADAR, no LORAN, and no GPS to find their target, all the while under constant threat of being seen by either Coasties - whose boats were armed-or Canadian customs agents. Cite-"***Freindly Fire Zone" A Fiercely Independent News Bureau***, 12 January, 2011, ***"Jake Freind's Story. The Life of a Jersey Shore Rumrunner."*** By Christopher Friend. ***Author's Note:.*** *For many years prior to the 1960's, an intermittent and dangerous sandbar existed close offshore to Long Beach Island, Atlantic City and as far south as Stone Harbor. At low tide, it was revealed with sometimes more than a foot of exposed sand, and at high tide, swimmers could walk upon it, only waist deep. In some locations, the bar was less than 200 yards from the beach and was very popular with bathers, as porpoises often swam near it, feeding in the shallows.*

6 **FBI Director, J. Edgar Hoover** was a closeted homosexual and reputed cross dresser with a gambling habit. The mob was privy to this information. Hoover had always insisted, "There is no organized crime." Cite-**Mickey**

Cohen, the Life and Crimes of L.A.'s Notorious Mobster, by Tere Tereba, ECW Press, pg. 77.

7 **Minnesota Fats.** ***Author's Note:*** *When Tuck had the opportunity to interview Minnesota Fats at the Resorts Casino in Atlantic City in 1985, Fats allowed Tuck to beat him in a game of eight ball and remarked that he remembered Sal as an up and coming player in the "old days" and that he (Sal) even resembled Paul Newman, who portrayed a "hustler" in the 1961 movie of the same name in which he (Fats) was played by Jackie Gleason. Willie Mosconi also verified Sal's expertise at the pool table.*

8 **Kate's Island Store** came into play in May of 1947 when Sal and 13 others were arrested by New Jersey State Police at a location "in the Shreve Street woods in Southampton Township." Described as "devotees of the cubes," they were arraigned before Justice of the Peace Jules Scheidecker in Easthampton and fined $5 with $5 costs each. *Cite-**Mt. Holly Herald***, May 2, 1947, pg 1. and ***Mount Holly Historical Society*** Photos; Kate's Island Store 1 & 2, from disc, ***"1025 Historical Photos of Mt. Holly, NJ."*** ***Author's Note:*** *Shreve Street, the road that leads one to Kate's Tract Road, the sole access to the bridge to the Island store, was a dirt road in 1947. The Island store had been the site of hundreds of craps games since the 1930's, and in the late 40's became the home of legendary landscape painter Hugh Campbell. Sal said, "Everybody in two counties knew about the games at Kate's."*

9 **Elkton** is the County seat of Cecil County, Maryland. It was formerly called Head of Elk because it is located at the navigational source of the Elk River, which flows into the nearby Chesapeake Bay. When northern states began to pass more restrictive marriage laws in the early 20th Century, Maryland did not. As a result, a number of Maryland towns near borders with other states became known as places to get married quickly and without many restrictions, or "Gretna Greens". Elkton, being the northeastern most county seat in Maryland (and thus closer to Philadelphia, New York, and New England), was particularly popular. It was a notorious Gretna Green for years; in its heyday, in the 1920s and 1930s, it was "the elopement capital of the East Coast" and thousands of marriages were performed there each year. A 48-hour waiting period was imposed in 1938, but Elkton continued to be a place to marry, and especially elope. Hundreds of people are still married in Elkton each year. Cite-***Historical Society of Cecil County*** (http://www.cchistory.org/factfile.htm) 6/25/2010

10 **Legend of the New Jersey Devil.** Most tellers of the legend of the Jersey Devil trace the devil back to Deborah Smith who emigrated from England in the 1700s to marry a Mr. Leeds. The Leeds family lived in the area of the NJ Pine Barrens (Leeds Point, Galloway Township, Atlantic County). Mrs. Leeds had given birth to 12 children and was about to give birth to her 13th. The story goes that Mrs. Leeds invoked the devil during a very difficult and painful labor and that when the baby was born, it either immediately, or very soon afterwards, (depending on the version of the story), grew into a full-grown devil and escaped from the house. **(Cite 1)** ***Author's Notes:*** *Most of the myths associated with Pinelands families; incest and interbreeding, ignorance and retardation can be attributed to a*

*published study in 1912, **"Kallikak Family,"** by Henry Herbert Goddard, PhD, Director of the Laboratory of the Training School of Vineland, New Jersey, for Feeble-minded Girls and Boys. The book describes in detail the testing procedures for determining the mental state of Deborah Kallikak and the generations of families that preceded and followed her. Although not entirely clear, it appears that classifications of "normal" or "feeble-minded" were created based on Mendel's laws and eugenic principles, popular at the time. Chapter 2 includes 18 pages of the Kallikuks in ancestral flow charts, each individual represented by a circled N (normal) or a black squared F (feeble-minded).* **(Cite 2)** - *The myth was reinforced by Elizabeth S. Kite, field worker, who stereotyped Pineys as "lazy, shiftless and feeble minded."***(Cite 3)** *Watson Buck, noted historian of Rancocas, narrates a tale of the Jersey Devil harassing a citizen returning home from the Centerton Inn in 1909 after a week of numerous sightings of the creature in that area. According to the tale, the flapping of wings and screaming by the devil as it landed roughly in 10 inches of newly fallen snow frightened the man so badly that he broke through the heavy door of Levi Atkinson's store, tearing it from its hinges.* ***(Cite 4)*** *(Cite 1)*- ***The New Jersey Historical Society*** 52 Park Place -Newark, NJ 07102 *(Cite 2)*- ***"Kallikak Family, A Study in the Heredity of Feeble-Mindedness"*** by Henry Herbert Goddard, PhD, Director, Laboratory of the Training School of Vineland, New Jersey, for Feeble-minded Girls and Boys, The MacMillan & Company, 1922 *(Cite 3)* - ***"The Survey," Vol XXXI Oct 1913 to Mar 1914,*** subtitled ***"Pineys" Today's Morons, Colonial outcasts, disowned Friends...revelers from Bonaparte's Court at Bordentown, and other sowers of wild oats."*** by Elizabeth S. Kite. Published by The New York Survey Associates, 105 East 22nd Street, NYC, NY. *(Cite 4)* ***"Watson Buck's Presentation,"*** as he gave it to the Rancocas Women's Club in 1962, transcribed by Nora Dunfee.

11 **Ibid, endnote 5. Rumrunning.**

12 ***Author's Note: Knucky Johnson's story,*** *now popularized by the HBO series, "Emerald City" attributed this killing to an intrigue among his gang members and rival associates. Tuck's father related the story as it is presented here just two days before he died in Burlington County Memorial Hospital in 1980. Although no actual newspaper reports could be found reporting the murder, the author had heard family accounts of it long before "Emerald City" was conceived, and considers the incidents' inclusion in the HBO story as vindication of Sal's narrative.*

13 **The San Domingo Tract** on Pine Street south and east of the Rancocas was named by the refugees from that island (Santo Domingo) who came to Mount Holly, no doubt at the suggestion of Steven Girard, after the uprising of slaves in the West Indies in 1791. William Richards built the house about 1820. Cite-***The History of Mount Holly,"*** by Henry C. Shinn, Published by the Mount Holly Herald, 1957, page 15, *and* ***"Historian Traces Origins of Mt. Holly's San Domingo,"*** by N. R. Ewan, Mount Holly Herald, September 14, 1950

14 **The Pine Barrens of New Jersey** are comprised of 1.4 million acres of pine forest in sandy soil. Aquifers retain an estimated 17.7 trillion gallons of fresh water under the soil. These aquifers are separated by less porous

silt and clay layers that prevent flow between aquifers. There are only a few aquifers beneath the Pine Barrens that can be used for domestic water use. From the oldest to youngest they are the Potomac-Raritan-Magothy, Englishtown, Wenonah/Mount Laurel, Piney Point and Kirkwood-Cohansey aquifer system. The most important aquifer is the Kirkwood-Cohansey aquifer, since it is the shallowest, and provides water to streams, rivers and wetlands. Cite-***Pinelands Preservation Alliance*,** 17 Pemberton Road, Southampton NJ 08088.

15 **The Blue Comet,** "The Seashore's Finest Train," a huge G3 Pacific locomotive and its first class passenger cars were painted bright blue and made daily runs between Jersey City and Atlantic City from 1929 through 1941. It had special coaches; observation, smoking and dining, all named for comets. In August of 1939, the Comet derailed in a severe rainstorm that dropped 14 inches of water in 4 hours and washed away the underpinnings of the track near Chatsworth. Thirty-two passengers received minor injuries. Cite-**Steam to Diesel in New Jersey,** and **http://www.njpinebarrens.com**

16 **The Tuckerton Stage Road.** At the mouth of the Great Egg Harbor was the old established port of Somers Point, which was also the scene of shipbuilding. In 1797 the new nation established a customs house increasing the town's importance as a port and a shipbuilding area. The sloops John Clark, John Wesley and J.F. Armstrong were built in this area. **(Cite 1)** The first Europeans that settled here followed this same route on foot and horseback to Camden. Eventually, this route needed to be widened to accommodate wagons and was named the Road to Little Egg Harbor. By 1791, Clam Town (because of the great mounds of clamshells left here by Indians) was designated as a port of entry for the United States by George Washington. At the time, it was the third largest port town in the Country, after Philadelphia and New York. Little Egg Harbor became a place of considerable commerce and prospered. In 1798, the town changed its name to Tuckerton...and the stage line became known as the Tuckerton Stage Road. **(Cite 2)** Further ease of travel had occurred in the early 1740's when the Mount Holly and Philadelphia Mail Stage began operating. *"The stage will leave Thomas Smith's Inn in Mount Holly every morning at seven o'clock, drive to Moorestown where the horses will be changed, and arrive at William Cooper's Ferry by 10 o'clock...the stage will leave at 3 o'clock and return to Mount Holly early in the evening".* **(Cite 3)**William Cooper's ferry to Philadelphia *was created in 1688 leaving from a dock near the intersections of the Newton Creek and Cooper River in what is now Collingswood, NJ.* **(Cite 4)***Cite 1*-From ***"Shipbuilding Along the Great Egg Harbor River"*** By Richard Roberts Crane. *Cite 2-* ***http://www.waymarking.com*** and ***June Sheridan***, Township Historian, Egg Harbor Township, 6647 West Jersey Avenue, Egg Harbor Township, NJ 08234. *Cite 3-****"The History of Mount Holly,"*** by Henry C. Shinn, Published by the Mount Holly Herald, 1957, page 35.*Cite 4-from an address by Charles S. Boyer to the Camden County Historical Society on October 11, 1911 recorded in "****Annals of Camden, No. 3, Old Ferries.***

17 **Rancocas Valley.** It is difficult to imagine the Rancocas River valley a vast wilderness with no Mount Holly, Hainesport, Rancocas or Centerton,

when Riverside, or Goat Town, was only sand hills and swamps, and with only Indian Wigwams to mark the sites of unnamed towns. This demands a nimble play of the imagination. Through the eyes of the first Europeans, the Eastern Shore of the Delaware from the Falls (Morrisville, PA) to the Capes (Cape May, Cape Henlopen), was a dense primeval forest. Today, it is difficult for us to picture in our minds this great expanse of timber that had never known an axe, thick, black soil, made of rotted leaves that had fallen for thousands of years, covered with undergrowth and thick with brambles. From this terrain sprang mighty oaks 60 or 80 feet up to the first limb. Among these great trees the lesser elbowed each other for living space and everywhere spreading over shrubs and low growing trees. Climbing in the branches of the highest, grape vines flung their tangled network. Great bogs formed by clogged streams or filling naturally undrained low places, grew rank with weeds and plants. By only by a few Indian paths, rarely over 18 inches wide and animal trails, could this wilderness be penetrated. There was a variety and abundance of wild life, such as is unknown anywhere on this continent today. This was the land to which Europeans were flocking; some for the adventure, for gold, for commerce, for settlement where they could freely worship God according to the dictates of conscience. Through a slash in the forest wall, the Rancocas River entered, peopled here and there by a small Indian tribe..., Excerpted from ***Watson Buck's Presentation***, A talk he gave to the Rancocas Women's Club in 1962. Transcripted by Nora Dunfee on http://www.rancocasNJ.org

18 **Cranberries** only grew wild in New Jersey before Benjamin Thomas established the state's first Cranberry bog in 1835. By 1862, the American Cranberry Exchange was the first organized agricultural exchange in the country, distributing Whitesbog cranberries, packaged under the American Beauty brand name. Elizabeth White cultivated the wild berries growing on the edge of the cranberry bogs, and collaborating with scientist Frederick Colville, cultivated the blueberry in 1916. South Jersey farmers also developed the first plow with a replaceable steel blade, were among the first to use and develop steam tractors, and of course cultivated tomatoes, working with Campbell Soup scientists. Cite-**South Jersey Farming,** by Cheryl Baisden, Arcadia Publishing, 2006, ISBN 0-7385-4497-3.

19 **Segregation** In 1908 the Samuel Aaron School was erected on Chestnut Street (in the colored section of town, called "sand hill") to educate the black children of the community. By 1940, educational conditions had improved for the white population of Mt. Holly, but the population of the colored elementary school aged students was still housed in the Aaron school until junior high school age with only two teachers. In 1949, however, a holdout by the colored families who had students attending the Chestnut Street School engendered a civil rights movement and provoked a special meeting of the Board of Education. Parents charged that the segregated Aaron School was substandard in its teaching efficiency because the two teachers were burdened with five grades, while white students passed the school every day to attend properly staffed classes at the all white Samuel Miller School. The Board reluctantly reassigned the 53 students, stating that they were disappointed that the situation was precipitated before they (the BOE) had

time to reach an "intelligent decision." The situation was complicated by the East Garden Street housing project, (Clover Hill Gardens) which would surely impact on the school population when completed.**(Cite 1)** The population of Mt. Holly in1940 was 6,892. The town experienced a burst of citizens in 1960, when it swelled to 13,271, but receded to 10,639 in 1990. **(Cite 2)** The area in which the Aaron School was located, the north and south sides of Washington Street, was known at different times as "Irishtown," "Sand Hill" and "Nigger Hill." Washington Street was originally called "The Great Road to Philadelphia," and later "Reynolds Street." **(Cite 3)** *Cite 1–**"Board Closes Aaron School to End Segregation,"*** The Mount Holly Herald, September 8, 1949, page 1. *Cite 2.-**New Jersey Labor Market Information, 1930-1990, Resident Population by Municipality,*** http://www.WaybackMachine.com *Cite 3-**"The History of Mount Holly,"*** by Henry C. Shinn, Published by the Mount Holly Herald, 1957, page 15ff.

20 **Relief 1930's.** As unemployment rates surged past 20 percent, Roosevelt argued that the Great Depression was a national peacetime emergency... During the First Hundred Days the Roosevelt Administration established the Federal Emergency Relief Administration (FERA). The FERA distributed federal monies to the states to be used to provide work relief or direct relief to households. The amounts distributed to each family were meant to help them reach a minimum standard of living. The actual payments often fell short of the maximum when relief officials, faced with large case loads and limited funds, cut payments to provide relief for more families. Between November 1933 and March 1935, the administration ran the Civil Works Administration, which immediately put up to 4 million people to work. When it ended, many people were transferred back to the FERA work relief jobs. **(Cite)-The Impact of Relief and Public Works Programs on Socioeconomic Welfare During the 1930s**, Fishback, Price V., Michael R. Haines, and Shawn Kantor, ***"Births, Deaths, and New Deal Relief During the Great Depression,"*** Review of Economics and Statistics 89 (February 2007): 1-14. ***Author's Note:*** *By the time the monies got down to local levels, it was doled out to the "most deserving" recipients, according to local politician's interpretation. The program only lasted a couple of years, but some people were helped. Edie Maye, too proud to risk the rejection, never applied.*

21 **Hobos.** "The gentlemen of the road" (Hobos) experienced their Golden Age with the onset of the great depression. It is believed that at one time there were over a million and a half hobos riding the freights, many of which were displaced white collar workers, dustbowl farmers and even abandoned children. The railroads by the 1930's stretched from the east to the west (New Jersey alone had 2,352 miles of track) offering to the desperate any chance of a return to dignity. The hobo lifestyle remained outside of mainstream society. They developed a cultural uniqueness and were seen not only as jobless men but as an icon of freedom in what was then a structured American society with millions of homeless drifting citizens. Hobos were exploited in the economic and industrial landscape of that time. They could fill a necessary role in the labor force as reserves, would easily adapt to the ever changing circumstances, and quickly be

driven off by law enforcement when no longer needed or wanted. **(Cite 1)** Eventually the economy began to recover and the railroads consolidated and became more streamlined. For the hobo, it signaled the end of an era. For America, the idealized image of the carefree train rider lived on. During the greatest heyday of hobo history, hobo "jungles" sprang up along the railroad tracks in nearly every community. These were transient shanty towns, where hobos would set up tents and build campfires for cooking. Everyone would bring whatever food they had and meals were prepared and shared. The hobo jungles were generally accepted as long as they stayed on the outskirts of towns and cities. Mt. Holly's biggest Hooverville was located east of the PRR track on the bank of the Rancocas near the Station Trestle, visible from Madison Avenue. **(Cite 2)** *Cite 1 - **Hub Pages, 20th Century History, The Great Depression** Cite 2 – **http://www.American-Rails.com*** Edited by the author.

22 ***Author's Note: "Peanuts" Rossell** was an alcoholic sign painter and pin striper of great talent. The rule of thumb was, "Don't offer Peanuts a drink or pay him until he's done." It was not unusual to see vehicles about town with unfinished advertising, a reminder that Peanuts, although well intentioned, could not resist a drink, and could not work after having one. Nearly every Mt. Holly business wore his beautiful sign work, on window glass, store fronts, signs or vehicles. The town pridefully boasted of its other itinerant artists, Mr. Wright, widely known for his pen and ink landscape sketches, Norman C. Reeves, a nationally known magazine illustrator, Betty Pease Gutman, illustrator of children's books, and of course, Hugh Campbell, landscape painter.*

23 ***Author's Note: Drummers**. Horse and wagon salesmen were common in the 1930's in Mt. Holly. Mr. Passalacqua, whose farm edged the town at the top of High Street, across from the Fairgrounds, traversed the neighborhoods throughout the summer growing season, offering fresh vegetables and fruits from the farm and his store on Main Street. Tom, whom Edie May attacked, was called "the Tin Man" and sold pots and pans and kitchen paraphernalia. There also was a fish monger, a knife and scissor salesman and sharpener, and a broom wagon. "Any old broo-ooms, new brooms for old..." was his cry. The streets were seldom silent, as delivery wagons and later, trucks from the Atlantic Tea Company, Charles' Chips, Abbott's Diary, Friehofer's Bread, Hollyford Ice and Coal and other companies competed for neighborhood sales.*

24 **Sam DeCavalcante** was frequently described as an "old school" Don when he inherited power as the boss of the family. The behavior of Robert DeNiro's character as a young father in Part 2 of the Godfather Trilogy reflects DeCavalcante's early concern and attention to friends and neighbors in the "burg." It was thought by many that he (DeCavalcante) was the exemplar for the Vito Corleone character. His conversations were wiretapped continuously for two years (called by the FBI the 'Goodfella Tapes') and his attitudes and one-liners became legendary in FBI circles. He was also known for philosophizing on about honor; he was known to say things like 'I'd give my life to my people' and 'honest people have no ethics'; and 'Those guys (judges) just won't stay fixed'. At times he was also quite paternalistic when

dealing with internal disputes. Cite-various sources: ***Wikipedia, Tumblr, Senate Committee hearings on Organized Crime in the U.S.**, **www. MafiaNJ.com***

25 ***Author's Note*: *the Burlington Diner*** *was a typically shaped prefabricated dining car restaurant that became extremely popular in New Jersey, which at one time had more than 550 diners across the state. Sheathed in enameled metal and art deco stainless steel, it was the popular gathering place directly in the center of the town, at the intersection of highway 25 (U.S. Route 130) and County Road 541. One of its specialties was grilled corned beef and Swiss cheese on rye, with French fries and cole slaw. The site is now occupied by Amy's Omelette Restaurant, the inside of which is styled Formica, like the original diner.* Cite-**Jersey Diners,** by Peter Genouese, p. 74.

26 **The Annenberg wire.** (Nationwide News) service, an extension of the Daily Racing Form, was the broadcast arm of the bible of horse racing and transmitted almost real time racing results across the country to 15,000 subscribers in 223 legitimate media outlets including any "pool rooms" that could afford it. ***(Cite 1)*** Pool rooms of the 1930's were bookie joints, taking numbers and horse bets, whereas shooting pool actually took place in a "billiards parlor." Typically a subscriber paid from $25 to $40 per week for the (wire) service, receiving the results of 29 racetracks. The service required the installation of an actual electric wire terminating at a teletype machine. When Annenberg was indicted for income tax evasion in 1939, he bowed out of the wire service, which was reorganized as the Continental Wire Service. ***(Cite 3)*** Sal, with Sam's influence and resources had the wire terminating in the back room of a downtown business, from which a "reader" would telephone or radio the results to the "setup," a portable horse parlor similar to, but smaller than, the one shown in the film, "The Sting." The setup was moved almost weekly among the 18 apartments Sal rented throughout Burlington, Riverside and Palmyra. ***(Cite 2 and Author's notes).*** Annenberg, who amassed a fortune, began as a newsboy for Randolph Hurst's Chicago Tribune. He and his brothers were so successful in terrorizing competition that Hurst made him Circulation Director for the Tribune, and he eventually began purchasing newspapers, including the Racing Form and The Daily Telegraph in 1922. ***(Cite 1)*** In the fifties, Bugsy Siegal created the Trans America Wire Service, competing with Annenberg (Continental) and muscling it into rooms, which, when confronted with two groups of thugs selling the same service, ended up purchasing both, rather than face the consequences. It was thought that among other things, the new wire service was a contributing factor in Siegel's assassination in 1947. ***(Cite 3)*** *Cite 1-* "***From Paperboy to Philanthropist***," Richard Smith, The New York Times, book review of "***Legacy,***" by Christopher Ogden, July 25, 1999. *Cite 2-**When Vice Was King: A History Of Northern Kentucky Gambling 1920-1970*** by Jim Linduff with Roy Klein and Larry Trapp. *Cite 3-**Mickey Cohen, the Life and Times of L.A.'s Notorious Mobster,*** by Tere Tereba, ECW Press, 2012. Edits by the author.

27 **The Mob in New Jersey.** Throughout criminal history New Jersey has always been divided territory, mainly between the five New York families and

the Philadelphia Family. However, one crew stays attached to New Jersey like no other, the DeCavalcante Family. Throughout the years it maintained strong relations with several of New York's Five Families, but being less powerful and smaller often brought them discredit and disregard from the New York mobsters as "the farmers". In either case the DeCavalcante family grew wealthy and violent, even giving inspiration to HBO's successful series "The Sopranos," which is widely inspired by this old Jersey mob. ***(Cite 1)*** The criminal organization's origins are believed to have begun with Gaspare D'Amico somewhere around 1910. D'Amico held that position, probably with the support of New York organizations, until 1937 when he retired. Not much is known of D'Amico and it seems he had little recognition. The next in line to take over was Stefano Badami. Badami had a relatively calm reign as boss until internal struggles lead to his murder in 1955. An organizational war raged during that period between the Newark and the Elizabeth factions, and although the violence subsided, the frictions between both sides would remain for several decades. His (Badami's) successor Phil Amari tried to calm things down again but eventually stepped down after only 2 years of service. Nicholas Delmore then managed the organization for 7 years before retiring, leaving the Family to his nephew, Simone DeCavalcante in 1964. DeCavalcante held a series of meetings to establish their territory. He controlled crews in Princeton, Newark and Trenton and used a plumbing supply store as his front. ***(Cite 2) Author's note:*** *Phil Amari retired to Sicily. Sam DeCavalcante "opened the books" for the first time in years, doubling the number of soldiers in the sixties. Joe Bonnano, incensed because he never received skim from the National Hotel in Cuba, demanded a share of skim from the Stardust and Tangiers casinos in Vegas, controlled by Accardo. The feud escalated to violence, as depicted in the movie, "Casino," and the Commission voted Bonnano out and brought DeCavalcante in to act as liaison with the exiled Boss. Other edits applied to correct grammar. Cite 1-www.lcndb.com,* La Casa Nostra Data Base and **"War of the Godfathers,"** by William Roemer, Jr. *Cite 2-**"Made Men, The Rise And Fall Story Of A New Jersey Mob Family,"*** Greg B. Smith, Berkeley Publishing, the Penquin Group (USA), 2003. *www.MafiaNJ.com*

28 **Ibid. endnote 25. Burlington Diner. *Author's note:*** *On several occasions when Tuck accompanied Sal to his "office," local police officers sat in the booth and chatted with Sal, and on one occasion, bought Tuck a serving of apple pie, ala mode.*

29 ***"Mom Wishmeyer's Good Old-Fashioned Mustard Plaster."*** This old-fashioned but very effective and safe home remedy is applied to the chest of those suffering lung congestion due to colds or chest infections. Mix flour, mustard, and water into a spreadable paste (Edie Maye added a thick black cough syrup to the recipe.) On wax paper or a disposable underpad with the absorbent side up, spread the flour/mustard paste evenly over this pad to within about an inch of the edges. Fold the pad with its mustard paste and heat it until hot but not scalding. Apply a little Vaseline to the patient's nipples and with the patient resting in bed, apply the hot mustard plaster to the chest with the wax paper or plastic of the underpad to the outside and the mustard paste in contact with the chest. Cover this with a warmed towel. Pull up the

bedclothes and settle the patient in for a rest...This is a very effective old-time remedy; it quickly relieves chest congestion caused by colds and other chest infections. Most people respond very well and are greatly improved by the next day. ***Author's note:*** *this is the remedy with noted addition used by Edie Maye to control Tuck's congestive onslaughts as a result of whooping cough attacks.* Cite- www.healthbeat news.com "***Healthbeat news, Pneumonia - Deadly But Preventable"*** By Dr. Myatt.

30 **The Numbers**. The game dates back at least to the beginning of the Italian lottery in 1530. "Policy shops," where bettors choose numbers, were in the United States prior to 1860. In 1875, a report of a select committee of the New York State Assembly stated that "the lowest, meanest, worst form ... [that] gambling takes in the city of New York, is what is known as policy playing." The game was also popular in Italian neighborhoods known as the "Italian lottery," and it was known in Cuban communities as bolita ("little ball"). By the early 20th century, the game was associated with poor communities, and could be played for as little as a penny. One of the game's attractions to low income and working class bettors was the ability to bet small amounts of money. Also, unlike state lotteries, bookies could extend credit to the bettor. In addition, policy winners could avoid paying income tax. Different policy banks would offer different rates, though a payoff of 600 to 1 was typical. Since the odds of winning were 1,000:1, the expected profit for racketeers was enormous. *Cite-"**By Chance a Winner, The History of Lotteries,"** by George Sullivan, Published by Dodd, Meade & Co, NYC, NY, 1972* ***Author's Note***: *The game was largely indigenous to African American populations until the rise of organized crime in the 1920's, when it was seen as a cash cow by the Italian mobsters. It was supplanted beginning in the 1970's by state operated lotteries, but the old "policy game" still flourishes in some ethnic neighborhoods in U.S. cities.*

31 **Indian Ann.** Ann, born in 1804, was the daughter of Chief Lasha (sometimes called Ash) Tamar, and was among a small number of her tribesmen that did not accept an invitation to relocate to Oneida Lake, New York. Local stories read that Ann met with a local white girl on the Bread and Cheese trail...and shared a lunch by a stream, which now bears a name from this lunch. Ann introduced Mary to her father, who escorted her back to town and recounted the lunch the girls shared to her family. The area is now called **Inawendiwin**, a word meaning "friendship," coined by Ann's father. It is known that Ann became a renowned basket weaver, and her wares are a treasured Pinelands find. It is not known when she began weaving, or when she met and married her first husband, Peter Green, a former slave. Little is known about how former slaves came to be in this area, it may have been from the famed Underground Railroad, or from a slave camp that was reputedly in the area (no evidence has ever been found). It is also not known when or how her first husband died. There is more known about Ann's second husband, John Roberts, who served in the Civil War, Company A, 22nd Regiment of Colored Troops. He would have been much her junior, as they married in 1864, when Ann would have been sixty-four years of age. Roberts died in a hospital in Yorktown, Virginia after serving thirteen months in the Union Army. After his death, Ann began receiving a

pension of $8 a month, increasing to $12 when she was eighty-two. That was considerable income for the time. John and Ann lived in a small frame house on Dingletown Road, not far from Indian Mills. There were seven children. Ann lived in this house until her death. Ann wore her hair in long thick braids, and smoked a clay pipe. She had a clock that needed winding with a key, but for some reason she was afraid to wind it herself, and often had local children perform this task for her. Her grave sits, appropriately, in the Tabernacle Cemetery, not far from the place where she lived. Each Memorial Day, the president of the Tabernacle Historical Society places flowers on her grave...memorial to the last of the Lenni Lenape tribe of the Pinelands. Cite-**Indian Ann, Indian Mills, NJ** - New Jersey Historical Markers on http://www.Waymarking.com ***Author's Note:*** *Camp Inawendiwin, operated by the Camden County Council Girl Scouts of America, is located there, but Ann could not be the last of her tribe, since she had seven children.*

32 **Spanish American War.** In the summer of 1898, the United States fought Spain in one of the shortest and most pathetically one-sided wars in modern history. The war led the United States to expand westward by defeating Mexico in 1846-48. This impulse toward imperialism took place as major European nations were establishing colonies throughout Africa. As a result of the Spanish-American War, the United States became a world power that controlled an empire stretching from the Caribbean Sea to the Far East. **(*Cite 1*)** The First New Jersey Volunteer Infantry served out its term of service in the continental U.S. Formed from the New Jersey National Guard, the unit was mustered into federal service between May 5 and 12, 1898 at Camp Voorhees, located at Sea Girt, New Jersey. At the time of its muster in, the regiment consisted of fifty-one officers and 949 enlisted men. On May 16, the regiment was ordered to Camp Alger located near Washington DC at Dunn Loring, Virginia. The regiment broke camp on May 19 to move to the new location. Camp Alger was a rather dusty, crowded, and unhealthy camp, with very unhealthy water. The men were subjected to malaria and typhoid fever **(*Cite 2*)**. *Cite 1-**Britannica Online Encyclopedia, 2012** Cite 2-**"The History of the 1st New Jersey Volunteer Infantry,"*** by Patrick McSherry, and ***The Spanish American War Centennial Website!*** www.spanamwar.com).

33 **U. S. Merchant Marine.** Young mariners trained at the U.S. Merchant Marine Academy, various state Maritime Academies, or the U.S. Maritime Service Training Stations. William Travers, 22, was captain of the SS James Ford Rhodes, while his 21 year old brother was first mate. The U.S. Maritime Service officially took youngsters who were 16 years-old. They took them with one eye, one leg, or heart problems. Many men who were too young or too old for the other services or who were physically unfit for the other services joined the Maritime Service and went in the Merchant Marine. During World War II, some gossip columnists claimed that merchant mariners were getting rich on outrageous salaries. In a 1943 letter to the American Legion, Admiral Telfair Knight of the War Shipping Administration compared salaries for equivalent positions in Navy and Merchant Marine, and found salaries to be equivalent or even higher for Navy personnel. In addition, the Navy offered outstanding benefits, including paid leave, disability and death benefits, free medical care for personnel and dependents, free uniforms, and a generous

retirement pension. Mariners signed on for each voyage which lasted until they returned to a U.S. port, which could be one year or more. They had no paid leave, no vacation and no pension. Countless mariners performed acts of bravery and heroism beyond the call of duty. The Distinguished Service Medal, the Merchant Marine's highest honor, was awarded to 140 mariners, of whom 7 were cadets from the U.S. Merchant Marine Academy. Ten ships were recipients of the Gallant Ship Award. ***(Cite 1)*** The memorial in Castine (at the Maine Marine Academy) states 6,895 merchant mariners—including 60 from Maine—plus 1,810 Armed Naval Guard members died in the war. An American Merchant Marine at War website puts the mariner figure closer to 9,300—or one of every 26 mariners, the highest casualty rate of any branch of the military in the war...Even so, merchant mariners returning from the war did not qualify for the G.I. Bill that enabled many vets to pursue higher education and other benefit programs. And it was not until 1988 that the U.S. government formally recognized World War II merchant marines as veterans. ***(Cite 2)*** *Cite 1-* http://www.usmm.org *Cite 2-**"Merchant Marine Vets Recognized,"*** Mike Francis, The Oregonian, 1999.

34 **The Red Men Association** was spawned of revolutionary zeal from the original Sons of Liberty, the colonists who dressed as "red men" (Indians) and dumped 346 chests of English tea into Boston harbor, protesting British tyranny (The Boston Tea Party). The patriotic group evolved through the American Revolution and splintered in the early 1800's into several small factions. At historic Fort Mifflin, Philadelphia's eastern defense on the Delaware River, they came together in 1813 and formed the Society of Red Men, which became the Improved Order of Red Men Association. With the formation of a national organization, the Improved Order of Red Men soon spread, and within 30 years there were State Great Councils in 21 states with a membership of over 150,000. The Order continued to grow and by the mid-1920s there were "tribes" in 46 states and territories with a membership totaling over one-half million. ***Cite*** - www.redmen.org.

35 **Setting up operations in a municipality.** Mr. PETERSON.* Usually a particular mob is tied up with the authorities of that particular jurisdiction, which gives them more or less a monopoly, so to speak. *In other words, a place doesn't operate unless they have the permission of the authorities.* Nobody is foolish enough to open a $250,000 establishment with the idea that maybe the authorities might find it the next day. In other words, they don't do that. They divide up the territory. It is a matter of record in Chicago years ago that they even had conferences between the gangsters to divide the territory. *When you get into somebody else's territory, then you are in trouble.* Take, for example, one particular area in Chicago a few years ago. Here is an accurate description of how a gambler operated in this particular area in Chicago. If you wanted to operate a gambling establishment, you first went to the ward committeeman. However, he did not have the final word in that particular ward. This is a few years ago. Mr. PETERSON. I am talking about that as an example. You asked how this thing operates. If you went to him and said, "I want to operate a place at such-and-such an address," the ward committeeman would say, "All right; I will think it over." The ward committeeman contacted the syndicate's representative. The

syndicate's representative in this particular area said either "He can go at that address" or "He can't go." If he can go, the syndicate gets 60 percent of the total profits. They put their own man in the place to make certain they get the 60 percent of the profits. All of the protection, everything, was handled by the syndicate. That was in this one district where we developed that information several years ago. *That is the way it operates.* (Cite 1) ***Cite 1-"Hearings before a Special Committee to Investigate Organized Crime in Interstate Commerce,"*** United States Senate, Eighty-first Congress, second session, pursuant to S. Res. 202 .. (1950) Para 181. ***Author's Note***: *In Mount Holly's case, there was no ward committeeman to approach, but the most powerful figure in the county with respect to the battle against "big time gambling" was local resident and future County Prosecutor Harold T. Parker, whose name was frequently in the news as a crusader against gambling and often claiming that it (gambling) didn't exist in his jurisdiction. In July of 1946, Parker announced "the county is faced with no problem on this score (organized gambling) at this time...we will continue to crack down on gambling."* ***(Mt. Holly Herald,*** *July 26, 1946, pg 1) He frequently rounded up the "criminals" involved in lottery slips and back room poker games. Mr. Parker was politically important, a major player in county politics.* ***Testimony of Virgil W. Peterson, Operating Director, Chicago Crime Commission, representing the American Municipal Association** before the Senate Committee.

36 **Paul John Carbo** (born Paolo Giovanni Carbo; August 10, 1904–November 9, 1976) better known as **"Frankie Carbo"** was a New York City mafia soldier in the Lucchese Crime family, who operated as a boxing promoter and a gunman with Murder, Inc. In 1959 he was sentenced to 25 years in federal prison, finally convicted for fight-fixing. It was widely reported that Kid Gavilan and Don Gordon, two prominent fighters of that era, were owned by Carbo, and that several big bouts had been fixed by Philadelphia's Blinky Palermo and Carbo, who was then known as the "Czar" of boxing. At the time he was convicted, he owned heavyweight champion Sonny Liston's contract. He was thought to have committed 17 murders, but was charged with only 5, all of which ended in acquittals. *Cite-***Bureau of Narcotics, Sam Giancana**, the United States Treasury Department. ***"Mafia: The Government's Secret File on Organized Crime. 2007,"*** Author: Bureau of Narcotics, The United States Treasury Department. (pg 85) ***Author's Note:*** *The five acquittals resulted from dead, missing or absent minded witnesses to Carbo's crimes. Although unsubstantiated, different sources also have attributed the 1947 death of Bugsy Segal in Los Angeles to Carbo, supposedly operating on the orders of Meyer Lansky and approved by the Commission. Tuck thought the unsolved Philadelphia murder of Joseph Brennen, who operated a casino in Roebling, NJ in 1942, might be the work of Carbo as well as the break in to the cottage on Garden Street. It is alleged by Earnest Volkman, in his book, "Gangbusters" that Carbo fixed the heavyweight title fight that catapulted Cassius Clay to the top of the boxing world, by arranging for Sonny Liston, whose contract he owned, not to answer the bell for the seventh round.*

37 **Gamblers Fined.** Sal was represented by Harold T. Parker, future county prosecutor and party leader. (**See endnote 35.**) With his counsel, the

originator and leader of the illegal casino operation was fined only $2000 and released with a reprimand regarding his role as the "Club Secretary" of the "Young Men's Social Club," his penalty the least of the principles, but more than the customers (gamblers), who were fined $25 each. Sal's partner, Tony, received a 1-1/2 to 3 year jail sentence. *Cite-**Mt. Holly Herald***, 4/25/41 and Thursdays thru 6/26/41, pgs. 1 and 8.

38 ***Author's Note:*** *According to Santo, Sal's younger brother, he, Apples and Sal left New Jersey together, Sal carrying a bankroll of $45,000 in cash, proceeds from the Casino. They traveled to Los Angeles, where Sal created the casino in the banquet room of Lucy's El Adobe restaurant. Upon leaving there, Sal went to Mexico and subsequently to Covington, KY to work the Yorkshire Club. It is certain that Covington and LA were definite stopovers in Sal's illegal casino career, but the sequence of events is difficult to pin down.*

39 ***Author's Note: The cost of the gaming equipment and setup at Red Men's Hall is*** *estimated in 1935 prices at approximately $10,000.00, which equates in 2012 to nearly $328,000.00. The author believes that Sal expected the casino closing to be temporary, and that his (Sal's) family's presence would bring some protection to the stored equipment investment, presenting at least the illusion that he or some of his associates were nearby. The Carbo raid was unauthorized by Sal's mob superiors, but the politicians accepting the Saturday payoffs had little or no chance to prevent it, exploiting the gamblers for a services they had neither the integrity, courage nor inclination to provide. Although Carbo was quite successful in intimidating prize fighters and fixing boxing matches, he lacked the organizational skills and personality to outfit and operate a carpet joint. He nevertheless coveted the equipment that Sal had acquired and tried unsuccessfully for years after to obtain it.* ***See endnote 35,*** *"Nobody is foolish enough to open a $250,000 establishment with the idea that maybe the authorities might find it the next day"*

40 ***Author's note:*** **The Buck Squires character** *is a composite of several police officers who were the stalwarts of law enforcement in 1930's Mt. Holly. Although Tuck had grown up believing that Buck had thwarted a robbery at the Farmer's bank, that story was largely mythical. Research revealed that Buck had interrupted a robbery attempt at the bank, causing the robbers to run away, but no heroics were involved. Tuck was witness to a different Officer shooting a tied rabid dog while holding him by the collar and inadvertently amputating one of his fingers at the second knuckle.*

41 The name **"Battle of the Atlantic"** was coined by Winston Churchill in February 1941. It has been called the "longest, largest, and most complex" naval battle in history. The campaign began immediately after the European war began and lasted six years. It involved thousands of ships in more than 100 convoy battles and perhaps 1,000 single-ship encounters, in a theatre covering thousands of square miles of ocean. The situation changed constantly, with one side or the other gaining advantage, as new weapons, tactics, counter-measures, and equipment were developed by both sides. The Allies gradually gained the upper hand, overcoming German surface raiders by the end of 1942 (withdrawn on Hitler's orders) and defeating the U-boats by mid-1943, though losses to U-boats continued to war's end. After the United States entered the war in December 1941, U-boats began patrolling

off the American East Coast and in the Gulf of Mexico, where they unleashed Operation Paukenschlag (Drumbeat) to destroy American shipping. In four months the Germans sank more than 360 ships, including the destroyer USS Jacob Jones. Caught off guard, the U.S. Navy had failed to adequately protect commercial coastal vessels, which were often gunned down by surfaced U-boats using East Coast city lights to silhouette their targets. *Cite-* ***"Oxford Companion to U.S. Military History,"*** U.S. Naval Operations in World War II: The North Atlantic by Samuel Eliot Morison, The Battle of the Atlantic: September 1939–May 1943, Vol. 1, 1947. ***Author's Note:*** *A little known fact is that New Jersey and other east coast yachtsmen created "The Corsair Fleet," an anti-submarine patrol organization that assisted the Navy and was supervised by the Coast Guard. American recreational sailboats were used as ships of war during WWII. "The Hooligan Navy" tells about the Corsair Fleet, a band of young yachtsmen and fishermen who were recruited into service - their vessels "armed" - so they could patrol the coastline of America's Eastern seaboard and, if necessary, engage Nazi U-boats. Most vessels carried machine guns and a few depth charges. The sailors and their sailing yachts were sent out so quickly the grey paint was still wet. Cite-"Good Old Boat Magazine" from their website.* (www.goodoldboat.com).

42 **Ibid endnote 19. Relief 1930.**

43 **Vincent "China" Skola** suspected in the 1942 murder of Joseph Brennan, Philadelphia mobster (***Camden Courier Post***, March 29, 1944, pg 1). "Big Time" gambling continued in South Jersey throughout the war years; Sal and his partner Tony were convicted and incarcerated in Cape May County for three months in 1944, after an arrest and fines in Wrightstown the previous year. Tony was arrested again for operating the "Hainesport Dart and Billiards Club," and sentenced to another 3 to 5 year stretch that same year. State Police made another successful raid on Kate's Island Store in 1947, rounding up a dozen craps players and Sal. In 1948, Police closed the "Penn Jersey Athletic Club" which occupied the second floor of an old Victorian at 22 Alden Street in Roebling. And in 1949, the persistent "Big Time" gamblers were once again indicted along with the chief of police and mayor of Maple Shade when their gambling den constructed of reinforced concrete with steel doors and "peep hole" windows was raided, pulling in 187 unhappy gamblers. Sal was not included. Cite-***The Mount Holly Herald,*** various issues, 1942 through 1949.

44 **Covington, KY** MAJOR CLUBS. The clubs listed as "major" are somewhat arbitrary, but represent establishments that played a significant role in the history of Northern Kentucky gambling. The **Beverly Hills** and the **Lookout House** became the top "carpet joints" run by the Cleveland Syndicate... Others, like the **Flamingo** and the **Yorkshire Club**[1], were run by the Eastern Syndicate[2] with agreement from Cleveland. The **Merchant's Club** and the **Primrose Club** had a longevity that deserves the title of "major." Other "major" clubs were **Glenn Hotel/Glenn Rendezvous**, **Glenn Schmidt's Playtorium/Snax Bar**, **Hi-De-Ho/19 Club**, and the **Primrose Club/Latin Quarter/Bluegrass Inn (*Cite 1*)** At approximately 2:40 a.m. on May 9, three city detectives burst into room 314 of the Glenn Hotel in Newport, Ky., which occupies the same building as an illegal gambling casino and strip-tease joint

called the Tropicana. In the room, the three cops found and arrested a man they later said was clad only in shirt and socks, and a woman with nothing on but an imitation-leopard negligee. The man was George Ratterman, the former Notre Dame and Cleveland Browns football star-and currently the reform candidate for sheriff of Campbell County, Ky., which includes Newport. The woman was a 26 year old, long-legged strip-tease named Juanita Hodges, who earns her living divesting herself of her clothing nightly in the Tropicana under the name April Flowers.***(Cite 2)*** *Cite 1* **-*"WHEN VICE WAS KING - A HISTORY OF NORTHERN KENTUCKY GAMBLING 1920-1970,"*** by Jim Linduff with Roy Klein and Larry Trapp. *Cite 2-*__*"The Great Kentucky Scandal"*__ by Bill Davidson, Look Magazine, October 24, 1961. ***Author's Notes:*** *A "Carpet joint" is an operation offering straight games, professional employees and pleasant surroundings; a "bust out joint" is the opposite, with crooked games and dealers whose total objective was to rip off the player and/or the house, often with collaboration of management. The cited story in Look Magazine chronicles the beginning of the end of a 60 year era of mob-controlled corruption in northern Kentucky, the straw that broke the camel's back being the clumsy attempt to frame George Ratterman, a newly elected reform sheriff, by feeding him knockout drops and photographing him naked with a stripper named April Flowers. The public were incensed by the treatment of the famous Notre Dame quarterback and aroused to back the reformers in ridding the county of the mobsters and prostitutes. With assistance from Governor Combs, the FBI, U.S. Attorney General Robert F. Kennedy and Chicago crime buster Elliot Ness, the result was a Campbell County Grand Jury, in September (1961), which indicted almost the entire Newport city government. It charged that 193 officials had conspired to obstruct justice by permitting widespread vice. Named in the indictments were the Mayor, the City Manager, three city Commissioners, George Gugel, retired police chief, a retired detective and six policemen.* ***Note 1*** *- Research reveals that it (Yorkshire Club) was the only club in the area with an operating history that spanned three generations at the same location, and also was known to have ties to eastern mobsters. Sal told Tuck that one of the box men that assisted in the "sting" was the grandson and son of boxmen (croupiers) who, as young men, had learned their trade in the same casino.* ***Note 2*** *- The "Eastern Syndicate" was Meyer Lansky and Bugsy Siegal, both alleged to own shares in the Yorkshire Club, and Moe Dalitz, who became a major player in early Las Vegas.*

45 **Resorts Casino Hotel** is a hotel and casino in Atlantic City, New Jersey. Resorts was the first legal casino hotel in Atlantic City, becoming the first approved casino outside of Nevada in the United States, when it opened on May 26, 1978, built on the site of the famous Haddon Hall (1869) hotel. The resort completed an expansion in 2004, adding the 27-story Rendezvous Tower, and underwent renovations in 2011, converting the resort to a Roaring Twenties theme. Cite – www.resortsac.com

46 **Tony Cornero Stralla.** (Governor Earl) Warren's adversary in this battle (of Santa Monica) was the (Gambling ship) Rex owner and operator, Anthony Cornero Stralla (known as Tony Cornero). Cornero had been a key Los Angeles rumrunner during prohibition, smuggling bootleg alcohol

on boats from Mexico and Canada. Cornero would become a major crime figure in Los Angeles for 25 years, yet remained a local player, refusing to ally himself with the East Coast or Chicago-based Cosa Nostra families. Without the extensive connections and protections of the syndicate, it was near impossible to maintain a land-based gambling operation. Instead, he operated on the high seas. Water taxies costing $0.25 shuttled passengers 3.1 miles to the palatial ship called the S.S. Rex. Unlike previous gambling operations, Cornero catered to a higher class of clientele. His LA Times ads claimed "all the thrills of Biarritz, Riviera, Monte Carlo, Cannes -surpassed!" He hired skywriters whose planes wrote, "Play at the S.S. Rex." ***(Cite 1***) The Corneros spent $31,000 to build the Meadows nightclub (in Las Vegas in 1930) and announced plans to add a fifty-room hotel, declaring their goal to make it the state's "finest resort." They brought in a producer who presented a floorshow called the "Meadows Revue," with a band known as the Meadow Larks. The (Cornero) brothers had decided to locate the club on Boulder Highway, which was the main route into Las Vegas for workers from the Boulder Dam (now Hoover Dam) project at the Nevada-Arizona border. In the early 1930s, the club's concert stage featured performers such as the Gumm Sisters, with a young girl named Frances Gumm, later known as Judy Garland. ***(Cite 2)*** *Cite 1 -**"The Era of the Gambling Ships & the Battle of Santa Monica Bay."*** The Los Angeles Almanac (http://www.laalmanac.com/history/hi06ee.htm). *Cite 2-**"O N E"*** -Online Nevada Encyclopedia, ***"Meadows Club,"*** by Jeff Burbank, www.onlinenevada.org. ***Author's Note:*** *Tony Cornero's ships were legal if outside the 3 mile limit; however, Attorney General Warren attempted to redefine how the limit was determined geographically and lost. He then attacked the water taxi service, forcing the gambling ships out of business. Cornero fought off boarding parties of deputies with fire hoses, and then was blockaded. He finally settled, saying after six weeks, he 'had to come ashore to get a haircut'. Cornero and his brothers became founding fathers of the Las Vegas Strip, creating two casinos; the Meadows (on Boulder Highway, near the new dam), which burned in 1935 and another, the Stardust, which opened after Cornero died of a heart attack while shooting craps in 1955.*

47 ***Author's Note:*** *Tuck could never confirm if these incidents were the reason for Sal's arrival in Hollywood. But Lucy's remains the only continuously operated restaurant since the 1940's directly across the street from a major movie studio's front gate, with a history of mob connections and activity. There is no question that Sal's casino existed in Lucy's Adobe restaurant. Santo, Sal's younger brother verified the casino across from Paramount's main gate at a family club dinner in 1994. Sal told Tuck that he was "sent to LA" by his boss, Sam Giancana, because "he had something for him (Sal) to do there."*

48 **Auto Production.** From early February 1942 through the end of 1944, nearly three years, essentially no cars were produced in the United States. In addition to a ban on the production and sale of cars for private use, residential and highway construction was halted, and driving for pleasure was banned. Strategic goods—including tires, gasoline, fuel oil, and sugar—were rationed beginning in 1942. Cutting back on private consumption of

these goods freed up material resources that were vital to the war effort. **Cite**-Excerpted from ***"Plan B 4.0 Mobilizing to Save Civilization,"*** by Lester R. Brown, from Chapter 10.

49 **Mayor LaGuardia.** "New York's most colorful mayor since Peter Stuyvesant." La Guardia was elected to an unprecedented three terms and served as mayor from 1934 to 1945. He wrested control of the city from the Tammany Hall political machine, which had dominated New York politics for more than 80 years. In 1934, he hefted a sledge hammer and led a search-and-destroy mission against mob boss Frank Costello's slot machines. **Cite-"Fiorello's Foggiani**," by John T. Correll, Air Force Magazine, June, 2010.

50 ***Author's Note: The annual tomato harvest*** *was a bonanza each year for high schoolers, hobos and low income families wanting to work. For dozens of Burlington County farmers, tomatoes were the most important crop and could be harvested from July through October. Pickers were hired and paid piecework at $0.10 to $0.25 per basket. Campbell Soup worked with local farmers to help them produce the perfect soup tomato. The Campbell Soup Company contracted with an estimated 2,000 growers per year, each farm producing and average of three to four tons of produce per delivery. The lines at the company loading dock often stretched for nine miles. Entrepreneurs ran used school buses through town early every morning, and to get work, one only had to flag the driver down. Trucks followed the pickers in the fields, and the tomato trucks were loaded into a pyramid of stacked baskets, sometimes 8 rows high. These trucks, often dangerously overloaded, made a steady convoy to the Campbell Soup loading docks in Camden that lasted for the entire harvest season. Cite-**South Jersey Farming**, by Cheryl L. Baidsen, Published by Arcadia Publishing, Charleston, SC, 2006. ISBN 0-7385-44973.*

51 **Ibid endnote 35. Setting up operations in a municipality.**

52 **Gas Rationing**. Gasoline was rationed on May 15, 1942 on the east coast and nationwide that December. The OPA (Office of Price Administration) issued various stickers to be affixed to the car's windshield, depending on need. To get your classification and ration stamps, you had to certify to a local board that you needed gas and owned no more than five tires. The 'A' sticker was issued to owners whose use of their cars was nonessential. Hand the pump jockey your Mileage Ration Book coupons and cash, and she (yes, female service station attendants) could sell you three or four gallons a week, no more. For nearly a year, 'A' stickered cars were not to be driven for pleasure at all. The green 'B' sticker was for driving deemed essential to the war effort; industrial war workers, for example, could purchase eight gallons a week. Red 'C' stickers indicated physicians, ministers, mail carriers and railroad workers, and incidentally were the most counterfeited type. 'T' was for truckers, and the rare 'X' sticker went to Members of Congress and other VIPs. Cite- ***www.PreWarBuick.com, "What They Didn't Teach You About World War II,"*** by Mike Wright, Presidio Press, 1998. ***Author's Note:*** *Sal's source of bogus gas ration stamps was most likely Tommy Lucchese, who specialized in a WWII black market for counterfeit rationing stamps and was soon to become a boss of one of the five families of New York. Sal's taxi business ran up to six cars continuously in addition to the V-12 Lincoln*

and V-16 Cadillac, gas guzzlers supreme. Lucchese became a member of the commission and during the fifties was allegedly the manipulator of prize fighters through gangster Frankie Carbo, Sal's nemesis who had robbed the Secret Casino at Red Men's Hall in 1941.

53 ***Author's Note: Pawn Shops*** *were illegal in New Jersey in the 1950's, but Sal was undeterred by the law. The painted window sign said "Wrightstown Jewelers." He actually had a few lower priced watches in one section of a showcase, but all of the rest of his merchandise was made up of "hocked" items. Sal skirted the law by requiring the customer to sell him the item, and buy it back within a certain time, or lose it. His interest rates ranged from 17 to 29%. Now legal in New Jersey, pawn brokers are licensed by the State and restrained to interest rates less than 31%.*

54 **Class of 1947 includes veterans.** The nine veterans receiving diplomas (from Mt. Holly High School, class of 1947) were William J Allen, Paul H. Baessler, and Frank A Ellis of Medford, Monte K Bennett, John W. English, Eugene F. Hasson and James McFarland of Mount Holly, Charles W. Porto of Lumberton and Albert F. Clark of Hainesport. The school graduated 108 students on June 13, 1947. Cite-**Mt. Holly Herald**, June 14, 1947, pg. 1.

55 **Guard Dogs.** In 1942, the Coast Guard recognized that the use of dogs, with their keen sense of smell and their ability to be trained for guard duty, would help enhance the (beach) patrols. The Coast Guard eventually received about 2,000 dogs for patrol duties. The dogs and their trainers were schooled on the 300-acre estate of P.A.B. Widener, at the Elkins Park Training Station in Pennsylvania. Others trained at Hilton Head, SC. The first dog patrols began at Brigantine Park, NJ, in August 1942. The dogs were so successful, that within a year, the animals and their handlers were on duty in all the districts. *Cite* - www.olive-drab.com/wardogs/WWII/beach patrol, *and* ***"Print in the Sand: The U.S. Coast Guard Beach Patrol During WW II"***, by Eleanor Bishop. ***Author's Note:*** *The Elkins Park training facility eventually became the nucleus of Widener College and University.*

56 **The New Jersey School for Feeble Minded Males.** The school still exists. The **Vineland Training School** is a non-profit organization in Vineland, New Jersey with the mission of educating the developmentally disabled so they can live independently. It has been a leader in research and testing. The Training School changed its name several times. Finally in 1988 the name "The Training School at Vineland" was restored. However, the literature also makes reference to the "Vineland Training School for Backward and Feeble-minded Children" and "Vineland Training School for Feeble-Minded Girls and Boys" and other variations. "The Kallikak Family," an influential book written by Dr. Goddard in 1912, described a scientific study of heredity and feeblemindedness conducted at the Training School. However, it has since been recognized that the book was mostly fiction and used flawed scientific theory. (**See endnote 10**.) Cite-www.vineland.org/history/trainingschool/fastfacts.

57 **Arnold Schenck.** ***Author's note:*** *Schenck was kidnapped, held without bail or representation and harassed for 75 days by police who were attempting to make him confess to the abduction and murder of the Lindbergh baby.* Cite-**"Master Detective. The Life and Times of Ellis Parker, America's**

Sherlock Holmes," by John Reisinger, Published by Citadel Press (Kensington Publishing Company, 850 Third Avenue, New York City, NY 10022), Chapter 8, ff.

58 ***Author's Note: Nelson Anderson****. Nelson often invited neighbors and especially children, to watch a volunteer crack a concrete mass balanced on his chest with a sledge hammer while he lay serenely on his bed of nails. He was known for pulling fire engines and locomotives with his teeth, and once allegedly performed a handstand atop the Lumberton water tower without benefit of nets or any safety equipment.*

59 **Ibid. endnote 53. Veterans in high school.**

60 **(Stanley) Dancer** emerged as one of harness racing's first modern driving stars in the early '50s and, over the years, became one of its wealthiest. As of the beginning of this month, (May, 1981) he had won 3,473 races and nearly $22 million in purses. He was the first driver to win $1 million in a single season (1964) and the trainer-driver of America's first standardbred millionaire (Cardigan Bay. 1968). He is the only trainer-driver to produce three Triple Crown winners: the trotters Nevele Pride (1968) and Super Bowl (1972) and the pacer Most Happy Fella (1970). And as the 1981 season warms up. Dancer may be the keeper of the most remarkable set of standardbreds ever assembled in one racing stable: the pacer French Chef and the trotters Smokin' Yankee, Panty Raid and Filet of Sole. They are all 3-year-olds; all set world records as 2-year-olds. Cite-***"Back In The Driver's Seat Again. The great harness horseman, Stanley Dancer, has had his ups and downs. Now he has a barnful of burners ready to go for the classic races."*** By Sandy Treadwell, Sports Illustrated Magazine, May 18, 1981 (excerpted). ***Author's Note:*** *Stanley's fame was still in his future when he gifted Tuck with a collie pup. Stanley, a troublesome student, graduated 8th grade only on the promise to the Principal that he would not attempt high school.*

61 **Mickey Shaughnessy** Mickey Shaughnessy, the Irish-American character actor best known for his portrayal of Elvis Presley's musical mentor in the rock n' roll classic "Jailhouse Rock" (1957), was born Joseph Michael Shaughnessy on August 5, 1920 in New York City. As a performer, the young Mickey made his bones on the Catskill Mountains tourist resort circuit. During a stint in the Army during World War II, Mickey appeared in a service revue. After being demobilized, he made his living making the rounds of the nightclub circuit with a comedy act. His breakthrough as an actor came with his debut in support of the legendary Judy Holliday and great meat n' potatoes character actor Aldo Ray in The Marrying Kind (1952). Shaughnessy signed a contract with Metro-Goldwyn-Mayer, which typecast him as dumb but likable lugs in such pictures as Designing Woman (1957). He was memorable as "the Duke" in The Adventures of Huckleberry Finn (1960) for MGM and even acted Jerry Lewis off of the silver screen as Jerry's wrassler-pal in Don't Give Up the Ship (1959). Other major pictures he appeared in were Academy Award-winning From Here to Eternity (1953), Until They Sail (1957) in support of up-and-coming Paul Newman, Frank Capra's disappointing final film Pocketful of Miracles (1961), and Henry Hathaway's comedic potboiler North to Alaska (1960) with John Wayne. He died in 1985 in Cape May Court House, NJ. Cite-www.Fandango.com

62 ***Author's Note: One Eye Irving.*** *The man's real name was Eli Newmark. Newmark, known as the "Slot Machine King" of Ocean County, NJ had a lengthy record, with arrests for illegal stills, gambling equipment and aiding and abetting. Abstracted stories in the New York Times January 07, 1932, and September 26, 1938 attesting to some of "One Eye Irving's exploits, follow: TOMS RIVER, N.J., Jan 6--Eli Newmark, so-called "slot machine king" of Ocean County, was sentenced to six years in the State prison and a fine of $1,500 by Judge Arthur German Gallagher. The prison, sentence, representing three of the eleven indictments to which Newmark pleaded guilty two weeks ago for possession of slot machines, was suspended. NEWARK, N.J., September 26, 1938, Eli Newmark of Lakewood, known for years as the "slot machine king" of Ocean County, who disappeared two years ago on the day he was to have appeared for sentence in Newark Federal court on a charge of operating an unregistered still in Ocean County, was arrested this afternoon in Island Park, L.I., as a fugitive and brought here for detention.* **Cite**-*NY Times pay articles index, Jan 07, 1932, and Sept 26, 1938 Sal's explanation of One Eye Irving's specialty (in an unguarded moment) was that "he breaks legs with a baseball bat."*

63 ***Author's Note: Freddy Fittipaldi*** *and Peter Pro were the only arrested persons carrying arms when the Casino at Red Men's Hall was raided in April of 1941. Was the bodyguard and second story man "Apples," really Fittipaldi? Verification is impossible, but Tuck was sure that Apples was never without his shoulder holstered pistol.*

64 **Japanese atrocities.** In December of 1937, the Japanese Imperial Army marched into China's capital city of Nanking and proceeded to murder 300,000 out of 600,000 civilians and soldiers in the city. The six weeks of carnage that followed would become known as the Rape of Nanking and represented the single worst atrocity during the World War II era in either the European or Pacific theaters of war. Cite - **The History Place™**, Genocide in the 20th Century (Website), and **"The Rape of Nanking,"** by Iris Chang, Published by BasicBooks, a subsidiary of Perseus Books, LLC, 1997, ISBN 0-465-06835-9.

65 **Hugh Campbell** was born December 4, 1905 in Atchison, Kansas. He moved to the Camden, New Jersey area when he was 10 years old. Hugh Campbell left a nine-to-five job in 1930's to pursue an artist's life. He jumped into his new life with nothing but determination and a "feeling" that he could paint. He had no formal training. Training himself was his first priority, which he did by drawing over 1,000,000 free-hand circles and then over 130,000 action sketches of people on the streets. But it was the fields around his boyhood fishing spots in Mount Holly where he felt the most at home. He commuted from Camden to Mount Holly regularly as he discovered that those fields and streets were the subject matter that he wanted to paint. He had no money and no place to stay so he would pitch a tent in a field and stay overnight. At one point the owner of Hack's Canoe Retreat told him that he didn't have to pitch a tent, he could come as often as he liked and stay as long as he liked in an unheated canoe barn at no charge He (the owner of Hack's) thought Hugh was going to stay a week or two, but he ended up staying seven years. In the 1940s Hugh Campbell bought an old tar paper

bicycle repair shop building for $150 and moved in on Kates Tract, in the Southampton woods on the banks of the Rancocas. In the late 1930s he became a vegetarian and began a Yoga discipline. He read extensively on the subject, teaching himself Hatha Yoga and practicing it daily much in the same way that he taught himself to draw and paint. In 1942 he met a teacher from India, Swami Yatiswarananda, who taught him about Vedanta, one of the world's most ancient religious philosophies and one of its broadest. Campbell studied with him until Yatiswarananda's return to India in 1948. He corresponded with his teacher for many years afterwards and continued with his Yoga practice. In 1962 he published a book called *Knock Vigorously to Be Heard*. The title was taken from the notice on his cabin door. It is filled with hometown humor, depression memories and spiritual observations, giving us revealing glimpses of an unusual man living in a small country town. His paintings and writings are a moving history of Mount Holly at mid century. Campbell stayed in the shack on Kates Tract until the mid-1980s when he was overcome by fumes from a faulty kerosene heater. After a stay in the hospital, he became a ward of the state and spent his last years in a nursing home. Cite-***Ask/Art, The Artist's Bluebook,*** by Lynn Lemyre, Visual Arts Coordinator, Burlington County Division of Cultural Affairs & Tourism. ***Author's Note:*** It *was not the owner of Hack's, but Mr. Katz, who owned Kate's Island Store and offered Hugh a place to stay. Mr. Campbell lived in his canoe barn on the island, accessible from Shreve Street. Hugh told Tuck that he lived there. Tuck saw him there many times and also paddling a Katz canoe in the Rancocas. Dick Lamb was the manager at Hack's and would have been the contact for any such arrangement there. Hugh may have stayed briefly at Hack's, which was in the downtown area on Mill Street, but was never seen there by the Author, who kept a canoe in the barn for four years. It was the author's experience that Mr. and Mrs. Hack were not very friendly people; the author doubts that they would make such an arrangement for a homeless man. Hugh told Tuck that he had lost a beautiful house on the beach in Margate, as well as his personal fortune because of the 1929 crash. Some shortening and editing by the author, who knew Mr. Campbell personally.*

66 **German POWs at Fort Dix**. Daniel Zimmerman, curator of the Fort Dix Museum, said they (German POW's) were housed in America, rather than England, because the United States had more space and food for them. He said of the 15,000 POWs who passed through Fort Dix, 3,000 to 4,000 were housed there. Some of the Dix prisoners worked at canning factories in or near Bridgeton, such as the P.J. Ritter Cannery. Others were sent to work at Seabrook Farms-then the largest processor of vegetables in the world. Zimmerman said the POWs included soldiers from other European countries that had been defeated by the German Army-like Slovenia, Austria and Yugoslavia. *Cite-* "More Fort Dix History" ***Posted by Filatore*** and ***"German POW's Worked in S.J."*** by Carol Comega, Courier Post Staff (Courier-PostOnLine.com)

67 **Peace Treaties with Japan and Germany.** The United States concluded a treaty ending the state of war between the United States and Japan in 1951 that included POW compensation provisions. In addition, the War Claims

Act (WCA) dealt with U.S. POWs held by all Axis powers, as well as civilian American internees of Japan. Since the United States did not conclude a peace treaty with Germany, only recently has compensation for some U.S. civilian internees of Germany been awarded ***(Cite 1).*** On 25 June 1950, the young Cold War suddenly turned hot, bloody and expensive. Within a few days, North Korea's invasion of South Korea brought about a UNs' "police action" against the aggressors. That immediately produced heavy military and naval involvement by the United States. ***(Cite 2).*** *Cite 1 -**"U.S. Prisoners of War and Civilian American Citizens Captured and Interned by Japan in World War II: The Issue of Compensation by Japan"*** The U.S. Navy Dept. Library, Cong. Research Service Report for Congress, Chapter: Peace Treaties with Japan and Germany. *Cite 2-**"The Korean War, June 1950 - July 1953"*** Introductory Overview and Special Image Selection, USN History & Heritage Cmd.

68 **Draft.** During the war in Korea, 1,529,539 men were drafted in the years 1950 to 1953. In 1951, the Universal Military Training and Service Act came into force by Congress. At that time, the age of the draftee was 18 years and required men to serve in the Army for 24 months. Married men were exempted from the draft system, but on 11 July 1953, President Eisenhower changed this rule, stopping this impartiality. Cite–http://www.**ehow.com/** about_6376851

69 **Brooklyn Navy Yard.** During World War II, the Brooklyn Navy Yard played a pivotal role in the American war effort–it built battleships and aircraft carriers, repaired over 5,000 ships, and sent troops and supplies to fronts across the globe. The tireless efforts of its 70,000 workers earned it the nickname "The Can-Do Yard." **(Cite 1)** The USS Missouri's sponsor was Miss Margaret Truman, daughter of Senator Harry S. Truman of the State of Missouri. The ship was the last battleship built at the New York Navy Yard and the last to be launched with ceremonies in the United States, on 29 January, 1944.**(Cite 2)** *Cite 1-**Brooklyn Navy Yard Center*** at bldg 92. *Cite* 2- Department Of The Navy-Naval Historical Center, 805 Kidder Breese SE, Washington Navy Yard, Washington DC 20374-5060. ***Author's Note:*** *The Brooklyn Navy Yard recommissioned the USS New Jersey for her first resurrection and battle assignments in Korea.*

70 **Drowning. *Author's Note:*** *The local paper put its own spin on the Zanphel boy's accident, implying blame to the town leaders for permitting swimming at an unguarded and "treacherous" beach, and claiming that the accident had elicited a "storm of protest" from citizens. It further exaggerated the quickness with which Charley was recovered, stating that he was grappled within 20 minutes. He had been in the water for nearly an hour when finally hooked. The story completely ignored the female tourists' presence at the beach, grounding her canoe right in the middle of the area where several children were playing, and sneaking ignobly off while the search was taking place. There was no hole into which Charley fell, only a beached canoe on which he struck his head while diving in the shallow water. It was the only drowning that ever occurred at the popular swimming spot, while Tuck was aware of at least two drownings at the guarded Mill Dam. Some specifics from the* ***Mt. Holly Herald***, Aug, 1942.

71 ***Author's Note:*** *In Jamestown, Virginia, at the site of the original Jamestown Colony, there is a life sized bronze statue of the Pohowton princess Pocahontas who saved John Smith from execution and went on to become his bride and live in England. She is depicted in Native American garb with both arms extended in greeting. Thousands of children and adults have taken pictures there, holding her hands, which are bright gold in color to the elbows, since the green patina is worn off by constant caress.*

72 **NATTC Memphis.** Millington Regional Jetport formerly known as Millington Municipal Airport is a public airport in the city of Millington, in Shelby County, Tennessee. The airport is located 16 miles north of Memphis. It was formerly known as *Naval Air Station Memphis* and it still provides support to military aircraft visiting the adjacent Naval Support Activity Mid-South... After the start of World War II, the Navy took over the property and bought an additional 1,279 acres for an air station and a technical training school... During the postwar period of the mid-1940s through the mid-1990s, NAS Memphis hosted numerous locally-based Naval Air Reserve and Marine Air Reserve flying squadrons, as well as a major naval air technical training center (NATTC Millington) that provided the bulk of enlisted aviation specialty training for the United States Navy and Marine Corps. Cite-**Millington Regional Jetport**, From Wikipedia, the free encyclopedia.

73 ***Author's Note:*** *USS Megara's specialized crew numbered 240 enlisted personnel, 20 officers, double the size for ordinary LST's, which were called "ninety and nines" for the usual crew size of nine officers, ninety enlisted personnel. The ship floated in only 11 feet of water and could take on water ballast to provide stability and dampen rolling. Cite: NAVsource Online, Service Ship Photo Archive.*

74 **Liberty Cuffs.** The patches (liberty cuffs) were sewn, usually by a uniform tailor using a hidden stitch. This resulted in a regulation looking uniform when the cuffs were in place and buttoned, but displayed when the sailor was on liberty and unbuttoned and rolled the cuff up one roll to display the fancy designs. Liberty cuffs were found all over the fleet, and in many state side uniform tailor shops. But they were most commonly made in Asian ports. In fact, the oldest versions of these fancy inside cuffs were often attributed to "China Sailors." The customizing of the inside of Navy blue jumpers dates back to the late 1800s. Cite-**Daniel D. Smith, SCPO, USNR** (Ret), Navy Dress Blues, **"Tailor-mades" and "Liberty Cuffs"** http://www. Navycollector.com. ***Author's Note:*** *It was common to similarly customize the underside of the neck flap with Asian dragon designs and the blouse, inserting a hidden zipper from the armpit to the waist on the left side to facilitate removal when the blouse was tailored to the sailor's exact chest and waist measurements. The final and most essential customizing was to replace the 13 button front flap with a hidden zipper. These elements were seen on Steve Mc Queen's uniform in "The Sand Pebbles," a film about a navy gunboat (The USS San Pablo) in China waters, loosely based on the exploits of the USS Panay, which was sunk in the Yangtze River during the communist uprising in China.*

75 **Mexican Divorce.** The Mexican General Population Act (*Ley General de Población*), which is a federal law and thus supreme in all (Mexican) states,

literally provides that no judicial or administrative authority may hear a divorce action involving non-Mexicans unless the corresponding petition for dissolution of marriage is filed together with a certificate issued by Mexico's Department of State, certifying the plaintiff's legal residency in Mexico and that the plaintiff's immigration status allows the filing. The Regulations of the Mexican General Population Act (Reglamento de la Ley General de Población), which explain and expand the provisions of the Mexican General Population Act, further provide that a Divorce Permit shall be granted only if the marital domicile was established in Mexico. Cite–***Assn of Corporate Counsel***, http://www.Lexology.com

76 **Ibid endnote 31. Indian Ann.** ***Author's note:*** *That Ann, the daughter of Chief Lasha, was the last of the tribe is ridiculous since she had seven children, and she must have many descendants living in the area today. See* ***"We Are Still Here!"*** *by John Norwood, a Nanticoke Lenni Lenepe historian.*

77 **Illegitimacy:** In many societies, people born out of wedlock did not have the same rights of inheritance as those within it, and in some societies, even the same civil rights. In the United Kingdom and the United States, as late as the 1960s and in certain social strata even up to today, extramarital birth has carried a social stigma. In previous centuries unwed mothers were forced by social pressure to give their children up for adoption. In other cases extramarital children have been reared by grandparents or married relatives as the "sisters," "brothers" or "cousins" of the unwed mothers. **Cite-**Wikipedia, the free encyclopedia, "***Family Law.***" **Author's *Note:*** *Doc Mc Donald, out of respect for Edie Maye, did not want to officially record an illegitimate birth and death, which would become public record.*

78 ***Author's Note:*** **Hollyford Ice and Coal Company.** *During Tuck's tenure at the Company (1952 – 1959), it was the sole supplier of ice to Mt. Holly and its environs. It also supplied sub stations at Pemberton and Toms River with regular truckload deliveries of 10 tons of 300 lb. blocks of ice. Tuck was one of approximately 15 employees who operated the freezing plant, stocked and defrosted the storage unit and prepared ice for retail sale as blocks, crushed (bagged) and sprayed (for vegetable trucks). The plant maintained several heavy trucks and five or six panel trucks for local delivery. Although refrigerators were fast becoming an essential appliance, many people were still unable to afford one, a major purchase. A 50 cent 50 pound block of ice would last a week in the average icebox. There were at least five regular routes for local deliveries from residences and apartments in downtown Mt. Holly to blueberry picker's shacks east of Pemberton and west to the Centerton Inn (Rancocas). The Company also supplied fuel oil, coal, cold storage and butchering for meats.*

79 **Pawn Shops**. **Ibid. endnote 52.**

PART II

80 **MATS.** The Military Air Transport Service (MATS) was a command of the U.S. Air Force from 1948-1965 shortly after the Air Force became an independent service branch. (1947). It was activated 1 June 1948. MATS was created by consolidating the Air Transport Command and the Naval Air Transport

Service under the control of the newly created United States Air Force (USAF). The first test of the newly created MATS was the Berlin Airlift-- "*OPERATION VITTLES*". The Soviets had blocked all surface transportation in the western part of Berlin. Railroads tracks were destroyed, barges were stopped on the rivers, and highways and roads blocked. The only avenue left was through the air. On June 26, 1948, the airlift began. MATS transports from around the globe began making their way to Germany, including two of the U.S. Navy's air transport squadrons assigned to MATS. This operation would continue for some 15 months until the Soviets lifted the blockade. MATS provided numerous humanitarian airlifts. Until 1965 MATS continued flying, globally offering servicemen free transportation wherever they flew. Cite: MATS: The Story of the Military Air Transport Command, by Stanley Ulannoff, published by the Watts Aerospace Library. Available on http://www.c141heaven.info/dotcom/matsbook_html.

81 **Mediterranean Storm.** ***Author's note:*** *In later years, Tuck had the opportunity to correspond with some of Cholly's shipmates, but only a few recalled this storm and although some verified the illnesses as described by Beersy, none verified the deaths he described. Cholly's alcoholism, combined with a reduced diet may have caused his situation and Beersy may have exaggerated in an attempt to spare Edie Maye's feelings. In any case, the illness and mistreatment in the Army hospital was real; Cholly was very sick when discharged.*

82 **Ribbon Creek.** On April 8, 1956, six Marine Corps recruits drowned in a disciplinary march into Ribbon Creek (Parris Island, SC). The aftermath caused an overhaul of (USMC) basic training. Matthew C. McKeon, the Parris Island drill instructor who received national attention when he was court-martialed after six of his recruits drowned during a disciplinary march into Ribbon Creek on April 8, 1956, has died at the age of 79. Ironically, he died on Veterans Day, Nov. 11, 2004. For days, news of the death of the man whose actions caused an overhaul of Marine Corps basic training – some say the demise of the "Old Corps" – (has) circulated by word of mouth and e-mail throughout the Marine Corps community. McKeon's obituary appeared in the Worcester (Mass.) Telegram & Gazette but without reference to the Ribbon Creek tragedy after the most publicized court martial in Marine Corps history. **Cite-*"Special to the Carolina Morning News,"*** By William H. Whitten, Ridgeland, SC, Nov., 2004.

Author's Note: *The McKeon affair took place barely two years after Tuck left Parris Island. Acts of brutality, such as punches and kicks to the face and body, dry shaving in a trash can while running in place or denial of food and sleep were commonplace at Parris Island; a part of the training. Even at Camp LeJuene, fleet Marines witnessed everyday beatings of "brig rats" in plain sight in the brig's wire-fenced yard, which was next to the mainside movie. Major General Chesty Puller, the most decorated and revered marine of modern times who testified at McKeon's courts-martial, told Tuck personally that the incident was "regrettable, but insufficient reason to crucify McKeon, who was doing only those things that all Drill Instructors do." Puller, who visited the Naval Academy and lunched with the marines of the Class of 1959 on his 1956 retirement tour, said that "the (Marine) Corps* *was changed forever." Marginal swimming instruction was part of the USMC training at the time.*

83 **Joe Blsphk.** ***Author's Note:*** *A character in Al Capp's comic strip, "Lil' Abner," Joe was a resident of Dogpatch who was followed by a raincloud where ever he went, continually rained on and always a recipient of bad luck.*

84 **Chesty Puller in Shanghai**. Puller went to the place where the Chinese were imprisoned, had his men set up two heavy machine gun emplacements, and drew his pistol on the Japanese officer in charge. The Japanese left without their prisoners. Cite-**"The U. S. Marine Corps Story,"** *J. Robert* Moskin, Chapter 2 of "Getting Ready, 1919 to 1941" pg 217. ***Author's Note:*** *The scuttlebutt about Camp Lejuene's brig commander was that he had served with Puller in Shanghai and had met FDR during his presidency. He was regarded as a legendary figure and famous locally for his bulldog, "Chesty."*

85 ***Author's Note: USNA curricula.*** *In 1955, the course of study at Navy was the same for all Midshipmen with the exception of a language elective. On the day that Tuck was sworn in, his schedule for the next four years was already set, even to class rooms in which the subjects were taught, as well as how many Middies were estimated to be bilged out each semester to meet a satisfactory graduation number for the class of 1959, based on experience. In 1957 elective majors were included in the curricula, including marine engineering, mechanical engineering and others. Current midshipmen may select majors from five classifications offering a total of 17 different areas of specialization, and a great deal of help is now offered middies with academic troubles. Navy has slowly been accepted as not only one of the most difficult schools in which to be accepted, but among the top ranked (17th in 2012) academic programs in the country. In 1955 most universities were unwilling to accept Naval Academy work as college credits. The class of 1959 graduated 798 on June 3, 1959. There were 299 non-graduates. The years following '59's graduation saw significant changes at Navy. The introduction of major/minor courses of study made marching to classes impractical, and that practice was abandoned. The Academy instituted verification of freshman equivalent courses from other educational institutions, and hazing practices were tempered. The Navy and Marine Corps memorial stadium was completed and dedicated. The first female Midshipman was graduated with the class of 1980. It was rumored among the class of 1959 that Midshipman W. C. Weber, who had measured the speed of light while a high school student, would receive some advanced instruction in Physics. Weber graduated with the class, went on to Cambridge University and co-authored a book on closed conformal vector fields.*

86 **USNTC/NAPS** –Though the focus of USNTC Bainbridge was recruit training, the Tome School for Boys campus was at the center of the decision to purchase the land and create Bainbridge (Naval Training Center). Hence the Navy sought a use for the school and in the earliest days officers used the school proper. A new purpose was developed in 1943 and 800 men were signed on for the first US Naval Academy Preparatory School program in the history of the US Navy. (Tome) Memorial Hall served as it did years prior, as the classroom facility, while the dormitory buildings of Harrison, Jackson, Madison and Van Buren housed the officer students...The US Navy brought

in Heavyweight Boxing Champion Gene Tunney as Athletic Director to bring in even more recruits, especially to NAPS and the fledgling military football teams, and other sports teams. Tunney was able to recruit such men as Stan Musial, Baseball hall of famer, and Charlie "Choo Choo" Justice, former Washington Redskin, to wear the Commodore uniform. Cite –***"Bainbridge Naval Training Center - Naval Academy Preparatory School or NAPS,"*** Town of Port Deposit, Erika L. Quesenbery, Administrator. From: http://www.bainbridgedevelopment.org. ***Author's Note:*** *By the time the Class of 1955 got there, the four luxurious "President's Mansions" had been absconded by the high ranking brass of USNTC and students were housed in barracks closest to the school and used the Training Center's enlisted mess. NAPS was moved in the 90's to Aquidneck Island, Newport, Rhode Island, where it now shares a campus with Naval War College and the Navy Undersea Warfare School. The Tome School campus, golf course and Naval Training Center, turned back to government control in the 1990's have reverted to their original state: overgrown, unkempt woods and fields.*

87 **Jack Phillips.** The President of the United States takes pride in presenting the Silver Star to Jack W. Phillips (0-77504), Captain, U.S. Marine Corps, for conspicuous gallantry and intrepidity in action while serving with Company G, 2d Battalion, 4th Marines, 3d Marine Division (Rein.), FMF in connection with combat operations against the enemy in the Republic of Vietnam on October 14, 1967. By his courage, aggressive fighting spirit, and steadfast devotion to duty in the face of extreme personal danger, Captain Phillips upheld the highest traditions to the U.S. Marine Corps and the United States Naval Service. He gallantry gave his life for his country. Home Town: Mission, Kansas. *Cite – http://www.togetherweserved.com.* ***Author's Note:*** *Jack and Tuck shared many liberties together, and at Christmas, 1955, they hitchhiked to Jack's home in Mission, KS, from Philadelphia.*

88 ***Author's Note: Navy Football.*** *Contrary to public opinion the military academies are active recruiters for their sports teams. All Navy alumni are encouraged to bring to the attention of the Athletic Department potential candidates for the sports teams. "Blue and Gold" alumni are recruited from alumni at large and coached in how to approach and talk to potential athlete scholars without violating any NCAA ethical regulations. Richard, who had achieved notoriety as a high school football and track star was approached by Navy personnel after becoming a marine, and then funneled into the NAPS track. Bob Reifsnyder, who gained All-America status at Navy, was recruited by alumni. While at Navy, Paul Brown visited the academy and attempted to lure Bob into resigning and joining his Cleveland Browns professional football team.*

89 **CEEB.** In the beginning, the CEEB (College Entrance Examination Board) was composed entirely of eastern colleges, thirty-five of which agreed to accept the board's tests in lieu of their own entrance examinations. The first

CEEB examinations—essay tests in chemistry, English, French, German, Greek, history, Latin, mathematics, and physics—were offered during the week of June 17, 1901, at sixty-seven locations in the United States and two in Europe. The first SAT was taken in 1926 by 8,040 college applicants, but for many years, it remained less popular than the CEEB's traditional essay examinations. That changed in 1942, when war intervened...In that year Princeton, Harvard, and Yale shifted to a wartime year round calendar of instruction. Currently, two college entrance exams are used for admissions, college placement, and scholarships: the SAT Reasoning Test (SAT) and the ACT. Cite–***Testing Testing: Social Consequences of the Examined Life.*** By Hanson, F. Allan, Berkeley, University of California Press, 1993.

90 **Paul Troast.** In 1953 Troast won the Republican nomination for Governor of New Jersey. Time Magazine wrote "county bosses... pushed him through a bitter, party-splitting primary last April. Troast, with no political experience, was known principally for his chairmanship of the commission that built the $220 million New Jersey Turnpike...Troast suffered his roundest wallop early in October, when newspapers broke the story that he (Troast) had asked New York's Tom Dewey to commute the sentence of Labor Extortionist Joey Fay". Seven major candidates had run in the primary, with Troast beating Malcolm Forbes by 47,000 votes. Initially favored, he lost to Robert B. Meyner by 154,000 votes. **(Cite 1)** He (Meyner) disclosed that his Republican opponent in 1953, Paul T. Troast, a wealthy building contractor, had written to Gov. Thomas E. Dewey of New York urging clemency for a labor racketeer, Joseph Fay, then in a New York prison. **(Cite 2)**- NEW JERSEY'S BIGGEST UPSET. The biggest surprise of the day came in New Jersey where the Democrats won the governorship for the first time in 10 years and added another fillip to their jubilation by sending a Democrat to Congress from a normally heavy Republican district. Democrat Robert B. Meyner, a country lawyer, defeated Republican Paul Troast in the gubernatorial contest by a vote of 959,669 to 805,750 just a year after Eisenhower swept the state by a 350,000 plurality...Political strategists saw possibly even greater significance in the upset victory scored by Democrat Harrison A. Williams, Jr. who defeated Republican George F. Hatfield by about 2,000 votes in the state's Sixth Congressional District, where a Republican won by 54.000 votes in 1952. **(Cite 3)** Williams, as a senior senator was later snared by the FBI in the famous Abscam entrapment. **(Cite 4)** *Cite 1*-**Time Magazine,** November 24, 1958 Cover story. *Cite 2*-***"Robert B. Meyner Is Dead at 81; Flamboyant New Jersey Governor,"*** By Wayne King, New York Times, Published: May 29, 1990. *Cite 3*-Pittsburgh Post-Gazette, November 5, 1953. Cite 4-**Gangbusters,** the Destruction of America's Last Great Mafia Dynasty, by Earnest Volkman, Published by Avon Books, 1998.

91 **Harold J. Adonis,** formerly an executive clerk to Governor Driscoll was named by a Bergen County Grand Jury for receiving a $228,000 bribe fund from racketeers in Fort Lee, Lodi and Cliffside Park (NJ). The funds were to induce state and local officials to cripple an investigation into gambling. Adonis has been overseas since 1949. Named with Adonis were his brother, Andrew, Willie Moretti (now deceased) and four John Does (Source dated January 5, 1960). ***(Cite 1). Author's Note: Gambling Renaissance.*** *One*

and two room brothel/casinos like the one in North Wildwood where Tuck stayed as a child were scheduled for most of the small towns, but larger municipalities had contracted with Sal for the use of Town Hall meeting rooms and other public spaces. Troast's success with the NJ Turnpike contract was the result of the mob ensuring that there would be no trouble with the unions. It appears that in return, he would attempt to maneuver a pardon for Joey Fey, a convicted Union racketeer and he would "look the other way" regarding gambling when elected Governor. Willie Moretti is named in some reports as the gangster who held a pistol to Tommy Dorsey's head to persuade him to release Frank Sinatra from his contract ***(Cite 2).*** *Cite 1-****"Special to The New York Times,"*** *Jan 5, 1960. Cite 2-http://www.AmericanMafiaHistory.com, et.al, re: "Willie Moretti"*

92 **Anacostia Naval Air Station** was merged with Bolling Air Force base in 1962 to JBAB (Joint Base Anascostia and Bolling). In the early 50's Anacostia hosted 11 different navy schools and research labs as well as naval reserve training squadrons. The navy accredits the facility to the discovery of radar in the 1930's when radio scientists noticed that large sailing ship anchored in the adjacent Anacostia River was interfering with radio transmissions. Due to its proximity to Reagan Airport and other airfields in the capitol, its runways were removed and the facility became a rotary wing airfield facility, hosting Marine One, the squadron of personal helicopters for the President. Cite – http://www.freeman.com/DC/airfields and http://www.DCmilitary.com

93 **Fixed Races.** Finally, (in 1976) it was alleged that certain individuals, including Winter, Martorano, James DeMetri, Charles DeMetri, and (Tony) Ciulla purchased a race horse, Spread The Word, for approximately $30,000, with the purpose of having the jockey hold it back so that it would finish poorly in several races; when the odds were high enough, it was to be entered in a race with inferior horses and allowed to win. To effectuate the scheme, several individuals would purchase large quantities of tickets on the fixed races. Others, including Winter, would make telephone calls in interstate commerce and discuss wagering information on those races. Winter, Martorano, Ciulla, and others drew up lists of New England independent bookmakers whom the group would cheat by betting with them on races the group had fixed, and the Las Vegas members of the enterprise, including Price and Goldenberg, would cheat Las Vegas independent bookmakers in the same way. Cite-***United States of America, Appellee, v. Howard T. Winter, (et.al.) Appellant***, United States Court of Appeals, First Circuit. ***Author's Note:*** *Tony Ciulla spent most of his adult life fixing races from the east to the west coast, coordinating his fixes with gangsters, bookies and race books across the country. Sal's involvement and explanations to Cholly in the 50's are a testament as to how long the gangsters got away with manipulating the biggest and best tracks in the country. This Cite, a federal criminal complaint in 1974, only addresses one particular scam, while fixing was occurring on a regular basis at many tracks, made possible by the slave-like conditions under which jockeys worked without fair payment or any semblance of job security or insurance against injury.*

94 **Serapis Flag.** At seven in the evening the *Bon Homme Richard* (Jones' ship; The Poor Richard) closed with the *Serapis,* and began one of the

most desperate conflicts on record. After a few broadsides they fouled and lay side by side until the fight was over. The *Serapis* let go an anchor to swing clear, but Jones lashed the two ships together to deprive the enemy of the advantage of his superior battery and sail power, and to prevent his retreat. Two of the *Richard's* eighteens had burst at the first fire, blowing up the deck and many of their crews. The fire of the *Serapis* silenced her opponent's main-deck battery, and crashed through her sides. Jones kept on fighting with a few light guns on the spar-deck, and musketry in the tops. A hand-grenade that was dropped from the main-yard of the *Richard* down a hatchway in the *Serapis* caused a terrible explosion on the lower deck. Jones drove back a boarding party, and the *Scarborough* struck her flag at half past ten at night. Each ship had nearly half her men killed or wounded...Benjamin Franklin commended "the sturdy, cool, and determined bravery" which Jones displayed in this action, and the victor was received with enthusiasm in France. Cite-Adapted from ***Appletons' Cyclopaedia of American Biography,*** **vol. 3.** New York, D. Appleton and Company, 1887. [See "Jones, John Paul," pp. 467-469.] ***Author's Note:*** *Jones, responding to Pearson's demand to surrender, replied, "I have not yet begun to fight!" The actual flag, which has red, white and blue stripes, hangs in Memorial Hall at USNA and is the flag under which Tuck was sworn and many Midshipmen are still sworn into the United States Navy.*

95 **Defectors.** (2) Former fleet sailors that disenroll from the Naval Academy/NAPS for reasons other than acceptance of a commission or a physical disability will revert to the enlisted status held immediately prior to entry to the Naval Academy/NAPS. Enlisted members will be required to complete the period of service for which they originally enlisted, and for which they have an obligation (any extension or reenlistment). Time served as a midshipman (Naval Academy) or midshipman candidate (NAPS) will be counted as time served under the original enlistment or period of obligated service. Cite- **OPNAVINST, Part 8(b) 2. Service Obligation.** U. S. Navy Operating Instructions for USNA and NAPS. ***Author's Note:*** *This regulation was suggested by Congressional action and appeared in Navy regulations after the defections from the NAPS class of 1955.*

96 **Bracing Up. Author's Note:** The other unfortunate Plebe who suffered with Tuck this early, but routine example of upper class harassment was Buddy Wellborn, whose father was an admiral. Buddy went on to become a class leader and received accolades for his play at fullback in his junior year, when Navy won the Cotton Bowl.

97 **IX-48: HIGHLAND LIGHT.** The Naval Academy took possession of the 68-foot cutter-rigged sloop on 19 Oct. 1940 as a donation from the estate of Dudley F. Wolfe, who had died trying to climb Mount K-2 in the Himalayas. She had been designed by Paine, Belknap & Skene and built in 1931 by George Lawley & Son of Neponset, Mass. The yacht arrived at the Academy on 26 Oct. 1940. On 17 March 1941 CNO recommended that she be designated "Unclassified" and retain her name. On 10 May 1941 BuShips assigned the symbol IX-48 to the vessel. She became the Academy's leading racing yacht and participated in ten Newport to Bermuda races between 1946 and 1964, by which time she was thoroughly outclassed by newer yachts. She

was sold in 1968 following the investigation of the faltering sailing program at the Naval Academy by the Fales Committee in the mid-1960s. Purchased by Anthony O. Mignano of Los Angeles, she became the passenger craft HIGHLAND LIGHT and was still in service in 1972. Cite-**USN BuShips.** ***Author's Note:*** *The big cutter eventually was outclassed, but not by much. Jacque Naveiux, former NAPS marine and midshipman crew member, reported in January, 2013 that "Jack Phillips, Dick Baldwin and I were the nucleus of the racing crew for three years on the Highland Light. She held the Bermuda race record from 1932 until 1956. The new record was set by Bolero which only beat the Highland Light record by an hour and twenty minutes. Our sailing coach was a math professor, Jim Abbott."*

98 **Alexander Haig.** *(b. Philadelphia, 2 Dec. 1924; d. Baltimore, MD, 20 Feb. 2010)* *US; General US army 1973 – 1979, Supreme Allied Commander Europe 1974 – 1979, White House Chief of Staff 1973 – 1974, Secretary of State 1981 – 1982* Haig was educated at West Point and graduated MA from Georgetown University, 1961. He joined the US army in 1947, serving in Korea 1950 – 1951 and Vietnam 1966 –1967. In 1973, promoted to the rank of General, he became Vice-Chief of Staff US Army Washington and worked as a junior adviser to Dr. Kissinger in the National Security Council. This latter post brought Haig to the attention of President Nixon, who appointed him White House Chief of Staff. After Nixon's resignation Haig returned to military duties as Supreme Allied Commander in Europe, 1974 – 1979. Retiring from active service in 1979, he took up a career in private consultancy. Cite-*Inner Circles: How America Changed the World, A Memoir,* Haig, Alexander M. Jr., with Charles McCarry, Published by Warner Books, New York, 1992. ***Author's Note:*** *Haig was Company advisor to the 11th Company at USNA in 1956. Naval officers on a 'flag' track were also sometimes assigned to USMA (West Point) in the same role. Cite-**USNA Lucky Bag, 1956, 11th Company.***

99 **Doris Miller.** Holder of the Navy Cross for outstanding bravery at Pearl Harbor, Hawaii, Ship's Cook Third Class Doris (Dorie) Miller was one of the earliest American heroes of World War II. Although at the time the U.S. Navy did not offer African Americans opportunities to rise above the menial labor of the mess hall, Miller took advantage of the chance fate gave him to distinguish himself in battle. But two years after his heroism at Pearl Harbor, he lost his life aboard the USS Liscome Bay in the Gilbert Islands in November of 1943. In addition to the Navy Cross, Miller was granted several other honors, including the Purple Heart Medal, the American Defense Service Medal, the Fleet Clasp, the Asiatic-Pacific Campaign Medal, and the World War II Victory Medal. On June 30, 1973, the USS Doris Miller, a frigate, was commissioned in his honor. In 2001, Academy Award winner, Cuba Gooding, Jr. played Miller in the film 'Pearl Harbor.' Cite-http://www.*nationalgeographic.com/usn/doris-miller.*

100 **Wes Phenegar.** The President of the United States takes pride in presenting the DISTINGUISHED

FLYING CROSS posthumously to CAPTAIN WESLEY R. PHENEGAR, JR. USMC. For service as set forth in the following CITATION: For heroism and extraordinary achievement while participating in aerial flight as Pilot of an A4E jet aircraft while attached to Headquarters and Maintenance Squadron 12 and flying with Marine Attack Squadron 223 in the Republic of Vietnam. On the morning of 13 August 1967, Captain Phenegar was scrambled from the "Hot Pad" as the leader of a two-plane flight with the assigned mission of providing emergency close air support for embattled Marines twenty miles northwest of Chu Lai. Approximately five minutes after becoming airborne, Captain Phenegar notified his wingman that he had developed engine problems and would be returning to Chu Lai. Immediately turning for home, he skillfully maneuvered his aircraft into position for a low altitude precautionary approach. While approximately five miles from the field, however, Captain Phenegar notified Chu Lai tower that his engine had failed completely and that he was planning to eject. With complete disregard for his own personal safety, he unhesitatingly directed his aircraft away from the congested Chu Lai airfield complex, all the while losing precious altitude at an alarming rate. Attempting unsuccessfully to eject, he was immediately aware of the severity of his situation. Committed now to a barely controllable forced "dead stick" landing, and realizing full well the hazard his combat loaded aircraft presented to the inhabitants of Sam Hai Hamlet which lay directly in his path, Captain Phenegar, exhibiting outstanding heroism and iron determination, maneuvered his disabled aircraft away from the populated area scant seconds before impact, saving countless innocent lives. Captain Phenegar's dauntless courage, expert aeronautical skill, and selfless devotion to duty reflected great credit upon himself and upheld the highest traditions of the Marine Corps and the United States Naval Service. He gallantly gave his life for his country. For the President, Paul R. Ignatius Secretary of the Navy. Cite-*http://www.Togetherweserved.com.* ***Author's Note:*** *Wes befriended Tuck as a Plebe and assisted him in his studies, enabling him to complete Plebe year. Both made their respective wrestling teams; Wes varsity,and Tuck the plebe team, they often practiced together and pushed each other to their limits.*

101 **Edgar Fahs Smith** was born in York, Pennsylvania and earned his college degree at Pennsylvania College at Gettysburg (now Gettysburg College) in 1874. He received his Ph.D. under Friedrich Wöhler at the University of Gottingen in 1876. Smith then returned to the United States and, in time, became associated with the University of Pennsylvania, as a professor of chemistry (1888-1911), as vice-provost (1899-1911) and then as provost (1911-1920). Smith's scientific research covered the fields of electrochemistry, the determination of atomic weights, and the rare-earth elements. Smith was a co-founder of the American Chemical Society's History of Chemistry division. He served three times as president of the American Chemical Society and was president of the American Philosophical Society (1902–1908) and the History of Science Society (1928). In 1898 Smith was elected to the National Academy of Sciences. Cite-***"The Nine Lives of Edgar Fahs Smith,"*** The Schoenberg Center for Electronic Text and Image, University of Pennsylvania Libraries. ***Author's Note:*** *Among his voluminous writings, Smith expounded*

on a Stream of Consciousness Philosophy (which preceded Dewey's) in a monograph, which was included in the Academy's collection and was the subject of Tuck's paper.

102 **Ibid endnote 95. Highland Light.**

103 ***Author's Note: Summer Cruise.*** *The Youngster class (Midshipmen entering their second year) and the First class (Midshipmen entering their last year) are divided among the ships assigned for a two month cruise. The ships include surface warfare ships: battleships, cruisers, and destroyers. In 1956 two task forces were required to accommodate the 700+ Midshipmen, each led by an Iowa Class battleship with 10 support ships. The other two classes of Midshipmen are divided into two groups: entering plebes attend plebe summer at USNA, midshipmen entering their third year were assigned to Marine Corps training units at USMC schools, submariner training in fleet boats or at Submarine School, Newport, Rhode Island, or aircraft operations on a fleet carrier. Data*: **Battleship New Jersey, an Illustrated History,** Paul Stillwell, The Naval Institute Press, Annapolis, MD, 1986, ISBN 0-87021-029-7.

104 **Ibid. endnote 101. USS New Jersey. *Author's Note:****This configuration (described by Tuck) was the last that was most true to Jersey's original design, which was significantly altered after her first decommissioning on 30 June, 1948. Mothballed at the Brooklyn Navy Yard, she was recommissioned in November, 1950 and served gallantly in the Korean theater until decommissioning in August, 1957, which occurred only a year after discharging Tuck and his group of Midshipmen in Norfolk. Further resurrections, each one involving tear down of her internal systems and replacement of engineering and armaments with up-to-date electronics, RADAR and weaponry, occurred in April 1968 and December 1982, until her retirement to a permanent berth in Camden, NJ. in September, 1999, the most decorated ship in the U.S. Navy. The heart of the original battleship, the 16 inch rifles and main propulsion units, remained intact with new aiming electronics throughout all of the renovations. Data from* **Battleship New Jersey, an Illustrated History,** by Paul Stillwell, **Ibid. endnotes 101,102.**

105 **Ibid. endnotes 101. 102. *USS New Jersey. Author's Note:*** *When the ship retired to her Camden, NJ berth, Tuck went aboard and found his way to the starboard inboard shaft alley, no mean feat since the entire propulsion spaces had been reconfigured. He was disappointed to find the oaken oil lubricated bearing blocks gone, where he had carved his initials in 1956, and the shaft now resting in new more durable inorganic bearings. Also missing was the grilled bridge on the fourth deck level which crossed above the open engine room spaces (comprised of the eight boilers and four turbines and auxiliary machinery). He was able to find number 2 engine room, where he had replaced injectors in a hot tub (boiler) while underway. His topside battle station, a gun control turret controlling 5 "quads" of 40 millimeter Bofers guns in gun tubs in the port, after quarter had been removed along with his aiming radar turret in the second renovation for Jersey's participation in the Vietnam War. In preparation as a museum ship, his sleeping quarters on the main deck level had been made into a display space. Data from Author's notes and* ***The Battleship New Jersey, From Birth to Berth,*** *by Carol Comega,*

published by Pediment Publishing Company, a division of the Pediment Group, Canada and the Courier Post Newspaper, Camden, NJ.

106 **Blue Whales.** The blue whale is the largest animal that ever lived on earth. It is also the loudest animal on earth. These enormous mammals eat tiny organisms, like plankton and krill, which they sieve through baleen. They live in pods (small groups), but are most often seen in pairs. These gray-blue whales have 2 blowholes and a 2-1/4 inch (5-30 cm) thick layer of blubber. Blue whales are rorqual whales, whales that have pleated throat grooves that allow their throat to expand during the huge intake of water during filter feeding. Blue whales have 50-70 throat grooves that run from the throat to mid-body. Their young are born after a one year gestation period and are usually about 25 feet in length. Females are larger than the males and have been known to reach 99 feet in length and live up to 90 years. Cite-***The Lives of Whales and Dolphins***, Richard C. Connor and Dawn Micklethwaite Peterson, Henry Holt & Company, 1994, ISBN 0-8050-1950-2.

107 **Americans in the U.K.** Two million American soldiers and airmen passed through Great Britain during the war. Many brits met by Midshipmen on the streets in 1956 harbored ill feelings towards the Americans, and some Mids were spat on and pelted with trash. However, many citizens were friendly. The country that had imported 50 billion tons of food annually was reduced by German U Boat activity to an average of 12 billion tons, causing strict rationing beginning in 1940 and not lifted until 1954, only two years prior to New Jersey's 1956 visit. 93,000 British civilians and nearly a half million servicemen (about the same number of servicemen as the U.S.) were killed during WWII. During the rationing, one of the most popular items traded on the black market was SPAM, brought to Britain by U.S. soldiers. Yet the American servicemen who arrived in Britain in preparation for the Normandy landings became renowned for more than their dubious canned meat. The English comedian Tommy Trinder famously referred to them as: "overpaid, oversexed and over here." ***Author's Note:*** *After spending time in Oslo, Norway, which was sparkling clean and populated with friendly people, Tuck's impression of London was that it was very dirty and overpopulated with political activists and prostitutes,* data from **The U.S. Marine Corps Story, Third Revised Edition,** by J. Robert Moskin.

108 **VAMARIE,** the IX-47: The 72-foot main trysail ketch was presented to the Naval Academy by Vadim S. Makaroff and accepted 11 Nov 1936. She had been designed by Jasper Morgan of Cox & Stephens, built in 1933 by Rasmussen in Lemwerder (Bremen), Germany, and named for Vadim and his wife Marie. Her original auxiliary power plant consisted of a wooden airplane propeller swung on a hub on the mizzenmast and connected by V-belts to a gasoline engine mounted on deck. (The Navy later fitted a conventional screw propeller.) The yacht was listed by BuShips as an unnumbered District Craft - Unclassified (YX) She was lost in Hurricane Betsy on 13 Sept 56 when her moorings in Annapolis harbor parted and she was pounded by a tug against a quay wall to leeward in the mouth of the Severn River. The damaged wreck was declared excess and demolished by 31 Jan 56. ***Author's Note:*** *Corrected data is underlined. BuShips and Navy Log each report Vamarie lost in 1954 in hurricane Hazel, but Tuck watched*

*her destruction from the Annapolis seawall during hurricane Betsy in August of 1956. Cite-**US Navy BuShips.***

109 **Ibid. endnote 100. Wes Phenegar.**

110 **Ribbon Creek.** In the year after the Parris Island "death march," 197 Drill Instructors were relieved for a variety of causes, and an emotional battle raged between Marine generals and many veteran officers and noncoms. Under public and Congressional pressure, the Marine Corps ordered an end to "hazing and maltreatment" of recruits. Cite-**The U.S. Marine Corps Story**, Part VII, Tumultuous Times 1953 – 1975, Chapter 2, page 597. ***Author's Note:*** *As a result of his trial, Sgt. McKeon spent 10 days in the brig, was reduced to private and dishonorably discharged. His original sentence had been for one year's imprisonment. It appeared that SSgt. Flowers was among those drill instructors who were disciplined as a result of the Ribbon Creek incident.*

111 ***Author's Note: College Credit transfer.*** *Tuck applied to The Philadelphia Museum School of Art, Drexel University, Glassboro University and Rutgers University, Camden upon returning home from USNA, and was told by all that absolutely no credits would be given for any of his Plebe (freshman) year academic work at Navy, regardless of his grades in the subjects (which were all passing). It was erroneously accepted in academia at the time that both Navy and West Point offered course work that was barely high school level and that the schools' regimens, requiring great memorization of facts and physical activity were substandard. The schools inexplicably were thought to be merely extensions of boot camps by college admission boards. Tuck's experience in civilian colleges after Navy (he attended four in the next 13 years) demonstrated exactly the opposite; the course content, loads and requirements were extremely easy compared to those at the USNA.*

112 **Sputnik.** History changed on October 4, 1957, when the Soviet Union successfully launched Sputnik I. The world's first artificial satellite was about the size of a beach ball (58 cm. or 22.8 inches in diameter), weighed only 83.6 kg. or 183.9 pounds, and took about 98 minutes to orbit the Earth on its elliptical path, emitting a beep signal every second. While the Sputnik launch was a single event, it marked the start of the space age and the U.S.-U.S.S.R space race. Cite–**http://www.History.NASA.com.**

113 **Ibid endnote 61. One Eyed Irving.**

114 **Glen Canyon Dam.** In 1957, (The Bureau of) Reclamation constructed a government camp close to the dam site in northeastern Arizona to house construction workers and their families and to provide community services. This community was later called Page in honor of Reclamation Commissioner John C. Page. (The Bureau of) Reclamation managed the community of Page during and after construction of the dam until the town was transferred to private ownership pursuant to the 1974 legislation authorizing incorporation. Page became an incorporated town on March 1, 1975. In order to construct the dam, the Colorado River had to be channeled around the site. With the river diverted, crews began work to excavate to the canyon's bedrock for the dam's foundation, and concrete placement began in June 1960. Work continued 24 hours a day until on September 13, 1963, (when) the last of over 400,000 buckets of concrete was placed. Glen

Canyon Dam emerged from bedrock incrementally, reaching a full height of 710 feet. The dam began impounding water in March 1963 when the diversion tunnels were closed and Lake Powell was born. It took 17 years for Lake Powell to completely fill for the first time. On June 22, 1980, Lake Powell reached elevation 3,700 feet, with a total capacity of over 26 million acre-feet. Cite-U.S. Department of Interior, U.S. Bureau of Reclamation, ***"Glen Canyon Dam"*** on http://www.USBR.gov.

115 **Page Casino.** A routine application to use the back room of a Page bar as a "social club" has exposed a complex fraud scheme that involved a wild attempt to install wide open gambling in Page with the perpetrators having the "bought blessing" of public officials, Cocominino County Attorney Lawrence T. Wren revealed today. The result, Wren said, is that three men—two New Jerseyans and a Washington, D.C. attorney—have been charged with felony fraud in a criminal complaint filed with Justice of the Peace James F. Brierly, and a cache of dismantled gambling equipment, found in the back room of Danny's Lounge at Page has been shipped back to Las Vegas, under the watchful eyes of the Federal Bureau of Investigation. The three charged with obtaining $7,500 under false pretenses—Wren said the case actually involved a total of $17,500—are Eli Newmark, 63, and (Salvatore Falconetti), 45, of New Jersey and attorney George Mc Grath, 51, of Washington, D. C. They are accused in two counts of defrauding Ray and Polly Carson of Las Vegas through fraudulent negotiations for the sale of the Page club at Page, which in fact had not been put up for sale by its owner, Lloyd Porter, at that time.

116 The Carsons, Wren said, have admitted being the ones who moved the store of assorted gambling equipment to Page and who "contemplated setting up a gambling operation there." He said they claimed they were assured that "local, state and Bureau of Reclamation officials and others up to and including Sen. (Carl) Heyden had been bought off," Wren added. However, Wren said, "absolutely no official has been even approached on the matter to my knowledge, and we have no evidence whatsoever that this claim that officials were 'bought off' is anything but spurious" Newmark is under the jurisdiction of New Jersey authorities and will have an extradition hearing in Trenton on Friday. Deputy Sheriff William Steele of Sedona is flying to the east coast this week to represent Arizona at the hearing...The Carsons said that they were informed "that everything was ready to go and the public officials had been bought off," Wren added. Wren said that when he heard the Carson's story, and after receiving the call from USBR officials, he notified the FBI which checked the shipment of gambling equipment from Page over the state line and back to Las Vegas. Wren said the Carsons told him the original idea broached by the defendants had been for them to buy the Page Club for legitimate purposes, but after the sale deal fell through, they brought up the gambling proposition at Danny's Lounge. Wren said that the gambling equipment found in Danny's back room was "in pieces" and consisted of various types of gaming apparatus, including craps tables. Cite-***"GAMING PLANS IN PAGE BARED,"*** By William Hoyt, From the Arizona Daily Sun, Wednesday, May 10, 1961. ***Author's Note:*** *Mob aliases abounded in Sal's Arizona: Tony Marinella, Sal's long time partner became "Blackjack Jones,"*

Ray Carson was introduced to Tuck as Mr. Paul, "The Oklahoma Kid," and of course, "One Eye Irving" was really Eli Newmark. According to Sal, he had distributed nearly $100,000 into the eager hands of the Senator and his flunkies, including the prosecutors and lawmen of several Counties. Tuck had no reason not to believe him. It was all about the whores brought in by the Kid and Blackjack. The entire text of the newspaper coverage of the event has been redacted here, since the length and complexity of the cover story supplied the press was overwhelming. The fraud story was created by USBR authorities with the cooperation of Ray Carson and his wife, who were not charged. The "disassembled gaming equipment" was in full operation on the night that Tuck visited Danny's Lounge. It is significant that Page was not even a municipality under Arizona law until 1975 (See 37-3). It was part of the dam project, administered entirely by USBR officials, all federal employees.

117 ***Author's Note: A Casino near a new dam.*** *The similarities of the attempted casino at Glen Canyon Dam to Tough Tony Cornero's casino ventures in Las Vegas (The Meadows Club on the road from the then new Boulder Dam) are probably coincidental, but remarkable. See endnote 112.*

118 **Gambling in Mississippi:** By 1932, the Isle of Caprice Resort, which featured a full blown casino three miles offshore in the Gulf of Mexico, was completely submerged, defeated by the shifting sands and tides of the Mississippi delta. Along the Mississippi Gulf Coast legal gambling continued at hotels such as the Pine Hills, the Edgewater Gulf, the Tivoli, the Buena Vista, and the White House. These hotels and many smaller establishments offered slot machines for their guests, along with other activities such as dancing and golfing...Gambling devices were more prevalent along the Gulf Coast and in Mississippi River towns, where gambling had historically existed, than in other sections of the state. Yet, elsewhere in the inland counties of Mississippi, road houses supplied back room gambling activity. Road houses visited by white people were generally called "honky-tonks," and those visited by blacks were called "juke joints." Because gambling was so profitable, the Broadwater Beach Hotel was built in 1938 specifically to cater to out-of-state and Mississippi gamblers who could afford to gamble. Throughout the 1940s and 1950s, gambling expanded and by 1950, the opening of U.S. Highway 90, the first four-lane super highway, boosted travel along the Coast, bringing In nightclubs lining Highway 90, and entertainers such as Elvis Presley, Jayne Mansfield, Andy Griffin, and Hank Williams Sr. Gambling and entertainment were everywhere along "The Strip." Cite- ***"Gambling in Mississippi," in Mississippi Encyclopedia, Center for Southern Studies,*** by Deanne S. Nuwer, University of Mississippi, Oxford, Mississippi, 2008.

119 **Ibid. endnote 112. Glen Canyon Dam.**

120 ***Author's Note: Page Casino.*** *Sal described to Tuck how he had paid off necessary politicians and USBR officials one by one when he (Tuck) first arrived in Phoenix. Several attorneys and USBR officials had traveled to Phoenix and met him at his motel for that purpose, according to Sal. A prerequisite to all payoffs to which Sal agreed was that no prostitutes would be permitted. Page was a tight knit and highly religious community. The continued emphasis on this aspect (of officials bought off) of the "conspiracy"*

by the Arizona lawyers and Police convinced Tuck that Sal had been telling the truth about the affair. ***See endnote 113.***

121 **Dragnet.** "We believe that this attempt to install gambling in Page was used merely as an inticement for a confidence game," he (Wren) added. At the moment, Wren said, Newmark is under the jurisdiction of New Jersey authorities and will have an extradition hearing in Trenton on Friday. Deputy Sheriff William Steele of Sedona is flying to the east coast this week to represent Arizona at the hearing. Newmark, Wren added, was fined $1,000 only last April 15 in New Jersey's Salem County Court for attempting to bribe a New Jersey state legislator to allow him to conduct gambling operations in Salem County. Newmark's record also includes a $25,000 fine 23 years ago, for violating federal liquor laws. Mc Grath, Wren said, waived a preliminary hearing here this morning through his local attorney, Dan Sloops, before Judge Brierly and has been released on his own recognizance. (Falconetti's) whereabouts are presently unknown, Wren added, although a bulletin on him has been sent out across the country. See **endnote 113.** *Cite -"****GAMING PLANS IN PAGE BARED,****"* By William Hoyt, From the Arizona Daily Sun, Wednesday, May 10, 1961. ***Author's Note*** *- Eight years later, Director Don Siegal and Clint Eastwood coincidentally brought to the screen the story of an Arizona Deputy Sheriff Coogan traveling east to New York to extradite fugitive prisoner Jimmy Ringerman in "Coogan's Bluff."*

122 **Texas Savvy.** ***Author's Note:*** *The car Tuck was driving was the first Mini Cooper (then called the Austin - Cooper, now called the Mini) sold on the east coast of the U.S., and featured the earliest front wheel drive integrated engine-transmission package offered to the U.S. driving public (the lone exceptions being the Cadillac Eldorado and the Cord). The mechanic at the Sweetwater, Texas, City Garage described it as "nothing more than Farmall tractor engine turned sideways" and diagnosed and performed a $28 valve job as soon as he got the parts from nearby Fort Worth.*

123 **Richard Dagampat**. Originally from the Hawaiian Islands, Dag came to the silver shores of the Severn after serving two years in the USMC. A dazzling pigskin carrier, it was not very long before he won the reputation as "Navy's scampering little fullback." His modesty, radiant personality, quick wittedness and broad smile, combined with his talent on the gridiron, landed him the job of captain of Navy's outstanding football team. A great guy both on and off the field, Dick's next touchdown may very well be made in a Navy jet. RICHARD M. DAGAMPAT Twelfth Company, Los Angeles.

Cite–"The Lucky Bag," *U.S. Naval Academy yearbook, 1959.* ***Author's Note:*** *This description from the USNA yearbook, projects Dag as a Navy jet pilot like his brother, a U.S. Air Force Captain, but Richard, although a phenomenal athlete, was unnerved by high speed aerobatic flight, and frustrated at the USMC's insistence that he continue playing football at Quantico, gave up his USMC commission and enrolled in the Air Force, where in spite of giving up his numbered placement in the hierarchy of USN*

officer rankdom, he enjoyed a successful career in administration and retired as an Air Force Colonel with a PhD.

124 **Pilonidal cysts**. Excessive pressure or repetitive trauma to the sacrococcygeal area is thought to predispose individuals to develop the cyst or to irritate an already existing pilonidal cyst. Cite–http://www.medicinehealth.com

125 ***DCSC. Author's Note:*** *The U.S. Army's Defense Construction and Supply Command, moved in the 1970's to St. Louis, MO. The Command prepared all of the parts, operations and instruction publications (manuals) for all items used by Army personnel.*

126 ***Florida Aircraft Plant. Author's Note:*** *The seeds were planted for an incursion of aircraft manufacturing by Howard Hughes and gave the phony Lanier Paraplane credibility. In 1956, Del Webb, the Nevada casino entrepreneur announced in a public press release in Miami that "the Howard Hughes Medical Institute has already made its beginning in Florida. It recently acquired part of the Richmond Naval Air Station (south of Miami)... and the medical institute was only the start of Hughes' program in Florida. Coming next would be a huge aircraft manufacturing plant-at a site to be selected-employing thousands of people" Cite –* ***Miami News****, April 9,1956.*

127 **Lanier Paraplane.** Prototype aircraft were built and flown, even at the Paris Air Show. The plane took off and landed at 25 mph but had a top speed and range equal to other light planes. The secret was in the wing design, which featured controllable openings in the topside of the wing that created vacuum spaces in flight, lifting the airplane. Combined with forward wing slots and very large flaps, the effect was a very slow and stable STOL aircraft, which for unknown reasons, never caught on with the flying public. A negative report circulated by Princeton engineers stated the plane had very high drag coefficients. **Sources.** Google **"Lanier Paraplane" (**http://www.Rexresearch.com**)** for pictures and specifications,and ***"Flight Tests of Lanier Paraplane, Aeronautical Report,"*** James Forrestal Research Center, Princeton University, NJ by C. D. Perkins, January, 1952.

128 **Mary Roebling.** (1905-1994) was the first woman in the United States to serve as president of a major commercial bank, the Trenton Trust Company, and the first female governor of the American Stock Exchange. Apart from her impressive business career, Roebling promoted equal rights for women, served as a civilian advisor to the military, and assisted numerous charitable and non-profit organizations in her native Trenton. Cite-***The Mary Roebling Papers,*** in Special Collections and University Archives, Rutgers University Libraries, New Brunswick, NJ ***Author's note:*** *Mary's second husband was Siegfried Roebling, whose family had long been prominent in engineering and cable manufacturing. He was a great-grandson of John A. Roebling, who designed the Brooklyn Bridge, and a grandson of Col. Washington A. Roebling, who completed its construction.*

129 **Beau Rivage Palace.** The Hotel Beau Rivage Palace in Lausanne, Switzerland is one of the most prestigious luxury hotels of the world. Located in Ouchy on the shores of Lake Geneva, it has been classed as one of the 50 best hotels in the world by the American Association of Travel Editors and the Légion d'Honneur du Voyage, and is regularly ranked among the top

hotels in Switzerland by several specialized publications. In 1923 the Treaty of Lausanne was signed at the Beau-Rivage Palace. In 2010, readers of Condé Nast Traveler judged the opulent Beau-Rivage Palace--where Lord Byron once stayed--the number two hotel in northern Europe. Cite-***The Conde Naste Traveler Book, 12 Edition***, Published by Penguin Books (USA) 2012, ISBN 13 978-0143112617.

130 **Swiss military service.** Military service is compulsory for every male Swiss. There is no civil service to substitute armed service (this was refused two times in a vote). Every male Swiss citizen has to go to the army unless physically or mentally handicapped or unless he can "prove" to a jury of officers that he has sound religious reasons for refusing to do service (Barras Law). Every soldier keeps his military outfit, his weapon, and war ammunition at home at all times. The ammunition is sealed. The weapon can be used for compulsory and voluntary shooting exercises, which are quite popular (also drawing large female participation). The ammunition shall only be opened in case of war. Cite-http://**stason.org/TULARC**/travel/swiss-switzerland/3-2-1-Switzerland-Militaryservice.html.

131 ***Author's Note: Virginia Hill,*** *Bugsy Siegal's girlfriend had opened Swiss Bank accounts in Geneva and signed a lease on an apartment there at approximately the same time that construction on the Las Vegas Flamingo gambling resort was experiencing losses in the millions. Familiarity with European banking and arbitrage was common with commission mobsters, but this coincident activity, in addition to Bugsy's attempt to put Continental Wire Service out of business and to take over mob activities in Los Angeles, may have sealed Bugsy's fate. Bugsy had left Virginia in charge of the Flamingo project while he was attempting to solidify his position as the top gangster in LA. Some sources state that Virginia returned the money after Bugsy's assassination.*

132 **Girard College,** endowed and founded by the provisions of Stephen Girard's 1831 Will, opened in 1848. Nearly all his seven million dollar estate was left to establish and operate a school for "poor, male, white, orphans." A Board of Directors of City Trusts was appointed to administer and assure that Girard's legacy was properly protected, wisely invested, and administered according to his instructions....Unique grounds, marble buildings, a mile long, ten-foot high wall, and a main building that resembles a Greek temple, are distinctive features of the College...it was the quality of its staff that made Girard College an outstanding educational institution. Forty four of its members had master degrees, seven had doctorates, several were engineers, and others had degrees in health education, and music. Nearly all the teachers and house parents had at least a bachelor's degree. Additionally, the staff included seven medical doctors, six registered nurses, and five dentists. This impressive list of skills and academic achievement was unmatched in any pre-college school, private or public...In 1941, there were 362 candidates for admission, all poor, male, white, and fatherless. Today, nearly none of the students fall into that category. Most of today's students are "functional orphans," a term coined by the courts to describe children from single-parent homes. In 1941, 78 percent of the new students stayed to graduate, whereas today hardly 50 percent stay to graduate. In 1941 the student population

was 1658, all boys, all white, and all orphans. Today there are about 600 students, a heterogeneous group of boys and girls of all races. The $1.7 million yearly operating costs for 1941 increased to $12 million in 1992. In 1941 the yearly expenditure per student was $1018. Today it is approximately $22,000. (Written in 1999) **Author's note:** *Stephen Girard, who started his fortune as a sea captain trading between New Jersey and the Caribbean Islands, lived in Mount Holly on Mill Street* Cite-***"Stephen Girard - The Man, His College and Estate"*** 2nd Edition, 1999, By Thomas J. DiFilippo, excerpts from Preface and text.

133 **The Mob in the Car Cloning business.** ***"Crime in the United States, 2000,"*** Uniform Crime Reports, Federal Bureau of Investigation, U.S. Dept. of Justice, ISBN 0-16-048756-0. Statistics from "***Byrd's Eye View,***" by Senator Robert C. Byrd, "***Organized Crime and the Stolen Car,***" Syndicated column, Sept. 8, 1971.

134 **Judith Campbell Exner** broke years of silence when she co-authored with People Magazine to reveal her romance with Jack Kennedy in the White House and her connections with mobsters introduced to her by Frank Sinatra, including Johnny Rosselli and Sam Giancana. *Cite-**"The Dark Side of Camelot,"*** by Kitty Kelley, People Magazine, Vol 29, No. 8, February 29, 1988.

135 ***Villa Venice.*** In the 1960s, mob boss Sam "Momo" Giancana ran a restaurant and night club on Milwaukee Avenue in Wheeling (Illinois) called the Villa Venice Supper Club. Located where Allgauer's Restaurant now sits, near the Des Plaines River, the Villa Venice had a boat landing with Venetian lanterns on the banks, where patrons could ride in a gondola. For an out-of-the-way club, the Villa Venice somehow got top-flight talent, including Frank Sinatra, Sammy Davis Jr. and Dean Martin, and then-popular singer Eddie Fisher. Sinatra's daughter Tina wrote in her book that to repay Giancana for help getting the union vote for John F. Kennedy in 1960, her father brought the Rat Pack to do several shows at the Villa Venice *(three shows a night for eight days).* One of the shows is still available on a CD, "The Rat Pack - Live at the Villa Venice." In 1967, the theater and restaurant burned down in a mysterious fire. Bill Hein, a member of the Wheeling Historical Society, was at the Rat Pack show. He said the club was gorgeous, with satin ceilings and tapestries, and the show was fabulous. Hein, a former volunteer firefighter in Wheeling, was also there the night Villa Venice burned down. "I've never seen anything go up so quick in my life," he said. Giancana was shot and killed while cooking in his basement kitchen in Oak Park in 1975. In the short time Villa Venice and its casino were open, according to crime magazine.com; the FBI estimated the supper club and gambling at the nearby Quonset Hut grossed over $3 million. Cite-***Chicago Daily Herald,*** JJ Flood. ***Author's Note:****-Antoinette Giancana suggests in her book,* ***"Mafia Princess"*** *that her father sold the Villa Venice before it burned, but also admits that her father, like Sal, never discussed his affairs in her presence, and she knew little about the Villa Venice and other details about his business. Kitty Kelley, in Sinatra's unauthorized biography suggests the club was just a hook (using Sinatra) to make quick money for Giancana, who stopped the entertainment and closed the casino within days of the last show by the "Rat Pack." A "bust out"*

occurs when the mob wheedles its way into partial or complete ownership of a business and then uses its credit and good name to make purchases which become black market sales items, bankrupting the business. The Coup de Grace is the inevitable fire and insurance payoff. Giancana may have sold the restaurant with the condition that Sal would remain Manager. Reports indicate that when the restaurant burned, conditions on the property, which had been a hog farm, reverted and created a horrible stench from the polluted canals. Data from ***"Wheeling Through the Years,"*** *Wheeling Historical Society, 1987, pg157.*

136 **Ibid. 32-3 Jack Phillips.** ***Author's Note:*** *According to Angelo, Jack was killed by an RPG (Rocket Propelled Grenade) fired by a Viet Cong soldier on the perimeter of the hand to hand fighting melee.*

137 **Florida mob.** Though Miami and South Florida has been host to mobsters from around the country, Florida has a homegrown Mafia family, based in Tampa. The Tampa (Santo Trafficante) family made its initial fortune in gambling, specifically bolita (Spanish for "little ball"), a numbers game popular in the ethnic enclave of Ybor City. The Tampa family also had no compunction about getting into the narcotics business. The island nation (Cuba) was a paradise and a playground for the mob and wealthy Americans who went there to gamble and indulge in other vices. This all changed when Castro seized power in 1959. The most famous Tampa Mafioso was Santo Trafficante Jr., who succeeded his father as boss of the family after Sr.'s death in 1954. Trafficante Jr. became one of the most respected Mafia leaders in the country, forging alliances with mobsters from the United States, Canada, Italy, Spain, and Southeast Asia. Trafficante died in 1987. *Cite-* ***"Santo Trafficante of Tampa-The Gulf Coast Connection"*** by Scott M. Deitche. ***Author's note:*** *Although Sal never explicitly mentioned operating (casinos) in the Gulf Coast area, Tuck's half brother was living evidence that he spent some time there. His association with the Trafficante's was obvious in his later banking connections in Tampa, and it seems logical in real time (looking back on the patterns of his life) that he somehow was involved with casino operations in the area, and car cloning from his "iron works".*

138 **Card Cheats** rarely work alone. Big action often brings what we call *crews;* a cheating organization. The roles are clearly determined just like a film script. The leader is known as the *captain*. He is the writer of the script. He has full responsibility over the *mob*, from role assignment to money sharing. The *mechanic* is the technician, the one with exceptional skills at the table. He is supposed to make the *move* at the right time (chip stealing, dice switching, card mucking, false shuffling, etc.). The *takeoff man* is the man who collects the money when the scam takes place. He bets and folds according to the captain's directives. The *inside man* is the employee (casino, clubs, private games, etc.) working for the crew. He provides significant information to the captain. The *support member* plays a lesser part in the organization, and the role is more flexible. This person can be a *turn*, like an attractive woman to distract the surveillance, a *relay*, who receives a signal from the cheat and sends it to the takeoff man, or an *advance man*, who finds a *sucker*. There is a thin line that separates the professional cheat and the expert, even though one plays the bad guy and the other one the good guy. As the renowned

cheat Walter Irving Scott once said: 'There isn't a card player who wouldn't cheat, if he knew how.' Once you possess the power, it can be tempting. But cheating remains a crime severely punished by the law. And some have paid with their lives. Cite-***"About cheating"*** by Marwan Mery, on http://www.cards-ex-pert.com

139 **Royal Flush Exhibition Poker Deal.** *The card trick that Sal demonstrated to Tuck was an old and well known magician's routine called Exhibition Poker Deal. The trick wasn't original with Nelson Downs. He said it was a favorite of Adrian Plate. Tom Boyer published his version, Klondike Poker, in 1926 in The Linking Ring (Vol IV, No. 1). He dealt seven hands, dealing a bottom card on the 14th and 28th cards. This gave everyone a full house. The performer than draws four cards to win with a straight flush. Ross Bertram resurrected it, publishing it under his own name as the Exhibition Poker Deal, in The Linking Ring (July 1930). Leslie Guest spotted that it was a variation of the Downs trick and added some notes of his own, including a story about throwing the unlucky thirteenth card away and the fact that the trick will not work if certain cards are showing on the bottom of the deck. Downs referred only to the Jack, but in fact there are more cards to look out for than that. Cite-**The Art of Magic***, by T. Nelson Downs, Published by Arthur P. Felsman, Chicago, IL, 1926 and *http://www.cards-expert.com.*

140 **Theodore Mc Keldin** for the third time ran for governor (of Maryland) in 1950. He was successful, defeating incumbent William Preston Lane, Jr. by the largest margin in state history up to that point. As governor, McKeldin endeavored to improve the state highway system, namely by establishing the Baltimore Beltway (now I-695), the Capitol Beltway (I-495), and the John Hanson Highway (US 50 between Washington, DC and Annapolis). Cite-**Wikipedia,** the Free Encyclopedia.

141 **Tampa Banking.** The owner of the Pittsburgh Maulers in the new league (USFL) was Edward J. DeBartolo, Sr., who was frequently under suspicion of mob ties. For example, the U.S. Customs Service had received information from one of its special agents, William F. Burda, in January 1981 that the DeBartolo organization 'through its control of particular state banks in the state of Florida is operating money-laundering schemes, realizing huge profits from narcotics, guns, skimming operations, and other organized-crime-related activities. This organization is reported to have ties to [Carlos] Marcello, [Santos] Trafficante, and [Meyer]Lansky and because of its enormous wealth and power has high-ranking political influence and affiliations...DeBartolo, who bought Metropolitan in 1975, owned 227,000 shares of stock in the bank. His position was so strong at the Metropolitan Bank that he, unilaterally, forced the bank's president to resign in 1981. Other board members had no say in the matter. Metropolitan collapsed in 1982. It was the largest bank failure in Florida history Cite-***"The DeBartolo Family and Organized Crime,"*** From ***"Interference: How Organized Crime Influences Professional Football"*** by Dan Moldea, Chapter 42, pp. 352-353: ***Author's Note -*** *Sal's connections to the Tampa mob allowed him to purchase up to $50,000.00 worth of cars at the wholesale auctions up to twice weekly, all on the bank's credit. At its peak, Sal's "Iron works" was selling (or cloning) 500 to 700 cars monthly.*

142 **Crown Jewels.** ***Author's Note:*** *Sal told Tuck that only two complete replica sets existed of the Crown Jewels of England, and each had cost $250,000 to create. Tuck ran into a part of the replica set of jewels display at a press conference at the Tropicana Casino in Atlantic City in the '80's. It was the diamonds display, which included replicas of the Hope diamond, the Star of India and other famous jewels. This group had accompanied the Replica set of the Crown Jewels of England in one of the smaller trucks.*

143 ***Author's note: Sam the Plumber****, or Sam the Count was known for his flashy apparel. He always looked the part of Italian royalty. All of suits were hand tailored in Italy, as well as his accessories, including shoes. In white summer attire, with a healthy sun tan from his frequent hideout vacations in Florida, he was a startling figure. Sam once chastised several of his soldiers who showed up at a family christening party without coats and ties, and sent them home to return in proper attire.*

144 **Coopersmith.** ***Author's Note:*** *Tuck considered it likely that the Cadillac was not stolen, after researching the history of auto theft in the latter part of the century. A common mob procedure was to approach owners of new autos on a long term lease, take possession of the car, re-title and resell it, while the original lessor reports It stolen and gets a replacement from his insurance, and a loner while he waits for it. This scam was very popular until the dealerships and leasing companies restructured their agreements to avoid it. Coopersmith was thought to have mob connections, according to the State Police.*

#